Education in Great Britain and Ireland

The Open University
Faculty of Educational Studies

Course Teams

Decision-making within British Educational Systems (E221)

Robert Bell
Gerald Fowler (Chairman)
Tony Gear
Robert Glaister
Donald Holms
Vincent Houghton
Ken Little
John Miller
Colin Morgan
Vera Morris
Jennifer Ozga
William Prescott
David Seligman
Alberto da Silva e Melo
Adam Westoby

Education, Economy and Politics (E352)

Robert Bell
Ben Cosin
Roger Dale
David Godwin
Donald Holms
Richard Hooper
John Jones
Christine King
Ken Little
Donald Mackinnon
William Prescott
Donald Swift (Chairman)
Peter Woods

Education in Great Britain and Ireland
A source book

Edited by
Robert Bell
Gerald Fowler
Ken Little
at The Open University

London & Boston
Routledge & Kegan Paul
in association with The Open University Press

First published 1973
by Routledge & Kegan Paul Ltd
Broadway House, 68–74 Carter Lane,
London EC4V 5EL and
9 Park Street,
Boston, Mass. 02108, U.S.A.
Printed in Great Britain by
Cox & Wyman Ltd, London, Reading and Fakenham
Selection and editorial matter © The Open University 1973
ISBN 0 7100 7517 0 (c)
ISBN 0 7100 7516 2 (p)
Library of Congress Catalog Card No. 72–95680

Contents

Preface

This volume is meant to be not so much a reader in what is now the conventional academic sense, but a source book for Open University students doing either of the Faculty of Educational Studies courses, Decision-making within British Educational Systems (E221) or Education, Economy and Politics (E352).

Its aim is, however, to break new ground in two respects; first, it probably represents the first attempt to bring together in one volume documentation concerning the educational systems, not merely in England and Wales but in all the constituent parts of these islands. Secondly, it attempts to bring together not merely official documents in the style of the invaluable collection by Maclure (*Educational Documents in England and Wales, 1816–1967*, Methuen, 1970) nor merely academic articles dealing with key topics. It attempts in addition to combine such conventional academic materials with further evidence such as newspaper articles, radio discussion and political statements so that all the various kinds of material that help to form public opinion on educational issues can be examined and assessed, and so that students are given an all-too-rare opportunity to study an amalgam of influential materials, instead of only those materials which are academically 'respectable'.

The contents provide the merest selection from those which could have been desirably included. Many major topics, such as adult education or the detailed discussion of teacher training, have had to be omitted on grounds of space, not because they are regarded as comparatively unimportant, but because they are either covered adequately in the course materials, or because their affairs are in such a state of flux that much of what would be included would be out of date by the time this volume appeared.

The volume in general is about the making of decisions, and the forces, financial, political, ideological and rhetorical, that produce climates of opinion. It must be seen as taking its place in a course structure, which elsewhere gives greater weight to the related philosophical and sociological issues. Nor should the volume be taken as an infallible source of 'facts'. Much of its content is opinion only and the editors take no responsibility for its accuracy—particularly in areas of controversy.

Acknowledgments

The Open University and the publishers would like to thank the following for permission to reproduce copyright material. All possible care has been taken to trace ownership of the selections included and to make full acknowledgment for their use.

Reading

1–7, 17, 35 © The Open University
8 Reprinted by permission of the *Roscoe Review* and the author.
9, 45 Reproduced by permission of the OECD, Paris.
10 From Schools Council's information leaflets, *A Brief History* and *Representation*. These and other leaflets on various aspects of the Council's work are free on application to Schools Council, 160 Great Portland Street, London W1N 6LL.
11 © Manchester University Press, 1970.
12 Reprinted by permission of Routledge & Kegan Paul Ltd and the author.
13 Reproduced by permission of the *Journal of Curriculum Studies*, Collins and the author.
14, 20, 28, 33, 36, 38, 39, 42 By permission of the Controller of Her Majesty's Stationery Office.
15, 32 By permission of the *Irish Times*.
16 Reprinted by permission of the author.
18 Reprinted by permission of the Jersey Teachers' Association.
19 Reprinted by permission of the Edinburgh and Midlothian Association for the Advancement of State Education and the author.
21 Editorial comments and selection reproduced by permission of The Clarendon Press, Oxford; © Robin Davis, 1967; © Routledge & Kegan Paul Ltd, 1962; © Routledge & Kegan Paul Ltd, 1957; © Victor Gollancz Ltd, 1966.
22 Reprinted by permission of *Comprehensive Education* (journal of the Campaign for Comprehensive Education), editor, Caroline Benn.
23 Reprinted by permission of the Fabian Society.
24 Reprinted by permission of the Conservative & Unionist Central Office and the Rt Hon. Edward Heath.
25 © Bow Publications Limited, 1967.
26 Reprinted by permission of the author.
27 Reproduced by permission of Dr Rhodes Boyson, Head of Highbury Grove School.
29, 31 Reproduced by permission of the editor, *Studies*.
30 Reproduced by permission of the Controller of the Stationery Office, Dublin, and the Department of Education, Dublin.
34, 49 Reproduced from *The Times* by permission.
37 Reprinted with the authority of the Labour Party.
40 © Edinburgh University Press, 1969.
41 © Victor Gollancz Ltd, 1964.
43, 46 These articles first appeared in *New Society*, the weekly review of the social sciences, 128 Long Acre, London W.C.2.
44, 47, 50 Reprinted from *Higher Education Review* by permission of Cornmarket Press Limited, London, and © Cornmarket Press Limited, 1969, 1970, 1971. *HER* is now published three times a year by Tyrrell Burgess Associates Ltd, Croydon.
48 © Tyrrell Burgess and the Contributors, 1971.

Section I   An introduction to the formal educational systems in the United Kingdom, the Irish Republic, the Isle of Man and the Channel Islands

Section I provides a beginner's guide to the formal educational systems in the United Kingdom, the Irish Republic, the Isle of Man and the Channel Islands. The authors, some academics and some educational journalists, naturally see the systems from their own point of view and elsewhere in this volume (as well as in the course units) students should not be surprised if they find disagreement with the positions stated here. Nevertheless, we feel that all seven articles provide a useful introduction for outsiders and a useful work of reference for students in the field of educational studies.

This introductory section ends with a somewhat light-hearted article by Dr Edmund Leach, Provost of King's College, Cambridge, discussing some of the beliefs underlying educational practice and attitude in England and, by infection, in other parts of the British Isles.

1   Education in England

Anne Corbett

The English educational system is notable for its diversity. Universities are autonomous; teachers have a great deal of professional freedom; and local education authorities, who administer the system, vary. One can argue about where these characteristics shade off from fact into fiction. For while the system is apparently the most decentralized and pragmatically organized in Europe, its more obvious features cannot totally conceal a tightly knit structure based on national controls.

This chapter outlines the structure of the English education system and notes some of the major educational controversies.

Administration

The legal basis of the system is the Education Act, 1944, and the amendments made by fourteen Acts between 1946 and 1972. The 1944 Act prescribes the duty of government, local education authorities and parents in a system which is compulsory for those aged five to sixteen, and which contains optional pre-school and post-school provision.

Schools in England and universities throughout Great Britain are the responsibility of the Secretary of State for Education and Science. Under the Act, the Secretary of State is responsible for securing the 'effective execution' of the 'national policy'. In other words, the Secretary of State does not control directly, but acts at one remove.

For example, education has a budget of over £2,000 million a year, making it second only to the health services and social security in its share of the gross national product. Direct expenditure by central government is only about 14 per cent of the total budget. Similarly the Secretary of State does not control the content of the curriculum or prescribe

Anne Corbett is an educational journalist.

textbooks. The Secretary of State does not run examinations or employ teachers. The Department of Education and Science is not concerned with the day-to-day administration of schools.

That is not to say that the Secretary of State does not have almost complete power if he chooses to exercise it. The Secretary of State can give directions to an authority acting 'unreasonably'; he can call for any information; he approves the short-list for chief education officer appointments. But in the normal course of events where local education authorities are concerned the Secretary of State acts as a checkpoint rather than an initiator. He has to approve changes in the use of schools. He sets minimum standards on pupil–teacher ratios. He controls capital expenditure and the supply of teachers. He maintains an oversight of educational standards through the inspectorate (Her Majesty's Inspectors of Schools or HMIs).

The style of the system, outside universities, is generally determined by the 163 local education authorities. These elected bodies are required, under the 1944 Act, to provide education in three successive stages (primary, secondary and further) and to 'contribute towards the spiritual, moral, mental and physical development of the community' by ensuring that 'efficient education throughout these stages shall be available to meet the needs of the population'. And, as far as is compatible with providing efficient education and avoiding unreasonable public expenditure, local education authorities are required to educate pupils in accordance with the wishes of their parents.

Beyond those general principles, local education authorities decide on the size and, generally, the organization of schools. They prescribe the level of textbook allowances. They make decisions on a whole lot of the non-statutory extras which often go to make the difference between a 'good' and 'bad' authority. They can employ extra teachers on a part-time basis. They decide on the scale of in-service training, how many local advisers and inspectors to employ, how many teachers' centres to set up. They decide how generously to support leisure-time and adult education.

Many people would argue that the roots of the system are even more local. There is an almost mythical belief in teachers' freedom. And schools do vary depending as much on the personality of the head-teacher and staff as the area the pupils come from. Teachers are not required to teach particular subjects other than religious education. Nor are they required to enter pupils for examinations.

However, parents are given duties under the Education Act, and, together with the duties imposed on the local education authorities, these act as constraints upon schools and teachers. Parents have the duty of ensuring that their children receive efficient education 'suitable to their age, ability and aptitude' between the ages of five and sixteen. Parents are also required to see that their children attend school regularly. Parents can, and do, complain, if schools maintained by local education authorities do not provide 'efficient' education.

Universities are outside this general pattern. The Secretary of State exercises his responsibilities through a buffer organization, the University Grants Committee. This is to enable public funds to be channelled to universities while still preserving their autonomy.

Finance

The financing of education illustrates the checks and balances between national and local interests in the system, and in the case of universities between national and academic interests. The local education authority service is financed on the concept of partnership. Historically the reasoning has been that the education service is responsible for the growth of individuals, the transmission of the nation's cultural inheritance and the progress of ideas; therefore it should not be controlled solely by a central authority. On the other hand, educational facilities should be equally available to all citizens, whichever part of the country they live in; therefore the central authority has some responsibility to contribute towards those facilities.

Current expenditure is financed by an element raised locally through the rates, and an element which comes from the government for all local services, known as the rate support grant. At present, the rate support grant makes up about 60 per cent of local authority expenditure on education. In theory local authorities are free to decide how to distribute it between different services. In practice the freedom is limited by two factors: the grant, which is made every two years, is decided on the basis of detailed bargaining with the local authority associations; and many of the large items of expenditure, like teachers' salaries, are determined by national agreements.

Some of the funds for education are then further redistributed by one authority to another. Authorities will trade among themselves in the provision of specialized facilities, like special schooling for handicapped children. And all the financing of non-university higher education is taken care of by a national pool, to which authorities contribute on a *per capita* basis for students resident in their area, and from which they draw if they run higher education courses.

Capital expenditure is determined by the Department of Education and Science. It gives loan sanction to authorities for particular projects.

Nearly all university incomes come from public funds. The government contributes about 70 per cent of their current income and 90 per cent of their capital programmes. With the exception of the Open University, which gets its share of public funds in the form of a direct grant from the Department of Education and Science, universities are financed through the University Grants Committee. The UGC distributes the grant for current expenditure, which is made every five years, to individual institutions. Universities, like the local authorities with the rate support grant, are free in theory to spend their grant as they wish. In practice they are likely to be constrained, because they too will have got their funds on the basis of detailed negotiation.

Compulsory schooling

Education is compulsory between the ages of five and sixteen. The minimum leaving age has been raised from fifteen to sixteen in 1972–3. Compulsory schooling is divided into a primary and secondary stage. The transition from primary to secondary schooling is normally made around the age of eleven. Since the Education Act, 1964, gave local education authorities the power to establish other ages of transfer, there are now areas in which the transition occurs when children are ten, twelve or thirteen.

Over 90 per cent of children attend schools which are wholly maintained by the local education authorities and at which no fees are charged. These include schools which for historical or religious reasons retain a majority of independent governors (see below). The education of about 5 per cent of the population is financed mainly by parents' contributions at either direct grant or independent schools.

The direct grant schools are a small group of 320 schools which span the state and independent systems. They receive a large part of their income in the form of a direct grant from the Department of Education and Science. These schools, which include some of the most prestigious grammar schools in the country, were given their status as a result of negotiations in the period 1947–51, and again in 1959, when the direct grant list was reopened. Direct grant schools have to award free places to at least a quarter of the pupils admitted to the school: these places are allocated by the governors or through the local education authority and are available only to pupils who have attended maintained or grant-aided primary schools for at least two years. Local education authorities may take up a larger proportion of free places, though they do not usually take up more than half. Parents pay the fees for the remaining places. Fees are based on a scale related to the parents' income.

Independent schools do not receive grants from public funds. But 10 per cent of the places in independent schools are paid for by the government or local education authorities (for children needing boarding education or for those needing some sort of facilities not available in the maintained sector). The schools also benefit from a number of fiscal privileges. Parents may reduce the cost of the fees by paying over a capital sum which attracts tax relief, or the fees may be covenanted. Schools which register as charities are exempt from tax on income other than their business profits, for example, and pay reduced rates. Most of the larger schools have charitable status. Independent schools have to be registered with the Department of

Table 1.1   Public authorities' educational expenditure   £ million

sector	1969–70			1970–71 provisional		
	current	*capital*	*total*	*current*	*capital*	*total*
Schools (England)						
Primary	380·4⎫			436·2⎫		
Secondary	422·1⎬	157·4	1,073·9	477·9⎬	205·9	1,250·9
Others, including nursery and special schools and grants to independent and direct grant schools, school health and transport	114·0⎭			130·9⎭		
Further education (England and Wales)	226·8	45·0	271·8	262·7	51·0	313·7
Teacher training (England and Wales)	92·3	7·8	100·1	102·0	7·6	109·6
Universities (Great Britain)	234·3	74·4	308·7	284·8	76·4	361·2
Other	84·4	6·2	90·6	97·5	6·7	104·2
School meals and milk (England) (excluding loan charges)	86·8	10·6	97·4	94·6	10·6	105·2
Total	1,641·1	301·4	1,942·5	1,886·6	358·2	2,244·8

Source: Education and Science in 1971 (HMSO).

Table 1.2   Schools, pupils and teachers, January 1970

	schools or departments	*full-time pupils*	*full-time teachers*	*part-time teachers*
Schools maintained by local education authorities:				
Primary	23,060	4,912,874	168,431	26,540
Secondary	5,385	3,045,974	157,619	28,063
Direct grant schools	315	129,069	7,887	1,382
Independent schools recognized as efficient	1,424	303,977	21,184	7,666
Other independent schools	1,351	109,811	6,551	5,134
All schools	32,900	8,597,451	370,022	69,841

Source: Statistics of Education (HMSO 1970) **1**.

Education and Science. They may ask to be 'recognized as efficient'. The 'Public Schools' are so recognized.

Dual system

The historical contribution of the religious bodies and city companies to public education is still reflected in the classification of schools. It was in 1833 that the government made its first grants to the voluntary bodies. In 1870 the government legislated for universal elementary education and set up school boards to start schools where no voluntary schools existed. In 1902 local education authorities took over from the school boards, and were given the responsibility of overseeing the efficiency of secular instruction in all schools, including voluntary schools. But they also became responsible for the maintenance of all schools. The 1944 Act marked a new stage in the balance between making voluntary schools viable, with the help of public funds, while allowing them to retain religious freedom; and in maintaining a Christian bias in the education of all children.

In the first place, under the 1944 Act, religious instruction was given compulsory status in county as well as voluntary schools. That makes it unique in the English school curriculum. All children are also expected to take part in communal daily prayers or some other act of corporate worship. The only exceptions are children whose parents have made the special effort of asking that they be withdrawn from prayers and religious education.

Second, voluntary schools were presented with a series of choices, the amount of money they would receive from public funds, varying in inverse proportion to the degree of independence they would be allowed for denominational religious instruction. There are just over 9,000 voluntary schools (6,400 Church of England, 2,500 Roman Catholic and a few Jewish schools, Methodist schools and others belonging to philanthropic bodies). Almost 4,000 became voluntary controlled schools, over 5,000 chose to become voluntary aided and 155 are special agreement schools.

At aided schools the voluntary body appoints two thirds of the managers or governors, and they are responsible for maintaining the exterior of the building, and for making improvements or alterations; the local education authority appoints the rest. Up to 80 per cent of approved expenditure can be recovered from the Department of Education and Science. The local education authority pays for the internal maintenance of the building, teachers' salaries and the general costs of running the school. Religious teaching and the appointment of teachers are controlled by the governors.

At controlled schools the voluntary body appoints only one third of the managers or governors, the local education authority appointing the majority. All maintenance and building costs are met by the local education authority. The voluntary body's influence is limited to the appointment of the headteacher and of the teachers appointed for religious instruction. The voluntary body managers or governors have to approve such appointments.

Special agreement schools are a hangover from the 1936 Education Act. They are like aided schools, except that they have got a government contribution of between 50 and 75 per cent towards the cost of building a new school.

The question of voluntary schools still arouses some passions. It is no longer a matter of religion. But some of the aided schools have caused widespread resentment because they have used their majority on governing bodies to resist local education authorities' reorganization plans. And the voluntary bodies themselves still say they are short of funds, and are currently pressing the government to increase their contribution towards capital costs.

Primary education

Primary education includes three age ranges: nursery for children under five years, infants from five to seven or eight, and juniors from seven or eight to eleven or twelve years. Attendance is voluntary, but much sought after, for children under five. They may attend one of the rare publicly maintained nursery schools, an independent nursery school, a pre-school playgroup, or increasingly a nursery class attached to a primary school.

There are 23,000 public sector primary schools. In January 1970 they had 4·9 million pupils. Nearly all these schools were for boys and girls together. About half had 100 pupils or less. Maximum class sizes as laid down by the Secretary of State are 30 for nursery schools and 40 for infant and junior classes.

Middle schools are now being set up by a number of authorities to span the gap between primary education, which is largely pupil-centred, and secondary education, which has traditionally been subject-centred. There were 136 in 1970. Those schools for pupils aged eight to twelve are regarded as primary schools for statistical purposes, those for pupils aged ten to thirteen are regarded as secondary schools, and those for pupils aged nine to thirteen may be either, at the local education authority's choice.

Secondary education

Secondary schools are generally much larger than primary schools. Over half have between 400 and 800 pupils. The largest schools have 2,000. There were 5,400 maintained secondary schools in 1970 with 3 million pupils, 178 direct grant schools with 119,000 pupils and 2,775 independent secondary schools, including the famous 'public' schools, with over 413,000 pupils. These are divided almost half and half between those the Department of Education recognizes as efficient and those it is merely prepared to register.

Maintained secondary schools may be organized in a variety of ways. The policy of the last Labour government was to move from the old division of grammar and secondary modern schools over to a non-selective comprehensive pattern. About 40 per cent of secondary school pupils are now in comprehensive schools of one sort or another.

In recent years an increasing proportion of pupils have been staying on beyond the minimum school-leaving age of fifteen. About 50 per cent were staying on voluntarily in 1970–1. The school-leaving age has been raised to sixteen from 1972–3.

Special education

Special education treatment is provided for children handicapped by deafness, blindness or other physical disabilities and for those who are educationally subnormal. Some handicapped children attend ordinary schools. About a third of the special schools are boarding schools. All require their pupils to stay one year beyond the minimum leaving age and a number provide a period of further education and pre-vocational training. In 1970 there were 986 special schools with 87,000 pupils.

Curriculum and examination

Since, with the exception of religious education, no subject is compulsory, the shape of the curriculum in any school depends on the balance between the pressures created by the examination system, the teachers, parents and local interests.

There are two main sets of public examinations for secondary school pupils, the General Certificate of Education and the Certificate of Secondary Education. More than half the pupils who leave school will have attempted the examinations and passed in at least one subject. The General Certificate of Education is run by seven boards based on the universities. It is taken at Ordinary Level (at sixteen years or so) and at Advanced Level (at eighteen or so) as a qualifying examination for higher education. The Certificate of Secondary Education is run by thirteen regional boards controlled by teachers. The highest grade in CSE (grade one) is regarded as equivalent to a GCE 'O' Level pass.

Efforts to change the curriculum, and indeed examinations, often arise from individual schools. Most national stimulus comes not from the Department of Education but from an independent body, the Schools Council. Widely representative of the education service, it is advisory to its members on curriculum. It has a special advisory role to the Secretary of State on examinations. Symbolically the Schools Council has a majority of teacher representatives on its governing body.

Further education

Although technically further education may cover any period of education beyond the minimum leaving age, it is generally taken to exclude those who remain at school and those studying at universities or colleges of education. Even in this restricted sense further education ranges from GCE courses, technical and commercial courses for operatives and craftsmen, to degree, including postgraduate courses. The term also covers evening courses. Courses reaching standards above GCE 'A' Level and the Ordinary National Diploma are regarded as 'advanced' and their students as in higher education.

The further education sector is based mainly in six types of college. There are two national colleges, established and financed jointly by the Department of Education and Science and an industry. They are intended to provide advanced technical studies for a particular industry. There are 30 polytechnics, which are designed as a local education authority complement to universities. They have full-time, part-time and sandwich students at all levels of higher education. Some of the polytechnics now incorporate colleges of art and colleges of education as well as their normal base of technical and commercial colleges. There are 112 art colleges, 45 agricultural colleges and 485 technical colleges and colleges of commerce known as 'other major establishments'. These usually draw their students from a local area and run many day courses. There are finally over 6,000 evening institutes with many leisure-time courses. Altogether there are 3·2 million further education students. Of these 1·4 million are in evening institutes and 1·4 million are on part-time day or evening vocational courses; 270,000 students are on full-time or sandwich courses. The proportion of full-time and sandwich students is growing.

Degree awards are made by the Council for National Academic Awards, which validates colleges to run degree courses, and London University, which is now enrolling a diminishing number of external students. Other advanced qualifications are conferred by professional institutions and joint committees representing the profession and academics.

Education and training of teachers

Colleges of education are the principal source of supply of qualified teachers for primary and secondary schools. (Teachers may also get their qualified status through a university department of education, or one of the few education departments in a college of further education.) There are 30 university departments of education, 157 colleges of education, 7 polytechnic departments of education, 13 art teacher training centres, 4 colleges of education for technical teachers and 19 other maintained colleges training teachers. In 1970 they had 119,000 students.

The normal course is three years. Some students go on to a fourth year in order to get a Bachelor of Education degree. Students already holding a university degree have to do a one-year course of professional education at a university or certain colleges of education.

The structure of teacher education and training is now being reviewed by the government, following the publication in 1972 of a report by a committee chaired by Lord James and appointed by the Secretary of State for Education and Science.

Universities

There are forty-three universities in Great Britain (of which one is in Wales and eight in Scotland), including the Open University. They each have a royal charter, which acknowledges their status and rights. They decide what students to admit, what staff to appoint, what to teach and in what conditions degrees will be awarded. Students do not, as in many continental countries, have an automatic right of entry if they hold the basic qualifications. The university decides – although it is likely to be on the basis of their performance in GCE. Universities' relations with the Government are conducted through the University Grants Committee (see p. 195).

In general a first degree may be taken in three years. There were in 1970 219,500 full-time students. Of these 39,000 were postgraduate. The numbers of university students have trebled since 1960, largely due to a government decision to implement the findings of the Robbins Committee Report, dealt with in a later section of this volume.

The Open University is unique in several respects. Catering overwhelmingly for mature students at a distance, its teaching methods are based on a combination of television, radio and correspondence courses, with short residential courses. It does not require formal academic qualifications for entry.

Teachers

Teachers are appointed by local education authorities or a school's governors or managers. They are not, as in many countries, civil servants.

Teachers in maintained schools must be approved as qualified by the Department of Education and Science. Completing a college of education course or a university course of professional training is the most usual way of getting qualified status.

Teachers are paid on national salary scales. In 1970 there were 334,400 full-time teachers and 48,000 part-time teachers in maintained schools. The pupil–teacher ratio was 27·4:1 in primary schools and 17·8:1 in secondary schools.

Controversies

Criticisms of falling educational standards or indiscipline in schools or student behaviour surface as items for educational news and argument. But politically there is remarkably little controversy on educational matters. The fact is that matters requiring the lion's share of resources—expanding higher education, increasing the supply of teachers in order to cut down the size of classes, improving school buildings—do not cause political divisions.

There is still some mileage in issues which the Conservative Party regards as a test of quality in the system and the Labour Party regards as inimical to quality. Two issues stand out: the position of independent and direct grant schools, and the reorganization of secondary education.

Although the famous independent 'public' schools and the highly academic direct grant schools take only 5 per cent or so of the population, their pupils take an enormous share of influential jobs. The Conservatives see direct grant schools as a vital ladder by which bright children can escape from the handicap of a poor

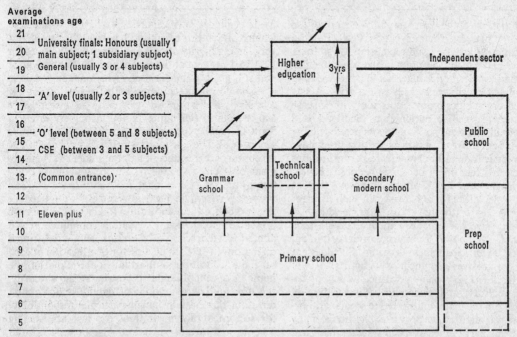

Figure 11. The English educational system

home. The Conservatives think parents should have the freedom to opt out of the maintained system. The Labour Party claims it would like to be able to abolish this privilege. So when the Labour Party said in July 1972 (in a document to be submitted to the party conference as the basis of a manifesto) that it wanted to abolish fee-paying in schools, and as an interim measure would propose a licensing system for independent schools and would make direct grant schools choose between maintained and independent status, there was predictably an outcry in *The Times* correspondence columns. Observers might however note that the public and direct grant schools generate more political talk than action.

The reorganization of secondary education—going comprehensive—has been taking place gradually and by local education authority initiative from the end of the 1950s. By 1964 three quarters of the authorities had at least one comprehensive school. In 1965 the Labour government introduced a policy of completely comprehensive secondary education. About 40 per cent of secondary school pupils are now in comprehensives as a result.

The Conservative Party, since coming into office in 1970, has effectively slowed reorganization. Authorities wanting to reorganize no longer submit development plans to the Secretary of State; they merely ask for approval for a change in the use of individual schools. This means that it is easy to keep selective schools out of reorganization plans. The Secretary of State also, while expanding the primary school building programme greatly, has cut down on secondary building. This makes it more difficult to introduce new schemes.

In any other sectors of the system the Conservatives give more emphasis to primary education whereas the Labour Party want more positive discrimination to favour deprived areas.

As for higher education, outside politics there is a great deal of criticism of the binary system, which leaves universities one side of the fence and polytechnics and colleges of education on the other, controlled by local education authorities. But there is no sign of either of the main political parties wishing to dismantle the present structure.

---

2 Education in Scotland

Colin MacLean

Scotland has over the years proudly exported the products and patterns of her education. Partly because this education enjoyed a good reputation for so long, Scots have had difficulty at times in accepting the idea that it may be in need of change. But in contemplating the possibility of change, which is being vigorously advocated on all sides today, Scots add to their sense of tradition a sensitive nationalism: Scotland is a nation within a nation, so many Scots are inevitably defensive about those attributes which they think have given distinctive colour or character to her institutions and which they fear might be submerged if her educational system were linked more closely to that of England and Wales. There is reason in such fear, for major decisions on the future of Scottish education can be and have been made without Scotland as a nation having any power to influence or even, it might be claimed, to anticipate these decisions. She does not have full control over her educational imports.

Even before 1872, when attendance at school became compulsory, and when the administration of schools was, in the main, transferred to secular authorities, there was an extensive provision of schools, many of them being part of the parochial system established

Colin MacLean is the Editor of *The Times Educational Supplement* (Scotland).

by law almost two centuries earlier. A distinctive feature of Scottish education has been the fact that a very large majority of children of nearly all classes (in 1971 95·8 per cent of the school population) have gone and still go to public schools, which are fully public and should not be confused with the English 'public schools', which are really private. In 1971 there were 640,000 pupils (including 12,400 at nursery level) in Scottish public primaries and 314,000 in public secondaries. These schools, which with only a very few exceptions are co-educational, are under the management of 4 city (Aberdeen, Dundee, Glasgow, Edinburgh) and 31 county or joint county councils. (The proposed reform in local government would reduce the number of local authorities to eleven.) Within the present 35 councils are education committees which administer the schools by means of a professional directorate. There is one director of education in each of these education authorities: depending on the numbers of schools and colleges run by the authority, the director has a number of deputy and assistant directors, these usually having particular responsibility for sectors of administration, for instance staffing schools, and further education. Also in the service of the authorities, varying in number and type of responsibility, are specialist advisers, supervisors, or organizers who have oversight of such areas or subjects as primary or secondary education, music, modern languages, and physical education. Most of these advisers etc. are involved in curriculum development, as are many of Her Majesty's Inspectors.

Scotland does not have local inspectors: it has only HMIs, some of them inspectors with responsibility for areas or districts. These inspectors act for the Scottish Education Department, which is responsible to the Scottish Secretary of State for the general supervision of the Scottish system of education, with the exception of the eight Scottish universities. The universities depend largely upon grants from the public purse which are made to all the British universities through the University Grants Committee: the Secretary of the Scottish Education Department is an assessor to this committee.

The legislation for Scottish education is separate from England's. The money for the running of the schools and colleges managed by Scotland's education authorities comes partly from national taxes through central government grants and partly from local rates.

A second and small group of Scottish schools, providing for about 2·5 per cent of the Scottish school population, are grant-aided, that is they receive grant aid from central government funds. This grant-aid goes to some residential special schools and to orphanages, but the group mainly identified by the title grant aided, and in some respects comparable to the English direct grant schools, is made up of nearly 30 secondary schools, most with primary departments attached to them, a few with nursery departments. (In 1971 there were 8,700 pupils at primary level and 13,000 at secondary level in these grant-aided schools.) These schools, run by boards of governors, are diverse in character: some take boarders, some do not; most are single sex, but among the others there are several degrees of co-education; they are scattered unevenly over Scotland, the largest group in one area being in Edinburgh (where the total school population in 1972 was 82,670, of which 7,412 (9 per cent) were in grant-aided schools and 5,884 (7·1 per cent) in independent schools). Some grant-aided schools have academic traditions, some have not; they are all selective in varying degrees and in different ways; a few fit within or partly within the framework of local authority provision, but not in the way that direct grant schools do in England.

The grant received by the Scottish grant-aided schools is a limited percentage maintenance grant, and this percentage varies widely among the schools. The rest of the money required for the running of these schools comes from endowments and from fees. (Within the Scottish education authorities there have been some fee-paying schools: the number of these schools has fallen in recent years, especially under pressure from Labour governments, local and national. Such schools have recently existed only in Edinburgh and Glasgow and their future in both cities is most uncertain.)

A few of the Scottish grant-aided schools have strong associations with—but by no means a monopoly of—what many people would say is one of Scotland's educational traditions, that of the academically able child from the poor home being encouraged by school and parent to apply himself earnestly to his education and to continue it beyond the statutory leaving age. Some of these schools still do this by means of bursaries or foundations. But since the Second World War, as the standard of local authority provision has improved, as the idea of comprehensive education has become established, and as the fees for grant-aided schools have risen (at the same time as the demand for places in many of the schools has increased), the grant-aided schools have been increasingly identified, for instance in local and national political debate, with privilege and selectivity—this word being used in its highly pejorative sense.

A small number of Scottish children (17,500 in 1971, some 1·7 per cent of the school population) go to fully independent schools which have no support from public funds. A few of these private schools, such as Edinburgh and Glasgow Academies, Fettes College (these three for boys only), Gordonstoun (now becoming co-educational), St Leonard's, in St Andrews, and St George's, in Edinburgh (both for girls), combine good academic standards with considerable social status, drawing their pupils almost exclusively from families of high income in Scotland and beyond. Such schools, however, stand somewhat apart from the rest of the Scottish education system, to the extent that some prepare pupils for English rather than for Scottish examinations; that in consequence they follow the English rather than the Scottish curricular pattern; and that some give more thought to entering pupils for Oxford and Cambridge rather than for Scottish universities. Whereas the comparable 'public' schools in England have been said to feed pupils to, and to hold some monopoly of entry to, many of the top places in English public life, these Scottish independent schools cannot be said to have played a role in any sense equivalent for Scotland. It should be noted that Scottish fee-paying schools are not the only schools which provide for boarders. Several authorities, rural and highland, provide hostels for secondary pupils (over 2,000 in 1971) who, because of the distances involved, must leave home to attend school. The hostels recently built in some areas offer living conditions more luxurious than are available to some pupils at expensive independent schools.

No sector of Scottish education, either at school or university level, could be said to have evolved a tradition of producing men to go and represent Scotland in parliament. This is partly why Scotland today has so few members of parliament who are particularly well informed about or preoccupied with the subject of education: this may in turn be partly why Scottish education is, as is generally claimed, run so much by civil servants in the SED. Scottish education has over the years come to accept a great degree of centralization, not least because the Scottish educational system has in any case been so unified, and also because it is a fairly convenient size for running as a national or regional unit.

Till recently Scottish education has been markedly unified in its teacher training. There has been a firm insistence upon the training itself: this has been provided for both primary and secondary teachers in colleges of education, of which Scotland has ten. The secondary teachers have normally attended the college for a year after they have taken a university degree or other comparable qualification (for instance in music or technical subjects), the primary teacher either doing the same or taking a three-year college diploma course. Scottish teacher associations have for some decades said that the objective must be an all-graduate profession. (In November 1971 at Scottish colleges of education 8,000 non-graduate students and 330 graduates were preparing for the primary diploma; 2,200 graduates and 1,800 non-graduates were preparing for the secondary diploma.)

Greater diversity in teacher training has been introduced in recent years to Scotland by two different types of degree course. Four-year BEd degree courses are being run jointly by colleges and universities. (In November 1971 there were 710 students in the first- and second-year stages of the BEd course; 80 in third- and fourth-year stages for primary qualifications, 310 in third- and fourth-year stages for secondary qualifications.) Other colleges are to run BEd courses approved by the Council for National Academic Awards. Also at Stirling University, where education is a subject studied at undergraduate level, teacher training may be combined with study for ordinary and honours degree courses.

While this new diversity in teacher training has been developed, the prospect of greater professional unity has been made possible through the setting up in 1966 of the General Teaching Council for Scotland. This council includes representatives of teachers (who are directly elected by teachers and who hold a majority of places), education authorities, post-school education, the churches and nominees of the Secretary of State: it makes proposals to the Secretary of State on standards of training for and entry to teaching in Scotland. Such entry was jealously guarded even before the council's formation. All Scottish teachers in local authority and grant-aided schools now have to be registered with the council, which has powers of discipline, including removal of a teacher's name from its register. The probationary system has been revised by the council: now headteachers in schools have oversight of new entrants to the profession and have the responsibility of reporting to the council on probationers' ability as teachers.

Another factor contributing to the unity of Scottish school education is its examination system, which used to be administered by the SED. Since 1965 the Scottish Certificate of Education Examination Board has been responsible for conducting examinations at two levels, the Ordinary Grade, which may be taken in the fourth secondary year or later, and the Higher Grade, which may be taken in the fifth year or later. Higher is awarded with A, B or C ranking: some pupils, especially those wishing to improve their prospects of university entry, resit the Higher in order to upgrade the ranking. In the sixth year, pupils may take a Certificate of Sixth Year Studies, also administered by the SCEEB: the original intention was that this should not become a required or even a recognized qualification for university entrance, but there are now conflicting views on this.

The Scottish universities no longer administer a preliminary examination of their own, and apart from those few schools (mostly independent) which enter pupils for one or other of the English 'O' and 'A' Level examinations, virtually all Scottish secondary schools today prepare pupils for the SCE.

Entry from school to university in Scotland is now usually at the end of this sixth secondary year, though a number of pupils still enter from the fifth. In Scottish schools there are six secondary years and seven primary, pupils normally beginning in P1 at the age of five and transferring from P7 to S1 at the age of 12. This means a slightly later move to secondary school than in England and a slightly earlier one to university.

Scotland's universities do not come directly under SED control, but the SED's control over most of school education and over all the rest of post-school education does mean that the SED can do much to determine the developing pattern of higher education in Scotland, quite apart from the fact that the SED is represented on the British University Grants Committee and that the SED (not the local authorities, as in England) administer all grants for Scottish university students.

Though there is something unmistakably Scottish about all of Scotland's eight universities, to some extent they all resist nationalist definition, and some university men in Scotland, whose loyalties to the Scottish pattern of school and university education have never been questioned, would offer strong resistance to the idea, for instance, of a separate UGC for Scotland: they would argue that, as things are, Scottish universities have the best of several worlds, and that the idea of their working together as a well-knit separate Scots team is somewhat irrelevant for in many ways and at many levels they have, and would wish to develop, strong links with universities outside Scotland.

There was a great degree of uniformity in Scottish universities so long as there were only the four ancient ones, St Andrews, Glasgow, Aberdeen and Edinburgh, and so long as their students came predominantly from Scotland (many of them still living at home while students). These universities educated virtually all of Scotland's doctors, lawyers, church ministers, and teachers. In their arts and science faculties students have for much of the past century worked towards either ordinary degrees (requiring a minimum of three years' study) or honours degrees (requiring four). A large number of the graduates have ordinary degrees, but for some years the ordinary degree has suffered a loss of prestige, while the honours courses have drawn most of the students who showed early signs of promise in particular subjects and who in some cases did not wish to tackle the broad ordinary course. This tendency has been thought to signify a drift towards the English system.

Recently the Scottish educational system, which used to require some width of study even from many of its specializing honours students, has won favourable mention from English commentators (Dainton for instance), but it is not clear how the arguments on width and depth will be resolved in Scotland. Much will depend on how the schools and universities work together and also on the extent to which and the way in which Scottish universities are affected by the influx of students from outside Scotland. Scotland now has eight universities. In October 1971 the full-time student population of the eight Scottish universities was about 38,000, nearly 6,800 (17·1 per cent) being from the rest of the UK, 2,500 (5·6) being from overseas. (In 1971–2 Aberdeen had 4,900 students, Dundee 2,700, Edinburgh 9,300, Glasgow 8,100, Heriot-Watt 2,200, St Andrews 2,700, Stirling 1,700, Strathclyde 5,600.) The number of these students whose homes were outside Scotland was over 9,000; the number of Scots students attending higher education establishments in England and Wales was about 2,500, and elsewhere about 100.

Though these eight universities have no long-established practice of providing student accommodation (except in the past fifty years at St Andrews) they are now providing many places in residences and student houses. Of the four ancient universities only Edinburgh and St Andrews before the past decade took many English students. Now in the eight there is a great variety of patterns of intake: in October 1971 Glasgow having compared with 7,200 Scots, 469 from the rest of the UK and 300 from overseas; Dundee having 1,213 Scots, 1,356 from the rest of the UK, and 130 from overseas. Because of the greater influx of students from outside Scotland, but also and even more because of the many changing demands upon, and fashions in, higher education today, there is great diversity of style among and within the eight universities.

At its best the Scottish university system has provided that liberal or liberating quality in education resulting from submission to a variety of disciplines, some subjects being obviously less to the student's liking than others. The strong ordinary degree course constituted a kind of comprehensive insurance policy and was therefore essentially different from the course chosen by the student who says he knows what he will both like and (for purposes of future employment and enrichment) need—this student may simply be doing what comes easily. The Scottish tradition at all levels has been tougher than that, often seeming to say that it was being short-term cruel to be long-term kind—an argument that is open to varying degrees of both

misrepresentation and self-deception. It is often easier for a university to build width on a comparatively narrow but strong school foundation. The school which proudly lets its pupils choose freely from a wide range of subjects may thereby be limiting the width of their university course unless the university is in turn prepared to increase the number of subjects it teaches at a basic or elementary level: the school with this policy may in some circumstances be limiting the pupil's prospects of entry to a university.

But there are other centres of post-school education to which pupils can proceed. One group are called Central Institutions. Ten of these are financed directly by the Secretary of State for Scotland, and three agricultural colleges are financed by the Department of Agriculture and Fisheries for Scotland. These Central Institutions offer a variety of courses, many leading to qualifications of degree level. In October 1971 there were 10,000 students at Central Institutions. These centres include colleges of technology, art, domestic science, one college of textiles, one nautical college and one academy of music and drama. At two of the institutions (in Aberdeen and Dundee) several areas of specialism are covered, so Scotland has a few near equivalents of England's polytechnics. There are also, for instance, in Edinburgh and Glasgow, polytechnics of a kind within the further education sector, which are run by local authorities. In recent years many further education colleges (some with a technical, others with a commercial bias) have been built in Scotland. Some of their courses cater for early leavers from the schools: the schools and further education colleges have some overlap in course content (for instance, many further education colleges prepare students for SCE examinations), but the colleges are essentially concerned with the provision of vocational education. In October 1971 15,600 full-time and 119,800 part-time students were taking vocational courses at Scottish further education colleges. (Also these colleges along with other agencies of adult education, contributed to the education—for recreational, cultural and leisure-time purposes—of over 164,000 adults.)

As the figures make clear, a large number of Scots pupils go from school to colleges of education, central institutions and further education colleges, but few complaints are heard about the school curriculum being dominated or determined by college attitudes and requirements. Such complaints have been common about the universities, which even now absorb a comparatively small proportion of the pupil output from schools—though this proportion has been higher in Scotland than in England. There is also strong feeling among some teachers against the idea of the pattern of school education being determined by the SCE examinations which the pupils may sit or, for that matter, by examinations of any kind. Much of this style of educational thinking has resulted from, or coincided with, the new ideologies of comprehensive education. To tackle these and other kindred problems the Consultative Committee on the Curriculum was

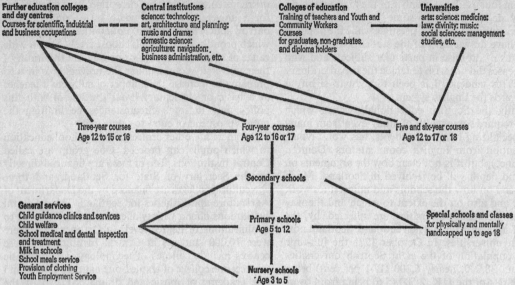

Figure 2.1   The Scottish educational system

set up by the Secretary of State for Scotland in 1965. Under the committee's aegis a series of reports have been issued, for instance on computers in schools, science education, and organization of courses leading to the SCE (this advocated that pupils working for examinations be assured of an appreciable proportion of school time for 'minority subjects', which would not be studied primarily for examination purposes).

The insistence that university entrance should not determine the pattern of secondary education has had a parallel in the argument that the pattern of secondary education should not determine that of primary. This argument has been made more meaningful, perhaps indeed it has been made possible, by the ending or relaxing of tests for transfer from primary to secondary: this change has been closely linked to the introduction of comprehensive education.

In 1965 a memorandum, 'Primary Education in Scotland', prepared by a committee representing schoolteachers, college staff and the inspectorate, advocated what may loosely be described as 'new methods' in primary education, the main adjustment recommended being—to use the idealistic jargon of the day—from a teacher-centred, formal-classroom approach to techniques which emphasize those relationships between teacher and class, especially between teacher and pupil, from which interested and pleasurable learning on the pupil's part can grow. Though the memorandum has had widespread effect, much of it beneficial, there has been undeniable resistance to it among teachers and indeed among parents and the public. Such resistance cannot be measured or defined, but one may claim that in Scotland it has had strength of a peculiarly Scottish kind; also that this resistance has had something in common with the marked resistance in Scotland to the raising of the school-leaving

age. Scots may have believed that education should be available to all, that for instance all should be drilled as thoroughly as possible in the three Rs, and that those who seemed likely to benefit from what is provided should be given every encouragement. But, one may argue, many Scots have been reluctant to believe that education could be expected to offer continuing benefits, much less pleasure, to all: education, they would say, is essentially a tough process: those administering it have an inevitably tough job; those subject to it must accept its toughness, but when after some years they show little sign of benefiting from its continuance, then they should be released from the ordeal. This attitude, which tends to set store by proven experience may be seen as merciful, or as down-to-earth and economic: clearly it offers some degree of resistance to experiment and innovation.

Part of the toughness of the Scottish school has been its corporal punishment, effected with the aid of a leather belt, administered to the pupil's hand. An official committee recently proposed a code on corporal punishment but it did not say how the code was to be enforced, nor did it venture to estimate how much corporal punishment is either needed or used in Scottish schools. Scots teachers are not yet required to keep punishment registers.

One distinctive feature of Scottish education has recently attracted much attention because of the fear that it is not simply recognizing but contributing to a division within the Scottish community. With the Education Act of 1872 the Church of Scotland and the Free Church of Scotland handed over most of their schools to the new state system of education, but the Roman Catholics remained outside, wishing to preserve their separate denominational identity. Then the Education Act of 1918 gave the Roman Catholics the guarantee that their denominational identity could be preserved within the state system. Now in several areas of Scotland, especially where there is a large Roman Catholic population, the local education committees manage and provide the entire financial support for Roman Catholic schools (over 400 in 1971) which nevertheless remain denominational and clearly separate. In the other schools run by local councils religious observances are held and instruction in religion is given (predominantly along Presbyterian or Protestant lines: the Presbyterian Church of Scotland is the established church in Scotland). Parents may withdraw their children from such observance or instruction; indeed the law permits a neighbourhood to elect for non-observance.

Religious instruction, however, is not—like other subjects in the school curriculum—subject to the inspection or approval of HMIs and the SCE Examination Board do not provide examinations in religious education at either 'O' or 'H' grade. A committee was appointed in 1968 by the Secretary of State for Scotland to review 'the current practice of Scottish schools (other than RC schools) with regard to moral and religious education and to make recommendations for its improvement'. The committee's report, published in March 1972, showed that religious education suffered considerable neglect and lack of status in the schools: no bold or clear recommendations to remedy this situation were made by the report. Part of the committee's difficulty lay in the fact that it was asked to consider moral as well as religious education.

Moral education had not hitherto been officially within the vocabulary of Scottish education, and in the report it was not given precise definition. However, the general concept of moral education has recently been much under discussion—though never satisfactorily defined or explored—in thinking about guidance in Scottish schools. Many secondary teachers now have guidance duties, and there are promoted posts in guidance, which incorporates careers, curriculum and personal help for the pupils. The need for such guidance has been argued partly because of the growing size and, therefore, it is feared, impersonality of secondary schools: but it has also been claimed that the new guidance is needed because of changes in society and the family.

In this attempt to show personal concern for the pupils we may see yet another aspect of the general ideology of comprehensive education. There was indeed a ruthless and rigid impersonality in the Scot-

tish system before comprehensive reorganization was introduced: many pupils, especially in the urban areas, had been streamed on transfer from primary schools into junior and senior secondary schools.

It will be apparent from much of the above—in relation, for instance, to fee-paying schools, to religious divisions and to comprehensive education—that in recent years Scottish education has at various points been involved in those social, educational, economic and ethical problems associated with the separation (or, put more emotionally, segregation) of different groups. The problem is to determine whether and how much this separation indicates that the wishes, needs and capabilities of individuals and groups are being carefully and tolerantly catered for, or on the other hand that people are by this distinctive treatment being labelled and therefore unfairly limited for life—this limitation meaning, in some cases, relegation to underprivilege, in others the assurance of advantage.

The problem is given edge and often irony by the fact that Scots themselves as a nation have difficulty in determining the nature of the disadvantage they may be enduring or the advantage they may be enjoying by maintaining a distinctive and to some extent separate system. There was a time when Gaelic was not thought a fit subject for study in Scottish schools or universities: it was not even tolerated as a language to be spoken in schools by Gaelic-speaking pupils. That old repressive attitude has gone, though too late for there to be much hope of major restoration of the language even in those areas where it survived longest. It is only recently too that much attention has been paid to the study, at either school or university level, of Scottish literature, language and history. All three have gained considerably in status in both schools and universities in the past two decades, but it is too early yet to say how the expansion may be expected to continue and with what effect.

The entry of Britain into the EEC may in a variety of ways stimulate a new self-assertion among Scots, but as with the Gaelic tongue the change in attitude may come too late. Because today Scotland cannot easily decide things for herself and develop them in distinctive ways, she may find that in extending the attention given to her literature, language and history she is creating a puzzling paradox for pupils and students, by laying increasing emphasis on the fact that Scotland used to be different, is becoming less different, and cannot expect to reverse the process.

3 Education in Wales

Ned Thomas

When we speak about the structure of Welsh education and the tensions within that structure, we are not dealing with a system brought into being by a Welsh nation-state, as we might be in other countries, nor even, as in Scotland, with a strong indigenous tradition going back to a time of political independence. Education Acts have dealt with 'England and Wales' as one unit, with marginal adjustments made after the main decisions have been taken.

Even when Welshmen have set up their own institutions, these have often been copies of an English prototype. Thus the University of Wales, set up by the Nonconformist leadership in 1872, is only marginally distinguishable in college organization from nineteenth-century English foundations.

The main tension in Welsh education, and increasingly so since the Second World War, has been between the norms of the 'received' system, and various kinds of pressure or protest in the name of a distinctive Welsh reality not felt to be adequately reflected in the system. The landmarks in development have been the setting up of specifically Welsh bodies, but the initiative for this has come from many quarters. Central government officials in Wales have sometimes shown more imagination than local authorities, but these have also provided some important initiatives. And sometimes it has been left to voluntary bodies to pioneer Welsh institutions which have later been adopted by the state system.

This chapter is by its nature concerned with specifically Welsh questions, but it is important at the outset to make one balancing point very strongly. Because of the strong connection with England, Welshmen have taken part in the struggles within the British education system. In government and parliament, as administrators, teachers, union leaders, and in the polling booth, Welsh people have usually thrown their weight for the extension of education to all, and for a generous attitude to public expenditure in this field.

In many of the ways in which local authorities might be judged on a UK basis, the great majority of Welsh education authorities perform exceedingly well: high and generous expenditure, a high proportion of young people staying on at school and going on to higher education. Cardiganshire, where average income is half the average UK *per capita* income, sends a higher proportion into higher education than any local authority in England or Wales. In the days before comprehensive schools were introduced, Wales had a very high proportion of children in grammar schools,

Ned Thomas is at the University College of Wales, Aberystwyth.

which no doubt had a bearing on the numbers staying on and going into higher education. It is probably less true in Wales that there is a great pool of talent hitherto untapped by a structurally undemocratic school system. Parental support for the school is good not only among the middle classes. Nor will it be forgotten that the first local education authority of all in England and Wales to establish a fully comprehensive school system was Anglesey.*

Yet this very example illustrates how easy it is to misinterpret Welsh radicalism in education as in other fields. Anglesey's commitment to comprehensive education was not a particularly ideological one. The great battles were fought, and the arguments developed, elsewhere, in London or Coventry. In Wales comprehensive schools have mostly fitted without much opposition into the pattern of a more socially homogeneous society which our history has produced; indeed, in rural Wales many secondary schools were *de facto* comprehensives before the term was heard of. Welshmen would not have been educational or political radicals on the British scene were it not that they came from a distinctive society with its own internal tensions, too complex to be assimilated to an abstract radicalism.

The core of the separate Welsh identity, in the absence of political and most other kinds of institution (at least until recently) has been the Welsh language. Up to the turn of the century it was spoken by a majority of the population, and today, although the proportion has fallen to 26 per cent or some 650,000 people within Wales (there may be a further 100,000 Welsh-speakers outside), it is still the language of everyday life for a large number, even a majority of people, over a large geographical area, while there are strong enclaves of Welsh-speakers in the more populated areas of south-east Wales. For many Welshmen who do not speak Welsh the language is still an important factor in their background and a badge of nationhood. Many of those who remember Welsh in their families strongly regret its loss.

For the Welsh-speaker the language is the form his consciousness of life takes; it records all that the community has done and created and suffered down the centuries. For the Welshman educated in his culture the language gives access to the fine early

---

* It is worth noting that by 1954 on average grammar school places were allotted by English authorities to some 20 per cent of the age-group. In Wales the figure was nearer 33 per cent. In Nottinghamshire and Northumberland 14 per cent of the age-group were allotted grammar school places. In Merioneth they went to 60 per cent.

poetry of the dark ages that followed the Roman withdrawal, the medieval court poetry, the folk, religious and mystical literature of succeeding centuries and the remarkable twentieth-century renaissance of poetry and drama. The language is itself a creation—the co-operative effort of ordinary Welsh people down the centuries has gone to make it—and while this is true of every language, it is a truth more immediately understood by a small language-group which feels threatened.

The first blow against Welsh was struck by the Act of Union of 1536 which proclaimed its intention 'to utterly extirp' the 'divers sinister usages' which constitute Welsh. From that time Welsh lost its official status and could not be used in the courts nor in dealings with public authority. The lines of patronage now ran to London, and inevitably the Welsh language came to be regarded as socially inferior. Although such grammar school education as existed in Wales in this period was, of course, in Latin, the gentry, who might proceed to Oxford or Cambridge, were quickly socialized so that they came to link their status and interest to those of their richer counterparts in England. The Anglican Church, which had English as its language, was the test of political loyalty for the gentry, and the common parishioners probably understood less of the service than they had of the Roman Catholic service in Latin.

It was not surprising that in these circumstances the educated tradition in Welsh should have worn very thin, while for the majority of people education in English was what one would expect in a poor agricultural area, with the added aggravation of the two-language situation. In 1845 a report published by the National Schools Society showed adults and children in Wales attending occasional schools for short periods, often learning by rote to read passages of English which they might not understand at all. To an outsider the Welsh language appeared a handicap. One of the Commissioners who prepared this report wrote:

Whether in the country or among the furnaces, the Welsh element is never found at the top of the social scale, nor in its own body does it exhibit much variety of gradation. In the country, the farmers are very small holders, in intelligence and capital nowise distinguishable from labourers. In the works, the Welsh workman never finds his way into the office. He never becomes either clerk or agent.

The conclusion drawn by a number of humane Englishmen from this was that Welsh people should be given the opportunity of abandoning Welsh and rising through the medium of English to the social surface. Matthew Arnold, poet, school inspector and author of a book on Celtic literature, could write: 'It must always be the desire of the government to render its dominions as far as possible, homogeneous. Sooner or later the differences of language between England and Wales will probably be effaced ... an

event which is socially and politically so desirable.' Although there was a strong sentimental attachment to the language in nineteenth-century Wales, which prevented Welshmen from agreeing with Arnold explicitly, the majority did not *act* as if they held an opposite view. When in 1870 the state intervened to institute universal elementary education, the great majority of articulate Welshmen accepted that this naturally meant education through the medium of English.

But meanwhile a kind of education in Welsh had been established which was, and remains, distinctive. The Nonconformist sects, and particularly the Calvinistic Methodists, who became such a force in Wales, were from the start committed to the language because of the personal emphasis in their presentation of Christianity. A man should be able to read his Bible, meditate it in his heart, and speak naturally about his religious experience in the *Seiat* or 'Society of Experience'. The Sunday School was set up to teach young and old alike to read and discuss in Welsh, and to this day there are adult as well as children's classes in the Welsh Sunday School. Although the overtones of pietism and respectability which later crept in belong to the Welsh world's *Ysgol Sul* as to the English 'Sunday School', it nevertheless stands in the minds of those with an experience of it as a free and democratic place, one of the few institutions we have been able to call our own, and earns a special loyalty, significantly connected with the language in the hymn:

Am yr Ysgol rad Sabothol
   Clos, clod i Dduw!
Ei buddioldeb sydd anrhaethol;
   Clod, clod i Dduw!
Ynddi cawn yr addysg gorau,
Addysg berffaith Llyfr y llyfrau
Am gael hwn yn iaith ein mamau,
   Clod, clod i Dduw!
(For the free Sunday School, praise be to God.
For its incomparable usefulness, praise be to God.
There we have the best of educations, the perfect
learning of the best of books, for having this in
the language of our mothers, Praise be to God.)

In the report of 1845 quoted earlier one of the commissioners wrote:

These Sunday Schools have been almost the sole, they are still the main and most congenial, centres of education. Through their agency the younger portion of the adult labouring classes in Wales can generally read, or are in the course of learning to read, the Scriptures in their mother tongue. A fifth of the entire population is returned as attending these schools.

Thus literacy in Welsh must have been quite well established by 1870, something that can also be reasonably deduced by the quantity of periodical literature, usually of a religious kind. The skills of the Welsh in public speaking, reading music and in literary composition, though connecting with earlier traditions, must also be largely ascribed to the training given in musical and literary societies attached to the chapels.

This whole area of activity can be interestingly regarded as a kind of counter-culture. What people learnt was to be for the good of their souls or for the immediate instruction and entertainment of the local community. It was not, and being in Welsh, *could* not be geared to getting on, rising socially, becoming richer. Herein, in retrospect, lies its great attraction, but also, as it turned out, its weakness.

With the establishment of universal state education came the development of the railways communicating with England, the English newspapers now became intelligible, and the general integration of Wales into England accelerated. Welsh people could and did become more socially and geographically mobile within Britain, escaping the hardship of life in Wales, where the economy was largely based on poor agriculture or else on heavy or extractive industries. The drives of Nonconformity towards self-denial and self-discipline became easily transposed, with the decline of the movement's early fire, into an ethic of hard work, planning ahead, prudence in the short term and a passion for self-advancement in the long term.

But this movement in turn produced strains and left scars which are still an important part of the present situation. Teachers used, and parents acquiesced in the use of, the notorious 'Welsh Not' so that their children might the sooner acquire English. The 'Not' was a stick or board hung round the neck of a child heard speaking Welsh. The child was allowed to pass it to someone else heard speaking the language, and at the end of the day whoever was in possession was punished. References to the 'Not' can be found throughout the nineteenth century, and almost exact parallels existed in Brittany and Provence.

Although this barbarity disappeared about the turn of the century, the attitude towards Welsh in the schools which it expressed has survived much longer and is not wholly dead even now. Welsh became a subject on the curriculum in secondary schools but until recently was scarcely ever a medium of instruction beyond primary level, though teachers and taught might all speak Welsh at home. The secondary school in Welsh-speaking areas was therefore, and to a certain extent remains, an island of Englishness, out of touch with the local community and its life. That this was anti-educational was realized early on by the Welsh inspectorate who have given every encouragement to the education of Welsh-speaking children through their own language. But progress has been slow because of the inferiority felt by older Welsh-speakers towards the language (the result of their own education) and because teachers in the same generations were never taught how to teach in Welsh.

These matters are so contemporary and political, and within so many people's personal experience, that they can form the subject of one of Dafydd Iwan's more popular satirical pop-songs, *The School Song*: here, every morning, the boy's mother calls him to breakfast in Welsh, it is Welsh he speaks to his first girl-friend when he meets her in the woods, and it is Welsh that Christ seems to speak when he reads the Bible in his Sunday School, but at School everything is in English except the occasional lesson of Welsh, which is called by its English name on the school timetable.

It is from this depreciation through the school system of a child's personality and family background that one strain in Welsh protest and political nationalism derives. Again there are interesting foreign parallels: it was the inferior treatment of Arabic and therefore of Arabic speakers in Algeria that first brought Algerian nationalists such as Belkacem Krim and Ferhat Abbas into conflict with the French authorities.

And there is a different sort of parallel in the English-speaking world and in England. The Northern school child taught to read all poetry with a 'good' accent—and never told that Wordsworth spoke with a Cumberland accent not so unlike his own; the child immured in the classroom learning lists of the kings and queens of England but never looking at the history of his own locality; the West Indian boy put into a school blazer under the scorching sun and made to recite 'Daffodils'—flowers that he has never seen; all these are part of the same pattern of alienation through education from the environment and the community. The presence of a separate language merely makes the gap more obvious.

English-speaking Welsh people are very much a part of this pattern. Lacking the Welsh language they lack access in many ways to the Welsh tradition, but there is nevertheless (and in some areas more than others) a strong difference of background that makes it difficult for people to enter wholly into English society; and the Welsh accent in English tends to be regarded as comic. In English-speaking areas too education has tended, particularly in the grammar schools, to be an exercise in taking people away from their roots. Thus Glyn Jones, the Anglo-Welsh writer, can say of his time at Merthyr Tydfil Grammar School in the second decade of this century:

> The establishment might have been in the middle of the Broads or up on the top of the Pennines for all the contact it had with the rich life of the community surrounding it. We had no school *eisteddfod*, we heard nothing of the turbulent industrial history of the town itself, nothing of its Welsh literary associations, nothing of its religious history.

The strains and alienations of the grammar school child who moves between two different worlds of values as he comes and goes between a working-class home and school are phenomena well chronicled in the English fifties. They occurred earlier in Wales because of the earlier increase in the numbers going on to higher education, and in a special and aggravated form where there was a different language at home. In what follows I am concerned with changes in the educational structure that have narrowed this gap. These changes however have their inner psychological dynamic. Welsh radicalism and educational radicalism —things that are part of the mythology and reputation of the Welsh—certainly contained a noble element of self-sacrifice, belief in self-development, and honour for true learning. But it was also subtly connected with the determination of a disadvantaged group to win for itself the same education, culture and way of life as the English middle classes, without stopping to ask whether this was really possible for them, or desirable ultimately. It is against this other face of radicalism that a reaction in favour of community values is now taking place.

But everything that we have put under the heading 'alienation' undoubtedly also has an institutional aspect. It can be argued that in legislation for 'England and Wales' the special needs of a bilingual country are inevitably treated as marginal, and that no number of advisory committees or Welsh sub-committees or even the administrative devolution of school and further education to the Welsh Department of Education in Cardiff (which has recently come about), can be a substitute for a community setting its own priorities through its elected representatives. I take this view, but must also admit that considerable advance has proved possible within the present overall framework.

The setting up of a Welsh Department of the Board of Education in 1907 was important because it meant that henceforward a number of people would discuss education with Wales as the unit of their concern. Reports and booklets were produced and the Welsh inspectorate was able to put local authorities in touch with each other's experience.

It was not until 1949 that the Welsh Joint Education Committee was set up, a body that has no comparable equivalent in England. It operates in any field it thinks fit, initiating research, agreeing on the location and financing of joint projects and institutions, commissioning textbooks, and acting as an examining board. It is a characteristically Welsh exercise in co-operation and democracy, with some of the slowness to move that is perhaps inseparable from this kind of co-operation. But again its importance is that it looks on Wales as the unit and focuses attention on our peculiar problems and needs.

1940 saw the establishment of UCAC (the Welsh initials of the National Union of Welsh Teachers). Though relatively small, the union is strong in certain Welsh-speaking areas such as Meirionydd and includes in its ranks some of the most influential Welsh teachers and headmasters. It permits dual membership with the British unions but is nevertheless felt by these to be a threat to their membership. It has gained representation on many of the advisory committees in Welsh education, submits evidence and prepares reports, but has perhaps been quite as influential by forcing the larger

unions, in self-defence, to pay more attention to Welsh matters and strengthen their Welsh sub-committees.

Quite as important in this emergent pattern as the strictly educational institutions are BBC Wales' radio and television services, and the ITV company's programmes, and also the Welsh Arts Council, now separate from the Arts Council of Great Britain. The Welsh Arts Council, for example, supports with grants a 'Writers in Schools' programme, which for the first time lets children talk to Welsh writers in both languages. Radio and television bring a certain amount of classic and contemporary Welsh writing, and also discussion of Welsh issues, to the public. If one is looking at education as a total process, then one must also mention the establishment of the Welsh National Opera, the two Welsh Theatre Companies (one in each language) and the Welsh Books Council which has vastly improved the quality and availability, and increased the numbers of books published in Wales, including school and children's books. With the same total view those who argue for a Welsh-language television channel point out that an estimated annual expenditure of £4m. is less than many local education authority budgets even in Wales, while the impact of television on children may well equal that of their schooling.

In the voluntary field one of the most important events was the founding of *Urdd Gobaith Cymru*, the Welsh youth movement, in 1922. This has branches in schools, villages and towns throughout Wales and a membership totalling 50,000. As well as local activities it runs a national youth *eisteddfod*, holiday camps by the sea and in the mountains, and in the pre-war years the *Urdd* pioneered youth holiday cruises. It now produces half a dozen magazines in Welsh, some for Welsh-learners specifically, and these are widely used in the schools. Perhaps its greatest importance, however, has been to bring young people from different parts of Wales together, thus creating a sense of shared experience in a Welsh environment that stays with them afterwards.

It was on the *Urdd* premises at Aberystwyth that the first Welsh primary school—a private one—was opened with seven pupils in 1939. This was the beginning of one of the most remarkable movements in Welsh, and perhaps British, educational history. In 1947 Llanelli opened the first local authority primary school, and was soon followed by Flintshire and Glamorgan, counties where Welsh primary schools are now common. It is also in these two counties that the first four bilingual secondary schools have been established. (A bilingual secondary school can be defined as one where the majority of subjects are taught through the medium of Welsh to all children, a number of other, usually scientific, subjects, being taught through English, but the whole social life of the school being in Welsh.)

The counties that set up these schools, soon to be followed by others, are overwhelmingly English-speaking, and this fact is interesting. English-speaking parents often choose to send their children to Welsh nursery, primary and secondary schools, while English-speaking councillors made the decisions which brought these schools out of the voluntary into the state system. So far bilingual secondary schools have turned out to be very good schools in other respects as well, and Wales is a place to which people come to study bilingualism in education. There is a modern and European air about the schools and one is reminded that to be an individual or a school or a nation with more than one language is not an uncommon phenomenon outside Britain.

In the Welsh-speaking areas change comes more slowly. The spread of population of rural areas makes it more difficult to offer parents a choice between bilingual and English-medium schools, and there is still a lot of resistance to the notion that Welsh-speaking children should have their education in Welsh, let alone that everyone in Wales might hope in the next generation to be bilingual.

The poor level of teaching Welsh as a foreign language has undoubtedly contributed to this resistance, but a National Language Unit has been established at Pontypridd and is turning out properly researched and structured audio-visual materials. Welsh has, however, the strong advantage of a nearly-phonetic spelling which allows children to learn to read very quickly.

Research into bilingualism, and special pilot projects, have shown people that bilingualism can help general performance and the acquisition of a third language, but research has also shown that parental attitudes are all-important in the acquisition of a second language within Wales.

A set of partially-related issues centres on the University of Wales. This institution was felt to belong to the people of Wales in the special sense that it was established by public subscription and door-to-door collection. It has also had a higher proportion than in English universities of students from the manual working-class. But in structure, apart from the fact that it consists of six colleges (until recently, four) loosely related within a federal system, it has been, as mentioned at the start of this essay, very like its English nineteenth-century counterparts. When it was established no one thought it necessary that any instruction should be offered through Welsh nor that the courses should have any particular relevance to Wales. Even in the departments of Welsh, lecturing was initially through English, but these departments soon developed a strong character of their own and in this century have employed people such as Sir John Morris-Jones, Saunders Lewis, D. Gwenallt Jones and R. Williams Parry, important writers and public figures beyond the confines of academic life. Other departments flourished under particular professors in a way that connected specifically with Welsh traditions; thus the establishment of a department of International Politics at Aberystwyth reflected the pacifist–internationalist strain in Welsh Nonconformist culture.

But almost any statement about the university has to be modified drastically in the light of what has happened in the years since 1955. University expansion, particularly following the Robbins Report, has meant that the various colleges of the university, instead of drawing some 80 per cent of their students from Wales, now draw 39 per cent, with 56 per cent coming from England and the remaining 5 per cent from abroad. While it is true that this imbalance is partly caused by the fact that so many Welsh students choose to go to English universities, it is also true that even if they did not and came to the University of Wales, they would still be far from taking up all the places that expansion has now created.

None of this is particularly worrying if the United Kingdom is taken as the unit, but if Wales is taken as the unit it does produce problems. Whether or not English-speaking Welshmen feel that the character of the colleges has changed, the Welsh-speaking student cannot help feeling this. From being present in the colleges in rather more than the proportion of the Welsh-speaking element to the whole Welsh community, Welsh-speaking students have moved to being a fraction of the total student body. This change is particularly noticeable at Bangor, where only 24 per cent of the student body come from Wales at all. Again the university college appears to be a foreign island in a strongly Welsh area.

Welsh-speaking students have reacted militantly and defensively. At Aberystwyth halls of residence for Welsh-speakers have been set up and there have been sit-ins against further expansion. But institutions have a growth-dynamic of their own, and moreover to resist expansion too easily comes to seem a negative policy of keeping people out of university education. More recently Welsh-speaking students have changed the object of their campaign, and now want to establish a Welsh-medium teaching college within one of the existing university colleges (probably Aberystwyth), having something like the relationship of an Oxbridge college to the university. This seems to be a logical and conflict-avoiding solution in a situation where the demand for Welsh-medium higher education will predictably increase with the rise of the bilingual secondary schools. Several university colleges have already made appointments to teach such subjects as French, philosophy and history through the medium of Welsh, and further funds have been earmarked.

The colleges of education can by today claim to be more representative of Wales than the university colleges. They have a more local catchment area, have adapted their syllabuses sooner to the Welsh environment, and are, through the schools, more directly in touch with the community. It is thanks to these colleges that young teachers have been arriving in the schools of Wales able to teach most subjects through Welsh, and with a knowledge of the Welsh background and of the communities in which they will work.

Behind all this discussion lies the general question: how far is education, and particularly university education, perhaps something universal and indivisible, above national and community needs; and how far is it something that starts from community needs and works out to the general? Does not the universalist view, like the community view, in fact reflect the notions of a particular community or class? And, beyond this, what *is* the unit of community, of *felt* community, and are the units different for different purposes, and how does one achieve a hierarchy of institutions that expresses people at different levels and gives their work and study relevance while also attaching them to the world-wide community of scholars?

The University of Wales, as mentioned, is a federal university, controlled ultimately, though colleges have extensive autonomy, by a large Council on which lay representatives of local authorities and other bodies predominate. This represents one kind of democracy in the university structure. But when this body comes into conflict with colleges in which non-Welsh people predominate among both staff and students, that same structure can also appear to be a denial of democracy. This is a real dilemma, and in the sixties strong moves were made, unsuccessfully, to defederalize the university.

But it can also be argued that the University of Wales has not taken full advantage of its federal structure to plan higher education on a rational basis. Expansion has been more or less at the whim of the individual colleges, yet as costs soar, particularly for science and technology departments, there is bound to be pressure towards forming centres of excellence in particular fields at particular universities, and the federal framework gives the University of Wales the perfect framework for doing this planning itself rather than having it done for it by the University Grants Committee.

And this brings us to the overall imbalance of higher education in Wales towards the arts. The roots of this lie very deep in national traditions, but one contributing factor was that same rush from the hardship of the Welsh nineteenth century to the security of the middle-class professions, particularly teaching. The immense over-production of teachers in Wales has meant the emigration of a high proportion of qualified Welshmen, and in the reaction against this we are now seeing for the first time in generations educated young Welsh people choosing to run bookshops, become accountants, start printing presses or craft shops or pubs, rather than follow the traditional paths of the Welsh teacher to Birmingham and London.

This chapter has turned in on a centre of activity that will not be familiar to most readers. They must be asked to believe that these tensions and arguments have for us, because of a different history, an excitement and importance such as that of, say, the comprehensive controversy in England. They fit, on the one hand, a pattern of psychological emergence for the people of Wales, and on the other, a pattern of institution building. But at the same time the questions that have arisen about the nature and definition of community, about relevance and alienation in education systems, are ones that are found far outside Wales and that are likely to be forced increasingly on everyone's attention.

---

4 Education in Northern Ireland

Margaret Sutherland

Administration

Since 1922 the educational system has been controlled by the Northern Ireland Ministry of Education. Before this, education in Ireland as a whole had been provided in voluntary schools with individual managers or management committees, and financial assistance from public funds had been received from the Commissioners of National Education (elementary schools), the Board of Intermediate Education (secondary schools), the Department of Agriculture and Technical Instruction (technical education): state supervision ensured simply that conditions for the payment of grants and elementary teachers' salaries were respected. In the Education Act of 1923 provision was made for eight local authorities which could appoint one or more education committees for their area; altogether eighteen committees were appointed. Since then local authorities have gradually become responsible for almost all the primary schools formerly managed by Protestants, for technical schools and colleges, and for a few grammar schools; they have provided many new primary schools and a large number of the newer type of secondary school, the secondary intermediate; they have also provided new technical colleges and some grammar schools. The structure of local authorities has also changed: in 1947 the number of education committees was reduced to eight—one for each local authority; by the 1972 Education and Libraries Act these are re-

Margaret Sutherland is Professor of Education at the University of Leeds.

placed by five area boards with responsibility for both educational services and library services within their areas, though the relationship between the local authority (the area board) and the Ministry seems likely to remain unchanged by the division into new administrative units.

In the fifty years of the Northern Ireland educational system there has thus been a tendency towards centralization as administration has passed from the original management committees for each school, or small group of schools, to local education authorities, whose numbers have been reduced from eighteen to eight to five. More central control has also come through educational expenditure: expenditure eligible for Ministry grants is subject to meeting Ministry conditions for approval. So far as the curriculum is concerned, the 11+ selection examinations conducted by the Ministry (1947–65) can be regarded as part of a centralizing trend; in secondary education, external examinations which were under Ministry control until very recently have been highly important especially since 1947 and have had a similarly standardizing effect. Visits by the Ministry's Inspectors have been frequent and, until fairly recently, of a formal kind, though now the Inspectorate in Northern Ireland, as elsewhere, has moved towards acting more as advisers or consultants. At the same time it must be noted that the local authorities have developed in confidence and importance since 1923; their grants to schools tend to standardize provision within their own areas and the establishment of links between them and maintained voluntary schools has newly added to their stature. The appointment of special advisers in individual school subjects by each local authority has encouraged distinctive developments within different authority areas. Thus the local authority contribution has made for some centralization within the local area while providing a counterbalance to centralization at Ministry level.

Dual system: finance

But to some extent there is a dual system of education in so far as Roman Catholic children at primary and secondary school level normally attend schools provided and managed by the Roman Catholic Church authorities; here parents and church have responsibilities for financing education. Yet support from public funds has always been given to voluntary schools and this public financial contribution has increased recently. Teachers' salaries in voluntary primary, special and secondary intermediate schools have been and are paid by the Ministry and LEAs; so are employers' contributions to superannuation and part of (or if the school is maintained, all) National Insurance contributions. In voluntary grammar schools a proportion of teachers' salaries, superannuation, National Insurance contributions is paid by the Ministry, which also gives a capitation grant based on the number of pupils in the school. Since 1947 Ministry grants of 65 per cent of capital costs for new building have been available; and local authorities have paid 65 per cent of approved expenditure in voluntary primary, intermediate and special schools. The system of 'four and two' committees introduced in the 1920s—i.e. school management committees having four representatives of the body providing the school and two representatives of the local authority— allowed full payment of running costs of such a school by the local authority and Ministry payment of 65 per cent equipment and external maintenance, but was viewed with some suspicion as a possible attempt to influence religious teaching in the schools and to acquire control over them. Few Roman Catholic primary schools took advantage of it. But in 1968 new provisions were made for 'maintained school' status in which voluntary primary and secondary intermediate and special schools accepting one third representation of local education authorities on their management committees receive 100 per cent maintenance and equipment costs from local education authorities and 80 per cent capital costs from the Ministry. Voluntary grammar schools accepting one third Ministry representatives on their boards of governors become eligible to receive 80 per cent capital costs (a provision of importance to voluntary schools of Protestant affiliation, as well as to Roman Catholic grammar schools). The maintained status offered by the 1968 Act has proved widely acceptable; by the end of 1971 382 out of 613 voluntary primary schools (62 per cent), 79 of 87 voluntary secondary intermediate schools (91 per cent) and 47 of 60 (Catholic

Financial aid to voluntary schools

Table 4.1A Voluntary primary, secondary intermediate, special nursery schools
(a) 'maintained' (one third LEA representatives on management committee)
(b) not maintained

	From LEA		From Ministry	
	(a)	(b)	(a)	(b)
Teachers' salaries			*100%	*100%
Employers' contributions to superannuation			*100%	*100%
Employers' contributions to national insurance			*100%	* 65%
Lighting, heating, cleaning, maintenance	100%	+65%		†(65)
Capital expenditure on premises			80%	65%
Equipment	100%			65%

† For non-maintained voluntary schools a distinction is made between internal and external maintenance: the LEA pays 65 per cent of internal maintenance, the Ministry pays 65 per cent of external maintenance.
* The Sixth Schedule of the 1947 Act listed certain 'specified items'. For these, expenditure, whether by Ministry or LEA in the first place, is pooled for Northern Ireland and an Exchequer contribution deducted; the Ministry pays 65 per cent of the remainder: from the remaining 35 per cent is deducted a Ministry of Development contribution; each LEA then pays a share of the remaining amount in proportion to the LEA's net annual valuation. Specified items include teachers' salaries (other than salaries of teachers in voluntary grammar schools), superannuation contributions and national insurance contributions.

Table *4.1B* Voluntary grammar schools

	From LEA	From Ministry		
	All voluntary grammar	*Group A (1/3)	Group A	Group B
	Tuition fees for qualified pupils			
Teachers' salaries	Two thirds of excess over £650 per teacher			
Superannuation (employers' contrib.)	50%	50%	50%	
National Insurance (employers' contrib.)	65%	65%	65%	
Capitation grant	Under age 15, £16.80: 15+, £21.50			
Capital expenditure on premises	80%	65%	—	
Equipment	80%	65%	65%	

*(1/3 i.e. having one-third Ministry representatives on Board of Governors.)

and Protestant) voluntary grammar schools (78 per cent) had taken up the offer. Schools remaining purely voluntary continue to receive the former amounts of assistance (see Table 1). There are only 8 entirely independent schools in Northern Ireland, having altogether some 600 pupils.

Dual system: curriculum

In Roman Catholic schools religious education is naturally in accordance with the teaching of their Church. Local authority ('county') schools are legally bound to provide for non-denominational religious instruction and collective worship. Parents have the right to withdraw their children from such religious observances. Teachers have the right to make a statutory declaration that from religious motives they do not wish to give such teaching or to participate in collective worship; they must then be excused from these activities without prejudice to their pay or professional condition. Local authorities must also grant to clergymen of denominations acceptable to the parents access to schools to teach religion, including denominational tenets, or to examine such teaching of religion.

Other differences may be found in the choice of 'foreign' languages taught or in the approach to history teaching. Irish is taught almost exclusively in Roman Catholic schools—though such teaching is not without problems in so far as Irish is not the home language and the choice between it and a foreign language more widely spoken in Europe is sometimes difficult; there are also some problems in finding textbooks to suit the region and the pupils' age level. In the Catholic schools there is usually more emphasis on teaching Irish legends and Irish history; the complaint is sometimes made that county schools and Protestant grammar schools tend to teach Irish history

mainly in the context of British history, from the English point of view. Again, there has been a problem of finding suitably unbiased textbooks but this problem has now been largely overcome. Other possible divergences lie in the choice of music (folk-songs) or literature to be studied in school; but in general such choices depend more on the attitudes of individual teachers than on school policies and cultural differences are more powerfully developed by factors in the home environments than by the curriculum of the schools.

Dual system: attempts to integrate

In spite of the separation of schools it should be recognized that some mainly Protestant schools do have some Roman Catholic pupils while a few Protestant pupils attend Roman Catholic schools; similarly there may be 'mixing' on school staffs. But such representation of the 'other' religion in a school tends to be in a small minority. Many teachers have been concerned about the separation of schools and efforts have been made—often with great success, though on a limited scale—to bring pupils of different religions together in extra-curricular activities such as conferences, school camps, community service.

Compulsory education: basic provisions

In most respects the school system resembles that of England though there has been also considerable Scottish influence in the schools and on the general system of education. Education is compulsory from the age of five to fifteen (five to sixteen from 1972 onwards). Some children enter school from the age of four, occasionally because parents want to see them well started towards selection for grammar school. The provision of nursery schools is small—only twenty-two, half of them in the Belfast area, though there are plans for increase here. At the other end of the age-range increasing numbers of pupils are remaining in full-time education after the minimum leaving age. The Youth Employment Service Board, an independent organization with eleven regional centres, financed mainly by the Ministry of Education, with some contributions from local education authorities, provides advice, help in finding employment and follow-up counselling both to young people leaving at the statutory minimum age and to older school leavers.

Primary education

There are 643 county and 613 voluntary primary schools. One of the problems of primary education is the existence of large numbers of small rural schools; as in other countries, the religious division contributes to this problem. 718 (57 per cent) primary schools have three or less than three teachers. A policy of centralizing has been followed in most areas but concern about long journeys for young children and possibilities of giving schools better equipment have caused some deliberate decisions to continue to maintain small schools. Some children in the primary age-group attend preparatory departments of grammar schools, occasionally as boarders in the school's boarding department. These prep departments have been much criticized as giving unfair advantages and probably guaranteeing places in grammar schools for children whose parents can pay prep school fees. But in fact only a very small proportion (2·5 per cent approx.) of children—some 5,000 out of a total of over 200,000 children in the appropriate age-groups—attend such schools.

Secondary education

Before the 1947 Act most children attended elementary schools up to the statutory leaving age. Those with academic interests and/or parents who preferred such education attended grammar schools from about the age of twelve; a limited number of local education authority scholarships to grammar schools was awarded annually on the result of an examination. Other children could enter, about age thirteen, technical schools which enjoyed a good reputation, especially in the country districts, for providing a valuable and useful education; competition for entry could be keen. These technical schools had—and technical education, like university education, still has—the added advantage of being undenominational, attended by young people from all religious backgrounds. In 1947 the fact that the majority (87 per cent) of grammar schools (67 out of 77) were under voluntary control, either of Roman Catholic authorities or of various bodies mainly Protestant in membership (but by no means all representing church authorities), complicated the proposed reorganization of the educational system. Although comprehensive secondary education was animatedly discussed at the time, the 1947 Act laid the foundations for what can be described as a typical tripartite system and did not provide—as the 1944 Act did in England—for an alternative of comprehensive schools. In Northern Ireland a process of selection at 11+ was to send academically gifted children to grammar schools; later selection would admit others to Technical Intermediate Schools, while a new kind of secondary school, similar to the English Secondary Modern, to be known as the Secondary Intermediate School, would receive the majority of the secondary school population. To overcome the problem of providing enough grammar school places, it was agreed that local authorities would pay 'scholarships' for any qualified children of their area admitted to a voluntary grammar school; voluntary grammar schools willing to reserve 80 per cent of their places for qualified pupils would also receive 65 per cent of capital expenditure—these were to be known as Group A schools; other voluntary grammar schools not willing to reserve that proportion of places for qualified pupils would not receive

capital costs grant but would still receive the scholarship fees paid for any qualified pupils they did admit—these were Group B schools. (Group A has proved increasingly popular; there are now only four Group B schools.) Voluntary grammar schools determine individually their tuition fees, subject to Ministry approval; in addition to these fees, which are covered by the scholarships paid for qualified pupils by local authorities, voluntary grammar schools (Group A) can charge parents a supplementary fee of up to £15 per annum to cover their share of capital costs; Group B schools can charge a higher supplementary fee.

Evolution of the secondary school system

This tripartite system has undergone considerable changes since its inception, especially where secondary intermediate schools are concerned. These schools, responding to demands from pupils, parents and teachers, have moved away from the original model of a four-year general, examination-free education for 'average' pupils. They have gradually included some commercial, technical and pre-apprenticeship courses on the one side and on the other have developed courses preparing for external examinations—initially RSA and College of Preceptors or Junior Technical Certificates; later the Junior Grammar School Certificate (formerly taken only after three or four years in grammar school) and eventually GCE 'O' Levels and 'A' Levels. (CSE courses of the N.W. England Board have also been introduced; the Northern Ireland CSE courses are expected to begin in 1973.) At one stage there were protests about alleged poaching on technical intermediate preserves and attempts were made to prevent this; but in the 1960s the decision was taken to phase out the technical intermediate schools and let the technical institutions of which they were normally a part concentrate on technical and further education after the basic school stage; from 33 in 1960, with over 4,000 pupils, technical intermediates in 1970–1 numbered 13 with 484 pupils. The academic courses in secondary intermediates (now designated simply 'secondary' schools—as distinct from grammar schools—in local parlance) still provide only a minority of the entrants for GCE examinations; nevertheless some of these schools are now at least quasi-comprehensive. In 1964 a White Paper, *Educational Development in Northern Ireland*, indicated willingness to encourage in these secondary schools developments 'designed to reduce the importance of selection'. A few country schools serving areas where qualified pupils lived far from the nearest grammar school have in fact been 'comprehensive' for many years. In other cases, notably in the new development area of Craigavon, a two-tier comprehensive system combining former grammar and intermediate schools has been introduced. A few new schools have been built to serve as comprehensives for their neighbourhood. There is much public enthusiasm for a change to a fully comprehensive system, but the voluntary grammar schools still cherish their traditions and freedom to choose their own pupils and staff; the problem of integrating them in a comprehensive system presents great difficulties.

Changes have also occurred within the grammar schools, not least being the large increase in numbers of grammar school places (from 15,662 in 1945–6 to 45,135 in 1969–70). Traditionally grammar schools prepared pupils for the Junior Certificate (taken after three or four years in the school) and Senior Certificate (taken two years later, about the age of seventeen or eighteen). The Senior Certificate, which served as entrance qualification for university and other higher education, was a 'group' certificate, requiring passes in six subjects chosen from specified groups of subjects. In 1952 'O' and 'A' Level examinations parallel to those of the English system were introduced and in 1963 the Northern Ireland GCE on a subject basis (i.e. awarded for any one or more passes) was introduced. The Junior Grammar School Certificate became progressively less important, though retaining some value as a secondary means of 'qualifying' and as a prestige symbol for secondary intermediate school pupils; in 1967 the Junior Technical Certificate examination was combined with it and in 1971 the Junior Certificate examination was held for the last time. These examinations were under the control of the Ministry of Education until 1970, when an autonomous Examinations Council was set up, linked with the Schools Council in England, and having two Boards, one responsible for the GCE (N.I.) and one for the CSE (N.I.). The Northern Ireland 'O' and 'A' Level examinations are conducted so as to maintain parity with the corresponding English examinations and cover approximately the same range of subjects.

Selection for secondary education

The selection procedure has also undergone considerable modification during the last twenty-five years. At first pupils were selected for grammar school on the basis of an external (Ministry administered) examination in English and arithmetic, plus two intelligence tests. After 1965 this was replaced by a procedure in which a school ranking order, based on records kept during the last three years at primary school, is standardized on verbal reasoning test scores to provide 'suitability quotients' for each child; these, added to the child's verbal reasoning quotients (in two tests) decide whether the child is declared qualified for grammar school, non-qualified or in the border-zone; border-zone children are then declared qualified or non-qualified on the basis of a scheme devised by their own local authority. Parents make individual application for a place for the child in the grammar school of their choice. Since the voluntary grammar schools can offer at least 20 per cent of their places to non-qualified children, parents able and willing to pay fees can usually obtain grammar school places for their non-qualified children. Throughout its existence the

selection procedure has been heatedly criticized—because of possible errors, emotional stress for children, the 'stigma of failure' and, before 1966, because of the cramming which the exam encouraged in primary schools. Even now there are complaints about coaching for verbal reasoning tests. Other complaints focus on socially divisive effects, which are the more probable because of the 'fee-paying loophole'. Admittedly there has been, since the beginning, a review procedure which enables pupils to be transferred to schools more suited to their aptitudes; but this has not satisfied all critics. Consequently there are many demands for the abolition of selection.

Further education

Institutions of Further and Technical Education (former technical colleges) provide a wide range of courses, day-time and evening classes, vocational and liberal studies. Students prepare, for example, for City and Guilds examinations, ONC, HNC or GCE qualifications. The Institutions also collaborate with the seven Industrial Training Boards in the provision of appropriate courses, and in Londonderry there is a one-year training course for teachers of commercial subjects. Three colleges under Ministry of Agriculture control provide agricultural education in the form of short courses, Certificate, Advanced Certificate, OND and HND courses. (Degrees in agriculture are taken at Queen's University, Belfast.) Belfast College of Technology has long been associated with Queen's University in teaching for applied science degrees; this association in the University Faculty of Applied Science and Technology was further strengthened by the Higher Technological Studies Act of 1954, which led to the Joint Authority linking city and university for the provision of such teaching; but this partnership has been dissolved on the creation of the Ulster College, the Northern Ireland Polytechnic, and teaching in Belfast College has returned to more typical municipal college activities.

The Ulster College

The proposal to establish this institution, which unites the former Belfast College of Art, the Belfast College of Domestic Science and the Ulster College for Physical Education (women) with a new Regional College of Science and Technology and a College of Commerce and Management, was made by the Lockwood Committee in its report, *Higher Education in Northern Ireland*, 1965. The committee expected beneficial effects from the integration of these studies and the mingling of students of different interests on the same campus. As yet the Ulster College exists largely in separate buildings, but the new Regional College of Technology is now functioning on the central site and a large variety of courses, leading in some cases to CNAA degrees, is being developed rapidly; at the same time studies in the various units of the College are being co-ordinated by a system of six faculties.

University education

More traditional higher education is provided at Queen's University, Belfast (founded in 1845 as a Queen's College, becoming in 1850 part of the Queen's University in Ireland and an independent university in 1908). The Lockwood Committee created a second university, the New University of Ulster at Coleraine. At the time of the Lockwood Report there was much controversy as to the need for a second university (but expansion of Queen's, which is now nearing the 7,000 mark, seemed better kept within limits) and as to its site; Magee University College, Londonderry, was then providing undergraduate studies recognized as equivalent to one year of study for a Queen's degree or two years for a degree of Trinity College, Dublin; but division of facilities for undergraduate studies has proved difficult and the university authorities decided in 1972 to use Magee as a continuing education centre for postgraduate courses and adult education. In the New University studies are organized in four schools —biological and environmental studies, physical sciences, social sciences and humanities; an education centre ranks as a fifth school and interacts with the others. New approaches to university teaching—e.g. units of credit, continuous assessment—are being enthusiastically developed. At Queen's the traditional division into faculties (nine in all) continues, though within this structure there is also considerable interest in new approaches to university teaching. Both universities are visited by the UGC, which advises the Northern Ireland Ministry of Education on their financing. The universities also participate in the UCCA scheme and receive students from other parts of the United Kingdom and overseas. Similarly many Northern Ireland students opt for higher education in other UK universities or follow a tradition of going to Trinity, Dublin or one of the Irish University Colleges. In all cases, student grants are available from local authorities in much the same way as in England.

Teacher education

Some specialist training is given in units of the Ulster College; three colleges in Belfast offer general training —the Ministry-provided Stanmillis College (men and women) and the Roman Catholic Colleges of St Mary's (women) and St Joseph's (men). These colleges offer a three-year certificate course, a four-year BEd (Queen's University) and a one-year course for graduates. The Queen's University department of education provides a one-year Diploma in Education training course for graduates, courses for the degree of MEd and supervision of MA or PhD work in educational topics. Since 1968 the three colleges and the department are linked through the University Institute of Education which presents students for recognition as

teachers; it also co-ordinates the non-graduate certificate courses in the colleges and provides in-service courses for teachers. The University Faculty of Education, which includes many college members, has responsibility for co-ordinating the college work for the BEd degree. It is noteworthy that a large proportion of students entering the colleges have university entrance qualifications and one third to one half of them enter BEd courses. A Teachers' Centre has also been developed by the university, initially dealing with science subjects, now providing discussions, displays, short courses in all subjects. In the New University of Ulster, in addition to in-service courses and conferences for serving teachers, the Education Centre provides a three-year certificate course of training for non-graduates and teaches both non-graduates and under-graduates; transfers may be made from the non-graduate to the graduating courses. Postgraduate studies in education are also pursued. Ministry of Education training scholarships are awarded to those accepted for training in any of these institutions or in colleges or university departments in other parts of the UK; similarly students from other areas are received. In the past, while it has been essential to have professional training for appointment to teach in a primary school (untrained graduates were not eligible), it has been possible for untrained graduates to teach in secondary intermediate and grammar schools; but all who graduate after December 1973 will have to have professional training before they can be appointed as teachers at any level in schools. Recognition of qualification to teach is now however a general recognition, whereas formerly it was (for secondary education) recognition in specified subjects; it is now left to schools to decide which subjects a teacher is competent to teach.

Community relations and education

Many believe that if schools were no longer for separate religious groups but brought together Roman Catholic and Protestant pupils and teachers the problems distorting community relations in Northern Ireland would be solved. But although public opinion polls have at times suggested a majority view in favour of this development it seems improbable that it would be accepted at present. Its implications have not always been clearly realized; the position of the religious teaching orders would—at least initially—lead to some uneasiness among some Protestant parents; staffs would be concerned about the safeguarding of their professional position during integration; and the fear of 'mixed marriages' resulting from school acquaintances is still strong. From the Roman Catholic point of view, the church authorities still reaffirm the necessity to have the whole school-day permeated by the right religious atmosphere and reassert their wish consequently to have all Roman Catholic children educated in Roman Catholic schools. Nevertheless there have been many efforts by teachers

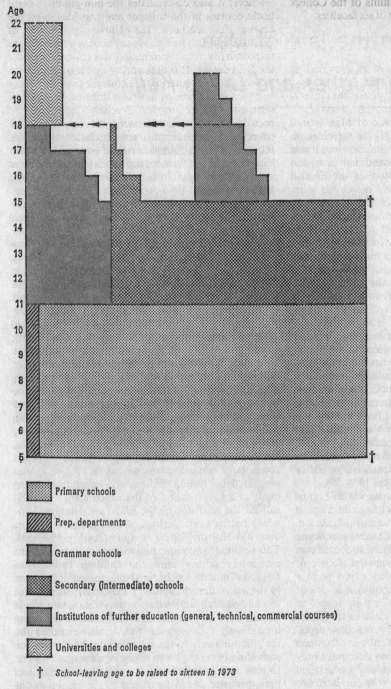

Primary schools

Prep. departments

Grammar schools

Secondary (intermediate) schools

Institutions of further education (general, technical, commercial courses)

Universities and colleges

† *School-leaving age to be raised to sixteen in 1973*

Figure 4.1

and by outside agencies to improve contacts between schools; the Unesco Committee, the Schools Curriculum Committee and projects supported by the Community Relations Commission have made some contributions to producing a better understanding at least in some groups of pupils. Teachers' conferences on methods and examinations similarly unite teachers of all denominations; there has even been collaboration in drawing up GCE and CSE syllabuses in religious education. So it is possible that such activities will gradually help to develop the wider tolerance and friendships which the country so greatly needs.

5 Education in the Isle of Man

Margot Cameron-Jones and Dollin Kelly

The history of education in the Isle of Man is well documented from the middle of the seventeenth century, which seems in some way ironical since it was at this time that the island's educational provision became the target of the attention of an English bishop who spoke no Manx. Long before his time, however, and as early as the thirteenth century, there is evidence that education was available to youths being trained for the Church and to certain other groups, and that it was provided by priests. In the sixteenth century the Manx clergy, for example, are reported to have been 'generally natives and have had the whole of their education in the island' (West, 1956-8) and in 1609 all the twenty-four members of the House of Keys signed their own names (Crampton, 1946-50). Petty schools, taught by laymen, and parochial schools, taught by the parish clergy, were in existence in the first half of the seventeenth century, and in 1634 a visitation of all the Manx parishes revealed that no unlicensed schoolmasters were keeping a school (Cubbon, 1926). At this time, there was no printed Manx, the first known written Manx being a manuscript translation of the Prayer Book in 1610 by a Welshman, Bishop Philips; though it is recorded that in 1658 at least one parson made translations, either of the Prayer Book or of the Bible, and also prepared his own manuscripts from which to teach his pupils to read in their own language (Crampton, 1946-50).

It was Bishop Barrow's decision (he was Bishop of Sodor and Man from 1663 to 1671) to make English the medium of instruction for the school population. Having assessed the people as for the most part 'loose and vicious' (Stenning, 1942-6, 1950), he supposed that 'the best way of cure would be to acquaint the people with the English tongue, so that they might be in a capacity to read the catechisms, and books of devotion: and for this purpose to set up an English School in every parish, and withal, to fit the children for higher learning, in a grammar school, which was also necessary' (Moore, 1900). But one hundred and fifty years after this, one third of the population still spoke only Manx and two thirds spoke, read and understood Manx better than English (Craine, 1946-50). Barrow's fund-raising and organizational skill were, however, formidable. He regained the tithes, called the Impropriate Fund, which had been lost to the Church at the Reformation, and used them to increase the stipends of his teaching clergy; he obtained, from the excise, £100 a year Royal Bounty, 'for the better maintenance of the poor vicars and schoolmasters' (Moore, 1900); he collected £600 from English sources (including Charles II), with which to promote education; and he willed land and raised a further fund to maintain three boys at an academic school when one was founded (Caine, 1942-6; Craine, 1946-50; Eason, 1966-8; Moore, 1900). It was due to his efforts that, by the end of the seventeenth century, an elementary school had been established in every parish.

In establishing parochial organization, Barrow made his educational demands upon the clergy themselves, by extending their functions to include compulsory teaching in the parochial schools, and the keeping of records of the families in their parishes and of their hopes for reforming them (Stenning, 1965). For parents, the first compulsion to educate their children derived from a civil source when Lord Derby issued an order to all his island tenants in 1672 that they should 'send their eldest sonnes and all other children to such pettie schools as they are capable, wherein if any doe fail or be remis . . . [they] shall not only be fined severely but their children be made incapable of bearing any office or place of trust . . . for want of such literature and education' (Crampton, 1946-50; Crellin, 1938; Cubbon, 1926; Quayle, 1946-50). But when the legislation which enforced compulsory education was passed in 1703-4, it was generated by Bishop Wilson, the enactments being made at a Convocation of the island clergy in 1703, ratified the next day by the island's legislature (Tynwald) and by Lord Derby, and proclaimed as law on Tynwald Hill the following June (Ashley, 1946-50). This statute required parents to send their children to elementary school until the children could read English distinctly, or 'be fined one shilling per quarter to the use of the schoolmaster'. There is evidence that this fine was duly imposed upon non-compliant parents (Crellin, 1938; Cubbon, 1926) at least in the years immediately following the Act. It also exceeded the fee paid quarterly to the schoolmaster by parents for each child being taught to read (sixpence quarterly) or to read and write (ninepence quarterly). Even at this time, however, families certified by the bishop as unable to pay fees, paid none (Ashley, 1946-50).

Like Barrow, Bishop Wilson was a vigorous and powerful incumbent of his office. Moore (1900) says of him that 'during the greater part of his episcopate, his biography is practically the history of the time'. And in addition to his personal resources, he deployed the power of a Church which, until the middle of his episcopacy, had, as an institution, more authority in Man than in England (and is the only diocese with a

Margot Cameron-Jones is a Research Fellow at the University of Dundee and Dollin Kelly is Headmaster at Santon School, Isle of Man.

Vicar-General to this day (Stenning, 1946–50)). The Manx Church was a separate national Church, though bound by canons passed at the Convocation of York (Kelly, 1956–8) and able, through its bishop, to present Bills to the island's Legislative Council. Bishop Wilson, for example, obtained an Act of Tynwald to make the rectors and vicars accountable for the books in the parish libraries which he founded. The Church also had judicial functions, performed by its ecclesiastical courts, and it had too the means of enforcing its decisions by the use of the ecclesiastical prison in Peel castle.

In the second quarter of the eighteenth century, during Wilson's bishopric (which lasted from 1698 to 1755), the influence of the Church began to lessen, its loss of authority beginning when Tynwald ruled that it was no longer legal for a bishop to use soldiers from the garrison to arrest and imprison persons sentenced by the ecclesiastical courts (Stenning, 1950). This ruling did not, of course, negate the 1703 Act, but despite this Act, and the by now well-established school provision, there followed from the middle of the eighteenth century a decline in standards of elementary education. This decline, manifested in an increase in illiteracy and school closure (Crampton, 1946–50; Kermode Parr, 1929) may be variously explained. As the power of the Church grew less, lay teachers, poorly paid and of more variable qualification than the clergy, taught in the petty schools (Craine 1955; Crampton, 1946–50): these teachers included 'maimed soldiers, retired mariners, tailors—in fact any person with sufficient knowledge to distinguish a round O from a crooked S and to wield a strong stick' (Crampton 1946–50). At this time, too, the Impropriate Fund, which contributed to the salaries of the teaching clergy, was claimed by the Duke of Athol and secured by him for twenty-two years (Cubbon, 1926). One Vicar was disciplined for keeping, perhaps for economic reasons, sheep, instead of children, in his school.

And during this period the language of instruction remained a cultural anomaly (Crampton, 1946–50; Moore, 1900). It was Church power which had earlier imposed, as the language of education, English, on a population which used only Manx for the purposes of daily life. This home-school disjunction was recognized by Bishop Wilson who, when imprisoned for a time during the Church–State struggle (Kinvig, 1950), began a translation of the Gospels into Manx. Wilson had learned Manx himself, sufficiently well to preach in it, and had written in 1698 that 'The English is not understood by two-thirds of the Island, though there is an English school in every parish: so hard is it to change the language of a whole country' (Craine, 1946–50). The matter of language also troubled Wilson's successor, Bishop Hildesley, who wrote to the Archbishop of York in 1772, 'They are taught to read ... the English Bibles: which numbers can do very roundly, while they scarce understand the meaning of a single sentence' (Crampton, 1946–50).

But by Hildesley's time, English was already beginning its ascendancy in some groups, and his tolerance of the Manx language attracted little support from the anglicized townspeople. He reported, 'This is, I believe, the only country in the world that is ashamed of and even inclined to extirpate, if it could, its own native tongue.' It was Hildesley who obtained funds for translations from English philanthropists and the SPCK. By 1773 an entire translation of the Bible, in three parts, had been produced, and this Bible remains the standard authority for the language (Craine, 1946–50). Despite this, and the production of a book of Common Prayer, a dictionary and a grammar, 'the end desired by Bishop Barrow—the abolition of Manx in favour of English—grew nearer year by year' (Craine, 1946–50). In 1816 the first Deemster (a judge) (Moore, 1961–2; Stenning, 1950), who spoke no Manx was appointed, and used an interpreter, and by the middle of the nineteenth century Manx[1] was seldom heard in the courts.

The first grammar schools on the island were the schools established in Castletown, probably in 1671 (Cubbon, 1926; Kermode Parr, 1929), and in Douglas in 1705 (Crampton, 1946–50). Both were set up by the efforts of the bishopric, which also authorized the extension of Ramsey School to a grammar school in 1743. In the eighteenth century there abounded, too, various private 'Academies', mostly in Douglas (Crampton, 1946–50), and other profit-making ventures which provided education beyond the elementary level, including, for example, tuition in navigation (Harrison, 1880). In Peel, however (where as early as 1658 the poor children had had their books and writing materials provided by the bequest of Philip Christian, a native of Peel who had become a prosperous London clothworker), the Grammar School (endowed in 1746) and the Mathematical School (endowed in 1763) were financed, and their masters housed and paid, by the bequests of private benefactors. It was also in this century that the charity of Lady Elizabeth Hastings established a fund to pay the teachers (not vicars) who taught in schools, and that, in 1772, the first woman teacher was licensed to work in a Parish School (though in 1764 there is a record of the licence given to the mistress of a free school (Garrard, 1967)) receiving, in Kirk Bride, 'such stipend as has formerly been allowed for a parish school'. This application of the principle of equal pay is, of course, consonant with the happy position traditionally occupied by Manx women in law (Quayle, 1946–50).

It would be difficult to make summary evaluative statements about education on the island in the nineteenth century. On the one hand, there are accounts (Kermode Parr, 1929) of poor attendances, dilapidated buildings and, according to a statistical account of 1847, many teachers reporting themselves so deep in poverty that they were 'obliged to follow other work'. On the other hand, it was at this time that the fees payable to parochial schoolmasters were raised, having remained fixed since 1704 (Moore, 1900); Sunday Schools were begun in 1803; a large Lancastrian school was founded for the poor children of Douglas; some parochial schools were funded by the National Society, and others received Imperial Parliament grants. An Act of Tynwald in 1851 empowered local vestries to levy rates for the support of the parochial and other schools, and, in the same century, the island's two public schools were founded in Castletown. In 1872 state intervention in education began when Tynwald passed the Public Elementary Education Act, which was followed by the 1892 Act making elementary education free. The 1872 Act was framed on the lines of the 1870 English Act, though it also obliged every elementary school, apart from Roman Catholic ones, to provide non-sectarian instruction in religious subjects. The Act's most important clause was that which incorporated the code of the English Education Department.

> In this way [wrote Moore in 1900] education in the Island is saved from becoming local in its character, and from falling below the standard prevailing in England. The Manx schools are, in effect, included in the great system governed by the Education Department at Whitehall. The same subjects are taught in them, the same inspectors visit them, and they are compelled to attain the same standard of efficiency as the English and Welsh schools.

Education on the island at that time, and now, might perhaps usefully be considered by reference not only to constitutional independence but also to institutional imitation. The Isle of Man is an independent sovereign country under the British Crown. Party politics, as that phrase is applied on the mainland, do not obtain. The island has its own judicial system which administers its own common or customary and statute law, with a High Court of Justice based upon the English system, but simplified. Its Justices of the Peace (Craine, 1964–6) some of them *ex officio*, are appointed by the Lord Chancellor of England, usually on the nomination of the Lieutenant-Governor, who is appointed by the British Crown. The island's legislature, called Tynwald, has two Houses. The Lower House, the House of Keys, is one of the oldest legislative assemblies in the world and consists of twenty-four members elected by the adult male and female population. The Upper House, called the Legislative Council, consists of the Lieutenant-Governor, the Bishop of Sodor and Man, the First Deemster, the Attorney-General and seven members appointed by the House of Keys. The Two Houses meet both separately and together. The island is not bound by Acts of the Imperial Parliament unless specifically mentioned in them, and any measure may be introduced by any member, either of the Keys or of the Council, and is usually read for the first time without a division. Bills, when they have passed both Houses, are signed by the members and sent for the Royal Assent, but even after the Assent is received a

Bill does not become law unless it is announced on the first Tynwald Day following. On Tynwald Day (5 July, Midsummer's Day in the pre-Gregorian calendar) the Bill is read out in English and in Manx on Tynwald Hill and becomes law when the certificate of promulgation is signed by the Lieutenant-Governor and the Speaker of the House of Keys.

The island is normally included in Westminster legislation pertaining to such matters as defence and foreign affairs, but it is legislatively independent in internal affairs, including its finance and education. Although the Isle of Man Education Act of 1949 does allow regulations made at Westminster to be put before Tynwald, Tynwald's power is vested in its ability to reject these measures. Thus, when the raising of the school-leaving age was considered by Tynwald, although it was accepted in principle, no scheme for effecting it will proceed until 1974. Other matters, currently of some interest on the mainland, are neither relevant nor salient. School milk, for example, has never been free on the island except to children certified by the Schools' Medical Officer as in medical need, and there are no conflicts over comprehensivization, which was effected by 1948, and is not, of course, defined as a party-political issue.

The education system is also administratively independent, its college of further education and college of domestic science, and its thirty-four primary and four secondary schools being controlled by the Board of Education, twenty-four of whose members are elected to office by the adult population of the island, and five of whose members are appointed by Tynwald. Her Majesty's Inspectors do make twice-yearly visits to the island's schools, and there is an HMI with particular responsibility for the Isle of Man, but the Inspectors' functions are now solely advisory and informative.

But the system, though legislatively and administratively independent *de jure*, is, however, *de facto* heavily influenced by the powerful mainland model. The 1949 Act itself, for example, is largely modelled on the English Act of 1944 and gives to primary and secondary education an organizational form (nursery education, primary school, and transfer to secondary at the age of eleven) similar to that of England and Wales. At the tertiary level, independence (both in the sense of separateness and in the sense of control) in some respects ceases. Various forms of vocational training are available. There are, for example, the colleges of further education and domestic science, and facilities for nurse-training and for legal and trade apprenticeships. But there is no local provision for teacher-training, or for other forms of higher education, and children seeking education at this level gain access to it through the examinations of the English Boards, and, having followed successfully the same examinable curricula, and used the same textbooks, as their mainland counterparts, are routed into the larger system. These forms of control are of a rather different order from Barrow's imposition, on Manx children, of English as a necessary sub-goal to spiritual salvation. But they derive, no less than Barrow's measures did, from the ascendancy and proximity of a powerful though benevolent neighbour.

In another way too, the English norm appears. That is in the estimated 10 per cent of the island's secondary school children who attend public schools. Headmasters in the state schools[2] report that transfer to island or mainland public schools normally occurs at or around the age of eleven. Only one headmaster (of a primary school) reported that no such transfers had occurred in his school during his headship of thirteen years; the others reported that these transfers did take place in small numbers annually, one head commenting that transferred pupils were mostly from the professional and business families and that they represented 'a fairly large proportion, considering the size of the community'. At the two public schools on the island itself (King William's College, with a roll of 365 boys, and the Buchan School, with a roll of 300 girls) some 50 per cent of the pupils are island-resident children, who either pay fees or win Board of Education scholarships[3] to attend these schools as boarding or day pupils.

In 1926 Cubbon, discussing Manx pride in King William's College, added, 'But I think we would be prouder still if it would be more national in its character and its ideals.' Comment on either the character or ideals of any school would be hazardous. But at King William's local studies are not a distinct part of the formal curriculum, though there is an active sixth-form Manx Society, and pupils' personal work in Manx studies is rewarded by prizes. The Buchan School, however, reports at least as much curricular and extra-curricular emphasis upon local studies[4] as the state schools do, and when asked the personal and educational value of local knowledge to her pupils the headmistress (who was born and went to school on the island) judged it to be 'very important' on both counts.

It is, of course, to the schools and to the teachers themselves which one must look for some of the evidence for distinctive forms of socialization and enculturation. Killip (1959–60) has touched upon these matters with reference to the early twentieth century:

Of subjects of Manx interest there is scarcely any mention. Some, though not all, of the teachers were English, and unsympathetic in their attitude, so that the dialect was frowned upon, and the language itself ignored, though in one school, in Surby, its existence was recognized to the extent that its use was forbidden. The child who on her father's knee had learned Ny Kirree fo Niaghtey [*The Sheep under the Snow*] and Mylecharane [*a folk ballad from Jurby*] to whom the old carval [carol] book was a familiar sight, and who had listened at the Oie'll Voirrey [*Christmas Eve Service*] to the old men droning their interminable verses, was soon made to understand that these things were of no real

significance, and compared with Spelling and Grammar and Mental Arithmetic were of very little account.

Now, however, things may go somewhat differently. 80 per cent of the state school headmasters report having had their own primary and secondary education on the island, the vast majority also being island born. And, on average, 70 per cent of their staff were either born and/or went to school on the island (at the Buchan School, the percentage is sixty). Only one head, when giving reasons for choosing his present appointment, responded without making a reference to the island. The responses of the other heads (including that of the Buchan School) seem to indicate a rather strong personal attachment to the Isle of Man, regard for its people and approval of its education system. The state heads' verbatim responses include the following:

'I was soon convinced that the future lay with the comprehensive system, and of course enjoyed being back in my native Island.' '. . . my love of the Isle of Man and good relationships with Manx people. I had taught in the London area and overseas and greatly prefer the pleasure of teaching in a small community in such an attractive setting. Manx pupils are responsive and able to reach very high standards of achievement.'[5] 'I married a Manx girl . . . of course the native "Manx" has high innate ability.' 'It is my home.' 'My home, love of the Island.' 'I was teaching in a large city (Sheffield) and although personally very happy there I preferred to bring up my family in the Isle of Man. I have not regretted the choice.' 'I felt that after five years I had carried out my obligations (to teach in Manchester) and returned to the Island.' 'I was forced by circumstances to teach on the Mainland for five years, always strongly resolved to return, which I did in 1955.'

Statements such as these do not seem to argue for the kinds of indifference or alienation which Killip (1959–60) reported for the early 1900s. But, of course, these statements, even though made by those who have authority in the island's schools, would be of little significance if no provision were made in the schools for the transmission of local knowledge. This provision is however reported, even from the secondary schools, though one might make some inference about the stratification of knowledge from the fact that in the secondary schools local studies are for the most part offered in the form of optional subjects and voluntary activities. All of the primary headmasters, however, report that local studies (including, in two respondent schools, the Manx language) are promoted as an important part of the integrated curriculum[6] and the respondent heads, both primary and secondary, rated local knowledge as 'important' or 'very important' to a pupil both personally and educationally.

Reported provision, of course, when unsupported by observational studies in the schools themselves and by research into the political attitudes and cultural values of the population, can be taken only as evidence of the schools' intended functions so far as the transmission of a corpus of distinctive local knowledge is concerned. But the heads' assertions can be taken as evidence that the heads do include local studies in their definitions of 'what counts as valid knowledge' (Bernstein, 1971), and their replies to open-ended items seemed to show that heads (with one exception) valued highly a knowledge of local matters, both as a cognitive base ('a child's knowledge is in the first place founded on the world around him') and as a distinctive agency of socialization. Examples of such free responses include:

'Obviously, we wish our children to be brought up to appreciate and we hope continue, where possible, Manx traditions.' 'Local knowledge ... gives the child a pride in his heritage.' 'The Manx heritage is something to do with character. I find Manx people proud of this heritage.' 'A knowledge of folklore, history, geography, natural history and perhaps particularly the love of music. This is the kind of

patriotism we should strive to maintain.' 'I attach some importance to an awareness of Manx identity and considerable importance to an awareness of freedom, not lightly won.'

Some care has been taken in this paper to refer to education on the Isle of Man, rather than to Manx education, and also to note that though legislatively independent and administratively distinct, the system is organizationally indistinguishable in many ways from the mainland system into which, at various tertiary levels, it finally feeds, with inevitable consequences for the examinable curriculum of the secondary schools. To assess the power of various informal agencies of socialization, large-scale research would be required. But so far as the formal system is concerned, the available evidence suggests that to identify what is distinctively Manx about education in the Isle of Man, one might point to the teachers' definitions of what counts as educational knowledge, and also to the curriculum, particularly in the primary schools.

Notes

1 Manx speakers: According to the Census of 1961, 165 in a population of approximately 50,000. The proportion is now rising.
2 Questionnaire Survey: In February 1972 an approach was made by letter, and personally, to the island's four secondary heads, to eight primary heads (of town and rural schools throughout the island), and to the two public schools. Three secondary and seven primary heads responded to the questionnaire, as did the headmistress of the Buchan School. The writers are grateful to these respondents, and especially to those who

also contributed additional informative material.
3 Arrangements described in 1950 (Stenning, 1950) as 'knocking off provincial angularities' for the children concerned.
4 Defined on the questionnaires as 'Manx history, affairs, geography, government, language and environment'.
5 Examination successes support this view.
6 The Local Studies Committee (of island teachers and the island's one educational adviser) provides teaching materials and in-service courses in this field.

References

Throughout, *JMM* refers to the *Journal of the Manx Museum*, and *IMNHAS* refers to the *Proceedings of the Isle of Man Natural History and Antiquarian Society*.

Ashley, A. (1946–50). The claims and needs of children in traditional Manx law and custom. *IMNHAS*, 5, no. 2, 358–67.
Bernstein, B. (1971). On the classification and framing of educational knowledge, in M. F. D. Young (ed.), *Knowledge and Control. New Directions for the Sociology of Education*. London, Collier-Macmillan.
Caine, P. W. (1942–6). Pages from seventeenth century Manx history. *IMNHAS*, 5, no. 1, 146–60.
Craine, D. (1946–50). The Bible in Manx. *IMNHAS*, 5, no. 2, 540–54.
Craine, D. (1955). *Manannan's Isle*. Manx Museum and National Trust.
Craine, J. H. (1964–6). The Justice of the Peace in the Isle of Man. *IMNHAS*, 7, no. 1, 120–27.
Crampton, N. V. (1946–50). Schools in Man. *IMNHAS*, 5, no. 2, 484–98.
Crellin, R. J. (1938). Unpublished documents in the Manx Museum. *JMM*, 4, no. 54, 35–44. (Compulsory education in Man 167 years before England, p. 44.)
Cubbon, W. (ed.). George Borrow's strange experiences

in Man: one of his manuscripts secured for the Museum. *JMM*, 4, no. 59, pp. 115–18.
Cubbon, W. (1926). Early schools and scholarship in Man. *IMNHAS*, 3, 106–29.
Eason, R. K. (1966–8). Survival of the see of Sodor and Man in the nineteenth century. *IMNHAS*, 7, no. 2, 232–47.
Garrard, L. S. (1967). Catherine Halsall's School, Castletown and the Finigan Family. *JMM*, 7, no. 83, 41–3.
Harrison, W. (ed.). (1880). *Manx Miscellanies*, 2, Manx Society. Journal of the Rev. John Gell, Chaplain of St Mark's, during his early seafaring life.
Kelly, B. H. (1956–8). Some reflections on church and state relations in the time of Bishop Wilson. *IMNHAS*, 6, no. 1, 324–51.
Killip, I. M. (1959–60). Unwillingly to school. *JMM*, 6, no. 76, 94–6.
Kinvig, R. H. (1950). *A History of the Isle of Man*. Liverpool University Press.
Moore, A. W. (1900). *A History of the Isle of Man*, London, T. Fisher Unwin.
Moore, R. B. (1961–2). The Deemsters and the Manx Courts of law. *JMM*, 6, no. 78, 155–60.
Kermode Parr, D. (1929). Pages in the history of Manx education. *Isle of Man Examiner*.

Quayle, E. L. (1946–50). Woman in Man. *IMNHAS*, **5**, no. 2, 296–304.

Stenning, E. H. (1942–6). The original lands of Bishop Barrow's trustees. *IMNHAS*, **5**, no. 1, 122–45.

Stenning, E. H. (1946–50). Manx Spiritual Laws. *IMNHAS*, **5**, no. 2, 287–95.

Stenning, E. H. (1950). *Isle of Man*. London, Hale.

Stenning, E. H. (1965). *Portrait of the Isle of Man*. London, Hale.

West, J. I. (1956–8). Sir Thomas Fairfax and the Isle of Man. *IMNHAS*, **6**, no. 1, 81–96.

6   Education in the Channel Islands

Dora M. Pickering

The Channel Islands lie about fifteen miles off the west coast of France and approximately a hundred miles from the south coast of England. The population varies a good deal according to the relative size of each Island:

Jersey	72,600
Guernsey	47,500
Alderney	1,500
Sark	525
Herm	One family and resident employees in shop, hotel and farm
Jethou	One family plus employees
Lihou	One family and visiting members of a summer school (Outward Bound type)

Many of the families living on the Islands claim Norman descent and a form of Norman-French is still spoken by some of the inhabitants. The Islands are divided into the bailiwicks of Jersey and Guernsey, each one possessing its own legal system and constitution, the latter based on the ancient laws of Normandy. Alderney and Sark, although within the bailiwick of Guernsey, possess their own constitution. Herm, Jethou and Lihou are leased from the Crown through Guernsey.

The states are autonomous in government, but in certain matters are subject to the Monarch in Privy Council, from whom all enactments of state must receive the Royal Assent. Her Majesty is represented by the Lieutenant-Governor, who is always a member of Her Majesty's Forces.

The English Department of Education and Science has no control over the educational policies in the Islands, but a member of the English inspectorate is invited over at regular intervals to inspect and comment on the facilities provided and the progress made in both bailiwicks. He is invited to comment as he chooses.

There are no political parties as such in the Channel Islands. Several officers of the States are appointed by the Home Office, some by the Crown, and the rectors

of the various parishes are included by virtue of their office. The remainder are elected officers (unpaid).

Until recently, French, but not Jersey-French or Guernsey-French, was the official language used in the court, states and churches. As late as 1948 the states minutes were kept in French, but later it was made optional. Radio, television and English-trained teachers have left but a few of the older folk remembering their once close ties with France. Nevertheless, many families have large numbers of French relatives, and there are considerable numbers of French agricultural labourers employed during the season. Attempts are being made to prevent the old *patois* from dying out, and a notable *Dictionnaire* has been compiled and published.[1]

Provision of education

Primary

Jersey	Entry at 6 years, reduced to entry during the child's 5th year in September 1972
Guernsey	Entry at 5 years
Alderney	Entry at 5 years
Sark	Entry at 5 years. Infants taken in for morning school only

Secondary

Jersey	States	Grammar	Hautlieu
		Secondary-Modern	St Helier Girls
			St Helier Boys
		co-ed.	Les Quennevais
	Public (in English sense)	Victoria College for Boys	
		Jersey College for Girls	
		The Convent F.C.J. (RC)	
		De La Salle College for Boys (RC)	
		Beaulieu Convent	
	Several good private schools		
Guernsey	States	Secondary-Modern	St Peter Port
			St Sampsons
			Les Beaucamps
			St Josephs (RC)

Dora M. Pickering works for the Jersey Education Service.

Guernsey	States	
contd.	*contd.*	Guernsey Grammar School for Girls
		Guernsey Grammar School for Boys
	Public	Elizabeth College for Boys
	(in English	The Ladies College for Girls
	sense)	Blanchelands College (RC)
		Vimera College (RC)
		Les Vauxbelets (RC)
	Several good private schools	

'Streaming and setting' in secondary schools

This varies greatly in degree from one school to another, at the discretion of the Heads (who are also permitted to make their own choice of staff in some schools to suit their own particular requirements). 'Setting' in an unstreamed school often takes place during the third year and is mainly confined to English, French, maths and science. At this stage pupils are given guidance for their fourth- and fifth-year options. The school-leaving age is fifteen except in Sark where it is fourteen. The Working Report submitted to the Jersey states in 1971 by the Jersey Teachers' Association (County Branch NUT) advocated to follow the English ROSLA. This was defeated in the subsequent states' debate. Similar strong opposition is shown against the idea of making Victoria College into a sixth-form college.

Tertiary education

There are no teacher training colleges, art colleges, polytechnics or universities on the Islands. Students are prepared for these and proceed to the mainland or to the Continent. Most colleges award travelling scholarships to Caen or Grenoble. The Jersey Education Committee and the Guernsey Education Council make grants where necessary but the difference between the English and Island income tax is taken into account when the grants are awarded, thus these are substantially less than the English grants.

Colleges of further education in both the large Islands offer various courses, and pupils who are early leavers are urged to make use of them. The day-continuation classes and the day release schemes are well supported. Twelve centres are used in addition to the main college buildings, the departments being divided into business and general studies, engineering and construction, catering and fashion and horticulture and agriculture. Similar courses are offered in Guernsey, including courses for registered states apprentices. The colleges provide facilities for a study centre for Jersey residents who have been enrolled for the Open university.

Private education

Both bailiwicks have a higher percentage of privately educated children than on the mainland. This is possibly as a result of:

(1) tradition;
(2) the large number of wealthy residents who prefer their children to be educated at public schools on the Island;
(3) The advantage of smaller classes;
(4) Parents whose children are unable to pass the entrance examinations to the college send them to private schools;
(5) Children can be accommodated on a five-day weekly basis as boarders, or as full boarders;
(6) Not all parents accept the idea of retarded and ESN children mingled with more able children in the states schools.

All nursery schools, playgroups and private schools must comply with states regulations and can be inspected at any time. The regulations are strictly enforced.

Number of registers of schools in Jersey

Primary	5–11 1971	States	5,449		
		Private	1,501	Total	6,950
Secondary	11–19 1971	States	3,245		
		Private	721	Total	3,966
Total	States primary and secondary schools in 1971				8,694
	Private schools				2,222
					10,916

This total of 11,000 children in attendance in all schools of all kinds is the largest ever recorded. In 1951 the number was slightly over 7,000.

The present system of education is based on decisions which were taken twenty years ago, one of which was to establish a selective school in Jersey. The cost per head is increasing rapidly in both secondary and primary areas. In Jersey there has been an increase of 300 children in the six to eleven age group attending private schools. However by 1977 there should be a total of approximately 5,200 primary school places in buildings new or modernized by the states since 1965. In 1970 the cost of education was £1·94 m., but estimates for 1972 are likely to exceed £2·69 m., an increase of more than 38 per cent in two years. The reasons which lie behind this large increase can be attributed to:

(1) Considerable extensions to buildings in hand;
(2) A rapid programme of further development;
(3) Unprecedented increase in the cost of land, building material, wages, salaries and school equipment.

Sark

Sark is unique. It is a direct survival from feudal times and the small population rely on three sources of income: tourism, agriculture and fishing. The Seigneur of Sark is Mrs Sybil Hathaway whose title is the Dame of Sark. She presides over the Court of Chief

Pleas. No building can be altered or erected without permission; with the exception of the Dame's powered bath chair, no powered vehicles except tractors are allowed, and she owns the only female dog on the Island.

For many years Sark has had two co-educational schools. One junior up to eleven plus and one senior. An infants' school is open during the mornings and it is hoped that it will soon be possible to increase this time to include afternoons. Children passing the selective examination go to the Guernsey grammar schools—their attendance and boarding fees paid by Sark (with parental contributions for part board). Many of the children of wealthy immigrants on Sark attend public schools in Britain.

Alderney

Alderney has one co-ed all-age school. Selected pupils go to Guernsey.

Staffing ratios

These are extremely generous by UK standards
Primary UK County Boroughs
    1969/70 28·4 pupils per teacher
      Jersey 22 „   „
Secondary UK County Boroughs
    1969/70 18·2 pupils per teacher
      Jersey 15 „   „

Experimental work in education

Some six years ago a new co-educational secondary modern school was opened in Jersey. It is modelled on the Cambridgeshire Village experiment with special emphasis on the needs of the community. When an expansion of the housing programme became inevitable, land which was unsuitable for agriculture adjacent to the airport was chosen. Several hundreds of comparatively low-priced houses and bungalows were built by the states and some private development took place in the same area, augmenting the houses already built there. A new shopping centre was added and in 1972 a church was built and a chapel converted to a synagogue. This larger complex demanded new educational facilities which would at the same time cater for the larger adult population and have a regular intake from the rural areas in the west of the island.

The school was built for 500 pupils. It now holds nearly 700 and further extensions are being added in 1972. A good library is attached – a branch of the public library in St Helier replacing a small mobile van—and used by pupils of the school as well as the general public. The adult community can attend both afternoon and evening classes; facilities are given for a welfare centre, the senior citizen's group, the local Women's Institute, the judo club, basketball team, and any other groups who wish to hire a hall or a room. Adult bridge clubs play during the afternoon on one day each week and all these activities go on throughout the normal school day. It is quite possible for a child to be in school with its mother, infant brother or sister and grandparents. Very small infants and toddlers are cared for in a creche by fourth and fifth year pupils as part of their home economics course (with adult supervision), whilst the mothers attend an afternoon class. Older children still at school over the age of fifteen may join the adult evening classes without payment. Originally the initial staff chosen by the headmaster were mainly experienced in both children's and adults' teaching, and were expected and encouraged to take an active part in the evening educational programme under the auspices of an adult tutor who also took occasional children's classes. Many still do so one or two evenings weekly, but the number of adult entries has increased so much that additional staff have had to be engaged for work on the adult side. In the 1971–2 session some 3,000 students enrolled. These evening students have an active Association, mainly for social purposes and many are also active participants in the PTA. Staff support both these groups by giving lectures, film shows, demonstrations and organizing charitable activities and fêtes etc.

The school's outdoor activities are closely connected with the Old Fort in St Aubin's Bay, which is a form of Outward Bound education. Children are taught sailing, canoeing, rock climbing and camping. Once a year the whole school is involved in an activities week during the summer term. Each member of staff chooses an activity in which he or she has a personal interest, and the children are invited to choose and enrol. The groups are composed of children of all ages and both sexes, although some special groups have to be more selective. The less able children are directed into something which is more directly geared to their limitations. Each teacher is responsible for about eighteen children, and should it be considered wiser to have two members of staff engaged in an activity such as camping, cycling on the Continent or skin-diving, they double up their numbers as far as possible. Overseas and out of the island trips are arranged, and activities such as bird watching, canoeing, heraldry, pottery, art, fashion and costume, reporting, photography, field studies, music, film-making, drama etc. are offered. Older children are encouraged to work with the old peoples' assistance group and the handicapped children, or to watch and study children at play.

In their last year at school, work-study is introduced and children leave school for one day a week to work with local firms or attend the horticulture and agriculture courses. School days are extended until 6.15 p.m. on four days per week for children who are taking CSE exams and children who expect to leave but who show interest in extra subjects. Some teachers are allowed compensatory time for these extended days; others are paid at the evening-class rate in excess.

For three years an interdisciplinary inquiry experiment was made with the assistance of Goldsmiths' College, London. This has gradually been phased out although some team-teaching still exists.

There is an abundance of equipment, PE, photographic, craft, visual aids, television on each floor, audio aids, musical instruments etc. and no expense has been spared to give this type of education a good chance to prove its worth.

Language problems present some difficulties since there are children who speak French at home, children of immigrant Continental season workers, and children of Portuguese, Spanish and Italian workers in the catering trades. There are also a number of retarded children and slow learners. (This may be the result of inter-breeding.) A noticeable number of Jersey-born children are left-handed and there are regular epidemics of glandular fever.

A high percentage of children have never left the island, some not even their own parishes. All are encouraged to do so, particularly to have residential experience outside their island. A very special relationship between teacher and pupil is necessary for this type of education and the line between friendship and familiarity is one which all must learn to appreciate; it is remarkable how many of our visitors comment upon the atmosphere which prevails throughout the school and this extends to staff relationships, which are excellent. It is difficult to assess the value and consequences of the experiment yet, we have much to learn as well as to teach and only time can answer the age-old question 'Is this the best way?' and the other one 'What next?'

Teachers

The policy in both bailiwicks is to recruit teachers from Britain and elsewhere as far as possible and very few island-born teachers until they have had considerable experience elsewhere. This is considered to be to the advantage of teachers and pupils alike. The native inhabitants would appear to tend to be rather parochial through habit, custom and intermarriage.

Salaries are paid in accordance with the current rates of salaries for teachers in primary and secondary schools and service in the Islands is recognized by the Department of Education and Science for superannuation purposes. There are strong links with the Seychelles Islands and a teacher-exchange scheme is in operation. There are further strong links with St Luke's College, Exeter, the University of Exeter and the University at Southampton, together with many others on the mainland.

College of education ideas are brought over by young teachers, but Heads are expected to sort out the chaff from the wheat and the teachers themselves tend to modify their ideas as they gain more experience and there are still many Jersey-born teachers in the schools who are rarely swayed by the prevailing winds of change. I cannot stress too greatly the built-in

characteristics of the Islanders, who put the welfare of the whole above all other considerations. This attitude appears to have largely died out in Britain or has become unfashionable. It may be one of the reasons why many English-born people such as myself prefer to live and work elsewhere. Many young teachers become accustomed to this outlook and those who do not are always free to leave.

Influence of teachers

During February 1971 an Educational Consultative Committee, composed of members of the Education Committee and representatives from the professional associations—NUT, NAS, PWT etc. was set up. This was advocated ten years ago, and it is regarded as a step forward towards greater understanding and as a vehicle for expression concerning present and future problems of education. In 1970 the local county branch of the NUT, known as the Jersey Teachers Association, produced a working report which was submitted to the Education Department and the States Committee. This included several proposals concerning future policies indicating that the JTA were in favour of ROSLA (which was not unanimous nor accepted by the NAS) and the lowering of the school-entry age to five.

Many visits have been made by all the interested parties to various establishments and schools in England to evaluate the worth of their systems to Jersey. Selective, comprehensive 11–16, the 3-tier system 5–9/9–13/13–18 and 5/10/10–14–18.

Influence of the press

There are no special correspondents for educational matters, but public meetings are well covered and so are states business and debates. It is noticeable that meetings of the newly formed Educational Consultative Committee are not made known, nor are their meetings reported upon afterwards.

Television

School broadcasts are made regularly on Channel Television. Programmes deal with many aspects of Channel Island life such as fishing, agriculture, history, landmarks, customs, myths, and are written locally.

Towards the future

Plans for expansion in all levels of education are in hand in both bailiwicks. In his economic 'Survey of Jersey', Mr G. C. Powell, who is the economic adviser to the states says of school-leavers:

> Leaving aside the marginal effects of immigrant families with children of school age, it is possible to be fairly definite about the number in the age group 15–18 in the next decade. The estimating of numbers who will leave school at a specific

age is more difficult, because of the growing tendency to stay on after the statutory age. The Education Committee, in its report to the States in 1969, estimated that it was to be expected that 75 per cent would stay on at school until the age

of 16 in 1978, compared with 55% in 1968, 40% until 17 compared with 28% in 1968, and 25% until 18 as compared with 16% in 1968. If local job opportunities are poor, children may stay on at school rather than take an unsatisfactory job.

Note

1 It must be remembered that during the last war, the Channel Islands were occupied by the Germans for some years. Alderney was completely evacuated; Guernsey's children were evacuated and all schools closed. Elizabeth

College moved *en masse* to the Peak District for five years. In Jersey, the colleges continued to function for a time, but were finally taken over by the occupying forces. All Channel Island children were required to learn German.

7 Education in the Republic of Ireland

John Horgan

Facts

Legislative basis

The scattered and unco-ordinated system of educational provision in the twenty-six counties of the Republic of Ireland prior to 1922 came under the direct control of the new state in two stages. In 1922 the work formerly carried out by the commissioners for intermediate education (secondary schools) and the commissioners for endowed schools (largely religious foundations) was assigned to the Minister of Education. The Department of Education as such was not created until 1924, under the Ministers and Secretaries Act of that year, when it was also given responsibility for the work formerly carried on by the Board of Technical Instruction, and that for Reformatory and Industrial Schools. The system inherited by the Department of Education in this way was essentially one devoted to the indirect subsidization of local or private educational initiatives, controlled by regulation rather than by legislation, and this is a pattern which has remained unaltered in many important respects to the present day. The only major legislative development since that time has been the establishment of a system of vocational schools under the Vocational Education Act 1930, which created thirty-eight local education committees to oversee the building of these schools and the education provided in them, subject to the general control of the Minister for Education and financed partly from central and partly from local government funds. Further developments in this sphere have included two Apprenticeship Acts (1931 and 1959), and the Vocational Education (Amendment) Act 1970, which provided for greater co-operation between the vocational and

John Horgan is a Member of Seanad Éireann and Education Correspondent of the *Irish Times*.

secondary sectors of post-primary education, notably in the joint provision of capital for new school buildings on the basis of shared control. In general, however, successive Ministers for Education have attempted to shape the development, rationalization and centralization of the educational system through their wide-ranging regulatory powers and through persuasion, resisting increasingly vocal demands for a codifying Education Act from teachers and managerial organizations.

Administration

The total picture is complex. At the primary level there are state-aided national schools and a small number of non-state-aided schools. Some of the state-aided national schools have 'secondary tops' providing post-primary courses. At the post-primary level there are vocational schools; private boarding and day secondary schools; comprehensive schools (established by the Department of Education in areas where post-primary educational provision was inadequate or non-existent); and community schools, which are being created by agreed mergers between educational interests in new urban areas or in rural centre formerly catered for by a number of small non-viable schools (two of these are due to open in September 1973; some thirty more are planned).

Management

National schools are administered under a managerial system which has remained essentially unchanged since the last century, when it was evolved as a compromise between often deeply opposed religious interest groups. Managers are usually local clergymen of different denominations (although the regulations do not preclude interdenominational or lay management), with the result that the system, although *de jure* non-denominational (any child may seek admittance to any national school), has become in practice strongly denominational. The manager employs—and dismisses—the teachers, and school sites are usually vested in bishops or other clerical representatives. There is a small number of private *preparatory* schools, both Catholic and Protestant, under lay management, charging fees. *Secondary* schools are privately owned and managed, the majority by Roman Catholic religious orders, and a minority by Roman Catholic or Protestant laymen or foundations. *Vocational* schools are administered by the vocational education committees, eight of whose fourteen members are usually elected by the local rating authority, and the remainder co-opted from other local interests. Each committee also has a chief executive officer, who is the link between the committee and the headmaster of each individual school. *Comprehensive* schools, whose origin dates back to 1963, are controlled by a three-man committee representative of local (usually denominational) interests, the VEC and the Department of Education, and is ultimately responsible to the Department. There is a small number of comprehensives with a different, and more strongly denominational, managerial structure, which are in effect denominational schools that have been transferred to the Department of Education. *Community* schools, although there is no fixed pattern, are controlled by a six-man committee composed of two representatives of merged or transferred secondary schools (usually one boys' school and one girl's school, both run by religious orders), two representatives of the merged vocational school (usually members of the VEC) and two elected parents. As in the case of comprehensive schools, the ultimate authority for these schools, especially in financial matters, is the Department of Education.

Finance

The state pays the total salaries of all teachers in national schools, together with a grant towards heating and cleaning of school premises. A variable contribution—usually 10 per cent—of the capital cost of new school buildings is, however, raised locally. The difficulties that this creates, particularly in mushrooming urban communities, are often considerable. In practice the financial burden is often so large that it can only be accepted by a religious order. Further sums, amounting to £10 per teacher in 1971–2 (with extra funds available at the discretion of the inspectorate), are payable in respect of school equipment. In other cases the money required is raised by local committees or by the school manager, who is usually a clergyman, Catholic or Protestant. Non-state-aided primary schools receive no state subsidy whatever.

The state pays the incremental salaries of all recognized teachers in vocational, secondary, comprehensive and community schools. In secondary schools a further payment is made to teachers by the managerial authorities, who are their contractual employers. Current expenditure in comprehensive and community schools is borne by the state. In vocational schools it comes partly from central funds and partly from local rates. In secondary schools it is subsidized from central funds (a) by way of capitation grants (£24 per senior pupil and £19 per junior pupil for first 100 pupils), and (b) by a further payment of £30 per pupil to schools who have forgone their fees and opted into the 'free post-primary education scheme' launched in 1967. Secondary schools which have opted into this scheme still frequently exact a regular 'voluntary' contribution from parents to help repay building debts previously incurred. Those outside the scheme continue to receive capitation grants but charge fees. The subsidy for Protestant education is differently organized: the Department pays a lump sum roughly equal to £30 for every Protestant child of post-primary school age to a joint committee, then distributes it, in accordance with a means test, to Protestant parents in order to subsidize their children's attendance at Protestant schools. The *per capita* subsidy to Protestant and Catholic children is therefore the same, but the higher cost of Protestant education, owing to the absence of any Protestant equivalent of the Roman Catholic religious orders, many of whose members have traditionally used their salaries to underwrite both capital and current expenditure in the schools under their control, has resulted in higher fees. As the rates of subsidy are determined by the amount needed to provide free education for Catholic children, it follows that Protestant parents, although in receipt of no less money, still have to make up the difference between the subsidy and their fee levels out of their own pockets. This has caused considerable controversy, and has led to the creation of so-called 'Protestant' comprehensives to provide totally free education for Protestant children in some areas. Capital costs of comprehensive schools are borne fully by the state. Capital costs of vocational schools are borne partly by the state and partly by the local authority. Capital costs of community schools are borne by the state (90 per cent) and by the various educational interests—local authorities, religious orders, etc.—whose schools are being merged in the new foundation (10 per cent). Under a scheme first introduced in 1966 capital grants for secondary schools are made available for approved projects in either of two ways: (a) if all or a portion of the costs are being met by way of a loan obtained from a source other than the Department, and repayable over a specified period of years with interest at an approved rate, the Minister will undertake to pay to the school authorities during the specified period an annual grant not exceeding 70 per cent of the annual repayments (principal and interest) on such loan as may have been obtained by the school authorities to meet the approved cost of the building or (b) the Minister may undertake to pay the total approved cost of building—70 per cent by way of grant and 30 per cent by way of loan repayable over fifteen years with interest at the rate current for loans from the Local Loans Fund.

Separate funds are available to secondary schools for science and other equipment for practical rooms (£150,000 in 1971–2) and to all post-primary schools for free books for pupils in need of them (£220,000 in 1971–2).

The school-going population

School attendance is compulsory between the ages of six and fourteen, but the raising of the school-leaving age to fifteen is due to take place in 1973. In addition, on 1 February 1971 there were 37,617 four-year-old and 57,674 five-year-old pupils enrolled in national schools. At the beginning of the 1970–1 school year, 90·8 per cent of national school pupils transferred to recognized post-primary schools, and 0·5 per cent to some other type of post-primary education. The estimated figures for the percentage of each age-group in full-time enrolment in education (February 1971) were: (15) 69·8 per cent (16) 55·2 per cent (17) 40·8 per cent and (18) 20·9 per cent. A small proportion of children remain at national school until age fifteen; equally, some leave before the legal school-leaving age. Of post-primary senior cycle school-leavers, an estimated 5·1 per cent enter all types of teacher training, 9·8 per cent go into further education, and 25·6 per cent into the universities (February 1971).

Curriculum

The curriculum of primary schools in the Irish Republic has been shaped by a number of political and educational factors, among them the national policy aimed at the restoration of the Irish language as a vernacular throughout the country, the existence of a compulsory Primary Certificate Examination between 1943 and 1967, and the overwhelmingly academic nature of the post-primary curriculum generally adopted by the church-controlled secondary schools, to which an overwhelming majority of Irish parents have traditionally sent their children. Irish has been a compulsory subject in primary schools since 1922. The Report of the Council of Education on the function and curriculum of the primary school, published in 1964, criticized the narrowness of the existing curriculum, and suggested a stress on practical subjects, but its defence of the concept (if not the actual practice) of the primary certificate examination ensured the domination of a subject-centred approach until the abolition of the examination and the almost simultaneous introduction of a new child-centred curriculum in 1971–2. The introduction of the new curriculum has posed immense problems, not least for teacher training and for the necessary reduction of class sizes, especially in the early years of schooling. It was in use experimentally in 600 schools by 1972. The Report of the Council of Education on the curriculum of secondary schools, published in 1960, approved of the courses then offered, but warned against over-specialization. 'The dominant purpose of our secondary schools' they stated categorically, 'is the inculcation of religious ideals and values.' This emphasis is a constant one in Irish education. It has found expression in the government publication *Ar ndáltai uile* (*All our Children*), 1969, which describes religion as one of the three 'most important subjects' in post-primary schools (the other two are civics and PE), and in numerous speeches by Ministers for Education at the opening of church-controlled secondary schools. Here, too, Irish became a matter of controversy. The creation of the community schools was closely linked to an experiment in curriculum development minimum based on a compulsory core of subjects and a range of optional subjects, assembled in different groups. A Department of Education attempt to make this compulsory throughout the system foundered on the rock of the secondary schools' resolute opposition, based in many cases on their unwillingness to abandon a narrow academic approach—an approach based, in turn, on university entrance curriculum. Thus, a student who wishes to enter an Irish university to acquire a degree in agriculture may not present agricultural science as a matriculation subject, since the universities do not recognize it as such: but he may present Greek. Similarly, an intending student for an engineering degree may present Hebrew as a matriculation subject, but not mechanical drawing. These and other anomalies have been the subject of a long-standing disagreement between the Department of Education and the university authorities: so far the universities have shown little willingness to compromise. All curricula are marred by the absence of project work and proper assessment techniques. Comprehensives still group to a certain extent. There are no important differences between the curriculum taught in Catholic and in Protestant schools. There is a fractional cross-over factor, in that some Catholic pupils attend Protestant schools, and vice versa: usually facilities for religious instruction are provided in such cases. In the vocational schools, which are non-denominational, clergymen of all denominations are afforded free access. There was until recently a marked difference between the curriculum provided by the secondary schools and that provided by the vocational schools, which were largely technical in orientation and in many cases did not prepare children for Leaving Certificate or University Matriculation examinations. The introduction of a 'technical leaving certificate' designed to end the cul-de-sac quality of vocational education proved a failure, and eventually the vocational school curriculum was expanded by the addition of grammar-school type subjects leading to the Leaving Certificate and Matriculation examinations. Curriculum development projects have been started in a number of areas, linked to experiments aimed at evaluating the traditional examination framework, and 1972 saw the formation of an independent Curriculum Development Association. Two individual developments are noteworthy:

the move away from a simplistic and often Anglophobe interpretation of history, and the projected introduction of philosophy as a senior cycle subject. There are four state examinations. The Day Group certificate, taken exclusively by vocational school students of fifteen plus is awarded to students who pass in a 'core' or group of two or three specified subjects and any number of a wide range of optional subjects. These results must include at least Grade D in each of the core subjects, Grade D in subjects tested by practical examination, and 30 per cent in oral Irish. The Intermediate Certificate is awarded, also at fifteen plus to candidates who reach at least Grade D in five or more subjects, one of which must normally be Irish. The Leaving Certificate is awarded, at seventeen plus to candidates who achieve Grade D in Irish and at least four other subjects. It may be acquired by accumulation. The Advanced Leaving Certificate is to be awarded (from 1972) to candidates of eighteen plus who achieve Grade D in one or more subjects: they must take a minimum of three subjects. All examinations except the Group Certificate can be taken in all post-primary schools.

Exams

There are four state examinations, and the university matriculation examinations.

The Day Group Certificate, or Day Vocational Certificate, is designed to meet entry qualifications for various apprenticeship schemes for children who leave school at the end of the junior cycle (fifteen plus). Because of its technical bias it is rarely if ever available in secondary schools. It consists of five different 'core' groups of subjects and a number of optional subjects. Because of its flexible and to a certain extent non-competitive nature it is the focus for a number of curriculum experiments. In 1971 9,475 pupils obtained this examination.

The Intermediate Certificate is designed to show that the fifteen plus pupil has completed a well-balanced course of general education, and to be an indication of his fitness for further education. Candidates must pass in five subjects, including Irish. In 1971 26,657 students obtained this certificate.

The Leaving Certificate is taken at seventeen plus in at least five subjects, including Irish. It is regarded as a test of achievement. Passes above a certain level, in certain subjects, give students exemptions in the equivalent matriculation subjects for university entrance. Certificates may be acquired on a cumulative basis. In 1971 16,764 students obtained this certificate.

The Advanced Leaving Certificate, to be taken at eighteen plus, is in at least three subjects: the certificate will be awarded to candidates who reach Grade D in one subject or more. The first students to sit for this examination will do so this summer (1972).

Further education

The regional technical colleges, the colleges of technology, and a number of other institutions providing courses in areas such as domestic science, commerce, retail distribution and management studies account for the bulk of further education provision in the Republic. It is a small but growing sector. In the past it prepared pupils largely for British qualifications. With the recent (1972) establishment of a Council for National Educational Awards—to include degree-level as well as non-degree-level courses—the attractiveness of these institutions has been enhanced. Another notable development has been the creation of the National Institute for Higher Education in Limerick, which will include facilities for the training of physical education teachers for the country as a whole but whose basic approach is geared both to degree-level and diploma-level students, in module-type courses, with a strong bias towards both technology and European studies. The first students will be accepted for the Institute in the autumn of 1972. Numbers are expected to rise to a total of about 5,000 in the near future.

University education

There are two universities in the Republic. Dublin University, which received its charter from Elizabeth I in 1591, has one college—Trinity College, Dublin. The National University of Ireland, founded in 1908 on the foundation of the old Queen's Colleges, has three colleges: one in Dublin, one in Cork and one in Galway; St Patrick's College, Maynooth, the national Roman Catholic seminary, is recognized by the university for degree-awarding purposes. There is an independent medical school, the Royal College of Surgeons in Ireland, founded in 1784, with a limited, high-level intake, much of it from abroad. The universities are independent institutions, but rely to an increasing extent on government funds for capital expansion and for subsidization of current expenditure. The state subsidy per university student (1972) is £527. This includes sums made available to the universities for capital purposes, but excludes money paid to holders of university grants, under a scheme based on a means test plus examination results. In 1971–2 £1,176,314 was paid to 4,333 students under this scheme, representing 21·4 per cent of the student body. An anomaly in this area is that the grants do not operate below the level of four Leaving Certificate honours, whereas a number of university faculties—notably arts—accept two honours as an admission qualification. With one exception, the number of students normally resident outside the state who are attending universities in the Republic is low. Non-Irish students in UCD in 1971–2, for example, amounted to no more than 193 out of a total of 7,966. The other colleges of the National University had less than 100 full-time foreign students between them. The exception is Trinity College, Dublin, which has traditionally had strong links with Northern Ireland (for many years all students at Magee University College in Derry completed their undergraduate courses in Trinity, before Magee's incorporation into the New

University of Ulster). At present some 20 per cent of admissions to Trinity is being reserved for students from Northern Ireland and the university authorities hope to increase this to 25 per cent. As recently as 1971 some 40 per cent of the graduates at this college were non-Irish. The decision to earmark a proportion of places for NI students is, therefore, not so much a limitation as an indication that the increasing enrolments from students resident in the Republic will not be allowed to prejudice the special relationship between the College and the North of Ireland. Another feature of Irish universities generally is the high proportion of students doing pass courses—approximately two and a half to three times as many as do honours. There is also a high failure rate in first arts examinations, especially in the colleges of the National University, sometimes approaching 40 per cent. The huge majority of undergraduate courses in arts, commerce, law, science etc. are three years in the NUI colleges (four in Trinity). Medicine and dentistry are five-year courses.

The whole university system is currently under revision, partly as a result of the findings of the Commission on Higher Education, 1960–7. The National University is to be divided into a number of independent colleges, but the existence of the Higher Education Authority (created on a statutory basis in 1972) provides a certain amount of co-ordination, both of development and of financing, and there may also be created a Conference of Irish Universities. It is unlikely that the traditional faculty and subject divisions within the colleges will be significantly altered in any way, but the need to rationalize the use of resources will probably result in the development of certain appropriate areas of specialization within each of the newly independent universities. In the early 1960s considerable interest was generated in a proposal to merge Trinity College, Dublin, with University College, Dublin, both on financial and on social grounds—to prevent unnecessary duplication of university resources in the capital city and to effect a fusion of cultural traditions represented by the Protestant heritage of TCD and the Catholic heritage of the theoretically non-denominational UCD. Increased admissions of Roman Catholic students to TCD however, coupled with the need for overall revision of the system, have modified these plans. So, inevitably, has growing academic opposition to the idea of a total merger as originally propounded by the Minister for Education.

Third-level reorganization

The almost moribund controversy about the projected merger between Trinity College and University College Dublin received a fresh fillip in July 1972 with the publication of a Higher Education Authority report on the issue. In broad terms, the HEA accepted a compromise agreement worked out by the authorities of the two colleges in 1970 in response to the govern-

ment's proposals. The only major difference was in medicine, where the HEA recommended the replacement of the existing three professorial units with a single unit. The university compromise envisaged the maintenance of the existing units. Under the HEA proposals the new joint medical school would be run by a statutory 'Conjoint Board' with equal representation from the two colleges, both of which would, as anticipated, become full universities in their own rights, together with the National University Colleges in Cork, Galway and Maynooth. The Conjoint Board would also supervise and facilitate the reorganization of certain faculties and their reallocation between the two institutions on the basis agreed in their 1970 compromise. The HEA also proposed the eventual establishment by the universities themselves of a non-statutory Conference of Irish Universities. Despite the appeal by the HEA for an early statement by the government to end the uncertainty which has plagued the universities since the report of the Commission on Higher Education (1960–7), progress is likely to be slow.

In a possibly more far-reaching report published at the same time the HEA proposed the creation of a new third-level institution with a strong technological bias in Dublin. This was in response to the plans of the City of Dublin vocational education committee for a polytechnic-type institution on a sixty-acre site outside the city. The HEA accepted the principle of a new institution, but pruned it rather drastically (removing art, music and teacher education, among other things, from the model) and expressed concern about the isolation of the site. They stressed, however, the need for technician education, and called for maximum mobility of both staff and students of engineering between university and non-university institutions.

Teacher education

Teacher education in Ireland is provided in the universities, in teacher training colleges, and in a number of other training institutions, catering for domestic science, woodwork, art, physical education, building science, mechanical engineering and motor engineering teachers. The majority of post-primary teachers have university degrees plus a Higher Diploma in Education (one-year course) acquired at postgraduate level. Primary teachers go to a training college on completion of a post-primary education (entrance is competitive, based on Leaving Certificate results, and entrance standards are generally higher than those for university admission) for a two-year course. University graduates may qualify as primary teachers on completion of a one-year course at training college: primary teacher qualifications allow a student exemption from a first-year degree course in some university faculties. Cross-over within the teaching profession is limited, except between the vocational and secondary schools. In some cases (e.g. H. Dip. in Ed.) all fees are payable by the students concerned. In others (e.g. two-year woodwork courses) students, who must be suitably qualified in the trades concerned, pay no fees and receive weekly maintenance allowances on a single/married scale. The Higher Education Authority has proposed (1970) the establishment of An Foras Oidechais, an independent teacher training authority, the extension of the primary teacher training course to three years, leading to a CNEA primary degree, and the deepening of the H. Dip. in Ed. course in the universities. Specialist teacher education, it has further recommended, should be located at the Limerick Institute. The Minister for Education has promised a three-year course for primary teachers, but has not said when this will happen or whether it will—as primary teachers insist—take place within a university framework.

Research

Research is still in many ways the poor relation of the Irish educational system. The major research effort was that devoted to the report on investment in education prepared in co-operation with OECD (1965). The most recent figures for research allocations included almost £40,000 for primary education, divided between the Research Unit in St Patrick's Training College, Dublin (£10,780) and a special project for inner-city education (£27,600). The allocation for research in the post-primary sphere for 1971–2 was £25,000. There are no specific allocations to research workers at third level, but research is carried out in the normal course of events by the university departments of education. There is, however, relatively little postgraduate work proper in education, as Irish university departments of education have had to concentrate their slender resources largely on the one-year diploma students.

Controversies

1. *Selection*

There is no selection for entry to vocational schools, community schools, or comprehensive schools and although there have been hints that Protestant children will get priority in certain comprehensive schools which have been established on the transfer of formerly Protestant secondary schools, it is not yet clear how this will work out in practice. A considerable number of secondary schools, however, have established selection procedures of one kind or another, usually in the form of an 'entrance examination' designed to assess the child's capacity to follow the type of academic course provided in these schools. The Department of Education, while defining its task as the provision of post-primary education for every pupil who seeks it, has said: 'The discharging of this task does not enable the Department to seek to control the enrolment procedures in individual schools.' Opposition to this practice—which has always

existed in one form or another—has been growing. It comes from parents, who see their children denied entry to local secondary schools while pupils from outside the catchment area are accepted; an additional anomaly is that a pupil who is refused entry to his local free post-primary school and who therefore has to travel to a post-primary school, secondary, vocational or comprehensive, which will accept him, does not receive a travel subsidy because of his proximity to a free school. It also comes from teachers in primary schools, partly because they resent the way in which the individual progress cards, which have taken the place of the old primary certificate examination, are disregarded by the secondary school authorities, partly because few if any of the entrance examinations are designed to take into account the nature and existence of the new curriculum in primary schools. In some areas the principle of selection is underwritten by the existence of national schools under the management of the same religious order which controls the secondary school: pupils attending such a national school have a higher chance of acceptance than those at primary schools which lack this link. Some secondary schools, in addition, have private, fee-paying preparatory departments from which entry into the secondary school is virtually assured. Opposition to all these practices is still not at a high enough level to have any noticeable effect. There is much support for them—and for streaming—in the organizations catering for post-primary teachers in the secondary schools (although not from the vocational teachers' organization).

2. *Rationalization and comprehensivization*

The unco-ordinated nature of the Irish educational system at both primary and post-primary level was the object of an intensive study on 'Investment in Education' carried out jointly by the Irish Department of Education and the OECD. It was published in 1965, the first study of its kind to be undertaken in Europe, and has provided the basis for all rationalization efforts since then.

(a) *Primary.* An intensive programme of primary school rationalization was embarked on. By 1972, for example, almost 1,000 one-teacher schools had been closed, together with a large number of two-teacher schools. This is a continuing process, as declining populations in rural areas reduce three-teacher schools to two-teacher status and make them vulnerable to closure. Transport schemes have been instituted for children thus affected—schemes which take the special problems of Protestant children in rural areas into account. There are still 1,561 two-teacher schools (February 1972). In February 1971 there were 6,733 pupils in one-teacher schools, 76,735 in two-teacher schools, and 67,599 in three-teacher schools. Local opposition to school closures has been expressed in a number of areas, notably Irish-speaking areas. A cognate problem is that of class size. In February 1971 almost half the total primary school population (233,506) was in classes of forty or over.

(b) *Post-primary.* The main findings of the Investment in Education Report were: (i) that there was likely to be a shortage of persons with suitable qualifications for the jobs available in Ireland in the 1970s; (ii) that there were great inequalities, based on social group and geographical location, in the participation of children in post-primary education at all levels; (iii) that the relative emphasis given to different subjects within the curriculum was not consistent with careers subsequently followed by the pupils; and (iv) that there were gaps in the efficiency of the educational system in terms of the pattern of use of existing educational resources. An early attempt to remedy some of these deficiencies was the establishment of the comprehensive schools. Later (1966) the government attempted to persuade post-primary schools in different rural and small town centres to participate in voluntary co-operation schemes: this had virtually no effect. Finally (1970) it came up with a plan for community schools, to be created by agreement rather than by legislation, in new buildings in the different centres. The community schools were to be co-educational, comprehensive and non-fee-paying with enrolments of 400–800 or even 1,100. A carrot-and-stick policy was adopted—and is still in force—to persuade schools to participate, involving refusal to sanction capital grants for additions to existing schools or for new private secondary schools, coupled with offers of generous representation on the boards of management of the new schools to the interests controlling the existing schools. To date the policy has not been a marked success. Some religious orders have objected to it on the grounds that it would force them to comprehensivize their overwhelmingly academic curriculum; others have objected on the grounds that it means surrendering part of their control over education. Teachers have objected because they are not represented on the boards of management of the new projected schools. Protestants (and some Catholics) have objected to the size of the role given to Catholic educational authorities in the new schools, but this has since been reduced, and the new schools have been deemed 'acceptable' by authoritative Protestant spokesmen. Overall, the lack of any regional framework, and the intense degree of centralization involved in the proposals, has also been widely criticized. Parents in the centres chosen for new community schools have also campaigned in many cases for the retention of the *status quo.* The general belief is that a school of 400–800 is too large, and that one of 200 is viable. The problem is a continuing one. Its extent— and the extent of the opposition to comprehensivization—can be gauged from the fact that the enrolment patterns in post-primary schools were, until comparatively recently, heavily weighted in favour of the secondary schools, in a ratio of 240-100. This was partly because of the social cachet of the secondary schools, partly because the academic curriculum they provided was a passport to university and the professions, while the vocational school curriculum was a cul-de-sac. Shortage of job opportunities for academically qualified school leavers, and raised university entrance requirements, together with the expansion of the vocational schools curricula towards the end of of the 1960s, have now produced an enrolment pattern which is roughly equally divided between the two types of school. With the establishment of the regional technical colleges, some of the glamour of the traditional academic curriculum may disappear, but nobody pretends that this will happen overnight. The raising of university entrance standards, coupled with the unemployability of the academically-educated child in a technician-starved economy, may well be powerful factors in this.

3. *Irish*

One of the first acts of the new government in 1922— at a time when the country was heading into a deep civil war—was to decree the compulsory teaching of Irish in national schools. In 1928–9 this was extended to post-primary schools where it was made a compulsory subject for the Leaving Certificate examination. Subsequently it became compulsory for entry to the civil service. The psychological effect of these requirements has to some extent overshadowed the reality. Less than 1 per cent of candidates fail their Leaving Certificates annually because of failure in Irish (failure rates in Irish as a subject are normally much lower than for mathematics); and in 1961–2 377 out of 385 people appointed to professional and technical posts in the public service were appointed without having the required Irish qualifications. It has been calculated that about 20 per cent of the population have a fair knowledge of the language, but it is not until comparatively recently that the political attempt to revive it was backed up by the appropriate educational research; for many years, for example, the unwillingness of protagonists of each of three main dialects to abandon their positions made it impossible to elaborate any form of Standard Irish (newsreaders from each area took it in turn to read the news in Irish on the radio). Opposition to the language revival policy has existed for many years in an unco-ordinated way. It might be argued that part of it stems from the Protestant/ Unionist tradition (a Protestant representative on the Council of Education signed a minority report objecting to the status of Irish in both the report on the primary and that on the secondary curriculum, in 1954 and 1960 respectively), but as against that some of the strongest supporters of that policy have also been Protestants. In more recent times, both opposition to the language, and a renewed enthusiasm for it, have been located primarily in the middle classes. A 'Language Freedom Movement' has been formed to campaign for the abolition of compulsory Irish in schools: its first public meeting was disrupted by pro-Irish members of the audience who demanded and finally received from the platform equal time to put their point of view. Concern has also been expressed by some Irish educationalists about the possible dangers of an undue stress on Irish in the primary school curriculum in areas, such as centre-city areas, where children are educationally at risk in any case, and one study—whose findings have been strenuously controverted—has attempted to show that the teaching of Irish in primary schools has affected children's performance in other areas in comparison with that of English children. Together with this must be considered the problems of the children and parents in the Irish-speaking areas of the country, mostly along the western seaboard, who constitute a linguistic minority of a very special kind in that their vernacular is officially designated as the national language. The Minister for Education has recently indicated (1972) that he is prepared to reconsider the compulsory aspects of the revival policy as long as he is sure that the language will not suffer thereby. Fine Gael, the main opposition party, has come out strongly against compulsion, at least at the post-primary level. A number of important, government-commissioned attitudinal surveys are currently in progress throughout the country in an attempt to provide the government with sociological material relevant to any future changes or developments in policy.

8 Education for what?

Edmund Leach

As a child I was accustomed, like other children, to ask a lot of silly questions and my parents, like other parents, gave in desperation a lot of silly answers. Some of those questions and answers have stuck in my memory: they formed a very basic part of my education. Here is a case in point. I recollect that when travelling in a crowded tram-car or train I was very systematically told that 'I must give up my seat to a lady'. When I said 'But why?', I would get versions of one of three answers: First: 'Because it's good manners.' (This of course is no answer at all, and merely produced another question 'Why is it good manners?') Second: 'Because it shows respect to women.' Third: 'Because women are the weaker sex and get tired from standing up.' The second and third answers to my question were often offered simultaneously, but it was a long time before I realized that they were mutually contradictory. Yet clearly, if I act towards a woman in such a way as to assert that she is weaker than I am, I am showing not respect but disrespect.

This trivial example illustrates the general theme which is intended to run right through what I am about to say. Our educational system teaches us one set of values explicitly, intentionally, and quite another set of values implicitly, unintentionally, and often the second set of values is exactly converse to the first. If you will bear this example in mind I think that you will see what I am getting at.

On reading through an earlier draft of this lecture it struck me that there is one very obvious criticism from which I had better try to defend myself right away. Much of my argument is concerned with the social class implications of the choices which all of us make in the course of our educational careers and it may well seem to some of you that, although my comments may have some relevance to Eton and King's College Cambridge, they could have no bearing on anything that goes on under the auspices of the University of Manchester. I don't believe that is true. Admittedly I talk from an Oxbridge rather than from a Redbrick or post-Robbins view of what the education of adults is all about, but I am not simply surveying the world from the roof of King's College Chapel. It is indeed central to my complaint that *all* the newer Universities in England, whether they are located in great cities like Manchester and Leeds or open fields like York and Canterbury, tend to take a distant view of Oxbridge dreaming spires as the model of what a University ought to be. If this is genuinely *not* the case, then no one could be more delighted than myself.

This lecture is sponsored by a University Department of Extra-Mural Studies and it is a pre-supposition of all such departments that Education is a good thing in itself, quantitatively as well as qualitatively. I am aware that 'adult education' now ramifies into all sorts of strange avenues but the general objective behind all these activities remains the same; it is to give some of the benefits which are supposed to come from a sixth form and University education to those who went into a job straight from school.

This optimistic faith that 'Education is good for you' like a daily apple or a bottle of Guinness is now shared by the whole world. Whether you are a peasant fisherman from Anguilla or a former headhunter

Source: Roscoe Review, Department of Extra-Mural Studies, University of Manchester (Autumn 1969). This was originally delivered as the fifth Roscoe lecture at the University of Manchester's Annual Reception for WEA and Extension students on 26 April 1969.
Dr Edmund Leach is Provost of King's College, Cambridge.

from Borneo, or a housewife from Salford makes no difference: you want your children to have 'more' education.

But why is this thing 'Education' so desirable? To the cynical observer, it does not seem at all obvious that formal schooling makes people happier or turns them into better world citizens. In my travels as an anthropologist I have on several occasions been able to observe the immediate consequences of the introduction of *elementary* education—i.e. reading, writing and arithmetic—among a previously illiterate population. The consequences are very striking; but they are socially extremely disruptive, and it is difficult to see why they should be rated as 'good'. Or to go to the other extreme: the population of the United States is at the present time by far the 'best educated' in the world in the sense that a far higher proportion of young people get a College-type education than in any other country. But do we really all want to become Americans? The American Way of Life is no doubt congenial to a great many people but it certainly isn't *my* idea of Heaven. So if we are to increase the *quantity* of education available to ordinary people in this country, what is supposed to be the advantage, and for whom?

Now this is an awkward question—and perhaps for some of you it gets rather near the bone. You see, so long as everyone is ready to agree that formal education is a good thing *in itself*—then the question 'But why do you want to have *more* education either for yourself or your children?' needs no answer. But as soon as I challenge that basic assumption and ask 'But *why* is education a good thing?', then you are pushed back to seek a justification, which must in the end boil down to one of self interest: 'I want more education because of what I shall get out of it.'

Well what will you get out of it? More knowledge? More pay? Higher social status? Greater happiness? It might be any of these things and much else besides. So let us ask that awkward question: Why do we think that education is a good thing? What do we expect to get out of it?

So far I have been using the word education in its ordinary colloquial meaning to denote the kind of formal training that goes on in schools and technical colleges and universities of various kinds. But you need to understand that education in this sense is an artificially narrow concept appropriate only to the peculiar conditions of our present age. The finished product of *any* educational system in *any* part of the world at *any* point in history is an adult human being who adopts a particular way of living because of what he has *learned*. But only a small part of this learning is likely to have been acquired formally as a consequence of going to school. Your total education as an adult Englishman includes everything which differentiates you from being, say, a Frenchman or an Italian, and most of it has been acquired in a quite *informal way*—it includes for example a wide range of quite unconscious 'habits', the way you talk, the way you walk, the way you sit down and stand up and how you use your arms when talking, the kinds of clothes you wear, the sorts of houses you live in, the way you eat your food and the sorts of food you eat, your manners, your values, your general way of life—*all* this is a product of education but very little of it came to you formally from any sort of schooling; mostly it was simply a matter of imitating others in the context of home or school or place of work.

And this is true of *every* kind of human society, primitive as well as sophisticated.

The way of life of the ordinary adult has to be learned; it doesn't come naturally, it is a product of education. But because this educational process of cultural transmission is very largely imitative it is always deeply conservative.

Even in a situation such as the present when, on the face of it, the teenage generation are trying to express their quite normal hostility to their parents by creating what *they* think of as a brand new culture of their own design, the outcome is entirely lacking in originality— every detail turns out to be a more or less conscious borrowing from the past—side whiskers from 1880, posters from 1895. The universal principle is that what was good enough for our ancestors must be good enough for us: the *right* way to behave *always* belongs to a tradition stemming from the past.

Remember that: I shall come back to it again presently. The ideas which we have about what is *right* so far as formal education is concerned belong to a tradition stemming from the past. Presently I shall take a look at this tradition but first let me make a different point.

If we take the very broad sociological view that, in human society as a whole, education signifies the total process of socialization—that is to say everything that is transmitted by learning from one generation to another then we can break down this very broad category into several components:

(1) *Habits*, which are learned informally at home or school or place of work
(2) *Skills*, learnt formally at school or by some other systematic form of training
(3) *Knowledge*, mainly acquired by conversation and by reading. We acquire 'knowledge' mainly because it is interesting. It has little utilitarian value.

When we break down our categories in this way we can see immediately that these different facets of the total educational process are mutually in competition. Any form of learning takes up time and if you exaggerate the time spent on formal school education then you will inevitably cut back on the more informal but perhaps equally valuable process of informal socialization. To take a case in point: Anyone who has ever had anything to do with university undergraduates must be aware of the problems posed by young men and women who are academically very advanced but socially and emotionally very backward. It isn't that they have had too little education; they have been educated with the wrong kind of mix. Many of my own past pupils would certainly have been much better adjusted to adult life if they had had much *less* academic pressure imposed upon them at school and spent more time just learning to know their fellow-men.

Such cases imply that whether we like it or not, we are faced with problems of evaluation. The issue is not simply: Is formal education a good thing? But rather: Is it *such* a good thing that in order to attain it we are always prepared to prejudice informal non-school education?

And from there we are led on to another kind of evaluation as well: How can we assess the merit of learning which is useless but interesting as against learning which is useful but dull?

In short we need to understand that whatever we do we shall always be learning something or other, but we have to make choices. How should we allocate our time between one kind of learning and another?

In our present circumstances this problem of choice does not arise at primary school level. A moderate degree of literacy has now come to be accepted as an essential component of our culture. The argument starts when we begin to consider the content of secondary and higher education, including all forms of adult training.

First there is the distinction between the acquisition of manual skills and book learning with the curious but deeply rooted bias which tends to make the latter superior to the former.

(In fact of course it is much *easier* to read about how to do something than to learn how to actually do it, and the high status of book learning is simply a hang-over from a much earlier period when skilled craftsmanship was common but elementary literacy very rare.)

Then within the esteemed category of 'things which we learn from books' there is the distinction between subjects which, potentially, have some practical utility, and this includes all the sciences, and subjects which are merely 'interesting' but which cannot have any practical consequences, e.g. all historical and literary studies. Here again for a great many people—the *less* the practicality the *higher* the prestige . . . all the humanities are better than all sciences, and all 'pure' sciences are better than any 'applied' sciences. Yet logic would surely argue just the other way round. On what possible basis could an historical study such as archaeology be evaluated as 'a good thing in itself'—good for what? What do people *really* get out of studying these subjects (and there are a great many of them), which can have no possible consequences for anyone? Is it knowledge that they are after, or personal enjoyment, or prestige, or just a degree—a kind of certificate of industrious intelligence?

So my question is serious: Education for what?

Let me repeat: The *right* way to behave always belongs to a tradition stemming from the past. Our approval of education is just such a case; let us look at the tradition.

Our assumption that scholastic education is good in itself is a residue of the history of English society—a society which for centuries past has placed tremendous emphasis on social class differentiation. One of the most insidious elements in the whole business is that all of us have been taught (not explicitly but implicitly) to set especially high value on those forms of education which are considered appropriate to a gentleman. Let us consider how this came about.

In medieval England there were three sectors of society which had an interest in formal schooling. Firstly there were the *clerks*—the Bureaucrats as we should now call them, but in those days primarily the Clergy and the Lawyers. They conducted their business in Latin and had a vested interest in obscurantism. They were a dominating influence in the Universities and their attitude to learning was based on reverence for established authority. The highest form of scholarship was to be able to write a new commentary on Aristotle. Radical criticism and inquisitiveness were strongly discouraged.

Secondly there were the *merchants*. They needed educated apprentices who could conduct correspondence and keep accounts. It was primarily the members of *this* social class who founded the numerous 'grammar schools' which started up all over the country in the fifteenth and sixteenth centuries. Unlike Winchester and Eton, which had been linked from the start with Oxford and Cambridge as a training ground for would-be *scholars*, the new grammar schools were what their name implies, places for teaching reading, writing and arithmetic to the sons of the middle class. But bear in mind that, at this period, the bulk of the population was quite illiterate so that to be able to read or write at all was itself a mark of prestige.

Finally there were the *aristocrats* in the great houses who cultivated learning as a kind of hobby—learning for learning's sake. A sixteenth-century Gentleman composed madrigals and wrote Latin sonnets with much the same kind of fluency as some of his modern successors complete *The Times* Crossword Puzzle before breakfast. The education of such people was, of set purpose, deeply impractical for it was an essential part of the definition of a gentleman that he did not have to work for his living.

This close association between erudition and aristocratic amateurism lasted right through until the end of the eighteenth century and has had a lasting significance. In class-conscious Britain it *still* provides the perfect answer to the sceptical: 'Scholarship and learning *must* be a good thing: look how the gentry approve of it.'

But the other side of this penny is that the scholarly education which was so much admired by the gentry during the late Renaissance period and afterwards was completely divorced from the great technological developments which were taking place at the same time. A great mathematician such as Newton could be immediately recognized and honoured because mathematics had been a part of the traditional learning right from the start, but innovations in the world of technology were left to the blacksmiths and the wheelwrights and other practical artisans. Such men could probably read and write but they never got anywhere near a University. Yet it was people of *this* kind who were ultimately the creators of the Industrial Revolution during the latter part of the eighteenth century and who thus provided the base from which the whole of our contemporary civilization has grown. Ironically, history gives them a relatively low ranking in the general scheme of things just because they were craftsmen rather than scholar gentlemen.

This class discrimination has persisted with tragic results. In the Universities of today you may meet with a whole series of subtle discriminations:

Arts versus Science.

Pure Science versus Applied Science.

Full-time students—(who know nothing of the great world outside) versus Part-time students (who are working for their living).

In every case prestige and virtue is felt to reside with the alienated and the impractical. Arts men are claimed to be more cultured than Scientists, Pure Science is more prestigious than Applied Science, Day students (full time) are more intelligent than Night students (part-time), Engineers are barely human.

I am not talking without some inside knowledge: I was both a student and a teacher at the London School of Economics (which runs night classes as well as day classes) before I became a Cambridge don and I took my first degree at Cambridge in Mathematics and Engineering.

But let us go back a bit. It was the eighteenth century Industrial Revolution which saw the birth of the Adult Education movement. The journeymen artisans who were experts at installing and maintaining the new machinery found their services in tremendous demand and aspired to better their social position. It was people such as these who were the highly motivated patrons of the newly established night schools and who educated themselves by omnivorous reading of absolutely anything they could get hold of. The objective was quite plain:—the upstarts wanted to break through the class barrier and achieve recognition as cultured gentlemen. The educational rat race had begun.

For those who were successful in this competition the rewards were glittering. I can speak rather definitely on this point because my own ancestors were people of precisely this sort. They had lived in the vicinity of Rochdale at least since the sixteenth century, but until the end of the eighteenth century none of them ever got above the copyhold farmer—small shopkeeper—artisan class. It so happens that a collection of letters and notebooks written by my great-great-grandfather during the period 1785–95 has survived. (This perhaps sounds like a telescoped pedigree but is explained by the fact that I myself was born on my father's 60th birthday.) In 1785 my great-great-grandfather was barely literate but he was evidently attending night school or else he was getting some coaching in calculations. He was also teaching himself correct letter-writing style out of a copy book. His technical skills were probably substantially less than those of a modern garage mechanic but he knew his value. Although he had no capital assets at all he already aspired to being a mill owner.

Forty years later his son is described in a parliamentary report as one of the leading cotton manufacturers in the country, and ten years later still (that is in 1835) letters from his granddaughters show that they had been very fully educated; they are worrying about whether their ball dresses are really in the latest Paris fashion and about other trivia of Manchester high society. Needless to say the boys of the next generation all went to public schools and one or two went on to the University and the Church. The family had made the grade.

Well that's one kind of answer to my question: Education for What? I hope you understand the moral of this personal anecdote. For my great-great-grandfather in 1785, primary education was a basic tool which he needed to get himself off the ground. But once the business enterprise had succeeded education became a symbol—a mark of social status; its content was then quite irrelevant, it was a means of exhibiting social class.

And let me be quite clear—this set of values is *still* a dominant factor in the pattern of English education. The persisting middle class support for fee paying Public Schools is a case in point. As to the motivations of those who attend WEA classes, well I really wouldn't know!

But let me go back to my history lesson. As the nineteenth century progressed ideas about what ought to go into education and who was entitled to get it gradually changed. So long as education was simply 'the mark of a gentleman' there was little or no specialization. The ideal then remained that of Renaissance Italy where Leonardo da Vinci had been artist, natural scientist, architect, engineer, ballistic expert all at once. There were English academic giants in the nineteenth century who were of comparable quality: W. Robertson Smith at different times held Professorial Chairs in Mathematics, Theology, Arabic, and Hebrew and edited the Encyclopaedia Britannica in his spare time.

Alas, *that* sort of academic achievement is no longer possible, but for people of less outstanding intelligence the *idea* of becoming an educated man in this all embracing sense is very attractive. It has the great merit that it is *not* an all or nothing procedure. Even if you are *not* the world's most outstanding expert at anything in particular you can still get a great deal of pleasure from knowing a certain amount about a wide area of human knowledge. In *this* kind of education no one ends up as a failure. It's a kind of education of which I personally approve and so also do most of you.

But unfortunately as things have now developed anyone who expressly sets out to educate himself in this broad fronted way only arouses contempt—he is an amateur, a dilettante. In University circles the 'serious scholar' is now required to be a specialist expert, and the whole educational machine has been redesigned so as to create such people. From the age of about ten onwards every child is constantly under pressure to make irreversible choices, which have the effect of narrowing down his or her academic interests. At each stage the prizes go to the pupil who concentrates on a narrow speciality. The boy or girl with wide ranging interests is always being pushed aside as 'not serious'. Those who are ultimately successful in this extraordinary competition become the supreme world experts in some minute corner of human knowledge but in the process they may have to abandon all other kinds of learning and 90 per cent of the fun.

The most pernicious aspect of this scheme of values is that extreme specialization is the goal set for *everyone*. Up to University level the whole educational system is now streamlined to suit the convenience of the tiny percentage of people who end up with Ph.D. Degrees right at the top of the specialist hierarchy. This means that, in so far as the ordinary pupil accepts the values which are implicit in the way he is taught, nearly everyone ends up by feeling himself to be a failure. Instead of teaching our pupils to feel pleased with themselves, no less than 90 per cent of those who are pushed right through the educational sausage machine are predestined to be labelled second rate or worse. Could anything be more absurd?

One of the corollaries of forcing pupils to specialize is that the proliferating departments and faculties in the Universities and other advanced educational institutes are themselves specialized and alienated from each other and have become subtly differentiated in terms of social prestige along the lines I have already indicated. Academic specialization and class consciousness are natural partners; by teaching the one we automatically instill the values of the other.

I hope you can see roughly what I am getting at. It is well established by now that a very high proportion of the population have the innate capacity to benefit from some variety of higher education if they choose to pursue such a goal, but this capability is a *general* not a special capability. If you want to become a musician or an artist or a poet it is just possible that you need to have *special* gifts, but to become a scholar or a scientist all you need is *general* capability. Mathematicians and ancient historians and molecular biologists are not different kinds of people—they are the same kind of people but they just happen to have specialized in different directions.

But why do people specialize in different directions?

As we grow up each potentially educated person is constantly being faced with choices: to work at examinations or not to work, to continue with schooling or take a job, to go to this University or that, to work at this subject or at that . . . How do we choose?

Our choices are *not* free. If we follow what we *think* are our private hunches, we are in fact being influenced unconsciously by the total values of the Culture within which we live. And it is just the same if we seek the advice of others, for that advice also will be biased by hidden prejudice inherent in the total system. Thus, if it is true, as I have suggested, that the whole system of English higher education is permeated through and through with implicit class-conscious assumptions, then these assumptions are bound to have the most complex feed-back consequences for the choices that are made by young men and women who are passing through the system. At the present time, as many of you will know, young people moving from school to university or polytechnic display a paradoxical disinclination to specialize in straight science: paradoxical because the monetary rewards which accrue to the trained scientist or engineer are very great; certainly very much greater than those which are likely to result from a degree or certificate in the social sciences which are currently so fashionable.

No doubt there are many complex reasons for this tendency:—One of these is that very few good scientists feed back into the teaching profession so that science is badly taught at school and is made to seem uninteresting. But there is more to it than that. On the humanities side also there has been a drastic shift of student preferences so that, in the older Universities anyway, Departments of Classics and History now find themselves overstaffed while Departments of Economics and Politics, Sociology and English Literature are crowded out.

The old guard academics regard this development as deplorable and tend to blame the students. They mutter darkly about lazy young men who choose soft options —though in point of fact (in so far as there is any evidence on these matters) it seems to be rather easier to get a good degree in some of the subjects which are shunned than in some of those which are crowded out. But there is also evidence that it is the newly fashionable departments of Economics and Politics, Sociology and English Literature which are the centres of the current student unrest.

Now two points deserve note. Firstly, these fashionable subjects have in the past all rated very low in the hierarchy of prestige; secondly, they all have it in common that they stimulate a sense of criticism of contemporary social conditions rather than a respect for the institutions which have been handed down from the past. I am suspicious of glib cause and effect 'explanations' of social phenomena, but one factor in all this, as it seems to me, is a deeply felt reaction against the class structure which is implicit in the established arrangements of the older Universities and which any education in the orthodox style of the past serves to reinforce.

Now here I am in a quandary for I am myself a part of the Establishment. How can the Provost of King's College, Cambridge, be other than an upholder of things as they are? And indeed, for the most part, I consider that the behaviour of the student revolutionaries is not only unpleasant but extremely stupid and yet, up to a point, I believe that the criticisms which they level against the system-as-it-is are quite justified.

You may have noticed that the only country which is ever praised by the revolutionary students is Maoist China; if they had actually been there they might be less enthusiastic but, in the present context, Maoism, as an *ideal*, has much to be said for it.

(Don't get alarmed, I am not just about to start off on a new lecture! This is where the threads begin to come together.)

I only want to make two points about Maoist China:
1 It is Mao Tze Tung, the self-educated peasant, who is still in the saddle and it is Liu Shao Chi, the academically trained Marxist theoretician, who used to be regarded as the brains of the Chinese communist party, who has failed.
2 In theory there is now a continuous interchange between the Universities and the villages and the workshops. University students are continually having to take time off from their University studies to go to work in factories or in the villages and the student population itself is supposed to be selected by committees of villagers and factory workers rather than by academic professors. The whole operation of University life is thus conceived as a glorified scheme of adult education.

Now I am quite sure that this is *not* how it works out in practice but the relevance for us is this:

Unquestionably the people who really matter in our own society (so far as the future is concerned)—the people who are going to decide whether life is to be physically tolerable or intolerable—are the applied scientists and the practical engineers. Consequently our educational concern must be *first* that our prestige system is such that people of the very highest calibre are drawn into practical professions of this sort, and *second* that they are people who have a *broad* understanding of the nature of society as a whole and that they are not just specialist experts in some tiny field. We still need people of the Renaissance mould—the would-be Leonardos.

In other words, in my own ideal Utopia, things would be just the other way on from what they usually are. It would be the practical men *not* the theoreticians who would get the prestige and the publicity and they would get a *broad* education. In contrast specialized education (which is now meted out to nearly everyone) would be cut right back and offered only to a small minority of eccentrics.

How would I set about it?

Well, on the specialist point, I would first of all abolish the Ph.D. altogether and I would eliminate nearly all research grants other than those in the pure and applied sciences. There is absolutely no justification for the State subsidy of scholarly self indulgence which is the present reward for a good first degree in English, or History, or Modern Languages.

The problem of the prestige hierarchy is much more difficult because we at present always give pride of place to students who work full-time and this inevitably creates the idea that the ivory tower kind of scholar who works in isolation from the world is a superior person, a member of an academic elite. Mind you, both the dons and the students like it that way. But *if* higher education is really intended to be a *training for adult life*, then surely it ought to be so organized that the young people concerned actually experience something of adult life in the process of being trained? The 'best' education ought to be reserved for those who are already earning their own living.

The logical implications of such a proposition are fairly drastic. For example the Cambridgeshire College of Arts and Technology ought to be rated a more prestigious institution than the ancient University of Cambridge. As things now stand this is not a probable development but my point is that it is a perfectly *possible* and in some ways *desirable* development. MIT (The Massachusetts Institute of Technology), which is an immediate neighbour of Harvard, has now outstripped its ancient neighbour in many fields even though thirty years or so ago it was little more than an Adult education technical school.

Where have we got to? Let me sum up.
1 Education is the total training of the adult. It starts the day you are born; it ends the day you are dead.
2 Every social system is by its nature conservative. Collectively it tries to reproduce itself. Our English social system is characterized by an extremely elaborate emphasis on social class difference. Our Educational system, as it now is, reinforces this class structure. That is what our educational system is about.
3 If you are satisfied with the existing class hierarchy then you do not need to worry about the educational system. It will continue to function much as it is functioning now—English society will evolve according to capitalist expectations and we shall all fetch up as fourth rate North Americans imbued with intense feelings of personal competitiveness.
4 If however you want to change the underlying structure of society then you need to think hard about some of the things that I have been talking about. The way our educational system creates categories of specialists who cannot communicate with one another and who are systematically *taught* that nearly everyone is second rate because only a tiny few can possibly achieve the ridiculous academic goals which are posed for all, and who are likewise *taught* that because of the gentlemanly traditions of the game there is something incompatible between being a student and a wage earner at the same time.

I am not myself a revolutionary. I do not believe that sudden changes ever make things better; they usually make things much worse and I am not suggesting that we should turn all our established conventions upside down overnight; but it is still possible to change things by degrees and if we have the insight to appreciate what is the *implicit* as distinct from the *explicit* in our educational procedures we may be able to push the system in a more sensible direction. Really it is all very obvious. You all know from your personal experience that the people with whom you can get on most easily are those who have had roughly the same upbringing as yourself—at home, at school, at work. If you want to maximize this sense of being able to get together, then you must minimize differentiation through specialization, not only difference between one kind of learned man and another, but between learned men and the rest. We need to stop teaching the student that he is a being of a special social class.

At school level the move towards Comprehensive Education is in the right direction but at the top end of the scale among the adults and near adults we may be playing the whole game the wrong way round. Influenced by academic snobbery, we have been starting up new universities galore and converting old established technical colleges into universities by a magical change of name. To what end? Some of the older members of this audience may have felt in recent months that the deplorable intolerance exhibited in student demonstrations is quite horribly reminiscent of Hitler's 'Brownshirts' in the early '30s. We should not be surprised! Without actually saying so we have been following closely in Hitler's footsteps. We have been systematically *teaching* our student adolescents that they form a superman elite—a race apart.

It might have been much better if we had left the old established Universities alone (as antiquated bastions of archaic learning) and concentrated on building up the status of the technical colleges into that of high-prestige technical institutes for the further training of adults who have already had some experience of what grown-up life is all about.

This perhaps is fantasy but one thing is quite certain . . . in a sane world the elitist status of places like King's College Cambridge would need to be severely deflated.

Section II The financing of education in Great Britain

Introduction to reading 9

In this article, written in 1964, John F. Embling, Deputy Under-Secretary of State, Department of Education and Science, provides a general account of how educational expenditure in England and Wales was then controlled. Since then the Welsh Office has opened a separate education department for the oversight of primary and secondary education. Further, there have been substantial changes in the way in which the grant from central government to local authorities is calculated: it remains, however, a general rather than a percentage grant.

9 Control over educational expenditure in England and Wales

John F. Embling

Introduction

It may be postulated that any rational system of financial controls will operate through some or all of the following techniques:

(i) The submission of estimates, whether on a simple annual basis or for a number of years, in a prescribed form which identifies main blocks of expenditure, e.g. salaries, maintenance, capital provision, equipment;

(ii) the scrutiny of estimates in the light of known facts and accepted standards of cost, with a separate assessment of the cost of proposed developments;

(iii) approval of the estimates by main subheads after necessary amendments;

(iv) continuing analysis of expenditures by sample checks in order to devise and maintain yardsticks of cost;

(v) rendering returns of actual expenditure for the approved period;

(vi) inspection and audit of accounts.

It is suggested that such a basic pattern is fundamental to good management and is reasonable, whether the cost is met partly or wholly by grants or subvention from another authority. The question of grants, e.g. from the central government to a local authority or a private agency, is a separate matter which may underline the need for good financial management but does not create it.

Good internal management should be distinguished

Source: *Financing of Education for Economic Growth*, Paris: OECD (1966). (Papers prepared for the Conference organized by the Directorate of Scientific Affairs of OECD, held in Paris, 21–24 September 1964.)

from control by an external body, the latter operating by the external body's participation in the function of management. The existing system of public expenditure on education in England and Wales[1] is examined in the light of this brief analysis.

The expenditure[2] falls into three main groups, shown in the summary table for the financial year 1962–3.

	£ million sterling	per-centage
Universities	119·4	10·8
Department of Education and Science	54·8	4·9
Local authorities	931·5	84·3
	1,105·7	100·0

Universities

About 70 per cent of the total income (apart from capital grants) of universities, is received in the form of continuing state grants, about 10 per cent from tuition and other fees paid by students (in a large number of cases with help from public funds), and the remainder from endowments and private sources and from research grants paid by the State. The greater part of the capital required for developing the universities is also found from government sources.

The arrangements for settling and paying the main State grants do not follow the usual pattern of government finance; they are founded on the fundamental importance attached to the freedom of the universities, the general nature and significance of which was described in Chapter XVI of the Robbins Report, which has been accepted by the government.

The key agency in these arrangements is the University Grants Committee, whose functions are:

To inquire into the financial needs of university education in Great Britain; to advise the government as to the application of any grants made by Parliament towards meeting them; to collect, examine and make available information relating to university education throughout the United Kingdom, and to assist, in consultation with the universities and other bodies concerned, the preparation and execution of such plans for the development of the universities as may from time to time be required in order to ensure that they are fully adequate to national needs.

The operation of the system is described in detail in Appendix IV of the Robbins Report, pages 5–13. In brief, it is the task of the Committee to advise the Department of Education and Science on the total grants required to run and develop the universities, and then to allocate between the universities the total sums which the government makes available. The Committee's recommendations concerning allocations are, by convention, regarded as binding.

The Exchequer grants fall into two main categories —non-recurrent (for capital development) and recurrent.

For non-recurrent expenditure the University Grants Committee, after assessing the needs of the universities, submits proposals to the Department for a building programme over one or a series of years, taking into account any general objectives for expansion of student numbers which the government may have adopted. The government then announces the overall programme which it is prepared to sanction, having regard to other claims for capital investment and the prospective state of the economy. It is the task of the Committee, and not of the Department, to decide how the funds made available should be distributed, what building projects should be approved, and to give guidance on methods of planning or building. The Committee's assistance to the universities, aimed at inducing them to obtain value for money, is increasing rapidly, and with the Department's encouragement is likely to increase still more. It is important to note that, in principle, such matters are the Committee's concern, although it is in close liaison with the Department and other government agencies, and its cost limits system is subject to government approval.

Recurrent grants are fixed at five-yearly intervals on the basis of proposals made by the individual universities. Detailed estimates are submitted by each university for each of the five years under consideration, and in the light of these and visits to the universities by members of the Grants Committee and their staff, the Committee presents its recommendations to the Department on the financial needs of the universities as a whole. These visits are an essential part of the Committee's work; they enable Committee members to inform the university authorities of essential national needs and to obtain the necessary detailed information about the universities as background to their discussions with the Department on the total sum to be made available for university development. The recommendations are considered by the government, which announces its decisions to Parliament. The Committee then divides the total sum made available among the universities. The quinquennial settlement thus arrived at may, on the proposal of the Committee and with the approval of the Government, be revised for upward price changes and changes in the salaries of academic staff, which are on scales approved by the government. 'Earmarked' recurrent grants for special development may also occasionally be made, but in principle the recurrent Exchequer Grant, once paid, is entirely at the university's disposal.

Although the issues made on the recommendation of the University Grants Committee are not subject to the normal detailed Parliamentary audit, and universities have a considerable measure of discretion in applying them, controls are not absent from the system. They are exerted primarily by the overall settlements for both current and capital expenditure which have been described; in addition, the University Grants Committee will sanction capital payments only for buildings designed within its cost limits and which it has approved in the context of its overall programme, and it also maintains norms for the equipment and furnishing of buildings; on the recurrent side the main items of expenditure—salaries and overheads— are governed by approved scales and staff ratios, and cost indices. In view of the rapidly growing expenditure on universities, the apparatus of the Committee is being enlarged and strengthened.

Direct educational expenditure by the Department

Educational administration (other than universities) is mainly the responsibility of locally elected authorities (which are also responsible for other services), but there are a number of functions carried out by the Department. The expenditures involved fall under one or other of the following heads.

Assistance to 'voluntary' institutions and organizations

Most public education is provided by public authorities in publicly owned institutions, but a substantial proportion is not. A number of primary and secondary schools (e.g. most of the famous and oddly named 'Public' schools, such as Eton, Harrow and Winchester) are completely independent and receive no assistance whatever from public funds, but there are about 9,000 primary and 900 secondary schools in England and Wales which, though owned by non-public ('voluntary') organizations, particularly the Church of England and the Roman Catholic Church, are regarded as part of the public system and of which all the current or most of the capital expenditure is met from public funds. Other schools are partly in and partly out of this system and receive some assistance with current costs. About one-third of the 150 teacher training colleges are provided by voluntary bodies (again, mainly the Churches) and the same is true of a large range of clubs for young people, adult education centres, sports and recreational organizations, many of which are in receipt of some grants.

Maintenance of national institutions

Particularly in the field of technical education there are a number of institutions giving advanced, and often highly specialized, courses which are more conveniently provided by the central government than by the local authorities which cover a relatively small area. Examples are the Colleges of Advanced Technology, soon to become universities; the College of Aeronautics, the Royal College of Art and the Colleges for Agricultural Engineering, Food Technology, Rubber Technology, etc.

Certain centralized functions

There are some functions which can be carried out only, or more appropriately, by the central department —grants to postgraduate university students, sponsoring and financing educational research, assistance to national bodies for general services of value to education, the payment of international subscriptions, e.g. to UNESCO.

There is, therefore, a complicated and varied collection of institutions and organizations which receive financial assistance from the Department. The form in which the assistance is given is equally varied, and can be any of the following:

(a) a *percentage* grant, in which the percentage of expenditure met by grant may be unchanging (even fixed by Parliament as in the case of building work at voluntary primary and secondary schools) or settled *ad hoc* according to the needs of the particular case;

(b) a *capitation* grant, in which a fixed payment is made for each student, as in the case of some independent secondary schools;

(c) a *deficiency* grant, by which the Department meets the balance of approved expenditure after account has been taken of fees, investment income and other resources;

(d) a *fixed* grant, by which the Department agrees to pay a fixed annual sum to an institution or body but undertakes no further commitment. This is usually in acknowledgment of general services rendered to education;

(e) a *negotiated ad hoc* payment, as for research contracts or to meet some emergency.

It may well be asked why there is such lack of uniformity in the grants which the Department makes and whether some rationalization would not conduce to economy and efficiency. The diversity lies in history,

in the fact that the different grants have grown up haphazardly during half a century, just as the grant-receiving institutions themselves have evolved with great variety over the years. The principal explanation undoubtedly lies in the voluntary element which plays so large and so rich a part of British life. Schools and other institutions and organizations were founded by voluntary effort and have proved their worth; then they found their obligations outstripping their resources and turned to the State for help. These and other situations have been met over the years by *ad hoc* measures without any consistent pattern, and though some greater uniformity could undoubtedly be achieved and might contribute to ease of administration, there is no inclination in educational or political circles to make any drastic change.

With such a wide range in the pattern of payments, there can be no uniformity in the degree of control which is exercised. A fixed grant or contract price is self-contained, it is arrived at after examination of the facts, including the other resources available to the recipient, and is an agreed figure. Subject to evidence that the grant is, in fact, being used for the purposes for which it is given, no further control is necessary. The same is true of a capitation grant, which is fixed or varied in the light of the institution's commitments and resources at the time in question, involving such examination of accounts and formal estimates as may be regarded as necessary; subsequently, it is merely a question of checking that the number of payments made matches the number of students in attendance.

With either a percentage grant or a deficiency grant the control process conforms more nearly to normal, for in either case there is the obligation to ensure that the net expenditure figures on which the grant is paid are accurate and reasonable. In such cases, therefore:

(i) estimates are obtained in standard form, examined and, after any necessary adjustment, approved in major sections;

(ii) actual expenditure figures are required, again in a prescribed form;

(iii) *ad hoc* investigations into costs are carried on from time to time;

(iv) accounts are open to examination by government auditors.

Stages (i) and (ii) are normally the responsibility of the administrative Branch concerned with the particular educational sector to which the institution belongs, e.g. Schools, Teacher Training, Technical Education. Scrutinizing the estimates is a matter partly of gauging the accuracy of the costing in the light of known yardsticks, but more often of deciding the justification or admissibility of a new educational development which has been proposed by the institution or organization and provisionally incorporated in the estimates. It is for the administrative branch to consider whether there is a sufficiently good case for accepting such additional developments, of which part or all of the cost would fall on public funds, and then to get such financial approvals within the Department as may be necessary. This scrutiny of the estimates is often a time-consuming operation, but it is an essential part of the control operation involving judgments on educational merits and on priorities.

To assist the administrators the Department maintains a Cost Investigation Unit, staffed by professional accountants, whose purpose is to help all those concerned with running educational institutions to achieve the maximum economy and efficiency compatible with the standards required and with varying circumstances. In particular, it assists with making the most effective use of costs data obtained from educational establishments through standardized annual returns and devises techniques for interpreting the resulting figures.

The most important function of the Unit is to instil a sense of cost consciousness amongst persons directly engaged in the administration of educational establishments and to help them to master the techniques of financial control. The general policy governing the administration of the establishments falls outside the Unit's province; it is, however, concerned with concentrating attention on securing value for money, taking into account the local conditions.

It would obviously be neither practical nor desirable to exercise continuous detailed control, which would in any case conflict with the aim of increasing cost consciousness among those responsible for management in the field. In pursuit of this aim several methods have been adopted:

(a) the dissemination of comparative information derived from standard forms of accounts from establishments performing reasonably similar functions;

(b) the scrutiny of these costing statements to determine acceptable levels of costs and to single out excessive variations;

(c) visits to individual establishments that appear typical as well as those where it appears that there is scope for improved management. The visits enable the reasons for apparently high or low costs to be evaluated and serve as a useful means of testing the application of new ideas;

(d) the organization of conferences for those directly concerned with the administration of establishments.

Whilst costing statistics themselves do not necessarily provide proof of efficient or extravagant management, they help to establish reasonable standards of expenditure under particular headings, and act as a signpost to elements needing further investigation. Where there is reason to question the variation from the relevant standard, the appropriate administrative branch of the Department may take the matter up by correspondence, or a member of the Unit may investigate on the spot. In many cases it is found that local circumstances may provide good reasons for the differences; in others it is often possible to identify a source of extravagance and to recommend means of improving the efficiency of the organization.

The Department is itself subject to the financial control of the Treasury (the British Ministry of Finance) through which the Annual Estimates to Parliament are submitted and whose approval is needed before any new service or substantially increased expenditure can be undertaken.

Finally, there is the role of the Exchequer and Audit Department, under the control of the Comptroller and Auditor General, who is an independent officer responsible directly to Parliament and whose main function is to ensure that government money has been spent on the purposes for which it was intended, without extravagance or waste, and under proper controls. The day-to-day work of checking departmental expenditure is done by Exchequer and Audit staff stationed permanently with the Department, engaged on a running audit of expenditure and discussing as necessary with the finance officers of the Department any doubts or queries which may arise during the course of the survey.

Government expenditure nowadays is so vast and so varied that the auditors have come to rely more and more on test checks and special studies, the results of which are incorporated each year in the Comptroller and Auditor General's Reports to Parliament, published annually and examined by the special Public Accounts Committee of the House of Commons. The Senior Administrative Officer of the Department may be summoned before the Public Accounts Committee for questioning about the Comptroller and Auditor General's Report; the proceedings and the ensuing report from the Committee to the House of Commons will also be published.

Local authority expenditure

As will be seen from the table at the beginning of this paper 84·3 per cent of educational expenditure is incurred by the 146 local education authorities. They maintain some 30,000 primary and secondary schools, 700 technical colleges, and over 100 teacher training colleges, and provide a wide range of educational services for children at school, for young people and for adults. They employ and pay teachers for the wide range of establishments as well as the doctors, dentists, nurses, architects, administrators and other specialists needed to run the services.

Until 1959 almost all these expenditures were assisted by the central government through grants which, after making some allowance for the different level of resources available to the individual authorities and for their differing commitments, met a fixed percentage of all expenditures. This percentage basis, which was introduced in 1918, has been valuable in encouraging authorities to develop the educational services, and the system was flexible in that it was possible to encourage progress in particular sectors by paying a preferential grant, as was done from 1952–9 for advanced technical education. But the percentage system was frequently criticized; as early as 1921 it was assailed as a 'money-spending device' and as reducing the central government to a position of impotence 'in either controlling expenditure, or affecting economies, once the policy had been determined.' Finally, it was criticized in 1958 'as an indiscriminating incentive to further expenditure' and also as carrying with it 'an aggravating amount of central checking and control of detail.'

The government therefore decided that a substantially larger part of the grant aid from the centre to local authorities should be in the form of general assistance and not be tied to specific services such as education or expressed as a percentage of expenditure on those services. By Act of Parliament the change was introduced from the financial year 1959–60 whereby a number of specific (mainly percentage) grants were replaced by a general grant, the amount of which was to be fixed in advance for a short period of years, though not necessarily at the same level for each year. The specific grants abolished included those for certain health services, child care, fire, town planning, but by far the largest and most important was that for education, amounting to 85 per cent of the total. The total grant was to be distributed among the major local authorities, i.e. all counties and county boroughs (who happen also to be the local education authorities), *not* according to expenditure but by reference to certain objective factors (population, school population, young children, old people, decline in population, sparsity of population, etc.).

Since April 1959 this system of general grant has been used as the method for giving central government assistance to the local authorities and there has been no grant relative to, or even identified with, educational expenditure. The fact remains that the educational element is the major part of the total field covered by the grant and that the number of pupils in school is a very important factor in determining its distribution.

Hitherto the grant has been fixed for periods of two years, i.e., 1959–60 and 1960–1; 1961–2 and 1962–3; 1963–4 and 1964–5. Negotiations will soon commence on what the grant should be for the period April 1965–March 1967. The procedure adopted is as follows:

(a) Each local education authority submits statements under a number of specified heads showing the latest available figures of actual expenditure on educational services, and its estimates of likely expenditure under these heads for the next two years, i.e., the next grant period.

(b) These estimates are scrutinized by the Department in the light of known facts about the school population, the available supply of teachers, building programmes and likely developments in the different educational sectors, the main purpose being to test the estimates for realism. This is particularly necessary in a situation where teachers and building resources are scarce; the sum of 146 separate local education authority estimates is apt to be inflated. Though there is no attempt to impose any particular pattern of development, it is also necessary to ensure that the total expenditure envisaged, though inevitably rising, is not on an unrealistically steep curve, given the limited national resources.

(c) Discussions are held between the Department and representatives of the local authorities to reach agreement if possible on any amendments to the total estimates figures, which are then submitted with the concurrence of the Treasury to the Ministry responsible for relations with Local Government and added to similar estimates for the other services in the ambit of the general grant.

(d) Discussions are held with the representatives of the local authorities on the amount of the total expenditure which shall be covered by the general grant, though the final decision rests, of course, with the government, which submits a White Paper and Order to Parliament for ratification. The proportion of expenditure met by grant for the relevant services is about 56 per cent; the operation of a 'rate deficiency grant' to help the poorer areas brings the overall percentage up to 62 per cent.

(e) The total grant is then divided among the authorities in accordance with the agreed objective factors. It will be noted that the grants payments are in respect of all the relevant services and that it is not possible to identify any of it as for educational purposes or to say, therefore, what share of the expenditure of the local education authorities as a whole, still less of any individual authority, is met by the State.

(f) The amount of the grant is fixed in relation to the levels of remuneration and prices current at the time; it can be supplemented during the grant period should there be unforeseen increases which could not reasonably be carried in full by the local authorities.

It is to be emphasized that this system does not, and is not intended to, involve government control of local expenditure. The estimates as accepted by the Department are used as the basis for determining the government's contribution towards that expenditure and the authority is free to spend more or less on its educational services as it sees fit, any difference accruing to, or being found from, the authority's separate local revenues, mainly taxes on occupied premises, known commonly as 'rates'. In fact, however, the differences are relatively small; in 1960–1 educational was £5·65 million less than estimated, in 1960–2 it was £4·95 million more, and in 1962–3 some £24 million more.

Control of educational expenditure therefore rests primarily with the local authority itself; it was, indeed, the government's objective in making the change over to general grant to encourage local responsibility and control. The elected council of each authority has its own machinery and qualified officers to enable it to follow the conventional procedures indicated above; estimates are prepared by the education staff and examined by the Education Committee; they are scrutinized by the authority's financial officers, submitted to the Finance Committee and finally approved by the authority itself, i.e. the elected County or Town Council. Final accounts are produced and are examined by an independent 'District Auditor' with regard to the legality and reasonableness of the expenditure, as well as accuracy and the avoidance of fraud. He is not an officer of the local authority but a member of an autonomous body of people attached to, though in practice independent of, the central government department which has particular responsibility for relations with local government. The basic principles of control are, therefore, observed; indeed, when the new system was introduced in 1959 fears were expressed that local control might be unduly severe and restrictive.

Local control over expenditure does not mean that the Department is without power or influence in such matters; its controls, however, are mainly with a view to the maintenance of educational standards and not primarily financial. One exception to this is school building: the Department not only prescribes minimum conditions which a school must satisfy and decides which schools may be provided, enlarged or substantially improved, but also fixes a maximum cost yardstick which must be observed. This, however, is exceptional and springs not from the desire to limit expenditure as such, but to get the maximum return from the limited amount of capital investment in educational building which can be permitted. In any case, there is room for manoeuvre, experiment and variety between the 'floor' of the regulations and the 'ceiling' of the cost limits.

One other direct control is the fixing of the number of full-time teachers that each authority may employ in primary and secondary schools; this, again, is not for financial purposes but for greater fairness in the distribution of the limited number of teachers available, and is devised in the interests of the less attractive areas of the country.

A major element in local education expenditure is teachers' salaries, over which the individual local authority has little control as they are fixed nationally in negotiations between representatives of the teachers and of the authorities and, if approved by the Secretary of State, are made obligatory on all authorities. (The arrangements for negotiating teachers' salaries are at present under review to see whether the Department should play a larger role than the simple acceptance or rejection allowed at present.)

Generally speaking, the function of the Department is not so much to control local authority expenditure as to secure adequate educational provision and to bring to the attention of the providing authorities needs that should be met. Its work is expansionist rather than restrictionist. At the same time, it has to bear in mind both the need to consider the general economy and the many other demands upon resources and to ensure that, so far as possible, the education service is not excessive and extravagant and that there is the maximum return for money spent. An important element in its work is, therefore, advice to authorities on economical provision, through such agencies as the Cost Investigation Unit already described and the Development Group in the Architects and Building Branch.

Conclusion

It will be seen that in the United Kingdom there is no central control of educational expenditure but a very diffuse and varied pattern of arrangements which is dictated partly by constitutional powers, partly by historical growth and partly by currently accepted doctrines. More than three-quarters of the educational expenditure is incurred by the local authorities, which are democratically elected bodies with their own means of financial control and which are left free to make their own decisions within the general framework of national educational policy without government control over detail. It is true that the particular system of general grant which allows this freedom is of recent introduction and was strongly resisted by many educationalists and the subject of political controversy. Many critics feared that educational progress would be obstructed by the general grant system. In fact, before the last election, the present government indicated their intention to alter the system. It remains to be seen whether the implementation of this undertaking involves a return to a percentage grant system similar to that which prevailed before 1959 and to arrangements for more detailed approvals by the central government of proposed local educational expenditure, or whether some new pattern of education grant emerges.

The arrangements for financing the universities, as described above, is outside any normal pattern of financial control, and whatever modification may be introduced as regards accountability to Parliament for money spent, is not likely to be substantially changed.

We are left, therefore, with the Department's own expenditure, a mere 4·9 per cent of the total, to which central control on the normal pattern could be regarded as appropriate. Even here departmental action is to some extent bound by Parliamentary decisions (e.g. that assistance to the providers of 'voluntary' schools in England and Wales should be a grant of 75 per cent with an obligation to lend the balance if the providers so request) but there remains a field in which the techniques of control by estimates, cost analysis and audit can be, and are, exercised.

The great variety in the type of payment made may seem unnecessarily wide and it must be admitted that it has no rational justification. Given, however, the force of tradition and the resistance of the grant-receiving institutions themselves to change, it is unlikely that any large-scale changes will be made within the foreseeable future.

Notes

1 Education in the United Kingdom (except for universities) is administered separately for England and Wales (Department of Education and Science), Scotland (Scottish Education Department) and Northern Ireland (Ministry of Education). For the sake of simplicity, this paper deals only with England and Wales (except for universities), though the system of financial control in Scotland differs only in detail.

2 Though the provision of meals and milk in schools is the responsibility of the local education authorities and the cost is reimbursed 100 per cent by the Department of Education and Science, it is regarded as 'welfare' and not as 'educational' expenditure.

Section III The schools and the curriculum

This section begins with an official statement on the history of the Schools Council and its membership. The Schools Council is the body responsible in England and Wales for the assessment and encouragement of curriculum development and for the overall organization of examinations. Its affairs are therefore a matter of considerable public discussion, and the two papers which follow, the extract from *Teachers and Politics*, by R. A. Manzer (a history of the work of the National Union of Teachers in the making of national education policy in England and Wales since 1944), and an article on the politics of educational knowledge, by Michael F. D. Young, highlight the major political and theoretical problems surrounding the Council's work.

10 The Schools Council: an official statement of history and representation (September 1971)

The Secondary School Examinations Council (SSEC) had been in existence since 1917, but during the latter part of its life the conviction had grown among its members that their usefulness was restricted by the necessity to consider examinations divorced from a study of the schools' curriculum. In 1962 the Minister of Education (Sir David Eccles) set up within his Ministry a Curriculum Study Group which brought together HM Inspectors, LEA Inspectors and Organizers, specialists from Institutes of Education, teachers and administrators. An object of the Group was to offer advice and information to the schools and technical services to the SSEC.

In July 1963 representatives of every educational interest met under the chairmanship of the Minister of Education (Sir Edward Boyle) to discuss the need for new co-operative machinery on schools curricula and examinations. The meeting appointed a Working Party under Sir John Lockwood, Chairman of the SSEC, to consider the question. The Lockwood Working Party reported to the Minister in March 1964 recommending the establishment of a Schools Council for the Curriculum and Examinations. In June 1964 a reconvened representative meeting adopted the Lockwood Report and invited the first Secretary of State for Education and Science (then Mr Quintin Hogg) to take the steps necessary to implement its recommendations.

The Schools Council came into being on 1 October 1964, its first Chairman being Sir John Maud. It took over the functions of the SSEC and of the Curricu-

lum Study Group, the staff of the latter forming its secretariat. Lockwood had recommended precise Terms of Reference and also a model Constitution (to be reviewed after three years) and both were adopted by the new Council. One of the most important recommendations which the Council adopted, and which still holds good, was that the membership of the Governing Council and its major committees should contain a majority of *teachers*.

In December 1966 the Council set up a Constitutional Review Working Party which reported in February 1968. A revised Constitution was adopted on 12 December 1968. This replaced the old Coordinating Committee and General Purposes Committee with the Programme Committee and Finance and Staff Committee. Under the Governing Council, the Programme Committee is now the main educational policy committee. Certain other changes were made in the committee structure with the object of improving the efficient conduct of Council business. Modifications were also made in the representation of member interests; these were aimed mainly at strengthening the teacher majority.

This new Constitution was the basis on which the Council was granted registration as a Charity early in 1969.

On 1 April 1970 the Council became an independent body, financed in equal parts by the DES and by the LEAs.

Teachers are represented on the main committees of

the Council through their associations which are member interest. The constitution insists that at least a majority of the members of each of the main Council committees shall be teachers.

Details of the membership of the Governing Council are given below. Representation on the other main committees of the Council is given in the constitution which is printed in full in Section 2 of the Annual Report.

GOVERNING COUNCIL

The Chairman of the Governing Council shall be appointed by the Secretary of State for Education and Science.

7. (2) The members of the Governing Council shall be:

(a) Seventy-five members, to be appointed as follows by the member interests specified below—

National Union of Teachers	17
Association of Head Masters	2
Association of Head Mistresses	2
Assistant Masters Association	3
Association of Assistant Mistresses	3
Association of Teachers in Technical Institutions	3
National Association of Schoolmasters	4
National Association of Head Teachers	3
Headmasters' Conference	1
Incorporated Association of Preparatory Schools	1
County Councils Association	2
Association of Municipal Corporations	2
Inner London Education Authority	1
Association of Education Committees	2
Welsh Joint Education Committee	2
Society of Education Officers	1
Church of England Board of Education Schools Council	1
Catholic Education Council	1
Free Church Federal Council	1
Committee of Vice-Chancellors and Principals of the Universities of the United Kingdom	4
Association of Principals of Technical Institutions	2
Association of Teachers in Colleges and Departments of Education	2
The University Council for the Education of Teachers	3
Council for National Academic Awards	1
National Foundation for Educational Research	1
GCE Examining Boards, acting jointly	1
CSE Examining Boards, acting jointly	1
National Association of Inspectors of Schools and Educational Organizers	1
Association of University Teachers	1
Trades Union Congress	1
Confederation of British Industry	1
National Confederation of Parent-Teacher Associations	1
Secretary of State for Education and Science	3

(b) Not more than ten co-optative members to be appointed by the Governing Council.

(c) The Chairman for the time being of Curriculum Steering Committees A, B and C and of the Schools Council Committee for Wales shall be ex-officio members if they are are not otherwise appointed as members under clause 2 (a) above.

At least a majority of the members of the Governing Council shall be teachers and at least two teacher members thereof shall be from schools in Wales.

11 The technical power of organized teachers

R. A. Manzer

An association of professional teachers like the National Union of Teachers performs two functions essential for the efficient administration of the educational system. First, it articulates and communicates to higher levels information about the provision of education in the schools which is indispensable to decision-making.[1] Secondly, it presents the personal needs and professional specifications that teachers

Source: R. A. Manzer, *Teachers and Politics*, Manchester University Press (1970).

expect the system to satisfy. Each of these functions makes the teachers' union a potential source of important decisional information; and, therefore, each can be converted into political influence.

The exercise of 'technical' power underlies the three case studies collected in this chapter. The involvement of press, Parliament, and politicians which characterized the exercise of 'electoral' power is here exchanged for advisory committees and bureaucrats; and policy outcomes are often the adjustments of several years of consultation and negotiation. The events leading up to the creation of the Certificate of Secondary Education illustrate how information about developments at the technical level is filtered through the organizational network of the teachers' union and fed into the national policy-making system. The events leading up to the creation of the Schools Council show how the NUT and the AEC were able to conserve the *status quo* and prevent an attempt by the Ministry to obtain a greater influence in curricular decisions. The lengthening of the period for teacher training from two years to three in 1960 represented the fulfilment of a policy objective which had been accepted in principle in the sub-government since 1944.

The technical power of organized teachers only explains the ability of the profession to intervene effectively in each of the cases that is described below. The rationale for the intervention in each case is the collective defence of traditional professional values in the face of changing demands on the educational system. The freedom of teachers in their class-rooms is a strongly-held professional value in England and Wales. As the *Schoolmaster* (30 September 1960) stated with respect to the Beloe Report,

> It has always been a source of pride to the profession, and a very proper one, that in this country the teacher has the inalienable right to decide what to teach, and how to teach it, and in so far as he is the best judge of the child's readiness to learn, when to teach.

The structure of external examinations and the nature of the school curriculum, considered below, are both matters which impinge directly on this freedom in the classroom. The problems of teacher supply serve to illustrate the manner in which a conflict between, on the one hand, the values of teachers with respect to the status of their profession and the education of children and, on the other hand, the view of outside groups with respect to the needs of the educational system can be translated into serious policy differences.

The three case studies illustrate the way in which the new institutions of the educational system may be affected by new demands. Where the new demands were successfully harmonized with traditional values of the profession, as defended by its 'technical' power, the Certificate of Secondary Education and the Schools Council were created. Where the new demands could not be reconciled with old values, the result was impasse with respect to policy output and a breakdown of the institution governing teacher supply, the National Advisory Council on the Training and Supply of Teachers.

Finally, the cases described in this chapter go beyond immediate educational issues to illustrate the relevance of English cultural norms for English Educational politics. The empirical quality which characterizes so much of British politics can be seen, for example, in the dispute about an external examina-

tion and its resolution at the point it threatened a traditional value. Again, the static quality of British political life is evident in the creation of the Schools Council to solve the problem of society's interest in curricular development. As one of the principals involved remarked, 'The Schools Council may not work, but it had to be tried first.' This measured approach to political change is one of the basic elements of British political life. Finally, all the aspects of 'muddling through' are apparent in the response to the introduction of auxiliaries into the classrooms. Behind the stalemate over the Department's proposal, some schools have resorted to part-time education; but many more have introduced auxiliaries into the schools anyway and a few local authorities have developed fairly elaborate policies governing their employment. Given time such developments in the schools will no doubt make the dispute between the Department and the NUT irrelevant on this particular issue and register another example of the pragmatic qualities of British public administration.

The creation of the certificate of secondary education

That whoever controls examinations controls the curriculum is one of the maxims of educational politics. The attitude of educationists to externally assessed examinations has altered considerably since the war and immediate postwar years. The manner of the change, its articulation, and its integration into educational policy decisions illustrates one pattern of educational policy-making.

The Crowther Committee's report in 1959 remarked that 'the most promising part of the educational system for experiments in new methods of teaching relatively difficult things will be in the middle streams of Modern schools—but only if they are left free from the cramping effects of a large-scale external examination'.[2] In the years 1939 to 1945 such a sentiment would have been considered relevant to all levels of secondary education.[3] In its memorandum to the Consultative Committee on the Education of Children up to Age Fifteen (Hadow Committee) in 1926, the NUT testified against the idea of an externally assessed leaving examination; and it continually criticized the School Certificate Examination in the interwar years. In 1946 complete abolition of external examinations was still the official policy of the Union but, as a result of the compromise over the first report of the SSEC, a reconstructed external examination (the General Certificate of Education) was accepted as suitable for students proceeding to further education.[4] Protected by the age limit of sixteen for entry to the GCE, after 1947 it was only the modern schools that were to be free from the 'cramping effects' of external examinations.

However sound on educational grounds the reaction against external examinations was before and after the 1944 Act, it ran counter to social and economic forces tending to make quasi-vocational studies, examinations, and paper qualifications more, rather than less, important.[5] Instead of being discarded as a temporary device (as the Norwood Committee of the SSEC hoped in 1943) or confined exclusively to students in selective courses (as the SSEC hoped in 1947), the GCE examination at the O-level grew steadily in influence and prestige; and the numbers taking it from all types of schools continued to rise. By 1959 one-third of the candidates for the GCE came from outside the grammar schools.[6]

At the same time entries increased to externally assessed examinations other than the GCE. A number of schools and local authorities established local school-leaving examinations, mainly for pupils completing a four-year course of secondary education. Experiments of this nature at the local level were welcomed by the Ministry's Circular 289 in 1955, but local examinations had only local currency. Consequently, increasing use was also made of the examinations of the larger and long-established, privately organized examining bodies.[7] Illustrative of their growth was the Beloe Committee's finding that the candidates for the examinations of the Royal Society of Arts increased from 3904 in 1958 to 6833 in 1959. These increases occurred in the face of the Minister's objections and in spite of difficulties the School Regulations put in the way of entering pupils for such examinations.[8] The demand for external examination was a 'mass movement' which developed outside the official governing institutions of the educational system, arising from the classroom level and persisting in spite of official disapproval. It was an educational development too widespread to be ignored indefinitely. Eventually it forced up for re-consideration and renewal the policy decisions taken after the war about the role of external examinations in non-selective schools. A sub-set of institutions which was instrumental in this process of policy change was the National Union of Teachers.

Acceptance of the initial report of the Secondary Schools Examinations Council in 1947 constituted a first, unobtrusive step in the change of opinion inside the NUT on the question of external examinations. Acceptance of the second report, permitting head teachers to enter pupils under the age of sixteen at their own discretion, was another. A third sign of changing attitudes was the increasing influence of the representations of the NUT Grammar School Committee. In 1951 the Union approved a resolution sponsored by the Grammar School Committee that the pass level of the GCE O-level had been established at too high a level and ought to be lowered. By 1954 the National Union of Teachers was demanding greater freedom for teachers to enter pupils for external examinations. In particular, it sought the withdrawal of the regulation that the minimum age for entering the GCE from a secondary modern school was sixteen. In the same year a resolution passed by the Union's Annual Conference called for increasing the output from the nation's secondary schools and contended that the

need should be met, in part, by 'enabling secondary modern schools to develop specialized courses, including courses leading to the General Certificate of Education and other desirable examinations where teachers deem them appropriate, by providing the necessary material and staffing conditions'. A year later the Executive still supported this resolution but opposed any attempt by local education authorities or other bodies to set up any new external examinations outside the GCE. On the recommendation of the Grammar School Committee, the Executive instructed the Union's representative on the SSEC to achieve a lower pass standard in the O-level examination and to oppose any proposal for a GCE level lower than the O-level.

In response to the dissatisfaction being expressed about opportunities for pupils in non-selective schools and the growing demand for a new kind of external examination for them, Circular 289, issued in July 1955, set out the Minister's own views as a basis for general discussion. It stated that the present standard of the GCE at both O-level and A-level should be maintained, that the establishment of any new general examinations of national standing for secondary schools or the widespread use of privately organized external examinations would be discouraged, and that the Grant Regulation which required school authorities not to enter any pupil under the age of sixteen for an external examination except the GCE would not be varied.

The Education Committee of the NUT after considering Circular 289, a report of the Grammar School Committee, and a report of discussion in a joint committee with the AEC, recommended to the Executive in January 1956 that the Ministry be supported in maintaining the present structure and standards of the GCE and in opposing the introduction of any new lower level external examination, but that the Grant Regulation which required school authorities not to enter anyone less than age sixteen for an external examination except the GCE should be amended. In advocating support for the present structure and standards of the GCE the Education Committee was plainly recommending a major change in the policy of the Union, which had since 1951 advocated lowering the O-level pass standard and making the GCE a more attractive and feasible objective for pupils of lesser ability. After some debate the change in policy was rejected by the Executive and an amendment to lower the standard of O-level passes was adopted twenty-two to fifteen. The closeness of the voting in the Executive on a proposed change in an established external examination suggests that the 'mass movement' had not yet gained a strong foothold in the governing institutions of the Union, particularly since the proposal in question had been official Union policy for five years.

In its comment on Circular 289 the SSEC, had recommended that an *ad hoc* committee be appointed to study the question of an external examination below the GCE; but, when the Minister sought the views of the SSEC, it declined to offer advice. Following the comments submitted on Circular 289, the Minister issued Circular 326 in July 1957 reaffirming that he would not vary the former circular without further information. At his request the Central Advisory Council (Crowther Committee) undertook to investigate the matter as part of its inquiry into the education of students aged fifteen to eighteen.

The policies advocated by the NUT before the Crowther Committee in respect of external examinations were essentially those produced in response to Circular 289, but behind them were important developments in attitude. The Union continued to oppose any new external examination, and it is clear there was wide support for this in the Union. The recommendation to make entry to the GCE and other external examinations easier had been Union policy for a number of years, but now it was definitely envisaged that lowering the passmark of the GCE O-level would be a first step in its gradual evolution into an external examination for average pupils.

> We believe that the tendency will be to move more
> and more away from 'O' level requirements
> [for university entrance, etc.] and to regard this
> level as satisfying the examination needs of the
> average, rather than the able pupil. It may also
> be added that the present pass mark is too high
> for some of the purposes for which the
> examination results should be used. If it were
> slightly lowered the examination results might
> prove more useful than they are at present.

The Union's brief to the Crowther Committee showed no great sense of urgency about coping with the rising demand for an external examination for average students, and this attitude was reflected in the conclusions of the Crowther Committee published in December 1959. The Committee admitted the strength of the pressure for a lower-level examination but concluded that 'to set about the construction of a national system of minor examinations would be to rush to the other extreme. The right course, in our view, for the next five years or so is to watch very closely the development of regional and local examinations and to postpone any question of a national system until the experience of these years is available to be assessed.'[9]

None the less, concern was now increasing in the teaching profession about the rapid growth of external examinations outside the GCE framework. The SSEC decided the matter was at last urgent enough for it to undertake its own inquiry, and a committee under the chairmanship of Robert Beloe was set to work in July 1958. Its report two years later was the decisive event in the creation of the new examination. The Beloe Committee foresaw that in five to ten years almost all schools would be entering pupils for external examinations and that examining below the GCE probably would become increasingly concentrated in the eight existing regional and national Examining Bodies. As the number of candidates increased and employers and users became familiar with the certificates, their syllabuses and papers would come to 'exercise great and perhaps decisive influence on the development of the schools'. The Crowther Committee had recommended five years' delay. The Beloe Committee believed that at the end of five years the situation would be only more dangerous and more difficult to remedy. It concluded that the Minister had to take the initiative by creating a new examination below the level of the GCE for pupils of average ability.

The reaction of the leadership of the NUT to the report of the Beloe Committee, as expressed in the *Schoolmaster* (30 September 1960), left no doubt that the Union's official policy of equivocation would now be altered. 'We are no longer exploring roads which can be easily abandoned. External examinations are with us in a big way, and they are here to stay. The question is no longer whether we approve or disapprove of them, but what we intend to do about them now that they are here.' The profession had to decide whether the curricula and organization of the schools should be left to outside examining bodies or 'whether they should remain where they rightly belong, in the hands of the teaching profession'.

There could be no doubt where the traditional interest of the profession and the Union lay. In December 1960 the Education Committee of the NUT, on the advice of its advisory committee, recommended the principle of a national examination on the lines suggested in the Beloe report be accepted as preferable to the existing multiplicity of examinations; and the Executive Committee adopted it as official Union policy.[10] In July 1961 the fourth report of the SSEC was sent to the Minister, advising the creation of a new examination. The Minister was not very happy about the decision he had to make, but the consensus which had been built up behind the proposal was so extensive that he had no choice but to accept. On 17 July 1961, he announced that, having to choose between prohibiting all examinations other than the GCE for non-selective schools and trying to improve the existing system along the lines proposed, he had decided on the latter course of action.

To the educator, the educational development growing out of the 'mass movement' at the technical level would seem the most important feature of this case. To the student of educational politics what is more interesting is the manner in which the inarticulate demand of this 'mass movement' was translated into official educational policy. This translation cannot be explained without reference to the institutions of the NUT. Inevitably, the upsurge of the secondary moderns towards an external examination was articulated through the institutions of the Union. In the Union's extended network of committees, panels, and branches the argument about external examinations went on; and the implications of official NUT policy, if not its language, gradually altered as a result. This leisurely process would no doubt have continued without a definite conclusion if the findings of the Beloe Committee had not placed the whole issue in a new context. The report of the Beloe Committee showed the 'movement up' virtually out of control, to such an extent that by strengthening the private Examining Bodies it was threatening the professional freedom of teachers. With a vital interest of the teachers suddenly at stake, the movement, too far gone to be reversed, had to be pressed to a conclusion which was educationally sound but which guaranteed the traditional freedom of the profession. The result was the Certificate of Secondary Education.

The secret garden of the curriculum

A prominent example in the early 1960s of the assertion of more positive administration by the Ministry was the creation of the Curriculum Study Group. Although concern on the part of the central authority for the content of education was not a new thing, in the recent past first the Board and then the Ministry had deliberately refrained from interfering with the direction of schools. Under the Education Act of 1944 the local authorities are competent to prescribe curricula, but they have imitated the lead given by the Ministry and left the matter largely to the professionals.

The Curriculum Study Group was originally conceived by Sir David Eccles. The first suggestion of a venture by the central authority into what Eccles described as 'the secret garden of the curriculum' came in the course of a debate in the House of Commons on the Crowther Committee's report on 21 March 1960. Expressing his regret that education debates were devoted exclusively to bricks and mortar and organization, Eccles stated that he would 'try to make the Ministry's voice heard rather more often and positively and no doubt more controversially' on what was taught in the schools and training colleges.

Because of divided opinion in the Inspectorate it was two years before the Curriculum Study Group was officially announced. When it came, the announcement was made without prior consultation with organized educational interests. The Group was to involve HMIs, administrators and experts coopted from the outside. It would provide a nucleus of full-time staff to organize and coordinate research studies. Its work would be linked with that of the universities, practising teachers, local authorities, research organizations, professional institutes, and others concerned with the content of education and examinations. Eccles envisaged the Group as a relatively small, 'commando-like unit', making raids into the curriculum. This was implied in the comparison of the proposed Curriculum Study Group to the Development Group in the Architects and Buildings Branch. Started after the war, the Development Group was highly successful in improving the development of school buildings by combining administrators, architects, quantity surveyors and HMIs into working

teams. Each team completed a project for an LEA and planned, tested ideas, and considered successes and failures. Like the Development Group, the Curriculum Study Group presumably would be invested with no greater authority than was merited by the quality of its contribution to the work of the education service as a whole. In the case of the Development Group this was considerable.

In a letter to the educational associations, the Permanent Secretary described the Curriculum Study Group as a response to the pressure of rapid change and increases in knowledge.

At a time characterized above all by the speed of change, we believe that the Ministry and Inspectorate have a useful contribution to make to thinking about the educational process, arising partly from the knowledge we obtain from the view we have of the whole of the educational field, partly from our contacts, through central government, with some of the mainsprings of change, and partly from our opportunity (which we share with some large local education authorities) to form interdisciplinary teams capable of bringing to bear on current and future problems a considerable concentration of skill and experience. And it seems to us peculiarly important that we should make this contribution where it is a matter—as it so often is today—of foreseeing changes before they become apparent on the ground, and of placing before our partners in the education service a range of possible solutions to future problems.

The recognition of the needs of an educational system expected to service a rapidly changing society, the dissatisfaction with the performance of the system according to established relationships, the desire to assert more strongly the role of the central administration as the leader in a period of change—all of which characterized the Ministry's changing attitude to teachers' salaries and supply—were also part of the Ministry's rationale for its intervention into the development of school curricula. It marked a definite departure in the Ministry's conception of its role in the formulation of an important area of educational policy. In more general terms, it involved the insertion of an agent of the community into what had previously been regarded almost entirely as a technical or administrative problem. As such, it was unlikely to go unchallenged by the educational interests.

The initial reaction of professional educators to the Curriculum Study Group was hostile.[11] There was fear that the prestige of the Minister behind any recommendations of the group would make them practically mandatory and uneasiness about the comparisons that were being drawn with the Development Group in school building, a policy area where the Ministry exercised a relatively large measure of control and direction. On the central issue of the interpretation of the educational needs of society there were two points of view. One regarded the existing system, where this was the function and responsibility of the head teacher, as the desirable pattern. External influences, which kept the schools thinking about curriculum changes and adaptations, impinged upon the head teacher and were translated by him, with the aid of his staff, into the life of the school. Parents, the local requirements of industry and commerce, the school governors and local councillors, his knowledge of the views of the Ministry and the Government, his professional colleagues, the church— all provided evidence for the head teacher and influenced the choices he made. According to this view, it was difficult to see what a Curriculum Study Group could do to help the head teacher improve the conclusions he made from the evidence already available.

The second view, held by Sir Ronald Gould and Sir William Alexander, accepted the argument that the interests of society were not being asserted strongly enough within the present pattern of curriculum formulation but disagreed with the Ministry about the desirable changes. Gould admitted that curriculum programming was not self-evidently the concern of teachers, but neither was it that of the Ministry. For this reason he objected strongly to the unilateral intervention of the Ministry without full use being made of the usual consultative machinery. Sir William Alexander went even further to see a threat of substantial change in the distribution of educational power. To prevent this and to safeguard the future, the Curriculum Study Group should be brought under a representative body. Local education authorities, teachers, and other relevant agencies of society could then be involved in determining the programme of the Curriculum Study Group. A representative body, like the NACTST or the SSEC, was 'a normal procedure in English education'; and, if the Minister wanted the cooperation of local authorities and teachers, he must set one up.

The Curriculum Study Group never did comprise 'experts' in the sense implied at its origins. Essentially, the members of the Group were HMIs and Ministry officials who tended to make judgements based on administrative experience rather than conduct research to illuminate choices. With a few exceptions, there were no experts in the Ministry or the Inspectorate of the type envisaged by the original proposals for the Group; and the number recruited from outside was negligible. This group of HMIs and Ministry officials was never large and produced little of the kind of material which had been expected. Far from being a research-oriented, commando-like unit, the Curriculum Study Group, lacking a common, binding interest, did not have even the cohesion of a departmental committee. It is difficult not to conclude that the 'projects' under its care would have been carried out just as easily if there had been no Curriculum Study Group and that the Group, if not exactly a fiction, was largely irrelevant.

The disappointing reality behind the image pro-jected by the Minister cannot be explained without knowing the divisions inside the Ministry on the issue, which combined with the uncooperative attitude of the educationists to block the development of the Group. The question is why the educationists were upset by the Curriculum Study Group in the first place. Both Sir Ronald Gould and Sir William Alexander accepted the basic premise of the Ministry in creating the Group, that the existing pattern was no longer satisfactory. The issue, as Gould put it, was not centralization but its form and extent. It was not the reality of the Curriculum Study Group but the principle of interference by the central authority in curricular matters that concerned Gould and Alexander. They insisted, for the sake of the future, that the principle by itself was unacceptable and unthinkable and could only be made so by the creation of a representative body. This continuing insistence on a representative body, even after the weakness of the Curriculum Study Group must have been known reflects the realization by Gould and Alexander that some kind of action was necessary, that the future should be safeguarded, and that any exertion of central control had to be made through a representative body if the balance of educational power was not to be seriously disturbed.

In May 1963 Sir Edward Boyle announced that a Schools Council would be formed along the lines of the representative body demanded by Gould and Alexander. It would cover all aspects of curriculum and examinations in primary and secondary schools, with the Curriculum Study Group serving as its secretariat. A committee was set up under the chairmanship of Sir John Lockwood to plan an organization for the Schools Council for the Curriculum and Examinations. Reporting in March 1964, the committee affirmed existing principles.[12] Schools would retain the fullest possible measure of responsibility for their own work within a framework reflecting the general interest of the community in the educational process and taking account of requirements of further education and professional organizations. There would be no career secretariat or study-team organization. The Council would be organized as a free association of partners, not advisory to the Ministry of Education alone, but to all its member interests. Members retained the right to take decisions affecting their own interests but would seek to coordinate decisions through the Schools Council. The Council's work would lead only to recommendations, supported by nothing more than the authority of good research. Teachers were assured a majority on the Council. As the *Teacher* (20 March) concluded, it was 'an organization which can cock a snook at the Ministry any time it likes, yet has no powers of dictation over the man in the classroom'.

The Curriculum Study Group, in theory at least, represented an attempt by some people in the Ministry of Education to take greater responsibility in an area of policy which had previously been left to the educationists. The terms on which that responsibility seemed to be demanded were unacceptable to the educationists. They wanted and, in the end, the Minister conceded the creation of a representative body independent of the Government. It was a concession completely in harmony with the traditional manner of developing national educational policy. It was equally a concession in harmony with the traditional practices of British public administration.[13] To be sure, there were a number of officials at the Ministry of Education who wanted to convert the Curriculum Study Group into the high-powered research unit it was advertised to be; but they lost out to their more conservative colleagues, supported by the educationists, who preferred to experiment carefully, to make no sudden departures, to try to assimilate the required adaptations within traditional practices.

Like the reconstruction of the management side of the Burnham Main Committee, the original constitution of the Schools Council merely legitimatized a long-established pattern of informal relationships among teachers and central and local administrators in the area of curricular development. In this sense it represented a genuine victory for the teachers and local administrators who had opposed the Curriculum Study Group. But the Schools Council did create a legitimate institutional location for debate about curriculum and established the right of the central administration to contribute to that debate. Thus the Department was left in a stronger position to affect curriculum than it had before the Curriculum Study Group was formed.

Given the circumstances it is not surprising that the Schools Council, created out of controversy, has continued to be controversial. No one denies that the bulletins and working papers produced by the Council's secretariat have been useful and even influential documents. The Organization for Economic Cooperation and Development in its *Curriculum Improvement and Educational Development* (1967) has gone so far as to suggest that other countries might find the Schools Council an appropriate model for an organization to promote curricular change. But for educational change in England and Wales the matter is not simple, for the distribution of power in the education sub-government is also at stake.

In November 1966 lengthy consideration of the functions of the Schools Council by the Executive of the National Union of Teachers revealed serious discontent with the operation of the Council. Both the size and the effectiveness of teacher representation on the Council and its committees were in question. From the founding of the Council the Union has tried without success to get greater teacher representation in general and, in particular, to have its own representation enlarged to reflect its predominance among the teachers' unions. The teachers on the Council and its committees have found themselves overwhelmed with paper (as one member complained, 'two pounds of documents two days before a meeting'),

unable to cope effectively with all the material confronting them, and thus unable to take the initiative themselves or to prevent its being taken by the Department of Education and Science. The problem has been compounded by the Union's failure so far to adapt its own organization to support its representatives appointed to the Council and its committees. In contrast with those members of the NUT Executive who see the Schools Council as 'power hungry', however, *The Times Educational Supplement* has argued (24 February 1967) that the reservations that greeted the birth of the Council in 1964 have led it to cast itself in a humble role that underestimates both the value and the urgency of its work. As a result it sees the Schools Council in danger of becoming excessively defensive and failing to provide the leadership necessary in this policy area.

Whether the Schools Council does provide leadership in curricular development, or not, the argument surrounding it is not ended. Advance and adaptation with the agreement of all important interests concerned is comfortable, but it is also notoriously slow. In a time demanding fairly quick responses to changing situations, where policy decisions must be renewed much more rapidly than previously, it is likely to be highly frustrating and costly as well. The criticism of the Schools Council reflects both the frustration of those wanting more rapid change and the discontent of those concerned to protect traditional values and prerogatives. That criticism is certain to continue as long as pressure for curricular change continues. But whatever the differences between teachers and administrators, they have been limited to the education sub-government. Common agreement that the broad interests of society need to be better represented and inserted more positively into the process of curriculum formation has not resulted in any effort to improve the representative function of the sub-government by going outside it, for example, to Members of Parliament. As a result the Schools Council may be regarded as an assertion of orthodoxy and, quite possibly, an opportunity lost.

The supply of teachers

Within the National Union of Teachers there exists a potential conflict between, on the one hand, teachers' ambitions to fulfil professional ideals and improve their status and, on the other, their view of the needs of the educational system in terms of teacher supply. In its external relations the Union confronts another, more serious, potential conflict between its professional aspirations and the view held by other groups of the needs of the educational system. This latter type of conflict appears to be a continuous situation where agreement is, at best, temporary because technical-level people and community agents have different functions and tend, not surprisingly, to see the problems of the educational system in the context of the function they serve.

The circumstances in which the conflict between aspirations and needs is of the former, internal type are fairly narrowly defined. A recent example was the acceptance by the National Union of Teachers in 1956 of a scheme for governing the distribution of teachers. Measures for affecting the distribution of teachers had been a feature of the educational scene for many years.[14] Before the Second World War the staffing establishments of each elementary school were reviewed annually by the Board of Education, primarily as a means of controlling educational expenditure. From 1941 to 1946 each local education authority was assigned a quota of newly trained teachers, who were required to spend at least one year in the service of their first employer. After 1948 arrangements were introduced to control the distribution of women teachers in infant schools, but early in 1956 this women teachers' scheme was discontinued. Local authorities were allowed complete freedom in the number of appointments they made, although those better placed were expected to exercise restraint in recruiting. During the year evidence of increasing maldistribution accumulated.

The NUT organized an *ad hoc* committee to examine the problem in July 1956, and in October the Ministry called for a conference of local authorities and teachers to consider corrective action. The *Schoolmaster* (12 October) remarked that

> in this crisis the Union has a three-fold
> responsibility. As a body of educationists it is
> profoundly concerned to avert a local break-down
> in the educational system. As an association of
> colleagues working for a common end it is
> equally concerned to relieve the hardship which
> the present position is inflicting on its members
> in the shortage areas. And as a national
> organization it must at all times have regard to
> the staffing and recruitment position at the
> national level. Its task, therefore, is to press for
> measures which will effectively help the short-
> staffed areas, but which will not rebound at the
> national level to damage the interests of all its
> members—including those in the shortage areas.

No solution emerged from the conference, but it was agreed that positive steps would have to be taken to improve the distribution of teachers. The proposals advanced by the NUT involved going outside the educational system to solve the problem.[15] The Minister insisted that it had to be solved inside the system with the resources presently available. This could only mean some form of rationing; but it was promised, as a condition of the Union's agreement, that the scheme would not entail the direction of teachers. In December after submitting it to both the teachers and the local authorities for comment and consultation, the Ministry issued Circular 318, which introduced a new method of alleviating maldistribution by setting each local authority a precise objective (a 'quota') by which to shape staffing policies.

The Union's initial support for the quota scheme is accounted for, first of all, by its recognition of the need for some remedial action and of the impossibility of securing resources outside the system. Secondly, it was believed in 1956 that control over the distribution of teachers would be needed only as a temporary expedient. Thirdly, considerable pressure for relief had developed inside the Union from local associations in disadvantaged areas like Birmingham.

In the event, expectations for the supply of teachers were disappointed. Persistent staffing difficulties have made it necessary to prolong the quota indefinitely. Despite some criticism of the scheme, the gap between the staffing standards of the best and worst placed authorities is half what it was in 1956; and the staffing standards of the great majority of authorities now fall within quite a narrow range of variation.[16] It is generally agreed that, so long as there are not enough teachers to go around, control of distribution needs to be continued to protect the shortage areas and avoid gross disparities in staffing standards. The local associations in shortage areas provide continuous pressure in the Union for such controls, and the quota scheme continues to be supported as the least of possible evils.

The achievement of a three-year course of training for teachers in 1960 was probably the outstanding improvement in quality in the educational system after the school-leaving age was raised in 1947. Like raising the school-leaving age, three-year training was a product, somewhat delayed, of the convergence of professional and political opinion around an agreed programme of educational reform in 1943.

Lengthening the teacher-training course to three years was first recommended in 1919 by a Committee of Principals of Training Colleges. It received increasing support throughout the interwar years, including the support of the NUT; and it was included among the recommendations of the McNair Committee in 1944. The McNair recommendation was accepted in principle by the Minister of Education with the observation that, in view of the urgent need for additional teachers, lengthening the normal course could not at that time be authorized. The Association of Teachers in Colleges and Departments of Education presented a plan, in 1950, for the gradual implementation of a three-year course; but the National Advisory Council on the Training and Supply of Teachers put it off on the grounds that any measure reducing recruitment before 1957 (when pressure in the schools from the high wartime birth rate was expected to decrease) could not be considered.

Early in 1955 the Advisory Council concluded that it was time to consider again the feasibility of introducing a three-year training programme. During the early 1950s the picture had seemed to change and the strain to be easing. In particular, the slowing down of recruitment after emergency training ended was less than expected; and wastage fell, as fewer teachers, especially married women, left the profession and more women returned to teaching than had been expected. A sub-committee was set up, which reported in March 1956; and the fifth report of the Advisory Council published in the same year recommended three-year training.

The report foresaw a rapid change in demand for teachers in the early 1960s. The number of children in school would be at its highest peak in the years 1958 to 1961. Thereafter, it would fall until 1967, when it would be four or five hundred thousand below 1961. At the same time it was assumed that the net annual increase in teachers would average seven thousand up to 1961 and six thousand thereafter. These expectations of an increase in the teaching force and a decrease in the number of school children, argued the Council, offered a unique opportunity to introduce three-year training. Some reduction in recruitment would be quite compatible with a continued reduction of the size of classes. The Council even went on to point out that there was a limit to the number of additional teachers which the schools could absorb and the country could afford in a period of declining school population. Without the introduction of the three-year course, it was not impossible that there would be some difficulty in the early 1960s, as there never had been in the 1950s, in maintaining full employment in the teaching profession.[17]

Given the situation with respect to teacher supply described by the Council and its own longstanding commitment to a three-year training course, the Government had little alternative but to accept the recommendation. The wide support the recommendation enjoyed among educationists, the lingering hostility of teachers to the Government over the Teachers Superannuation Bill, and a desire to soften the anti-education image the block grant promised to create—all contributed to the Government's positive decision. In June 1957 Lord Hailsham announced that training would be extended to three years for the class entering the colleges in September 1960.

The enthusiasm which greeted the Minister's announcement did not last long. It soon became clear that the assumptions of the Advisory Council about wastage in the profession and the size of the school population were hopelessly wrong. In February 1958, Sir Edward Boyle announced that wastage had grown rapidly. The net increase in teachers had dropped to just over five thousand in 1957 compared with an average of 6,500 over the previous seven years. Despite this falsification of optimistic estimates about teacher recruitment, the Government remained committed to the 'great forward project' of three-year training. There could be no going back, Boyle insisted, on this piece of forward policy which had been deliberately announced in both Houses.

Despite some argument from outsiders that a reduction in the size of classes was the main priority and that three-year training must now be postponed, there is no evidence the Government ever seriously considered changing its policy. At no time does a Government relish the charge that it has broken a pledge to an important sector of the community.[18] Probably a postponement of three-year training would have been welcomed by the Government if the educational pressure groups had advocated it. The National Union of Teachers, the Association of Teachers in Colleges and Departments of Education, and the Institutes of Education in the universities all continued to support three-year training and oppose any postponement. In the circumstances the Government made no attempt to reverse established policy.

Since 1959 the Government has been increasing its programme of training-college expansion at a remarkable rate. Each year the programme has had to be revised upwards, but targets have been achieved with considerable success. The National Advisory Council on the Training and Supply of Teachers had urged an expansion of the colleges to 36,000 by 1962; and, after some hesitation, the Government accepted this figure as the target for 1964. By 1961, the promise was revised to 54,000 places by 1966. In fact, the number of students in training colleges increased from 31,000 in 1959–60 to 54,000 in 1963–4. In October 1962 the Advisory Council recommended a target of 80,000 students at training colleges by 1971; and this was accepted by the Government in January 1963. In 1966–7 the number of students in the colleges was 84,000. In February 1965 the recommendation of the Robbins Committee for 40,000 entrants to the colleges in 1973 was accepted; and the National Advisory Council urged in its ninth report that this target be achieved two years earlier. In 1966–7 there were over 33,000 entrants to the colleges, a figure the Robbins Committee anticipated by 1971 and the NACTST for 1969. Thus, expansion has been remarkable, running well ahead of the targets and involving a sharp increase in expenditures. Monetary outlays on training teachers in the Colleges of Education rose from £5·6 million in 1955 to about £23·1 million in 1965 or, in real terms, from £4·2 million to about £11·0 million.[19]

With the expansion of the teachers' training colleges a change has occurred in the attitude of the Government to the supply of teachers. However much the Government and the Union might agree on the commitment to an expanded educational programme, the Government's approach to the problem of teacher supply must also include an efficient use of every means of increasing and effectively deploying teaching personnel. Just as meeting the demand for an expanding educational system has involved both increasing teachers' salaries and allocating expenditure on salaries in more efficient directions, so the demand for teaching manpower has had to be met by a combination of expansion and reallocation of resources inside the system. As in the case of salaries, the efforts by the Government to solve the problem have led to conflict with the teachers. The disagreement over the employment of auxiliary teachers to ease the shortages in the classroom is a useful example of an impasse over policy produced by a conflict between professional aspirations and the realities of public economy.

In May 1961 the Minister of Education proposed in the House of Commons that, to go some way to meet the shortages disclosed by the Advisory Council, auxiliary assistants should be employed in the primary schools. They would be young girls who wanted to work with children or married women who had raised their families and could now help in the schools by 1965. The NUT immediately announced its opposition to helpers doing any teaching. It deplored the Minister's failure to consult the Advisory Council and insisted that the only solution was to expand the teacher training programme on the scale outlined by the NACTST and to restore the cuts in university grants to increase the number of teachers available from the universities.

A year later Eccles wrote to the chairman of the Advisory Council suggesting the employment of more part-time teachers in the schools, short-service employment for some women teachers and the creation of some sort of auxiliary service. After some hesitation the Council rejected the suggestions. In September 1962 the NUT Executive issued a policy statement on the use of ancillaries in the schools. It stated that certain categories of ancillaries were necessary, but none was capable of the education of children or should have any part in a teacher's duties. The Union's statement of policy made it plain that its conception of school helpers did not involve them in any teaching duties, and this continues to be the official Union view.

An increase in the number of ancillary helpers outside the classroom of the kind envisaged in the Union's policy statement would decrease the burden on, but not greatly ease the shortage of, qualified teachers inside the classroom. Despite equivocation about the extent of the teaching duties to be undertaken by auxiliaries, there is no doubt that Ministry proposals involved them doing some teaching under the direction of qualified teachers. Proponents of an auxiliary service contend that teachers would thus become managers, and their prestige would be increased. Teachers are not convinced. First, as Sir Ronald Gould has pointed out, there is no accepted division of functions in teaching, as there is in other professions where auxiliary assistance is employed. Much of the force of feeling against the proposal among members of the Union derives from a fear that semi-qualified auxiliaries would blur the line between qualified and unqualified teachers and undermine the hard-won status and self-esteem of the teaching profession. Secondly, supervision, it is argued, would tend to fall on the youngest and most inexperienced members of the teaching profession. It is also regarded as questionable whether suitable women would be attracted by a salary much less than the existing minimum for a qualified teacher. Thirdly, teachers believe that the delivery of pupils into the hands of 'child minders' must be resisted in the interests of the children. Replying to a leading article on the subject in *The Economist*, Fred Jarvis, an official of the Union wrote:[20]

We differ from you not on the seriousness of the teacher shortage but on what needs to be done. Apparently you see the problem only in terms of getting children from a place called home to a place called school and making sure that there is somebody to look after them. The NUT's concern is for the quality of the education received by the child. It therefore takes a different view on the employment of auxiliaries.

Three policy changes could be made to ease the teacher supply problem: raise the age of entry to primary school from five to six, introduce auxiliaries into the classrooms, or settle for part-time education. The first is rejected as inadequate and unacceptable by all concerned. The second is rejected by the teachers. To them education on a part-time basis is preferable to handing pupils over to 'child minders'. Their critics 'can imagine no policy, and no other trumped-up expedient, that would more wickedly aggravate the existing disadvantages suffered by children in the parts of the nation least favoured with modern housing or modern schools'.[21]

The dilemma between policy based on educational considerations and policy reflecting economic considerations is obvious. The advocates of an economic approach, including appropriately enough *The Economist*, contend that 'trained teachers, that scarcest of resources, must be deployed with the maximum efficiency. The refined instrument must be used for fine tasks. The less fine tasks must be done by less expensively sharpened tools.' Turning the teacher into a kind of manager, however, involves recasting the traditional role of the teacher, which gives him a direct, personal relationship *in loco parentis* with each individual child in his class. It is this educational tradition and situation which, ultimately, the teachers aim to protect. In all the debate, the National Union of Teachers has often come under strong attack. The unstated assumption in all the criticism seems to be that the Union's official policy misrepresents the true attitudes of teachers to helpers inside the classroom, but there is no good evidence that this is the case. The Ministry was not prepared to assume it. Nor was it prepared to alienate the teachers by forcing auxiliaries upon them.

Teachers are called upon to relax their traditional attitude to some kind of help inside the classroom, among other reasons, because this traditional attitude no longer corresponds to urban realities. The force of this argument cannot be denied. For as far ahead as can be seen, there will not be an abundant supply of teachers. The Secretary of State (Crosland) has pointed out that, if help is not given in the classroom, teaching will simply collapse in certain areas for lack of teachers. The Secretary's responsibility as an agent of the community could thus conceivably lead him to impose auxiliaries on the teachers. Equally, he might be forced to adopt the expedient, acceptable to teachers, of part-time education. In the meantime, a very real conflict of social and educational values is being worked out inside the educational system.

It is interesting to observe the effect of this change of circumstances on the National Advisory Council on the Training and Supply of Teachers. The conciliatory style of its deliberations and the consequent unanimity of its recommendations, which characterized the first decade of its operations, have given way to internal divisions too serious to be submerged. In the eighth report of the Council (1962) a group of distinguished members dissented from the recommendation that the period of teacher training be eventually raised to four years, expressing their dissatisfaction with the arguments for professional unity and parity with other professions adduced by the majority of the Council. The ninth report of the Council showed it to be deeply divided over the use of auxiliaries in the schools and over the introduction of a four-term year for the teacher-training colleges proposed by Sir William Alexander. The Chairman, Mr Alan Bullock, resigned as a result of the strong disagreement in the Council, which he felt unable to resolve; and the Secretary of State has so far refused to reconstitute the Council despite considerable pressure to do so from the teachers. The pressure of an expanding educational system has thus not only created policy dilemmas; it has also put traditional policy-making procedures in the education sub-government under a severe strain which they could hardly have been expected to bear when they were devised many years ago.

The ninth report of the NACTST also revealed its political incapacity. The report indicates that the teaching force of 360,000 in 1963 in all kinds of educational institutions would have to nearly double to maintain current policy objectives and grow to 750,000 if primary classes are to be reduced to a maximum size of thirty pupils. Plainly, as the Council concluded, a teaching force would be required which far outstrips all other professions in its combination of sheer size

and fully professional standards of qualification. In respect of size it could only be compared with the labour force employed in certain of the country's major industries. Yet, reporting in such a context, the Advisory Council completely disregarded the manpower demands on other sectors. The report admitted, for example, that to build up and sustain such a teaching force would require about half the annual output of the higher educational system. It specifically refused to consider whether this demand was too much. Its recommendations were devised and advanced in what amounted to a social vacuum. The Council failed to proceed from its recognition that old standards like class sizes of thirty in secondary schools are outmoded and that pupil-teacher ratios are more relevant to the consideration that these ratios could intentionally be allowed to rise as a matter of social policy and to the problem of what would be the organizational and educational implications if they were.

Essentially, the Department of Education and Science was getting policy advice from a body which was no longer in a position to give it. The Council did not know what was the politically relevant framework within which to make its recommendations regarding educational policy. It was neither functionally responsible nor psychologically disposed to settle such questions for itself. Since it included no members responsible to the community for devising such a political framework, such as Members of Parliament, it was not even equipped to effect a reasonably approximate substitute. Accordingly, its advice became either largely irrelevant, where its political assumptions were unjustified, or at most provided sectional support for the Minister in his contest for funds with the Treasury and other departments. In either case, the Advisory Council, used to proceeding by consultation on the basis of an agreed set of priorities, found itself unable to resolve the tensions created by the pressures of a rising demand for education and with its usefulness pretty much at an end.

Notes

1 For an analysis of the educational system in terms of its 'technical', 'managerial', and 'institutional' functions, see Talcott Parsons, *Structure and Process in Modern Societies* (Chicago Free Press 1960), 59–96.
2 Ministry of Education, Central Advisory Council (Crowther Committee), *15 to 18*, I (London: HMSO 1959), 94.
3 William Taylor, *The Secondary Modern School* (London: Faber & Faber 1963), 128.
4 Ministry of Education, Secondary Schools Examinations Council, *Examinations in Secondary Schools* (London: HMSO 1947), 5.
5 Taylor, op. cit., 104–5.
6 Ministry of Education, Secondary Schools Examinations Council (Beloe Committee), *Secondary School Examinations Other than the GCE* (London: HMSO 1960), 9.
7 The eight most important named by the Beloe Committee are Royal Society of Arts, College of Preceptors, London Chamber of Commerce, City and Guilds of London Institute, Union of Lancashire and Cheshire Institutes, Union of Educational Institutions, Northern Counties Technical Examinations Council, and East Midland Educational Union.
8 Outside the GCE pupils under the age of sixteen could only be entered for external examinations privately by their parents, who bore any expense involved.
9 Crowther Committee, op. cit., 85.
10 The Union continued to remind the Minister and the SSEC that it was Union policy to slightly lower the pass.

standard of the GCE O-level and that, if this were done, a new examination might not be necessary. There was no support for this compromise and it was not pressed.

11 See the comments of spokesmen for the educational interests in reaction to a paper by D. H. Morrell, 'The freedom of the teacher in relation to research and development work in the area of curriculum and examinations', *Educational Research*, **5** (February 1963), 83–103. This study is not concerned to delineate the internal politics and decision-making of the Ministry, but the contribution of Mr Morrell to the Ministry's curriculum initiatives cannot be underestimated. Mr Morrell was Joint Head of the Curriculum Study Group and later associated with the Schools Council. He came to the CSG from the Development Group in the Architects and Buildings Branch. Before that he was private secretary to Sir David Eccles.

12 Great Britain, Ministry of Education, *Report of the Working Party on the Schools Curricula and Examinations* (London: HMSO 1964), 9–10.

13 See Brian Chapman, *British Government Observed* (London: George Allen & Unwin 1963).

14 See Ministry of Education, 'Teachers on Quota', *Reports on Education*, no. 8 (February 1964).

15 The NUT proposed that men teachers finished with professional training should be released from the national service and men finishing professional training in 1957 and later should be deferred. To get them into shortage areas there should be resort to incentives but not direction. The Union suggested assistance by the local authorities in obtaining housing, priority in nursery accommodation for children of married women teachers, and improved working conditions in the classroom. It rejected a quota system or financial incentives. It did indicate its willingness to examine carefully and without prejudice any system of establishments or quotas which might be proposed, an expressed willingness to negotiate which suggests it had little confidence in the acceptability of its own proposals.

16 The local education authorities with the highest ratios of pupils per full-time teacher in 1968–9 were Bootle 27·2, Derby 27·2, Ipswich 27·2, Birmingham 27·1, Nottingham 27·1, Leicester 27·1. Those with the lowest were Breconshire 20·2, Montgomeryshire 19·6, Cardiganshire 19·6, Merioneth 19·2, Radnorshire 18·6, Isles of Scilly 11·6. (Source: *Teacher*, 23 February 1968, 3.)

17 Ministry of Education, National Advisory Council on the Training and Supply of Teachers, *Three Year Training for Teachers* (5th report; London: HMSO 1956), 11.

18 Peter Self and Herbert J. Storing, *The State and the Farmer* (London: George Allen & Unwin 1962).

19 John Vaizey and John Sheehan, *Resources for Education* (London: George Allen & Unwin 1968), 93.

20 *The Economist*, 19 September 1964, 1077.

21 *The Economist*, 12 September 1964, 996.

12 On the politics of educational knowledge: some preliminary considerations with particular reference to the Schools Council

Michael F. D. Young

Abstract

An attempt is made to raise some preliminary implications of recognizing the 'political' character of education and definitions of educational knowledge in particular, by taking the Schools Council as a case study. Following a brief review of some existing approaches to the politics and control of education, and a specification of the possible significance of the Schools Council as a critical case, a more detailed critique of current orthodoxies is presented as exemplified in Manzer's study *Teachers and Politics*. This leads to an alternative perspective in which three critical issues are examined: 1. teacher control and autonomy; 2. legitimation of knowledge; 3. types of child and the differentiation of curricula.

The links between the issues and their implication for treating the separation of 'politics' from both 'education' and 'educational research' as themselves sociological questions, are considered.

Source: Economy and Society (1972), **1** (2), 194–215.

A weakness of much sociological research and 'theorizing' about education has been that it has failed to treat as problematic the categories used by educators. This implies that a sociological approach to education needs to begin by treating definitions of education as the product of social arrangements. More specifically, 'subjects' (Musgrove 1968) and schools (Cicourel and Kitsuse 1963) are viewed not as fact but as the products of the activities of educational personnel, and the language of education (with its terms like ability, achievement, motivation, innovation, etc.), becomes viewed as a vocabulary of motives (Mills 1940) used in particular contexts.

A further implication, that is central to the issues

raised in this paper, is the assumption that 'education' is a label with political and ideological connotations.[1] Thus all 'educational' issues are viewed as 'political' in that they involve decisions (or non-decisions [Bachrach and Baratz 1963]) about priorities in contexts where there is differential access to resources, both of economic support and cognitive legitimacy.[2] Most educators[3] do not perceive educational matters as political in this sense, and in their writings and public statements appear concerned to emphasize a distinction between 'educational' and 'political',[4] and the need to decide things on 'educational grounds'.[5] Such statements are conceived here as claims for the legitimacy of particular definitions of 'educational' made by those in a position to assert their 'non political' character.

The purpose of this paper therefore is to explore the implications of these proposals and some of the research questions they give rise to. It is divided into two main parts.

1 Some comments on two existing approaches to the 'control' of education, which serve to emphasize the necessity of focusing on definitions of educational knowledge that are maintained in particular settings, followed by a brief account of some features of a particular setting, the Schools Council.[6] A statement of the rationale for treating it as a potentially critical case leads on to an examination of the assumptions underlying the one available account of its development and activities in Manzer's (1970) study of the National Union of Teachers.
2 An alternative perspective that is developed from the preceding critique, which leads to a focus on three main issues underlying both specific questions about Schools Council and more general questions concerning the political character of education:

   (i)   Teacher autonomy and control.
   (ii) Curriculum project styles and the legitimation of educational knowledge.
   (iii) definitions of 'types of child' and their implications for the differentiation of curricula.

The 'control of education': some existing approaches

Research into the control[7] of education is still, as Banks (1968) reported, almost non-existent. In the way she, and more recently Musgrove (1971), set up the discussion, we are not taken much further with suggestions about how it might develop. Banks focuses on the very general issue of the degree of decentralization of decision-making but does not point to the specific issues about which 'decisions' are made or the process involved that might be open to empirical enquiry. This question might be explored fruitfully in a comparative study of say, French and English teachers. The former participate in a system that is highly centralized, but which at least one case study suggests allows considerable areas of discretion (Wylie 1961). The latter as will be referred to later, participate in a

formally decentralized system. However, the extent of this 'decentralization', in practice, would appear to be limited by the way English teachers perceive the examination systems and accept existing academic and institutional hierarchies. This was eloquently demonstrated to me recently when a group of teachers were complaining about their CSE Board (*a teacher-based* exam system, but no one present knew who the teachers on the Board were or how they were selected).[8]

Musgrove (1971), in asserting that 'contemporary research reveals the impotence of schools', and defining the problem (whose problem?) as the expansion of their power, evades both the substantive question of 'power to do what?', and the theoretical and empirical problems of what might be meant either to the sociologist or the teacher by the notion of 'impotence'.

An alternative approach, which did not take as a 'given' particular definitions of educational knowledge, is suggested in the latter section of this paper. This focuses on how priorities for 'curriculum development' are defined which would involve exploring the definitions of educational knowledge that are held by different groups. One can view these priorities as constituted in the interaction, in particular settings, of agents of educational support (primarily those from business, local government and the Ministry, who are in a position to allocate resources), and of educational practice (teachers). One such setting is the Schools Council. It is suggested that an enquiry of this kind might point to how one might explore linkages between the financing, control and practice of education more generally, which at present can only be hinted at.[9]

The Schools Council

In spite of its annual reports, monthly newsletter and voluminous publications, remarkably little is known beyond 'official histories' of how it operates. However there are certain features which are worth emphasizing at this stage, which give some indication of what its significance might be.

Firstly, it is an agency which has spent £4·3m since its inception in 1964, at present spends on both 'projects' and administration approximately £1m a year, and increasingly as the Nuffield Foundation has withdrawn from research in education, has become the *only* source of funds for curriculum development projects in primary and secondary schools. Furthermore, it not only has significant advisory powers over the forms of CSE and GCE 'O' level examining,[10] but it is able to veto any new proposals for courses to be examined at 'A' level.[11] Thus in a very real sense the Schools Council activities define educational priorities and the limits of certain kinds of educational change. Secondly, of the 111 projects reported in the Schools Council document, *Projects*, in June 1971, seventy-six were situated in Universities, eleven in Colleges of Education and two in schools. It would be unjustified to infer too much from figures such as these, but they would seem to be an indication of at least one largely unquestioned assumption, 'educational research is best done in Universities'. A third point to note from the Schools Council's Annual Reports is that of the £3m spent by the Schools Council up to 1970; £660,500 was committed to proposals in which particular ability-groupings are *explicitly* referred to, but only £97,000 was committed to projects *specifically* referring to 'mixed ability' teaching. These figures are at least some indication that a change towards curricula based on non-hierarchical conceptions of ability is not a high Schools Council priority. Each of these features of Schools Council activity, linked to the questions raised in the last part of the paper concerning teachers' autonomy, the legitimation of 'subjects' and institutional hierarchies, and the assumptions made about 'types of children', are no more than possible illustrations of potential areas of enquiry.

A critique of Manzer's model of 'educational politics', and its application to the Schools Council

In view of the little interest shown by sociologists or political scientists in the politics of education, it is not surprising that Manzer's (1970) study of 'educational politics'[12] should have become so widely quoted, well received and in 'educational circles' almost definitive. What is more significant is the way in which his own analysis appears to be an explication of many of the shared understandings held by educational personnel. This becomes apparent when one reads an account such as Nisbet's (1971).[13] Though containing none of the familiar concepts of the 'systems theory' used by Manzer, the implicit model of explanation is very similar. It is therefore primarily because it makes it possible to examine the tacit assumptions of both official histories and educationalists' accounts that it seems useful to begin by looking in some detail at Manzer's theoretical framework, before making some tentative alternative suggestions.

Manzer's book is a study of British education after 1944 as a 'political system', and in particular the role of the National Union of Teachers in this system. The section of the book of major concern for this paper is his account of the origins and development of the Schools Council as a case study in 'educational politics'. His theoretical framework (drawn from the 'political system' theorists—such as Easton (1953)) and the assumptions implicit in it can be outlined as follows:

Political culture is seen as a relatively persistent set of common values. Manzer characterizes the values of the British political culture as 'support of evolutionary changes', 'hesitant support for innovation', 'education as a good', 'commitment to maintaining a public education system', and governmental right to 'interpret community needs'. The problem arises when the 'common values' referred to are postulated and then used as an explanation of the maintenance of a particular order. If one moves from the very general level of 'support of evolutionary changes', to more

substantive values, these can only be seen as constructed and legitimated by groups with common concerns in particular historical contexts; these have *to be explained* not used as explanations.

Political structure. The British political structure is conceived of as 'pluralist', which implies sets of relatively autonomous 'sub-governments' of education, housing, health, etc. These structures represent agreed definitions of the limits of 'educational (or housing) politics'. They are seen as serving to translate in a relatively unproblematic way changing 'demands for education' (inputs), which are generated through wider social and economic changes, into 'educational policies' (out-puts).[14] However, the assumptions on which such a 'pluralistic' view of English politics rely are as dogmatic and naive assertions as the idea of some conspiratorial ruling class. Each remains closed to questions about the origins and persistence of particular definitions of 'educational politics', and of the distinctions between 'educational' and 'political' in terms of which educators want 'education kept out of politics'. Furthermore an input/output model of education is just as vulnerable in relation to the Schools Council as Cicourel and Kitsuse (1963) have shown it to be in connection with the social class determinants of college-going in the USA. In the latter case it was demonstrated that the high proportion of college achievers among upper class groups was 'produced' through the routine practices of high school personnel. Similarly it would be necessary in the case of the Schools Council to show the processes of interaction involved among the different groups, and not just assume an unproblematic translation of assumed 'demand' into 'policy'.

The 'educational sub-government' (teachers, local authorities and Ministry) is described as acting as a self-regulating 'adaptive system', with the major concerns of the three groups being to maintain any existing power balance within the values defined by the 'educational culture'. Thus, 'educational politics' are removed from 'macro-politics', and analysed as an autonomous system. Manzer views the values of the educational culture as the expression of the wider political culture that defines the legitimate rights of the three main interest groups referred to above. As with his concept of political culture, values are imputed and used as explanations. If, however, one views a belief in professional autonomy, not as an expression of the 'educational culture' with a relatively fixed meaning, but as a product of teachers' particular historical and social circumstances, then this also becomes a topic of enquiry rather than an explanation of teachers' corporate actions.

In terms of Manzer's model, the origin and development of the Schools Council is viewed as a process of 'structural differentiation' which can be summarized as follows:

1 The central government initiative in forming the Curriculum Study Group,[15] which Manzer 'accounts

for' in terms of 'demands' external to the system. As this was perceived by local authority associations and teachers' unions[16] as illegitimate interference, the system 'adapted' and a new structure was created (the Schools Council).

3 This structure through the limits of its sphere of action (only powers to 'recommend'), its legal autonomy from central government, and the teacher majorities built into its constitution, recognized both the 'new needs' of the society and the traditional rights of the members of the 'educational sub-government'. The formally defined objectives of the Council were to 'keep under review curricula, teaching methods and examinations. ... It should produce recommendations which were agreed by all member interests concerned. But they would still be *recommendations . . .*' (HMSO 1964) (my italics).

Like all functional analyses, we are presented with an account that seems plausible enough and is accepted to a large extent though not explicitly in the Nisbet report already referred to and by the 'member interests', whether in DES reports, statements by teacher unions, local authority representatives, or Council officials (Caston 1971). Everything is made to seem understandable and non-problematic, provided you accept the original assumptions.

Let us look briefly at three critical elements of Manzer's account:

a. The assumed 'adaptation' processes

If one does not, like Manzer, start from an equilibrium model of an educational system, the Ministry's ready 'adaptations' to criticisms of the Curriculum Study Group by forming the Schools Council raises quite different questions which he does not consider. If the 'reality' of a teacher-controlled curriculum was in question, then the Schools Council might in this situation serve to maintain this 'reality'. One can only speculate on the implications of teachers, pupils and parents finding that perhaps 'what was taught was *not* really decided by teachers (except in a very limited way), and politics *did* enter in'. Conceivably the response might be an attempt to assert collective influence through which each group might come to question the whole hierarchical structure of English curricula.

b. His characterization of 'teacher politics' between the wars.

The period between 1920 and 1940 is described by Manzer as one in which teachers as a group were 'responsible', 'idealistic', and 'autonomous'. Except that it provides a neat contrast to his 'pathological' model of contemporary education, one is led to ask what kind of account this might be. In apparently equating a lack of union militancy with responsibility,

a concern for the 'underprivileged' with 'idealism,' and for protecting 'professional rights' with 'autonomy', we are told more about the values implicit in Manzer's perspective than about the activities of teachers in their discussions about curricula. Manzer relies on this account to be able to claim that changes were little more than the formalizing of existing processes of negotiation about curricula. However, terms like 'negotiation' and 'cooperation' hide just the processes that need to be understood, and evade the issues about how 'demands' like 'more scientists' and 'less specialization in the VIth form' come to be defined. A description of discussions about the curriculum in English education prior to the creation of the Schools Council is one of the informal processes of consultation that Manzer refers to. As suggested, it is important to his account, and would seem to be a characteristic of the biological analogy underlying structural differentiation models of change, that what appears like a change is in fact a modification and elaboration of what was already there. In this case the informal processes still go on, but in a new context (the Schools Council).

c. Accounts of the influence of 'demand' on 'policy'

Manzer claims to describe the influence of increases in the demand for education on policies. However, persistences and changes in curricula and examinations remain just as much a mystery as before, and the expenditure priorities of the Schools Council of about £1m per annum are left unexplained. They are presumably a product of some inevitable process or of a series of 'acts of faith, followed by trial and error', as Wrigley (1970) puts it. Manzer's plausible 'redescription' creates problems even within its own terms as it cannot account for the differences and lack of consensus on 'desirable policies' among teachers and administrators. He is thus led to a kind of 'social pathology' model to account for what he calls the 'sickness' of British education. The 'causes' of the 'illness' are primarily lack of leadership, in the Ministry and among the unions (pp. 52 and 149–150— lack of leadership is reflected in the irresponsibility of salary claims, imposed on the leadership by union members). Its symptoms are a failure to 'go far enough fast enough to do more than gradually shift the balance of English Education to the needs of a more technologically oriented society' (p. 161). Again the familiar, rather naive, technological determinism is apparent, a characteristic of functionalist accounts of change ably criticized by Goldthorpe (1964).

The basic weakness of Manzer's approach is characteristic of the 'systems' perspective that he uses, that is not uncommon among those who write about education. He manages to make problems unproblematic and thus fails to raise questions for research or the hypotheses that require data to support them that might generate new enquiries. I would suggest that it is the uncritical though, doubtless not conscious, acceptance of assumptions like Manzer's that has contributed to the aridness of much discussion about the Schools Council. It has either been criticized for being 'power hungry' (usually by the unions), or defensive and lacking a coherent policy (usually by academics). Again such criticisms are more informative about the critics than about how competing priorities in education come to be defined or resolved.

The advantage of presenting the functional analysis in some detail is that it enables one to see what has to be taken for granted or 'given', for such an approach to be accepted as an explanation at all. If one conceives of the assumptions implicit in such concepts as 'political culture', etc., as 'produced conditions', rather than 'given', then one can begin to see why such a model of explanation is so limited and how a whole set of questions that might have been raised are not. Questions about the content of education which provided the context in which discussions about curricula were given meaning are avoided, as are the particular economic circumstances of the time. It would be valuable, for instance, to examine why the legitimacy of various conceptions of hierarchically differentiated education do not appear to have been questioned. The 'informal consultations', which were the precursors of the Schools Council, presupposed as 'given' these definitions of education and academic knowledge which were themselves historical products.

An alternative perspective

Much of this paper so far has been concerned with an elaboration of a critique of the functionalist model of 'change' in education as used in a particular case. The thrust of the argument can be summarized by a claim that sociological questions for research in education (or politics or industry for that matter) can only be posed by not accepting the ideas and institutions of the system that those involved in it are constrained to take for granted. This is as true for an institution like the Schools Council as it is for categories like teacher and pupil or even what counts as education, ability and achievement. An alternative perspective to the system model is implicit in the critique, and one of the limitations of this paper is that it is only hinted at, rather than made explicit.

It must incorporate the way those involved in 'education' give meaning to their activities and to the curricular material that they construct or that is made available. These meanings will vary with the context, from classroom to staff meeting or union conference to Schools Council committee. However, this is not enough; classrooms, staff meetings, union conferences and Council committees as contexts of interaction, all in part *take their meaning* from the wider social and economic structure. How these 'levels' and 'contexts' of explanation are linked is a central question to any sociological enquiry and can only be guessed at prior to research. Suggestions about these

links are more likely to arise out of research into particular problems with both 'levels' in mind.

It was suggested at the beginning of this paper, that we consider what counts as education as socially and historically constructed. This process points to an analysis of what are perceived as the dominant definitions of educational knowledge by different groups at particular times. This takes us back to the political nature of education, and the opportunity of some groups to restrict access to the records or information that would be necessary for this kind of research. This question would have to be asked within a broader framework that treated as 'to be explained' the definitions of 'political' and 'legitimate autonomy', which gave meaning, to quote one of Manzer's sources to 'the actual as well as inalienable right of teachers to teach what they liked, how and when'. One problem that might be explored, assuming this to be a view widely held by practising teachers and not just an example of union rhetoric, is to question how it is possible that the university-dominated Examination Boards are accepted by teachers as legitimate definers of 'what ought to be taught' and are not seen as posing a threat to this 'inalienable right'. A remaining difficulty not recognized by Manzer and to some extent evaded in this paper is that teachers are not a homogeneous group and the meaning of 'rights' is likely to be very different when say a Grammar School teacher involved primarily in VIth form work is compared to a middle school general subjects teacher.

An examination of the ways in which different groups have been involved in attempts to redefine what counted as education might shed light on one of the more significant aspects of the Schools Council's priorities. Its projects have, to a large extent reflected an acceptance of the academic/non-academic distinction as characterizing two kinds of knowledge, suitable for two distinct groups of children and associated with fairly distinct occupational rewards. This is illustrated not so much in the early priority given by the Council to problems of 'the extra year' and the 'Newsom Child', but in how these problems were defined. If one conceives of the 'early leaver' or 'Newsom child', not in terms of this group of children's 'characteristics', but as 'products' of the dynamics of the school system of a particular society, quite different 'problems' are raised. One gets some indications from the 'Young School Leavers' working papers, whether in science, mathematics or the humanities, and in Nisbet's comment that 'the increasing numbers of pupils in full time education . . . resulted in a situation where the traditional curriculum was unsuited to *many* secondary school pupils' (my italics).

If we draw together the strands of the argument of this section so far, an alternative perspective, which focuses on the socially constructed character of educational knowledge, will direct our attention to three questions which have largely gone unasked up till now:

1 What is the political or social meaning of teachers 'having control' over what they teach or 'being controlled'?

2 How are existing educational hierarchies (both 'subject' and institutional) maintained and legitimated?

3 What are the social characteristics of the distinctions made between different types of child and different 'curricula'?

We shall take these questions, in the context of the Schools Council though clearly they have much wider implications.

1. Teacher control and autonomy

It is worth exploring the possible meanings of 'teacher autonomy' in relation to the Schools Council. The Nisbet Report documents what is at least the rhetoric of the rights of teachers to decide the content of what they teach, and how it has been supported not only by teachers, but by local authorities, Schools Council personnel, and civil servants. However, what it actually means is uncertain, and in the absence of research one can only raise some questions.

On the evidence of NUT policy statements it would appear that the Union, and therefore presumably its representatives on the Schools Council, while having specific policies on the abolition of the 11+ and on examinations, does not have any policies at all on curricula, streaming or the form of organization of secondary education. The implication is that professional autonomy involves having a union policy in what is seen as an area of professional expertise (an example is whether or not children should take a selection test or an examination). Whether however, the issue concerns the individual teacher selecting syllabuses, textbooks, etc., or the individual headmaster planning the grouping of children and timetable of his school, then for the Union to have a policy would itself be an infringement of professional autonomy. This is a highly individualistic notion of autonomy, and is expressed in such public statements of teachers' unions as that 'the Schools Council should not be able to legislate to teachers what they should teach'. If teacher members of the Schools Council do attach this meaning to autonomy, it would seem to raise questions about the significance of the teacher majorities on committees, which will be taken up in more detail later; in particular it would seem doubtful whether in terms of this notion of autonomy they can do more than respond to initiatives from elsewhere. This may well leave teachers, while 'in theory' protected from imposition by the Schools Council (or anyone else), 'in practice' accepting that the initiative for developing new courses and materials comes from project directors, Schools Council officials, academics, and publishing companies. Some reference has already been made, and one finds frequent mention in public statements, to the 'teacher majorities' on all the Schools Council committees except the Finance Committee.[17] However the power that these majorities are assumed to imply depends on what may often be a very heterogeneous group of teachers from different unions voting as a block.[18] It is equally possible that they may see themselves as union representatives first[19] and teachers (independently of what and who they teach) second.[20] Furthermore if the meaning of autonomy is defined by the teachers, as has been suggested earlier, primarily as defending teachers' right *not* to use Schools Council material, then the consequences for committee members who have to generate priorities, make recommendations, and provide rationales for particular projects would appear uncertain. What, we would need to ask, are the legitimizing categories that members use to accept or reject proposals? It may be appropriate here to raise some of the problems associated with the term autonomy which have recurred in this paper. Prior to an empirical enquiry into the areas where different groups of teachers perceive differing areas of discretion over their activities and the accounts of the constraints that they give, it might be better to dispense with the term though not with the questions it raises. Like most school systems, English education is pervaded with various constraints which teachers may not perceive as such, as they are seen as 'legitimate'. 'Expert' knowledge (as will be taken up later), respect for 'academics' as selectors of students, and the relative 'fairness' of the examination system are examples. I would suggest that it is in the interrelations of social and economic circumstances and the context these have provided for the development of beliefs in these legitimacies that the problematic nature of what has been referred to as the 'freedom of the teacher', or 'teacher autonomy' might be best examined.

An alternative approach to the problem of the nature and origin of curricular initiatives, would be to start by examining empirically what is seen to count as an 'initiative' or 'innovation'. This would suggest that the Schools Council, by making recommendations within currently accepted definitions of knowledge and ability, may either be disregarded or be perceived by teachers as one of the constraints on change not unlike the Examination Boards. The sanctions available in this case are not the power to 'fail' pupils, but the control of resources which enables members of the Schools Council to become in effect, definers of what is to count as innovation. A more satisfactory answer to this whole question could only be found through having much more direct access to the Schools Council at work. Whatever the other advantages, the limitations in this context of the appointment of a part-time research professor are apparent when one looks at what is no more than another 'official' account that he provides (Wrigley 1970). If we take the question of teacher control out of the context of the Schools Council, we find a Ministry memorandum (MOE 1962) justifying some form of intervention in the following way:

The tradition of substantial *laissez-faire* in curriculum matters . . . becomes a means whereby . . . teachers are forced to respond to events they cannot control.

The implied question then becomes, who does control the events referred to? The implication of this, theoretically, is a view of curricula as 'political products', in the sense that 'what is taught' is an expression of current legitimacies as to what is valued knowledge, and how they are distributed. To take an extreme case, it would only need the assertion of teachers' 'inalienable right' to, say, 'not teach maths', for the *constraints* on the teacher to be more apparent than his *freedom*. However it is only by rejecting the widely-held tacit consensus that 'education is good' and 'we all know what education ought to be', that social or political constraints can be distinguished from legal, traditional or constitutional freedoms. This does not necessarily imply that all teachers subscribe to similar definitions of 'a good education', but it does suggest that rights and freedoms are socially defined in terms of particular definitions of education, and that in terms of alternative definitions, notions of freedom and autonomy may have a very restricted meaning.

In order to examine the possible nature of the constraints on teachers who may believe that they have 'rights' as traditionally defined, it becomes necessary to question what is taken for granted in most educational practice, writing and research. This is not only that 'schooling is good', but that 'we all know what a good school is'.[21] It is through starting from the opposite assumption 'that all schooling as we know it is harmful' that Illich (1971) is able to raise fundamental questions about the 'political' character of contemporary education.

A revealing quotation from a Schools Council official addressing a group of headmasters suggests links between the question of teacher control of the Schools Council and the legitimation of kinds of knowledge. The official is quoted in Nisbet's report as saying 'the Council has *no authority over teachers*. It may—and indeed I hope it does sometimes carry a certain amount of professional consensus, and *a great deal of the kind of authority which comes with organized knowledge*' (my italics). The question that this raises is that the speaker appears to be tacitly assuming that he and his audience all know and agree what 'organized knowledge' is and that the legitimacy of its authority is unquestioned. What the quotation does suggest is the kind of data one might look for to illustrate how the activities of the Schools Council are but one example of the hierarchical assumptions about what counts as knowledge that are held by educational personnel. A further illustration can be found in the Foreword to Working Paper 33 'Choosing a Curriculum for the Young School leaver'. The writer states '*At the outset* there was no firm intention of producing a report of the conference for publication: there were no *authoritative* speakers present, *only* people working on develop-

ment projects' (my italics). Questioning the legitimacy of 'curriculum development projects' as 'organized knowledge', and linking this to the concepts that teachers have of their autonomy, would seem an important way to begin to explore the meaning of teacher participation in the work of the Schools Council. We know little of the processes through which teachers get selected through unions and other sources for the Council's committees. A study of the career patterns of teachers who have been involved in projects, working parties and committees would seem an important extension of this; one might also study types of project sponsorship as a way of approaching the social and economic basis of particular definitions of education. Similarly, we know little of the processes by which projects become legitimized as '*organized*' knowledge, through the support of local authorities and industry or being 'housed' by universities, and through the elevation of project directors to professorial status.

2. Legitimation of 'subject' and institutional hierarchies

Most accounts of Schools Council activities see one of its purposes as a centre for discussion and debate. However this, as so often, while on a general level true, begs just the question that needs to be asked; what are the legitimate alternatives that define the terms of the discussion? For no one would suggest they are not limited (see note 21). One would want to know how far the various conferences of 'academic educators' (Hirst and Peters, among others), which are 'written up' as working papers, provide guide lines for the defining of 'problems' and 'priorities' (see Schools Council Working Paper 12). Perhaps the age and subject distinctions of the *Steering* and *Advisory* Committees provide institutional constraints on what is developed or discussed and for whom.[22] In having official representatives from 'subject associations', whose 'right to speak about their subject', would appear to be largely accepted, the Schools Council structure contributes to the maintenance of 'subjects' as 'educational realities',[23] and defines the distinctions in terms of which debates about 'integration'[24] and 'the slow learner' are likely to take place. Clearly one would need to know something of the educational background and ideas of participants in various conferences and working parties—as well as the characteristics of the Council as a particular institutional context (how do practising teachers act in relation to 'academics', HMI's, and Ministry personnel?), in order to begin an explanation of what is debated and what is not, and the possible meanings of such debates in terms of maintaining academic legitimacies.

The question of 'academic legitimacy' leads us to one of the more neglected sets of social processes, which Bourdieu (1968) discusses and to which an enquiry into types of curriculum project might contribute. The problem is how various kinds of intellectual activity gain and maintain institutional support. It is related to the question, opened up by Horton (1967), but hardly considered by sociologists, of the relation between what is treated as 'theoretical' and 'practical' knowledge, how in different contexts the legitimation of 'theory' or 'practice' is called on, and also how 'theoretical' or 'practical' knowledge may be defined as legitimate for different types of child (see (3) later). Nisbet, in the report already referred to, distinguishes two broad classes of Schools Council development projects, based on what I shall call 'academic expertise' and those based on 'good practice'. It is not suggested that all of the hundred projects sponsored by the Schools Council can be classed as one or the other, or that it may not be possible to develop other more sophisticated classifications. However the distinction does appear to have two advantages. Firstly it is simple and appears to be based on what the practitioners think they are doing. Secondly it does suggest ways of asking questions about the educational philosophies and epistemologies underlying the projects. More specifically it raises questions about 'the range of specific meanings given to the intuitively understood elements that make up the components of schooling'.[25]

The distinction, then points not only to how particular projects are legitimated in different contexts, but also to the relation between the social position and occupational career of those involved and their conceptions of 'what a curriculum development project is.'

The 'academic expertise' style characterizes those projects, particularly in the sciences and mathematics which draw on university 'subject experts', who start with a fairly explicit idea of 'what ought to be learnt'. In these projects the fundamental 'structure' of 'what is to be learnt' is not in question, because the academic experts involved in the project are also in a position to be the definers of this 'structure'.[26] The typical project therefore consists of developing teaching and learning materials which reflect these ideas and using field trials in schools to modify them in light of how teachers find they 'work'. In contrast to this 'style' is the 'good practice' style, which appears to draw on an older English educational tradition carried out earlier almost entirely by the Inspectorate. These projects (the Middle School Curriculum, English in the Middle Years, and Social Studies (8–13) are examples) rely on those involved having some implicit notion of 'good practice', with which they can identify such practices in schools. The project therefore consists of collecting together and ordering samples of 'good practice' for dissemination to the schools. The possible differences and similarities in the underlying assumptions can only be hinted at here without a detailed investigation of particular projects.

The 'academic expertise' style depends on a fairly explicit definition of the 'structure of a subject'; it rests on a clear distinction between knower and known, and therefore between *what* has to be taught and *how* it is taught. The model of the teacher, then, is a kind of technologist (used in a very general sense). The criteria used to define those aspects of the child, such as age and measured 'ability', that are explicitly taken account of in the construction of teaching materials, are limited and fairly specific.

As criteria of success are fairly rigorously 'subject-defined', failure will be likely to be seen in terms either of the materials' unsuitability for particular children (Nuffield Science), or in terms of attributes of the children. It is entailed in these subject-defined criteria that such projects will operate with typically hierarchical concepts of knowledge and ability, and though they appear to be likely in areas of the curriculum with fairly explicit 'logics', as in mathematics and science, investigation might well suggest similar philosophies underlying projects in other fields, particularly for the 'less able'. There is a paradox indicated in how this style has been characterized, that would be worth exploring empirically. It has been implied that the assumptions about knowledge of the 'academic expertise' style define what is seen as relevant knowledge 'of' and 'by' the pupils in the construction of project material; relevant knowledge 'of' the pupils would be restricted to age and 'future studies' (for example] a major criterion of relevance for the new 'integrated science' project has been, 'will pupils be able to go on to single subjects (physics, chemistry and biology) at 'A' level?'). Pupil science, for example, is only 'relevant' when incorporated into 'subject' science. However, one would speculate that the failure or inappropriateness of these projects may be explained by those involved, whether project developers or teachers, by drawing on 'knowledge' that has no explicit subject definitions of relevance. This suggests that this style does in practice carry with it a model of the child that incorporates many features that are not made formally explicit.

I am suggesting, that, although in the new 'O' level science syllabuses one finds few explicit references to what might be significant or relevant to different children's own non-school experience, implicit in the activity of construction of 'suitable' teaching materials is a concept of the kind of child the materials will be suitable for.

Focusing on the model of the typical child or children held by those involved in this style of project, could be one way of raising more general questions about social and political definitions of knowledge. It may not be without significance, to take an example, that the early working papers that formed the basis of the Nuffield 'O' levels in Physics, Chemistry and Biology were drawn up by members of the then Science Masters Association (now the Association for Science Education), which was founded by a group of Eton Science masters and has drawn its membership largely from independent, voluntary aided and direct grant grammar schools.

The underlying assumptions, particularly the notion of what counts as knowledge, of the 'good practice' style are less easy to postulate, partly because they are far less explicit. With its major emphasis on the exemplar of good practice, this style necessarily entails less emphasis on the cognitive aspects of 'practice', and more on the personal involvement of the learner,[27] and an educational philosophy that is pragmatic and empiricist. The questions any enquiry would ask then are, firstly, what are the exemplars of 'good practice', and what are the tacit criteria used to identify them? If they cannot, as has been suggested, be made formally explicit, how are the 'ropes' of good practice learnt by pupils and student teachers? The second point is to consider the implications of the definitions of knowledge characteristic of the 'academic expertise' style, where the 'knowledge', not the teacher, is treated as the exemplar; how different in this context is the process of learning or not learning the 'academic ropes'? With the exception of one study (Reisman *et al.*, 1970), sociological enquiry into education hardly seems to have raised these questions. Furthermore, an understanding of the processes involved in 'reconstructing' the 'good practice' of a sample of teachers' logics in use (to borrow Kaplan's distinction) which are then made available to other teachers would need much more detailed investigation.

It would not be surprising, given the common social and economic context in which they are generated, if there were significant similarities as well as the differences in educational philosophies of the two project styles that have been referred to. The 'academic expertise' style takes for granted the basic structure of academic 'subjects' while the 'good practice' style does not question the practice of 'good' teachers. Thus each makes implicit assumptions about the autonomy of educational knowledge from the society of which the educational institutions are a part. In this way both project styles may contribute to maintaining for educators the 'reality' of 'something that really *is* education' and the 'non-political' character of education.

To be able to suggest any explanations about how Schools Council priorities might be determined would seem premature without any access to records or committees. Council officials tend to claim that decisions rest on 'the quality of the proposals', and that they represent no balance across subjects, or age groups. However, though it is not easy to infer from the patterns of expenditure an alternative explanation, it would appear somewhat naive to accept at face value such statements from officials of an organization so strongly committed to not having a policy. This does not imply that such statements were not believed to be true, or that given the categories that they were working with (Languages, Science, English, Mathematics, Humanities, etc.) they were not true. The point is that we would want to try and ask how are the categories themselves constituted,[28] and how might they influence the conception of available alternatives.

3. Types of child and types of knowledge

The Schools Council has had explicit priorities for projects specifically directed to 'the young school leaver'. Furthermore in Geography, Science and Maths, there are two separate projects, that can be broadly characterized as for the 'academic' and for the 'non-academic' child. The assumption made therefore is that the 'majority' are incapable of succeeding in academic courses, and at the examinations associated with such courses. Therefore different kinds of courses with different kinds of examinations must be organized for them. The maintenance of these distinctions has been a central if unpublicized aspect of the Schools Council activity; it has links to the two previous questions discussed, and implications both within the schools system and outside it. A glance at the teaching materials or working papers in the 'Young School Leaver' series (and a detailed analysis would be an important task for the sociologist) would suggest that whatever use teachers may make of such documents, the authors claim to be contributing to what they see as a critical 'teacher problem'—the control and occupying of time of increasing numbers of children who would rather not be in school at all. Even if they are not made specific use of in the schools they confirm and legitimate the distinctions on which they are based, and thus also provide legitimacy for existing subject and institutional hierarchies and the assumptions about competence and ability that they imply. Within the schools the distinct courses make the feasibility of mobility between courses seem 'for all practical purposes' to be impossible. Outside of schools the distinction becomes (at the extreme) between those courses that are qualifications for further schooling or particular jobs, and those courses that are qualifications for jobs that do not require qualifications, or no jobs. It is suggested therefore that the Schools Council, through its legitimation of curricula that might be characterized in Bourdieu's terms as based on class cultures, together with the schools, maintain the class structure of which they are a reflection. The task of a politics of educational knowledge, is then, in the context of this paper, not only the empirical study of such legitimations as 'academic expertise' and 'good practice', but also the construction of possible alternative models reflecting different assumptions about knowledge, learning and ability.

To conclude then, an attempt has been made to examine some of the implications of recognizing the political character of education by drawing on a sociology of knowledge perspective and focusing on a particular institution, the Schools Council. Some readers of this paper, whether they be teachers or sociologists or both, may well ask: why bother with the Schools Council?—it does not have any influence anyway. Whether or not this is true is beside the point, though the sale of over half a million copies of 'Mathematics in the Primary School'—its first curriculum bulletin— and the increasing numbers of commercial companies signing contracts to publish Schools Council material would suggest that it is not. What is important, and in the widest sense what this paper is about, is to try to show how enquiries that start by considering education as a social category cannot be separated from a perspective which conceives of what is taught as a 'political' question. The former treat as problematic, and therefore as topics for enquiry, the social meanings that make the interaction between educational personnel in different contexts possible. The latter emphasizes the distribution of power which limits access to some contexts and some meanings and not others. Thus not only education but educational research is political; to put it crudely, dossiers on children are available, but Department of Education and Schools Council minutes are not; teachers in classrooms are observable, the Programme Committee of the Schools Council is not. It is not surprising therefore that in this, as in other fields of sociological enquiry, we get detailed information about the subordinate group (in this case children), but only

speculation or official histories of the activities of those who control their educational destinies. The parallel with recent criticisms of research into race relations is not hard to see. It has frequently been suggested that the separation of the sociology of knowledge from the sociological study of education has impoverished both. Perhaps a further suggestion is that a similar impoverishment has been a product of maintaining the distinction between education and politics, whether in sociology or anywhere else. However these speculations about the control and accessibility of knowledge may raise even more fundamental questions that are implicit, if not central to the sociological enquiries suggested in this paper. What kind of model of education is implicit is an alternative to one based on agreed definitions of expertise and good practice? What kind of model of society is implied where all or none are experts or good practitioners and there is no differential opportunity to avoid 'being researched', when, as it were, the researchers and controllers are researched?

Notes

1 This point is a major focus of the work of Paulo Freire (1970a; 1970b).

2 This term is taken from Bourdieu (1967; 1968), who in a series of papers has examined the relationship between kinds of educational institution and the structures implicit in various kinds of intellectual activity and modes of thought.

3 The use of this 'global' term is not intended to imply any necessary consensus among a very heterogeneous group. It is merely a convenient way of referring to those who have a direct and officially defined responsibility for educational matters—teachers, union officials, administrators and academics.

4 Paradoxically this was also true of the overtly political debate between the Black Paper supporters (Cox and Dyson 1969) and their opponents Rubinstein and Stoneman (1970) (among others), most of whom limit the terms of political debate to 'who gets education?' rather than the political character of education itself.

5 That there are such grounds is very much part of the 'vocabulary of motives' (Mills 1940), referred to earlier, of those who write about, administer and practise education. The 'reality' of 'educational grounds' forms part of the tacit assumptions of all government reports and recent discussions about examinations and secondary school reorganization. They enable those involved to perceive their discussions as insulated from the political and economic context in which they take place.

6 The Schools Council for Curriculum and Examinations was established in October 1964, on the lines recommended by the Lockwood Report (Ministry of Education 1964), with representatives from the teachers' unions, local authority associations and others. Details of its constitution, official policy and the scope of the projects it has sponsored can be found in its Annual Reports (Schools Council 1969; 1970).

7 Banks (1968) in her chapter, 'Who controls our schools?', avoids making explicit what is meant by control. In this paper I shall use it in the way discussed

in the introduction to Young (1971) when I draw explicitly on the ideas of Dawe (1970). It points to questions about how and by whom is meaning given to education.

8 It would be naive to suppose that classroom teachers, in effect, ever thought they would control the Certificate of Secondary Education, in spite of its constitution which emphasized its regional basis, independence from the universities, and the process of nomination to the regional Boards through the teacher unions. This examination system was specifically set up for those children not able to reach General Certificate of Education (the university controlled system) standards. The fact, therefore that it maintained rather than questioned existing academic legitimacies with regard to the crucial question of access to higher education, may account for the universities' lack of active interest. Whether they will remain similarly detached during the projected discussions about amalgamating the two exam systems remains to be seen.

9 Whether, and what it means to say that the Schools Council has *influenced* educational practice remains an empirical question. The lack of follow-up research and the inaccessibility of the Council to 'being researched' will be taken up later in the paper. Two points are worth mentioning here:

 i. The concern of the Council with the raising of the school leaving age has enabled schools to have a new claim on resources, though which section of the school population are in practice the beneficiaries remains to be seen.

 ii. The fate 'in the schools' of projects like the Humanities Curriculum Project (which was explicitly set up to provide material for 'children of average and below average ability') is uncertain, though the willingness of local authorities to sponsor in-service courses on the project material may be significant. The wider question this raises is whether some projects are more actively 'sponsored' than others.

10 Not only does the Council have specific committees (see n. 17) concerned with GCE and CSE examining, but 36 per cent (85) of the references to Schools Council projects refer to examining, mostly CSE (Schools Council 1971).

11 Nisbet (1971) mentions that 20 of the 84 'A' Level syllabuses considered between 1968–70 were not approved, though we have no information as to the criteria of approval used.

12 It is important to distinguish between Manzer's (1970) use of the term politics and that used in this paper, referred to earlier. The use in this paper is more akin to that of Dexter (1964) and Postman (1970), while Manzer's definition 'politics is the process by which social values are authoritatively allocated' (op. cit., p. 1) presupposes the consensus on values that it is the aim of this paper to treat as problematic.

13 I am very grateful to Professor Nisbet for lending me a copy of his report prior to publication. Though it reads rather like an 'official history', it is useful in being carefully documented often from not readily accessible sources.

14 By implication, what counts as 'education' is not questioned.

15 A small group of 'experts', drawn mainly from the Ministry and the Inspectorate and set up in 1962.

16 It would be more accurate to say the leaders of the teachers' unions and local authority associations, as Manzer is only able to document *their* public statements.

17 The Constitution of the Schools Council lays down that all committees except the Finance Committee

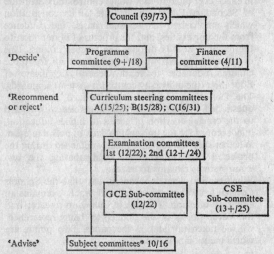

'Decide'

'Recommend or reject'

'Advise'

(*Art, classics, craft, English, geography, history, home economics, modern languages, music, physical education, maths, religious education, science, social science, general studies.)

Note Numbers refer to proportions of *teacher union* representatives.

Two points are worth mentioning here:

i. Each potential 'project' is considered twice at each level, but can be rejected on the first or second 'round' by the Programme Committee.

ii. The teacher majorities are in all cases small, so for the committees to be at least 'formally' teacher-controlled, a high level of teacher attendance is assumed.

should have a majority of teacher representatives. The significance of the distinction made concerning the Finance Committee is uncertain, though Schools Council personnel would undoubtedly see it as subordinate to the 'teacher controlled' Programme Committee. A summary picture of the Council's formal structure is presented at the foot of column 1 and is adapted from *Dialogue*, no. 1, the Schools Council's Newsletter.

18 For instance the nine teacher 'representatives' on the key Programme Committee come from five different unions, which in other contexts are competing for legitimacy and new members.

19 The question still remains as to how 'representative' the teachers' representatives are. They may tend to be union office holders, or potential office holders, and therefore in this context what 'representativeness' means remains uncertain.

20 After a year or more of meetings they may even come to see themselves as primarily 'Schools Council men'. A possibility suggested by the most recent 'official' account of the aims and activities of the Schools Council (Caston 1971).

21 The 'Raising of the School Leaving Age' programme illustrates this. The whole question of compulsory school attendance for all for 11 years from 5–16 has only been discussed in terms of finding activities that are 'relevant' for the 'young school leaver' (itself an unexamined social category). More specific examples are how Working Paper 33, 'Choosing a curriculum for the Young School Leaver', and the Welsh Committee's 'Another Year—to endure or enjoy?' have an image of the characteristics and future occupational position of the 'type' of child under discussion, a point taken up in the final section in this paper.

22 The Steering Committees are the three Curriculum Committees referred to in n. 17. They are distinguished by overlapping age categories which define their responsibilities (A—from 12–13; B from 11–16; C from 14–18). B and C also supervise the examination Committees responsible, respectively for CSE and 'O' level, and 'A' level. One might speculate that members come to conceive of their groups of children as, partly, separate problems, with C Committee members being predominantly concerned with 'academic' children and B Committee members with 'non-academic' children. The Advisory Committees are those associated largely with the traditional subjects of the curriculum (see n. 23).

23 A very crude index of support for this can be obtained from an analysis of the Schools Council Project list produced by its Library and Information Centre. There are 161 references to what are usually called school subjects. Of these 84 (52 per cent) refer to science, English and maths, 28 (17 per cent) refer to geography, history and French, but only 7 (4 per cent) to home economics, technical drawing, health and handicraft.

24 The conference in June 1971 on the Integration of the Social Sciences in the Sixth Form at Norwich, whatever its outcome, reflected in its conception the group of 'subject' representatives that are represented on the Schools Council 'Social Science' Advisory Committee, and so, what one might call the Schools Council definition of 'Social Science'.

25 The quotation is takens from Westbury and Steiner's (1971) paper, where they make an interesting com-

parison between the assumptions of two quite different approaches to curriculum development; Bereiter and Engelman's 'compensatory education' programme, and Dennison's (1969) description of his First Street School.

26 This notion of structure was first used by Bruner (1960). Its implications have been examined by Kleiband (1964), who suggests that it has become a source of legitimacy for various 'subject associations' to gain economic support; he also suggests how the idea of 'structure' is related to an unquestioned acceptance of the disjunctions between school and non-school knowledge.

27 For example in the 1969–70 Schools Council report, the reference to the 'Middle Years of Schooling' project emphasized the 'needs of the children . . . and ease of transition from primary to secondary education' (p. 13); likewise in Working Paper 33, the project 'Arts and the Adolescent' emphasized the intention to 'study art education to pinpoint key factors effecting *success in terms of pupil response*', p. 33 (my italics).

28 To view these categories as 'normative orders' (Blum 1970), is only to pose the problem. Empirically it would lead to an enquiry into what members of different committees take for granted in making these distinctions appear 'obvious'.

Acknowledgment

I should like to thank Basil Bernstein, Brian Davies, Nell Keddie and Elizabeth McGovern for their helpful comments and criticisms of earlier drafts of this paper. The final revision owes much to Elizabeth McGovern's suggestions and her careful reading of an earlier draft.

References

Bachrach, P. and Baratz, M. S. (1963). Decisions and non-decisions; an analytical framework. *American Political Science Review*, **57** (3).

Banks, Olive (1968). *The Sociology of Education*. London: Batsford.

Blum, Alan (1970). The corpus of knowledge as a normative order, in *Theoretical Sociology*, ed. J. McKinney and E. Tiryakian. New York: Appleton Century Croft. Also in Young, Michael F. D. (1971).

Bourdieu, Pierre (1967). Systems of education and systems of thought. *International Social Science Journal*, **19** (3).

Bourdieu, Pierre (1968). Intellectual field and creative project. *Social Science Information*, **8**, (2) (both papers available in Young, Michael, F. D. (1971).)

Bruner, Jerome S. (1960). *The Process of Education*. Cambridge, Mass.: Harvard University Press and New York: Random House Vintage Books.

Caston, Geoffrey (1971). The Schools Council in context. *Journal of Curriculum Studies*, **3**, May.

Cicourel, A. V. and Kitsuse, J. I. (1963). *The Educational Decision Makers*. Indianapolis: Bobbs Merrill.

Cox, C. E. and Dyson, A. E. (1969). *Black Papers 1 and 2*. Critical Quarterly.

Dawe, Alan (1970). The two sociologies. *British Journal of Sociology*, **21** (2).

Dexter, Lewis (1964). The politics and sociology of stupidity, in *The Other Side*, ed. Howard S. Becker. New York: Free Press.

Dennison, George (1969). *The Lives of Children*. New York: Random House.

Easton, David (1953). *The Political System*. New York: Alfred A. Knopf.

Freire, Paulo (1970a). The adult literacy process. *Harvard Educational Review*, **40** (2).

Freire, Paulo (1970b). *Pedagogy of the Oppressed*. New York: Herder and Herder.

Goldthorpe, John (1964). Social stratification in industrial societies, in *Sociological Review Monograph*, no. 8, ed. P. Halmos.

HMSO (1964). *Report of the Working Party on Schools Curricula and Examinations*.

Horton, Robin (1967). African traditional thought and Western science, *Africa*, **67**, and in Young, Michael F. D. (1971).

Illich, Ivan (1971). *Deschooling Society*. London: Calder & Boyars.

Kleiband, H. (1964). Structure of the disciplines as an educational slogan. *Teachers College Record*, **66**.

Manzer, R. A. (1970). *Teachers and Politics*. Manchester University Press.

Mills, C. W. (1940). Situated actions and vocabularies of motive. *American Sociological Review*, **4** (5).

Musgrove, F. W. (1968). The sociologist's contribution to the curriculum, in *Changing the Curriculum*, ed. J. Kerr. London: UNIBOOKS.

Musgrove, F. W. (1971). *Patterns of Power and Authority in English Education*. London: Methuen.

Nisbet, J. (1971). Unpublished report for the OECD, 'The Schools Council'.

Postman, Neil (1970). The politics of reading. *Harvard Educational Review*, **40** (2).

Reisman, D., Gusfield, J. and Gamson, Z. (1970). *Academic Values and Mass Education*. New York: Doubleday.

Rubinstein, D. and Stoneman, C. (1970) (eds.). *Education for Democracy*. Penguin Books.

Schools Council (1971). Schools Council Projects; Information Centre/Library (mimeographed).

Westbury, I. and Steiner, W. (1971). A discipline in search of its problems. *School Review*, February.

Wylie, Lawrence (1961). *Village in the Vaucluse*, Cambridge, Mass.: Harvard University Press.

Wrigley, J. (1970). The Schools Council, in J. Butcher and H. B. Pont (eds.), *Educational Research in Britain*, **2**, University of London Press.

Young, Michael F. D. (ed.) (1971). *Knowledge and Control: New Directions for the Sociology of Education*. London: Collier-Macmillan.

Introduction to readings 13–16

The following four readings deal with different aspects of curriculum development in Scotland, Wales and Ireland. In the first of these Professor John Nisbet outlines the situation in Scotland.

In present circumstances, all parts of Britain and Ireland tend to share common curriculum problems, and there is great similarity between the approaches practised in the different systems. However, as the articles in section I have demonstrated, there is one problem shared by Wales and Ireland—that of institutionalized bilingualism. Horgan and Thomas have already discussed some of the issues, but in the items which follow three further views are presented. The first, by J. R. Webster, forms part of an article in the 1870 centenary issue of *Trends in Education*, the periodical published occasionally by the Department of Education and Science. However, the Department is careful to indicate that opinions expressed in this issue are the writer's own and not necessarily those of the Department.

The article by Professor Devlin appeared in the *Irish Times* at a time of considerable discussion of the future of Irish in Irish schools, following an indication from the Minister in the Fianna Fail government, that his party was contemplating joining the main opposition parties in seeking an end to the compulsory nature of Irish teaching in schools. It presents what may be termed a scholarly nationalist view. It is in contrast with the rather less sympathetic but possibly more realistic view taken by Anthony Weir in the article from *Fortnight*, a news magazine with a wide circulation among moderate opinion in Northern Ireland, where the Dublin government's policies on the encouragement of Irish speaking have long produced scepticism, even among many of those sympathetic to the cause of Irish unity.

13 Curriculum development in Scotland

John Nisbet

'The danger of making comparisons is that one easily falls into the trap of exaggerating differences. Examiners, with their fondness for the "compare and contrast" type of question, know only too well what ingenuity can be used in discovering distinctions where none exist. Similarities can be overlooked because they are too obvious. ... The temptation is not merely to describe the differences which exist but to try to explain them.'[1] The pattern of curriculum development in Scotland is certainly different from that in England, and it is tempting to explain the contrast in terms of differences, in both size and character, between the educational systems of the two countries. Scotland is a small country, with only some 3,180 schools supported wholly or partly by public funds. Its educational system is more tightly knit: over 98 per cent of children attend the public schools (in the literal and Scottish use of the term). The smaller unit can

function on a less formal basis, for consultation takes place between people who know each other and meet together frequently. In consequence, some changes can be introduced quickly and easily. Revision of the secondary school mathematics curriculum in Scotland began in 1963; in 1969 over 70 per cent of schools are being examined on the new syllabus, and in 1970 the figure will be 98 per cent.[2] Another consequence is that the process of change is seldom adequately documented, so that it is difficult for those outside the system to know precisely what has happened. Two recent publications have helped to fill in the details of recent developments. In *Scottish Education Looks Ahead*,[3] the Senior Chief Inspector has outlined the machinery of change in Scottish education, and two members of the inspectorate have described the changes in English and mathematics. The *First Report* 1965–8[4] of the Consultative Committee on the Curriculum gives a comprehensive review of the whole range of curriculum development in Scotland, and provides an opportunity to make comparisons with the Schools Council report, *The First Three Years*.[5]

Source: Journal of Curriculum Studies (1970), **2** (1), 5–10.
John Nisbet is Professor of Education at the University of Aberdeen.

The Consultative Committee on the Curriculum is the Scottish equivalent of the Schools Council. In both Scotland and England, a considerable amount of work in curriculum development was under way before any formal national co-ordinating body was set up. But whereas the Schools Council was established with a large measure of financial and administrative independence, the Scottish Consultative Committee is a Committee of the Scottish Education Department, with the Secretary of the Department as its chairman. 'The Consultative Committee, as an advisory body with no executive functions, has no staff of its own and secretarial services are provided by officers of the Scottish Education Department. The work of enquiry and curriculum development has been carried out almost wholly by HM Inspectors and teachers in schools, colleges of education and universities.'[6] Perhaps appropriately, the Scottish arrangement would appear to be economic of funds. Costs are absorbed by other parts of the educational system, but if they could be separately accounted, it seems likely that the total cost of curriculum development in Scotland would fall well below the traditional eleven-eightieths, which used to serve as a basis for the ratio of Scottish to English expenditure on education. Whereas the report of the Schools Council lists research projects costing a total of over two million pounds, the report of the Consultative Committee does not mention money at all.

The twenty-four members of the Scottish Consultative Committee on the Curriculum are 'appointed as individuals—for their personal knowledge and experience—rather than as representatives of particular organizations'.[7] However, it is not by chance that nine of the members are teachers in schools, together with one from a technical college and one from an art college, while four are from the inspectorate and two are officers of the Scottish Education Department (the Secretary and one under-secretary). The Principals of three of the ten Scottish colleges of education are members; in Scotland, the colleges of education are financed directly by the Scottish Education Department. The other four members are: a director of education, a professor of chemistry, a professor of French and a banker. The Committee is thus very much an organ of the central authority in partnership with the teachers. At least the teaching profession cannot complain of over-representation of outside interests or of domination by the universities. For its independence and freedom of action, the Committee must rely on the independence of mind of its members, and on the frequent and consistent disclaimers by the Scottish Education Department of any wish to encroach on the teachers' freedom in curricular matters. 'The Committee's terms of reference require it to maintain a general oversight over the school curriculum, both primary and secondary; (and) to draw attention of the Secretary of State to any aspect of the curriculum, whether general or particular, which seems to call for consideration by specialist bodies. ... Neither the Secretary of State nor the Scottish Education Department has any direct responsibility for the school curriculum. Education authorities ... acting with the advice of the heads of their schools and their teachers, decide what shall, or shall not, be taught in their schools ... and it is for them to decide whether or not to accept any advice which is offered to them.'[8]

But the essential guarantee against interference by the central authority is the method of working which the Committee has adopted—the small working party, comprising a majority of practising teachers and inspectors, with college of education lecturers and occasionally a university teacher or other adviser. In 1955 the first working party on this model was set up to review the curriculum of the senior secondary school. The recommendations of their report in 1959 led to the introduction of the Ordinary grade in the Scottish Certificate of Education in 1962. Previously, memoranda of advice on the curriculum had been drafted by the inspectorate—for example, *The Primary School in Scotland* (1950), *Junior Secondary Education* (1955) and a series of papers on individual secondary school subjects issued between 1950 and 1961. This was the basis also of the memorandum, *Primary Education in Scotland*, which was published in 1965. Increasingly, however, the working party structure has been favoured, and more than twenty such groups have been formed in the past ten years.

A description of the work of one such group is given by A. G. Robertson,[9] formerly HMI and chairman of the Mathematics Syllabus Committee from 1963 to 1968. The appointment of the Mathematics Syllabus Committee followed from a report by a previous Departmental committee on mathematics, which had reviewed recent changes in university honours courses in mathematics. The new committee was given both a broad remit and a precise task: 'to review the school mathematics syllabus and to initiate in a number of schools experimental work on the introduction of certain aspects of modern mathematics.' The committee comprised fifteen principal teachers of mathematics in secondary schools, two principal lecturers in mathematics from colleges of education and four inspectors; later, three university lecturers were added to the membership. In April 1964, twelve months after its formation, the committee published draft syllabuses for the O grade in mathematics of the Scottish Certificate of Education. An experimental text with teachers' notes began its trials in fifteen pilot schools in session 1963–4, and the following session forty-five other schools joined in the experiment, thus involving a total of some seven thousand pupils. Seven books were planned to cover the three and a half years of study to O grade. Book I was written in the spring of 1964, printed in the summer and used in the experimental schools in the autumn. The remaining books were written in quick succession, two more being added eventually to take the course up to Higher grade (Scottish fifth year of secondary school). In-service courses and the supply of appropriate equipment to schools were also organized. Robertson[10] describes the task involved:

> At any one time from 1964 to 1968 then, the committee was revising one book, testing the subsequent book in the series, and writing the one to follow that. Most chapters for the experimental book went through three or four draft stages before being accepted by the group as a whole. The committee met about six times each year, held several two-day conferences, and worked through sub-committees from time to time. Debate and discussion were often strenuous, sometimes heated, but rarely acrimonious; the endpoints in the syllabus construction and associated writing were invariably compromises between the various extremes and shades of opinion. A reasonably close liaison between the Syllabus Committee and the sixty schools was maintained over the years by means of visits, conferences, questionnaires, newsletters and correspondence.

The resulting series[11] has had international success, special editions being prepared for Australia, South Africa, Holland, Germany, Sweden and Norway.

A number of working parties on this pattern had been set up before the appointment of the Consultative Committee; others have been appointed since. Some deal with subjects in breadth, English, science, classics, art, physical education; others with specific aspects, decimal currency and the metric system, computers and the school; others again with specific applications, modern studies for non-certificate classes, and integrated science syllabus as a common course in the first two years of secondary education.

In the field of English, a more extensive network of activities has been established. The co-ordinating body is the Central Committee on English, appointed in 1966 with eleven members (four school teachers, two university professors, two college lecturers, two local authority advisers and an inspector as chairman). Their remit is to 'promote research and development in the teaching of English at all levels'. The Central Committee has seventeen local development committees, which in turn have set up study groups to deal with particular aspects. To improve communication and act as a clearing house and resource centre, the Centre of Information on the Teaching of English has been established in Moray House College of Education, Edinburgh, with college staff serving on a part-time basis. This Centre issues regular newsletters, one of which provides a detailed description of the Central Committee's activities.[12]

It will be clear from this account that the various working parties and committees differ among themselves in their organization and procedure, so that it is difficult to write in general terms about curriculum development in Scotland. In some subjects, physics, chemistry and mathematics, for example, syllabuses have changed substantially—and, most would agree, for the better. Curricula in other subjects, such as geography, have been changing without the aid of any formal curriculum development organization. New ideas have been put forward in classics and English: whether these will affect the content of teaching in schools seems to depend on the content of future SCE examination papers more than on the persuasion of teachers. In other subjects, working parties have not yet had time to produce reports. But the production of reports is only the first step in the process of curricular change, as the *First Report*[13] recognizes. 'There must be some follow-up locally and nationally, if in the end the work of teachers in all parts of the country is to be influenced and, the Committee hopes, improved, by the changes and developments proposed.'

Curriculum development, however, is slow in arousing genuine involvement of teachers, though Scotland is not unique in this problem. Perhaps the Scottish educational pattern is too authoritarian at heart, so that it is unrealistic to expect teachers to show initiative or to do anything other than wait for a strong lead from the centre. With the concentration of effort in the hands of small working parties, one looks in vain for growth at the grass roots. Provision for discussion and development of the reports issued—through local groups in teachers' centres and through in-service training—is still far from adequate. Also, some of the reports are of a kind which is hardly likely to stimulate discussion. Built up from the experience and considered opinion of practising teachers, they can readily encourage the best of current practice. They can also too easily slip into the hortatory style of *Suggestions for Teachers*, or lay themselves open to criticism that they are just the old 'projects and activity' in a new glossy wrapping. The experimental sequence of defining objectives, designing appropriate materials and method, trials in schools, evaluation and feedback, has not been widely applied in Scotland. The Schools Council type of project has been adopted by the English Committee, but not by the others. The working party procedure keeps our feet firmly on the ground, and there are few in Scotland who would object. Nevertheless, there is a danger that a group of busy practical people may be too unreceptive of unconventional ideas which, though unpractical, are often a stimulus to re-thinking about important fundamental issues and are effective at least in provoking controversies and starting discussion.

The major achievement of the Scottish Education Department so far in this area has been its success in starting up the process of curriculum development, without arousing uneasiness or discontent among the teachers. In so far as teachers are aware at all of what is going on, they seem to welcome their new role of partnership with the inspectors and the colleges of education in this task. Some of the criticisms which have been made above must ring a familiar note to English readers. But those who know the Scottish system will recognize that the procedure which has evolved is peculiarly well suited to the Scottish situation. Educational problems know no frontiers, but educational institutions are not exportable. The Schools Council structure is probably too cumbersome for a country with one-tenth the population of England; and one cannot imagine the Scottish working party of twelve to fourteen members (the average size) being

acceptable as a nationally representative group in England. Curriculum development in Scotland is practical and down-to-earth; its reports are economical of words; and the provision is relatively inexpensive—three characteristically Scottish virtues, or faults?

Notes

1 G. S. Osborne, *Scottish and English Schools* (London: Longman, 1966), 307.
2 J. Nisbet (ed.), *Scottish Education Looks Ahead* (Edinburgh: Chambers, 1969), 87.
3 Op. cit., 1–10, 59–73, 74–90.
4 Scottish Education Department, *Consultative Committee on the Curriculum: First Report 1965–8* (Edinburgh: HMSO, 1969).
5 Schools Council, *The First Three Years* (London: HMSO, 1968).

6 *First Report 1965–8*, 6.
7 Ibid., 5.
8 Ibid.
9 *Scottish Education Looks Ahead*, ch. 6.
10 Ibid., 80–1.
11 *Modern Mathematics in Schools* (Edinburgh: Chambers).
12 W. A. Gatherer, The Central Committee on English: a report (*CITE Newsletter*, 1 (2), 3–5, May 1968).
13 *First Report 1965–8*, p. 6.

Professor Nisbet now adds the following comment (July 1972):

The main development in Scotland since this article was written is the establishment of other centres on the lines of the Centre for Information on the Teaching of English. So far, three centres have been set up, in colleges of education, for mathematics and science, modern languages and social subjects, each supported by a Central Committee. *The Second Report 1968–71* of the Consultative Committee on the Curriculum (HMSO 1972) comments:

It became clear . . . that it was not enough for a working party to be set up on an individual

subject and to report and for subsequent development to be unsupervised. Some form of permanent machinery was needed to keep under review all aspects of the curriculum in individual subjects.

The problem still remains of persuading teachers to adopt the practices recommended by the working parties: the fear is that the working party reports will gather dust beside the many other exhortations to good practice, while teachers continue as before. The Scottish arrangements, like those in other countries, have not yet bridged the gap between recommendation and implementation.

14 Curriculum development in Wales

J. R. Webster

Before 1907 the main concern of Welsh nonconformist leaders had been to create a national system of education which they controlled and which gave every Welsh child the possibility of social advancement. With the formation of the Department, the question of the control of schools became largely a dead issue, and controversy moved from administrative problems to the school curriculum. For this change Owen M. Edwards, the first chief inspector for Wales, is almost entirely responsible. Edwards's career from a Merionethshire farmstead to a Fellowship at Lincoln College,

Source: Centenary issue of *Trends in Education*, HMSO (1970).
J. R. Webster is Dean of the Faculty of Education, University College of North Wales.

Oxford, was all that the most ambitious nonconformist parent could wish for. Yet Edwards's own educational philosophy was strangely at odds with those of his countrymen. A disciple of Ruskin, he saw schools as existing to enrich their local communities. He took seriously Ruskin's view that there should be differentiation between the curricula of schools according to their locality—in cities, in the countryside, near the sea, or, as Edwards would have added, in areas where the Welsh language predominated. His greatest dread was to see a Wales 'full of clerks and teachers' who had lost touch with their locality, its language and its culture. During his time at Lincoln College, Edwards produced a flood of Welsh language books and periodicals. When he became Chief Inspector his main concern was to see that Welsh was studied for its own sake, and not, as its most ardent advocates had suggested up to that time, as a means of teaching English more proficiently.

The impact of Edwards's views was immediate. The first separate Code for Wales in 1907 stated that the Board of Education wished 'that every Welsh teacher should realize the educational value of the Welsh language, and of its literature, which from its wealth of romance and lyric is peculiarly adapted to the education of the young'. The new regulations for secondary schools in Wales were even more specific. 'In districts where Welsh is spoken the language, or one of the languages other than English, should be Welsh. Any of the subjects in the curriculum may, where the local needs make it desirable, be taught in Welsh.'

These minutes set the tone for the Welsh Department's policy. Officials and inspectors have, to the present day, followed Edwards's liberal, and perhaps rather idealistic, educational philosophy. Bilingualism has been the cornerstone of government policy. This official view has been supported by the reports of all the committees that have studied the language problem in Wales—from the Departmental Committee Report on *Welsh in Education and Life* (1927) to the Central Advisory Council (Gittins) report on the primary schools (1968). It is perhaps the most astonishing feature of education in Wales in the twentieth century that a bilingual policy has been imposed from above on a largely indifferent, and occasionally hostile, population. Local authorities have to be more sensitive to parents' wishes than the central government, and in the economically ruinous Thirties, in particular, they were forced to take a utilitarian view. Authorities have thus varied greatly in the extent to which they actively encouraged the teaching of Welsh, some doing no more than vaguely suggesting that they were making 'appropriate provision'. The Central Advisory Council reports (1953) on the place of English and Welsh in the schools of Wales analyse the problems of the local authorities exactly. 'In very many cases,' they note, 'the members of the authorities are themselves, like most of us, products of the outmoded policy of the early part of this century, and in addition have experienced those economic difficulties that account for much of the disinclination to afford the Welsh language its proper place. Moreover, they are far more delicate assessors of the current public opinion than the Ministry of Education . . . they need to be careful not to advance too far beyond the reach of those to whom they are responsible.'

This 'careful' policy is undoubtedly one of the factors that caused the proportion of the population of Wales who could speak Welsh to drop from 50 per cent in 1901 to 26 per cent in 1961. Public opinion, however, has not remained static. In recent years Wales has shared in the general affluence of Great Britain, but, to many successful Welshmen, affluence has not been sufficient compensation for losing their language and their cultural identity. Nationalism in Wales has found most support amongst the middle class intelligentsia—the products of the University of Wales and of Welsh intermediate schools. It was middle class parents who first established Welsh medium primary schools in anglicized areas. Some local education authorities, responding to the change in public opinion, established in the Forties and Fifties their own Welsh schools, and later at least three authorities have established Welsh medium secondary schools. Many authorities have now developed a much more positive language policy and have appointed language organizers to ensure its implementation. The Welsh Joint Education Committee, which took over from the Central Welsh Board in 1948, has been particularly influential in the production of Welsh books and teaching materials. Recently it has been helped in this work by the Schools Council Welsh Committee, who have initiated a number of research and development projects in the teaching of Welsh. This work has culminated in the creation of a National Language Unit by the Welsh Joint Education Committee to carry out comprehensive research into the teaching of Welsh as a second language. All this activity has resulted in pressure being put on the University of Wales to make large scale provision for courses through the medium of Welsh. Such provision has already been made by two of the Welsh colleges of education.

It would, however, be a mistake to exaggerate the strength of the Welsh language movement. A parental attitude survey carried out for the Gittins committee showed that perhaps as many as a third of the parents of primary school children in Wales were indifferent to Welsh, although the committee was certain that few people were hostile to it and would wish the language to die. The members of the committee (with one exception) were adamant that a full bilingual policy should be implemented throughout Wales. The Secretary of State for Education and Science agrees with this view. In a circular issued in March 1969, he recalled that, as a result of the Central Advisory Council report published in 1953, all but three Welsh authorities adopted a bilingual policy, but that 'practice in the schools has not always followed precept'. The Secretary of State seemed to agree with the Gittins Report that there has been some breakdown in communication between authorities and schools. To remedy the situation he suggested that local authorities implement the Gittins suggestion that they should once again review and publish their language policies, taking into account the views of teachers and the wishes of parents. They should ensure that their policies were 'clearly stated and sufficiently flexible to meet the varying linguistic needs within their areas' and were 'well understood in the schools'. Moreover, the Department was prepared to make additional teachers available to authorities so that they need not be thwarted by lack of staff in implementing their language policies. For many years a substantial addition had been made to the teachers' quota of some Welsh authorities and the Secretary of State was prepared to consider even further requests. He was also prepared to consider proposals for establishing new 'Welsh' schools where they were needed, and suggested that where such schools were impracticable the possibility should be investigated of establishing sets or groups so that pupils whose mother tongue was Welsh could be taught Welsh as a first language and receive instruction through the medium of Welsh. There should also be a more general spread of bilingual education to the first two years of the secondary school, and experimental bilingual schools should be established where the first language was English but where Welsh was introduced gradually and progressively. These schools, the Secretary of State agreed with the Gittins committee, could 'serve as growth points for bilingual education'.

This circular is undoubtedly one of the most positive and detailed statements made by a Minister on the teaching of Welsh. It is as yet too soon to assess either the changes local authorities have made to their language policies or the reaction of parents to them. Whether or not these policies will have any lasting effect in stemming the tide of anglicization it will only be possible to discern when the bicentenary of the 1870 Education Act is being celebrated. What is certain is that education in Wales has developed during the past 100 years in a direction which Henry Richard and his colleagues, listening to the debate on the 1870 Education Bill, could never have imagined.

15 Thinking about Irish

Brendan Devlin

Some recent remarks by the Minister of Education, speaking on RTE (Radio-Telefis Eireann), bring the problem of Irish in the educational system back into the news. Mr Faulkner's dilemma is that he would like to take the compulsion out of Irish in the school, while fearing that to make it optional would expose it to fatal social and economic pressures. Even his hint of a possible change of policy is liable to set a match to another of those violent arguments from prearranged positions which too often surround issues of profound importance to the community.

It is a pity that the effect of antics of this kind has been to generate an almost impenetrable boredom and weariness in the public mind at the very mention of the language problem. It is a pity because there is, like it or not, an unresolved problem and a problem of which the solution depends on a number of basic judgments about the nature of this country and of the community which lives in it. The question should in fact be the object of serious and sustained reflection by all the responsible citizens.

Unfortunately, of course, the obstacles to reflection of this kind are many and all the more difficult to isolate because they are so often bound up with the development of one's own personality, or with the casual assumptions of public opinion. Social status can make the Irish revival look like an effort to impose an uncouth and rustic way of life. Political allegiance can represent it as a party device for discrimination. A job lost because of an oral test, a sadistic teacher, can have a traumatic effect on a person and on his immediate circle. The worry, usually unnecessary, of passing an examination seems to anaesthetize most of our school-going population to the authentic values inherent in this culture of ours. Or uncritical commitment can blind people to the obvious problems of a language revival policy. We can think of some purpose about the whole business only when we try to rid ourselves of predispositions of this kind.

The questions which must be asked initially in this discussion are two: what kind of thinking led to the present policy? And is this thinking still valid today?

The Irish language revival policy was of course a direct result of the movement for self-government and regarded as a vital part of it by virtually all the leaders of the 1916–21 period. Pearse in *The Murder Machine* wanted to 'restore Irish as the vernacular of a free Ireland': Arthur Griffith believed in the 'necessity of making Irish again the common language of this nation', and Michael Collins held that 'until we have it again on our tongues and in our minds we are not free'. This objective was based on the ideas of the Gaelic League, as indeed the entire national movement was, animated by the League's enthusiasm. Perhaps the most effective statements of this attitude are found in the writings of D. P. Moran, polemicist of the League's heyday. He took what he called 'Davis's comprehensive idea of the Irish people as a composite race drawn from various sources' and he envisaged turning the Irish community into something it certainly was not at the end of the nineteenth century, 'a strong positive entity', capable as it had been in earlier centuries of absorbing and assimilating. This for him could be achieved only by casting the nation anew in the mould of the Gaelic tradition—which he held to be the

Source: Irish Times, 1 and 5 June 1972.
Brendan Devlin is Professor of French at St Patrick's College, Maynooth.

'matrix' of the very idea of Irishness. As Daniel Corkery was to express it in 1943, the Irish mind had to be restored to a sense of solidarity with its past by restoring what is 'chief-mode' or 'mother form', the Irish language.

Such was the objective and the idea on which it was based. Add to this the exaggerated notions about the importance of the school in language situations which seem to have been current in the early years of the State and the result is the oddly narrow language policy which the people with more realism perhaps than their rulers, have reduced to 'compulsory Irish'.

What relevance have these preoccupations to the Ireland of the seventies? Paradoxically enough, they may seem a good deal less remote than they did in the confident sixties. For even those who feel no involvement in hazy cultural issues, the hard-headed, the practical-minded, pragmatic and forward-looking businessmen or politicians or just plain people trying to make ends meet, these too will admit that Irish life will be shadowed for some time to come by the Northern problem and by our relations with Britain and Europe. These raise questions about our sovereignty, about our ability to heal divisions, questions which in fact demand a re-statement of our national identity and its implications in the cultural, political and legal fields.

Most of the debate, of course, is concentrated on devising new legal and political structures to ensure a harmonious future. But even within our own shores, this raises painful questions about our identity. Doesn't common sense indicate that the Irish language policy divides us even further from the Protestant North-East—or is Mr Ernest Blythe right in saying that its abandonment only convinces Protestants that southern separatism is based on Catholicism and nothing else? Are there any convincing reasons for the existence of an independent Irish State other than cultural ones, and is Gaelic culture not the richest and most distinctive in our inheritance? Is teaching Irish not a criminal waste of energy and money, when we should be teaching French and German? What use is Irish anyhow?

Instead of trying to answer questions like this piecemeal in the space available, we must go straight to the heart of the matter and point out that a community animated by a sense of identity is in itself an extremely valuable thing. The sociological reality of nationality must be sharply distinguished from the mystical nationalism of the last century. It is incontrovertible that it discharges the important function of providing a pattern of living for the individual. It gives him values that he can hold to, access to an accumulated historical experience, a sense of permanence and security.

Now the essence of this consciousness of belonging, of this valuable sense of identity and continuity, lies in the process by which the system of values, or the culture, is handed on from generation to generation. The process of tradition, as we call it, installs the individual in his community and its effectiveness in creating a vital community depends on the confidence of those handing it on and the trust of those receiving it. In this each succeeding generation comes to realize that it is not alone, that it is a link in a chain bearing the trust of dead generations and the hope of those yet unborn. Tradition touches a very profound aspect of the human tradition: man the learner, capable of communion with the past and future, and thereby in some sense overcoming the transitory nature of his own individual existence.

It is the vitality, the self-confidence and self-awareness of this tradition which produces a vital and creative community and consequently individual vision and enterprise. I say 'self-awareness' because the trust which is fundamental should be no blind acceptance of a sacred deposit but the result of a constant re-assessment in the light of new experience. One of the difficulties of modern Ireland is a tendency to see 'traditions' as inherited treasures to be kept intact like a miser's hoard. The 'Not an inch' attitude can be found in many areas of the national life. In fact, such immobility is a sign of insecurity and decay, not a warrant of strength.

This vision of a 'tradition' as a personal heritage of unchanged and unchanging values to which an unconditional loyalty is owed is a divisive tendency in our circumstances, because of the past these 'traditions' have often been bitterly hostile to each other. Possibly the central problem of modern Ireland is to devise a framework which will encourage these various 'traditions' to grow gradually into a consensus of unity. It would, however, be ultimately sterile to set about this in a spirit of horse-trading compromise, with all sides agreeing to drop some of their cherished values. The result would be impoverishment and a culture of the least common denominator, devoid of the power to excite loyal adherence. For while change is the mark of a vital culture, if it means the absorption of what is new, change which is merely a rejection of inherited values can easily undermine the sense of security and confidence.

It is in the light of fundamental considerations of this kind that the issue of the Irish language must be considered and practical decisions about it taken. Our first objective can be nothing other than ensuring a self-confident community in this island, one which exerts an attractive influence on the individual and stimulates his self-fulfilment. This in turn is founded on the determined acceptance of an Irish identity, of an evolving consensus about certain basic values. One of the fundamental values of any culture is language, if only because it is the chief means of transmitting that culture. The issue before the Irish people, North and South, is what is to be done with this distinctive language which has hung on in this country to our own day. We must weigh the question carefully because we are not alone in our decision: those whose language it was in the past live on in us in some sense and we will be deciding who, if anyone, will have it as their own in the future.

The question of 'compulsory' Irish can be adequately resolved only in the context of a general review of the problem of language both within this country and in its international situation. This language problem is, in turn, part of a more general cultural situation and has to be considered in that light. Part of our difficulties stem from the fact that moulders of opinion and policy-makers in this country do not sufficiently grasp these facts.

The cultural situation of this country, and we must consciously speak of the whole island, is that of many small countries which have been subjected to the influence of powerful neighbours. The result has been a weakening of the sense of being an individual entity, with attendant causes and symptoms like internal political and religious conflict; confusion about the constituent elements of identity; insecurity and consequent self-dramatization. Our fundamental task is not merely the saving of the past but the building of a future, the construction of a 'new Ireland', to borrow the expression launched recently by Mr Richard Ferguson (a former Ulster Unionist member of the Northern Ireland parliament). This can only be an evolutionary process, and a difficult and painful one it will be, as we can see from the need to reconcile such violent contrasts as the national separatist tradition and the Ulster Protestant, itself a particularism relying for its self-determination on a political link with Britain. This 'new Ireland' must not only be in a state of steady evolution towards inward integration, but it must also define itself in relation to its neighbours, particularly in the new Europe.

One major difficulty in working towards such a 'new Ireland' is that we can only guess at what it might be like. We should, I think, realize that it must be designed to attract eventually the willing adherence of the large majority of people. If this is to be so, it should not begin by shedding any element of our inheritance which significant numbers of people feel strongly about, because to that extent it will alienate those people. The total abandonment of the Irish language revival would be a mistake if only for this reason. It is dangerous to renounce too easily, genuine ideals which have sustained men in the past. The argument that the revival further alienates the Northern Protestant needs closer looking at. What the Northern fears is discrimination in the name of Irish, and it is for politicians and parliamentary draughtsmen to devise ways of protecting one part of ourselves without alienating another. The overriding objective must always be the achievement of a vital and creative culture, a pole of attraction and not of repulsion.

Even without the context of the Republic, however, there is an urgent need for new language policies. Here again it is not a question of abandoning, but rather of new achievement. The English language, for example, is of considerable practical importance (quite apart from its cultural aspect) whether for the businessman

dealing with world trade or the IDA offering an English-speaking labour supply to attract industrialists from abroad. Yet it must also be a matter for concern that it should be the chief language of our representatives abroad, particularly in the European context. Surely a variety of political considerations would urge that we opt for French and see to it that our representatives are at ease in that language.

As for the problem of Irish in our educational systems, the basic objective again must be to hand on to our youth the tradition of Irishness in a way with which they can identify and which will offer them an inspiration and a challenge. The question is to what extent the Irish language is essential to that tradition: and subsequently, what role should we aim at giving it in the national life and what means must be taken to that end?

It would seem that if a relatively small cultural unit like our own is to survive, our educational system must see to it that all young people be made acquainted with our tradition and made acquainted with it in a way which involves them personally as a vital link in the chain. This clearly implies the teaching of the historical manifestations of that tradition, whether in political and social change, in ideas and art, or in literature. It is very probable that the Irish language is essential to any vital grasp of the full extent of our historical tradition and for a thousand years the authentic voices of that past are found in the literature to which it is the key. Not to mention the probability that the very effort to build the future which we have been speaking of will itself force us to a more intimate awareness of the past which has produced us.

The aim of reviving Irish as a general medium of communication goes further than this of course and implies a different attitude to both our past and future. It would seem in principle to be a most desirable contribution to a new Irish culture, for a distinctive language is a very precious constituent of cultural originality. It should not be presented, on the other hand, as an absolute *sine qua non* for Irish survival, as has been done in the past; but it is equally wrong to see that a culture without a significant role for a living Irish language will be, and will see itself to be, a very different tradition, because no longer in intimate contact of mind with a huge area of its past. The Gaelic League ideal of the Irish language as the great uniter of the disparate elements of Irish culture remains a noble and enlightened ideal, but after the mistakes of two generations its achievement will demand a much more intelligent policy than has ever been envisaged.

We need a cultural policy, and specifically a languages policy, to fit our circumstances and few thinking people will shed any tears at the dismantling of the present apparatus if it is replaced by some intelligent and honest commitment. The English language is in no danger of being lost (though it needs better teaching). The Irish language problem will solve itself in a generation or two by the disappearance of Irish unless we have the will to find a real role for it. Technically speaking, this 'new Ireland' has to be bilingual to accommodate our various inheritances: but the practical problem is to develop what the linguists call a diglossia, or pattern of the use of language, in which Irish finds a significant and increasingly substantial part to play.

One of the essential tools for this purpose is an independent institute of scientific investigation engaged in the planning and constant review of the methods and aims of our policy in regard to language. Without such a scientific basis, discussion tends to turn on mere personal impression. There are, however, one or two things which can be clearly seen even at this stage. For one, communities and individuals whose preferred language is Irish should not be deprived of the facility of using it to the greatest reasonable extent.

This would entail a sincere commitment on the part of public servants, for example, in certain areas or perhaps in certain offices, or reasonable efforts on the part of business concerns in the same direction. Correspondingly, those who are convinced of the essential value of the Irish language to our culture must urgently re-think their philosophy and set about bringing others to their point of view and giving them sympathetic encouragement. As to 'compulsory' Irish, the ideal answer is to see to it that everyone absorbs our full cultural heritage in a personal way and without a sense of compulsion. Compulsion, after all, is largely in the mind and prejudice is often its root cause. The dilemma is to avoid trucking to such prejudice while ensuring that Irish should not be a cause of genuine disability to the individual.

16   Irish Newspeak

Anthony Weir

Since Independence, governments in the twenty-six counties* have tried by various means to 'preserve' the Irish language—or, at least, to halt its rapid decline. It is obvious to everyone that they have failed, failed for many reasons, one of the most important being that they tried too hard.

To make Irish virtually a compulsory subject in schools might have seemed to many people to be an admirable way of nipping decline in the bud and introducing young people to 'their' language; but in practice it has failed, partly because of appalling teaching-methods, and partly because of competing pressures from without: mass sub-culture from England and America, a rejection of traditional rural values, and the complete collapse of Irish rural society.

The Irish language has in the past fifty years (and even before) become something less than a language—more a sort of Gaelic Newspeak: a government jargon ritually pronounced, like Latin at the Mass, in public notices and over the government and capitalist-controlled air. Anyone who listens to the monotonous gobbledygook of 'An Nuacht'† for the first time would not be greatly encouraged to learn the language of saints and scholars.

The language question is, of course, fraught with nationalistic overtones. Irish is 'our' language (whoever 'we' may be). It is a 'pure', Gaelic and Catholic tongue. It is our duty to Holy Ireland to speak it.

Consequently, it becomes not so much a language, more a symbolic noise as worthy of serious attention as 'The Soldier's Song'* or 'God Save the Queen'. Few who learn Irish as a second language are interested in it *as a language*—to compare it with English, or French, or Greek—or, for that matter, with Welsh, Manx, Cornish or Scottish Gaelic. Few people are at all interested in the richness of its vocabulary, not only in 'rural' words, but in subtleties of abstract thought not possible of expression in English, or even in French or German. It is merely a verbal Tricolour to be waved (or waived) when occasion demands.

Ireland, of course, is not the only country to have problems of language. Across the sea in 'foreign' (but Celtic) Wales, the Welsh Language Society battles on with similar grim and humourless determination. In Norway, where for centuries the literary language has been basically Danish spoken with a Swedish accent, they have now seized upon an old dialect unchanged since the Danish take-over of Norway in the fourteenth century, and proclaimed it 'New Norwegian', the official Language of the People (Landsmaal as opposed to the currently-spoken language of the people, Riksmaal)—with the result that this fine dialect has been pulled about and stuffed, just like Irish, with bureaucratic zeal, to provide 'ethnic' words for 'polymerization', 'pre-empt' and 'disseminated sclerosis'.

In the Central African Republic, Sango has been transformed from a local dialect to a half-understood commercial and bureaucratic Newspeak. The story

Source: Fortnight, 25 July 1972.

*The Irish Republic.

†'The News' (i.e. in Irish on radio and television).

*The National Anthem of the Republic.

is repeated in other countries throughout the colonized world—for the language problem is one of the many dregs left behind by the colonial tide. 'New Norwegian' (Ny-Norsk) and the new 'Irish' fail for the same reason that Esperanto fails. They live not on their own terms, but merely by decree.

In the North of Ireland, the opposite approach has produced a similar result. The BBC, so anxious of late to broadcast in Welsh and Scottish Gaelic, has not only up to May of 1972 ignored the Irish language altogether (four programmes half in Irish were broadcast in May 1972 for the first time in 40 years), but very rarely, since it started up in Belfast in 1932, has it put out a programme of Irish music or folklore. Certainly the BBC in Ulster has always been and still is regarded as a Protestant-Radio-For-A-Protestant-People ('Catholics listen to RTE* anyway'!) In the past ten years Belfast has put out lamentably few programmes on Irish folkways (the monthly 'Country Window' and a dozen programmes on folk customs, hiring fairs, folk medicines and charms, and so on— all of them, I should add, excellent); and it is left to Radio 3 in London to broadcast programmes of Irish music. By and large, the nearest the BBC in Belfast has got to 'ethnic' broadcasting has been David Curry's travesty called 'Irish Rhythms'—despite a large archive of folk songs and instrumental music. Since the trouble in Northern Ireland started in 1969, the BBC has begun to realize that it has not served ALL the people of Northern Ireland. And even now it is the old refrain: 'too little too late'.

In defiance of the Protestant Parliament and a submissive radio, Irish as a second language exists in the North because it is taught in the separatist Catholic schools, and because of its unfortunate (if natural) link with Nationalism. This is not helped by the fact that Irish is not taught generally in State or in Protestant Voluntary ('Public') schools.

So, north and south of the artificial Border, Irish flourishes like a plastic flower in a cottage window neither natural nor organic—nor, for that matter, living at all. It is just as ludicrous to hear Irish spoken in a Belfast (English-language) accent as it is to hear the clipped Dublin jargon of RTE. It is only in the Gaeltachta,† heavily subsidized by Dublin, that the language survives in marginally less self-conscious and more natural health. The best that can be hoped for is to keep the Gaeltachta from shrinking, without turning them into Wild West Reservations For The Native Irish, as has been the tendency hitherto.

BBC Radio 4 broadcasts several hours every week of Scottish Gaelic, which is of course very similar to the Ulster form of Irish, and very much *more* similar to it than the Belfast, Derry or Dublin Nationalist

*Radio-Telefís Eireann (the Dublin television service).
†Areas where, for the majority of the population Irish is the first language.

Sound. It is easily received in Ulster by any moderately-good wireless set. If we want to hear a Gaelic language spoken unselfconsciously and beautifully, or would hear Gaelic music far from RTE's intermittent transmitters, we must tune in to Scotland. (Gaelic-speaking Scots may have different views on the quality of their programmes, however!)

If Irish is to flourish as an organic language, it must cease to be an official and chauvinistic jargon in the South, and a mere means of dissent in the North. It must not be abused as an educational requirement, for both it and the Irish suffer thereby. And, since RTE has abysmally failed to promote it above the soap advertisements as a living language, perhaps the BBC in the North might speak peace unto nations and (if necessary) import someone from Scotland to give the many people in the Six Counties who are interested in the language (not all of them Catholic, or Nationalist either) half an hour a week of Donegal (or Hebridean) speakers. And how about an Introduction To Irish course on the same lines as that broadcast in Wales?

But even should this miracle happen, the language is as doomed as 'New Norwegian' and Esperanto—to a slow death by facelessness and plastic surgery and 'spelling reform'. It is already like a geriatric millionaire kept grotesquely alive by multiple transplants and massive injections of (the wrong) drugs; or like a lobotomized scapegoat preserved as a helpless vegetable for the false pride of 'patriots' and the edification of a misguided society.

It is doomed because throughout the whole island the traditional values, culture, attitudes and way of life have rapidly disappeared under the lucrative onslaught of American and British capitalism—TV, commercial radio, mass-circulation newspapers, the cinema, mechanization, cost-effectiveness, rich relations in the USA, 'gombeen-men', and the owners of village 'supermarkets' (who buy potatoes locally and send them to Dublin for packing, and sell potatoes at twice the price to their neighbours in order 'to keep prices and supplies stable'); disappeared also under a wave of almost totalitarian educationalization of the people. (Education, to paraphrase Bismarck, makes people malleable. But not native-speakers.)

The all-too-domitable Irishry, Irish language and Irish ways have died because people and politicians in Ireland, in Britain and the USA have made much money out of what they are pleased to call 'progress'. It is futile to try and keep the tongue talking when the brain is cut out—or (to change the metaphor) to preserve a language in holy oil.

We may as well speak Astronaut English as IRA and Árd Fhéis* Irish in a country whose heart has been cut out and traded in as a down-payment on a plastic, atomic-powered one.

*Party Conference (literally, high festival!).

Introduction to reading 17

One of the major agencies for producing change in the curriculum, as well as for providing central control of content and standards, is the external examination system. The new Certificate of Secondary Education was designed with the intention of maximizing teacher participation in the framing and conducting of the examinations at the end of the secondary school course, but the long established 'academic courses' for the General Certificate of Education, still run by boards officially under the auspices of the universities, are more open to the charge of ignoring both innovatory ideas and the views of the class teachers in the schools where the examinations are being taken. In this transcript of a radio broadcast of the Open University course E.283, William Bott of the Southern Universities Matriculation Board, and Richard Christopher of the Joint Matriculation Board (connected with five north of England universities) discuss with Robert Bell, lecturer in Educational Studies at the Open University, the question of curriculum change in the context of the GCE examination boards.

17 The question of curriculum change in the context of GCE examination boards

Unit title:	*Perspectives on Innovation*
Radio Programme title:	Exam boards and curriculum change
Producer:	Ken Little
Presenter:	Robert Bell
Contributors:	William Bott and Richard Christopher
Recording:	Monday 8 November 1971 10.00– 13.00

BELL: In much of the discussion of the curriculum there sometimes seems to be too ready an assumption that innovation is a matter of decision-making simply for the teacher, the school or the local education authority. In fact, of course, curriculum change may be helped or hindered in a major way by bodies quite outside the local situation, such as the Schools Broadcasting Authorities or the publishers of school textbooks. But to most of the teachers in the secondary school the major outside influence always seems to be the external examination board. During the past half century schoolteachers have been acquiring a greater and greater say in the framing of the syllabuses, but the exam board must also bear in mind the demand of

Source: Course E.283, 'The curriculum: context, design and development', Faculty of Educational Studies, the Open University.

employers or of teachers in other educational institutions for which the board's certificates act as entrance qualifications. To discuss the role of the examination boards in curriculum change I have with me in the studio Richard Christopher, Secretary of the Joint Matriculation Board in Manchester, and William Bott, Secretary of the Southern Universities Joint Board in Bristol. Mr Christopher, most of the boards have the name of a university in their title, does this imply that they're not really autonomous, that they're under the control of the university, or perhaps under the control of the government?

CHRISTOPHER: It's true of course that all the examining boards, the GCE boards functioning in England, had their origin in the universities. My own board, for example, is connected with five universities, but it's quite wrong to imply from this that they are controlled by the universities. They are, in effect, controlled by the schools, but there is this crossplay, this interplay of ideas between universities and schools which makes them a valuable ground for starting innovations of the kind we're now discussing.

BELL: Mr Bott, you don't think that the government still exercises some veiled control over what the boards do, for example through the Schools Council?

BOTT: No, the only control which the Schools Council has in effect is at advanced level where the new syllabus or extensive review of an existing syllabus has to obtain the approval of the Schools Council before it can be introduced, but this applies only now to advanced level.

BELL: And you don't think that government could be one of the bodies that is preventing approval on the part of the Schools Council?

BOTT: Oh no, not at all.

CHRISTOPHER: It's true that in terms of syllabus development the boards are autonomous, but we mustn't forget that the framework in which they operate is laid down by the Schools Council, which advises the Department of Education and Science, so there is one constraint in that the framework is laid down from above.

BELL: And you don't think the people above use that framework as a way of control?

CHRISTOPHER: No, but it is used in important areas such as what gradings may be allowed, for example, at 'O' level and 'A' level and what sort of examination in general it is to be, but not in terms of what syllabus innovation, curriculum development, is to be.

BELL: Well now it's sometimes said that when schools want to change, the examination board is unsympathetic because there are difficulties. When the move for change comes from the schools, what sort of things are likely to get in the way of meeting the schools' demands?

CHRISTOPHER: I think that the main difficulties are to what extent it is practicable, because one must always bear in mind that practicality and cost have to be taken into account, also the need to work to timetables.

BOTT: As a small board, the Southern Board is able to meet the teachers who actually prepare and present candidates. We have a series of subject meetings going on at the moment in the autumn term, in which every head of every recognized school is invited to send a teacher to a meeting at our headquarters, and the function of these meetings is to discuss the syllabus and to listen to proposals for change from teachers present there.

BELL: Well now, there was the case in one board I believe, where, for example, classics teachers had put forward suggestions for a new syllabus, but this was not possible because of a veto from a local university. How would you react to this story?

CHRISTOPHER: This of course was in Scotland. In England I can quote a case in which my own board has introduced an alternative syllabus in 'A' level French which isn't entirely approved by all universities, but the board has gone forward with it nevertheless because it is approved by the schools, and indeed comes to us through innovation on the part of the schools.

BELL: Well now, what happens when the universities

or other bodies want a change in the syllabus and the schools aren't happy; what in fact happens in this case?

CHRISTOPHER: Well, all the boards have machinery which represents both the schools and the professional associations and the teaching associations. Our subject committees and other committees have representation of all these sides; they meet together and discuss what it is that they want to do.

BELL: But are there not cases where the demands of the schools and the demands of the universities are incompatible?

CHRISTOPHER: Ah now we're speaking of universities. Well I would say that the effect of the demands of the universities on the school examinations is much less than it is supposed to be. What really counts is what the schools want.

BELL: But what happens in the end if there is actual disagreement, I mean there must be some cases where there is disagreement?

CHRISTOPHER: I have given you one instance in which there was some disagreement about an alternative syllabus, our syllabus in 'A' level French, but the syllabus has gone ahead.

BELL: So in other words it's always ... you feel it's always the teachers who win in the end, the schoolteachers who win in the end?

CHRISTOPHER: I think so.

BELL: Do you agree with that, Mr Bott?

BOTT: Oh yes, entirely, I can give illustrations. Some years ago we introduced the use of atlases in examinations for geography and one or two of the senior university members on the geography panel were rather doubtful about the wisdom of it, but the teachers and myself were keen to put it in, and we literally introduced it over the wishes of the university members of the panel who said in effect, 'Well, this is really a matter for the schools, I don't entirely like it, but let's see how it goes; if the schools want it they shall have it.'

BELL: So neither of you can think of cases where universities or other bodies have actually vetoed change?

BOTT: There's never been one in the fifteen, sixteen years that I've been a Secretary.

CHRISTOPHER: No, and it just isn't taken into account. I'd like to give you an example of one of our innovations—in 'A' level engineering science. This was introduced by the board as an alternative to 'A' level physics. Without taking into account whether it would be acceptable or not, it was introduced, and we then asked the universities whether they would accept it as an alternative to 'A' level physics.

BELL: But does this mean that you feel that most of the

initiatives come from the schools or do most of them come from the universities?

CHRISTOPHER: Many innovations come from the boards because of the influence of the university element on the board. We must face it that much of the imaginative thinking comes from the universities. I think Mr Bott would probably agree.

BOTT: Well yes. You've got to bear in mind that the universities collectively represent the biggest reservoir of academic knowledge in this country, and it stands to common sense that if you have, for example, a physics panel, you need a few progressively minded professors of physics to bring the teachers literally up to date.

BELL: You don't think the teachers see the university attitude as being a patronizing one?

BOTT: Oh, not at all. In fact the teachers enjoy the participation of the university members and they benefit from the sort of know-how which the university people can present. Our own advanced-level physics syllabus, for example, has been undergoing review in the past three years very largely at the hands of the chairman, who is a professor of physics in one of our universities.

BELL: Now these are innovating professors you're talking about; you can't think of any examples where there are professors who are dragging their feet or perhaps slowing down the rate of change?

CHRISTOPHER: I wanted to make this point, that the university people who are interested in GCE examining work are not ivory-tower academics. They are people, many of whom have taught in schools, many of them are working in departments of education, they are thoroughly in touch with what goes on in schools, and so far as we are concerned, valuable though they are, they are a minority in the decision-making because of the . . . they are in the minority on my board's committees.

BELL: And you can't think of any examples of professors as reactionary in the decision-making?

CHRISTOPHER: Well now, we have been talking as we went along about the machinery whereby the board takes account of curriculum change. Are there any other points about this machinery that either of you would like to add? Mr Bott?

BOTT: In the sense that any school is free to put up its own syllabus, or indeed a new subject for examination if it wishes to do so, but of course it must meet the comparability that is essential between a standard syllabus in the same subject or a comparable syllabus in a different subject. That is the only, as it were, criterion. The other one of course is the one that Christopher mentioned earlier—the question of cost and one of the, as it were, crude facts of examining life is this: that you cannot have a ready-made suit at a

certain price and a tailor-made one at the same price. If the school has a tailor-made syllabus it must inevitably be more expensive for that school.

CHRISTOPHER: I want to stress this point of cost; it's very important. Our 'A' level engineering science is an important innovation. We've been examining for three years, we still have only just over a hundred candidates. We are running at a very heavy loss. This is a clear case of a board which is not only innovating but backing an innovation in terms of hard cash.

BELL: So you feel that money really is a major factor in the way in which the boards can cope with curriculum change?

CHRISTOPHER: It is one which always has to be taken into account, but in my experience the boards are always ready to put forward the money for something which is worth while.

BOTT: Yes.

BELL: There is just one point that has been made to us by headmasters, and that is that sometimes it's not the examination board with which they quarrel, but the use to which the examination board's examinations are put by other bodies, such as employers who are specifying the number of subjects which must be taken. Would you agree with this as a general rule, that sometimes you are maligned for what is really somebody else's fault?

BOTT: We'll always agree with that of course.

CHRISTOPHER: We reflect the society in which he have to work, it's an acquisitive society. We put far too much store by a piece of paper and certificates. I think you're right in saying that much of the criticism of examining boards is a criticism of the society in which they operate.

BELL: Well now, could we put this in more general terms? Do you feel that your boards should only reflect change that has already taken place or that other people want to take place, or should it in fact initiate change, should be a major way in which the system can be renewed?

CHRISTOPHER: They must initiate. It's essential. Without the help of the board's many developments, such as for example Nuffield Science could never have got off the ground.

BELL: How do . . .

BOTT: This is our experience as well. The initiation of major changes or new syllabus can come from both the teachers and from university members, and I can quote to you examples of both. For example, at ordinary level we've a subject called 'World Affairs Since 1945'. Now this was put up to us about five years ago by one of our schools as their own syllabus. We liked it and we introduced our schools to it and the result is now that it's gone into our regulations and there are several hundred candidates. On the other side, certain subjects, for example social and economic history, have recently had an entirely new syllabus produced by one of the university members, but always this syllabus is first introduced to the teachers; their opinions on it are sought and only after they have considered it carefully and had a look at specimen papers does it go to the panel which in turn recommends the board to accept it or reject it.

BELL: And do you feel that the board should wait until an experiment has actually appeared to succeed, or do you feel that the board should be involved in the early stages of the experiment, for example one of the Schools Council projects?

BOTT: It's very wise to get in early because quite often projects are run by keen teachers who tend to overlook the facts of examining life. We have mentioned cost. Another very important one is the provision of examiners.

BOTT: Now any man who is going to be an examiner must be well-qualified and well experienced, and if possible continuing as a practising teacher, because the great majority of examiners are. And one of the factors that must be borne in mind in devising any examination is whether you can get the people at the time to deal with the work which has to be done.

BELL: But is there not a danger with your examiners that some of them will have been appointed and will be there more or less permanently and will therefore reflect ideas that may have gone out of date? Mr Christopher.

CHRISTOPHER: No, examiners are not permanent appointments. They change, they are deliberately changed at regular intervals. Furthermore, it mustn't be thought that an examiner sets a question paper; it's sent to the printer and that is that. The examiners —and they work in groups rather than as individuals— draft question papers which are then dealt with by, in our case, by preparatory sub-committees on which there is a majority of teachers in our schools, who decide on the final form of the paper. Syllabus formulation is carried out on the same lines. The examiners play a small, very important, part—but a small part— in the total effort.

BELL: But is there not a danger that there will be insurmountable political problems in getting rid of an examiner who is no longer in touch with things?

BOTT: No, we have none at all. We . . . our examiners are all appointed annually, and the conditions of appointment is for this year. In practice the great majority are reappointed annually, and where a man is unsatisfactory he is not reappointed. It's really quite simple.

BELL: But what happens if there is a genuine disagreement between teachers—if they were split 50-50 on some policy—or if, for example, the universities were genuinely disagreeing about something and there were, you know, good points to be made on either side?

BOTT: Well, I think all those concerned with examining boards appreciate that the candidate is the person that they are really concerned with. And I've never found any situation, either at a subject meeting or a panel, that didn't eventually resolve itself in terms of what the candidate needs. The thinking of the panel can be turned so that the syllabus or the method of examining, whatever it is, has to be adjusted to what the candidate actually needs.

CHRISTOPHER: I would like to stress the importance of what Mr Bott has said. We mustn't think of the GCE examination as a battleground—universities versus schools. It's a co-operative effort in which both sides see the problems to be met and help to meet them.

BELL: But are there not some occasions when there is a demand for straight qualifications of a purely assessing kind, where in fact the teacher wishes to do something of a rather more innovative and open-ended kind?

BOTT: There are no problems because, as you know, if a teacher in a school wants a syllabus which reflects his particular point of view he can have it as a Mode 2 syllabus. That is to say, he provides the syllabus, the board provides the examination. It's true that this mode has never been very popular, but it exists; it always has existed.

BELL: But the universities wouldn't accept it necessarily as an entrance qualification would they, or some other body?

CHRISTOPHER: Well, in my experience they do accept. We have a certain amount of experience of this because my board happens to be both an examining body and a matriculating body. That is to say, it lays down the general requirement for admission to its five universities, and it approves its own syllabuses for this purpose.

BOTT: Yes, our experience is the same. But one must always bear in mind the final rejection or acceptance of an advanced-level syllabus, which is what you are talking about is a matter for the universities and the Schools Council. And, for example, we have a syllabus called 'Modern History and Contemporary Society', which is rather different from anything else any other board does, and this had to have about three years to-ing and fro-ing with the Schools Council before we got it in. But now it's in; it is accepted by universities as comparable to any other advanced-level history.

BELL: So it would appear that the boards have in fact developed a system whereby the needs of their various clients—that is the teachers and the people who are using their examinations for purposes, for example, of matriculation—can be reconciled. And in fact it seems to me from what you have said that the major problems which the board faces are the same major problems that are faced by teachers and all the other people involved in curriculum innovation. That is the problems of money. Thank you, gentlemen.

The extract from the 1970 Education Report of the Jersey Teachers' Association provides not merely a summary of proposals for nursery education and development in the Channel Islands, but also a useful account of current thinking about nursery education on the mainland itself. It also, incidentally, provides a reminder of how the smaller systems of education within the British Isles are continually being influenced by the example of the richer, major system of England itself. Most of the information and suggestions contained in it were the result of visits to England and the perusal of English materials by keen innovators in the Jersey Teachers' Association.

The Plowden Report on Primary Education (HMSO 1967) was not meant to deal with the peculiar problems of Scottish primary education with its very different career structure, its different age-groupings and its different approaches to such issues as streaming and corporal punishment. A report published in 1965 makes recommendations very similar to those in the Plowden Report, though it was much more specifically curricular in its recommendations and had much in common with the recent new primary school curriculum issued in the Irish Republic. There is, however, a common belief among some Scottish teachers and parents that this report, *Primary Education in Scotland*, has not yet had its maximal influence, and that there still exists a great discrepancy between aims and achievement. This anxiety over the unevenness of primary school provision in a large city, Edinburgh, is reflected in the following extracts from a booklet prepared by the Edinburgh and Midlothian Branch of the Council for the Advancement of State Education. We print a self-explanatory introduction plus an account of a number of typical schools from the hundred or so described in its pages. There is good evidence that the variety of provision which it displays would also be found in large English cities of similar size.

The introduction to the Guide provides some interesting comments on the provision of information for parents by British local authorities and schools.

The guide to Edinburgh primary schools was published in 1968 and it is of course important to remember that the conditions in individual schools have changed considerably since then. Edinburgh Corporation has, for example, decided to abolish fee-paying in the primary school sector. Nevertheless its inclusion does serve a useful purpose, that of reminding the reader that there is considerable variety of provision within the same authority and that a stereotype derived from statistics and generalized statements (however justified) can be extremely deceptive in terms of individual institutions.

18 Nursery education: a Head Start Programme teaching disadvantaged children in the pre-school

There was no statement in the Jersey Education Report of 1969 on Nursery Schools or Nursery Classes.

Approximately 80% of Jersey children begin their schooling before their sixth birthday. The remaining 20% constitute at present an under-privileged section of the community. Even if the law is amended to make attendance compulsory at 5 and sufficient places made available, there would still remain a problem regarding certain groups of children—those who may be

Source: Education Report, Jersey Teachers' Association (1970).

described as disadvantaged for one or more of the following reasons:

(i) Socio-economic status of the family
(ii) Medical and/or psychiatric problems in the family
(iii) Size of family
(iv) Absence of a parent from the home
(v) Working mothers

All known studies of 3 to 5 year old children from

lower socio-economic backgrounds have shown a far greater proportion to be retarded or of below average intellectual ability compared to other groups. Many, deprived of the opportunity of cultural learning in the home, are not able to profit as well as others when they do go to school. The inappropriate social behaviour of disadvantaged children is another aspect of this cultural deprivation in the home.

To overcome this deprivation a pre-school programme is required, for even by 3 or 4 years of age these disadvantaged children are already seriously behind other children in the aptitudes necessary for success in school, and they must somehow make up this lost ground before they enter their first school.

Educationists agree on the paramount importance of the first four years of the child's life to his future intellectual development. The provision of free nursery education would thus prove a worthwhile investment. Particularly relevant in this context are two quotations from the University of Exeter Institute's booklet 'Themes in Education No. 14':

(i) 'The effect of the environment is greatest in the earlier, more rapid period of development.'

(ii) 'this indicates that for a child who is slow to read, the chances on average become less with advancing years.'

There is no doubt that children who have been to a good Nursery Class enter the Infants' School with a more friendly and confident approach, emphasizing once again that a radical departure from established practices of early childhood education is needed for the disadvantaged child. However, the normal Reception Class only complements the influence of a good home; it does not replace it. It is therefore inadequate as a compensatory programme for disadvantaged children.

For many reasons, parents in Jersey want their children to attend school before the age of 5 years, and there are long waiting lists at St. Helier Day Nursery and Grands Vaux Nursery. A great many children attend some kind of nursery or play group for which their parents pay fees. Many of the remainder are children of families at risk and for whom the payment of fees is impossible. This hard core of disadvantaged children constitutes a seriously under-privileged class.

Public Relations are of particular importance, for some parents may see an interim 'Head Start' Programme as an instrument of segregation because only selected children are enrolled in it. This should be dealt with both individually and through publicity media.

Language is the key to a Head Start Programme. The Infants' School teacher more or less speaks the language of the intensive pre-school programme and therefore it is of vital importance that teachers of the classes under discussion should be Nursery-Infant trained; a minimum of 5 years teaching experience is needed and there should be further in-service courses related to this work. Each teacher should have not more than 20 children per half day and needs two aides.

Separate buildings for such pre-school groups are ideal, but if for financial or other reasons this is not immediately possible, temporary buildings suitably equipped and associated with new primary schools could provide the urgently needed basic facilities for an interim period.

On the question of Nursery provision, it seems that some confusion arises over the difference between the function of a Nursery School/Class and a Day Nursery. The latter is no more than, for want of a better word, a crèche, where children, usually of working mothers, are cared for and kept occupied. A Nursery School/Class is a professional educational establishment where children of pre-school age are gradually sympathetically and carefully introduced into the educational system.

It seems obvious that with the growth of estates and the tendency towards high blocks of flats, Nursery Class provision in Jersey must become an essential and vital part of a fully integrated educational structure.

19   A guide to Edinburgh primary schools

This guide to Edinburgh Corporation primary schools has been compiled by members of the Edinburgh and Midlothian Association for the Advancement of State Education. Almost without exception, all the information it contains is taken either from material published by Edinburgh Corporation itself and the local newspapers, or from personal observations of the schools involved.

But why have a guide to Edinburgh primary schools at all? Here is what a recent booklet, 'Parent/Teacher Relations in Primary Schools', by the Department of Education and Science has to say:

Most local education authorities regard it as an important duty to inform parents and the public about the local structures of the education service and to guide parents when crucial decisions have to be made for their children . . . Rather few have yet drawn up comparable publications describing primary schools for issue to parents before or on the first admission of their children.

Not only do we feel that Edinburgh parents will welcome such a guide as this. So too will Edinburgh's many teachers, whether they have always lived here or have recently moved to the area, or whether they are still training at one of Edinburgh's Colleges of Education and thinking about applying for their first post.

Most fee-paying schools offer some kind of brochure or prospectus, often expensively printed and containing photographs and illustrations, about themselves for the information and guidance of parents. This is a guide only to the corporation primary schools which, in Edinburgh, offer no such service. Although in one or two exceptional cases handouts have been provided by individual schools, for the most part parents in Edinburgh are forced to rely largely on hearsay, or to make a trip to the Education offices in St. Giles Street to get information.

Ideally, the parent who wishes to know about any school should visit it. Those responsible for this guide hope that one of its effects will be to encourage parents to visit corporation schools and see for themselves. At present this is not often done.

And even supposing the parent does visit the Education offices, or better still, the school, he has very little prior knowledge to go on and has only a vague idea of what to look for and what questions to ask. Answers, even when questions of a factual nature are put, are not always available. It was surprising, for example, how difficult it was to discover how old a school building was or what was the staff turnover.

We believe it is not enough for a headmaster simply to state that he is available for consultation whenever a parent wishes to make an appointment to see him, or once a year to hold an open day when parents can queue to meet their children's teachers. This is the normal practice, and we feel it is not sufficient. The primary schools and the education office should actively encourage parental inquiry and participation, invite the parents in to look round and meet the staff, ask for comments and assistance, visit homes, and declare a partnership between parents and schools for the benefit of the children. One way to begin is to make information about the schools readily available. To quote the Department of Education and Science once again:

> Local education authorities usually issue pamphlets or leaflets explaining to parents the schools that are available and how children are allocated to them ... Some booklets give a fairly detailed description of all the schools in an area; they may be issued to all parents, be available at the primary schools for parents to see, on display in local libraries, or available on request from the Education office.

This guide aims to indicate some questions a parent should ask about Edinburgh primary schools, as well as to provide answers in advance to general questions of a factual nature. The hope is that when the parent visits the primary school, he will go with an idea of what to expect and what to look for. If he already knows something about the school, he can devote more attention to judging for himself things that no factual, objective guide can cover:

Are relationships between staff and children easy or formal?
Are the staff easily accessible to parents?
Are you permitted to remain sometimes with a new or nervous child?
What is the 'feel' of the school—friendly, authoritarian?
Do the teachers' ideas seem to be old-fashioned, progressive?

Each parent has to decide for himself with his own child in mind about questions such as these and sometimes more than just one visit to the school is desirable.

It has not been easy to gather what information the guide contains about Edinburgh Corporation primary schools. When this project was begun over 2 years ago, unexpected difficulties were encountered. The result is that the guide has taken longer to prepare and is less detailed than was at first intended.

Information about individual schools is set out in the following way:

1. The name of the school, in alphabetical order, followed by the address and telephone number. Where the address is obscure, the name of a more well-known nearby street or area is given. This is followed by the name and degree qualification, if any, of the headmaster, or headmistress, and of the infant mistress. A few schools are too small to warrant having an infant mistress and in such cases only the head's name appears. Where the persons in these posts have been recent appointments, this is indicated in the written description and mention is usually made of what school the head or infant mistress came from.

2. The hours of the school are given next, showing the time allowed for the mid-day meal. It is advisable to contact the school itself for further information about the meals service, such as whether the meals are cooked on the premises or not or what they consist of. The first two years, during which children are in the infant school, have shorter hours as a rule than do the rest, the juniors, in years three to seven. First year means about five-years-old and third year means about seven-years-old. In schools where there are nursery classes, mention is made of their hours too. Contact the school for further details.

3. Numbers are given next in tabulated form for (a) the number of pupils in the school, (b) the number of full-time teachers, (c) the number of classrooms, (d) the number of classes, and (e) the average class size. The number of pupils in the school, the school roll, is taken from figures published by Edinburgh Corporation for the last school year, 1968–9, and is rounded to a multiple of five. Below, in the written description, mention is usually made of whether the roll is rising or steady or falling. The headmaster or headmistress is not included in the number of full-time teachers but the infant mistress is. Where there are other teachers part-time or for adjustment classes, their presence is indicated below in the written description of the

school. The number of classrooms is useful for comparison with the number of classes to see how crowded or open a school may be. In the number may be included some classrooms in an annexe or a hut and where this is the case, mention is made of it in the written description. Other rooms such as halls or sewing rooms are mentioned there too. The average class size is arrived at by adding all the class sizes, which gives the school roll, and dividing by the number of classes.

For comparison with the rest of the schools in Edinburgh, the average roll in all corporation primary schools is nearly exactly 490 pupils. For all corporation primary schools the average class size is 33·9 pupils per class. Since there are some ninety of these schools, these figures will not vary greatly from one year to the next by the opening or closing of one or two schools.

For each school in addition to the average class size the number of pupils in the largest and smallest classes is given as well for an indication of the spread of numbers. Otherwise the average size could occasionally be misleading. The preciseness of the numbers is already misleading in the sense that from day to day individual comings and goings may change them. However, some figure must be set down and we feel that so long as this fact is remembered the indication of the general sizes is worth the chance of small errors existing from time to time. According to the Education (Scotland) Act, no primary class should contain more than 45 pupils, and very few do, although a great many do contain more than forty pupils, which is the limit in England.

> If the head teacher is to have a chance of exercising adequately his educational responsibilities as they are described in the next chapter, the roll of the primary school should not exceed 600.

The above quotation comes from a 1965 report, *Primary Education in Scotland* (HMSO). The next quotation comes from the Plowden Report (HMSO, 1967):

> Teachers must be able to prescribe and provide for each child what he needs. We do not believe that any but exceptional teachers can know, in this sense, more than about 30 children and their parents. We, therefore, recommend that the maximum size of primary class should be reduced and that within the primary schools classes for the youngest pupils should be the smallest.

4. Other information is given in a written descriptive paragraph about each school. Here will be found a note about the age and, where pertinent, appearance of the school. In many cases children are not all taught in the main building, for which a date may be known, but in huts in the playground or on another site altogether. A very large proportion of schools in Edinburgh feature these temporary hutment buildings or transportable units, some of which have been there for a long time, as annexes. Where there are special facilities, such as swimming baths or libraries, mention is made of them.

> It is possible to get a good education in a building which is very nearly a slum, but it is obviously worth considering the age and state of repair, and adequacy of the school buildings.

The above quotation comes from a Penguin book by Tyrrell Burgess called *A Guide to English Schools*, the section titled, 'How to judge a school' (1964). The following quotation about school buildings is from *Public Education in Scotland* (HMSO, 1967).

> There are still to be seen some of the structures with narrow pointed windows provided before 1872 and during years following the establishment of the School Boards. The interiors were gloomy, and the rooms, which were lofty but unceiled, were difficult to heat and inconveniently arranged. ... During the later years of the last century and the early years of the present, the normal type of school building was that in which the classrooms were grouped round a central hall, which was sometimes little more than an enlarged corridor. A school so planned was compact and therefore comparatively cheap to build and to heat and was much better lighted than the earlier type. But some of the rooms necessarily had a sunless aspect, ventilation was poor and the central hall was most unsatisfactory for physical education as the floor could not be kept clean and the noise was disturbing to the surrounding classes.

In addition to mention of the school building, further information about the staff is given. The staff are what makes a school and they are the most difficult factor to assess. Good teachers, and there are a great many of them, do a good job regardless of the quality of the pupils and the age of the building. However, measuring how good a teacher is or how good a school staff are is notoriously difficult and rather than resort, as some guides to schools in other cities have done, to popularity ratings, we felt it best to remain objective and present what facts we could and let these facts speak for themselves. For each school in this guide the number of full-time teachers is supplemented by a note about how many of them are graduates and how many are men. Many parents will consider it important that there be men on the staff of a primary school. Primary teachers are not required to be graduates, and mere possession of a university degree does not necessarily make a better teacher. Another way to assess the staff of a school is to look at the turnover rate. For this reason we have listed for each school the number of teachers new to it last year and the year before. The figures for a single year taken alone could be deceptive. The turnover may seem large in growing schools simply because more teachers are required. An adjustment teacher is engaged part- or full-time in many schools to help children who are having particular difficulty in, say, reading or arithmetic. Where these and other relief teachers exist, mention is made of the fact. Beyond this we regret it is not possible fairly to do justice to the numbers of excellent teachers in corporation primary schools.

Still further to information about pupils, staff and buildings, one of the other indications we have included in this guide is one about parental involvement. Where there is a parents' or a parent/teacher association the name and address of its secretary or president and that individual's telephone number is given where possible. This can be a useful source of further information to a parent, but it is, of course, no substitute for a personal visit to the school. So far as the curriculum goes, it is best to contact each school for details. All the corporation primary schools in Edinburgh teach French, therefore this fact is mentioned here in the introduction rather than repeated for each school. Mention is made of the fact where applicable that a school uses the initial teaching alphabet for early reading work. Some primary schools use a new Nuffield mathematics scheme and these are mentioned too. So too are those which use a technique of vertical grouping in their infant departments. This means that in some classes there are children of different ages instead of the usual horizontal grouping with all the children of the same age. This is sometimes called family grouping and when pupils leave the class at the top for another, a new lot of younger ones is taken in at the bottom of the age range in the class. Any other information considered relevant and obtainable and verifiable has been included.

Abbeyhill School

Abbey Street (junction of London Rd., and Easter Rd.), Edinburgh 7.
Telephone 661-3054.

Headmaster   John C. Neill, M.A.
Infant Mistress   Mabel Lobban.

Hours: 9.10 to 12.00 and 1.20 to 3.00, first two years.
     9.00 to 12.15 and 1.30 to 3.30, years three to seven.

Numbers: *Roll Staff Classrooms Classes Avg. Size*
         400   13   16   13   30·6

Abbeyhill is one of the very old schools in Edinburgh. The school was officially opened in 1881. The building stands at the end of a cul-de-sac, closely surrounded by other buildings. The playground is small and surfaced with asphalt. The school roll is shrinking and last year's total was the first time it has been below 400 for many years. The largest class this year has 37 pupils and the smallest 22. Of the 13 teachers, 1 is an adjustment teacher, there is 1 man and 2 are graduates. A 14th teacher comes once a week. 4 are new to the school this year and 2 last year. In addition to the 16 classrooms there are 2 halls, 1 of which is used for dining, and a sewing room. Abbeyhill is one of 4

corporation primary schools which has a swimming bath. It is shared with 7 other primary schools and a secondary school. There is a Parents' Association whose secretary is Mr. J. Reid, 13 Lilyhill Terrace, Edinburgh 8; telephone 661-1675.

Broomhouse School

Saughton Road, Edinburgh 11. Telephone 443-3783.

Headmaster   James A. Gowans, M.A., F.E.I.S.
Infant Mistress   Kathleen A. Dougall

Hours: 8.55 to 12.00 and 1.25 to 3.00, first two years.
     8.55 to 12.15 and 1.25 to 3.30, years three to seven.

Numbers: *Roll Staff Classrooms Classes Avg. Size*
         650   17   17   16   40·6

An increase in roll over the past 4 years makes this school larger than average. The average class size is the fifth largest of Edinburgh Corporation primary schools, the largest class having 45 pupils and the smallest 33 this year. 1 of the 17 teachers is a graduate this year and there is one man. 5 are new to the school this year and 4 last year. One of the staff is a full-time adjustment teacher, and another part-time. 3 of the classrooms are in an annexe and there is also a hall, a tutorial room, a sewing room and a general purposes room. This is one of 8 primary schools in Edinburgh using the Nuffield mathematics scheme. It stands near a main road in open surroundings with nearby fields. The school was opened in 1955.

Colinton School

Thorburn Road, (off Colinton Road) Edinburgh 13. Telephone COL-2667.
Redford Place (annexe behind Redford Barracks). Telephone 441-1946.

Headmaster   Donald MacDonald, M.A.
Infant Mistress   Muriel M. Smith.

Hours: 9.00 to 12.00 and 1.15 to 2.45, first two years.
     8.55 to 12.10 and 1.15 to 3.15, years three to seven.

Numbers: *Roll Staff Classrooms Classes Avg. Size*
         400   13   14   12   30·8

Already small in size, this school has three parts, 3 classes being taught temporarily at Dreghorn Camp this year. The average class size is well below the city average, the largest class with 39 pupils and the smallest with 25. All but 8 of the staff are new to the school this year, and 3 of them new last year. There are no graduates and one man. The headmaster came to the school from Craiglockhart in 1968. The annexe has a hall and two dining areas and is of recent construction. The main building dates from before 1890 and has a hall which is used as a gymnasium and a sewing room.

Flora Stevenson School

Comely Bank, Edinburgh 4. Telephone 332–1604.

Headmaster   James H. Scobie, M.A.
Infant Mistress   Jessie McI. Stewart.

Hours: 9.00 to 3.00, nursery classes.
        9.00 to 12.00 and 1.30 to 3.00, first two years.
        9.00 to 12.15 and 1.30 to 3.30, years three to
        seven.

Numbers:

Roll	Staff	Classrooms	Classes	Avg. Size
575	18	18	17	33·8

Except this year, the roll at the school has decreased gradually in the past 6 years making it slightly over average in size. The average class size is just below the city average, the largest class this year having 44 pupils and the smallest having 22. The headmaster came to the school in 1967 from the post of headmaster at James Gillespie's Boys' School, 1 of the staff is new to the school this year and 2 last year. There is a full-time adjustment teacher, 7 of the staff are graduates and there is 1 man. The 2 nursery classes, each with about 30 children, were begun in 1967. The buildings, which stand at a busy roundabout, date from 1900 and have a sewing room, an adjustment room, a film and T.V. room, an art room, a French room, a singing room, a hall and a medical room. The president of the Parent/Teacher Association is Mr. D. Leach, 10 Orchard Brae Avenue, Edinburgh 4. Telephone 332–6466.

Fort School

North Fort Street, Leith, Edinburgh 6. Telephone 554–7101.

Headmaster   Charles Baillie, M.A.
Infant Mistress   Mrs Margaret Dyer.

Hours: 9.10 to 12.05 and 1.20 to 3.00, first two years.
        8.55 to 12.10 and 1.25 to 3.25, years three to
        seven.

Numbers:

Roll	Staff	Classrooms	Classes	Avg. Size
565	18	17	17	33·3

This school is gradually growing larger, this year's roll being slightly over the city average, whereas the average class size is slightly under the city average. The largest class this year has 40 pupils and the smallest has 30. 2 of the teachers are men and 4 are graduates, 7 new to the school, and one new last year. The Infant Mistress, and the Deputy Headmaster, took their posts in 1967. There is a full-time adjustment teacher. A new school was built in 1960 replacing the old one across the street which dated from 1886. It has a sewing room, an adjustment room, a room for dining and projects, rooms for viola and music and drama, and a room for assembly and physical education. 3 classrooms are in an annexe. 6 of the classrooms have fitted experimental carpeting and there is a Parents' Association which may be contacted via the school.

Holy Cross Academy primary department

Craighall Road, Edinburgh 5. Telephone 552–1972.

Headmaster   James V. Gaffney, M.A., Ph.D.
Infant Mistress   Mrs Beatrice Westlake.

Hours: 9.00 to 11.45 and 1.10 to 3.00, first two years.
        9.00 to 12.00 and 1.10 to 3.30, years three to
        seven.

Numbers:

Roll	Staff	Classrooms	Classes	Avg. Size
525	14	14	14	37·5

This is one of six Edinburgh Corporation fee-paying primary schools. The fees are £12 per year, books included. It is a Roman Catholic school for both sexes and slightly over average in size, the roll having remained about the same for the past 6 years. This year the largest class has 39 pupils and the smallest has 33. The average class size this year is eighth largest of all the corporation primary schools. There is a part-time teacher who relieves the Infant Mistress one day per week and one of the teachers is a nun, none of the staff being new to the school this year and 1 new last year. The staff this year include one man who is also the only graduate. The school was newly opened in 1965, across the street from Holy Cross Academy, with a grass and asphalt playground. The secretary of the Parent/Teacher Association is Mr. P. Mansfield, 15 Denham Green Place, Edinburgh 5. Telephone 552–5295.

Hyvots Bank School

Gilmerton Dykes Drive, Edinburgh 9. Telephone 664–2740.

Headmaster   Robert W. Munro, T.D.
Infant Mistress   Muriel O. Jack.

Hours: 9.00 to 12.00 and 1.25 to 2.55, first two years.
        9.00 to 12.15 and 1.25 to 3.25, years three to
        seven.

Numbers:

Roll	Staff	Classrooms	Classes	Avg. Size
400	12	16	12	33·5

The school roll has steadily decreased over the past 5 years, and it is now below average in overall size. The average class size is also below average, the largest class this year having 38 pupils and the smallest 24. The Headmaster and Infant Mistress both were appointed in 1967, 5 of the staff being new to the school this year and 1 last year. One is a man and there are 5 graduates, there is a full-time adjustment teacher. This is the only corporation primary school both to participate in the Nuffield mathematics scheme and to use the initial teaching alphabet for reading in some classes. The school was opened in 1957 and is built mainly of cellular plastic panelling on a concrete raft. It has a hall and a library and stands well away from the road in grassy playgrounds. There is a Parent/Teacher Association which may be contacted via the school.

Much greater controversy has been generated in all parts of these islands by issues concerned with secondary education, than with either primary or tertiary, and we begin by reproducing the account of the secondary education system in England and Wales given in the second report of the Public Schools Commission, whose remit was to discuss the ways in which independent and direct grant grammar schools could be more readily integrated into the general educational system.

20   The secondary education system in England and Wales

42. In this second Part of our Report we describe the changing system of education to which our own proposals, presented in the third Part, must be applied. This Chapter and the next deal with secondary education in England and Wales, pointing out some of the main changes at work within this system, and tracing the new patterns of comprehensive education now taking shape. Then, in two chapters on the direct grant schools and the independent day schools, we describe the sectors we have been asked to study.

International comparisons

43. Schools in different countries have developed in different ways from different origins. But the educational systems of the urban, industrial economies are now on the move in response to increasingly similar pressures and in pursuit of increasingly similar goals. Before examining our own system we should look abroad, note this country's peculiar strengths and weaknesses, and see what can be learnt from the experience of other countries. It is to Europe, North America, Australia and Japan that we shall look. Such comparisons, if they are to be presented briefly, must be painted with a broad brush in generalizations which obliterate the finer points and omit the many reservations and qualifications which a longer account would include. A more thorough study of the evidence about other countries can be found in Appendix 5.*

44. Compulsory education begins about a year earlier in Britain than in most urban, industrial countries. But elsewhere substantial proportions of children go to nursery schools of some kind before the compulsory age: that is a pattern which tends to favour children who already have most advantages, for it is they who are more likely to start early.

45. At the age of eleven most of our children enter a school in which they will remain until the end of their school days. In most other countries the transfer to secondary education comes later; and in many there is a break at age 15 or 16 when children go to upper secondary schools of some kind. In this country the pupils who stay on to complete their course normally take public examinations at 16 and 18, and they specialize earlier and more severely than children in other countries. Elsewhere there is usually only one public examination, taken at the end of secondary education, and pupils over the age of 16 will usually be studying 5, 6 or more subjects. Here they are studying only 2, 3 or (more rarely) 4 subjects for examination purposes, although they do study others as a matter of general education.

46. Heads of schools in this country probably have greater freedom to shape the character of their schools than they would have in most other countries. But this independence is limited in practice by the system of public examinations. Not only do these examinations at present come twice in the school career, but they are in the main conducted by external examiners, whereas in many other countries they are conducted mainly by the children's own teachers. Thus in British schools entering pupils for public examinations there is less variety in the curriculum than might be expected. In primary schools, now that eleven-plus selection tests are disappearing, there is more genuine freedom and greater variety.

Source: Report on Independent Day Schools and Direct Grant Grammar Schools, Public Schools Commission Second Report, HMSO (1970), **1**, chs 2–4, 21–57.

47. In this country there is little explicitly vocational education for children of school age, apart from shorthand, typing and commercial classes for girls in their last years at school. In many other European countries there are more frankly vocational courses alongside the academic streams in the later stages of secondary education, sometimes starting with children as young as thirteen. Many of our young school leavers complain about the lack of vocational content in their studies and the apparent irrelevance of their work to life outside school.[1] Yet a narrow, vocational education is clearly to be avoided at school. It may be that the raising of the school leaving age will eventually lead us to the right balance.

48. Although most countries have what could be termed independent schools—often catering for larger proportions of children than our own independent sector—in no other country have they the prestige and influence that the English independent schools have. The more famous of our independent schools are more closely linked to the upper income groups in society and play a more significant role in the country's class and power structures than the independent schools of other countries. One result is that many of the most influential parents in this country do not rely on the schools maintained by the State and are not personally involved in them.

49. The most striking feature of the British system, when compared with those of other countries, is the heavy loss of pupils at the minimum leaving age. Comparisons between the proportions of pupils staying on at school in different countries, with different educational systems and presenting statistics in different ways, must be hazardous. Figure 20.1 offers only a rough guide. Nevertheless one conclusion can reasonably be drawn from the figures—that smaller proportions of our children are still at school between the ages of 16 and 18 than would be found in almost any comparable economy. Comparison of such figures is complicated by the fact that many young people in these age groups are in this country and in Scotland educated in colleges of further education for which comparable figures are not available from other countries. But the effect of any errors arising from this gap in the statistics is small. Even if full-time students in colleges of further education are added to this country's figures, and their counterparts in other countries ignored, our place in the rank order shown in Figure 20.1 is scarcely altered. The proportion of children remaining at school in Britain has risen considerably since 1965–6, the year adopted for Figure 20.1. Data for later years are not available for all the other countries appearing in this comparison, but it is clear that staying-on rates are rising fast in most places. Thus, if data for more recent years are used for all countries, our place in the rank order shown in the Figure is unlikely to change greatly.

50. Since they start a year earlier, pupils in this country who stay on at school will generally have had one more year of education by the time they reach the age of 16 or 17 than their counterparts elsewhere. It is tempting to assume that they will therefore be a year ahead of children in other countries in their general intellectual development. We have found no evidence to support this view. A study of mathematical attainments at the ages of 13 and 17–18 in twelve countries[2] suggests, for this subject, that children who start at age five have no advantage over those who start at age six. This study also suggests that our average attainment in mathematics among pupils still in school is close to the averages for other countries. But our results showed a greater spread from top to bottom than most; i.e. our good performers are very good but we have far too many bad performers. These results are for mathematics only and might well be different for other subjects. If they are repeated in studies now being made of attainments in other subjects, they would show that our earlier start warrants no complacency about the small proportion staying on at school after the minimum leaving age. Neither could we assume that an earlier start justifies earlier selection and differentiation.

51. In general, the proportion of a country's age group attaining the highest standards by the age of 17 or 18 appears to depend heavily on the proportion who continue their education to this age. Early selection and early specialization, if they are achieved at the cost of high wastage from school at ages 15–16, tend to *reduce* the numbers attaining these high standards.

52. When European education first took shape the majority of children were not expected to pursue their schooling far. Each country has therefore had to incorporate schools which originally met the needs of different social classes into a national system for all children. First, the aim has been secondary education, with fairer opportunities of higher education, for all children. It is after this has been achieved that something akin to our own movement towards comprehensive education takes place. It is no longer enough to give children opportunities to compete for entry to the more academic forms of secondary education: they must be enabled and persuaded to take their education as far as they can. The United States of America, Australia, Japan, Sweden, Norway, France and the East European countries all have or will shortly have largely comprehensive educational systems, up to age 15 or 16 at least. Other countries (Denmark and Italy, for example) have introduced or are introducing, common schooling up to the age of 14. Other countries (Germany and Israel, for example) are experimenting with forms of comprehensive schooling or (as in Austria) with ways of making parallel systems more flexible and facilitating transfer between schools after the age of selection. All are engaged in the movement towards comprehensive education.

53. We examine the experience of other countries again in chapter 14* where we discuss the education of the most gifted children. We now turn to the system of secondary education in England and Wales. It is a system in movement, and our description therefore

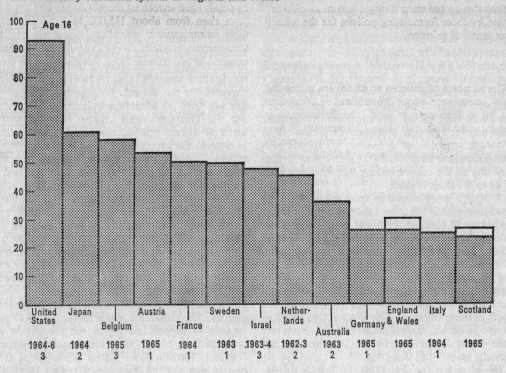

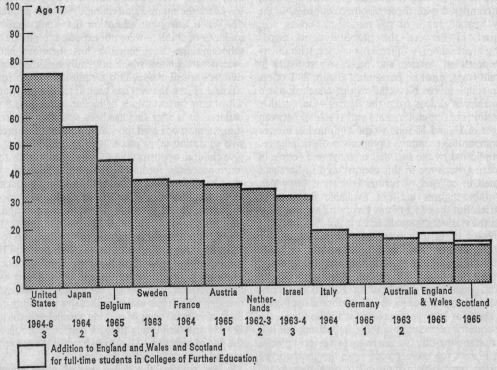

Figure 20.1 Boys and girls at school as a percentage of age group in total population in developed countries

Sources: 1. *Development of Secondary Education Trends and Implications* (OECD 1969).
   2. *International Study of Achievements in Mathematics.* 1 Torsten Husén.
   3. Statistics provided by overseas Education Departments. England and Wales from 1965 Statistics of Education Part I. Scotland from Scottish Educational Statistics 1965 and the Scottish Education Department.

concentrates on the main changes that must be borne in mind by those formulating policies for the schools in our terms of reference.

Pupils

54. The numbers of children at school are increasing. In 1947 there were about 5·6 million: in 1968 there were 8·1 million and in 1980, the Department of Education and Science estimates, the number will have gone up to 10·2 million. If past trends continue, independent schools as a whole will take both a declining proportion of these pupils and a declining number, though the number in schools recognized as efficient remains steady. The maintained primary and secondary schools must therefore take the increase in numbers, as they have done in the past. The Department estimates that, in 1980, maintained schools will have 9·6 million pupils. Of these, 4·2 million are expected to be in maintained secondary schools (unless some transfer to further education establishments) compared with 2·9 million in 1968. Thus in the twelve years from 1968 to 1980 the Department expects that there will be two million more pupils in maintained schools, 1·3 million of them in secondary schools. It is against this background that we have considered the future of the 100,000 pupils in direct grant upper schools and the 79,500 secondary day pupils in independent schools which are recognized as efficient.

The growth of sixth forms

55. It is in the sixth forms that the most dramatic growth is taking place. In twenty years, the numbers of pupils aged sixteen or more who are still at school have risen from about 115,000 to 373,000. Taking those in maintained[3] schools only, the rise has been even steeper, from 75,000 to 297,000—an increase of nearly 300 per cent. Part of this growth can be explained by increasing numbers in the age groups concerned, and part by the growing proportion of pupils who go to maintained schools. But most of the growth is due to the rising proportion staying on at school. In maintained grammar schools, where the opportunity of staying beyond the minimum leaving age has been more generally available compared with other maintained schools, the proportion staying until the age of 17 or over has grown from less than a third to nearly two-thirds. Figure 20.2 traces the growth in numbers of pupils aged 16 and over in maintained schools, and gives comparable figures for direct grant and independent recognized efficient schools. The figures are for January of the year concerned, and most of the pupils will be six months older by the time they leave school. Figure 20.3 shows how the percentage of seventeen-year-olds in maintained schools has grown, alongside comparable data for direct grant schools and independent recognized efficient schools.

56. Most striking of all has been the expansion in the numbers of full-time students under 18 in colleges of further education. In 1947 there were about 21,000; in 1968 there were 97,000. Gone is the dominance of evening classes which characterized these colleges twenty years ago. Alongside the 18 per cent of the 16–18 age group who were at school in 1968, there were another 5 per cent attending further education colleges full-time. In the same year some 16 per cent of the 16–18 age group attended part-time day courses and some

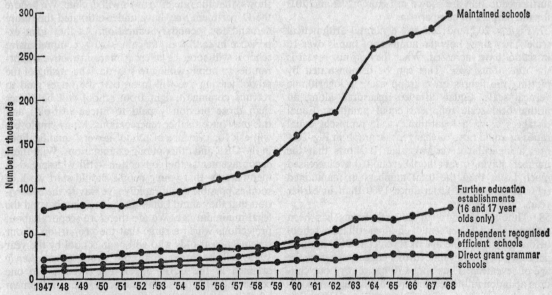

Figure 20.2 Pupils aged sixteen and over in different types of educational establishment

Source: Department of Education and Science returns.
Note: The figures for further education establishments are in respect of full-time students only. Students in national colleges of advanced technology and those on short full-time courses have been excluded.

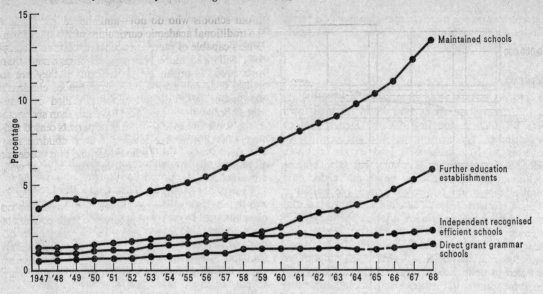

Figure 20.3 Seventeen-year-old pupils in maintained, direct grant and recognized efficient independent schools and full-time seventeen-year-old students in grant-aided establishments of further education, as percentages of all seventeen-year-olds in the age-group (1947–68)

Source: Department of Education and Science Statistics.
Note: The figures for further education establishments are in respect of full-time students only. Students in national colleges and colleges of advanced technology and those on short full-time courses have been excluded.

6 per cent attended evening classes at the colleges. A further 7·4 per cent attended classes at evening institutes. (Some pupils attending both day and evening classes will be counted twice in these percentages.) The numbers of sixteen and seventeen-year-olds and the percentages of seventeen-year-olds in colleges of further education are shown in Figures 20.2 and 20.3 for the purpose of comparison.

57. Figures 20.2 and 20.3 use a normal arithmetical scale. They show how the numbers of pupils over 16 in school have increased. What they do not reveal is the *rate of increase*. This can be demonstrated by plotting the figures on a graph using a logarithmic vertical scale. Equal distances measured along an arithmetical scale represent equal numbers. Equal distances along a logarithmic scale represent equal ratios or equal rates of change. The graph in Fig. 20.4 uses a logarithmic vertical scale. It shows that the numbers staying on at school beyond 16 have increased much faster than the total numbers in maintained schools, and much faster since 1960 than in earlier years.

58. Although the growth in sixth forms has been striking, about 77 per cent of children still leave school before they reach the age of seventeen. Only about 8 per cent go on to full-time further education before the age of seventeen. Thus about 70 per cent of our children abandon full-time education by this age. According to the projections of the Department of Education and Science, the proportion of 17-year-olds in school will rise from about 19 per cent in January 1969 to about 40 per cent by January 1990. These estimates do

not specifically allow for the effects of comprehensive reorganization or the secondary effects of raising the school leaving age to 16 in 1972–3. But the Department believe their projections offer a reasonable representation of the likely overall consequences of these and other influences. Their estimates assume, as Fig. 20.5 shows, that the rate of growth will decline. We believe the Department may have under-estimated the future demand for secondary education. As they gain experience in sixth form teaching, many comprehensive schools will soon be offering more attractive opportunities to pupils willing to stay on. The raising of the school leaving age will mean that the wages paid to recruits coming straight from school will be higher than those previously paid to fifteen-year-olds and this may have further repercussions. Many employers will ask for evidence of school leavers' qualifications in the CSE and other public examinations. With these encouragements, the convention—still widespread in many areas—that young people should start work as soon as possible could rapidly give way to the convention that they should take their education beyond the legal minimum age. We are therefore sceptical about projections which assume that the proportion of our seventeen-year-olds who will be in school by the year 1990 will be lower than the proportions *already* attained in the USA, Japan and Sweden. No one concerned with the social and economic development of this country can be complacent about such an assumption.

59. The pattern of staying on varies. Rather more boys than girls are still in school at the age of seventeen

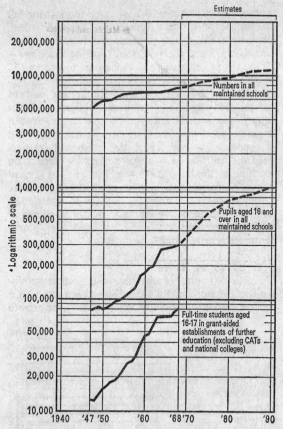

Figure 20.4 All pupils and those aged sixteen and over in maintained schools and students aged sixteen and seventeen in grant-aided establishments of further education

Source: Department of Education and Science Statistics.
Notes: 1. Solid lines indicate actual figures.
     2. Dotted lines indicate estimated figures.
     3. Estimates of further education students in the 16–17 age group are not available.
     4. The figures for maintained schools exclude pupils in special schools.

(16·8 per cent compared with 15·4 per cent at January, 1968). Regional differences are even greater. Only one pupil in eight is still at school at the age of seventeen (at January, 1968) in the North, North West and East Anglia, compared with one in five in the South East and Wales. The differences between maintained and non-maintained schools also stand out. Figs. 20.6 and 7 illustrate these differences. Table 11 in chapter 4* compares the patterns of staying on at direct grant and other schools.

60. Although most of the children now continuing at school to the age of seventeen and eighteen are 'first generation sixth formers' whose parents left school much earlier, the majority of them do well at the work traditionally expected of an academic sixth form. The proportions of sixth formers who take 'A' level examinations and gain two or more passes have risen. 'More' has not meant 'worse'. But already there are growing numbers of sixteen and seventeen-year-olds

in our schools who do not—and should not—follow the traditional academic curriculum of the sixth form. Others capable of pursuing academic courses successfully will need more help and encouragement than their predecessors in the sixth forms if they are to realize their full potential. Among school children's families in which parents have unskilled or semi-skilled occupations, one third have less than six books in the home and over four-fifths of parents ceased full-time education at age fourteen.[4] Such children may not give of their best if schools assume that academic teaching has the support and understanding of well-educated parents.

61. The expectations of teachers are as important as the morale of their pupils. Some recent research on primary school children suggests that the confidence teachers have in their pupils' abilities can have exceedingly important effects on their progress.[5] 'Boys and girls', as the Plowden Report said, 'tend to live up to, or down to, their reputations.'[6] Teachers who are

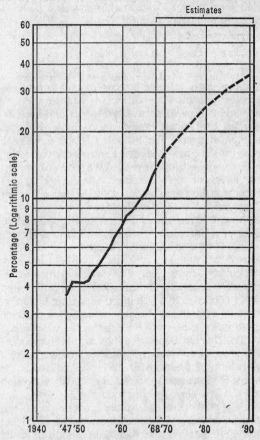

Figure 20.5 Seventeen-year-olds in maintained schools as a percentage of all seventeen-year-olds

Notes: 1. Solid line indicates actual figures.
     2. Dotted line indicates estimated figures.
Source: Department of Education and Science Statistics (1947–68), estimated figures Statistics 1968, Volume 1, Table 45.

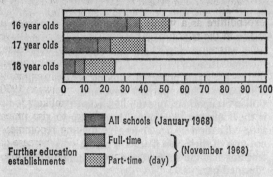

16 year olds
17 year olds
18 year olds

0 10 20 30 40 50 60 70 80 90 100

All schools (January 1968)

Further education
establishments

Full-time
Part-time (day) } (November 1968)

Figure 20.6 Percentage of the sixteen, seventeen and eighteen age-groups at school and further education establishments

Source: Statistics of Education, 1968.

to work successfully amidst the sixth form explosion must be capable of stimulating the interest, drive and confidence of pupils who would not feel at home in the more traditional sixth form.

The work of the schools

62. The revolution in teaching methods which began in the primary schools is now spreading into the secondary schools. Pilot schemes for 'Nuffield Science', the various New Mathematics Projects and the Humanities Curriculum Project are examples of more widespread trends. The Schools Council provides a focus for these new ideas and a framework for testing them and publicizing the results. We have not attempted to evaluate these experiments, but it is clear that teaching in secondary schools could be changed out of all recognition in the next decade.

63. It must be recognized that too many pupils regard much of their secondary school work as irrelevant or boring. The Schools Council's inquiry we have quoted showed that young people who left school early were particularly dissatisfied. The whole structure of secondary education and the systems of further and higher education to which it is related must be fundamentally reappraised if more of these young people are to make good use of a longer formal education.

64. The Dainton Committee showed that the proportion of sixth formers studying science has been falling.[7] More critical questions are being asked about the degree of specialization needed in secondary education and the age when specialization should begin. New forms of public examinations are being proposed. The work of colleges of further education can no longer develop in isolation from that of the schools: in many places there is a large measure of overlap between the two sectors, and some pupils of an age to work in schools feel more at home and work more successfully in the colleges.

65. New technologies are developing in the classroom. Audio-visual aids have been common for many years —models, projectors and radio, for example—but

more recent developments have come too fast for full assessment or full use in schools. Tape recorders, language laboratories, programmed learning, closed circuit television, computerized teaching machines— all are becoming available. Video-tape recorders will soon be widely used. These and other devices will enormously increase the scope, flexibility and costs of secondary education. Equipment budgets and the supply of skilled and enthusiastic practitioners are not as yet keeping pace. Thus far, there is no evidence that mechanical aids will reduce the number of teachers needed, but they will make a growing impact on teaching methods; and the teaching unit—at present almost uniformly the class or set—will become more flexible, ranging from large groups to individuals working independently on their own, sometimes at school, sometimes in public libraries or 'scarce resources centres', and sometimes at home.

Resources

66. In 1946–7 public expenditure on education amounted to £194 million. By 1956–7 it had grown to £626 million, and by 1966–7 to £1,694 million. The growth

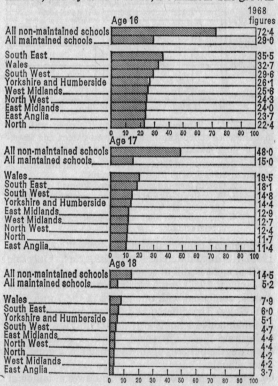

	1968 figures
Age 16	
All non-maintained schools	72·4
All maintained schools	29·0
South East	35·5
Wales	32·7
South West	29·6
Yorkshire and Humberside	26·1
West Midlands	25·6
North West	24·3
East Midlands	24·0
East Anglia	23·7
North	22·4
Age 17	
All non-maintained schools	48·0
All maintained schools	15·0
Wales	19·5
South East	18·1
South West	14·8
Yorkshire and Humberside	14·4
East Midlands	12·9
West Midlands	12·7
North West	12·4
North	11·7
East Anglia	11·4
Age 18	
All non-maintained schools	14·5
All maintained schools	5·2
Wales	7·9
South East	6·0
Yorkshire and Humberside	5·1
South West	4·7
East Midlands	4·4
North West	4·4
North	4·2
West Midlands	4·2
East Anglia	3·7

Figure 20.7 Percentage of pupils remaining at school to various ages in each region

Source: Statistics of Education, 1968, **1**, Table 9.
Notes: 1. Figures for regions are for maintained schools only.
    2. Percentages represent the number of pupils aged 16, 17 or 18 in January 1968 expressed as percentages of the number of pupils aged 13 years, 3, 4 or 5 years earlier respectively.

in these figures is due in part to a fall in money value, and they include large increases in expenditure on higher and further education; but they also reflect a large increase in the call which the maintained system is making on national resources. 'The share of national resources used by the education service in the United Kingdom in the mid-sixties was $5\frac{1}{2}$ per cent compared with $3\frac{1}{2}$ per cent of considerably smaller resources ten years earlier.'[8]

67. The increases in the numbers of pupils in the next decade or so will call for further large increases in expenditure. To provide the new places required for secondary pupils alone will cost at least £615 million at present day prices, without making any allowances for the new places required through shifts of population and replacement of old and unsatisfactory buildings. Current costs for secondary pupils were over £400 million in 1967–8 and could well double by 1980. In her paper 'Education and Finance' (IMTA 1969), Dr Kathleen Ollerenshaw predicted that public expenditure on education as a whole would rise so that by 1980 it would be equivalent to about 8 per cent of the Gross National Product; today it is about 6 per cent. Working on a rather different basis we would also conclude that if present policies are sustained, and recommendations like those of the Plowden Committee were carried through, over 8 per cent of the nation's productive capacity would be devoted to education by 1980. This assumes a 3 per cent growth rate in productivity and in salaries in the education system. On top of that it would be necessary to finance transfer items such as student grants.

68. While expenditure on secondary education has risen, its share in the total educational budget has fallen as the following table shows:

Table 20.1 Percentage breakdown of total educational expenditure

	1959/1960	1967/1968
Nursery schools	0·3	0·2
Primary schools	26·9	24·0
Secondary schools	34·8	29·3
Special schools	2·1	2·2
Further and adult education	10·2	12·5
Training of teachers; tuition costs	1·1	2·4
Universities*	6·8	11·3
Other expenditure	17·8	18·2
	100·0	100·0

Source: Statistics of Education, 1968.

* Including colleges of advanced technology from 1965–6 formerly included in further and adult education.

The country's recent economic difficulties have led to a check on the rate of growth of educational expenditure. Rate Support Grant for 1969–70 has been fixed by the Government on the basis that local authority expenditure as a whole is not expected to exceed a figure in the region of 3 per cent in real terms above what was agreed for 1968–9. Within this total increase, education expenditure is expected to increase by about $3\frac{3}{4}$ per cent in real terms. A similar increase in expenditure on education has been allowed for between 1970 and 1971. The education authorities are unlikely to be able to allow educational expenditure to rise much above this level. Clearly anyone making recommendations which would call for a substantial increase in public expenditure must not expect to see them implemented in the immediate future.

69. The post-war years have been a period of great activity in school building, but much of this work has had to be devoted to providing new places for the growing school population and to meeting needs arising from internal migration to new centres of housing. Meanwhile many schools are overdue for replacement: the School Building Survey carried out in 1962 showed that at that time three out of every eight secondary schools were in buildings, erected before 1918. Because of this pressure on limited resources, the construction of large, purpose-built, all-through comprehensives will often be impossible, and the scope for organizing comprehensive education through tiering schemes which link schools catering for different parts of the secondary age range is already being more carefully considered. If reorganization is to proceed as quickly as possible and the best use is to be made of scarce teachers and expensive equipment, there will have to be many different patterns of comprehensive education, and this diversity is already appearing.

Teachers

70. Although the number of pupils at maintained schools has grown from 5 million in January 1947 to nearly 8 million in January 1968, the supply of teachers has risen even faster. The ratio of full-time teachers to pupils has improved from 1:27·0 in 1947 to 1:24·6 in 1968 and in addition part-time teachers are making a growing contribution. The proportion of secondary classes with more than 30 pupils has been reduced from about a half to just over a third. What is more, new non-graduate teachers now have at least three years' training instead of the one or two years which was usual in 1947.

71. What about the future? Forecasting the numbers of teachers is even harder than forecasting the numbers to be taught. There were 316,000 qualified teachers in maintained schools in 1968. Estimates of future numbers depend on assumptions about the proportions of school leavers and graduates who will enter the profession, about the numbers who will leave teaching and return to it, and about the financial ability of authorities to employ the teachers needed. We cannot be confident about any of these assumptions. The Department, in the least optimistic of its forecasts, concludes that by 1980 the supply of qualified teachers will

improve sufficiently to reduce the overall qualified teacher ratio from 1:23·9 in 1968 to below 1:20·0. This forecast, though pessimistic about the supply of teachers, may underestimate the numbers of pupils to be taught, as we explained in paragraph 58.

72. As schools are at present organized, sixth form teaching requires more staff than the teaching of younger pupils. The growth in sixth form numbers has not so far produced economies in cost per pupil because the range of subjects which pupils can take has extended and in general the size of teaching groups has not risen. Sixth form teaching calls for a high proportion of graduate teachers. In 1968, there were about 62,000 full-time graduate teachers in maintained primary and secondary schools. The total full-time qualified teaching force in those schools is about 297,000. On the more conservative of two hypotheses examined by the Department, the numbers of graduates will increase to about 132,000 by 1980—including 35,000 Bachelors of Education—out of 456,000 full-time qualified teachers.[9] The proportion of graduates in the total teaching force of maintained schools will increase from just over 20 per cent in 1968 to very nearly 29 per cent in 1980. It must not, of course, be assumed that all the extra graduates will go into secondary education. Indeed, the Plowden Committee called for more graduates in primary schools.

73. The number of graduates could increase generally yet still leave shortages in certain subjects and for certain aspects of school life. Mathematics and Science graduates are those most often mentioned in this connection. The Department estimates that the numbers of graduate teachers in these subjects will rise from 16,600 in 1968 to over 24,000 in 1980, an increase of 45 per cent. Although this is less than the increase in graduate teachers from other disciplines, it could still be sufficient to keep pace with increasing numbers of pupils. But a greater proportion of their time may have to be devoted to teaching sixth formers taking these subjects since it is numbers in this age group which will rise most rapidly.

74. One of the fears frequently expressed to us has been that despite expected improvements in overall staffing ratios, comprehensive reorganization will lead to smaller and less economic sixth forms without enough graduate teachers. There are many patterns of comprehensive organization, involving schools which deal with different age ranges. But whatever the pattern, we think that by 1980 sixth forms will very seldom be fed from less than six forms of entry. An all-through comprehensive school with six forms of entry would today have about 1,000 pupils. By 1980 such a school would be larger because more pupils will stay on into the sixth. Moreover many schools will be based on more than six forms of entry. Therefore if there are 4·2 million secondary age pupils in maintained schools in 1980, there will probably not be more than about 4,000 sixth forms. If nine out of ten full-time graduate teachers are in secondary schools (as in 1967) and five out of six of them spend some of their time in sixth form teaching (as was the case in grammar schools in 1965) then there would be an average of 25 to each sixth form and about five of them would have degrees in science or mathematics. If sixth forms were fed from an average of eight forms of entry, there would be an average of 32 graduates per sixth form, six of them having science or mathematics degrees. Grammar schools in 1968 had an average of 20 full-time graduates, spending some of their time teaching sixth formers, nine of them having degrees in science or mathematics. Thus sixth forms of the 1980's could have more graduates, in total, than the grammar school sixth forms have at present—and appreciably more than those now available to the 29 per cent of 'A' level candidates who work in maintained schools other than grammar schools. But the proportions of mathematicians and scientists among sixth form teachers may decline. Special steps may be required to ensure that teachers with the scarcest skills concentrate their efforts on the pupils who need their help most.

75. The expansion of sixth form numbers and studies is putting, and will continue to put, a tremendous strain on the profession. It calls for more teachers with advanced academic qualifications in a wider variety of subjects, and more counselling and careers guidance among pupils. Meanwhile teachers of some subjects too often work with classes of no more than five or six pupils. There will be increasing pressures on schools to make more economical use of their skills. Critical questions will be asked about small sixth forms, and the barriers between separate schools may have to be broken down. Other countries contending with the same problems have had to reorganize the staffing and structure of schools, giving greater responsibilities and higher pay to some of those at the top of the profession, introducing more aides and technical assistants, and building more closely integrated systems of secondary education linking the work of different schools.

Administration and organization

76. Much of the 1944 Act was taken up with the problem of denominational differences, and little attention was given to what proved to be one of the dominant educational controversies of the last twenty years, namely the *kind* of school which should be provided for secondary pupils. The central government is now seldom concerned with mediating between the denominations: they generally take a common line in pursuit of common aims. It has, however, been much involved in differences between parents and local education authorities over choice of secondary schools. Thus far, it has been sparing in its use of the powers of direct action given by the Act: co-operation has been the keynote in relations between the Department of Education and Science and the local education authorities as shown by the variety of provision and policies in different areas. But the tensions inherent in relationships between central and local authorities

have been sharpened by comprehensive reorganization. An Education Bill which would exert growing pressure on local authorities to reorganize their secondary schools in accordance with central government policies is now being prepared.[10]

77. There have been slight changes in the numbers of local education authorities in the last few years and some boundaries have been altered, but the system remains substantially as it was left by the 1944 Act. The report of the Royal Commission on Local Government seems likely to change all that. If acted upon by the Government, it will lead to a drastic reduction in the number of local education authorities, and a great increase in the numbers of schools that most of them administer.

78. Such a reform is bound to have repercussions on the government of schools. The governing bodies of secondary schools, which the 1944 Act requires local education authorities to set up, vary enormously in their composition, in the powers they wield and in their effectiveness. The study made by the London University Institute of Education Research Unit[11] detected a major difference between county boroughs and counties. The former tend to favour closer control of schools by officers acting for elected representatives. The latter, covering larger areas, are more apt to delegate responsibility. The Royal Commission recommended that, in the main, the education authorities should be larger units, and that school governing bodies should have more powers and represent people in their locality more effectively. We hope this will enhance the quality and standing of school governors. That, in turn, will affect governors' relationships with the heads and teaching staff of schools and with local education authorities.

Conclusion

79. A few of the points made in this brief survey must be re-emphasized before we go further. First, the most striking feature of sixth form education in this country is that the great majority of our children do not have it: to give them, and the country, a fair chance in a competitive world, we must enable far more young people to take their education much further. To do that we must contend with scarcities of staff in some of the specializations in which advanced teaching will be needed, scarcities of buildings suitable for use as all-through comprehensive schools, and the growing complexity and cost of the equipment required for secondary education. We must also inspire the interest and motivation of growing numbers of young people who have not been accustomed to a traditional academic curriculum from the age of eleven and do not share the aspirations or the social advantages of the traditional sixth former. These pressures will compel us to reappraise many of our assumptions, both about comprehensive schools and about grammar schools. Within a comprehensive system we shall need the help of good schools of every kind if we are to attain our aims.

80. The cost of any proposals we make must be carefully weighed: the objectives to which the Government is already committed will call for the diversion to education of a growing proportion of the national product. Although the supply of teachers will improve, there are likely to be shortages in particular subjects. For this reason, and in order to make efficient use of the money available, the scarcer and more highly qualified teachers must be deployed to the best advantage. Unless the standards demanded for sixth form study change completely, the days of small, isolated sixth forms are numbered. Sixth formers will have to be concentrated in larger units, either in large comprehensive schools starting at ages 11 to 13, or in schools starting at 14, 15 or 16. Alternatively, or in addition, education from 15 or 16 onwards may be more closely linked with further education.

81. The administration of education and the organization of schools must be sufficiently flexible to cope with new developments and needs. They must ensure that scarce resources are used to the full and not duplicated wastefully at several institutions. This may call for the establishment of 'scarce resources centres' serving several schools and containing, for example, language laboratories and computer units. Alternatively these scarce resources may have to become more mobile. The barriers between schools (and colleges of further education) must be broken down. In future, areas served by several schools will constitute the basic unit for the more closely co-ordinated planning of secondary education. Yet the independence and vitality of teaching within these groups of schools must somehow be preserved.

Comprehensive reorganization

82. We have been asked to consider how schools 'can participate in the movement towards comprehensive reorganization'. In this chapter we describe the progress of the movement and the forms it is taking.

83. The idea of the comprehensive school is not a new one. As long ago as 1947 the Ministry of Education found it necessary to define it (in Circular 144). It was described as a school 'intended to cater for all the secondary education of all the children in a given area without an organization in three sides' (that is to say without separate grammar, secondary modern and technical departments). In 1950 the Ministry of Education's statistics showed 10 comprehensive secondary schools. By January 1965 there were 262. These schools had developed from initiatives taken by local education authorities. Under a Conservative administration, the Ministry of Education accepted proposals for comprehensive schools in country districts and in areas of extensive new housing but generally resisted proposals to establish new comprehensive schools which involved the closure of existing grammar schools.[12]

84. At the 1964 general election the Labour Party was returned to power pledged 'to reorganize the State

secondary schools on comprehensive lines, in order to end the segregation by the eleven-plus examination.'[13] The Labour Government accordingly, on the 21st January, 1965, moved a motion, which by virtue of its majority in the House of Commons was agreed:

That this House, conscious of the need to raise educational standards at all levels, and regretting that the realization of this objective is impeded by the separation of children into different types of secondary schools, notes with approval the efforts of local authorities to reorganize secondary education on comprehensive lines which will preserve all that is valuable in grammar school education for those children who now receive it and make it available to more children; recognizes that the method and timing of such reorganization should vary to meet local needs; and believes that the time is now ripe for a declaration of national policy.

Circular 10/65

85. The next step was the appearance in July, 1965, of Circular 10/65 which asked local education authorities to send in plans for reorganizing secondary education in their areas on comprehensive lines and gave guidance about the methods for achieving reorganization. The Circular stated that the Government's objective was to end selection at 11+ and to eliminate segregation in secondary education. While progress was to be as rapid as possible it was not to be achieved by the adoption of plans whose educational disadvantages more than outweighed the benefits expected from comprehensive schooling.

86. The forms of comprehensive reorganization to be adopted should depend on local circumstances and a local authority could propose more than one form in its area. Six main forms were identified:

(i) The all-through comprehensive school with an age range of 11–18.

(ii) A two-tier system whereby *all* pupils transfer at 11 to a junior comprehensive school and *all* go on at 13 or 14 to a senior comprehensive school.

(iii) A two-tier system under which *all* pupils on leaving primary school transfer to a junior comprehensive school, but at the age of 13 or 14 *some* pupils move on to a senior school while *the remainder* stay on in the same school. Most of these systems fall into two groups: in one, the comprehensive school which all pupils enter after leaving primary school provides no course terminating in a public examination, and normally keeps pupils only until 15; in the other, this school provides GCE and CSE courses, keeps pupils at least until 16, and encourages transfer at the appropriate stage to the sixth form of a senior school.

(iv) A two-tier system in which *all* pupils on leaving primary school transfer to a junior comprehensive

school. At the age of 13 or 14 *all* pupils have a choice between a senior school catering for those who expect to stay at school well beyond the compulsory age, and a senior school catering for those who do not.

(v) Comprehensive schools with an age range of 11 to 16 combined with sixth form colleges for pupils over 16.

(vi) A system of middle schools which straddle the primary/secondary age ranges. Under this system pupils transfer from a primary school at the age of 8 or 9 to a comprehensive school with an age range of 8 to 12 or 9 to 13. From this middle school they move on to a comprehensive school with an age range of 12 or 13 to 18.

87. The Circular said that plans based on alternatives (iii) or (iv) would only be acceptable as a temporary stage of reorganization because they separated children into different schools according to their different aims and aptitudes. The first proposal, for all-through schools, should be adopted wherever possible. Sixth form colleges were viewed with caution and middle school arrangements were to be approved only in a few experimental schemes. But the following year the Secretary of State issued a new Circular (13/66) in which he stated that proposals for reorganization based on a middle school system were fully acceptable and would be considered on their merits along with the other types. The various long-term solutions recommended are shown in Figure 20.8.

88. Circular 10/65 stated that comprehensive schools should create communities in which pupils of all abilities and with differing interests and backgrounds would be encouraged to mix with each other, gaining stimulus from their contacts, and learning tolerance and understanding in the process. Some neighbourhoods, it was recognized, would produce too few pupils with high attainments and aspirations, and the authorities were urged to ensure, when determining catchment areas, that schools serve as broad a mixture of abilities and social classes as possible.

89. Local authorities were urged to start discussions with the governors of voluntary and direct grant schools. It was hoped that the governors of the direct grant schools would be ready to consider changes in curriculum and in method and age of entry to enable their schools to participate fully in the local authority's scheme.

Reorganization plans

90. In response to the Circular most authorities prepared plans for the reorganization of secondary schools in their areas. By December 1969, schemes of reorganization had been approved for 129 out of 163 local education authorities; 108 of these covered the whole or the greater part of the area. Of the remaining authorities, the plans of 12 were under consideration and 6 had yet to produce a plan. The plans of 11

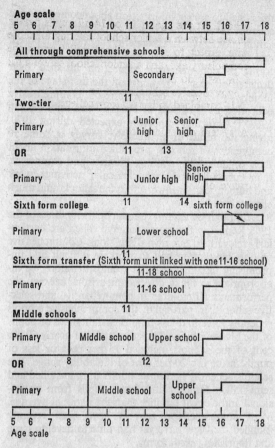

Age scale

5 6 7 8 9 10 11 12 13 14 15 16 17 18

All through comprehensive schools

| Primary | Secondary |

Two-tier 11

| Primary | Junior high | Senior high |

OR 11   13

| Primary | Junior high | Senior high |

Sixth form college 11   14 sixth form college

| Primary | Lower school |

Sixth form transfer (Sixth form unit linked with one 11-16 school) 11

| 11-18 school |
| Primary | 11-16 school |

Middle schools 11

| Primary | Middle school | Upper school |

OR 8   12

| Primary | Middle school | Upper school |

5 6 7 8 9 10 11 12 13 14 15 16 17 18
Age scale

Figure 20.8 Patterns of comprehensive organization

authorities had been rejected, of whom 8 had not yet submitted revised proposals and 3 had declined to do so. A further 5 have declined to submit any scheme.

91. Table 20.2 shows the number of authorities which have chosen various types of organization for their long-term plan where this has been approved (where long-term plans have not been approved authorities have been classified according to their approved short-term plans). The all-through school with an age range of 11–18 is the most popular, chosen by 62 authorities. Various kinds of middle school system have been chosen by 52 authorities, and two-tier arrangements by 32. Taken together, schemes which involve some sort of a break or transfer at 13 or 14 are more popular than all-through 11–18 schools, but they include a great many variations. Schemes involving transfer at 16 are less popular, at least at present. The schemes involving a break or transfer at 13 or 14 and those with one at 16 figure more prominently in schemes approved in the last two years than previously, and it may be that this marks the beginning of a trend away from the 11–18 school. The shortage of highly qualified teachers and the rapidly expanding numbers of pupils staying on at school after the age of sixteen are impelling authorities to search for ways of concen-

trating their sixth form resources. Some are looking at the possibility of educating all pupils over the age of 16 at colleges of further education. Others are considering the possibility of linking and co-ordinating the sixth form work of groups of comprehensive schools so that each specializes in particular fields. The pattern is complicated and changing; it may develop a good deal further in unforeseen ways.

92. The figures in Table 20.2 are for plans approved but not necessarily implemented. Some schemes cover county and voluntary controlled schools only, and do not settle the role of voluntary aided schools. The speed of implementation often depends on the availability of teachers and of resources for capital expenditure, and for this reason a number of plans set no firm date for completion or the date proposed is far in the future—20 years hence or more. When a school is reorganized it may be some years before it becomes comprehensive. For example, a grammar school being reorganized as a comprehensive school will normally start with an unselected entry in the first form only, the following year the first two forms would be unselected and so on. It would not be fully developed as a comprehensive school until the seventh year after taking its first unselected entry.

Table 20.2 Patterns of comprehensive organization chosen by local education authorities (as at December 1969)

	Number of authorities
All-through comprehensive schools (11–18)	62
Schemes including 11–16 schools	
11–16 with sixth form college to follow	18
11–16 schools working in concert with 11–18 'mushroom' schools to which pupils transfer at 16	24
*11–16 schools working in concert with 13–18 schools to which *some* of the pupils in the 11–16 schools transfer at 13 on parental choice	4
*11–16 schools working in concert with 14–18 'mushroom' schools to which pupils transfer at 16	2
Total	48
Two-tier arrangements	
Transfer at 14 (11–14+14–18)	22
Transfer at 13 (11–13+13–18)	2
*13–18 schools to which *some* pupils transfer on parental choice at 13 from 11–16 schools	4
11–13 schools from which *some* pupils transfer to 13–16 schools and the *others* to 13–18 schools according to parental choice	2
*11–14+14–18 'mushroom' schools to which pupils can transfer at 16 from 11–16 schools	2
Total	32
Middle school arrangements	
9–13+13–18	29
8–12+12–18	11
10–13+13–18	5
*8–12+12–16 with sixth form college to follow	7
Total	52
Sixth form colleges	
*Following 11–16 schools	18
*Following middle school arrangements (8–12+12–16)	7
Total	25

Source: Department of Education and Science.
Notes: 1. When an authority has had both a short-term and a long-term scheme approved, it is the long-term scheme which has been used for the table.
  2. Some authorities have more than one type of scheme, either in different parts of their areas or as between county and denominational schools. The schemes of such authorities will therefore appear under more than one heading.
  3. The sixth form college schemes include schemes at Exeter and Barnstaple for the provision of all post-16 work in the local college of further education.
  4. Schemes marked with an asterisk appear more than once in the table.

Aided schools

93. The reorganization of the voluntary aided schools presents special difficulties. In the first place these schools tend to be small in size, so that building is usually needed before they can become part of a comprehensive system. The arrangements for the financing of new building in a voluntary aided school demand a contribution from the voluntary body which it may not be willing or able to produce, especially if it has already incurred such expenditure for earlier (and possibly very recent) reorganization of all-age schools. The distinctive status of the voluntary aided schools makes merging with county schools difficult. Two-tier arrangements often seem to provide a convenient solution but they may not suit the voluntary body or the authority. No voluntary aided school which is unwilling to adopt a comprehensive role can be compelled by law to do so. If the local authority so proposes and the Secretary of State agrees, it may cease to maintain the school. But even if resources for building a new county school were readily available, few authorities would consider taking such action against a local school. In any case the churches which are responsible for most of the voluntary aided schools have declared that they are not in principle opposed to comprehensive reorganization and are working with many local authorities to introduce comprehensive schemes as soon as possible.

Survey of comprehensive schools

94. In 1966 the National Foundation for Educational Research in collaboration with the School of Education of the University of Manchester was commissioned to collect information about comprehensive schools, to chart the growth of comprehensive education and the practical educational problems it posed, and to devise means for measuring how far various forms of comprehensive education attained their declared objectives. A report on the first stage of the inquiry—a factual description of comprehensive education as it existed in 1965–6—was published in 1968.[14] A further report is expected during 1970, giving the result of an intensive survey of some 50 comprehensive schools, providing information about their organization, staffing, libraries and equipment, their curricular and extra-curricular activities, work and human relationships within the schools, and much else besides.

95. Although we cannot summarize the findings of the 1968 Report, a few points emerge which are particularly relevant to our own discussions. Comprehensive schools have often had to work in difficult and unpromising circumstances. It would, therefore, be inappropriate to make direct comparisons between the performance of children in comprehensive and selective schools. In particular, the comprehensive schools generally have had less than their fair share of pupils of the highest ability. Thus the intake of nearly 60 per cent of the schools included 15 per cent or less of pupils in the top 20 per cent of the ability range. The schools generally had more pupils from unskilled and semi-skilled families and fewer pupils from professional and clerical families than the national average. Most comprehensive schools have been recently founded, and few have yet had time to develop large and flourishing sixth forms.

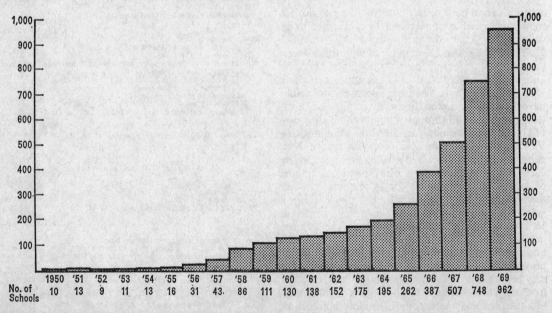

Figure 20.9 Growth in the numbers of comprehensive schools 1950–69
Source: Statistics of Education.

Variety of approach

96. The Government did not ask authorities to adopt any particular pattern of comprehensive education. The possibilities were listed and discussed and the authorities were asked to decide what form suited their particular circumstances. This means that re-organization is being tackled in many different ways. The comprehensive system is not by any means a monolithic system. Schools may be single-sex or co-educational, they provide for diverse age ranges, and they are linked with other schools in all sorts of different ways. Within the school, too, there is great variety of organization and approach. Different policies are followed on streaming, banding, setting and the mixing of abilities, on teaching methods and discipline; even the basic aims and principles of the schools vary.

Conclusion

97. It is now over four years since Circular 10/65 was published. What progress has been made? The number of comprehensive schools was already growing then and this trend has been greatly accelerated since. Figure 20.9 shows how the number of comprehensive schools has risen in the last two decades. Nevertheless, nearly three-quarters of secondary school children are still in schools not yet reorganized, and many of the remainder are in comprehensive schools which will only gradually offer them the full range of opportunities which comprehensive education is designed to provide.

98. Progress will depend on the resources available, the support of parents, and the determination and skill of central and local authorities, school governors and teachers. The variety of patterns already evolving makes it clear that schools cannot be classified as 'comprehensive'—still less evaluated—in isolation from the local system of education in which they work. It is these systems which are becoming comprehensive, and there are many different parts which schools can play within such systems.

Table 20.3 Comprehensive schools

	1965	1966	1967	1968	1969
Number of comprehensive schools	262	387	507	745	962
Number of pupils	239,619	312,281	407,475	604,428	772,612
Average of pupils per school	915	808	804	810	803
Percentage of total maintained secondary school population	8·5%	11·1%	14·4%	20·9%	26·1%
Number of authorities operating some comprehensive schools	48	57	72	81	94

Source: Statistics of Education.

Notes

1 See *Young School Leavers*, Schools Council Enquiry (HMSO 1968), paras 107 and 126.
2 *International Study of Achievement in Mathematics*, ed. Torsten Husen (John Wiley 1967).
3 i.e. county, voluntary aided, voluntary controlled and special agreement schools.
4 *Young School Leavers*, paras 191 and 192.
5 See for example, Professor Rosenthal's and Dr Jacobson's work on 'Teacher Expectations for the Disadvantaged', *Scientific American* (April 1968) and *French from Eight: A National Experiment*, by Clare Burstall (NFER 1968).
6 *Children and their Primary Schools*, para. 413.
*These refer to the original document.

7 *Enquiry into the Flow of Candidates in Science and Technology into Higher Education* (HMSO 1968), Figure 5.
8 Quoted from the 1966 Annual Report of the Department of Education and Science. para. 2, p. 9.
9 See Statistics of Education, 1967, **4**, Table 45.
10 Presented to Parliament on 4 February 1970.
11 *Research Studies 6—School Management and Government*, G. Baron and D. A. Howell (HMSO 1968).
12 See *Secondary Education for All* (HMSO 1958).
13 See 'Signposts for the Sixties', the Labour Party, 1961.
14 *Comprehensive Education in England and Wales*, T. G. Monks (NFER 1968).

Major controversy in the secondary education sector, both in the United Kingdom and in the Irish Republic has tended to centre on the decision taken (everywhere except in Northern Ireland) to move towards a system of comprehensive reorganization. This has provoked an initial re-examination of the case for and against the selective schools themselves, and in the four extracts which follow, the cases for and against, first the grammar school, and then the secondary modern school, in England and Wales are examined.

One key document in the battle for the introduction of comprehensive education has been a pamphlet by Professor Peter Townsend, which was widely circulated by those attempting to persuade local authorities to change their policies. It is printed alongside an extract from Tract 411 of the Labour Party's Fabian Society, in which Dennis Marsden examines the question from a rather different though socialist point of view.

The three extracts which follow represent Conservative party viewpoints on major educational issues in the late 1960s, and particularly on the issue of comprehensive schools. The first is a speech by the leader of the party in 1967. This is followed by part of a memorandum giving the views of the 'left-wing' Bow Group; and third, we include an extract from a pamphlet produced by an education spokesman for the 'right-wing' Monday Club.

One group which viewed the move towards comprehensive secondary education with grave misgivings was the all-party group producing the Black Papers on Education, sponsored by the editors of the *Critical Quarterly*. One of the contributors to Black Paper 2 was Rhodes Boyson, headmaster of an actual comprehensive school run by the Inner London Education Authority.

21 Twentieth-century state education in England and Wales: an examination of the case for and against (i) the grammar school (ii) the secondary modern school[1]

The case for the grammar school

Robin Davis, *The Grammar School* (Penguin, 1967)

The challenge to the idea of segregated secondary education has led to considerable attention being paid to the nature of the grammar school.

This article gives a justification for the specialized type of education provided by such schools.

Robin Davis has been, since 1946, on the staff of Merchant Taylors' School, Northwood.

The approach of the grammar school is still, in the main, academic. Many of the subjects it teaches, though superficially useless, are of value in training the mind and developing personality. The demand for

Source: Twentieth-Century State Education, F. Field and P. Haikin (eds), Oxford University Press (1971).

1 Designed for promoting discussion of current topics among students at Southwark College for Further Education.

such trained minds in the adult world is fully established and steadily growing. For example the following is extracted from an advertisement for an intermediate post in a nationalized industry: 'The work requires clear thought, and eye for the relevant point, and the ability to draft quickly, in logical sequence and in plain English.' No mention here of particular knowledge or experience—indeed it is not clear, out of context, which nationalized industry is concerned, and it might well apply to any. Nor could one prescribe any one subject or course of training that would provide the qualities sought. The subject matters less than the approach, and this is, in effect, the academic approach, which broadly means treating a subject of little or no obvious practical value as tremendously important and worth while for its own sake. Now one of the hardest tasks of a teacher is to make a child on the threshold of secondary education see this. With some it is well nigh impossible, but it is easier with children of initial reading interest and ability, the prerequisite of which is usually a certain degree of intelligence and the

116

consequence a readiness and desire to think and criticize for its own sake. The approach of the grammar school is therefore literary rather than practical— a 'sit down and think' school for 'sit down and think' children. One consequence of this is its apparently somewhat limited curriculum. Compared with the vast range of subjects offered at a large comprehensive school the grammar school resembles a one-man business competing with an educational supermarket. Yet paradoxically this is its strength. Offer a boy of eleven or thirteen a choice between commerce and Greek, or let a girl of similar age choose between typing and trigonometry and who can blame each, with their limited vision in a materialist world, for choosing the former option often enough, when they are 'first generation grammar school pupils', with their parents' blessing. For the 'sit down and think' child there is much to be said, on the long view, for such options as commerce and typing just not being available. Both choice of subject and standards of work are involved here ... In the words of a grammar school master, 'academically we drive, and only in the later years do the pupils realize why they have been driven'.

If the approach of the grammar school is academic to match the needs of the grammar school mind, its method of teaching is also distinctive. That this should be so is perhaps best seen by considering the different character of teaching in the modern schools. Here the approach is more graphic and often more imaginative and experimental than in grammar schools. Visual and other teaching aids are, or should be, more extensively used and there is need for the teachers to be more concerned with and enterprising in the presentation of their subject. As a comprehensive school headmaster put it 'they can't just preach, they really have to teach'. Now there is nothing wrong with preaching provided that you have an audience more or less prepared to listen, and here is the crux. By and large the grammar school child really does want to learn, though youthful pride would seldom admit it. But with the secondary modern child the teacher first has to persuade his class to want to learn before they can even begin to think about learning. Motivation must precede instruction, and often enough the former is a longer and more frustrating process than the latter.

But if the grammar school approach to and method of learning is *different*, how far are we justified in suggesting that it is in some way *superior*? This word has two main uses: first, to convey that something is intrinsically better, and secondly, that it carries a higher status. Now things that are 'superior' in the first sense usually cost more, as when we speak of a 'Superior quality cloth'. In this sense a grammar school education is often more expensive in two ways. First, most of its staff and certainly a larger proportion than in a secondary modern school, are graduates, and this means the payment of graduate allowances and usually a more lavish scale of special responsibility posts. Secondly the pupil-teacher ratio in grammar schools is more favourable, on average 17–1 against 20–1 in modern schools. The average size of classes is roughly the same (28·4 and 28·6 respectively) but the larger sixth forms in grammar schools, with their smaller teaching groups, makes the overall ratio more favourable to them. But this is not always so and should not necessarily be so. For one thing, in many areas, as we have seen it is the secondary modern schools that have the new buildings and equipment, so that in terms of capital expenditure the balance has been redressed.

But even where grammar school education does not cost more it is often regarded as 'superior' in some other sense. To some it may seem it is better absolutely. When we speak of an 'educated man' we usually think of someone who has had a grammar school type education.

Values

The values of the grammar school are classless and inseparable from an academic education, and if the working class want those values, it is for them to come some of the way to meet them. And in honour to them many of them do. Neither of my own parents had more than a basic elementary education, and my grandparents were respectively a bricklayer and a farm labourer. I could have no help in the home with knowledge or cultural background for my grammar school course. But I did have, like many others, wisdom, understanding and encouragement. There was no resentment or criticism of my grammar school and its values—only an exaggerated and at times embarrassing deference. There is no reason why the 'working class', if we must use that term, should not be something more mobile than a rock in its relationship with the grammar schools—and in any case it is a rock which seems to be steadily disappearing. Why should it prove less capable of assimilating grammar school values than of acquiring a taste for consumer durables and holidays abroad, both hitherto regarded through economic necessity or social inertia, as the exclusive preserve of the middle and upper classes? To object to or seek to change grammar school values of one class is rather like going to France and objecting to the right-hand rule of the road or *priorité à droite* or feeling resentment because the French speak French. The British working class have enough sense and flexibility to recognize this. ...

The case for the grammar school crystallizes into a case for educational efficiency ... There is such a thing as the 'grammar school mind' which the nation needs and other nations covet, and selection, for all the propaganda against it, is the best way so far devised to identify such minds and give them the kind of education that will develop their full potential. To call that education 'superior', though politically specious, is misleading; and to claim that the ethos of the grammar school conflicts with that of the working class is to make an out-of-date and class-obsessed generalization that is unfair both to the schools and to the working class itself. The traditional values and approach of the grammar school, despite plausible demands for modernization, are still relevant to the world of today. And, paradoxically, to preserve a system that appears to be socially divisive is the best road to educational efficiency, while social engineering through reorganization invites stagnation or decline.

Grammar school values

Brian Jackson and Dennis Marsden, *Education and the Working Class* (Routledge & Kegan Paul 1962)

The second extract taken from a study of 88 working-class children who completed a grammar school course reveals the difficulties some had in adjusting to the school and considers the conflict met by many working-class children between the values of the school and those of the neighbourhood.

Out of the children 48 spoke clearly of themselves as being identified with the school 'I was very much an establishment man. I was all establishment man!' whereas 15 were just as clear that they had declared *against* the school, and 25 held some intermediate position. Being *against* school did not necessarily mean being against school *work*. For all kinds of children, interest here was intense and success of supreme importance.

We pay a great deal of attention to the children who refused to accept the school. This is because we believe that they often represent the very large numbers of gifted working-class children who abandon grammar school at 16, and do not progress (as well they might) on to university and the professional life. Certainly the children we spoke to remembered large numbers of dissident pupils up to the fifth form, but few of these remained at school after this, and only a minority fall on our sample. The rebels left.

Who are the ones who *did* remain, and who especially are in this inner group of 15, who stand out uncompromisingly against the grammar school ethos? Five of the 15 come from 'sunken middle-class' homes; eight have fathers doing unskilled or semi-skilled work; 11 live in rented homes. Lightly sketched in like this we see that they come from all ranges of our sample, with perhaps a slight emphasis away from the very top reaches of the working class.

The essential choice which these 88 children faced in the early grammar school years was one between school and neighbourhood. Some children had begun with few neighbourhood links, and for them this was no crisis. But the others who found themselves firmly, or sporadically, against the school were boys and girls who were still involved in neighbourhood life, and who preserved their other style of living. It was more than a matter of joining a youth club rather than the school scout troop; it had to do with deep differences in response, feeling, judgment—which recoiled against common images of 'dominance' or 'leadership': school

uniform, teachers' gowns, prefects, the Honours Board, the First Eleven, the Scout Troop, the School Corps, Speech Day, Morning Assembly, Expected Public Decorum. The children who drew back from this spent their evenings in youth clubs, or with cycling groups or roaming the parks and streets in large inclusive gangs.

Their friendships, touching on middle-class children at school, centred around others in exactly their own situation and linked up with local children who had not passed the selection examination. Their basic loyalties were local loyalties. School was interesting and work was important, but for all that it was *only* 'Just where I went to learn things'. To the fuller social life it was hardly relevant. . . .

Meanwhile difficulties were arising within school. There was the school uniform . . . The children who objected so strongly to school uniform were not the poorest children by any means. It seemed as if the objection was aimed at all those aspects of 'school' that did not have to do with 'work', but had to do with the school as an alternative community, as a particular code of living together and growing up. . . .

Almost any official side of the school was rejected by these children. They would not join the school corps, they would not join the school scouts. Nor would they even buy the school magazine. 'All the way down the school I'd refuse to buy the school magazine. I wasn't interested in buying it and I wasn't even interested in looking at it. I wasn't the only one, no. There were quite a bunch of us and the masters would come and bark at you and tell you how ashamed they were and how you were letting the side down, but I wouldn't buy it. And even when other kids bought it I wouldn't go and look at their copy.' It was odd to hear these consistent incidents in which children—often quite shy children—had taken a painful stand against the school over something which must have looked quite trivial to the teachers. Again it was not a case of the lack of money, though this might reinforce a stand, and it was not that the children could themselves explain why they were having nothing to do with this or that aspect of the grammar school. All they could say was, 'I won't', and stick.

On the other hand, it was by no means clear that the school understood either, and often there was the sense of two strange worlds finding themselves side by side, yet with neither fully aware of the other's difference. Head teachers saw that some boys and girls retained neighbourhood links through youth clubs and similar bodies. Most tried to dissuade their pupils from membership. Speeches were made in assembly suggesting that youth clubs really belonged to secondary modern school children and should be left to them. For grammar school children there was the school community with its societies and homework.

And daily from the teachers came a host of warnings, injunctions, suggestions, that spoke of the gulf existing. Working-class children felt themselves being separated from their kind. The choice between school and neighbourhood was faced daily in small concrete incidents. For the teachers these incidents were merely part of the pattern of manners, part of that training in 'tone' which distinguished the grammar school from the general community. They were honourably conceived and held, but for the child something much more central to his living was being locally but continually strained. 'She said you weren't allowed to eat ice-cream or sweets in the street. All sorts of silly things like that you'd have done *naturally*.'

We recorded a lot of evidence about the school's insensitivity and the child's hypersensitivity; the school's determination to hand on the grammar school modes, to spread its standards as the best and the only standards, and the child's awkward, clumsy and stubborn desire to preserve the other ways, to remain 'natural'. This gaucherie soon moved into rudeness, tactlessness and the impolite.

Tribute to the secondary modern school
R. M. T. Kneebone, *I Work in a Secondary Modern School* (Routledge & Kegan Paul 1957)

R. Kneebone, headmaster of Beckfield County Secondary Modern School, York, outlines what he considers to be the aims and purposes of the secondary modern school.

It would be true to say that no harder work and no more original thinking has been done anywhere than in secondary modern schools since their establishment just over ten years ago. It would be equally true to say that this has never been realized by the public. It is driving many secondary modern schools, mistakenly as I think, to seek recognition and esteem by creating within their schools examination streams and by entering pupils for external examinations.

We have a clear enough purpose. It is to take each child educationally as far as it can go—that means striving after true standards—and not neglect body and spirit. We do that, but because we have no examination results to show no other results can be seen. I will try to bring some of them within view of willing eyes.

Through the able work of our neighbouring primary schools the children who reach us are literate. Many are slow or even backward for the usual reasons of health, broken schooling, heredity and environment. They speak badly, read with little understanding, set their work down unintelligibly and resist attention. We work, as our primary school colleagues before us have done, to build confidence and win co-operation. We have our minor successes. Visitors tell us how well the children respond to questions and how eager they are to explain what they are doing or writing, even if it is not very good. With no other incentives than the highest—the desire to do their best for the children in our school—my teachers try every known method until at last there is something to build on. Suddenly a child who had no fluency in reading and writing finds himself able to do a little better and the improvement begins. There are those who say that these children should be turned out of school at fourteen to the labouring jobs for which alone they are fitted. That is not my view. Their work improves and so do they.

They are in our school during the most trying period of emotional and physical development in their lives. As we have had such a large proportion of children of secondary school age in our modern schools it stands to reason that we must expect most of the problems. Some of the children in difficulty because of emotional disturbance during adolescence have no strong support out of school and depend very much upon the care and help that we can give them. I have in mind several cases of children who were steered clear of juvenile court proceedings by the practical sympathy of teachers who made them work and gave them good advice. I can think of many cases of children with no training in courtesy or consideration who have learnt something of both before they have left us. The protection that we offer in school is continued with good effect in Junior Evening Schools and Youth Clubs. The public may think of secondary modern schools as breakwaters rather than lighthouses, but they should admit that because of us there are calmer waters ahead.

If we aim to improve work and behaviour we also offer our children the chance of acquiring a sense of responsibility. Senior pupils in grammar schools at 17 or 18 years will be prefects, captains of games or leaders of school societies. It would seem that the hierarchy in comprehensive schools will hardly come from the pupils leaving at fifteen. In the secondary modern school we have our opportunity and our pupils respond well to it. They are ready for responsibility and enjoy it, misusing their power sometimes but learning to assume care of a class or cloakroom with practice. They become smarter in appearance and walk with befitting dignity. They have a new sense of power in their developing physical condition; they have experienced using their authority in school games and clubs. We are in a position to tone down the over-exuberant and strengthen the nervous and uncertain. They are learning control over their speech, movement, opinions and feelings, each an education in itself. They are taking the first steps in self discipline.

We demand the highest standard of work of which the children are capable. Seven out of every ten children leaving the primary schools continue their education in the secondary modern school. We take them as they are and try to help them to develop a right attitude to work, to people and to themselves.

Critics make rare play with our children's educational ability, with their behaviour, taste and manners. They exaggerate, of course, and their exaggerations fall on willing ears. We can say with truth that some of our children are the equal in what the public easily recognizes as educational ability of some children already benefiting from the prestige accorded grammar school education. We can say that in character, effort, bearing and disposition we have many children who will prove to be the decent citizens playing leading parts in factories, offices and shops. We have children of lower educational and social status who merit no less attention than any other child in any other kind of school. Only devoted service from our teachers can help with these children. . . .

It is my intention to pay tribute to secondary modern teachers in this and every school. No social prestige attends our efforts. New schools and new equipment have lent strength to our work, but our main strength must come from the spirit with which we approach our work and the belief that remains in us after years of hard striving in the face sometimes of ridicule and often of doubt.

We are preparing children not for examinations but for life. We teach facts. We seek to establish values. We work hard and long believing that what we are doing is as important in the fullest sense as teaching potential state scholars. We go to bed tired. We rise to face another day. We go into our morning assembly. We look around. Incentives? Here before us are five hundred incentives.

Shortcomings in the secondary modern school
John Partridge, *Life in a Secondary Modern School* (Gollancz 1966)

This article describes the routine of a secondary modern school in a new well-equipped building. The author summarizes what he considers to be its chief defects.

John Partridge was a teacher in such a school and is now teaching educational sociology at a college of education.

I do not think that anyone could say that Middle School was offering any kind of satisfactory education, from whatever point of view one chooses to define 'education'. How one views the life and work of this school depends, of course, upon one's basic assumptions. If one accepts the view that these are children of poor ability who are just incapable of serious work, who dislike school and play about because of their low intelligence quotients, who are best occupied playing sport or engaging in other non-academic activities, who are not of the material to rise out of their degrading lower-class habits and attitudes, and who are for all these reasons best sent out to work at an early age; then, perhaps, Middle-School style education is making the best of a bad job; it isn't too good, but after all it is the best that can be done with the material.

These are, sometimes, the attitudes of the teachers in Middle School. It's always education for someone else's children. One senior colleague said bluntly, 'Well, you wouldn't send your kid here, would you?'

However, there are some in Middle School whose basic assumptions differ from those of the pessimists, if so they can be called. These teachers recognize clearly how inadequate the education is, and how low the all-round standards in the school are. But they do not accept that this is inevitable and assert that all boys (and girls) are educable given the right encouragement and conditions. These men tend to see reform in political colours, claiming that the low standards in Middle School are due most importantly to the lack of adequate provision in the past for teacher training and general educational facilities. These are the kind of teachers who take their classroom teaching most seriously and who try to do their best for any 'D' or 'C' stream with which they are entrusted. Most admit that there is likely to be little improvement in either this type of education generally, or in their own personal lot, unless it is imposed from above by a Government with a different set of national priorities. Those who think along such lines may not be in a strong majority in Middle School, but at least they do differ in that they see improvement as possible in the near future.

Whatever the assumptions of the staff as to the nature and purpose and possible lines for improvement of the education proffered here, there is no disagreement about the low standards. In each 'D' class, there are boys who can neither read nor write; in the first-year 'D' class there may be fifteen who cannot, but by the time they have reached the third- and fourth-year classes, there may be only six or seven who still have a far below average reading age. I think it is fair to say that some five to ten per cent of each year group in Middle School are to all intents and purposes illiterate. In ascending order of literacy, the next group is a large one composed of the remainder of the 'D' boys and most of the 'C' boys. This large group have below average reading ages, but at least they can make sense out of simple prose, and show some progress during their three to four years in the school. But they will have difficulty in writing short letters or straightforward narratives; they tend not to be able to spell, neither to punctuate nor construct sentences. This means that some forty-five per cent or nearly half the boys here have not really acquired the essential tools for learning after between six and ten years at school. It hardly needs to be added that their grasp of any subject requiring literacy is inevitably poor.

A few boys in the 'C' stream, perhaps most of the 'B' stream, and the lower half of the 'A' stream, are boys who can read, in many cases well, and they are able to write comprehensible English. These boys may have mastered the tools of literacy, and of course they turn out some good work; some may be very good at certain subjects; there are those who show aptitude for woodwork or art, or for English composition. But the overall impression, however, is one of disinterest. These boys, who represent the most literate group of boys, bar one, in Middle School, seem steadily to lose interest the nearer draws the day for them to leave. The first- and second-year boys who belong in this group, and indeed most of the younger ones in all the streams show to some degree the natural inquisitiveness of children. But by the time they have reached the third year of their secondary education, they begin to worry about what they will do when they leave school; and because much of their school work appears to them irrelevant to this central concern in their lives, then they begin to lose any interest they might once have had in their classroom instruction. These boys are more articulate than their less literate fellows as well as more realistic about the limited range of opportunities open to them. These are the boys who want to get away from school and to get on with what seems to them to matter most—finding an agreeable, well-paid, interesting and secure job. These are the boys who say there would be no point in staying on at school until sixteen, because then they would have to compete with better educated Grammar school leavers of the same age who would get all the best jobs. These are sometimes the boys who are tempted to join the Forces as 'boy entrants' to learn a skilled trade. These are the boys who know what they want and seek the freedom, denied them at school, to wear tight jeans and pointed shoes, to grow their hair long and to listen to the Beatles.

Our most erudite boys are the ten or fifteen who compose the top half of the 'A' stream. These are the boys who do well in the Secondary Modern leaving certificate, who will pass certain subjects in the GCE O-level examination, and for whose benefit much of the school time-table is designed. Some of them will go on to Technical Colleges or even Universities, but at the same time they leave Middle School too young to have acquired more than a basic grounding in certain narrowly defined subjects, and even as representing the best educated boys in this school they are not, perhaps, well fitted for the adult world.

22   The argument for comprehensive schools

Peter Townsend

Much of the evidence collected by sociologists, social psychologists and educationists about ability in relation to schooling and educational achievement in recent years suggests that Britain should abandon the tripartite structure of secondary schooling and develop comprehensive schools. The existing structure rests on three broad assumptions; that levels of ability remain roughly constant, at least from the age of ten or eleven; that only a small proportion of children, say a fifth or a quarter, are capable of benefiting from an 'academic' type of secondary education; and that it is possible to teach children to higher educational standards when they are separated into different types of school according to their ability. Few social scientists would now accept any of these assumptions and I shall discuss them in turn.

1. A constant level of ability. The results of intelligence tests and other tests of ability are treated with more caution and scepticism than formerly. The IQ reflects verbal and arithmetical skills rather than qualities of creativity, industriousness and good judgment. Test scores have been found to be only crudely approximate because some children vary by up to 25 or 30 points. Vernon concludes 'One should never think of a child's IQ (or other test result) as accurate to 1 per cent. Rather, an IQ of, say, 95 should be thought of as a kind of region or general level ... Over several years, say from six to ten or from 11 to 15, the most we can say is there is a fair certainty (i.e. 10 to 1) of its lying between 80 and 110.' It is disturbing to compare this kind of statement by an expert with the comparative rigidity of streaming in primary schools and the low rates of transfer between different types of secondary school.

2. Proportion suitable for university, the small 'academic' minority. Many more children than has been supposed are capable of benefiting from an academic type of education. The reports of the Crowther and Robbins Committees both showed there were huge reserves of ability in the population. In 1961 the number obtaining university entry qualifications was just under 7 per cent for both sexes, and was just under 9 per cent for boys only. The Crowther Report indicates, on the basis of a survey of army recruits, that the figure of 9 per cent could be raised to 16 per cent if the same fraction of able working- as upper middle-class children were successful. The Committee quoted careful Swedish calculations which suggested that at least 28 per cent of young people could gain the equivalent of British university entry qualifications. Half of each age-group in California already enter higher education. The figure would probably come down to about 25 to 30 per cent to represent the numbers obtaining the equivalent of British university entry qualifications. The United States Office of Education accepts an estimate that 50 per cent of each

Source: Comprehensive Education (journal of the Campaign for Comprehensive Education) (1965).
Peter Townsend is Professor at the University of Essex.

age-group in the entire United States will be entering higher education around 1970. Persson gives a figure of 40 per cent passing the university entrance test in Oslo. The Robbins Committee was unable to 'specify an upper limit' for this country. The Committee said only that the percentage of each age-group in England and Wales with entry qualifications was likely to grow from 6·9 in 1961 to 10·8 in 1973 and 14·5 in 1985. On present trends, untapped ability was 'most unlikely to be fully mobilized within the next 20 years'. There is no reason why we should doubt that 40 per cent of our children have the capacity to take a university course, and perhaps another 20 or 30 per cent at least five subjects in the GCE at O-level. I say this because good teaching over a number of years may not only help to raise children's verbal and arithmetical skills and so their IQ, but allow them to reach unexpectedly high educational standards.

11+ failures. A recent study of 1,000 boys who did not succeed at the 11+ examination but went to public schools showed that 75 per cent passed the GCE at O-level in five or more subjects (compared with 56 per cent of all grammar school leavers) and about a third of them passed two subjects at A-level. Between a fifth and a quarter went on to university. These successes may be brought about by social and cultural influences at home, however, as well as by good teaching in the classroom. Bernstein and others have begun to show that middle-class children not only have the well-known advantage of parental encouragement and more opportunity for quiet study; they are also introduced to conceptual frameworks through the 'formal' language as well as the public language that is used in the home environment. If we could overcome the handicaps of poverty, bad housing and lack of certain kinds of stimulus, far more working-class children of 'lesser ability' could be given an academic secondary education.

Many of our ideas about the pattern of individual ability are derived unconsciously from the social structure. The belief that only a fifth or a quarter of the population are capable of performing professional, managerial and clerical jobs reflects the fact that only a quarter are in fact engaged in such jobs. The grammar school type of education reflects the fact that only 20 per cent do in fact have such an education. Brian Jackson has drawn attention to the irony of the arrangements that are made for streaming children in primary schools. The streaming is usually into three groups—upper, middle and lower—reflecting the division into social classes among the population at large. Even when the school is large enough to have nine classes in each group, there are not nine streams, just three streams, with three classes in each stream. This streaming is perhaps reflected in many facets of national life. We may think we are streaming children according to their ability when we are in fact dividing them up into groups which are mirror-images of the social classes they will belong to, and which indicate the social roles they will perform in adult life.

3. **The brightest not held back.** Finally, the third assumption of separate schools suiting separate abilities. The division into three broad types of secondary school from the age of eleven, and streaming even before eleven, can be criticized severely. The Stockholm experiments provided the first really strong academic evidence in favour of the comprehensive system. Broadly speaking, they showed that in comprehensive schools children of higher academic ability perform at least as well as, and the children of lower ability rather better than, they do in segregated schools. Studies so far carried out in Britain point to the same conclusion, though among those of lower ability improvements are now uniform. In some comprehensive schools very high proportions of children are taking examinations at O-level and are entering sixth forms. The evidence in favour of unstreamed classes in primary schools also suggests it is wrong to suppose that bright children are 'held back' and dull children inhibited from trying in each other's presence.

Segregation into physically distinct schools at eleven is still advocated by some local authorities and can no longer be justified except as an expedient until changes can be made. Such authorities are like surgeons who fail to heed the warnings of a Lister. The flow of information from educational sociology in particular is difficult to ignore. When parents of children who are admitted to secondary modern schools begin to understand the shortcomings of selection at eleven and have more knowledge of the educational process, the corridors of Town Hall power will really begin to hum.

The *minimum* arguments for comprehensive schools are therefore that the majority of children can profit from an academic type of education until at least sixteen; that since children's performance varies so uncertainly from year to year, decisions about those qualifying for sixth-form work and higher education should be postponed to as late a stage as possible, and that the educational standards of the brightest children can be maintained but those of the academically weaker children significantly improved.

To these I would add a number of *social* arguments, which are really educational arguments in the widest sense. More children not only have access to a wide range of skills—from turning a lathe to learning Russian. They have access to a wide cross-section of children, who have different cultural backgrounds and different kinds of talent. In my humble belief this is richly educative. Children will be better equipped to communicate with individuals at all social levels and, perhaps, a shade more comprehending of society and its problems than otherwise they might have been.

But, finally, we need to recognize that in applying the comprehensive principle to the school system we are doing no more than breaking with the past so that we can make a fresh start. We are not solving all our educational problems, only adopting a framework which will make the task easier. There are rigidly separate streams in some comprehensive schools with little movement between one stream and another. Curricular and extra-curricular activities are devised so that there is a minimum of social interaction. There is scope for sharp argument and experiment about the

forms of comprehensive schooling. But at least there will be a minimum fulfilment of the principle of equality of educational opportunity and a corporate social unity which may even spill over into adult life.

23 Politicians, equality and comprehensives

Dennis Marsden

The persistence of educational inequality in 1964

The dimensions of educational inequality in the twentieth century, against which we may measure the achievements and problems of the Labour Party up to 1964, may be summarized as follows. After the 1902 Education Act had officially permitted state secondary education, but of a grammar school type only, with a subsequent backing of scholarships and free places, the flow of working-class boys receiving secondary education increased from virtually 0 to 10 per cent before World War Two: at that time almost 15 per cent of all boys of secondary school age went to grammar or independent schools, but only 40 per cent of the boys' grammar school intake was working class.[1] Only 1·7 per cent of manual workers' sons reached university. The situation of working-class girls was, of course, even poorer educationally.

After the 1944 Education Act, abolition of grammar school fees and an overall expansion of selective school places resulted in about 15 per cent of working-class boys attending grammar schools: there were now about 23 per cent of the secondary school population in grammar and independent school places, and the proportion of the grammar school intake which was working class had risen to 56 per cent. Yet now only 1·6 per cent of manual workers' sons reached university. Meanwhile almost half of all middle-class boys went to independent or grammar schools, and almost a quarter went to university.

In fact, the post-war attempts to open up education had tended to bring into the grammar schools and the few technical schools only the *most able* sons of the *skilled* workers, and by no means all the working-class children whose measured ability should have entitled them to a place. And having entered grammar school many children still left at or before the sixth-form threshold, which now replaced the 11 plus as a barrier to highly achieving working-class children. Altogether, as has been demonstrated by the Crowther Report,[2] half the nation's top ability boys had left school at the age of 16 or younger, and this huge wastage occurred

mainly in the working class. Could we but develop working-class potential to the same degree as that of the middle-class child we would need to double and treble the provision of university places. It has been said that there is enough talent here to provide top staff for another Britain.

One cause of these inequalities of educational opportunity was the large regional variation in selective and other school provision. The policy of 'roofs over heads' (that is concentrating on building new schools for the expanding and migrating population rather than renovating old schools) had led to growing inequality between north and south, city centre areas and the new suburbia. A NUT survey published in 1962 had shown that a quarter of all primary schools and a sixth of all secondary schools should be rebuilt.[3] The Newsom Report in 1963 found only 21 per cent of secondary modern schools 'generally up to present standards', and as many as 41 per cent of schools 'seriously deficient in many respects'.[4] Schools on council estates or in new towns were considerably better than those in mining areas, one-third of the former achieving an excellent score and only one in ten a very poor score, compared with the mining area schools where none were rated excellent and one in six scored very badly. Some areas were so bad that the Report made the hitherto novel suggestion that they should be made priorities for spending, a recommendation which was later strongly reinforced by the Plowden Committee's report on primary education. The Plowden Report confirmed the NUT Survey's findings and made the staggering estimate that to bring all primary schools up to an acceptable standard £588 million would need to be spent: almost three-quarters of a million primary school children were in school buildings put up before 1875.[5] We can see what good use the Conservatives and Mrs Thatcher have made of this particular inequality in de-fusing the comprehensive debate. Associated all too closely with these inequalities of building provision were the inequalities in staffing, since poor schools in poor areas have what the Newsom Report described as 'poor holding power'. Conditions of educational deprivation substantially mirrored conditions in the surrounding catchment areas.

Overall, Brian Simon calculated one indicator of edu-

Source: Politicians, Equality and Comprehensives, Fabian Tract 411, Fabian Society (1971), 11–21; reprinted in *Labour and Inequality*, ed. Peter Townsend and Nicholas Bosanquet (Fabian Society, 1972), pp. 118–28.

cational inequality, by region, sex and school provision, showing that a middle-class Cardiganshire boy had 180 times as much chance of reaching university as the daughter of a West Ham unskilled labourer.[6]

Such inequalities cannot, however, be entirely attributed to unequal provision of educational resources. Early in the 1960s evidence was mounting to show the very early influence of social class and inequality on a child's *educability*—that is, on the child's acquisition of those skills and abilities which enable him to do well in school. The complex influence of such environmental factors on the child's skills and motivation and disposition handicaps him in school.

The two major areas of loss to the educational system could thus be identified in the early 1960s as the early years before five, when most children are not provided with schooling, and the threshold of the sixth form, where some schools lose almost two thirds of their pupils. Evidently secondary school reorganization without expenditure in other areas of policy would not solve all these problems of educational inequality.

Patently, when Labour came into office in 1964, almost sixty years of the Party's struggle for educational equality had achieved virtually no reduction in educational differentials. Nevertheless, in view of what we are now learning about inbuilt trends in our society towards greater inequality, it may even be a matter for congratulating the Labour Party that the working-class share in the expansion of educational expenditure did not actually decline over this period. For the discovery of continuing and possibly growing inequality in education was paralleled by the rediscovery of inequalities in other areas of the social services, for example, housing, the health service, and the social security system.

Comprehensive reorganization in 1964

By 1964 Labour should have been prepared for the Party's first major piece of educational legislation, and should also have been preparing to deal with inequality in other areas of policy. The failure of the 1944 Education Act to achieve greater equality, even on a narrow definition, had been repeatedly demonstrated. The distorting influence of private and grammar school education was manifest, and indeed struck at the base of egalitarianism. The form of common secondary education had been debated since the twenties, and working comprehensive schools—albeit struggling to 'coexist' with grammar schools—had been in operation for a decade. Comprehensive reorganization had been the official policy for thirteen years. But again, as in 1945, the Party was unprepared with its own legislation (with less excuse this time), and existing patterns and trends in education were accepted.

It is true that there were more formidable political and practical obstacles than in 1945, largely through Labour's failure to seize the earlier opportunities, and also at first there was only a small political majority.

But it might be argued that a really imaginative educational programme could have won support (and the same might be said of the 1970 election). This would have required careful handling, of course, for unfortunately the new educational needs and opportunities which, it had been asserted, were created by social and technological change did not emerge in demands either by parents or industrialists for a switch to comprehensives. Rather the public looked to a slight improvement of the schools they knew: as late as 1967 a much quoted *New Society* poll which ostensibly gave 52 per cent of the population in favour of 'comprehensive' schooling also revealed in two other questions that only 16 per cent would choose a comprehensive school for their own child, and 76 per cent wanted to retain the grammar schools.[7] As David Donnison rightly observed in his commentary on these figures, this was not a vote for comprehensive education so much as a vote against the secondary modern schools. Moreover a poll of this kind does not indicate the strength of the choices. Pro-grammar school marches of local citizens, teachers and pupils, were the only marks of political agitation about the comprehensive school, and it seems very likely that the support for the grammar school was far more vehement and practical than any wishy-washy poll preference. A further problem, indicated by the poll, was that the educational debate was still obscure so that its details might play little part in the electorate's calculations. Claims of a mandate for comprehensives were therefore so much eyewash. Nevertheless a determined campaign to abolish 11 plus and the secondary modern school would have made sound electoral sense and is indeed proving effective in shifting reluctant Conservative councils today, in Richmond and Bedford.[8] Moreover at this time the public schools, although never stronger, were again growing uncomfortable about their social élitism and were once again flirting with the idea of some deal with the state.

The Labour Party also inherited a large balance of payments deficit in 1964, but lack of cash was not the main obstacle to comprehensive reorganization. Educational expenditure expanded more rapidly than any sector of the economy apart from natural gas, and money could have been found for comprehensive reorganization had the Labour Party been prepared to take the step of choosing priorities—which might, for example, have meant holding back the decision just taken by the Conservatives to expand a largely middle-class higher education sector.[9] The major influence of the cash shortage should have been only to cause more serious thought to be given about tailoring reorganization to the use of existing buildings in tiering schemes such as that of Leicestershire. The further problems created by the lateness of the Plowden Committee's recommendation for the age of transfer from primary schools, the single-sex schools and church education, also indicated complex local tailoring, but not a major barrier to progress.

It was characteristic of Labour's remoteness from

education that a problem which did not receive sufficient attention was that the attempt to combine secondary education under one roof involved the fusion of two sets of teachers who had maintained a careful social distance from one another for the last hundred years. Teachers resented the demonstration of the state's power over their working conditions, and there were genuine worries over the assimilation of career structures and the disappearance or raising of qualification standards for jobs. Extensive and public information services at both national and local level, and consultations with teachers, were therefore essential. The same was true for parents, and especially for local Labour councillors who could have controlled the details of many comprehensive schemes. In the event an understaffed and under-budgeted Transport House did not even know who represented Labour on the local education committees.

Legislation was all the more necessary because, although the Minister of Education's powers had grown large (in spite of attempts to build in countervailing mechanisms), they were unspecific in key respects. In line with comfortable Conservative consensus philosophies, the powers were extensively delegated to local power groups; and, most important, the Minister could not directly specify the form of secondary education and had only the weapon of power to approve new schools. (We can see a notable example of this decentralized rule in Mrs Thatcher, who not only withdrew Circular 10/65 but has said that she will not approve local schemes as a whole but only plans for individual schools.) A clear national statement of goals in legislation was evidently needed before any substantial educational change could be brought about.

Labour's failure to legislate had its roots in the failures of perception and will described earlier: the leadership was still quite prepared to live with the grammar and the public schools. And there is evidence of a lack of commitment to the ideal of reducing inequality in society. There was a failure to appreciate that economic and structural changes left to themselves will not reduce and may increase inequality. Labour politicians had apparently developed an overpowering coyness about taking any action which would curb or interfere with the existing maldistribution of power or resources.

As a result the direct grant schools have continued to receive state support and to create problems for local comprehensive schemes into the 1970s, although here was an area easily within the Labour Government's control. And yet again the issue of the public schools was fluffed. A policy of integration was available, but instead there was a Commission because the Party could not resolve its own internal difficulties. This was revealed as a sham when the advice of its research workers, to the effect that the schools could not and would not in any meaningful sense be 'integrated', was ignored in producing the final recommendations for integration (Royston Lambert and his research team felt impelled to put out to the press a note disowning the Report). There was some interference with the tax evasion whereby parents paid children's fees, but other forms of support from the government have been untouched and Eton is, ludicrously, still a charity.

The ineffectuality of circular 10/65

Labour's lack of commitment to equality and manifest unpreparedness in educational policy emerges most clearly from a study of the strategy adopted in comprehensive reorganization. The new Labour Government chose unconvincingly to define itself as responding to an overwhelming spontaneous 'grass roots' movement, which merely required to be regulated in the interests of coherence, much as the 1944 Act had regulated secondary reorganization, but which needed little central guidance. The assistance of such a 'grass roots' movement was indeed necessary, but to pretend that it was actually there was either a gross misreading or misrepresentation of the facts.

Whatever else Labour learned from the first postwar spell in office, it should have been manifest that controversial change could not be entrusted to the DES to accomplish. Yet this is substantially what happened. Lacking a policy, Labour may have adopted suggestions from the civil servants, and the device of Circular 10/65 was used to request, but not to require, local authorities to prepare plans for the reorganization of secondary education on comprehensive lines. A year later Circular 10/66 also made it clear that funds would not be provided for reorganization, but added teeth to the earlier Circular by refusing to sanction building on bipartite lines. Above all, in January 1968 the postponement of the raising of the school-leaving age struck a major blow against reorganization, since the measure would have brought much-needed funds for building new schools on comprehensive lines. In 1970 a bill to outlaw the 11 plus was defeated by Labour's negligence and by the running out of time.

A lack of central guidance and definition appears clearly from the form of circular 10/65 itself. No commitment was made to comprehensive reorganization, the Circular merely commenting on six schemes which had been tried out by local authorities. Some of the schemes were not even comprehensive in that they retained parental 'choice' of transfer into an academic sector, a choice exercised mainly by middle class parents. Middle schools, the one scheme which was feasible without rebuilding, were at first explicitly discouraged (although this injunction was later withdrawn). Throughout, the civil servants behaved as if there were no controversy. It has been pointed out that certain actions of the new Department of Education and Science seemed to assume the permanent co-existence of comprehensives with the bipartite structure: for example, no ongoing research to evaluate the comprehensive school has been undertaken, and research projects on timetabling and allocation procedures have continued to deal only with the selective system, as though comprehensives will always be peripheral.[10]

Anthony Crosland may have hoped that slow changes at local level would provoke less hostility and permit time for the education of the public. Comprehensive schemes are proving difficult to reverse (although not to subvert). It is arguable that, with another spell in office and reorganization plans for most of the country secure, Labour could have isolated a few recalcitrant authorities and used all available sanctions to bring them into line. But the issue was already hotly controversial, and no programme of public education was undertaken—indeed the only successful one seems to be the establishment of comprehensive schools. Moreover time was not on Labour's side in that public pressures against the 11 plus were on the whole diminishing: secondary selection was shifting away from the 11 plus single shot examination and becoming more secret and more unfair, *but less disliked*. It was the *exam* rather than selection itself which people disliked.[11] Authorities such as Essex have now switched to verbal reasoning tests, and teachers' judgments which are biased against the working class.[12]

Thus the expectation that handing over the problem of redistribution to local authorities would damp down opposition seems naïve. In the event there has been a long drawn-out quarrel, rather than a short sharp one.

For all its shortcomings, this comprehensives policy had some results. There are now more comprehensive schools, including more fully comprehensive ones, than there would have been without a Labour government in office. Authorities who were cautiously moving towards the change were encouraged to produce plans, and with some reluctant authorities the small weight of the Circular's request may have tipped the balance or bluffed them into reorganizing. The discussion of comprehensive education and the establishment of more schools has also apparently won some support: current figures in a poll which correctly asks the question of whether the respondent prefers the comprehensive system to the continuation of grammar *and* secondary modern schools shows 46 per cent for comprehensives as opposed to 37 per cent in favour of bipartitism, with 17 per cent 'don't knows', the bulk of support being in areas where schools have been established.[13] From the new schools we are gaining more valuable experience of the practical working out of the comprehensive principle, information which has been badly needed and which no amount of discussion could have afforded.

But now that the dust has settled, the dimensions of the changes can be seen to be disappointing when compared with the expectations aroused by Harold Wilson's hundred days. The Circular was unsuccessfully challenged in the courts,[14] but reluctant authorities found that they need not openly oppose the Department; they had merely to engage in endless 'consultations' or to submit a scheme which moved towards comprehensive education at a vanishingly slow pace. So pathetically eager, or incompetent, was the DES that the official statistics relating to the speed of reorganization were worthless: they included such items as plans for which no date of completion was ever fixed, partial plans, and plans which were selective in principle but which were never required to become comprehensive.[15] The rate of change was artificially inflated by counting authorities rather than the proportion of school pupils involved in schemes. As a result, for accurate information the public had to turn to the Comprehensive Schools Committee, the major private pressure group campaigning for reorganization. Much of the behaviour of officials in inflating the figures and accepting non-comprehensive schemes is, however, explicable in a less than Machiavellian way, by the fact that sheer pressure of work on the DES necessitated the extensive delegation of the vetting of plans to officials who neither understood the aims of comprehensive education nor perceived when these were in fact being flouted in particular schemes.

For a while after Labour came to office the number of comprehensive schools expanded at a faster rate, from 262 in 1965, to 387 in 1966, 507 in 1967, 745 in 1968, 960 in 1969, 1,150 in 1970 and a projection of 1,275 for 1971.[16] Nevertheless, by 1970 when Labour went out of office and Circular 10/65 was immediately withdrawn by Mrs Thatcher, only 10 per cent of all secondary school children were in schools with an unselective intake. One third of secondary school pupils were in schools called 'comprehensive', but these were still skimmed, sometimes by as much as the top 20 per cent of their ability range: they should not be permitted the description 'comprehensive' in some instances. The comprehensives are still missing on average the top 5 per cent of the ability range, and at the moment despite rising numbers of schools this proportion is not changing.[17] By the end of Labour's spell in office it was clear that a number of large and very influential authorities like Birmingham were determined not to reorganize, and that a new Act would be necessary to compel genuine planning for comprehensives. In fact over the years 1961 to 1969 the percentage of the secondary age populations in grammar schools dropped hardly at all.[18] Thus far comprehensives had merely upgraded secondary modern schools.

Equality and the neighbourhood school

Circular 10/65 had failed because it ignored the obstacles created for the redistribution of educational resources by the existing unequal distribution of resources and power at the local level. In the debates of 1964 Labour ducked the issue of redistribution most obviously in relation to the neighbourhood school concept. In fact the issue of redistribution of educational and other resources crystallizes in the neighbourhood school. As Benn and Simon have pointed out, the bulk of the population have always gone—and will continue to go in the foreseeable future—to 'neighbourhood' schools, the old elementary schools, and the sometimes not so new secondary modern schools, and often the grammar schools. The 'community school' ideal comes up against its severest political obstacle in the inequality and class segregation of large urban areas, for here there is no balanced community mix, and the populations of such areas suffer, not merely from educational deprivations, but from a shortage of many other types of resources. Comprehensive schools alone could not hope, and should never have been asked, to solve such problems alone.

The effect of the debate about neighbourhood comprehensives was to focus attention on the fact that if schools were zoned to neighbourhoods and parental choice was restricted to those zones, some pupils who had formerly gone to grammar schools would have to share the comparative deprivations of the secondary modern schools: the few bright working-class children whom the state now 'rescues' from such conditions would be 'contaminated' by the education it provides for the residue. Meanwhile, the superior resources of the former selective and new suburban schools would often be even more overtly devoted to a predominantly middle-class population. Yet instead of seeing the moral that the comprehensive school must be part of a wider attack on inequality, the debate turned to give the impression that the comprehensive school would *create* inequality. Both the Labour and Conservative Parties evaded the issue, but it was the Conservatives who were able to exploit inequality to defeat the neighbourhood school concept.

Thereafter there was a switch in the DES's presentation of the comprehensive school from that of a school serving the population of a neighbourhood to a school which, Labour allowed it to appear, would engineer equality by containing within its walls a balanced social mix of children. The ideology of this alternative definition of comprehensive education is that where 'social engineering' schemes operate the catchment areas are drawn and the intakes of the school adjusted in other ways (by bussing, by allocation according to bands of ability, and so on) to form as representative a social cross section as possible, the schools thus being required to undertake the social mixing which radicals desire but which market forces inhibit. Students of the new towns policy will see a close parallel in the ideology here.[19] In fact, of course, as Benn and Simon have shown, in the large majority of cases the dilemma is not acute and carefully drawn boundaries do not flout local communities, claims for whose existence can in any case be sometimes over optimistic. The problem remains, significantly, a feature of our larger cities like London, which almost alone has tried to operate a banding scheme.

It is important to note that it was at this point that community school and social engineering definitions of the comprehensive officially diverge. All earlier Ministry documents had defined a comprehensive school as a school providing secondary education for all the pupils in a given area. But after 1965 the definition frequently put forward by the DES was merely a school in which pupils of all abilities and social classes are represented. As Caroline Benn has pointed out, even the official research commissioned by the DES could not decide by what criteria to define comprehensiveness.[20]

Equality and the local power struggle

Having evaded the issue of redistribution at national level the Labour Party then proceeded to evade it at local level. Without any guidance they handed over to local councils and local education authorities the hot potatoes of drawing the catchment areas of the schools and determining by how much parental choice should be restricted. In these two issues lie the bases of redistribution, which is undoubtedly why they generate so much noise and why, with the abrogation of central authority, there were such unequal local struggles.

We are only just beginning to piece together reports of the mess. There were wide variations in willingness to reorganize, and splits opened up not only between the opposing local political parties but within the Labour Party itself, the unconvinced older members clinging to 'their' grammar schools. To a striking degree some Labour councillors are out of key with even the limited advances of central policy, a phenomenon only partly explained by the lack of information and co-ordination within the Party, and more expressive of the peculiar propensity of some natural conservatives to operate under a Labour banner.

Depending on the quality and commitment of the local councillors and particularly upon the persuasion and experience of the Local Education Officer, the participants in the debate might be more or less well briefed. Some councils gathered a great deal of evidence and visited widely to look at existing schemes; but others were merely fed by the Education Officer with all the most negative evidence on reorganization. In the absence of evidence the argument could not but be 'doctrinaire' on both sides. On the other hand, as examples of what a good Education Officer can do with councils which are not markedly radical we have only to look at Sir Alec Clegg in the West Riding, and the Mason Plan in Leicestershire.

Without clear central guidance the councils also varied in the extent to which they consulted local teachers and parents. One study indicates that the teachers' unions voted in different ways in different areas, to some extent depending on the branch members' ages, for the younger NUT teachers backed 'egalitarian' aims while the older teachers were more concerned with the possible disruption of career lines. However in none of the four areas studied did the teachers' opinions materially alter the final plans.[21]

The greatest mockery was in the pretence of parental 'consultation'. Minority groups of middle-class grammar school supporters and teachers were much more active and articulate, and they were better served by the press. The behaviour of middle-class parents appears sometimes to have been very much affected by the proportion of grammar school places in the area: for instance a shortage of grammar schools in Richmond meant that 25 per cent of children were in fee-paying schools, a fact which evidently helped to power local middle-class resentment of the state selective system.[22] But in the majority of areas the middle class were well served by the grammar schools and were reluctant to relinquish segregated education for their children.

The verdict of a comparative study of the two areas, Gateshead and Darlington, is worth quoting in detail.[23] The authors conclude that in Darlington the grammar school supporters were able to influence the form of the plans to some extent, while the hardest battle for the comprehensive principle was fought between different members of the Labour Party, the final plan being the work of the Chief Education Officer. In Gateshead, without a middle class, where a Labour council had long been in favour of comprehensives, the constraint was the problem created by the early reorganization of education on bipartite lines. Councillors and the Education Officer worked together, and the final plan appears to have been influenced more by the configuration of school buildings and the geography of Gateshead than by pressure groups. It may be that only where power is evenly balanced can external groups influence the decisions. The authors of the study conclude that 'consultation' functioned mainly as a valuable pill sweetener. The truth is, of course, that it is difficult for 'consultation' or 'participation' to take place where bodies of teachers and parents are radically split in their opinions and differ very greatly in local power. What was needed here was a strong central definition within which these local discussions could have been educative.

The resulting local comprehensive schemes display a range of aims lying between a 'meritocratic' concern to preserve the grammar school ethos and more explicit social engineering or neighbourhood school schemes. For example, different schemes can be seen to be more or less concerned with speed, with the retention of selectivity at sixth-form level, with the sometimes conflicting aims of providing all schools with sixth-form work yet conserving scarce sixth-form staff (a problem with a thoroughgoing set of eleven to eighteen schools), and with opening up the schools to the community.

Almost three fifths of the schools have an age range from eleven or twelve to eighteen years, a small proportion of these schools taking pupils at sixth-form level from other schools.[24] Another fifth have an age range of eleven or twelve to sixteen years, and these are more typically old secondary modern schools. One in fourteen schools is an upper school, from thirteen or fourteen, or a sixth-form college. There are two types of sixth-form college, with selective or non-selective entry, and there are now interesting proposals for linking the sixth form with the local College of Technology, a development which is frustrated by the separate administrative structure of the schools. One in seven schools, approximately, is a lower school, taking pupils from eleven to thirteen, fourteen or fifteen years only. Only 27 per cent have been purpose-built, and 23 per cent of schools occupy more than one site. Most interest is now being shown in the sixth form college, and plans submitted by 1968 indicated that in future only 38 per cent would be all through schools, 25 per cent would be tiered, and 32 per cent would have separate sixth forms.[25]

But the overall design of the schemes tells us nothing of the inbuilt dynamic of change in the comprehensive ethos, and the social and intellectual achievements of the schools. Are we yet in a position to say that the schools are 'successful' in achieving anyone's goals? To answer this question we must take a rather more strenuous and sceptical look at the aims and the evidence than has yet been attempted by the bulk of political supporters of the comprehensive school.

Notes

1 J. Floud, 'Social class factors in educational achievement', in A. H. Halsey (ed.), *Ability and Educational Opportunity* (OECD 1961), 34–7, 91–109.
2 *15–18* (HMSO 1959).
3 *The State of our Schools* (NUT 1962).
4 *Half our Future* (HMSO 1963), 258.
5 *Children and their Primary Schools* (HMSO 1967), 389, 391.
6 *Inequalities in Education* (CASE 1965).
7 'Education and opinion', *New Society* (26 October 1967).
8 See *The Times Educational Supplement*, 25 (1970); *Comprehensive Education*, 10 (1968).
9 *Planning for Education in 1980*, Fabian Research Series, 282.
10 C. Benn and B. Simon., 40–1.
11 D. Marsden, *Where*, 9.
12 P. E. Vernon (ed.), *Secondary School Selection* (NFER 1957).
13 *Comprehensive Education*, 14 (spring 1970).
14 R. Batley, O. O.'Brien and H. Parris, *Going Comprehensive* (Routledge & Kegan Paul 1970), 11–14.
15 C. Benn, *Comprehensive Reorganisation Survey* (CSC 1968–9).
16 Benn and Simon, op. cit., 58.
17 ibid.
18 *Social Trends* (HMSO 1970), 124.
19 B. Heraud, 'New Towns: the end of a dream', *New Society*, 302 (1968).
20 C. Benn, op. cit., reviewing Monk's survey; *Comprehensive Education*, 10.
21 P. E. Peterson, 'The politics of comprehensive education in British cities', paper given to American Political Science Association.
22 *Comprehensive Education*, 10 and 13.
23 R. Batley *et al.*, op. cit.
24 Benn and Simon, op. cit., 72.
25 ibid.

24 Extracts from a speech by the Rt Hon. Edward Heath, MP, to the National Advisory Committee on Education, 1967

It is nearly a hundred years since education in this country was revolutionized by Forster's great Elementary Education Act. I believe that the revolution confronting our educational system today and in the next few years is as far reaching and fundamental as when the first major advance towards universal education was made in this country in 1870.

In fact there are a number of revolutions in education going on at the same time.

There is the revolution in teaching techniques and curricula.

The material revolution, which has seen an unexampled replacement of old schools in the past twenty years.

The social revolution which has caused us to switch the emphasis to education for the underprivileged.

The political revolution with its trend towards equal opportunity and what I consider to be an undesirable trend towards egalitarianism.

The revolution in knowledge which has put a strain on our schools and on our universities to match and keep up with modern technical and technological advance.

And there is the revolution in ideology threatening the erosion of accepted standards and values.

These are the revolutions with which any Government and any Minister of Education has to cope. These are the revolutions which we in the Conservative Party have kept firmly in our minds in formulating the policies which will guide us when we return to office.

Primary education

The foundation of our education system is, of course, the primary school. I can only endorse Lady Plowden's assertion that those foundations must be strong enough to bear 'the superstructure of secondary education'.

British primary education as it has developed in the last thirty years or so is admired all over the world. The Plowden Report acknowledged the success of the progressive methods which are constantly being developed by far-sighted education authorities and ingenious teachers. But too many primary school teachers are still having to struggle against the handicaps of nineteenth-century buildings and classes of forty to fifty.

Perhaps the most ambitious proposal in Plowden

which has attracted much attention, is the one for a large extension of nursery education. I agree that this is important. But the cost of implementing the Plowden proposals in this field would amount on the capital side alone to £100 million. I am sure, therefore, that if we want to see, as we do, an expansion of nursery education, it is right to support the minority report which advocates a parental contribution to the costs of nursery education by all those who can afford to pay one.

Secondary education

The Conservative Party has constantly enunciated the principle which is implicit in Lord Butler's great 1944 Act that all young people should have the opportunity to receive the kind of education that enables each of them to travel along the road of education as far as their ability and perseverance can carry them.

I believe that our society, and especially the parents, expect our educational system to ensure that the potential abilities and creative talents of the young people of our nation are developed to the full. It is the manner in which schools can best be organized for this purpose, and not what type of education the children receive, that constitutes the great debate of secondary education today.

I want to make it clear that we accept the trend of educational opinion against selection at eleven-plus. By selection I mean the process of classifying children according to their IQ and separating them into different types of school at too early an age.

Of course there has to be selection or grouping by ability at some stage or other if we are to do justice to children's differing needs and abilities. It has never been a Conservative principle that in order to achieve this, children have to be segregated in different institutions. If, however, the transfer from primary to secondary education is now to be made without selection, this is bound to entail some reorganization of the structure of secondary education, at least in the earlier stages.

Because the organization of education in their areas is the prerogative of local authorities, we have always said that the pattern of reorganization is a matter to be settled by them in consultation with parents and teachers. It should not be imposed by dictation from the Secretary of State for Education. Local authorities know their own areas best and are responsible for working out their own schemes. In this the parents must have their say.

Source: Given on 17 June 1967 at Overseas House, St James's, SW1.

The grammar schools, both the ancient foundations and those established in the last fifty or sixty years, have made a magnificent contribution to our educational progress and our national well-being. It is right that we should be so concerned about their future. Yet the grammar schools themselves have changed many times in their history, long or short, whilst at the same time maintaining their characteristics of a broad liberal education and high standards. It has been this readiness to change and adapt themselves which has enabled them to keep pace with the sociological as well as the technological developments of the twentieth century.

I am not going to try to give a single answer to the secondary education problems of millions of different children in hundreds of different areas. And I believe it would be presumptuous and wrong for any minister or any government to lay down a single solution, for clearly what is right for one cannot be right for all. What we will do is to set out the guidelines—to establish the criteria on which a sensible reorganization of secondary education may be based. But in the last resort it is the local authorities who must be free to judge in the context of local needs and conditions and in the light of local views.

What should be these criteria of judgment?

First, is the scheme genuinely in the interest of the children themselves? And not only in the interest of children ten or twenty years hence, but those who have to be educated under the scheme meanwhile?

Second, is the scheme one which will attract first-class teaching staff?

Third, will it avoid using up resources which might be better utilized for the improvement of primary education?

Fourth, does it fit the existing buildings, or will it involve trying to agglomerate widely separated buildings into a single school?

Fifth, what will be its effect on the sixth forms? Clearly we cannot afford any decline in sixth-form standards, as a number of vice-chancellors have recently reminded us.

Sixth, does it make adequate provision for the brightest children, for example, by ensuring that they will have the opportunity to clear the O-level hurdle in four years rather than five, and to be transferred for their A-level work to a sixth form which stretches their abilities to the full?

Conservative-controlled authorities rightly look upon reorganization as a reform which, if it is to be worth while, needs careful planning and should not be rushed. The Conservative Party remains firmly opposed to the rapid and universal imposition of comprehensive reorganization.

The Labour government is putting pressure on authorities to reorganize quickly, but the resources to do the job properly are just not available. The result has been a large number of ill-thought out, hasty and makeshift schemes. These are bogus comprehensive schemes. To take schools where the buildings are widely separated, mix them all up, let the children and staff traipse between them, and call the result comprehensive education is absolute nonsense. These schemes will almost certainly demoralize the staff and harm the education of the pupils beyond redress. They are being rushed through, often against the wishes of teachers and parents, purely to meet an unnecessary political deadline. It is right, therefore, that the new Conservative education authorities should look again at the plans that were drawn up by Labour education committees.

If our sense of priorities is right we must obviously concentrate on those aspects of the reorganization of secondary education. But do not let us forget the important role in the system which is played by the direct grant school. It is Conservative policy that local authorities should be encouraged, and should themselves encourage parents, to take up available places in direct grant schools for those children who would benefit from going to them. I am sure that the high standard of sixth-form work that they provide can continue to make a vital contribution to our pattern of education.

Conservatives do not believe that education should be a state monopoly. Our attitude on independent schools is quite clear. We believe that the best of them provide a valuable cross-check on curriculum development and new teaching methods.

We also believe that in a free society every parent should have the right to choose what kind of recognized education a child should have in accordance with its needs and abilities. To assert this right it is not merely necessary that the choice should remain open to them: it is also necessary to resist deliberate discrimination against the independent schools which would narrow the choice and restrict the freedom to make it.

What do we want from education? What are the hopes and ambitions of the parents and of the children? Perhaps a fair chance to qualify for good jobs, and for their share of the nation's prosperity. There is nothing wrong in that. It is quite natural that this should loom large in their aspirations.

But it is not the only thing. Parents also want their children to have the chance to develop their potential, to find fulfilment for their talents and to be able to respond to the challenges and the opportunities of the world in which they live. Educational opportunity therefore must not be regarded just as a prize for the talented few, but as a source of personal fulfilment which all should have the opportunity to enjoy.

Perhaps in the past there has been a tendency on the part of governments and teachers to concentrate too much on the ablest children and not enough on the average. This tendency is now being corrected, and rightly so. But we must be sure that in concentrating on those who have not had a chance in the past we do not neglect those who could and should be excelling. To the challenge of the revolution in education to which I referred at the beginning I add one other which confronts politicians and teachers alike. It is the

challenge of widening opportunity without sacrificing the abilities of the best.

25 Conservatives and comprehensives

Simon Jenkins

The Conservative attitude

The Tory Party's policy on comprehensive education has undergone a definite change in the past decade. The approach of the 1958 White Paper on secondary education,[1] which was the vigorous development of the secondary modern schools towards 'parity of esteem' with grammar schools, has now become Mr Heath's recent 'it has never been a Conservative principle that in order to achieve [selection or grouping by ability] children have to be segregated in different institutions'.

Conservative spokesmen at local and national level have recognized that the principle of early selection which underlies the grammar/modern distinction is no longer viable, educationally or electorally. It is interesting that this was often realized earlier by local councillors more in touch with the views of experts, teachers and parents than by the politicians at the national level. A major factor in this was certainly the great success, and local popularity, of the new purpose-built comprehensive schools that were springing up even before reorganization began on a national level in 1965. A grudging acceptance of 'the good comprehensive school' crept into Tory speeches in the early sixties—but this was a far cry from the acceptance of the most basic point about the comprehensive school: the ending of eleven-plus selection, and with it an acceptance of a change in the character of the grammar schools at least in their lower forms. It was not until the Party conference in Blackpool last year that the Party's education spokesman, Sir Edward Boyle, categorically stated that 'the Conservative Party has accepted the weight of evidence against selection as early as eleven or twelve'. In doing so, he accepted the case for some form of secondary education (defined as education beyond the age of eleven) on comprehensive lines beyond that age. The full implications of this on the old tripartite system were further developed by Mr Heath in his major policy speech on education in June. He stated: 'If the transfer from primary to secondary education is now to be made without selection, this is bound to entail some reorganization of the structure of secondary education, at least at the early stages.' He accepted that this would mean changes in the status

of grammar schools which had 'changed many times in their history, long or short, whilst at the same time maintaining their characteristics of a broad liberal education and high standards'. 'What is essential,' he went on, 'is that in the process these outstanding characteristics which have served us so well in the past are kept for the future.' He then suggested various ways of preserving the essential identity of the grammar schools within a reorganized pattern.

The tone of both Sir Edward's and Mr Heath's contributions to the comprehensive debate have been those of the traditional Conservative. While bending to the winds of educational reform, generated more within the education service itself than by any political party, they have demanded safeguards to preserve what may be considered best in the old system and also appealed for less haste and more caution. As such they have served as a valuable antidote to the educational confusion and administrative chaos that has resulted in many areas from Labour's 'headlong rush'. And it has meant that the Party can pick up some political capital from such ludicrous consequences of haste as Manchester's appointments row or the Enfield Grammar court case. It has been a very good position to hold when in opposition.

The Conservative Party is now no longer in opposition. In the vast majority of education authorities in the country it is in power. And the secondary school system in England and Wales is going through a crucial period of change—one that has been initiated by the Socialists in the wrong way and largely for the wrong reasons. The irony is that it will be administered largely by Conservatives. They have the opportunity now to make a distinctive mark on it by developing it their way.

What this means

The Conservative Party is now firmly and rightly committed to the ending of the old system of secondary education based on the eleven-plus examination. This system was a bad one: it constricted primary school curricula and debilitated the teaching of the weaker primary streams in preparation for the eleven-plus which, although as accurate as any test could be, inevitably made mistakes which had disastrous effects on children's futures; worst of all, it branded as public

Source: 'Conservatives and comprehensives', a Bow Group Memorandum, Conservative Political Centre (1967), 8–12.

failures nearly 60 per cent of the nation's children at the early age of eleven so that many lost all motivation to succeed educationally. The result was that secondary moderns in many cases could do little but keep them occupied until the age of fifteen. The old ideal of parity of esteem between grammar and secondary moderns was inevitably a farce. Contrary to much belief the system was a denial of parental choice—it was the results of the exam which dictated which type of school a child went to. And by the early sixties the whole rationale behind the selective system—that children had different predictable aptitudes that required different types of institution—had become a nonsense. The encouragement given by the Conservative White Paper on secondary education in 1958 to modern schools to develop O-level courses and academic studies merely rubbed in their widely recognized status as poor-men's grammar schools. The fact that considerable numbers of modern schools produced very creditable GCE results just added point to the question—why select?

The act of selection by an education authority is the making of a choice for a child: the point of comprehensive education is that this choice need not be made as early as 11 since once it is made it closes certain avenues of opportunity to him, in practice if not in theory. Any believer in equality of opportunity should oppose the categorization of children into successes and failures until they are more ready to choose for themselves. There is no reason in educational theory why this need be done at all. The reasons why we find we must separate children at some stage of secondary education are basically practical: first, ability differences entail some differentiation in teaching and in courses studied; second, children separate themselves after a certain age by going out to work or by staying on to gain higher qualifications; third, it is not necessarily economical to provide all types of course for the complete secondary age range under one roof, particularly at the sixth-form level where good teachers are scarce and facilities expensive. And fourth, however much local authorities may wish to emulate the grand new comprehensive schools with lavish accommodation and excellent GCE results, we have got to make do with the buildings, the equipment and the staff we have. We cannot wish into existence a complete new national system of schools specially designed or teachers specially trained, to take account of each change in educational thinking.

This pragmatism is vital at present. It must be recognized that the object of reorganization should be to promote a greater equality of opportunity among school children and to prevent the undoubted waste of talent, and thus of vital national resources, that has been occurring in the past. The Conservatives have at no time used the arguments in defence of comprehensive education that have been the driving force behind Labour's reformers—that it will end the socially divisive system that went before. Even if such social engineering were a legitimate object of educational

reform, it is already clear that it is a futile exercise. Comprehensive schools neither are, nor are likely to be, harmonious social mixes—indeed the growth of neighbourhood schools could well add fuel to the flames of Labour's class war. Nor is a Conservative approach to reorganization tainted by the bitterness that many Socialists feel towards the grammar schools. The treatment of grammar school heads in areas like Manchester and the gratuitous insults that have been hurled across committee chambers at defenders of these institutions have been a public disgrace. The result has been that plans are being implemented in the name of comprehensive education that will neither achieve the benefits that have been promised from them, nor even succeed in maintaining the standards that existed before. For these reasons the Conservatives must look thoroughly at previous Labour schemes and judge them by their own criteria.

What are these criteria?

1. The new secondary school system must maintain the highest of the standards that existed in the old. It is not good enough to accept some lowering at the top, as the price for a tremendous improvement at the bottom. There is nothing incompatible about the ending of eleven-plus selection and the maintenance of high academic standards, though to look at many Labour plans one might think so.

2. This means that particular attention must be paid to the deployment of highly qualified staff and of specialized buildings and equipment. The success of reorganization will be largely dependent on the size of the resources we can afford to devote to it, and the efficiency with which they are allocated. This is very important. It is absurd to pretend, as some authorities seem to be doing, that some day soon all their financial prayers will be answered and ample staff, buildings and equipment will materialize.

3. The fact that resources throughout the education system are scarce—and that the Government stupidly refuses to devote more money for the purpose of reorganization—means that it will all take much longer than the Government seems to think, unless we are prepared to sacrifice the education of those children at present going through the secondary schools. The downright bad interim schemes—often involving two-year 'educational transit camps' (as in Bradford) should be stopped, and transitional timetables revised.

4. It is a vital principle that educational reform will be doomed to failure if it is not carried out with the full consultation and support of all those affected. If recent educational research has shown anything, it is the importance to educational achievement of parental support on the one hand and sympathetic teaching on the other. If parents and teachers are not taken into the fullest confidence on the future of their schools, their support will not be forthcoming. This may mean

public rows and vigorous pressure group activity—but it will be far healthier to the education service than the *fait accompli* from a secret working party that has been whipped through the local council. Teachers in particular, whose jobs can be radically changed by these reforms, must play a major part in discussions.

Note

1 *Secondary Education for All: A New Drive*, HMSO, Cmnd 604.

26 Stop nationalizing our schools

Clive Buckmaster

Plans for the future

Realism and common sense

Unless we are going to become a nation of committee men and women unable to take decisions other than by the bureaucratic method of caucus consensus, we must resist the Socialists' declared intentions to integrate the entire educational system by their traditional ideology of levelling down. We must adhere firmly to the philosophic concept that wholly free state schemes produce in the end a mediocre service and professional resentment, as the case of the present National Health Service illustrates all too well. We must give to those who genuinely desire it a chance to participate in an expanded independent sector where they can have a financial stake, however small in what is after all a joint venture between the state, the school and themselves. This is surely preferable to handing over the children to the mercy of a left-wing oligarchy which is too engrossed in the perpetuation of Socialist ideals to permit any parental participation whatever.

There is no doubt that the basic character and spirit of our young people remains as sound as it ever was. If the country was faced with a grave national emergency the 'weirdies', hippies, beatniks, and self-styled anarchists would soon shed their attempts to draw attention to themselves and would once again rally to the national cause.

Since the war successive Governments have, with the very best of intentions done everything possible to give the young people the maximum opportunities to take their place in society as they grow older. This is sound enough—unfortunately however state aid has on occasions been superfluous and has not always been put to the best advantage. A good father will give his children the maximum encouragement and financial aid to give them the incentive to make the best of their abilities but he will not spoil them by giving them pocket money whenever they ask for it.

We as a nation must realize that it is not the function of the state to provide the individual with a comfortable living in order that earnings may be used as pocket money for non-essentials. Whilst every effort must be made to give the maximum opportunity and encouragement to all, individual success will only come by personal effort and sacrifice.

Basic aims

In order to form the basis of a constructive policy in line with present-day conditions it is essential to declare the following basic aims:

1 To preserve all aspects of our national heritage which have proved to be successful in the past (e.g. the Public and Grammar Schools).
2 To ensure that the limited resources so painfully extracted from the community are applied to vital necessities instead of being squandered, either on unnecessary trimmings which are frequently unconnected with real educational needs, or on affluent parents who don't need, and in many cases don't want the same level of subsidy.
3 To re-organize educational finance with a view to lowering costs at both national and local level.
4 To ensure that any changes made in the existing system are of benefit to the individual child and not to perpetuate political ideologies.

Most Conservatives wholeheartedly support in principle the present basic structure of our Public Schools. However many are conscious of the fact that the existing high fees are outside the range of the pockets of many parents in the lower and even the middle income groups. At the present time those who like the system but who cannot possibly afford the fees have no alternative but to accept what the state has to

Source: 'Stop nationalizing our schools', the Monday Club, 10–17 (no date on pamphlet.)

offer which is in most cases the nearest Comprehensive School. In order to overcome this difficulty it is logical that the independent sector should be substantially extended and that public funds should be made available in the form of fee remissions to parents according to individual needs. As a pre-requisite to this plan it is essential that the conditions governing direct grant schools are suitably amended after thirty-three years.

The basic concept of giving free places and ancillary allowances to those in genuine need, together with a pay-as-you-can-afford scheme for those more fortunate should be maintained but present day arrangements must be geared to suit changing conditions.

The recommended changes are as follows:

1 That completely free places should only be given to children of parents who are considered to be unable to make a contribution without undue hardship.
2 The Government capitation grant should be withdrawn altogether and replaced by reasonably generous fee remissions (through the Department of Education and Science) to cover the difference between what the parent can reasonably be expected to pay and the full economic fee. (In cases where extra funds for capital works are required Government loans to the governing bodies might be considered if the necessary finance is available.)
3 Local Authorities would be responsible for providing ancillary allowances in cases where need is proved. No discrimination should be made between children who have attended state primary or private preparatory schools.
4 The subsidy on school meals should be withdrawn and granted only where need is proved.
5 A limited number of genuine academic scholarships should be given by Local Authorities as a reward for exceptional merit irrespective of individual means and regardless of where the candidates received their primary education. These would take the form of educational vouchers given to parents.
6 A nominal enrolment charge of 10/– per term should be imposed for all entries.
7 Entry should be by common entrance examination preferably at thirteen plus with the option to individual governing bodies to make variations to suit local conditions.
8 Since the Government capitation grant is to be withdrawn these schools would hereafter be referred to as direct aid schools.

Bridging the gulf

On the basis of these alterations it is recommended that a substantial number of old established Grammar Schools be transferred from the control of the Local Authorities to the independent sector, and, with the existing direct grant schools be given direct aid status with completely independent boards of governors. The governors of voluntary aided schools would be given the choice of electing to take direct aid status or remaining in the state system, in which case they would have to comply with individual local arrangements. Voluntary controlled Grammar Schools, whose governors are elected by the LEAs would be given direct aid status at the discretion of the Minister if he considered it was in the best interests of parents and teachers concerned in any particular area. This would be irrespective of whether the school formed, or was scheduled to form part of a comprehensive unit. All considerations being equal preference should be given to those schools who originally applied for but were refused direct grant status.

It is to be hoped that many of these direct aid schools will provide boarding facilities. It is often claimed, with ample justification that it is easier to inculcate a spirit of responsibility and leadership if children are resident at the school. At present state boarding schools are available to children of split families, or where parents are abroad; children from normal happy homes must not be at a disadvantage.

It is impossible at this juncture to estimate how many schools would become direct aid if these proposals were to be accepted. The ultimate aim should be at least one for each sex in every catchment area where sufficient numbers of children with the required ability and aptitude are available; however the British public is invariably averse to sudden radical change, and therefore progress must not be too hasty.

Many of these direct aid schools will be required to cater for the purely academic element who must be allowed to develop their skills in that field, but there is a strong case for providing similar facilities for the child with plenty of common sense but who is not academically brilliant. It is therefore reasonable to suggest that direct aid Modern (or Comprehensive) schools be developed in the course of time to suit this particular type of child.

Existing arrangements whereby certain Local Authorities provide a number of free places to Public Schools should be encouraged but local committees should be asked to apply the fixed income scale to all parents, as otherwise certain children would have an unfair advantage because of their place of residence.

The new state system

The present state system is far too cumbersome and complicated. At the instigation of the present Government changes have been rushed through with scant regard for the wishes of parents and teachers alike. Individual schools are rapidly becoming computerized educational sausage machines, which invariably restrict individual initiative and thus cause increasing frustration to all concerned.

If the above proposals are accepted, Local Authorities will find that within a few years they are relieved of the responsibility of administering a substantial number of former Secondary Schools which have become direct aid. They will therefore be able to operate a streamlined system with greater ease and efficiency than hitherto.

The Conservative party believes that Local Authorities should be allowed to arrange their own educational patterns, but in accordance with reasonably defined and flexible guide lines. There is no reason why this principle should be altered unless it is considered that educational standards are being seriously impaired.

Whilst to the Conservative way of thinking it would be preferable if Local Authorities were to offer parents the widest possible choice, e.g. Academic, Technical, Comprehensive or Modern, local committees must be allowed to arrange their own schemes even if this means 'all through' Comprehensive Schools. When sufficient direct aid schools are in operation there will in any case be a very wide degree of choice for parents.

In recent months there has been considerable support within the Conservative party for the introduction of sixth form colleges to cater for high fliers in the comprehensive system. It is presumed that the advocates of this idea intend that existing Grammar Schools be utilized for this purpose. Under the scheme already suggested high fliers will be catered for earlier and better in the new direct aid schools (the outstanding successes of direct grant schools hitherto is universally accepted) and consequently recourse to sixth form colleges should be confined mainly to rural areas where individual state schools are not big enough to have their own sixth form.

It is a matter of great regret that so many Modern Schools are currently being absorbed into the comprehensive system. In recent years the standard of these schools has been raised considerably, and, as has been mentioned earlier, there is a good deal of resentment on the part of parents when they are deprived of their autonomy.

It must be accepted that those children who are not academically inclined should be allowed to progress at their own pace. This cannot be achieved by comprehensive streaming. It is to be hoped that non-academic subjects (including arts and crafts) will be increasingly available to those who have neither the ability or desire to continue even a semi-academic course especially in the company of brighter children.

No true Conservative will tolerate undue interference from Whitehall, but in view of the chaos already caused by amalgamating Grammar and Modern Schools into Comprehensive units, it is, on balance considered advisable that a future Conservative administration should not only prohibit future amalgamations but should take immediate steps to dismantle those already in operation except in cases where the two schools are on the same premises or where it is considered that such alterations would be against the interests of all concerned.

No one would deny that these moves would cause temporary dislocation and a degree of criticism. If however a Government is determined to maintain the highest educational standards in the future it cannot tolerate measures which it considers undesirable and incapable of improvement.

In order to raise the general standard of education in Secondary Schools it is imperative that more attention is given to improving primary schools (many of which will become middle or intermediate schools where three tier patterns are adopted). The Conservatives have a very good record in this respect, but with the Government's mad rush to reorganize Secondary Schools and the subsequent financial cuts caused by devaluation, it is unlikely that the recommendations of the Plowden Committee will be fully implemented for some time. It is the duty of any Government to ensure that available funds are used strictly in accordance with educational needs. Primary Schools are a very high priority.

Educational finance

The streamlining of the state system should facilitate the ever thorny question of educational finance. Since the new direct aid schools would derive almost all their finance from parental and exchequer contribution, they would not be incumbent on Local Authorities to any extent. It is therefore logical that exchequer grants to the latter should be reduced if not correspondingly.

It is generally accepted that the exchequer should provide the lion's share of funds for essentially national services, while local projects should be mainly financed from rate revenue. There is therefore a good case for advocating that educational finance be reorganized on the following lines:

1 That 100% grants be provided by the exchequer for: University buildings, teacher training establishments and teacher training.
2 That grants of 90% be provided for all major capital works and large extensions to existing schools.
3 That a separate block grant be made on a fixed *per capita* basis (except in remote areas where additional funds are considered reasonable) for all other educational requirements including teachers' salaries. The balance of the funds would be found from rate revenue.

Rate borne expenditure would therefore be much more constant as between the various Local Authorities and this should prevent undue extravagance by some at the expense of others. The subsidy on school meals should be withdrawn altogether and reallocated to those who have proved need by individual application.

There should also be a much stricter allocation of funds for incidental allowances i.e. transport, stationery etc. Most Conservative Controlled Councils are carrying out a war on waste; funds allocated in the disguise of 'essential educational expenditure' and other supplementary estimates should be subjected to more vigorous scrutiny than hitherto.

The need to maintain large empires of administrative

staff to proliferate Parkinson's law must be discouraged, and the entire administrative machinery must be severely pruned within the bounds of reasonable credibility. Above all divisional executives, which have never served any useful purpose should be abolished altogether.

Parental contribution

Nothing is more calculated to bring about verbal atrophy in a politician than a suggestion, however ill founded, that he or she intends to bring back the means test. This is no doubt why so many Conservatives often appear to be ill at ease when discussing differential social benefits. The old means test was introduced during the economic blizzard in the mid thirties. Investigations were made, not only into the applicant's personal income, savings and possessions, but also the earning capacity of the families and close relations. At the time this scrutiny may have been justified, but nobody would wish to resort to the same measures today. As far as can be judged there is little or no antipathy on the part of fee paying parents at direct grant schools even when they see their affluent neighbours being presented with free places. On the contrary the enormous waiting lists suggest precisely the reverse. There is surely no more subjectivity of the individual in completing the fixed income forms than there is in applying for an income tax rebate.

With a substantial increase in the number of parents making contributions towards fees in accordance with individual circumstances, a more simple method of individual assessment would save a great deal of time and expense. Consideration therefore might be given to the idea whereby parents were assessed on their net annual income after allowances have been deducted. This would ensure that individual circumstances were fully taken into account. It would therefore be perfectly possible to calculate the maximum contribution for each parent (irrespective of how many children he or she had at the same school in any one year) on the basis of a varying percentage of net income. If the tax authorities were to provide on request forms supplying this information each year, a sliding scale could be prepared on a national basis. The contributions should be carefully assessed from time to time according to the general standard of living. These should neither be too high to cause unnecessary hardship, nor too generous to encourage indolence. The ambitious individual who is prepared to work harder and consequently earn more should not be too heavily penalized.

There would be, as indeed there is now, an overwhelming case for individual income tax relief either on the parental contribution or on the economic cost of a place at a state school whichever is the lower.

Putting the message across

Few will question the necessity to increase the supply of scientists and technicians to cater for the increasing technological advance in modern society. Few ought to question the value of administrators, educators, and leaders with a wide cultural background who are prepared to accept responsibility at all levels, and can thus maintain the richness and variety of our civilization.

If we as a nation are to continue to produce leaders in all aspects of our national affairs we must obtain the maximum amount of diversification in our educational system—available to all sections of the community. Whilst we must maintain and improve existing standards so as to provide equal opportunities, it is nevertheless of paramount importance to ensure that each and every parent has the greatest possible degree of choice for their children—this is fundamental.

The Conservatives are pledged, when they are returned to power, to cut taxation, to direct financial aid for social services according to individual need, and to give encouragement to the weaker members of society to stand on their own feet. These proposals are excellent; the existing policy for putting these principles into practice, especially in the case of education leaves very much to be desired. No political party that shrinks from carrying out reforms which it believes to be necessary is worthy of the respect of the individual elector.

There are many shrewd propagandists in the Socialist and Communist parties who realize that the greatest political danger they have to face is a policy of genuine Conservatism. Quite naturally it is in their own interests to employ such emotive expressions as fascist, racist, right-wing and means test in the hope that they will frighten the Conservatives into modifying their policies until there is little difference between the two—this is what they seek to achieve.

If the above proposals were to be accepted there is not the slightest doubt that accusations would be made that the Tories were determined to wreck the educational system by resorting to a policy of class prejudice. Every Socialist speaker would invent lies and distortions of the truth to frighten the more gullible electors.

This is where the Conservatives must stand firm in defence of their basic principles and beliefs, and when the dust settles there is little doubt that the new education act will be popular with the vast majority of the people.

It would appear that many of those connected with present day policies consider themselves to be perpetually committed to the idea that the decision to abolish fees in state schools, contained in the 1944 act is sacrosanct. Whilst it is logical these days that there should be a limited re-imposition of fees for parents in the middle and higher income groups it is surely better to achieve this by persuasion rather than compulsion. There is a growing dislike on the part of many of the electors of being treated like paupers and having their hard won earnings milched in taxation and rates. The increasing antipathy towards indiscriminate family allowances is a good example of this. This is why it is intended to give parents the opportunity of opting out of the state system if they so desire in return for a contribution within their resources towards the cost of the children's schooling.

It must be realized that parents of today are not in the least interested in the miasma of political statistics, however accurate and however impressive they may be to the party organization. Their only concern is for the future of their own children. They have sampled Socialism and they are regretting it; they are not prepared to stomach a weakened dose of the same mixture.

Basic principles must never be compromised, but they should be applied in such a way as to give the maximum diversification possible in order to ensure the sanctity of choice for the individual.

---

27   The essential conditions for the success of a comprehensive school

Rhodes Boyson

Just as truth may be the first casualty in war, it can be an early casualty in any social or religious outburst from men looking for simple solutions for the problems of their time. A search for complete equality, combined with a vague Rousseautic belief that all men left unhampered are good, has brought the pressure for full secondary comprehensification for social ends, for non-streaming and the adoption of so-called 'progressive' and non-academic methods of teaching or non-teaching. This egalitarian movement driven forward by adult men and women with the sad simplicity of the militant students has made reasonable men of varied opinions jump for cover and could eventually lead to a back-lash in which what is good in comprehensive schools in certain situations is ignored, and the enlightenment which can often come from the limited use of discovery methods is itself suspect.

'Progressive' errors

There is no doubt that the 11+ test made considerable mistakes, that very many secondary modern school pupils can undertake academic work and that the arrangements for transfer within the tripartite system were unsatisfactory. My five years as a secondary modern school class teacher and five as a secondary modern school head convinced me that the view that secondary schools were equal but different was poppycock. The recent Schools Council Enquiry into Young School Leavers shows that parents see schools largely as places which train their sons and daughters for better jobs and in this basic requirement the secondary modern schools were and would remain inferior to grammar schools. The only secondary modern schools which approached in status the grammar schools were the ones which copied the grammar school's academic ethic, sat external examinations and through good discipline, an attractive uniform, some exclusiveness of

Source: Black Paper, 2, Critical Quarterly (1969).

intake, and the creation of tradition, became respected locally. The secondary modern schools with progressive methods, rural science, much art and music and freedom of development endeared themselves to no-one other than the vaguely idealistic, unworldly and levitating types so well represented and influential amongst education officials and advisers.

A natural development of the changing situation in secondary education in the 1950s and early 1960s was that more and more secondary modern schools reacting to local circumstances built up their pride and prestige by winning considerable successes in 'O' and even 'A' levels of the GCE and this brought growing numbers in their fifth and sixth forms. This meant that the 11+ was becoming less critical and many parents became happy to allow their sons and daughters to join secondary modern schools where the academic pace was slower than at the local grammar school but where academic values were nurtured. Indeed it is probable that pupils with an IQ of 90–110 could actually achieve better academic results in such secondary modern schools where the pace was more suitable. The tripartite system was thus being bridged by secondary modern schools becoming partially academic institutions, the very thing the progressives and the slogan chanters were opposed to since they really wanted the end of academic institutions as such. The very last thing this lobby wanted was an increased emphasis on objective academic standards which could come from men of good-will in all parties supporting not only this new development in secondary modern schools but concluding, like many of us who taught at this time, that comprehensive schools based on increased academic opportunities could be the best way of maximizing the academic talent of the country.

Thus the social egalitarians stepped in and clamoured for comprehensive secondary schools for social and not academic reasons, gained the ear of the Labour

Party and, disastrously for British education and possibly the Labour Party, made comprehensives a party political issue. This and not the first edition of the Black Paper was perhaps the blackest day in British education in the last hundred years and the academics, the Tories and the hard-liners in the Labour Party were to blame for being outmanoeuvred. Neighbourhood comprehensive schools would in the view of the egalitarians end the class system by educating the Duke's son and the docker's son in the same school and, in an unstreamed school, in the very same class. It is a pity that the advocates for such schools did not look on the map and note that the Duke and the docker lived in different places.

Highbury Grove School: a comprehensive described

By this time I had been the head of a secondary modern, a creamed comprehensive and a grammar school and I looked for an opportunity to open a new comprehensive in new buildings to try to see what could be achieved both in academic results and in unifying in one large institution various types of pupil. In 1966 I got my opportunity and I was determined to develop a full academic tradition in a disciplined and regulated framework where the arts and sporting activities flourished but where boys, staff, and parents knew that the standards of achievement and the percentage pass rates mattered. I was well aware that education and schools were and should remain a preparation for life and should not be confused with life itself as believed by many sociologists.

The social egalitarians had done their work so well that to succeed as an academic comprehensive school the parents, staff and boys had to be brought to recognize clearly that in our school academic values mattered. This applied to all boys including the C streamers who should be encouraged to stay on into the fifth and sixth forms to sit CSE and GCE 'O' level subjects. Each head of department was made responsible for the standards of work in his subject and the level of examination passes. Examination results were published for all staff and Governors to see and the local press listed our successes in examinations and our university entries. Each department could follow whatever teaching method it wished provided it obtained good examination results. The timetable was so arranged that for the first three years there were 90 boys in an A band, 120 in a B band and 30 in a C band in each year. The A band equated with 'O' level possibility boys, the B band with CSE possibility boys and the C band boys required much remedial work. Movement between bands was facilitated by a common curriculum for all bands throughout the first three years apart from a second foreign language being introduced in the A band in the second year. All boys do one foreign language. A common syllabus and curriculum allowed for movement whilst subjects could be taught in greater depth in the A than the B bands and in the B than in the C bands. Each

department could decide if it wished to stream within the band as all the boys in one band went to the same subject together. All departments now teach unstreamed within the band in the first year and most stream in the second and third years within the bands. In the fourth and fifth years boys opt for subjects irrespective of band, go to subjects together and are taught in sets at their ability level.

Thus in our school academic disciplines and achievements are nurtured and respected, all boys are taught at their ability and speed and there is flexibility and movement within the school. The parents and area respect the achievements of the school. Under the ILEA system parents opt for any one school on their first choice and some 17% go to grammar schools, but we are oversubscribed in all ability bands, including the grammar school band. This is a clear vote of confidence in the academic possibilities of comprehensive schools where academic values are nurtured. That parents prefer their top ability boys coming to us rather than local grammar schools is significant of their view of our standards. Some thirty boys from our Islington school go to university and further education each year, some 45 sit 'A' levels, 90 sit 'O' levels and 100 CSE out of an intake of 240 in an area which is educationally deprived.

We desired the school to succeed academically but also to be a place where the individual mattered and felt that he belonged and wasn't being processed in a sausage machine. Civilized values and tolerant concern for individuals are vital. No person can know and be responsible for 1,400 boys. Thus we split the school into six vertical houses and a sixth form under separate masters with wide delegated powers. This was made possible since our buildings had six general purpose dining halls each with a master's study attached and a sixth form area with common room and coffee bar, separate sixth form study and classrooms and a sixth form master's room. We decided on a House and not year system since this facilitated minor sporting events, gave more of a family atmosphere and spread out the work of Housemasters equally throughout the year whereas under a year system each year master is busy or slack in turn. Each Housemaster has a half teaching timetable which he fulfils in the houseroom and he thoroughly knows the 200 boys in his House and their parents and he is responsible for the academic and social progress of all his boys. The house-room is home for all boys, opens at 8.30 a.m., for canteens at morning break, for lunch and recreation in the lunch break and until 5 or 5.30 p.m. in the evenings for reading and recreation. There are even weekly or twice weekly evening clubs run by staff and parents in each House. Parent associations exist only at the House level. Boys in each House enter from the same primary schools each year, each House taking schools with varied social backgrounds. Thus boys and parents know each other and boys and parents in other years in their House when they enter the school, and primary school staffs are attached to and take an interest in their houses. The House is a real unit and everything apart from academic teaching, school sport and school societies happens within it, and to the boy and parent it is the unit to which they belong. Sixth formers are for duties and leadership in Houses but they basically live in the sixth form block and the sixth form master supervises their academic courses and pastoral care. House Assembly twice a week is balanced by full School Assembly three times a week to make sure the school is pulled together.

All teachers apart from the four senior staff belong to Houses and take tutor groups within them. A mixed group of twenty-five boys from all bands in the first to the fourth year constitutes each tutor group and boys stay in the same group from the time they enter the school until the fifth year. Fifth year boys and sixth form boys have each separate tutor groups within the Houses, since at this stage they often need specialized attention and their interests are far removed from first year boys.

Thus pastoral units within the House are small and both boys and staff in tutor group and House belong to a unit small enough for all to know and be known. By this method we gain the academic and faculty advantages of a large school with the social unity of a small school: it is almost like collegiate life at Oxbridge alongside university faculties and lectures.

Conditions of comprehensive success

The conditions of our success academically and in pastoral care are I think five and these could have bearing when decisions are to be made as to whether or not to introduce a comprehensive system. These are:

1 basing the new school in an established area on a well-respected existing school;
2 erecting special buildings on the one site;
3 a balanced ability intake;
4 a school of at least 1,400 pupils;
5 good staffing both in qualifications and with senior men of sufficient stature to be able to take decisions yet delegate responsibility.

1. The general public gains over many years a firm impression of the various local schools, an impression which is probably the most valuable assessment of their worth and use to the community. If a comprehensive school is made from the expansion of a highly respected academic school then there is every likelihood that the local populace will associate the new school with its predecessor and this will provide it not only with a fund of goodwill but will establish it as an academic school unless or until the new school through its own failure destroys this reputation.
2. The need for buildings on one site seems obvious and to call one school a school separated in buildings up to and beyond a mile apart, and to walk children backwards and forwards in long crocodiles is to sacrifice children and schools for vague social ends. It is also important that a comprehensive school is built as

such and is not converted from buildings erected for another purpose. The specialist accommodation in each subject should be together so that a head of department can properly supervise and inspire his department, watch his staff and boys, and be able to move equipment easily between different classrooms. There must be pastoral living blocks in one place whether the school is organized on a House or year system. A proper House system cannot be organized without housemasters' studies opening on to their house rooms with full catering facilities and even attached toilets. Toilets scattered around the building to satisfy the wishes of far-away medical officers lessen the concentration of facilities in the houses and provide ideal opportunities for the work of some fourth year 'wreckers'. There must also be roomy corridors for the movement of hundreds of boys.

Pressure for the creation of a comprehensive system to satisfy political beliefs is producing a hotch-potch and completely confused secondary educational system in this country. It is not only the cynics who have noticed that the system adopted in most areas was not decided on merit but on the availability of buildings. This is an equal travesty of educational opportunity as was the fact that under the tripartite system the number of pupils considered suitable for academic education in any area in any year was almost always the number required to fill the grammar school places, be this 10 per cent or 60 per cent of the local children. The complete mix-up in the present system with children in different areas transferring at all ages into lower, middle and secondary schools will be a serious handicap to the mobility of labour now parents of all classes are concerned about the future of their children and come more and more to realize the chaos which is spreading further over the secondary scene.

3. A balanced ability intake is essential. Each local authority has the choice of a bipartite system of grammar and secondary modern schools or of full comprehensive schools in its area. One cannot have grammar schools alongside comprehensive schools or the latter will be nothing but misnamed secondary modern schools. This is the error of ILEA which could eventually damage very seriously the support for truly comprehensive schools. If ILEA intends to keep 10–15 per cent of its pupils attending grammar schools then it can probably organize twenty comprehensive schools in various parts of London and keep the rest as secondary modern schools. These would then all be viable within their own definition of being and this could possibly be the widest form of consumer choice that any authority could produce. At the moment in London there are probably 20 genuine comprehensive schools which are being seriously handicapped on intake to try to save enough academic pupils for the remaining huge secondary modern schools which are labelled as comprehensives to prevent their intake being worse than respectable secondary modern schools in other counties. This is

seriously affecting the name and future of comprehensive schools in London, and the furore which arose on this in the national and educational press last year was simply an attempt by the genuine comprehensive schools to claim a right to take an intake balanced in each ability group equal to the balance throughout London. This seemed and seems the only definition of a comprehensive school which has real meaning.

4. A comprehensive school with a sixth form must be large enough to carry some 45–50 boys in each of the lower and upper sixth on two and three 'A' level courses. This, as the recent ILEA report has shown, is the minimum number of boys required if ten to twelve 'A' level subjects are to be offered and taught in economic teaching groups. If there is no sixth form in a comprehensive school then such a school will not attract the best qualified graduates whose exciting teaching of lower streams brings boys to desire to become scholars from a young age. No sixth form would probably mean a slowing down of lower school learning amongst the brightest pupils.

An upper and a lower academic sixth of 45 boys each requires a school with an entry of 360 boys each year if one accepts the present figure that an eighth of an age group can take two or more 'A' levels. This will mean a school of 2,000. If one expects the percentage of boys capable of 2 'A' level courses to rise to 20 per cent in the next few years and settle at this figure then a school of 1,400 with a fully balanced ability intake would bring an academic sixth form of sufficient size. Such a school can be smaller in a favoured town like a south coast resort or would need to be larger in a town with bad housing and a history of deprivation. To attempt to meet the fear which people have of the size required for all-through comprehensive schools by cutting them to schools of below 1,000 is to court eventual failure or uneconomic sixth form classes whilst to break such schools up by horizontal divisions and transfers at 13, 14 or 16 is to destroy the unity of secondary school learning and bring another decline in educational standards. Good comprehensive schools generally mean large comprehensive schools and they can only be reduced in size at great risk. The fact that on the 1st January, 1967 the average size comprehensive school had only 800 pupils and a total sixth of only 57/58 students shows that this problem of the necessary size has not been faced.

5. Good staffing will only follow a balanced intake, a large academic sixth and good buildings. Recent books and articles have stressed the special attributes required from senior staff in the new large schools. Lack of men of calibre at the top can ruin a school even faster than can the search for gimmick progressive methods. It is arguable that weak men will search for such gimmicks to hide their inability to achieve objective and traditional standards of achievement. It is also arguable that the only heads and teachers who can introduce 'progressive' methods with satisfactory results are those who can best use traditional methods and don't need to change.

Comprehensive headships

Comprehensive school leadership, senior positions and class-room teaching ask a great deal from the men chosen. It is far more difficult to impress a unity on such a school than it is at other large schools like Manchester Grammar School, Dulwich College and Eton where the objects to be achieved for all pupils are narrower and better understood. A comprehensive head should be a scholar of repute respected by his academic staff and brightest sixth formers: he must be a fine administrator able to delegate and keep the lines of decision and communication in his school open and clear and he must have sympathy and understanding with all pupils from the brightest to the educationally sub-normal. I do not think that these demands of comprehensive school headship have really been generally understood and to transpose men into such headships who have limited experience of certain types of pupil or wide gaps of understanding or will-power will mean a break down and as at Rome under such conditions minor Emperors will arise in Egypt and Gaul according to the strength of the staff. It is possible that eventually a form of collective leadership will arise amongst Heads of Department and Housemasters but this has serious risks of too much talk, delay tactics, stagnation or power struggles and internal political intrigues. A leader must lead and a head cannot as yet be deposed and he must lead permanently.

Comprehensive teachers

Class teaching in a comprehensive school also demands great versatility. Unlike other professions a class teacher has to become the non-specialist. To take a fast 'A' level GCE group and then transfer to a remedial group or a group of fourth year rebellious leavers is to ask a great deal from a teacher. Staff may specialize in one section of the school but they must teach some time in the week at all levels or there will be banding of staff on a graduate/non-graduate level. The staff who joined the early comprehensives were zealots who were prepared for this but it is only the most skilled and dedicated teacher who can achieve such teaching with complete satisfaction, irrespective of where his specialization lies. No wonder some comprehensives do contract out by banding their teachers. The state school Housemaster with his wide powers is also a new form of teacher but well-trained and well-led I think that such men can be found in sufficient numbers: fewer of them are required than there are class teachers.

Perils of discovery methods and student power

One final point. In comprehensive and all types of schools a stand must be taken against the wide spread of discovery methods, integrated days, permissive approaches and all the new Gods. When the educational correspondent of *The Times* takes for granted that the sixth form of the 1970s will react against the restrictions of the traditional sixth form it is time to call a halt. Student power wants stopping before it becomes infant or baby power which would be no more ridiculous than some of the demands of student power. It is time our society realized the need for most of its traditional values, and decided to stand by them. Education, like welfare, is not a right but a privilege to be paid for by the rest of the community to which the student or welfare recipient owes an obligation.

Discovery methods though useful in stimulating the mind are dangerous if people grow up thinking that they can in their life-time discover what it has taken 10,000 years of human history to achieve. Men are arrogant to believe that this can be achieved for its only result would be to revive the dark ages. People must learn the theorems of Euclid and the grammar of a foreign language. Traditional methods of study are generally short cuts to knowledge. Many new methods have been introduced as experiment for experiment's sake and to help bored teachers, not bored children.

The attempt to achieve understanding by all pupils of the rules behind Mathematics and other subjects can often fail because most pupils rightly see education as a tool and not an end in itself and want to use logarithms for their future work without worrying as to why they give the right result. Most men and women will not become great scholars but simply wish to use knowledge. It is possible that some children are less

confused by drill than by explanation that is beyond their understanding. It is good that pupils should understand the reasons for long division but not if it means they get their sums wrong. A girl does not want to get out her 'discovery blocks' every time she wishes to pay her shopping bill; she simply wants to add up quickly. Tables in the modern age can perhaps be rehabilitated as 'programming the human computer'.

Learning needs discipline, not the atmosphere of a Butlin's Holiday camp. Great scholars, good salesmen, reliable operatives need to be trained from birth to finish a task, not to give up when they are bored, and they must realize the real prize is the final achievement, not fun on the way. The International Survey of Achievement in Mathematics showed that what matters is what goes on in schools not how you organize them. This is the real issue and the battle goes on from primary schools through secondary schools to universities. Comprehensive schools, like the new universities, are, however, new creations without the discipline of tradition and they need special care that they do not simply become platforms for every gimmick, every social theorist and every disruption of our age. If they become such platforms we shall never know whether they could have been a means of extending academic education to more of their age group, and in twenty years' time we shall be re-introducing a tripartite or bipartite system again.

Introduction to reading 28

In the 1970s attention has tended to turn away from the comprehensive education controversy to the less controversial but equally challenging problem of preparing for the raising of the school leaving age in England, Scotland and Wales to sixteen. What follows is an official report on the progress made by March 1972.

28 Progress report on RSLA

[Local education authorities were requested in a Circular to submit reports to the Department on their state of preparedness for raising the school leaving age (RSLA). Detailed analysis of the replies from all the English authorities shows a general picture of considerable activity and of soundly based preparations. In most cases the information given provides encouraging evidence of authorities' actions and intentions and there are a number of good local initiatives. This report summarizes the national position in England. Some examples are quoted to illustrate common activities.]

Buildings

Authorities were given considerable freedom in the way in which they could use their RSLA building allocation, and the reports show wide variations in practice. Many decided to provide special RSLA units, based on the Department's Building Bulletin No. 32. Suggestions in this Bulletin included designs for combining normal teaching accommodation with flexible teaching spaces, thus allowing specialist and practical facilities to be provided. Designs in the Bulletin were planned with the educational needs of non-academic 15-year-old children in mind. Nottingham and Redbridge for example have spent virtually all their allocations on this type of construction, and Hampshire have gone to pains to ensure that their new teaching spaces are 'as unlike conventional classrooms as ingenuity can make them'. Surrey have designed their own RSLA unit based on Building Bulletin 32, and this incorporates practical craft

Source: Reports on Education, HMSO (March 1972), 73.

accommodation, a general science laboratory, a project room, seminar/tutorial rooms, a study/library area and dining facilities. An alternative plan provides facilities for a girls' home economics room where group activities such as home decorating, child care, home budgeting and cooking can be undertaken. On the other hand, some authorities have felt that the accommodation needs of new fifth-form pupils can best be met by incorporating suitable provision in secondary major building projects. Northampton for example are planning to use all their allocation to provide one new upper school. In general, authorities have been planning their secondary major building projects in recent years with RSLA in mind. In such cases, it has sometimes been possible to use RSLA money to provide such extra facilities as a sports hall (in Bradford) and drama facilities (in Bexley).

A number of authorities have planned the use of their RSLA allocation to fit in with comprehensive reorganization. This has meant, in some areas, using it at primary schools, or at prospective middle schools, in order to prepare for raising the age of transfer to secondary education (and thus reducing the secondary school population). In Oxford, for instance, RSLA and reorganization are closely connected and some new building has been done at primary schools in preparation for a change in the age of transfer from 11 to 13.

Most authorities have submitted details of the timing of their projects. A few indicated that they may need to provide temporary accommodation in 1973/74 pending the completion of major projects but in the vast majority of cases building work is well in hand and will be completed in time.

A few authorities, such as Somerset and Bucking-

142

hamshire, are planning some of their RSLA projects in conjunction with Youth Service projects. This will provide schools with social facilities for use by pupils during the day, and by the Youth Service during the evening, and will help the schools become a focal point in the community.

Supply of teachers

Generally speaking authorities are confident that the pupil/teacher ratio can be maintained, and many plan to continue the improvement that has been taking place in recent years. A number have plans to begin enrolling the additional teachers who will be required before the effect of RSLA is felt, in order to allow time for curriculum development work and to facilitate the release of serving teachers for in-service training.

Some authorities refer specifically in their reports to their intention of appointing teachers to posts of special responsibility for RSLA, and to the recognition of these additional responsibilities by Burnham increments and in some cases head of department status. A few have stressed the need to recruit experienced teachers for work with RSLA pupils, and some indicate their aim to recruit teachers to work with junior children, thus releasing more experienced teachers for work with the RSLA age-group. Some authorities, such as Rutland and the West Riding of Yorkshire, have also appointed education officers or advisers to have specific responsibility for co-ordinating RSLA preparations.

A few authorities mention that close consideration is being given to the implications of RSLA for their school welfare services. Manchester, for example, consider that they will need additional education welfare officers, and they are also planning to strengthen the psychological and child guidance services. Cumberland also will be strengthening their school welfare staff. In the West Riding of Yorkshire the results of a survey on the causes of vandalism and violence in relation to disturbed pupils is expected to be useful, and an assistant education officer has been appointed to have special responsibility for this survey. The reports do not, however, refer to anticipated behavioural problems as being in any way a major issue. In general rural authorities do not anticipate disciplinary difficulties and one has gone so far as to comment that its principal publicity problem will be to offset the harmful effects of the 'gloomy predictions of national pundits' which it does not consider to be applicable to its circumstances.

In-service training

Some authorities have been active in the field of teacher preparation for RSLA for a number of years, and most are now embarked upon programmes of in-service teacher preparation. Durham's preparations, for example, began following the publication of the Newsom Report in 1963, and work in Somerset and Liverpool was initiated by the publication of Schools Council Working Paper No. 2 in 1965. RSLA preparation has fitted naturally into the in-service programmes of the larger authorities: Leeds and Wolverhampton are two authorities which supplied brochures of training activities, which in most cases take the form of conferences, subject meetings, and courses run by the Area Training Organization and HM Inspectorate. Most authorities have established RSLA working parties of teachers and advisers, and these have developed ideas for new courses and produced working papers for circulation to secondary assistant teachers. In some areas, inter-school discussion has so far been mainly for head teachers and senior assistants/heads of departments, and the dissemination of information to other assistant teachers involved has been their responsibility. On the other hand a few authorities, such as Cumberland and Southend, have held a series of conferences for many or all of the secondary assistant teachers likely to be involved in teaching the RSLA age-group.

Teacher training has often centred on the local teachers' centres, where outside speakers have addressed meetings, and teacher discussions on a variety of topics have taken place. Talks about those Schools Council projects particularly suited to the needs of RSLA pupils have been given in many areas by officers of the Schools Council, and several authorities had previews of the BBC series of RSLA programmes for teachers. These programmes are being used as the basis for discussion in a large number of areas and many authorities are using audio-visual equipment to bring the programmes to as many teachers as possible. The emphasis in the teacher training courses arranged by authorities is usually being placed on the need to plan for a coherent secondary course, to break down traditional subject disciplines, and to involve contact with the outside world wherever possible. As part of their training programmes, one or two authorities have arranged short exchanges for teachers in industry and have arranged visits to schools where new methods are already being tried.

Newcastle, Croydon and Bromley are among those authorities which have sent substantial manuals prepared by working parties of teachers and advisers which contain analyses of RSLA objectives and suggestions for new course material. These include books for both pupils and teachers, films, places to visit and outside speakers. Wolverhampton have sent two substantial documents, one a *Handbook of Outdoor Education*, and the other a *Handbook of Audio-Visual Resources*. Both contain much useful information.

The Schools Council

Schools Council working papers and projects have formed the basis of most of the preparations in the field of curriculum development. The initial impetus was given by the publication of Schools Council Working Paper No. 2 and the publication in 1971 of the summary of projects *Schools Council and the Young School Leaver* has supplied many authorities with ideas for new work in the curriculum development field. Many authorities are involved in one or more of the Schools Council projects. In Hereford-shire, for example, work is being done in schools on the humanities, secondary mathematics, secondary science, technology and home economics projects, while Stockport have work in progress in the humanities, technology, social education and 'mathematics for the majority' projects. In many cases Schools Council officers have been active in assisting with preparations for the centres and have addressed area conferences, and meetings at teachers' centres and individual schools.

Teachers' centres

There are now about 450 teachers' centres in England, and many have full-time wardens—often with considerable secondary experience. Most authorities report that centres are acting as the focus for training and discussion. A number are developing their role as centres for new teaching resources, particularly audio-visual equipment. Besides subject discussions and talks by outside speakers, centres arrange for relevant films to be shown, and demonstrations of new ideas and equipment to be given. Many are planning to act as viewing/listening centres for the BBC RSLA series.

New courses

A number of new courses have emerged, some aimed at examinations and others designed to cater for the non-academic fourth and fifth-year pupil. Many authorities recognize that new Certificate of Secondary Education courses—especially CSE Mode 3—can provide an incentive to pupils who would otherwise lack one. Bristol, for example, is formulating a CSE Mode 3 course in social studies, while in Wolver-hampton and Bath a CSE course in computer studies is planned. Most authorities who are now operating Mode 3 courses are seeking ways of extending their scope.

Entirely new courses that are not aimed towards examinations are also being developed in a number of areas. In Grimsby, for example, a course on 'cosme-tology' (the analysis and production of cosmetics) is very popular with girls, while in Birkenhead and Chester courses based on the study of personal relationships have developed.

Some areas have adapted the idea of courses for non-examination pupils with a view to enabling pupils to leave with some form of qualification. In Swindon in Wiltshire a 'record of personal achievement' scheme has been developed, and this is being adopted by other authorities including the Isle of Wight and Norwich, where the intention is to assess pupils for a 'certificate of endeavour'. Many of these courses are outward-looking in nature and wherever possible there is close involvement with the community—often by social work with young children or the elderly. Some reports stress the importance of the role that residential experience away from the home environment can play, especially with children from disadvantaged areas. Wolverhampton has a number of residential centres and standing camps in Staffordshire, Shropshire, and North Wales where a variety of outdoor pursuits are available, including mountain climbing, sailing, and canoeing. Cumberland, the Isle of Wight, and the ILEA are other authorities with a programme of residential experience in their own centres.

A few authorities make special mention of arrangements to allocate additional resources to assist with the new materials necessary for RSLA work. Bristol is allocating an additional per capita grant in 1972/73 for pupils likely to be affected by RSLA, and have plans to increase this in the next year. Wolverhampton have a regular 'journey and visit' allowance for all schools, and have recently tried an experiment of injecting additional capitation for resources into four disadvantaged secondary modern schools in pre-dominantly immigrant areas, while co-ordinating curriculum development between all four—an experiment that is considered to be working successfully. The West Riding of Yorkshire and the Isle of Wight are other authorities making special provision for additional resources, and Grimsby have plans to do so. Several reports refer to schemes for making additional resources available specifically to extend the range of outside visits for RSLA pupils—often enabling schools to purchase their own vehicles. Those authorities who do have plans for providing additional finance stress how vital they feel that additional resources—especially audio-visual facilities—will be in establishing new courses.

Guidance on careers and courses

Many reports stress the increasing importance of careers counselling for RSLA pupils. Most schools now have a staff member with special responsibility for careers guidance and many reports refer to close co-operation with careers guidance officers—often to arrange careers conferences and conventions for both pupils and parents, as well as visits and outside speakers. A number of reports speak of special efforts to incorporate in new building work suitable accommodation for careers interviews and displays of careers material, and it is clear that a general effort has been made in recent years to up-grade the status of the careers teacher in schools. Many authorities have area organizations of careers teachers, which meet regularly for discussion of local careers opportunities and meetings with local employers, and in some cases attachments to local industry to study conditions at first hand are arranged. Some reports such as those from Newham and Sutton speak of recently completed surveys of the careers guidance service which are resulting in the expansion of the service and the adoption of new procedures. In a number of areas there have been recommendations that careers work should feature regularly in the timetable, although this appears slow to develop.

Work experience schemes form part of many authorities' arrangements for careers guidance, and almost all those authorities who have schemes operating stress their desire to see legislative amendment make such schemes possible for 15-year old pupils after RSLA. Some authorities indicate that they would like to see developments in this direction as soon as the legal obstacles have been cleared away.

Most authorities already give information about post-16 courses to those in their last years at school. There are a number of different approaches to this, including careers officers in schools, youth tutors with responsibility for both careers guidance and counselling arrangements generally, youth employment service and careers guidance officers, and in some cases speakers from further education establishments who visit schools regularly. Practical methods of stimulating interest in the opportunities afforded by the further education service include visits, talks and acquainting pupils with the facilities in colleges by arranging linked courses with the colleges for the pupils.

Linked courses

Most reports mention that linked courses with further education colleges are already running and others say that courses are in the planning stage. The majority of linked courses have a vocational flavour, but they are neither full nor complete vocational courses and do not in themselves lead to vocational qualifications. The aim is to introduce young people, within the context of a continuing general education, to vocational knowledge, skills and techniques. The range of topics of the courses reported is very wide and often make use of local opportunities (for example, links with agricultural colleges in Norfolk and the East Riding of Yorkshire). Among the most common topics for linked courses relevant to the needs of RSLA pupils are engineering (including motor vehicle work), business studies, careers 'taster' courses, pre-nursing, and construction work. One authority (Sutton) is looking, in conjunction with neighbouring authorities, into the

question of how to develop a wider variety of linked course opportunities for girls, since many of the linked courses currently available seem predominantly, though not exclusively, of interest to boys. Little information about the length of courses is given, but it appears that most courses are arranged on the basis of one whole day, or one or two half-days, per week release. Some authorities are arranging their linked courses in module form—the advantage of this being that after following the first six week module a pupil can then choose either to go on to the next module in the series, or to begin a course in another subject area. An interesting example of this arrangement exists in Birkenhead where two further education units have been formed as part of the authority's reorganization programme—one to be based on a technical college and one on the college of art. One unit is to offer linked course modules of a vocational nature, while at the college of art there will be opportunities for pupils to do craft work and experiment in art forms not usually available at schools. A pilot scheme of the latter involving three-dimensional art, design, advertising, and drama has proved extremely popular.

Several authorities report on administrative machinery specifically to co-ordinate consideration and development of linked courses. Bristol, for example, have established three 'boards of studies' in different subject areas, each of which will contain a member of the careers advisory service. In the Isle of Wight a co-ordinating committee of high schools and technical college staff has been established, and in the West Riding of Yorkshire the county has been divided into four areas, each with its own advisory team.

Publicity and information

The Department has made leaflets and posters available to local education authorities, most of whom are also running their own local publicity campaigns.

Many of the reports refer to the use of the DES publicity material and most authorities will be concentrating on school-based publicity. A few authorities will be basing their own leaflet on the material in the DES publication, and will take the opportunity to give information to parents on local developments. Regular contact with parents at school speech days and open days will enable them to be informed of RSLA arrangements, and a number of authorities have already written to parents. Efforts are being made in many areas to interest the local press, radio and television services in RSLA.

Introduction to readings 29–32

The 1960s were also a time of revolutionary change in secondary education in the Irish Republic. The article from *Studies* by Sean O'Connor has been regarded since its publication as a key document in all discussions of the package of reforms generally accepted as resulting from the economic changes in the life of the Republic during the early 1960s. It is followed by the official statements of 1970, which sparked off the considerable controversy surrounding the notion of 'community schools', a form of comprehensive school, suggested (possibly as the result of World Bank proposals) for the development of secondary education in certain Irish towns. The controversies which arose concerning community schools raised once more important issues in the field of educational control, such as the extent of central ministerial control over individual schools, and the extent to which one particular religious denomination should be allowed to dominate decision-making in a community whose schools had previously been organized on denominational lines. It also, however, raised issues recalling those in England, in that many academically orientated schools found themselves being drawn into organizational unity with schools similar in make-up and aim to the English secondary moderns. The extract from The Dáil Reports (which precedes the document issued by the Minister) reflects the air of mystery and controversy which, the parliamentary opposition felt, surrounded the first appearance of a document with such far-reaching consequences.

During the period of political controversy and violence which has bedevilled the life of Northern Ireland since 1968 great emphasis has been laid on the political significance of religious segregation throughout the primary and secondary school systems. In his article, J. F. Fulton of St. Joseph's College, Belfast reminds us that such denominational divisions are not peculiar to Northern Ireland and are indeed found in countries such as Scotland, where political divisions tend to transcend denominational boundaries.

In an *Irish Times* report of 11 July 1972 Father Denis Faul (a well-known political and religious controversialist) claimed that the question of denominational schools was really twentieth on the list of the problems besetting Northern Ireland, though his view would hardly be shared by others.

In the short article which follows that of Fulton, Peppy Barlow draws attention to what she regards as the far greater problem of selective secondary education which has not so far been as widely abandoned in Northern Ireland as elsewhere in the United Kingdom.

29 Post-primary education now and in the future[1]

Sean O'Connor

The last five years have been a time of rapid change in the educational scene in Ireland, particularly at the second, or post-primary level. The process of change at post-primary level began in May 1963 when the Minister for Education, Dr P. J. Hillery, made public certain proposals affecting this level. These proposals were based on the decision to provide some measure of post-primary education for all children and rejected the notion of selection by eleven-plus examination or otherwise. There were four main proposals: the establishment of Comprehensive Schools; the provision of Regional Technical Colleges; the introduction of the Common Intermediate Certificate and of the Technical Leaving Certificate. The planning of the

comprehensive schools and the regional technical colleges began at once but because of the time-lag inherent in any building project the first three comprehensive schools—at Cootehill, Carraroe and Shannon —were not opened until September 1966, while the first six regional technical colleges will not open until September 1969.

Dr Hillery, too, initiated, in 1962, the most important investigation of Irish education yet attempted. With the co-operation of the Organization for Economic Co-operation and Development (OECD) he set up a team of experts to survey and report on the Irish educational system and to assess the future demands for educational facilities at the different levels. The report of the team—*Investment in Education*—has received international acclaim. For us at home it has signposted the direction of educational reform and, by highlighting our deficiencies,

Source: Studies (autumn 1968), 233–51.
Sean O'Connor is Assistant Secretary, Department of Education, Dublin.

has offered a challenge that cannot be ignored.

In January, 1966, Mr George Colley, then Minister for Education, sent a personal letter to the authorities of each secondary and vocational school in the country asking for co-operation between the two existing post-primary systems and for a conscious effort to break down the barriers which had hitherto existed between the two systems. Following on this, the Department of Education undertook a survey of post-primary educational facilities in the country and produced a report for each county. The report supplied a substantial body of statistics about actual pupil enrolment in each school centre, about the kind and extent of the facilities provided in each centre, about future enrolment and facility requirements. In addition, the report offered specific suggestions for co-operation between schools and set out the criteria on which viability would be judged. These reports were circulated to all school authorities and discussed on two fronts: at county-level meetings where all the educational interests in the county were represented and at local meetings where the problems posed for particular areas were discussed in more detail. In this way, the school authorities and the public generally were involved in the educational planning process and a channel of communication was opened up between the Department and the local interests immediately involved. These confrontations were tremendously valuable in that they provided a two-way exchange of information and ideas and helped to promote an identity of interests and a common approach to the task of meeting future requirements and finding acceptable solutions to the problems exposed.

The 'O'Malley Scheme'

The Investment in Education Report has stressed the fact that participation in post-primary education was very strongly influenced by two factors: (*a*) the social group to which the child's parents belonged and (*b*) the distance of the child's home from the nearest post-primary school. To overcome the disabilities involved for children who are adversely affected by these factors and in order to facilitate the implementation of the Government's declared intention of raising the school-leaving age to 15 by 1970, the late Mr O'Malley introduced his Free Post-Primary Education Scheme, the main features of which were: (*a*) the payment of a supplemental grant to secondary schools which agreed to discontinue charging school fees; (*b*) the abolition of school fees in comprehensive schools, vocational schools and secondary tops; (*c*) the provision of free transport for children living more than three miles from their nearest post-primary school; (*d*) the provision of free books to those children whose parents might otherwise find it difficult to meet the cost involved.

The increase in participation at post-primary school level in recent years can be noted from the following table:

ENROLMENTS IN POST-PRIMARY SCHOOLS

Year	Secondary schools	Secondary tops*	Vocational schools	Total
1957–8	66,221	6,021	23,816	96,058
1962–3	84,916	6,789	29,689	121,394
1966–7	103,558	7,125	38,200	148,883
1967–8	118,557	6,636	41,666	166,859

* A 'secondary top' is a small secondary-level department grafted on to an existing primary.

The same trend can be noted by looking at the situation from another angle. The number of pupils who left primary schools and who were not subsequently enrolled in post-primary schools has been estimated as follows:

School year	Number	School year	Number
1964–5	18,000	1966–7	10,000
1965–6	15,000	1967–8	5,000

New Leaving Certificate programmes

Mr Lenihan has recently announced agreed proposals in regard to the revised structure of the Leaving Certificate programme. The main purpose of the revision was to broaden the scope of the programme, particularly in regard to technical and commercial subjects, and to introduce a modest degree of specialization at this level. Related subjects will be arranged in groups and each student will be required to study a number of subjects (at least three) from within a single group. Subject grouping will be introduced on a voluntary basis from 1969, with the intention that grouping will be compulsory from 1972 onwards. However, before compulsory grouping is introduced the whole question will be re-examined in the light of experience of its voluntary operation. A three-year Leaving Certificate course is considered desirable but it was thought unwise to introduce a three-year course at this stage as it might militate against the greater participation at senior-cycle level which we seek. A third-year course and examination—to be known as the Advanced Certificate course—will, however, be provided for examination from 1972 onwards for those who wish to take it on a voluntary basis. In the light of our experience of this measure, it will be possible to consider at a later stage whether the duration of the Leaving Certificate course might be extended to three years. The standard of the third-year course and examination will be such that it should be undertaken only by those who obtain high gradings at the Leaving Certificate examination and the Minister is leaving it to good sense and school counselling to decide as to the students who will proceed to this course.

Guidance service: building plans

The Department's Psychological Service has established the nucleus of a guidance service in the state comprehensive schools and in secondary schools which offer comprehensive facilities. The service is being extended by the recruitment of additional educational psychologists and will be available for all post-primary schools eventually. The guidance service is being organized as a two-tier service, the first tier in the school being provided by a member of the school staff selected by the school for the purpose and the second tier by the Department's psychologists. Instruction to the selected teachers is being given by way of a series of summer courses and subsequent on-the-job training.

The developments of the past five years have created a considerable demand for additional accommodation and this accommodation has to be provided at a time when much of the existing accommodation, particularly on the secondary school side, would also need to be replaced. Projected capital expenditure over the next five years in the building of secondary, vocational and comprehensive schools comes to the not inconsiderable total of more than £20 million and to that we must add another £7 million for the new Regional Technical Colleges.

A programme of this magnitude makes very heavy demands on our available capital resources and we must ensure that the best possible return is obtained in terms of school places provided. A Post-Primary Building Unit has been established within the Department. This Unit handles all post-primary school building and will have available to it both educational and architectural expertise. The establishment of the Unit enables a unified approach to be made to the planning of all schools, will facilitate the standardization of building procedures and will make practicable an overall system of cost planning and control. The Unit has drawn up a list of priorities from the hundreds of building applications at present before the Department and is implementing a phased programme over the next five years, dealing first with cases of greatest need. Prefabricated or system building will have a significant role to play and there should be greater opportunity for the development of such systems within a major building programme. The feasibility of introducing standardized components and having bulk tendering for such components is under consideration. The Unit will pay considerable attention to questions of design and lay-out. For our schools of the future, greater flexibility in the use of classroom space will be essential if the introduction of new techniques such as group-teaching and team-teaching is to be facilitated. Ideas are only now evolving but the signs are that we shall be moving more and more away from the idea of one teacher/one class and towards the idea of larger or smaller groups as occasion may demand. All of this means that in planning future school buildings we must start with the basic idea of a series of large spaces capable of being used as such or of being divided to meet the needs of groups of varying sizes.

University student grants

Mr Lenihan has also recently announced a new scheme of student grants at university level to replace existing local authority scholarship schemes. The main purpose of these grants is to ensure that no pupil of ability will be denied access to third-level education because of the inability of his parents to pay for it. To be eligible for assistance a pupil must obtain four honours at Leaving Certificate and the size of the grant varies according to the income of the child's parents, allowance being made for the number of children in the family. The maximum rate of grant is £175 a year for those living in or near a university town and £300 a year for those in other areas. Where the family income is £1,200 a year or less, the full grant will be payable. Thereafter the grants are scaled downwards according to income and size of family. Criticism has been offered that the scheme does not go far enough: the important thing is that it is there and that it has been drafted in such a way that any of its provisions can be modified as circumstances warrant. It is estimated that approximately 1,000 pupils will benefit under the scheme in the academic year 1968–9. This compares with approximately 275 local-authority scholarships awarded in 1967–8.

A full-time Audio-Visual Aids Officer has recently been appointed in the Department and an Audio-Visual Aids Unit is in process of being built up. In addition to providing the Department with expert advice on audio-visual aids, this officer is available to advise school managers, teachers and local education authorities on all aspects of teaching aids. A sum of £10,000 has been provided in the Department's Estimates for 1968–9 for the introduction on an experimental basis of audio-visual aids in a number of selected schools.

The Department is encouraging research into various aspects of education. A sum of £20,000 has been allocated for this purpose in the current financial year. These funds are allocated to university departments or other interested bodies to aid specific research projects. A committee has been set up to assess applications for aid, review progress of grant-aided projects and consider means of disseminating the results obtained. Projects under way at present relate to examinations, social attitudes to education (employers, schools, parents), disadvantaged children and building design.

For the first time, a technical assistance scheme has been introduced. The scheme provides for the payment of the cost of projects involving visits abroad by officers of the Department or by persons nominated by managerial bodies and teachers' organizations for the purpose of attending non-Government type conferences and studying or investigating any particular facet of education in other countries. It also provides for the bringing in of experts from abroad to advise on particular educational problems. The assistance available under the scheme makes it possible for those involved in education in this country to keep abreast of developments abroad and to study such developments on the spot with a view to judging their relevance to our circumstances.

The aim of recent developments

All of these developments are very desirable in themselves but have they any overall aim or purpose? The answer is that they are directed to the achieving of two fundamental purposes which each of the last four Ministers for Education has stressed from time to time. These are (1) equality of educational opportunity for all and (2) the fashioning of education so that it is responsive to the aptitudes and interests of the individual pupil. The first aim has little value without the second.

Let us look at it first from the point of view of the pupil. Arrangements have been made under which pupils will normally advance to a higher grade each year in the primary school and no pupil will be held back in the same grade more than once in his primary-school career. With the raising of the school-leaving age to 15-plus, this will mean that the great majority of children will have at least three years' post-primary education and no child will have less than two years in a post-primary school. This, then, is the first consideration, that *all* children must be catered for at the post-primary level. Another consideration is that traditionally our secondary schools have concentrated heavily on academic subjects and our vocational schools have, similarly, devoted their attention mainly to practical subjects. A child who went into one or other type of school had to take what it offered and if he proved unsuitable or had no bent for what he was doing, the only alternatives offered him were either to leave full-time education altogether or to slog ahead at something from which he derived little benefit. The comprehensive school idea is designed to overcome these difficulties. A broad curriculum embracing academic, scientific, practical and artistic subjects is provided. A pupil has a choice of options within each of these areas and the three-year period up to Intermediate Certificate is a period of observation during which a pupil's aptitude and ability can be assessed by his teachers with the professional help of the Department's psychologists. At the end of the Intermediate Certificate course meaningful advice can then be tendered to the pupil and his parents, advice which they can take into account in deciding what he should do next.

Re-organizing the school systems

Let us now look at this from the point of view of the organization of our schools. The provision of a broad range of subjects necessarily entails the provision of adequate facilities for the teaching of those subjects, in terms of teachers, building and equipment. The availability of options means that the standard class size will be broken down into smaller units for particular optional subjects. If we are to make any reasonable attempt to get the best use of available resources,

there must be a minimum size below which a school cannot be regarded as viable. The standard suggested by the Department in the county reports already referred to was very modest indeed, a minimum annual intake of 50 pupils for a junior-cycle school (up to Intermediate Certificate level). However, small schools have been traditional in Ireland, primarily because co-education was frowned on but partly because of the division of post-primary education into two separate and water-tight systems and partly because of the necessity of having schools readily accessible to pupils. With the introduction of the free-transport scheme, the force of the latter consideration is considerably weakened and the developing spirit of co-operation between our two post-primary systems should in time eliminate the complications arising from having two systems. A fair measure of success has attended the efforts to rationalize our post-primary school system. A number of very small schools have closed and various ways and means have been devised by which secondary and vocational schools can co-operate effectively with one another in order that the resources and expertise of both systems may be pooled to provide comprehensive facilities for the children of an area.

The introduction of the Common Intermediate Certificate eliminated the dead-end aspect of vocational school education which, heretofore, was seldom more than a two-year full-time course leading to the Day Group Certificate. These schools now provide a wide curriculum leading to Intermediate Certificate. The establishment of the Regional Technical Colleges and the inclusion in the new Leaving Certificate programme of the science, applied science and commerce groupings will further accentuate the trend towards a wider curriculum in the vocational school. Both of our post-primary school systems now provide outlets to higher education and growing co-operation between them will be essential, particularly at Leaving Certificate level.

The very wide range of subjects covered by the five groupings of the new Leaving Certificate programmes will emphasize the necessity for larger school units and for close co-operation between Secondary and Vocational schools. If guidance work is to be effective in practice, it will mean that all five groupings must be readily available in each area and that pupils must not be forced to take a particular grouping because the one of their choice is not available in the centre which they have been attending. This problem is under consideration at present and the Department's thinking on it will be set out in a second series of county reports which will be issued shortly. These reports will be discussed with the school authorities and with parents at local level and it is hoped in this way to secure a broad measure of agreement on what requires to be done. It seems clear, however, that a number of centres which have traditionally taught up to Leaving Certificate level will not be large enough to service the full grouping demand of the new Leaving Certificate programme and that some of them will in future be junior-cycle centres only. Even in centres with a reasonably large number of pupils, co-operation between secondary and vocational schools will be essential and the question of establishing senior-cycle schools in such centres under joint management may well have to be considered (see Appendix).

The greater identification of schools with the areas in which they are located would have obvious advantages from the point of view of social and community development. The equipment provided in the schools is too often not available outside of ordinary school hours and it seems wrong that such fine facilities should be locked up early in the evening and altogether over the holiday periods. Were such facilities made available to both children and adults outside of ordinary school hours they could be of considerable benefit to the community generally. One would hope that the possibilities of this will be more widely appreciated from now on and genuine efforts made to overcome such practical difficulties as may arise.

The future

What of the future?
Before venturing on to that quaking bog I must insert a personal note. Up to this point I have tried to set out the reforms introduced by the four Ministers who have held office since 1963, and to give the reasons for their policy decisions. From this point on I am speaking my own mind and the responsibility for everything I say is mine alone. Neither the Minister for Education nor his Department is accountable for any opinion, speculation or forecast that I may offer.

Let us take first of all the raising of the age of compulsory attendance at school. The Government has indicated that it intends to raise the age limit from 14 to 15 by 1970. Already, about two-thirds of the 14–15 age group are in school—the proportion may be higher when the 1967–8 statistics are available—so that the provision of school places for the remainder will not be beyond us. The real problem is with us already: how to cope with the greatly increased participation in second-level education in relation to the kind and quality of instruction required for the varying interests and aptitudes of a greater ability span. What about the children who are so disenchanted with our educational system that by the age of twelve all they want from it is to get out? What can you hope to do for them in the three years to 15 during which the law will require them to remain at school? You can, if you dare, let them linger in the back ends of primary classes until the day of release comes; this we do now and shrug off our responsibility by reminding ourselves that they had equal opportunity with all the others. Had they, though?

Reform of primary schools

Reform must begin at the primary level because here the foundation is laid. We must accept and act on what we all know—that children differ in capacity, in their approach to learning, in their motivation towards schooling, in their home environment, in drive and ambition. Education must be centred on the individual child; but do we do this when, in the face of the diversity offered by any substantial group of children, we provide a syllabus so detailed that limits are drawn and standards set for each of the six grades of primary education. I suspect that my ideal primary school is a place of organized chaos because the more I think about it the more difficult I find setting limits to its activities.

We have buried without regret the Primary Certificate examination. Let us now bury, again without regret, the present National School Curriculum. Of course, we must have a curriculum. Before he leaves the primary school a child should have some awareness of God and of basic morality; he should have learned to read, to write, to enumerate; he should have learned to use his hand as well as his eye; he should know something about his community, his place in it and his responsibility to it, the places of others in it and the community's place in Irish society. That should be enough and we should fashion our new curriculum around these objectives but so draw it that every child can be stimulated and encouraged by it, whether he gallops, trots, ambles, walks or crawls. This is not an easy task, but it is a task that must be faced.

But a new curriculum is not enough. We must look critically at the physical structure of our schools. Can we make any real progress in the stimulation and development of initiative, however flexible the curriculum we offer, in the face of the solid concrete with which we surround each little group of children? We must really experiment in school building, not just juggle boxes around. We have done very little as yet. Perhaps this was to our advantage because there must be coincident flexibility in curriculum and teaching methods as well as in physical structure in any such experiment.

Teacher training

Finally, and most important of all, there is the teacher. He must control, direct and develop the initiative and creative activity of each of his pupils and this demands that he himself be adaptable and prepared to experiment in his approach to teaching. If his training was formal and stilted, he cannot be otherwise than formal and stilted in his teaching.

Ever since World War II there has been a continuing evaluation of the aims and objects of education and of the methods used in imparting it. The demands created by the new sociological patterns now emerging, the demands of an increasingly technical society—all these bear down to a greater or lesser degree on educational activity at all levels. The patterns are continually changing.

To meet the demands of this changing society new

experiments in teaching methods and in learning programmes are proceeding; new theories are being offered, new technical aids appear. The results of all these activities are being channelled through the teacher to the student. The teacher must therefore be aware of and understand what is going on so that he can transfer to his students the benefits of the new ideas.

Because of the increasing demands on the teacher a tendency is developing to extend more and more his initial training. This, to my mind, is a mistake. The emergence of new concepts in science, the social and technological changes—all are so profound and are happening so rapidly that, if the educational sector is to keep pace with them, once-for-all training for the teacher can no longer be tolerated. Many of the methods and skills he has learned will become out-of-date in a short time. An adequate course of initial training must be given—and lest I be misunderstood, I do not regard a course of combined personal education and teacher training, covering a mere two years, as adequate—but this should be followed at stated intervals, say five years, by intensive refresher courses covering two to three months.

There are about 20,000 teachers in the first and second levels of education, so that the re-training programme would be a considerable undertaking. Only an institute of education in a university, adequately staffed and with its own research facilities, could offer re-training courses of this kind on a sufficient scale.

Leaving Certificate courses

The curriculum in the second-level schools has, as I have said earlier, been under examination in recent months. There has been very little fuss about the new syllabuses for the Intermediate Certificate Examination but the proposals for change in the structure of the Leaving Certificate course have come under heavy fire, particularly from certain members of the teaching staff of the National University.

Criticism is necessary and must continue; but it must be reasoned and constructive criticism, not just a reactionary cry against change. Because there must be change. We are in a new situation and what was passable before—though no more than that—is no longer so. We need the skills and abilities of all our people, and we must foster and develop these skills and abilities by all the means in our power. Because we have taken our stand on this and have widened the range of subject options for all students, the cry has been raised that we are neglecting the clever student. Students are educated in schools and I have yet to hear of any school that neglects its clever students. It may not offer the desirable options but it does not spare any effort in encouraging the clever student. The passion for streaming that grips our Irish schools springs, as I think, from the fear—in my view mistaken—that the bright students might be retarded if mixed with students less bright.

I do not say that the present proposals of the Minister in regard to the Leaving Certificate course and examination offer the answers to our problems. Time will tell. But they are a radical departure from the system that held sway for forty years and because continuing re-appraisal is implicit in the proposals one can be hopeful about the future. Indeed if there is radical curriculum reform at primary level—as there must be—then there will be need for further and perhaps more radical curriculum and syllabus reform at both Intermediate and Leaving Certificate level.

Examinations

Public examinations are the bogeymen of the second-level system. There are two—the Intermediate Certificate examination at the end of the third year and the Leaving Certificate examination at the end of the fifth year. They are achievement tests, or, more accurately, memory tests, and their form is totally unrealistic, particularly in the language area. Who, in real life, would contemplate writing an essay or attacking a problem without the appropriate reference material? Who cares whether or not the student can name the speaker of that immortal line, 'I am not bound to please thee with my answers'? We have gone to absurd extremes in memory testing; it would be a good thing now to give priority to comprehension and the intelligent use of information.

We are not alone in our dissatisfaction with the form and manner of examinations. Even as tests of achievement they are not particularly good while they are almost useless as predictors of initiative and creativity. But we must have some form of examination—at least until technological progress offers something better—and so experimentation in examination techniques must be undertaken. Fortunately, other European countries are engaged in reappraisal and experiment and we can profit from their experience and, as we should, join in the reappraisal and experiment. We could do this at Intermediate Certificate level for a start. It would be interesting to set up a limited experiment involving teaching assessment, the traditional examination process and, for example, the 'multiple answer' assessment system. Our difficulty is, of course, that we have very few people skilled in the preparation of multiple-answer tests; we will remain that way until we begin to use these tests.

I look forward with great interest to the results of the research into certain aspects of the Leaving Certificate examination which is being undertaken, with the support of the Department of Education, by Rev. John Macnamara, C.M., Ph.D., Lecturer at St Patrick's Training College, and Dr George Madaus of Boston College. The report is expected before the end of the year. I look forward, too, to the report of the seminar on examinations to be held in Oxford in July this year.

Nobody would essay to forecast at this point how

the quality of education will be improved in the future. We can, and we must, look for greater efficiency in the factors that bear on the quality of second-level education. We must improve the training and re-training of teachers; we must offer a wide choice of subject options to the pupil; we must offer an adequate guidance service to pupil and parent; we must provide an adequate supply of teaching-aids and equipment. At all times the curriculum and syllabus must be kept under scrutiny because these must accommodate themselves to the expansion of knowledge and, in addition, reflect the social needs of the community. To the extent that we do these things so can we expect that the quality of the education provided will improve.

University entrance and school programmes

I have no intention of discussing higher education in this paper but there are two aspects of university entrance requirements which make me uneasy about the success of our plans to expand curriculum choice so as to cater for varying aptitudes and interests. The first is the Local Authorities (Higher Education) Act, 1968, under which grants from State and Local Authority funds are to be made to students who obtain a general pass and four honours at the Leaving Certificate Examination. There is a means condition attached, also, but that is not my concern here.

Four honours is a reasonably demanding standard as last year's result would show; of the 17,000 candidates who took the Leaving Certificate Examination in 1967, 1,923 got four honours. For all but the very bright, four honours will be a tough task. While I would reject in present circumstances any suggestion that the standard should be lower, I am a little apprehensive of the consequent effect on the schools. Parental pressure will be strong—and the schools' public image will be an added incentive—to limit the range of subjects at Leaving Certificate level to the minimum—five—which the student must present for the examination. Already, the concern for examination results overrides all else in many of our schools. Now that the prizes have been increased fourfold and the competition is no longer between pupils but 'against the clock', the hunger for examination results will be fiercer than ever, I fear. What is to happen to the non-examination subjects and the other activities that are characteristic of the good school? These, much more than rigid examination syllabuses, offer scope for the development of enterprise and initiative in the student whether through project or other activity outside formal instruction—and these qualities are the main determinants of future success in adult life. Perhaps I am unduly pessimistic but I do not see how, without help, a school will be able to hold out against the pressures for the exclusion of all but the examination subjects. The school must get support and it seems to me that support must take the form of regulation.

Regulations should be imposed only where there is no alternative and where the need is compelling.

Should my fears prove well grounded then the need will be great enough to warrant remedy by regulation. The average weekly school time is about 28 hours. The regulation I suggest would prohibit giving more than, say, four and one-half hours (six class periods of 45 minutes) of that time to any single subject. An exception might be made for honours mathematics because this, if statistics are any index, is the toughest course of all and is consequently in the greatest danger of being shunned. Already only a small number of applicants take the honours papers in mathematics; still fewer reach honours standard.

I am well aware that the regulation would be ignored or circumvented by some schools: I am suggesting it because I think it might be useful to those school authorities who believe that there is more to education than examination results.

My second point concerns the university entrance examination. The National University accepts for Matriculation only those subjects in which courses are offered at the university. This seems quite fair and sensible at first sight, but let me point out that during his undergraduate course no student takes all five subjects offered for Matriculation. I am not pleading for a reduction in the number of subjects: I am asking that all subjects of the Leaving Certificate have equal value for purposes of Matriculation. The famous Texan surgeon, Dr de Bakey, said in an interview recently that his great skill was due in considerable part to the fact that from an early age his mother taught him to sew very neatly. Sewing is part of the Domestic Science course for the Leaving Certificate. Again, would anybody deny that a good course in Art would be useful to a future architect, for example? Art and Music are, to my mind, among the most valuable courses a school can offer but Art is not acceptable for Matriculation. I could go on.

The National University of Ireland requires the following subjects for Matriculation—Irish, English, Latin or Greek or a modern continental language and any two others from a selected list. Because of the prestige of the university and because a very substantial number of Leaving Certificate pupils aspire to university education the Matriculation requirements excessively dominate the curriculum. There is little point in encouraging a potential university student to develop his interests and aptitudes if the subjects of his interest do not tally with university requirements. The banner of the 'broad general education' was unfurled again when the proposals for grouping at Leaving Certificate level were announced. This grouping is on three subjects out of the six or seven usually taken and a choice of five groups is offered. N U I demands a concentration on three out of five subjects and that in one group only—the language group.

Co-education

One of the issues which has assumed considerable importance because of our pressure for larger schools is that of co-education. I feel I should give some space to it.

Ireland and East Germany are, as far as I can ascertain, the only two countries in Europe where the population is stationary or falling. Ours has been falling because heretofore there has not been sufficient job-opportunity for all our people. Our industrial growth rate for the past year (about four per cent) was satisfactory but the increased production required to maintain that growth, and thus to reverse the population trend, will make ever greater demands on the abilities and technical skills of our people. Already the signs are there that in a few years the Irish educational sector will not be able to meet the demands of an increasingly technical society.

Our educational system—at both primary and post-primary level—has developed as a hodge-podge of very small units. Transport difficulties do not provide the complete explanation because in many of our towns we find three or more Secondary Schools together with a Vocational School. To seek to provide in each of these small units adequate facilities for language, science and technical studies would be sheer extravagance. Our national resources are modest and we must not waste them. Yet, even if we dare ignore the rights of the child, our national interest demands that these facilities be available to all our children.

It is beyond the potential of the country to sustain inadequate schools—and adequacy must be assessed by economic as well as by educational criteria. Schools must be brought together so as to establish units viable by present-day educational standards. Single community schools are the rational requirement in most centres outside the large urban areas. Yet, though we have made progress in some respects in the matter of co-operation, we have made no significant gains in our drive for community schools. Maybe we did not try hard enough last time.

One of the major obstacles has been the attitude of Church authorities to co-education. In some dioceses it is not tolerated at all; in many of the others it is a thing of last resort. Religious orders, by and large, oppose co-education. It is not uncommon to find two girls' secondary schools and a boys' school in a centre where the pupil potential is such as to warrant only one school. The difficulty here is apparent at once: a single school would make the presence of all but one of the Orders unnecessary and the natural reluctance to leave a community where one had given service for a long time is understandable. Nowhere, yet, has joint management of a single school been attempted by two religious orders, though, in two areas to my knowledge, there are proposals for such joint management.

It seems clear that education is being adversely affected by institutional considerations not related to education. There are arguments for and against co-education but these are relevant only in centres where the pupil potential is large enough to enable the school authorities to follow their own inclinations, without disadvantage to educational objectives. My concern is with the very many areas where the educational advantage requires co-education. To persist in opposition to co-education in such areas is entirely unreasonable, and detrimental both to the individual student and to the community. It is significant that, in a number of dioceses, co-education is now acceptable in practice.

Church and State in education

Finally I come to what I think is the most important of all the problems facing us. In a general and imprecise way I would term it the problem of Church/State relations in respect to education. It is not a very satisfactory term but it will serve to indicate the principal parties concerned.

In the school year 1966–7 there were 586 recognized secondary schools in the country and 485 of these were conducted by religious of the Catholic Church. These 485 schools had a pupil population of 91,909 out of a total pupil population of 103,558. In the same year the number of secondary teachers receiving State salary—including probationers—was 4,891 and of these 2,728 were lay teachers; there were, in addition, 1,986 unfilled posts. A small number of these unfilled posts may have arisen because teachers of specific subjects were not available, but I believe I am on firm ground in suggesting that the great bulk of the vacancies arose because the religious authorities were not able to staff them with their own people and could not afford to take lay teachers because of the obligation to pay school salaries of £300–£400 each.

Thus, though they have charge of about 89 per cent of all Secondary school pupils the religious bodies provide only about 31 per cent of the authorized teaching power. The figures I give about teachers relate to all secondary schools but it is safe to assume that even in their own schools the percentage of religious to total staff would be less than 40 per cent if all posts were filled. It is easy enough to explain how this situation arose.

Prior to 1963 the State gave no specific contribution towards the building of secondary schools. The Church provided the great bulk of the schools and put into them all the religious that were available. Because school buildings are costly, particularly when designed to cater for large numbers, few laymen could afford to compete, though a small number did (I speak only of schools for Catholic pupils). The lay schools usually had their beginnings in dwelling-houses and catered for small numbers. In 1966–7 there were 56 secondary schools under Catholic lay management with a total enrolment of 5,231 pupils.

It is right, then, to stress that were it not for the Catholic Church the provision of secondary education would have been very scant indeed. One must readily concede that great sacrifices were made by Religious Orders for the benefit of Irish education.

Since 1963 the situation has changed. Now the State

will give 100 per cent grant on approved building costs, 70 per cent as outright gift and 30 per cent as loan repayable over fifteen years. Grants will be allowed only where a pupil enrolment of 150, as a minimum, may be expected within five or six years.

Strangely enough the effect of this State assistance has been to freeze out the layman altogether. At £400 a pupil place £100,000 will build a school for 250 pupils—a modest enough target. The amount of the repayable loan is £30,000, too much for any lay teacher, however ambitious. So that, in effect, the Church has been given a monopoly in relation to secondary schools for Catholic pupils.

The increased participation in post-primary education has created a demand for new schools and for extension of existing schools. In Dublin alone, it is estimated that 20,000 additional pupil places will be needed by 1970.

There would seem to be a shrinkage in vocations for the priesthood and for the teaching Brothers. With an increasing enrolment in all post-primary schools the spread of religious over total teaching staff will be thinner than before. Yet, though they are unable to staff the schools they already own, they propose to establish more and better schools wherever the pupil potential shows an increase.

There is another side to it. The lay secondary teacher remains always the hired man. His responsibility ends at the classroom door. He is consulted with, of course, because he may have something of value to offer, but he is never part of the decision-making. If he wants authority so that he may innovate, experiment, he must go elsewhere. The findings of the recent salary tribunal, if accepted, will not of themselves change the real situation. It is a frustrating situation for the good teacher. Is the situation responsible, at least in part, for keeping the high-class graduate out of education? The vocational schools have not yet reached their full stature and still rank as junior schools; in a couple of years, when they have senior cycles as well as junior, these schools will be able to offer responsibility and challenge to the able and ambitious lay teacher.

I lay stress on these things because I believe a change must be made; otherwise there will be an explosion, maybe sooner than later. No one wants to push the religious out of education; that would be disastrous, in my opinion. But I want them in it as partners, not always as masters.

I believe that there is need for dialogue at the highest level between Church and State on the problems in education now surfacing. Unless some measure of agreement is arrived at in the near future as to objectives and the means of reaching them, educational advance at both primary and post-primary levels will be hindered. The dialogue must be frank and must range over a wide area. The prospects for education are good, but only if the major providers are in harmony.

Appendix: criteria for size of future post-primary schools[2]

It is proposed by the Department that as far as possible every post-primary centre should offer both academic and technical subjects 'so that each pupil will have the opportunity of choosing the subjects best suited to his individual aptitudes'. The minimum requirement would be a two-form entry: about 50 pupils making an enrolment of about 150 pupils in six classes in the junior cycle (i.e. the three-year course to the Intermediate Certificate). *Areas that cannot provide an entry of this size would best be served by transport to another centre.* In the long term, therefore, it is proposed that existing schools that are not viable by these standards should be closed; in the short term, to ease the strain on resources, they would be retained, unless the numbers attending are very low indeed.

It is considered that a school with about 150 pupils in the junior cycle would be unlikely to have more than about 50 in the senior cycle (two years leading to Leaving Certificate), i.e. 25 in each year of the course. This number is considered too small to support any but a very restricted curriculum. In order to provide an adequate senior cycle, with provision for other than a purely academic course, the minimum annual intake of pupils into the junior cycle should be of the order of 80 to 100. *A major educational centre would, therefore, be one which would have a minimum pupil potential per year of 80 to 100 and would have available, as a minimum, accommodation for 320 to 400 pupils. A junior centre, on the other hand, would be one which would have an annual potential intake of about 50 and would provide post-primary education to the Intermediate Certificate examination level only; for the senior cycle, pupils would be transported to a major centre.* The average-sized administrative area known as a County should have three or four major centres depending on the school population.

A centre is regarded as a post-primary centre if it has any one (or more) of the following: a boys' secondary school, a girls' secondary school or a vocational school. It need not have full secondary and vocational facilities for boys and girls. Estimates of the annual potential available for entry to post-primary schools in each such existing centre have been made. The Department's planning with regard to the development, or otherwise, of the centres is based on these estimates and other relevant statistics, and the application to them of the criteria just set out. The proposals which emerge in this way show which existing schools it is thought necessary to 'phase out' or limit in facilities, and which ones will be designated for development. The accompanying table indicates the number of existing schools which might be affected by this re-organization.

Financing secondary schools
Capital cost

There is no state-owned secondary school system in Ireland. Except for three new comprehensive schools,

Post-primary schools 1967–8

Number of pupils	Number of schools									
	Secondary[1]				Voca-tional[2]	Secondary tops				All post-primary[3]
	Boys'	Girls'	Mixed	Total	Total	Boys'	Girls'	Mixed	Total	Total
1–149	101	92	60	253	119	2	25	4	31	403
150–249	56	93	34	183	60	1	9	—	10	253
250–350	42	48	1	91	30	—	5	—	5	126
over 350	38	27	3	68	6	—	1	—	1	75
Total	237	260	98	595	215	3	40	4	47	857

Notes
1. In the case of secondary schools all pupils are included whether 'recognized' or not.
2. In the case of vocational schools only whole-time day students, second level, are included.
3. There are in addition 3 comprehensive, mixed, schools, of which one is in the 150–249 category and 2 have over 350 pupils.
These figures, which are published by courtesy of the Department of Education, are provisional and subject to revision.

all existing secondary schools have been provided by private interests, mainly the teaching orders and diocesan authorities of the Catholic Church. 'Building Grants to Secondary Schools' appeared in the Public Accounts for the first time in 1966–7 (at £124,000). The secondary school enrolment of the previous year, 98,000, represented an investment by the school owners, without government subsidy, of £40 million (at replacement cost of £400 per pupil-place). This does not include residential accommodation for the 25 per cent of pupils who were in boarding schools. Almost 40,000 new places, replacement cost £16 million, had been provided in the ten years 1956–66. Government grants towards a portion of the cost of new school buildings are now being made available. The full cost of the local authority controlled vocational schools (38,000 places in 1966–7) has always been met from central and local authority funds.

Current cost

The State subsidizes the running costs of secondary schools. It pays a capitation grant for each 'recognized' pupil. There is an agreed salary scale for teachers and the State pays what is called the 'incremental' portion of the salaries of a fixed quota of teachers, requiring the schools to pay an additional 'basic' salary to lay teachers, to bring the whole salary up to the scale. Religious teachers, not being paid the 'basic' salary, effectively subsidize the system. The Lynch Report estimated that state assistance constituted 71 per cent of school income (excluding boarding costs) for 1961–2, and fees (of which 75 per cent were then under £20 per annum) 21 per cent. Since the last school year the majority of day schools are not charging fees, receiving instead an additional grant of £25 per pupil, under the 'O'Malley Scheme'. In the financial year 1966–7, incremental salaries paid by the State were equivalent to £39 per pupil, and capitation grants to approximately £14. Basic salaries foregone by religious teachers would have come to £8 per head of the pupils in their schools. Total state expenditure on secondary schools in 1966–7 was £6,750,000 plus a proportion of Civil Service overheads.

Notes

1 The Editor of *Studies* has made the following comment: This article was first published in *Studies*, the Irish quarterly review, along with comments on it by religious managers of secondary schools in Ireland, lay-teachers, parents and university educators. The second part of the article, described by Mr O'Connor as his personal view, was claimed to be a statement of previously undisclosed Departmental policy for the future of Irish schools. Notably, the commentators in *Studies* disputed Mr O'Connor's figures for unfilled teaching posts and the reasons he gave for vacancies, and disagreed with his picture of the lay teachers' position. His concept of the place of religious education in the schools was challenged by both Protestant and Catholic Church representatives. The authoritarianism, secrecy and failure of the Department to consult the educators was criticized, as—on the other hand—was the absence of a single representative body to speak with authority for the multiple interests of the Catholic Church in the educational field in Ireland. The full symposium can be found in *Studies*, vol. 57, no. 227 (autumn 1968), and has been reprinted as *Post-Primary Education: Now and in the Future* (Dublin: The Talbot Press, 1968).

2 This expansion of Mr O'Connor's necessarily summary paragraph has been adapted from documents issued by the Department. Editor, *Studies*.

This extract from the Dáil Reports reflects the air of mystery and controversy which, the parliamentary opposition felt, surrounded the first appearance of a document with such far-reaching consequences.

Mr Cosgrave asked the Minister for Education if he will state to whom a circular entitled Community Schools, dated October 1970 and issued from his Department, was addressed; and if it reflects Government policy.

MR FAULKNER [Minister for Education]: On numerous occasions in this House and also in An Seanad I have referred to the necessity to secure in every area of the country post-primary educational provision which would be such as to cater for the aptitude and ability of all the pupils in the area. I referred in this respect also to the necessity to establish larger school units as no small school could by itself provide the range of subjects and facilities which would be required. The memorandum . . . was in the nature of a working document, not a circular. It brought together in a form suitable for discussion my ideas as to how what I had in mind could be achieved by the establishment of community schools. As a preliminary to the discussion with interested parties which would be necessary copies of the memorandum were sent to the Catholic hierarchy.

MR COSGRAVE: Can the Minister state if there was any reason why the memorandum or circular was unsigned other than having the notice of the Department of Education at the bottom of the memorandum.

MR FAULKNER: There was no particular reason. (Extract from Dáil Reports, 18 November 1970, cols. 1613–14.)

Community schools

1 The creation of community schools must be viewed against the background of Government policy in relation to post-primary schools and in particular the following aspects of that policy:

(a) the provision of free post-primary education for all children irrespective of ability and without the use of selection procedures on transfer from primary to post-primary;

(b) the elimination of the barriers between secondary and vocational schools and the creation of a unified post-primary system of education;

(c) the provision of comprehensive facilities in each area of the country so as to cater for the varying

Source: Department of Education, Dublin, October 1970.

aptitudes and abilities of pupils and to provide reasonable equality of educational opportunity for all our children irrespective of the area of the country in which they reside or the means of their parents;

(d) the elimination of overlapping and duplication in the provision of teachers, buildings and equipment so that the available resources in manpower and finance may be utilized to best advantage and so make resources available to improve the level of services in our post-primary schools.

2 The optimum size for a post-primary school is a matter to which a lot of attention has been given both here and elsewhere. The Advisory Councils for Dublin and Cork have recommended the creation of school units of 400 to 800 pupils. OECD expressed the view a few years ago that the absolute minimum size was probably around the 450 mark. The Department's experience has been that in terms of the level of facilities which can be provided at a tolerable cost level, the optimum size is around 800 pupils. Generally the Department has accepted the views of the Dublin and Cork Advisory Councils and aims at the creation of school units of 400 to 800 pupils. It is accepted that given the present distribution of post-primary schools in this country, it will not always be possible, at any rate in the foreseeable future, to create school units of 400 to 800 pupils everywhere but there are a number of small towns throughout the country which at present have two or three post-primary schools with a total enrolment of something between 400 and 800 pupils. It is felt that in such areas a single post-primary school, if it could be achieved, would provide a better level of service to the area while at the same time removing the divisions that at present exist in our post-primary sectors and the difficulties to which these give rise.

3 On another level, there is growing acceptance throughout the world that education is a life-long process and that second chance education must be provided at all levels. It would seem clear, therefore, that there will be very substantial development of adult education facilities over the next decade. Allied with this, there is in all countries a growing community consciousness and an increasing demand for school facilities (hall, gymnasia, meeting rooms, playing fields, swimming pools, etc.) to be made available out of school-hours to voluntary organizations and the adult community generally.

4 Community schools are seen as resulting from the amalgamation of existing secondary and vocational schools or in city areas from the development of individual single schools instead of the traditional development of separate secondary and vocational schools. These schools would provide a reasonably full range

of courses leading to Group Certificate, Intermediate Certificate and Leaving Certificate. The community school would provide adult education facilities in the area and subject to reasonable safeguards against abuse or damage to buildings, equipment, etc. would make facilities available to voluntary organizations and to the adult community generally.

5 The community school would be governed by a Board of Management consisting of representatives of the secondary school managers and the local Vocational Education Committee with an independent Chairman who might be the Bishop of the Diocese or other agreed Chairman or with the Chairmanship rotating amongst the representative members of the Board. The representation of any particular interest would vary depending on the circumstances of each case and would be a matter for negotiation with the interests involved. It might prove possible to include representatives of parents or industrial/commercial interests but this would be by way of nomination of the educational authorities involved or by some other way which was agreed by them in the course of negotiations. The site and buildings would be vested in trustees nominated by the parties involved.

6 The Board of Management would be responsible for the administration of the school and its educational policy. The Board would be solely responsible for the appointment of staff, including Principals, Vice-Principals and other posts of responsibility, subject to the usual Departmental regulations in regard to qualifications, overall quota of teachers, number, types and rates of pay to non-teaching staff. In the case of amalgamations existing permanent staff in the schools being amalgamated would be offered assimilation on to the staff of the community school if they applied for it. Rates of salary and allowances would be those applicable to secondary and vocational schools under the latest arrangements.

7 The capital costs involved (site, buildings, equipment, furniture, playing facilities) would be met in full out of public funds subject to an agreed local contribution. This local contribution would be a matter for negotiation in each individual case.

8 The current costs of running the school would be met by the Board of Management which would be funded directly and in full by the Department of Education. This Department favours an arrangement under which a budget would be agreed annually in advance with the Board of Management and within the limits of that budget the Board would be free to decide how best to utilize the funds at its disposal. The Board would be free, if it thought fit, to supplement its receipts by such local contributions as it might be possible for it to raise for general or specific purposes. The Board's accounts would be subject to audit by the Comptroller and Auditor General in so far as expenditure of public funds was concerned.

31 Some reflections on Catholic schools in Northern Ireland

John F. Fulton

It is natural that, in the situation following the recent disturbances in Northern Ireland, which have once again focused world attention on the Province, the education system should come in for close scrutiny. Many contend that the dual educational system which operates in Northern Ireland causes or at least contributes significantly to the divisions in the community along religious lines. It is important for many reasons that this debate should not be conducted on a polemical level. As the editors of the 1966 *World Year Book of Education*, which is entirely devoted to the whole question of church-state relations in education, have warned, 'These are difficult issues and ones which, though dormant in some countries, are in many a major question. Progress must be made through facing them

Source: *Studies* (winter 1969), 341–56.

honestly, thinking strenuously, and seeking solutions in understanding and generosity.'[1]

This article will look at some of these issues in an exploratory way, and also give a short historical account of their presentation in Northern Ireland.

Parental rights

Article 16(3) of the Universal Declaration of Human Rights states that 'The family is the natural and fundamental group unit of society and has the right to protection from society and from the State.'

Among many others, such diverse figures as Pope Pius XI and Herbert Spencer have testified to this. Spencer wrote, 'As the family comes before the State in order of time, or when it has ceased to be, whereas the State is possible only by the bringing up of children it follows that the duties of the parent demand closer attention than those of the citizen . . . the welfare of the family underlies the welfare of society.'[2]

Article 26(3) of the Universal Declaration states: 'Every person has the right to education . . . The parents have as a priority the right to choose the kind of education to be given to their children.' These admirable sentiments were reaffirmed by the signatories to the Additional Protocol of the European Convention, safeguarding human rights and individual freedoms—'No person shall be denied the right to education . . . In the exercise of any function which it assumes in relation to education and to teaching, the State shall respect the rights of parents to ensure such education and teaching in conformity with their own religious and philosophical convictions.'[3] As Voeltzel has rightly shown, there are two rights mentioned in these extracts—one, the right to education which is universally recognized, but this is meaningless unless it is made clear 'who can and must decide what the education shall be'.[4] The child himself cannot choose. All the signatories to the Universal Declaration of Human Rights have affirmed the rights of parents in this respect.

The controversy between the rights of the individual and those of the State is an old one. In the specifically educational context, the problem can be viewed as a continuum with extreme individualism and extreme statism at either end. Extreme individualism is now of only historical significance. Before the latter half of the nineteenth century, when political and economic thinking was dominated by laissez-faire, any intrusion by the State into educational matters was viewed with abhorrence. Spencer, seeing the sole function of the State as a protector of rights, devoted in his Social Statics 'more space to his attack on statism in education than to any other phase of governmental interference.'[5] John Stuart Mill was less extreme. Although no protagonist of state education—he regarded it as 'a mere contrivance for moulding people to be exactly like one another'[6]—he felt that the State had a role to play, if for no other reason than to ensure that no child was denied the benefits of schooling on account of erring or careless parents. However, he did insist that in administering compulsory education, the greatest care should be taken not to impose on children religious teaching at variance with their parents' wishes. Mill's views had a profound influence on the education acts passed in Great Britain during the last thirty years of the nineteenth century and out of this legislation grew the compromise dual system, that is a system of state schools, developing side by side with voluntary schools, which were controlled and administered by religious bodies of different denominations.

The statist philosophy which asserts that the State's role in education is paramount, is by no means a twentieth-century phenomenon. Plato's Republic is perhaps the most extreme account of state domination. La Chalotais, also, expressed this view very forcibly:

'I claim for the nation an education dependent upon the State alone, because education belongs essentially to the State, because every nation has an inalienable and imprescriptible right to instruct its members, because in short the children of the State should be brought up by those who are members of the State.'[7] Nevertheless the problem of state control is an important one in our times. Communist education is its most extreme modern manifestation. A former member of the Czechoslovakian Ministry of Information claimed for the State 'the right . . . to educate all children, to administer and conduct the whole school education and . . . to conduct all state education inside and outside schools, in the spirit of our ideology, in the spirit of the scientific truth of Marxism—Leninism.'[8] However, advocacy of complete state control of education is by no means confined to Communists as can be seen by the fact that the Russian delegate to the United Nations did not lack support for his views when he spoke in the debate on Article 26 of the Universal Declaration of Human Rights.[9]

Various factors have contributed to the acceptance by a number of people of the primacy of the State in the control and administration of education, for example, the concept of education as an instrument of social and economic policy. But perhaps most important of all is the increasing cost of education, which is more and more placing the State in the position of being the only agency which can provide the finance necessary to support modern education. Dubay argues that John Dewey was able to avoid the logic of his own arguments only at the expense of being self-contradictory. His educational writings seem to imply 'a governmentally sponsored system of schools', while in his philosophical treatise, *The Public and Its Problems*, he describes 'government in the individualist tradition.'[10]

The political philosophy of state control of education is neatly summed up in the following extract from Alexander Meiklejohn's book, *Education between Two Worlds*: 'The first statement of Rousseau has said that, when men form a State they give everything into its hands. The second statement corrects this by saying that men have nothing to give, except as the State has already given it to them. Men have no rights: they have no property: they are not men, except as they are citizens of a politically organized community. That assertion seems to me to go to the very roots of a public system of education. If it is true, then we may be able to see how a government can plan and administer a teaching enterprise suitable to the life of a democratic community. The agency which creates the community may well undertake to teach what it is and does. The agency which is human reason in action may teach its members how to live reasonably.'[11]

The position of the Catholic Church

The Catholic Church eschews both of these extreme views. In the Decree on Christian Education, the

Fathers of Vatican Council II, having commended the universal recognition given to the right of all men to be educated, go on to point out that there are three major agencies in education, the parents (family), the State, and the Church.

Parents Since parents share in the creative act of God to give their children life, they receive their obligations and responsibilities directly from God. This basic principle of the 'rights of parents to have their children educated according to their conscience'[12] is the very core of the Church's teaching on education. As the Vatican Council asserted, 'They (the parents) have a most solemn obligation to educate their offspring. Hence, parents must be acknowledged as the first and foremost educators of their children.'[13]

Accordingly, the argument quoted earlier, advocating the primacy of the State in education, consequent on the principle that the child is first a citizen before he is a person, is energetically rejected.

It is often thought that the Catholic Church is concerned only with the rights of Catholic parents. This is not so. So strenuously does the Church defend the rights of parents in the sphere of education, that as Bishop Butler pointed out, sanction would never be given to the compulsory reception by, for example, the children of Jewish parents, 'of a form of religious education that does not meet with their parents' approval.'[14]

State The natural end of the State, the civil society, is the common temporal good of all its members. Its function in education, say the Vatican Council Fathers, is 'to promote the education of the young in several ways: namely, by overseeing the duties and rights of parents and of others who have a role in education, and by providing them with assistance; by implementing the principle of subsidiarity and completing the task of education, with attention to parental wishes, whenever the efforts of parents and of other groups are insufficient; and moreover by building its own schools and institutes, as the common good may demand.'[15] Particularly in a democracy, where the maintenance of freedom and the security of civil institutions depend, to a large extent, on the ability of the citizens to exercise their responsibilities to the full, the State is right to insist on compulsory education in order that adequate standards can be attained. Although this is almost invariably done by providing schools in which education is given free—this is administratively convenient—it could be also carried out by subsidizing parents in order that they may be able to pay school fees—this is not so administratively convenient. The State's function, therefore, is to help parents to fulfil their responsibilities, but this does not mean that it can usurp their rights. 'Except on the totalitarian premise that the creature is totally the creature of the State and has duties but no rights in regard to it, the obligation of government is to help parents obtain for their children the education that the parents want, not the education that the government wants.'[16] Even in those schools established and

directly controlled by the State, it must be remembered that, since the school is the auxiliary of the family and not of the State, the school exists to help the parents carry out their obligations more readily than they could otherwise do.

Church The Church claims the right to teach, 'not merely because she deserves recognition as a human society capable of educating, but most of all because she has the responsibility of announcing the way of salvation to all men, of communicating the life of Christ to those who believe, and of assisting them with ceaseless concern so that they may grow into the fullness of that same life.'[17] Thus, although the Church carries out its teaching functions principally through her clergy and in church buildings, she also, as the 'guardian of those theological truths, and the moral principles that follow from them, which it is the purpose of education to fulfil,'[18] establishes and runs schools in the service of its members, and so enables them, in a pluralistic society, to educate their children according to their conscience.

The relationship between the respective roles of the parents and of the bishops and priests of the Roman Catholic Church in relation to education has very often been misunderstood. The implication of Mrs Margaret Knight's remark regarding the position in England that 'the pressure for Catholic education does not come primarily from parents, but from the hierarchy,'[19] is that the hierarchy acted, if not in defiance of parental wishes, at least without any backing from them. It should be pointed out incidentally that it was not the hierarchy who made the running but the Catholic Education Council, a council which includes laymen. The relationship between the clergy and the parents is admirably summed up by Fr Ranwez, S. J. He says, 'It is within the Church and in functional dependence on her that parents exercise their responsibilities in the domain of Christian education. It is not a delegation but a participation in the motherhood of the Church. Put another way, the Church's motherhood is fully exercised over small children by their parents who are the very presence of the Church for them.'[20] Fr Leetham points out that 'they are excused the duty of sending children to Catholic schools if there is no Catholic school in the neighbourhood.' He adds, 'They are not bound to send their children to a Catholic school whose inferior standards would be a handicap to the child's future. In such a case, the parents' responsibility for the religious and moral instruction of their children becomes more grave.'[21] The role of the hierarchy is to lay down norms and issue directives. In forbidding parents to send children to schools other than Catholic schools without the consent of the local ordinary the Church is not assuming parental rights, but simply instructing parents how best to fulfil their natural duties. 'The responsibility still rests with the parents: the Church's law, in accordance with the true function of all law, is a guide to the proper fulfilment of that responsibility.'[22]

These are the principles which are outlined in the

Declaration on Christian Education and, as the Council Fathers pointed out, 'they will have to be developed at greater length by a special post-Conciliar Commission and applied by Episcopal Conferences to varying local situations.'[23]

Scotland and the Netherlands

There has been no uniformity throughout the world in solving the problem of church-state relations in education. Scotland, for example, has evolved a system unique in Western Europe. For the past four hundred years Scotland has been a predominantly Presbyterian country with small Roman Catholic and Episcopalian minorities. At present Catholics represent about 16 per cent of the population. The Education Act of 1872 established for children from five to thirteen years of age a state system of compulsory primary education administered by small locally elected school boards. A parliamentary grant of seven and sixpence per pupil was made on condition that no part of it was used for religious instruction. Almost all the school boards decided that in schools under their control, religious instruction which was 'to be financed out of the local education rate',[24] should be Presbyterian. Catholics and Episcopalians opted out of the system. The rising costs and the recognition that the position was inequitable led to a change in 1897, when a parliamentary grant of three shillings per pupil was made to the denominational schools. However, since the grant for each pupil at the state schools was simultaneously raised to sixteen shillings, there was in fact very little amelioration of the position in the confessional schools. The guarantee of equal opportunity could not be fulfilled, for there was a great difference between the state schools and those outside the state system. For this reason the local education authorities wanted to end the system of administrative dualism by getting control of all the schools.

The Catholic hierarchy insisted that education given in the schools would continue to be a Catholic education. As Beales points out, 'the only possible guarantee was that the teachers in (the transferred schools) . . . must continue to be Catholics.'[25] In effect, this was the substance of the agreement that was reached. The local education authorities administer and finance the Catholic schools which were handed over to them. Two statutory safeguards were secured, namely, (1) all teachers appointed must be approved as regards belief and character by the Church, and (2) religious instruction should continue to be given, the time allotted to it to be not less than before transference. The local education authorities appoint the teachers from 'lists of applicants who have already satisfied the bishops as to their religious qualification';[26] otherwise the local education authorities have control over the appointment, conditions of service and dismissal of teachers. The Scottish Episcopal Church authorities subscribed to the same agreement and also transferred their schools. Craigie, writing in the 1966 Year Book of Education says that the system 'has worked without change (since 1918) and to everybody's satisfaction; no one would now lightly seek to have it changed. There is today no discernible difference between the public and the "transferred" schools, whether primary or secondary, in buildings, staffing, equipment, educational standards and achievement, or status, and as a result the bitterness of religious acrimony is wholly absent from Scottish education.'[27]

In the Netherlands, which is entirely different from Scotland from the point of view of the religious affiliations of its people (Roman Catholic 40 per cent, Dutch Reformed Church 28 per cent, Calvinist Churches 9 per cent and 18 per cent disclaim adherence to any religion), the problems associated with church-state relations seem to have been satisfactorily solved. The achievement of financial parity between the State and voluntary (church) schools has been based on the rights of parents to obtain for their children 'schools with the religious background they desire'.[28] Of the present position in the Netherlands, Idenburg has this to say: 'The whole legislation is a system of checks and balances, the object contemplated being to ensure the spiritual freedom of the governing bodies and so of the parents on the one hand and on the other hand to prevent an unjust burden being placed on public funds and to guarantee a reasonable standard of education. . . . We in the Netherlands have taken the risk of diversity and it would seem that we have not done too badly.'[29]

Northern Ireland

In Northern Ireland, the dual system has evolved in a different way. When the Northern Ireland Ministry of Education was established in 1921, it appointed the Lynn Committee 'to enquire and report on the existing organization and administration of educational services in Northern Ireland, and to make such recommendations as may be considered necessary for the proper co-ordination and effective carrying out of these services'. The Committee issued two reports, an interim one in 1922 and a final one in 1923. The most far-reaching suggestion, at least from the point of view of administration and control, was the proposal to decentralize the administration of the education service, which had hitherto been the function of central boards, and to establish local education authorities for this purpose. The recommended change was provided for in the 1923 Education Act.

As regards future development, an equally crucial change was what might be called the 'secularization' of the educational system. For, although the local education authorities were required 'to afford opportunities for catechetical instruction according to the tenets of the religious denomination of the parents of children attending any public elementary school, being a provided or transferred school, and for other religious instruction to which those parents do not object', they were expressly forbidden by Section 26 of the Act 'to provide religious instruction in any such elementary school as aforesaid'. They were also forbidden to take religion into account when appointing teachers. Both these provisions were unacceptable to all the Churches.

The Protestant Churches wanted a guarantee that not only would Protestant teachers be appointed to the transferred schools but also that they would be required to give religious instruction, and until these questions were settled they refused to transfer their schools. An attempt was made to meet this demand by an Amendment Act passed in 1925, but while this Act removed the prohibition on the local education authorities with regard to the provision of religious instruction, no obligation was placed on the authorities to provide it nor on the teachers to teach it. This was unacceptable. After further agitation, another Amendment Act, which altered the situation completely was passed in 1930. The local education authorities were, by Section 4 of the Act, required 'to provide Bible instruction, should the parents of not less than ten children who are in regular attendance at such school make application to the Education Authority for that purpose'. Furthermore the teachers were obliged to give the instruction if required to do so. It was only after the 1930 Act had been passed that the Protestant Churches were wholly satisfied and felt able to transfer their schools.

From this brief survey it is clear that the 1925 and 1930 Amendment Acts had changed the situation in a fundamental way and the new legislation was at variance with the philosophy underlying the proposals of the Lynn Committee and that of the drafters of the 1923 Act, especially with regard to the public financing of the school system. Campbell, in an admirable survey, suggested that 'the main object of the 1930 Amendment Act would seem to have been to safeguard the Protestant religion in the state schools'.[30] The state schools envisaged by the Lynn Committee were secular schools, but by the passing of the 1925 and 1930 Acts, they became, in effect, Protestant schools. In this connection it is important to note that 'the superseded managers of transferred or replaced schools and their successors in office should have authority to nominate not less than half the members of local school management committees, which were given important rights in regard to the appointment of teachers'.[31] A further development was that by the 1930 Act grants amounting to 50 per cent were made available for the replacement, extension and repair of voluntary schools.

The 1947 Education Act, under the provisions of which the present educational system is governed and administered, altered fundamentally the position which prevailed after the 1930 legislation, and thus the conflicts of the 1920s were resurrected. With the decision that the 1930 Act, requiring a teacher to give religious instruction, was *ultra vires* the 1920 Government of Ireland Act, the Government abolished this requirement and inserted in the 1947 Act a conscience clause enabling teachers to be excused from giving religious instruction on the grounds of conscience. The Protestant Churches, who had transferred their schools without compensation after the 1930 Act, considered that the Government had gone back on its word. It was, as Dr Corkey put it, 'a raw deal for the Protestant Churches and a betrayal of the Protestant community'.[32]

Since the major aim of the 1947 Act was to provide secondary education for all, new schools had to be provided and the number of places in existing schools had to be greatly increased. This applied particularly to places in grammar schools, most of which were, and still are, under voluntary management. In order to carry out its policy, the Government either had to bring existing voluntary schools under local education authority control or alternatively it had to provide finance by increasing the rate of grants from the 50 per cent at which it stood. Because, as the White Paper which preceded the 1947 Act pointed out, of the fear that some schools 'would be disposed to sever their connection with the public system of education and assume completely independent status',[33] that is the status of the English public schools, the Government chose the latter alternative and increased the rate of grant to 65 per cent. The 65 per cent was applicable to all voluntary schools, not only grammar but primary and secondary intermediate also.

Until 1968, the position was that the Government paid 65 per cent of the cost of new schools, of the extension and/or alteration of existing ones, of equipment and of external maintenance. It also paid 65 per cent of the employers' contributions for teachers under the National Insurance Acts, and the manager or governing body paid the remainder. The local education authority paid 65 per cent of the approved expenditure incurred on heating, lighting, cleaning and internal maintenance. If the school was under a 'four and two' committee, the local education authority paid 100 per cent of this expenditure and the employers' National Insurance contribution was fully paid.

In 1967, a White Paper, *Local Education Authorities and Voluntary Schools* was published. It proposed that voluntary schools which accepted one-third public representation on their management committees would be designated 'maintained' schools and would be eligible for 80 per cent building and extension grants and 100 per cent maintenance grants. Those who did not accept maintained status would continue as before. In the case of primary and secondary schools, the public representatives would be appointed by the local education authorities and in the case of grammar schools by the Ministry of Education. Despite their fears and criticisms, outlined in a statement in January, 1968,[34] the Catholic bishops decided to give the new scheme a trial by transferring some of the schools. Up to the present rather 'more than one-third of the Catholic schools in Northern Ireland . . . have adopted maintained status'.[35]

Catholic schools

The Catholic school is an institutional affirmation of a philosophy of life and indeed it is an institutional protest that this type of school will provide something which can only be provided in this setting. This is not a rejection of the state school as giving a secular education inferior to Catholic schools, but rather it is 'a choice of something qualitatively different'.[36] In any discussion of the aims of education, it is important to be clear about what we mean by education. In the broad sense, education refers to the bringing up of children and adolescents and is not to be confused with formal education of schooling. Education is concerned, therefore, with the individual and no aspect of the indivisible human personality can be neglected. As Monsignor Johnson has said, 'Our physical health, our economic well-being, our social and civic relations, our cultural development, all are bound up in the most intimate manner with our moral and spiritual progress. To educate the child, consequently, means to promote his growth in all these spheres'.[37]

It would be extremely convenient if we could parcel out a part of education to a particular agency and let it carry out its function independently of the rest. For example, to the Church we could allot moral and spiritual development, to the home physical health and economic well-being, to the school intellectual development and so on. But this is obviously absurd. It is the child, the individual, who comes to school, not just his intellect, and thus the school has to be concerned with his total development, although the emphasis it places on each aspect of development will be different from any other educative agency. Consequently, for the Catholic the ultimate aim of the church-related school is that every pupil should 'know, love and serve God in this life and be happy with him for ever in the next'.[38]

In trying to determine the purpose of the Catholic school in this context, American Catholic educators have introduced the concept of the primary proximate aim of the school and there are differences of opinion about this. There are three basic positions on the primary proximate purpose of the Catholic school, namely the moralist, the intellectualist and the prudentialist. The moralist view holds that moral teaching, which includes not only religious instruction but 'the active encouragement of living a spiritual life'[39] is the primary proximate goal of the school. Pope Pius XI is often quoted in support of this view but, as Fr McCluskey, S.J.,[40] has clearly shown, the Holy Father was speaking of total education which has its end in 'eternal vision of the essence of God' and not of formal education in school.

Those who subscribe to the intellectual position contend that the primary proximate purpose of the school is the intellectual development of the pupil. It has a large number of supporters among the clergy concerned with education in the USA. Its basic weakness is that intellectualists 'tend to think of a . . . student more as a disembodied intellect than as a person'.[41] Schools, in fact, do not develop intellects but personalities.

The prudentialist view, which merges the best elements of the other two with important new elements, maintains that the primary proximate purpose of the Catholic school at all levels is to develop within the student 'knowledge and action coequally, (that is) to foster development of the student's mind and will'.[42] Put another way, it sees truth as the primary proximate object of the school. Maritain stresses the educational importance of truth: 'Truth is the inspiring force needed in the education of youth—truth rather than erudition and self-consciousness—all-pervading truth rather than the objectively isolated truth at which each of the diverse sciences aims.'[43] Possession of truth leads to Christian wisdom, a concept explained by Pope Pius XI: 'The true Christian, the product of Christian education, is simply the supernatural man: the man who feels, judges and acts always and consistently in accordance with right reason enlightened by the example and teaching of Jesus Christ.'[44]

It seems to the writer that adherence to the intellectualist position implies that a separate Catholic school system is not necessary although many intellectualists will not accept this conclusion. All that is required is a state secular school, with separate facilities for religious instruction. The supporters of the moralist and prudentialist positions, on the other hand, 'believe that the religious pervasiveness and thrust of the Catholic school are the essential characteristics which differentiate it from the state school'.[45] Many clergymen of other denominations agree that the secular school with Sunday school is an inadequate substitute for an ongoing day school. As Johnson said, 'Recently Protestants and Jews have evinced great interest in the religious school as an instrument of general education. Many turn to it with reluctance because of a deep devotion to the public school. But it seems to them that if the public school must be maintained at the price of a thorough-going dualism between the religious and the secular, the cost is too great'.[46] Dr Milne, Secretary of the Board of Education, General Synod of the Church of Ireland, answering those who would seek 'to eliminate the religious element from education altogether, or at best . . . consign it to a marginal area of visiting clergymen,' has pointed out that 'such attitudes presuppose a total change in the policy of . . . the Church of Ireland'.[47] Despite Wall's[48] assertion that in education the position of ultimate neutralism is difficult if not impossible to sustain, some governments have adopted, in the name of neutralism, a policy of excluding religious teaching from state schools and consequently have effectively secularized the schools. Others, for example in England and Wales, have recognized the value of commitment and have attempted to teach an 'agreed syllabus' in religious education. Yet, many devout Christians expressed forcibly to the Plowden Committee their desire for 'more convincedly Christian teaching than in present circumstances they sometimes get'.[49] Beales, in a recent article, refers to 'the ethical chaos in England's county schools'.[50] According to Brugmans, 'the philosophic tenor . . . (of the state school) is ill-defined and unclear'.[51]

Most educators would agree with Wall that 'the moral education of children is not something that can be treated apart from normal growth and education'.[52] Furthermore, the Church has never accepted any dichotomy between morals and religion. A representative of the Catholic Education Council of England and Wales in a comment concerning moral behaviour wrote in evidence to UNESCO, 'It is I suppose possible to teach children to behave socially without any reference to God and our duties towards Him, but if a child asks why one should behave socially, it is surely difficult to give him a satisfactory answer on the principles of a non-religious deontology. . . . One can teach children to do what is right for the love of God. The principle of morality then is no mere categorical imperative but a strong and vivid love for the person of Christ'.[53] It is necessary, certainly, to take account of sound psychological principles in the moral education of children and adolescents, but 'the content and inspiration of that education will be drawn from the moral, philosophic and religious belief of the educators, parents and teachers'.[54]

Community divisions

It has been said that, by maintaining a separate school system, the Catholic Church contributes significantly to divisions in the community. It has been further suggested that this separation breeds in the pupils undesirable social attitudes. It is not a problem unique to Northern Ireland, but because of the divisions in this community it has a crucial pertinence here. Is it true that a divided society is a necessary consequence of having separate county and voluntary school systems? If it is, then the Catholic Church will have to re-examine its position very carefully indeed, for (it seems to the writer) no person or institution can, except in the most extreme circumstances (when the State is anti-religion), accept responsibility for destroying community spirit and for perpetuating community divisions. Furthermore, it is quite as unhelpful to make a wholly negative response to this charge as it is to accept its validity uncritically. Its seriousness demands that it be examined in a way which does justice to its importance.

In education, as in other social sciences, the only satisfactory method of finding answers to questions of this nature is experimental research. As far as one is aware, there is no experimental evidence that a system of church-related schools parallel to the state system results in a divided community. In reporting a very comprehensive survey, two Americans, Greeley and Rossi, concluded, 'We could find no evidence that the products of such a separate system were less involved in community activities, less likely to have friends from other religious groups, more intolerant in their attitudes, or less likely to achieve occupationally or academically. On the contrary we found that they were slightly more successful in the world of study and work and, after the breaking point of college, much more tolerant. The achievement, and perhaps even the tolerance, seems to be related to the degree to which a young person was integrated into his religious sub-culture during adolescence'.[55] The authors of another study stated, 'We could find no evidence that parochial schools tend to alienate individual Catholics from their communities . . . Parochial school Catholics were as involved in community affairs as anyone else of comparable occupational position'.[56] If it is found that this last statement is not true for Northern Ireland, it would seem to suggest that the causal factors are other than educational ones. Recent research is very scanty but what little there is confirms these findings. It is true that these studies are exclusively non-European in origin and for that reason may not be either directly or wholly applicable to Northern Ireland. Nevertheless the research does suggest that social divisiveness is not a necessary consequence of the dual system.

However the position of the Catholic Church on the question of schools should not be sustained solely on the defence that they do not create community divisions. The case for the retention of Catholic schools is whether they are effective or not in attaining the goals for which they were established. One of the most undesirable effects of the astringent and polemical tone of the argument regarding the divisions alleged to have been caused by Catholic schools, is that the defensive reaction to it has inhibited for far too long the necessary reappraisal of the assumptions and implications and the examination of the practices and effectiveness of Catholic schools in Northern Ireland. Once again it is necessary to look overseas for research findings. The experimental findings agree on two conclusions, namely that (a) attendance at Catholic schools will foster and consolidate the Christian life of children whose parents have provided a strong religious home background and (b) the schools' ability to compensate for a weak religious home background is very limited indeed.[57] On the basis of this admittedly scanty empirical research evidence regarding the effectiveness of Catholic schools, the conclusion would seem to be that the present structural dualism be maintained, with as Fr Nicholas has said 'whatever modifications come to seem strategically or economically most wise'.[58]

The cultural divisions apparent in the community and mirrored in the schools show the difficulties of trying to consider educational problems apart from their cultural and political context. There seems to be no doubt that the divisions in Northern Ireland are rooted in the community rather than in the schools. As the Irish National Teachers' Organization wrote in evidence to Lord Stonham, 'It must . . . be recognized that given the peculiar politico-sectarian problems in Northern Ireland this area is not likely to become a pioneer in the field of interdenominational education'.[59]

None of this absolves the schools from their

responsibilities. Clearly, education, at least for co-existence, is a paramount necessity. But more than this is required. The promotion of all possible out-of-school contacts, not only at student but at staff level (e.g. teacher exchange on a term or year basis) must be energetically pursued. Furthermore, as one who favours the introduction of a non-selective secondary school system and leans towards the sixth-form college as a solution to the problems of secondary school reorganization, the writer believes that co-operative institutional experiments at sixth-form level may have some merit. As the Vatican Council pointed out, 'Since this same spirit (of co-operation) is most necessary in educational work, every effort should be made to see that suitable co-ordination is fostered between various Catholic schools, and that between these schools and others that kind of collaboration develops which the well-being of the whole human family demands'.[60] (Apart from the question of interdenominational co-operation, it is worth noting that there has been only very limited co-operation between Catholic grammar and Catholic secondary schools and virtually none among Catholic grammar schools themselves. This is surprising when one considers not only the economies of scale that could be effected, but more important, the opportunity afforded to raise the quality of the education given, particularly at sixth-form level.)

This essay is meant to be exploratory of the issues only. It could not be otherwise. More information and thus more research is needed. By this is meant not only empirical researches, although these are important. If Tillich is right that the problem of church schools 'is the problem of the relationship of Christianity and culture generally and Christianity and education especially,'[61] then at least as important is theological and philosophical investigation of these questions. What is needed in our educational discourse is, as Fr Nicholas has written, 'a team of theologians aware of empirical questions and social scientists sensitive to theological issues'.[62]

Notes

1 R. F. Goodings and J. A. Lauwerys, in G. Z. Bereday and J. A. Lauwerys (eds), *The World Year Book of Education* (London: Evans 1966), 18.

2 Cf. R. G. O'Brien, 'Parents and Education', *Catholic Education* (1955), **1**, 8.

3 R. Voeltzel, in Bereday and Lauwerys, op. cit., 217.

4 Ibid., 218.

5 T. Dubay, *The Philosophy of the State as Educator* (Milwaukee: Bruce 1959), 35.

6 J. S. Mill, *On Liberty* (London: Parker 1859)—quoted by J. S. Brubacher, *A History of the Problems of Education* (New York: McGraw Hill 1966), 519.

7 Cf. Goodings and Lauwerys, op. cit., 6.

8 Cf. O'Brien, op. cit., 11.

9 Ibid., 12.

10 Dubay, op. cit., 30.

11 A. Meiklejohn, *Education between Two Worlds* (New York: Harper 1942)—quoted by Dubay, op. cit., **51.**

12 A. C. F. Beales, in A. V. Judges (ed.), *Looking Forward in Education* (London: Faber 1955), 83.

13 Vatican Council, *Declaration on Christian Education* (1965), part 3.

14 Dom Christopher Butler, in Dom Ralph Russell (ed.) *Essays in Reconstruction* (London: Sheed & Ward 1946), 64.

15 Vatican Council Declaration, part 3.

16 H. Johnston, *A Philosophy of Education* (New York: McGraw Hill 1963), 323.

17 Vatican Council Declaration, part 3.

18 Beales, op. cit., 83–4.

19 M. Knight, 'Should the State back Religious Education?', *New Society* (21 July 1966), **199**, 84.

20 P. Ranwez, S.J., 'Family Religious Training', *Lumen Vitae* (1966), **21**, 144.

21 C. Leetham, *Catholic Education* (Abingdon, Berks.: Catholic Social Guild 1965), 24.

22 O'Brien, op. cit., 18.

23 Vatican Council Declaration, part 1.

24 J. Craigie, in Bereday and Lauwerys, op. cit., 323.

25 Beales, op. cit., 89.

26 Ibid.

27 Craigie, op. cit., 324–5.

28 P. J. Idenburg, in Bereday and Lauwerys, op. cit., 79.

29 Idenburg, op. cit., 89.

30 J. J. Campbell, *Catholic Schools* (Belfast: Fallons 1964), 16.

31 Government of Northern Ireland, *Public Education in Northern Ireland* (Belfast: HMSO 1964), 8–9.

32 Cf. Campbell, op. cit., 18.

33 Ibid., 10.

34 A Statement by the Catholic Bishops on The Education Bill (1968).

35 Irish National Teachers' Organization, Northern Committee, Memorandum of Evidence submitted to Lord Stonham (1969), 8.

36 N. G. McCluskey, S.J., *Catholic Viewpoint on Education* (New York: Doubleday 1962), 34.

37 G. Johnson, in Sr Mary Joan, O.P. and Sr Mary Nona, O.P., *Guiding Growth in Christian Social Living* (Washington D.C.: Catholic University of America Press)—quoted by Johnston, op. cit., 84.

38 J. M. Lee, *Principles and Methods of Secondary Education* (New York: McGraw Hill 1963), 55.

39 Lee, op. cit., 56.

40 Cf. McCluskey, op. cit., 61–3.

41 Lee, op. cit., 62.

42 J. M. Lee (1965). 'Some Reflections on American Catholic Education', paper given at Katholische Akademie, Bayern, 7.

43 J. Maritain, *Education at the Crossroads* (New Haven: Yale Univ. Press 1964), 62.

44 P. Pius XI, Encyclical: *Divini Illius Magistri* (London: CTS 1929), para. 120.

45 Lee, op. cit., 8.

46 F. E. Johnson, 'Church, State and School', *Education* (1951), **71**—quoted by J. H. Fichter, S.J., *Parochial Schools: A Sociological Survey* (New York: Doubleday 1964), 44–5.

47 K. Milne, Comment on article on Post-Primary Education. *Studies* (1968) **57** (227), 269.

48 W. D. Wall, *Education and Mental Health* (London: Harrap 1955), 86 n. 1.

49 Central Advisory Council for Education, *Children and their Primary Schools* (Plowden Report) (London: HMSO 1966), para. 567(a).

50 A. C. F. Beales, 'The Schools Debate', *Catholic Education Today* (1967), **1** (2) 13.

51 H. Brugmans, 'School and State', *Catholic Education*, **1** (1955), 5.

52 Wall: op. cit., p. 96.

53 Ibid., n. 1.

54 Ibid.

55 A. M. Greeley and P. H. Rossi, *The Education of Catholic Americans* (Chicago: Aldine Press 1966), 229.

56 Rossi and Rossi, quoted by McCluskey, loc. cit.

57 Cf. (a) Greeley and Rossi, op. cit. (b) R. A. Neuwien, *Catholic Schools in Action* (Notre Dame Univ. Press 1966). (c) A. L. Phillips, 'Bringing up Christians in Australia' (report of researches by Dr Hans Mol), *Tablet* (16 December 1967), 1302–4.

58 K. F. Nicholas, 'Basis of Catholic Education', *Catholic Education—Handbook of the Catholic Education Council for England and Wales*, London (1969), 25.

59 Irish National Teachers' Organization, op. cit., 12.

60 Vatican Council Declaration, para. 12.

61 P. Tillich, *The Theology of Culture*, quoted in B. Tucker (ed.), *Catholic Education in a Secular Society* (London: Sheed & Ward 1968), 44.

62 Nicholas, op. cit., 27.

Postscript

This paper was written in 1968 and some of its emphases no longer represent accurately the views of the writer. While some work relevant to the issues discussed above has been done in the interim, it has made little impact on the quality of the debate which is still mainly carried on at a level which begs fundamental philosophical and social questions concerning the aims of schooling, the nature of education and of society. Terms are used with little regard for precise definitions and for the examination of basic assumptions.

If few clear-cut answers have been found, at least some educationists and social scientists are beginning to ask themselves searching questions, some specific to Northern Ireland, others of wider application, e.g.

1 How far can the schools in Northern Ireland, both in terms of curriculum and of organization be held to have failed in one of their primary aims?

2 How effective are the schools in doing what they are said to do? How could alternative arrangements be evaluated?

3 Are there any states other than totalitarian where the reasons for a divided system are no longer relevant?

4 In countries where the problems are more or less satisfactorily solved, what institutional arrangements have been made?

5 What specific responsibilities do schools have in societies where strong communal tensions exist?

6 If insufficient common ground exists for a single system to be operated, what positive steps should be taken in terms of (a) curriculum (b) inter-school relations, and (c) teacher education?

In some of these areas, notably that of the curriculum, action has already been taken. The Institute of Education at Queen's University, Belfast is undertaking a schools curriculum development project concerned with community relations with the aid of a grant of £50,000 over 3–3½ years from the Community Relations Commission.

References

The following researches and reports should be valuable to those who wish to study the matter further.

Salters, J. (1970). Attitudes towards society in Roman Catholic and Protestant school children in Belfast—M.Ed Dissertation—Queen's University, Belfast, Library

Malone, J. H. (1972). Schools Project in Community Relations, Write to the author, Department of Education, Queen's University, Belfast BT7 1NN

St Joseph's College of Education (1971). Aspects of Catholic Education—Available from the college, Belfast BT11 9GA

Russell, J. L. (1972). Civic Education in Northern Ireland—Report to the Community Relations Commission Bryson House, Belfast 2

Community Relations Commission (Expected Jan 1973). A register of research on problems associated with the conflict in Northern Ireland.

32   Perpetuating the myth

Peppy Barlow

[Is integrated education the most important schools question in the North? Peppy Barlow doesn't think so.]

Religious integration in schools is often made to seem *the* educational issue in Northern Ireland. More often than not, however, it is used as a political stick with which to beat the Catholic community or as a diversionary measure when much more pertinent educational issues, like the persistence of a selective secondary system, are being raised.

Certainly it would be very comforting and convenient to have children of different religious persuasions mixing freely between the hours of 9 and 4 but it is hardly a realistic proposition. The Catholic educators, rightly or wrongly, feel that education cannot be separated from the religious atmosphere of the schools and are unlikely to sacrifice what little administrative independence they have in Northern Ireland before similar Catholic establishments in other countries, notably Britain and the USA. Protestants calling for integrated education usually mean Catholic children going to State schools, not their children being taught by nuns and Christian Brothers, or even by Catholic lay teachers.

Since the 1968 Education Act (Northern Ireland) the Catholic school managements have, in any case, shown considerable willingness in taking up maintained status, to the extent of about 70% of the primary schools and nearly 100% secondary. This involves accommodating two local authority representatives on a management committee of six (the other four being nominees of the school management) in exchange for 80% capital grants on building and 100% maintenance—as against a voluntary status which only entitled them to 65% grants but no local authority representation.

Selection exam

Beyond the semi-independent Catholic sector there is a powerful body of voluntary grammar schools, more Protestant than Catholic, upholding a selective system which does much more educational damage than any religious divisions, and is an anachronism in a country which 'officially' claims to be part of the UK.

Primary schools, faced with the constrictions placed on their teaching methods by a selection exam at 11 have always deplored it, even in cases where their obvious success at getting children into grammar

Source: Irish Times, 22 February 1972.

school met with parental approval. Secondary schools, now being encouraged by local authorities to make provision for secondary school exams like the Certificate of Secondary Education, the GCE, 'O' and 'A' level, and being increasingly pushed into the public eye under the label 'comprehensive', feel that the eleven-plus undermines their attempts to provide the kind of education they would like.

They are forced to play the dubious game of chasing exam results because this is the measure most parents look for, and many schools have achieved amazing results with an intake of 'non-qualifiers' who were designated 'non-exam material' at the age of 11. Forty-three 'A' levels, gleaned from such an intake in one large Belfast secondary school, is not uncommon, and there are certainly many pupils staying on past the school leaving age who would have left automatically ten years ago, mainly because there would have been no provision past 15 in their secondary schools.

However, this is not the true measure of their achievement. Confronted with children who need more than academic training, secondary schools have probably always been more aware of the realities of life than the grammar schools. Now they are coming into their own with methods of school organization and education that place the emphasis firmly on the individual needs of the pupil and the problems he will have to face in the outside world. Basically this means trying to give the school a less authoritarian, more humane aspect and providing endless opportunities for communication and expression.

On the administrative side many secondary schools are following the lead of Orangefield, a boys' secondary school on the outskirts of Belfast where John Malone pioneered a system of student counsellors—an idea which was further developed by John Malone during his time with the Community Relations Commission last year in the appointment of two youth counsellors in schools which were likely to have a high percentage of early leavers. The latter are people who spend only a third of their time in school and will remain in contact with leavers right into their first jobs.

Field centres

Beyond this there is a general promotion of outside activities which has involved the establishment of field centres, mostly on the initiative of the schools themselves, the encouragement of project work and individual expression both in and outside the classroom. In the case of Orangefield it has meant more successful entrants to the *Daily Mirror* essay competition than any other school in the UK.

On the whole their kind of approach brings the secondary schools into close contact with the community and many secondary heads will tell you how thrilled parents are when they find the school taking an active interest in their children and themselves as individuals.

These kind of developments make the secondary schools the centre of educational initiative and gives them a right to be resentful when the top 30% ability group is creamed off into institutions which lack these attitudes and often neglect the range of subjects offered by the secondary schools because of the emphasis placed on 'academic excellence'. Even a school as large as Methodist College, with 1,620 secondary pupils and a sixth form of 470, has so far neglected the practical subjects which are by no means irrelevant even to pupils of obvious academic ability. And this is a liberal school as grammar schools go.

In fact no one is suggesting that the grammar schools haven't done a fine job to date, and in Belfast, where housing is as socially segregated as it is religiously, it can be argued that they achieve a limited degree of social mix where secondary schools, confined to a catchment area, do not. But it makes no sense to perpetuate a system based on the *myth* that only a certain percentage of the population is capable of academic attainment when this limits the educational opportunities of all concerned and certainly keeps the middle classes out of their neighbourhood secondary school.

Political lobby

The grammar school lobby has been described by one despondent secondary head as 'second only to the Orange Order' in its political influence at Stormont, and much of its strength lies in the weakness of middle-class opposition. The middle classes in Northern Ireland have never had to face the consequences of selection because the grammar schools are allowed to take 20% non-qualifiers as fee payers—a matter of £60 a year which will probably be a one-off expense as pupils are reassessed at the end of the first year and may become eligible for a local authority grant. Further to this, children who pass the qualifying exam in an area where there is only secondary or comprehensive schooling available can claim the right to grammar school education and the local authority is obliged to pay travelling and even boarding expenses to make this possible. Consequently no truly comprehensive scheme can be instituted by a local authority and there is no real pressure for it among the politically vocal.

In spite of this, however, the structure is beginning to show signs of weakening. The Ministry of Education at Stormont declared a tentative interest in non-selective experiments eight years ago and since has not authorized the building of new grammar schools. And the Headmasters' Association, which represents the independent sector, is reported to be mulling over ways of fitting into a three-tier system, possibly as sixth-form colleges, if the dreadful day should ever dawn. The local authorities who are inclined towards the non-selective also seem to favour this arrangement as a way of using existing accommodation.

There has also been a significant move made by the 'experts'. The members of an advisory council on education, set up by the Ministry of Education to examine ways of improving *The Existing Selection Procedure*, refused to accept their brief on the grounds that they disapproved of the principle of selection until they were assured that they could go on to study alternative non-selective systems. And the teachers' organization, INTO, had voted to withdraw co-operation in the selection procedure after 1972, although as a union with a largely Catholic membership officials fear that this will be seen as a political 'knock the Government' move rather than an expression of educational principle.

Minor pressures like this can probably be safely ignored by Stormont for some time to come. But there is considerably more hope in the fact that parents are beginning to vote with their children's feet. The 'qualified' intake into secondary schools is on the increase and one mother I met told a very revealing story. She has three daughters. The eldest qualified and went to grammar school but got headaches under the pressure of exams. So she took her away at 15, a time when she could have left school altogether, and sent her to a secondary school where she got six 'O' levels, including commerce, and now has a good secretarial job which she enjoys. The second daughter also qualified and survived the grammar school but advised her mother not to send the youngest there on the grounds that 'it's not the kind of school for our sort and you have to be good to keep up or they don't bother with you'. The youngest was duly put down for the secondary school even before taking the selection exam.

Greater interest

Quite apart from the fact that this parent obviously felt that the secondary school took a greater interest in her daughters and herself as individuals, she also pointed out that they were getting better facilities for less expense. Grammar schools are authorized to charge a nominal fee of £8 a year to all pupils and in this case charged extra for things like ingredients for domestic science classes. The secondary school charged no fees, cookery classes cost 10p a week, and there was a much more realistic range of subjects.

Both schools in question were Catholic and so were the children, but the educational issues are the same in either sector. It seems so pointless to pursue subjects like integrated education which will take years to resolve when there is so much else to be done. When the selection procedure in the province was changed in

1964 from a conventional exam to the use of a verbal reasoning test and teachers' assessment it was found that Catholics suddenly equalled their Protestant counterparts in the proportion of children qualifying.

Get rid of selection and the non-qualifiers might get a better chance. Selection has, after all, only ever served to underline class advantages. It has never had very much to do with education.

This section of the volume ends with an article on the English public schools by Philip Venning from *The Times Educational Supplement* of 23 June 1972, in which he suggests that the whole approach of such schools' defenders, as well as of their administrators, has tended to change during the late 1960s and early 1970s. As a prologue to the Venning article, we print a significant paragraph from a report of some thirty years earlier by the so-called Fleming Committee appointed by the President of the Board of Education in July 1942 to investigate possible ways of integrating public schools with the general educational system. Its rhetoric is of some interest, both as historical evidence of attitudes which Venning now suggests are dying, and as early evidence of developments which have continued.

The publication of the Venning article sparked off considerable controversy in the paper's correspondence column, though this was more concerned with the ideological issues involved than with the facts as presented.

33 The public schools and the general educational system

113. But no mere analysis of the characteristics of the Public Schools can be expected to do justice to them. Like any other institutions which have an ancient history it would be as false to dwell only on their traditional customs, as it would to neglect the effect, often quite unconscious, of their associations with the past. A true picture of the Public Schools would have to include a reference to the annual Latin Play at Westminster, performed today as laid down in the Statutes of 1560, and also to such an undertaking as the performance of Mr Bernard Shaw's *St Joan* by the boys of one of the older schools to audiences in Strasbourg, Nancy and Paris in the spring of 1939. It would pay attention as much to the educational experiments in work on the land carried out at a very recent foundation, such as Bryanston, as to the rules of Fives at Eton, where the Court in which the game is played is a faithful representation of the space between the buttresses of the fifteenth century Chapel. It would have to take account of the Greek iambics written in Sixth Book at Winchester as well as the work in the Metal Shops at Oundle, without forgetting the Science taught at the one school or the Classics at the other, and it would have to consider the buildings of the Public Schools from the Chapels of the founders at Winchester or Eton to those of more recent years at Giggleswick, Lancing and Stowe, and to the War Memorial Chapel at Charterhouse completed sixteen years ago. At least the Public Schools have made of themselves real communities, and there may be seen in the education they offer a definite sense of purpose. During the last hundred years they have preserved for English education a belief in the value of humane studies, in the need for a training in responsibility, and in the essential part to be played by religion in education. But we do not feel it our duty to pass any final judgment on the merits and failings of these schools. We are satisfied that there are many in this country who would agree that the education they provide is of value and that by means of boarding schools, old or new, those who wish their children to have this kind of education should have the opportunity of obtaining it. We have framed our proposals in the belief that new schools must be provided which will absorb and no doubt enrich the Boarding School tradition and that the old schools should be enabled to remedy the most serious weakness in the education which they offer, derived from the fact that at present they too often concern themselves with children coming from only a limited section of society.

Source: Report of the Committee on Public Schools appointed by the President of the Board of Education in July 1942, HMSO, 44–51, 96–8.

34 Survival of the public schools

Philip Venning

There is a renewed feeling of optimism in the boys' public schools. A change of government has worked wonders, but this is not the whole story.

The middle and late sixties were among the blackest years in public school history. The schools were under attack from many directions. The Public Schools Commission was an overt political threat to their existence. Academic competition from the grammar schools hotted up. A new youth culture questioned their internal stability.

Costs rose steeply, bringing with them sharp rises in fees, and to make matters worse political, academic, cultural and economic threats came at a time when a kink in the population curve brought a sudden drop in the number of 13-year-olds from whom their entrants were drawn.

It was a bad time. Many of their enemies concluded that the schools were going down—that all that had to be done was leave them alone and watch them fade away.

A few very small independent schools did fold, but the public schools as a whole fought back. The result was to speed up far-reaching changes which had already begun, and bring about an anxious self-analysis out of which the schools have emerged, if not cocky, at least a good deal more confident.

The political question mark remains: it looks as if the Labour Party will enter the next election committed to the abolition of the public schools. But they have lived with this threat for a period of years, and the schools show little sign of allowing it to sap their morale.

Quite consciously they have concentrated on putting their present house in order, without paying too much attention to threats from socialist critics or the undoubted worries of those within their own ranks who feel guilty about the schools' narrow social base.

This then, is the thesis of this article. In part it can be substantiated by the outward indicators: pupil enrolments, staffing, university entrance results, academic achievements, economic survival. In part it depends on going round listening to what headmasters say and looking at the changes which are obvious to a visitor's eye.

One dangerous tremor which rattled the system was when public schoolboys began to reject the privileged position which was the very essence of it.

The new cult of youth, the rise of the Beatles, Carnaby Street, 'satire', and later on the student protest in the universities, produced a very different

Source: *The Times Educational Supplement*, 23 June 1972.

kind of boy from the one the schools were used to.

Mature earlier, less willing to accept established authority, keener to assert their own life style, the products of this revolution could not be suppressed in the customary ways, even if schools had stubbornly tried to do so. The hard core rebels left as soon as they could; but most of those who remained were also affected.

Parents were relieved that the schools were bearing the brunt of it (this, after all, was what they were paying for). But many, too, had come to agree with their sons' view of rigorous living conditions and petty restrictions.

And the more realistic among them had seen that unless the schools changed it would be impossible to persuade the boys to stay on after 'O' level.

The schools, in turn, had been forced by declining applications to look at the demands of parents in a new light. Parents became people to woo, instead of keeping at arm's length; and as more and more boys came from homes within a car journey of the school, parents, and particularly mothers, started to have growing influence.

The relative ease with which reform accelerated in response to these pressures owed a good deal to a sympathetic attitude to change in many schools. The headmasters can claim some of the credit. One group even claims that it was a new breed of headmasters that provided both the catalyst and driving force for change.

According to this theory, the young heads, appointed in the sixties, had been forced out of the Victorian mould. Instead of going straight from public school to Oxbridge and back to public school teaching, they had fought in the war. Returning to their schools, they were critical of what they saw, and once in power they pushed through reform.

But, in fact, many of the new men were surprisingly similar to the old style heads both in background and experience. 'Absolute old fossils, a great many of them', said one head. Though there are fewer clergymen in their ranks—this was true by the thirties—their influence lingers. The boys claim that several heads still feel at their best in the pulpit of the school chapel.

Much of the change in the schools was quite patently not the result of any inspired forward thinking by the heads; a great deal was thrust on them. But they all profess to be glad at having acted as midwives.

Success for a headmaster still depended, to some extent at least, on acting out the part of a great man, but the idea of a great man was changing. Doggedly upholding the old ways had come to look foolish, unashamed egotism and pomposity had ceased to be respectable.

But it was a mistake to carry the trend too far. Some of the most successful liberal reform was set in motion by some of the most orthodox-seeming of the new headmasters.

Faced with common difficulties, a new spirit of co-operation was born between the heads. 'In the past headmasters used to hide their problems under the carpet', one headmaster said. 'They have now learned they can all benefit from each other, even though they remain rivals.' After an evening at one of the dining clubs to which many of them belong, heads would return to their schools primed with new ideas.

Co-operation spurred competition—if one school started planning a sixth-form centre, it was pretty certain that the neighbouring schools would quickly do the same, or build some other attraction.

But it was easy to gain support for new buildings. For other aspects of reform, the support of the house-masters was usually crucial.

In most schools the house was the real unit of power, controlling most of the way of life within the school—how much fagging, cold baths, petty restrictions, and beating by prefects, for example. In many of the older, better known schools, the housemasters backed by senior staff, were the main opponents of a reforming head. Only after an all-out clash with the houses could liberalization struggle through.

No headmaster will deny that the sixties were difficult for the large and famous schools as well as the smaller, less well known.

In 1947 9 per cent of all school children were in private education. Twenty years later the proportion had dropped to 5·5 per cent. But the public school numbers continued to expand. From 1946 to 1961 they had increased by 32 per cent, then, in the next decade, growth slackened to 5·3 per cent.

In the 39 largest boarding schools the growth was less rapid: 23 per cent between 1946 and 1961, and only 4·4 per cent from 1961 to 1971.

Part of this growth was undoubtedly attributable to the high numbers of 13-year-olds in the population—the postwar baby boom. But by the middle and late sixties the number had plummeted by nearly 100,000.

Some headmasters are convinced that it was the population drop, pure and simple, which was the cause of all their troubles. Averaged out there was a large proportionate drop in the number of applications, and it came at a time when most schools could ill afford the loss of fee income. 'Even the top schools were not turning away boys in 1965', admitted one headmaster.

Rapidly rising costs could only be offset by annual increases in fees (many headmasters are amazed that there has been no concerted parental opposition to regular rises). Between 1952 and 1968 boarding fees in the whole private sector rose by 130 per cent, and day fees by 160 per cent, according to a survey by Howard Glennerster in 1970. At the same time the consumer price index went up by only about 60 per cent.

In 1969 there were ten schools with boarding fees of more than £650 a year: by 1972 there were ten (not the same ten) with fees over £800 a year.

'Fees are increasing at an alarming rate and parents are beginning to realize that they must make provision for the payment of such fees at the earliest opportunity. So they are turning to insurance companies', an insurance consultant reports. In the past five years special school fee schemes have been introduced enabling fees to be reduced in effect to as little as £300 a year.

The main reason for the rise has been increases in teachers' salaries, a heavy bill for public schools where both numbers and qualifications of staff are high. These increases tend to affect the small school relatively more heavily. Maintenance costs have also risen, with all the expensive new buildings and the facilities installed in the past 10 years.

There is little room for saving, nor do the schools want to cut. High staffing ratios are considered to be their most important single attraction. Increasingly schools are looking for labour-saving machinery on the domestic side—Wellington is considering washing machines for the boys to do their own laundry.

But any such economies will be slight, and the great uncertainty remains—if fees carry on rising faster than the cost of living, and there is every reason to think they will, are parents still going to think it worth paying for a private education?

By 1980, if present trends continue, fees might be up to £1,600 a year. Even with expanded and more elaborate insurance schemes the burden is bound to grow. Surely headmasters ask themselves, a point will come when the middle classes will say no.

Many schools seem to be staking all on making themselves more attractive by expanding the range of activities offered: when economic constraints would suggest curtailing them. Some schools may come to concentrate more on intensive tuition, becoming in effect larger versions of the professional crammers.

A few schools, notably the nine Clarendon schools,[1] have been cushioned by the income from endowments, but over half of all public schools have none at all. Averaged out, endowments and grants (from religious bodies, for example) only make up about 5 per cent of public school income. Very little is directly used to lower fees. More usually it goes towards capital projects.

Undoubtedly the massive modernization programme of the late fifties and sixties was a strain on resources; some schools could sell land to raise money, others looked at ways of mortgaging their buildings (worth £4m Sherborne estimates).

The Industrial Fund for the Advancement of Scientific Education helped many schools to build new laboratories; but the bulk of the money came from appeals to parents and old boys. Between 1960 and 1972 66 independent schools (boys and girls) raised about £12m, and the figure for all boys' public schools is probably between £15m and £20m.

The appeals are not once and for all; they are becoming more frequent and more ambitious. Oundle is in the process of launching an appeal for £1m. Sherborne is one of several schools on to their second appeal within 15 years.'The school is like an industrial plant', said the headmaster, at a meeting urging old boys to pay up once again. 'It becomes obsolete, there is competition from the maintained sector, and from other public schools, and standards of life are changing.'

Far from being frantic cries for help, the appeals reflect the returning confidence. The population figures are climbing back, and headmasters have started reporting that comprehensive reorganization is inducing a number of grammar school parents to take their sons out of the maintained sector.

A public school headmaster said: 'Parents come to me and say they want a school where their boy will be given some attention and where there is order in the classroom.'

The number of these refugees from the state system is tiny, and the smaller, cheaper schools probably benefit most. But the larger schools are also receiving these applicants. One famous school, for example, has recently admitted the son of the local plasterer, who had become worried when gypsy boys were reported to have moved into the local school with knives.

In spite of fears about their future, the public schools have made little sustained effort to recruit from the maintained sector. Most pay lip service to the idea of admitting a token number of boys from primary schools. Some probably are admitting a few more, but this is being offset by the action of local education authorities such as Solihull, which is withdrawing its assisted places at Solihull School, and ILEA which has stopped advertising special scholarship places at St Paul's.

The public schools' lack of enthusiasm, the headmasters say, stems from the fact that teaching methods in primary and preparatory school are so different that the primary schoolboy needs months of individual tuition to bring him up to the standard of his contemporaries in the range of subjects public schoolboys study at 13.

The changing attitudes of the middle classes show up most in the decline in the popularity of boarding. As parents began to value the schools as much for their academic as their character building, one of the central tenets of the system became seriously questioned.

Increasing boarding fees certainly played a part. Many parents decided that it was not worth scrimping and saving to send a boy away to school. Far better, they concluded, to spend the money on keeping up the family standard of living.

'The chance to travel abroad or own a boat is much more use to a boy than sleeping in dormitories,' said the mother of a day boy. And parents are beginning to think that they, not the school, are the people equipped to see their sons through adolescence.

The trend away from boarding set in after the war, but has been growing. Between 1946 and 1961 the number of boarders in HMC[2] independent schools went up by 28·6 per cent, compared with a 46·1 per cent increase in the number of day boys. Since then the number of boarders has stayed the same while the number of day boys continued rising. By last year they had increased another 16·3 per cent.

Inevitably the smallest schools are suffering most (the cost of accommodating a boy is much the same however famous or insignificant the school), but even the 39 largest HMC boarding schools have had a struggle to keep up their boarding numbers. In the past 10 years the number of boarders in these schools went up by only 1·76 per cent. Eight of them had a reduction in boarders and in seven others boarding numbers have been static or shown a slight, short fall. In the same period the number of boarders in the 16 predominantly day schools dropped from 1,002 to 902.

The schools have become more regional. Every school reports that a high proportion of its intake now comes from within 50 miles, an easy car journey away. In its prospectus, Tonbridge includes a map showing the towns in a 50-mile radius of the school.

The boys have also reacted against boarding. Responding to this a number of schools have made their boarding rules more flexible (following pioneering work done by Sevenoaks).

Some have introduced weekly or fortnightly boarding, others have allowed boys to opt for a year or two of boarding at whatever stage they wish. Boys can go to parties at weekends and keep up a more normal outside life. With more liberal sixth forms and a vast new range of extra-curricular activities, some senior day boys are choosing to board.

One mainly day school in the Midlands reports that its boarding numbers dropped from 104 to 49 in the late sixties, but after introducing a more flexible system they have crept back to 72 and are still rising ('in spite of the fact that I refuse to admit boarders who are not as academically good as the day boys', the headmaster added).

Few headmasters would now try to sell boarding as an essential part of the public school experience, but they point to hopeful signs: with business travelling abroad increasing (and the Common Market is bound to accelerate this) the need for boarding may return. The disappearing Commonwealth may be replaced by the international business community.

A return to boarding would be invigorated if firms were to help parents meet the boarding fees, allowing fathers to travel abroad or even move to head office (there is some evidence that firms have begun to do so, but no one admits it).

If there is not this return, the future of the smallish school miles from anywhere looks bleak; while those near a centre of population will almost certainly survive and prosper by admitting a growing number of day boys.

But the smaller schools have not been sitting back

waiting to go bankrupt. Faced with a mounting number of empty beds, they started looking round for new kinds of boarder. Girls seemed to be the obvious answer.

Marlborough had already attracted publicity when it took on senior girls as an experiment (though not for economic reasons). At the same time many girls' schools were finding it harder to offer adequate sixth-form work, and had started approaching the nearby boys' schools with plans for co-operation.

Other financially stronger schools quickly realized they were missing out on a selling point. Parents liked the idea (it dampened worries about homosexuality): it made the sixth form more attractive to boys; and permitted a wider scope for sixth-form studies.

Within a few years schools as varied as Charter-house and Taunton, Canford and Gordonstoun, had announced plans to admit girls. But the number so far has been minute: by 1971 the total number of girls in HMC independent schools was 409, or 0·7 per cent of the total number of boys. Of these 166 were boarders, 193 were full-time day girls, and 50 were part-timers, coming to the boys' school for lessons but returning to their own boarding school for the night.

People who expected girls to bale the schools out were wrong. Proportionately the greatest number of girl boarders are in the 39 largest schools. Eight of the largest schools experienced a drop in numbers in the sixties, but only two tried to make it up by admitting girls. One had a drop of 6¼ per cent in boys which they partially offset, by a 2¾ per cent intake of girls; the other school had a 1 per cent drop in boarders, offset by a 6 per cent intake of girls.

Because the number of girls in any school has been so small, their effect has been small. 'Which is why I am against having fewer than 100 girls', said the head-master of an all boys school. 'It is just not fair on the girls.'

How much the girls are a gimmick and how much a future mainstay of the boys' public school system is hard to tell—at the present rate of admission it will be a long time before many schools are truly coeducational. Opposition to boarding for girls seems to be growing faster than for boys, and if growth is to come anywhere it will almost certainly be in day girls. A typical public school of the future might well be one-third boy boarders, one-third day boys, and one-third day girls.

Another way of making up numbers would have been to admit more foreign boys, sons of Middle Eastern bankers, and American oil men. The public schools have always accepted a handful of overseas boys (all those sons of maharajahs), and headmasters have always been proud of the different influences they bring.

But with the exception of one or two schools which have deliberately developed their overseas connexions, most have not responded by packing their beds with foreigners. This has been left to the very small, sometimes unrecognized independent schools, where more than half the intake can be from abroad.

When the film *If* appeared in the late 60s, it looked as if the public school system had been given another shove down the slippery slope. Though exaggerated to the point of fantasy, it bore too many stylized resemblances to schools in an earlier generation for comfort.

But even in the short time since *If* came out, many of these resemblances have greatly decreased.

The new reformation was largely triggered by prefects and senior boys, the first products of the youth revolution. By the early sixties prefects were coming to their housemasters refusing to beat junior boys, and declining to exercise their authority in other ways. Almost overnight boy beating disappeared (it probably does survive on a very diminished scale, but head-masters seldom admit to it).

Fagging[3] still kept on in about a quarter of the public schools, quickly came to an end in the others. 'Senior boys just didn't want their shoes spotlessly clean, or their lavatory seats warmed for them by junior boys', a recent sixth-former explained. Where fagging does remain, it is often restricted to community work.

Early morning cold baths, already abolished in many schools, disappeared unmourned.

In the long term the collapse of the 'blood system' was partly responsible: when the games idols could no longer be guaranteed a university place and work was becoming much more important, they lost their position as natural power figures within the schools.

A new generation of prefects took over, often those who stay on longest, but increasingly those more suited to the job. A few schools have even started electing their prefects. Solihull has also introduced a lower rank of deputy—with no privilege, only responsibility, but which still attracts volunteers.

Even the most critical staff and boys agree that a more mature attitude to authority and prefectship has emerged in the past 5 or 10 years. 'So-and-so is wet' was the old approach; instead we now have 'so-and-so is being left out' said one headmaster.

Gradually the new approach is permeating the whole school—the headmaster's dealings with staff, and the staff's dealings with boys.

A housemaster at Winchester describes it in an issue of *Conference*, the HMC magazine: his predecessors 'were presiding over a system which made many men, and broke some. The line was "If you can't take a joke you shouldn't have joined. We are not altering the system for you my lad." We, on the other hand, try (I don't say we succeed) to interfere with the system the whole time to see that no one is broken. It is more tiring'.

Greater informality has been encouraged by 'central feeding'—many schools now operate a cafeteria, where the headmaster and staff queue alongside the boys (at least when journalists are about), in place of the traditional house dining halls, dominated by housemaster, oak tables, silver cups, and grace. Though usually justified on the grounds of economy, it has proved to be one of the strongest solvents of the house system, and has been much contested by traditionalists.

The elimination of many of the petty restrictions and privileges upon which the authority system used to depend entirely altered the atmosphere of the schools. Which button is done up, whether you are allowed an umbrella or not, trivial distinctions have become much less important in most schools. In a few they continue: 'It is a useful incentive to boys after finishing their "O" levels', said one more traditional headmaster.

But in spite of liberalization, it would be wrong to pretend that everything is harmony and enlightenment, and it is not surprising that the latest generation of boys are unconvinced by 'you've never had it so good'. Boys are maturing earlier, and 15- and 16-year-olds can cause trouble.

This is clearly shown by up-to-date findings by the Bloxham Project Research Unit, Oxford, which was set up in 1969 to look at the ways the boarding schools communicate Christian ideas and values. Though one in four boys in their sample public schools agreed strongly that the way authority is organized works well, two in five agreed strongly that there was too much concern with power and authority in the school.

At both boarding and day schools about two in five boys agreed strongly that generally relationships between staff and pupils were easy and friendly; but one in four were convinced there was little trust between pupils and members of staff.

Many of the old sources of friction remain, notably hair. Most headmasters relaxed their restrictions and follow a policy of containment. 'But there is much less argument about it than there was in the sixties', said one headmaster.

School uniform is still in force in about 95 per cent of schools but stiff collars and dark suits have largely given way to sports jackets and even blazers, and in the evenings and at weekends, jeans and sweaters are now common.

Living conditions are much less of a cause for complaint. The latest guide to the public schools reads more like a holiday brochure: 'Every boy has his own room, efficiently heated, with hot and cold water.' In fact, draughty dormitories with splintery floors can still be found, though for sixth formers individual study bedrooms are now widespread.

Sixth-form centres are being tried in perhaps a score of schools. 'Here with a resident warden, the most senior boys can concentrate on academic studies in a university ambience for their final terms, after they have given service to their houses, and at a time when it is important to recognize their adult needs', is how Cranleigh describes its sixth-form centre.

But many headmasters are reluctant to separate their senior boys from the rest of the school, nor do the boys usually want it.

Flexible boarding and the end of many petty restrictions were part of the new package offered to sixth formers; study bedrooms and a junior common room with bar and television was another. Though

smoking and spirits drinking is normally forbidden, even some of the most conservative schools have introduced bars for the seniors. Eton has had bars for many years.

The end of the 'blood system' was closely linked with the dethronement of rugger and cricket. Its position was often deliberately eroded in the weakening of the house system. Fierce and sometimes fanatical interhouse rivalry in sport was for years fuelled by diehard housemaster and prefects who saw their job as hammering house spirit into each generation of new boys.

Reforming headmasters found this the hardest nut to crack. Interhouse competition has survived, but sport competition is now normally organized on a school basis ('and the improvement in the atmosphere in the houses is remarkable' commented one headmaster).

Most schools keep games compulsory. But boys are steadily being given the chance to choose between a very much wider range of both major and minor sports. Soccer is appearing as an option, usually in response to pressure from the boys.

Headmasters on the whole favour the diversity. It fits in well with the new philosophy of the public schools that boys should be encouraged to do passably well at something rather than fail the customary challenges.

One of the first casualties of the reforms was the Combined Cadet Force,[4] now voluntary in about half the public schools, obligatory for a minimum of three terms in the rest. The CCF was anyway much reduced by the Army's desire to cut costs—they didn't think it contributed to national defence. Square bashing has largely disappeared in favour of Outward Bound type activities—camp-craft, first aid, map reading and canoeing. In many of the schools where the corps is genuinely voluntary up to a third or more of the school may belong.

As an alternative (and boys have to choose one) a staggering variety of outdoor activities has blossomed —for example, upkeep of the school grounds, vehicle maintenance, building, forestry, driving, farming, local history projects and most significant of all, social service.

The speed with which each school took up community work depended a good deal on geography—those in or near towns became involved much more quickly. The work is much the same as that done in state schools, painting old people's rooms, or digging their gardens, reading to the blind, or visiting the handicapped. Local environment work is also catching on fast.

No one could have been more pleased with this development than the headmasters. Here at last was an updated version of the traditional idea of service, and an outward sign that the schools were not indifferent to their surrounding community.

Enthusiasm also grew as public school religion and the school chapel declined. There are still one or two boarding schools where chapel is compulsory more than once a day; and many retain compulsory house prayers. But in general there is more flexibility over chapel going than there was a few years ago. In a few schools senior boys are entitled to discuss the sermon with the visiting preacher.

In its place has grown a revised version of the traditional doctrine of the whole man, which includes an almost Maoist devotion to the idea that academic studies should be tempered with both culture and practical skills. Partly for this reason and partly to give each boy more of a chance to excel, art, music, drama and handicrafts have started flourishing as never before.

Philistinism is a charge that the public schools are determined to destroy. Though improvements in art and music began well before the sixties, most of the building of new art schools and music blocks took place in the past 10 years. As one headmaster pointed out: 'Art and music are a much more genuine method of sublimation than running round a track.'

Schools such as Bryanston have taken steps to encourage local people to join in these cultural activities, particularly music. The headmaster of Wellington hopes to see the school develop as a centre of excellence within the area, attracting local people both to enjoy and participate in art, music and drama.

But in spite of these contacts, and the good impression usually created by social work, relations between schools and their surrounding areas remain fairly remote. For the boys this has been frustrating—the youth revolution bridges the class barrier. A common interest in pop music or football has meant that fewer boys are anxious to stand out from their contemporaries in the maintained schools. Some headmasters complain that one of the first victims has been the public school accent.

The frustration with the lack of contact is shown up by the Bloxham research, which found that nearly half the boys in the boarding school sample are unsatisfied with the amount of contact the school has with the outside world. In the day schools it was only a quarter.

There are exceptions: several schools are beginning to co-operate with their local grammar or comprehensive school, and Solihull School is one of a number using the local technical college to teach more unusual subjects. Some schools such as Kings School, Bruton, even make use of the youth employment and child guidance services.

But the biggest pressure of all has been the escalating competition for university places with the grammar schools. It affected the great schools every bit as much as the lesser.

With the universities calling the academic tune, all efforts were concentrated on 'A' levels. The younger boys were not totally neglected—new mathematics were born in the public schools; but pressure for examination results robbed many schools of the chance for much more curriculum development. It is a rare public school which does not expect all its boys to be university material (even the 11-plus failures).

The race with the grammar schools seems to have left little energy for updating and widening the curriculum. Classics—the cornerstone of the traditional public school—were downgraded, especially after Oxbridge dropped a Latin requirement. Virtually all schools kept up a certain amount of compulsory English and divinity in the sixth form; and a few new optional subjects such as Russian or economics were brought in to counteract the rigid arts or science 'A' level choice that all but a few schools were operating.

In 1963 only 4·3 per cent of boys in recognized independent schools took combinations of subjects at 'A' level which bridge the arts science divide, compared with 7·9 per cent in grammar schools.

But this is changing—the swing from science was much more marked in the public schools than elsewhere; and boys, staff and parents were coming to resent the narrowness.

A public school prospectus today will emphasize that specialization is delayed for as long as possible. 'One of the principal aims of the curriculum is to avoid over-early specialization', reads one. It will say that the curriculum has been completely revised within the past six or eight years. It will boast that unlikely 'A' level combinations are possible, even welcome.

But in spite of the intentions, the proportion doing mixed arts, and science 'A' levels is still fairly small. In 1969 it had only risen to 13·7 per cent, while in the grammar schools it was 17·3 per cent, and in the comprehensives 17·2 per cent. Almost certainly the proportion is higher in the public schools with larger sixth forms, and better means of coping with complicated and conflicting timetables. However, several headmasters admit to being secretly proud that the traditional subjects and combinations have held their own ('real work', they call it).

Mixed 'A' levels may have been slow to come in, but a leavening of the 'A' level diet was not. Some of the fiercest competition between public schools is now expressed in the wide range of different, and sometimes bizarre, options they offer their sixth formers.

At Bradfield the range of choice includes statistics, astronomy, anthropology, play production and philology. Blundell's offers American history, the Greek World, political theory, archaeology and architecture while St John's Leatherhead, offers philosophy, Mediaeval Latin, classical drama and New Testament Greek. Elsewhere boys can be introduced to geology, mechanical drawing, or psychology. Work with computers is common.

In most schools a sixth former will spend up to a quarter or a third of his timetable away from his specialism. A boy will find it difficult to escape from current affairs lectures, for example, and at Merchant Taylors' all sixth formers do a course in general economics.

The Use of English examination has ensured that most scientists emerge moderately literate; but within the last few years several schools have started insisting that their arts 'A' level students do some science.

Gresham's encourages boys in the arts sixth who are good mathematicians to take modern maths as a third 'A' level 'to fit them for management in an industrial and computerized society'. These days, the idea of 'the whole man' includes culture and practical skills.

But the accent on preparation for the future has some curious anomalies. Most notable has been the neglect of language teaching beyond 'O' level. The public schools were quick to install language laboratories as soon as they came in, but because of the 'A'-level system, not many boys do much serious language study after 'O'-level. Most schools have the normal links with schools abroad.

On the whole the schools have steered clear of the more unorthodox 'A' level subjects, such as archaeology, offered by boards other than the beloved Oxford and Cambridge. But business studies, pioneered by Marlborough, is a new arrival which is rapidly becoming popular; Malvern advertises preliminary medical work, and Ipswich School has just built an engineering laboratory where boys can work for engineering 'A'-level.

The need to make sixth-form work more attractive to the boys prompted a good deal of revision of the timetable. Though a small proportion of boys had always left school at 'O'-level to do 'A'-levels at the local technical college, at the height of the youth revolution, the idea of leaving school to take 'A'-levels at a technical college or a crammer suddenly became more popular.

Between 1966 and 1970 the proportion of those leavers who left recognized independent schools under 16 to go to technical college rose from 5·7 per cent to 12·4 per cent.

Headmasters now claim that because of the reforms the trend has been halted and in some cases reversed. One of the top 10 schools had only one boy leave for a local tech last year, compared with a higher number a few years ago. Another, equally famous, had only 10 leave.

Fears that all this trendy change would affect 'A'-level results proved groundless. Figures for the independent HMC schools on their own are not available but those for all recognized independent schools are a guide.

The proportion of leavers with either two or three 'A'-level passes did not change in either the grammar or the independent schools between 1966 and 1970. In the former it remained at about 36 per cent, in the latter about 43 per cent. However, during the period there was a noticeable increase in the proportion of public school leavers who had three 'A'-level passes ('four 'A'-levels are definitely not allowed', said one headmaster smugly). Many schools say their results showed a remarkable improvement after liberalization.

They can point to the traditional goal—Oxbridge awards—which are still dominated by the independent and direct grant schools. Wholly independent schools have had between 5 and 8 of the top 10 places in the league table over the past 6 years. Most of the famous public schools do fairly well, though even the best have had bad years. The upheavals within the schools had little obvious effect on the number of awards secured.

In spite of congratulating themselves on acknowledging the existence of polytechnics and advanced further education, recognized independent schools send very few on to CNAA degree work (rising from 1·5 per cent of leavers in 1966 to 2·7 per cent in 1970). The number going on to HND/HNC work increased from 170 to 260 in the same period.

In spite of increasing numbers going on to higher education, there has been a real boom in careers advice in the schools, something which was totally inadequate in the bygone days when the old boy network was infinitely more useful than any amount of vocational guidance. This appears to be an area where the independent sector is a few steps ahead of the state system: most schools now make use of the Public School Appointments Bureau, which has mushroomed in the past two years.

The PSAB has found that the changes in the schools have tended to force public school leavers into much more clearly definable types.

There are those who want further qualifications with an eye on a safe position in the professions, and those who 'want to do something creative' and normally end up as don't knows. Between 1963 and 1970 the don't knows rose from 11·0 per cent of leavers to 19·4 per cent.

However, the top ten most popular careers show little change (except that banking has now been replaced by economics). The high position of engineering is an interesting comment on the myth that the public schools tend to be pure arts, or pure science-oriented. Does it perhaps reflect shrewd advice about how to get a university place?

The tendency to imitate Oxbridge is reflected in the number of schools that boast a tutorial system, particularly after 'O'-levels. Sometimes the weekly meeting with the tutor is little more than a hello and goodbye affair: but schools are beginning to use them as a real way of giving a boy some individual help with his work.

Public schools have never offered specifically remedial work, or spent over much time on the needs of the non-academic boy. Instead they have concentrated on small classes, if necessary including special classes for those with little chance of exam success. At some time during any 24 hours a boy is guaranteed individual attention. This is what parents pay for and what at least one headmaster believes 'is the only justification for the public school system'.

Pupil–teacher ratios in boarding schools are notoriously hard to measure: but undoubtedly remain more favourable than in any maintained school (except in certain sixth-form classes).

In recognized independent schools for boys, ignoring those with primary departments, the ratio has been improving very gradually: in 1963 it was 11·5 falling

Appendix

Table I

Size of public schools

All HMC Independent Schools

	1946	1961	1971
Boys Boarding	27,922	35,346	35,347
Day Boys	11,038	16,129	18,812
Total	38,960	51,457	54,159

Top 39 HMC Boarding Schools

	1946	1961	1971
Boys Boarding	16,737	20,340	20,698
Day Boys	1,138	1,598	2,262
Total	17,875	21,938	22,960

Sixth form subjects studied
Percentage of total in 6th form

	Recognized Boys				Grammar			
	Independent							
	Maths/ Science	Other	Mixed	Non A Level	Maths/ Science	Other	Mixed	Non A Level
1969	37.0	46.4	13.7	2.8	43.9	37.1	17.3	1.7
1966	41.7	50.0	7.0	2.6	49.1	37.2	12.1	1.5
1963	46.5	46.5	4.3	2.7	54.8	34.9	7.9	2.4

A Level results of leavers
(Thousands)

	No subject tried	0	1	2	3	4 or more	Total
				Passes			
1970							
Rec. Indep.	4.79	1.00	1.50	2.17	4.33	1.05	14.84
Grammar	20.99	2.70	4.30	7.06	10.67	3.16	48.88
1968							
Rec. Indep.	4.93	0.87	1.31	2.46	4.35	1.15	15.08
Grammar	22.73	2.63	4.27	6.99	12.79	3.50	52.92
1966							
Rec Indep.	5.86	1.15	1.38	2.85	4.02	0.77	15.98
Grammar	27.90	2.72	4.76	7.24	13.75	3.64	60.01

Destination of leavers from
recognized Independent Schools

Percentage of leavers going to:

	1966	1967	1968	1969	1970
All Universities	28.0	27.1	30.3	29.2	27.8
Oxbridge	9.4	8.4	8.9	10.0	8.1
Colleges of education	1.3	1.2	1.4	1.2	1.2
Employment	50.3	47.4	43.2	43.0	40.5
Number of leavers going to:					
Oxbridge	1510	1280	1340	1540	1200
Number going to polytechnics and advanced further education					
CNAA Degree work	240	260	470	320	410
HND/HNC	170	280	230	170	260
% of leavers doing					
CNAA degree work	1.5	1.7	3.0	2.1	2.7

Top Ten most popular careers for public school boys

	% of leavers in 1970	Previous position			
		1968	1965	1963	1960
1. Engineering	10.3	1	1	1	1
2. Science	6.8	2	2	2	3
3. Commerce/Industry	6.0	3	3	3	2
4. Medicine	5.0	4	4	4	6
5. Law	5.0	5	5	6	8
6. Accountancy	3.1	6	7	5	5
7. Agriculture	3.1	8	8	8	4
8. Teaching	2.1	7	9	9	10
9. Economics	2.0	10	—	—	—
10. Services	1.9	9	6	7	7

to 11·3 in 1964, 11·1 in 1966 and to 11·0 in 1968, 69 and 70. (For statistical reasons it appears a bit lower than it probably is.) In 1970 the highest was in schools in Greater London where it was 13·1; the lowest in the South West with a ratio of 10·00:1.

The great improvements in education in the maintained sector do not seem to have starved the public schools of their top quality staff. The independent sector has always attracted some of the best qualified teachers, and though headmasters report that the top

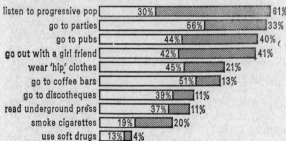

	To some extent	To a great extent
listen to progressive pop	30%	61%
go to parties	56%	33%
go to pubs	44%	40%
go out with a girl friend	42%	41%
wear 'hip' clothes	45%	21%
go to coffee bars	51%	13%
go to discotheques	39%	11%
read underground press	37%	11%
smoke cigarettes	19%	20%
use soft drugs	13%	4%

☐ To some extent

▨ To a great extent

Figure 34.1 Public schoolboys and the youth culture (Bloxham Project findings)

Note

All but one of the sample schools are Headmasters Conference Schools (HMC).

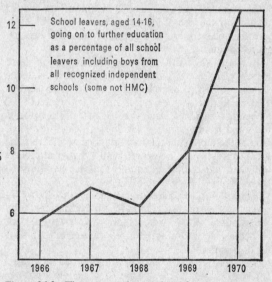

School leavers, aged 14-16, going on to further education as a percentage of all school leavers including boys from all recognized independent schools (some not HMC)

Figure 34.2 The move to leave school for the tech

staff are often harder to find, they claim they are still to be found.

But younger men seem reluctant to take on the near total commitment to the school that the job was always expected to entail—they prefer living an outside life to spending all their time running societies or coaching rowing.

The first report of the Public Schools Commission concluded: 'It remains true—and it could not but remain true—that their activities are based on the assumptions and aspirations of the British middle class, from which their pupils come and upon which their fees depend. The changes the schools are undergoing mirror and no doubt to some extent are mirrored by changes in the expectations and outlook of the middle classes: what has not changed is the existence of the intimate relation between the two.'

Whether the fundamental nature of the schools has changed is a matter of debate. But whatever the answer, all outward appearances suggest the schools are thriving on it.

Notes

1 These were the nine schools dealt with in the Clarendon Commission's Report of 1864—Eton, Winchester, Westminster, Charterhouse, St Paul's, Merchant Taylors', Harrow, Rugby and Shrewsbury.
2 Headmasters Conference—the main representative body of the principals of public schools.
3 The system whereby younger boys performed domestic tasks for older boys.
4 The Combined Cadet Force ostensibly provided combined training for all three services—but mainly for the army.

References

Glennerster, H. and Wilson, G. (1970). *Paying for Private Schools* (LSE Studies in Education). Allen Lane.
Bloxham Project Research Unit (spring 1972). *Trust in School: No and Yes.* Obtainable from 15 Norham Gardens, Oxford.

Section IV   Further and higher education

35 Further education

Gerald Fowler

Perhaps every system of public education must have its forgotten sector. In England and Wales such a sector is further education, the name used to subsume the variety of provision made by public authorities for the full-time and part-time education of those who have left school (whether at the statutory school-leaving age or later), other than that conducted in universities or colleges of education. The *aficionados* of FE passionately debate seemingly obscure details of its administration and course-structure, and their work is widely known and largely understood in industry and in some of the professions: educationists working in other sectors, in the schools almost as much as in the universities, have little interest in, and less understanding of further education, and often seem to regard it with an unjustifiable scorn. Its image is only now ceasing to be that of the 'night school' serving the workforce of the sooty industrial towns. Its teachers even have their own trade union, the Association of Teachers in Technical Institutions (ATTI), linked with, but separate from, the National Union of Teachers. Yet there are over 700 colleges in the further education sector, and in autumn 1970 they could muster 3,181,000 students (an increase of 1,260,000 in fifteen years) in England and Wales alone.

The statutory basis for the provision of further education by local education authorities in England and Wales is section 41 of the 1944 Education Act,[1] which laid upon them the duty of securing 'the provision for their area of adequate facilities for further education, that is to say:

(a) full-time and part-time education for persons over compulsory school age; and

(b) leisure-time occupation, in such organized cultural training and recreative activities as are suited to their requirements, for any persons over compulsory school age who are able and willing to profit by the facilities provided for that purpose.'

The duties and powers of the LEAs extended only to the provision of facilities in accordance with 'schemes of further education' or at 'county colleges'.

County colleges were to provide for the compulsory continued education of those who had left school, until they reached the age of eighteen, for one whole day or two half days a week for forty-four weeks of the year, or the equivalent in continuous periods of attendance.[2] They have never been established, and despite recommendations made in the Crowther Report (1959)[3] for the phased introduction of compulsory day-release attendance at such colleges, it now seems unlikely that they ever will be, even if the continued education of young workers is ultimately required by law. It would now be provided in existing further education colleges. This was the second abortive attempt to secure compulsory continued education. The 'Fisher' Education Act of 1918 and the Education Act of 1921 (sections 75–9)[4] provided for compulsory attendance for 320 hours each year at 'day continuation schools', but the 'appointed day' for the operation of these provisions was fixed for only nine areas of the country, and the scheme failed in them all except one, Rugby, which had a proud record of innovation in this field between the two World Wars.

Authorities were required to submit 'schemes of further education' to the Minister by 31 March 1948.[5] Such schemes took effect only after approval by the Minister, perhaps with modifications, and could subsequently be amended or extended. Authorities had to take account, in preparing such schemes, of facilities provided in their areas by other bodies, and must consult such bodies and neighbouring LEAs.[6] Further education has however expanded so rapidly in the postwar period that the concept of a 'scheme' of further education for each area now seems misleading. Consultations with other LEAs and with industrial interests now normally take place through the Regional Advisory Councils (RACs) for further education, on which all bodies with an interest in further and higher education are represented.

Section 41 of the 1944 Act read in isolation would seem to suggest that the school education of those staying on beyond the age of compulsory attendance would fall within the definition of further education. They are however covered by the definition of 'secondary education' (section 8) and of 'senior pupil' (section 114) given in the Act.[7] Thus, the Act sanctioned a system of dual provision, in the schools and in further education, for those above the age of compulsory school attendance but below the age of nineteen.

If further education overlaps the secondary schools, it also overlaps the universities and other institutions of higher education. The Further Education Regulations (1969)[8] cover voluntary as well as maintained establishments, and provision is made for grant to them by either LEAs or the Secretary of State. 'Further education' thus subsumes the Cranfield Institute of Technology, formerly the College of Aeronautics, and the Royal College of Art (both of which—since 1969 and 1967 respectively—hold Royal Charters empowering them to award degrees, but are grant-aided by the Department of Education and Science), the Royal Academy and the Royal College of Music, as well as the polytechnics, which offer courses primarily when not solely at a higher education level. The 1966 White Paper announcing the intended establishment of the polytechnics was significantly subtitled *Higher Education in the Further Education System*.[9]

FE thus includes the provision of courses of vocational training and of general education at any level, up to the postgraduate, provided only that students have passed the age of compulsory school attendance. Even that is not the end of the story, since sub-section (b) of section 41 of the 1944 Act covered provision for 'leisure-time activities'. Another section of the Act[10] gave LEAs the power to establish, maintain, or manage camps, holiday classes, playing fields, play centres and the like, 'at which facilities for recreation and for . . . [social and physical] training . . . are available for persons for whom primary, secondary, or further education is provided by the authority', and four years later the requirement that the provision of such education should be made by that same authority was removed. The Secretary of State is empowered to supplement the provision of the LEAs by grant-aid towards the establishment of facilities for social and physical recreation of adults otherwise unconnected with further education.[11] Grants may also be made by him (or her) towards the teaching costs of courses of adult education provided by a 'responsible body', defined as a university, a university college, a committee of such institutions, or of a national association or of its districts.[12]

'Further education' may thus be held to embrace the youth service on the one hand and much of adult education on the other, together with activities as disparate as those conducted at play centres or at recreational complexes. It is not the purpose of this article to consider either the youth service (for an understanding of the development of which readers should turn to the Albemarle Report and the more recent report of the Youth Service Development Council),[13] or the adult education work of the Workers' Educational Association or of the university extra-mural departments. In adult education, however, the work of the evening institutes, offering mainly non-vocational courses, covers a range of students wider than that of any other division of the education system. In 1970 there were 1,421,796 students enrolled at the institutes (roughly two women for every man), of whom 228,327 were under eighteen, but 1,103,661 over twenty-one. These numbers may be compared with the 139,038 enrolled for university extra-mural courses, and the 107,285 for courses provided by the WEA. Courses are offered in subjects stretching from dressmaking and cookery through Chinese and Hindi to car maintenance and carpentry.

The work of the institutes is a ready victim for economy cuts, since it is usually seen as peripheral to the main body of local authority educational provision. The economic crisis of the late 1960s resulted in a reduction of the number of courses offered by some authorities, and an increase in the fee charged for attendance by others. Yet by 1970 the number of students enrolled in the institutes exceeded the 1967 total, the previous highest, with a sharp increase (66,000) in students over twenty-one. It seems unlikely that the advent of the Open University,[14] initially offering only degree courses, will sap the demand for adult education met by the institutes and the 'responsible bodies', but the organization of this area of education, fragmented and too easy to prune, seems intrinsically unsatisfactory. The report of the Russell Committee, appointed to make recommendations for its development, it still awaited.

So far this account of further education has dealt only with England and Wales. In Scotland and Northern Ireland the legislative framework is different, but similar. Scotland however includes in its further education provision both further education courses offered by colleges of education, and the work of the central institutions, directly funded by the Scottish Education Department and mounting courses at levels ranging up to first degree and postgraduate.[15] In 1969 there were approximately 3,455,000 students enrolled on courses of further education, including non-vocational courses, in the United Kingdom.

No area of British education has expanded so explosively since the war as full-time further education. In autumn 1938 the last annual enrolment before the Second World War was of some 20,000 full-timers. By 1955 they had become 64,000, and ten years later 187,000. In 1970 there were 274,000. These figures include students on 'sandwich' courses, which are essentially full-time courses with intercalated and integrated periods of practical training or experience.

Students in England and Wales only are included here: the comparable 1969 figure for the United Kingdom was 295,000. It has been by the successful provision of full-time and sandwich courses at the higher levels that colleges have earned 'promotion' out of the further education system. Thus, the former colleges of advanced technology (CATs) and their Scottish counterparts, which entered the university system in 1964–6, still had only two full-time or sandwich students for every three on other types of course as late as 1962; two years later the proportion was already 9:7, and since the colleges received their charters the slow wasting of the part-timers has become galloping consumption.[16]

The primary concern of this article is not with those colleges which have from time to time been separated into a special category at the pinnacle of the further education system, like the CATs from 1956–7 until they became universities. The thirty polytechnics, of which all save one had been formally designated by mid-1972 are for example now best considered, along with the universities and the colleges of education, as part of the planned national provision of higher education, although their government and financing and the regulations under which they operate are similar to those of other further education colleges.[17]

Since the mid-1950s local authority maintained colleges have been graded as local, area, or regional colleges: the first catered mainly for students below the age of nineteen, the second offered similar courses together with other more advanced work, while the regional colleges were primarily concerned with higher level work, much of it full-time. In practice, some of the 'area' colleges came to have as much or more of a 'regional' flavour, and to offer as many advanced courses as regional colleges. It is these advanced courses, full-time and part-time, degree (whether a degree of the Council for National Academic Awards or an external degree of the University of London),[18] higher professional (e.g. the Associateship of the Royal Institute of British Architects or of the Institute of Builders or of one of the professional bodies in accountancy), or the Higher National Certificate or Diploma (HNC and HND) in science, engineering, or business studies, or even the college's own Diploma or Associateship, which overlap in level and content the work of the polytechnics and universities—even though they co-exist in the same establishment with craft or GCE 'O' Level courses for sixteen-year-olds. The 1966 White Paper which foreshadowed the designation of the polytechnics, and which outlined a policy of concentrating advanced work in these centres, together with the rising academic standard of entry demanded by the professions and an occasional snobbishness about where their courses shall be offered, has made it more difficult for the non-polytechnic colleges to start new courses of higher education. Yet many such courses still run. By no means all of the specialist colleges offering courses in the visual arts leading to the Diploma award of the National Council for Diplomas in Art and Design have been absorbed into polytechnics.[19]

The financial arrangements for further education and the system of remuneration of its teachers, both encourage colleges to seek to develop advanced work. Since courses could never be offered in all subjects at all levels in every local authority area, arrangements were developed for the reimbursement of authorities providing further education courses (the 'providing authorities') for those living in the areas of other authorities (the 'sending authorities').[20] Granted only that the sending authority has consented to the provision of a course, the providing authority may recover from it the full cost for all such students. Such an arrangement would lead to interminable wrangles about the true cost, were there not an arbiter. This role is played by the Committee on Inter-Authority Financial Adjustment in Respect of Further Education, which recommends from time to time appropriate recoupment payments for courses of all types and levels. There are three broad levels of course, distinguished by academic standard. Yet even with such recoupment arrangements, the cost of providing specialist staff and facilities for many advanced courses would bear heavily on smaller authorities, and when a course may of its very nature attract students from a national rather than a local or regional catchment area, it would be an arduous task to secure the consent of every authority. Thus, the cost of providing most advanced courses—of a standard higher than GCE 'A' Level—may be recouped from a pool to which all authorities contribute according to a set formula based upon the school population and the rateable value of property within each authority's area ('poolable' courses).[21] This means that there is at least a theoretical incentive to an authority and a college to develop advanced work, since it costs them little or nothing to do it, and in due course of time enough such work may establish for the college a national reputation, if not a claim for 'promotion' to polytechnic status. Even the recoupment system for lower level work can encourage the staff of a college to seek to mount a course for which they know there is inadequate demand in the area of its maintaining authority. Here is one reason for the continuing 'entrepreneurial' character of further education.

It may be asked why further education teachers should be such gluttons for extra work. Dedication, academic ambition, sensitivity to the needs of local industry or society may all provide a partial explanation. But the salary scheme established through national negotiating machinery (the Burnham Further Education Committee)[22] helps too. While there are basic salary-scales for each grade of lecturer, the proportion of staff within a department who may be appointed or promoted to senior posts, and the salaries of heads of departments and of principals and vice-principals, are based upon, not the quality of their work or its social value, but a pointing system which is weighted in favour of the higher graded courses. A head of department may wish to expand the provision of the courses and upgrade the level of the work for which he is responsible from wholly honourable motives, but he may also sometimes be aware that success will bring financial reward. Further, his lecturers know that their promotion from one grade to another (and there are five grades of lecturer) may turn upon the same factors. The system has other weaknesses: it requires less teaching from senior than from junior lecturers (the higher your skill the less you will be required to use it), and it can reward teachers who devote themselves to 'administration'—sometimes work that could be as well done by a competent clerk—more highly than teachers who concentrate on teaching. Its most conspicuous weakness however is that its central principle is that of payment by head-count, with some heads deemed to weigh more than others, irrespective of the difficulty or desirability of feeding them with the *pabulum* available.

The counter-side of the incentives to expansion built into further education is the complex structure of course-approval which has evolved. Before a college can offer a new course it requires the support of its maintaining authority. The proposal will then normally go before the appropriate committee of the Regional Advisory Council. If it secures the blessing of the Council, it will still often require the approval of the Secretary of State, which will be given in his or her name by the Regional Staff Inspector (a member of Her Majesty's Inspectorate). That may be the end of the story, if the course leads to a college award. If however it leads to an externally validated qualification, the approval of the appropriate awarding body must be sought, perhaps only for the college to run the course, perhaps for the syllabuses it will use and the staff who will teach them: there are a host of such bodies, especially in education for the professions. Or it may be that there would be no point in the college offering the course, since there will be few students, unless success in it is accepted by another educational institution as giving admission to a further course with a higher or more useful terminal qualification, or by a professional body as giving exemption from some part of the requirements for its own award. Alternatively, it may be necessary to ensure that a local or national employer will 'sponsor' students (that is, pay their fees, if no more, and perhaps provide related industrial experience), or will at least release them from work, to attend the course.

Even if the course is offered and students enrolled, it does not follow that it will ever run. The college may itself decide that the number of students does not justify the expenditure of time, effort, and money in running the course. It may even be that the unexpected expansion of numbers on other courses means that there is no room for the students and no one to teach them. More commonly, the college will be directed to stop the course, and possibly to transfer the students (if they are willing) to another college

nearby, by the Regional Staff Inspector (RSI). The National Advisory Council for Education for Industry and Commerce established after the last war, concerned itself in the 1960s with means of securing the most economical use of further education facilities. In particular it adopted criteria for the viability of higher level further education courses which were based upon the number of students enrolled, and are known, from the chairman of the sub-committee which recommended them, as the 'Pilkington numbers'.[23] The RSI will use this yardstick when deciding to close a course, although he will normally take account of the good of the students too. Even then an authority may wish to make representations to the Secretary of State, or even, in a fit of civic pride or sheer pigheadedness, persist in running a course in defiance of every instruction to close it. If the virtue of further education is that it is as flexible as a rubber hose, and highly sensitive to social demand, the corresponding vice is that it is also a maze, through which only the old and experienced are likely to find their way without error!

Although the complexity of the rules governing further education seems to favour the entrepreneurial style of management at local authority and college level, the government structure of colleges is changing in the direction of greater collectivism, with increased autonomy for the governing body financially and for the teaching and student community educationally and academically. Circular 7/70 of the Department of Education and Science,[24] issued in April 1970, extended to other further education colleges the arrangements already made for the polytechnics (and for colleges of education). It recommended that local authority members should form only a minority of the governing body, perhaps no more than a quarter, while the principal and at least two other staff members, and students where this is thought appropriate (especially in colleges with a significant proportion of students over eighteen), together with representatives of local industry, commerce, and education, should also have seats upon it. The governors should be empowered to exercise financial virement within heads of expenditure once annual estimates have been approved by the authority. Internally, educational policy was to be a matter for the academic board, on which senior staff would sit as of right, together with elected representatives of the staff, and perhaps of the students. The chief administrative officer of the college should replace the chief education officer of the authority both as clerk to the governors and as head of the internal 'administration'. While the draft Articles of Government contain elements of the traditional autocratic system of management,[25] they are essentially designed to ensure staff and student participation and interaction in policy-making, and freedom from detailed external control. The contradiction between these objectives and those implicit in the salary arrangements and course-approval system for further education seems clear.

A wide diversity of educational provision in the local, area, and regional colleges of further education results from this structure of control. No two colleges look the same or offer exactly the same range of courses. Buildings are rarely all of the same era; they have been built or acquired by steady accretion as further education has continued its unpredictable expansion. Many colleges still have some ancient 'annexes'—old schools, factories, mills, houses, even a hospital—pressed into service in a crisis of accommodation which turns out to be chronic. Similarly most colleges have their 'local' courses, sometimes reflecting a demand in the local community or the zeal of individual members of staff, but sometimes little more than the last historical relic of a once great but moribund industry.

Full-time courses found everywhere in England and Wales include those leading to the General Certificate of Education. By 1970 there were 31,110 students working full-time for GCE 'A' Levels. Most of them were of the same age-group as those taking 'A' Levels in the schools. At Ordinary Level, there were 32,160 full-time students. Full-time 'A' Level students have doubled in number over the past seven years, but numbers of 'O' Level students have increased very much more slowly. The figures show that young people beyond the compulsory school age, but still able if they so desired to study full-time at school, have increasingly voted with their feet for further education, with its often freer and more adult atmosphere. At the same time more of those who have taken 'O' Levels or the Certificate of Secondary Education (CSE) at schools which still have no sixth form have continued their studies in further education colleges.

Full-time students of the fifteen to seventeen age-group in the colleges totalled 114,000 in 1970. It follows that even if all the full-time GCE students were assumed to be of this age, there would still be over 50,000 other full-time students in the colleges of an age at which they were still eligible to attend schools. This development has occurred at the same time as more schools have sought to provide non-GCE courses for pupils wishing to stay beyond the compulsory school age. If schools and colleges were to develop in competition with each other, the consequences would be grave, both economically, where provision was wastefully duplicated, and educationally, when there was consequent omission of other provision in both sectors.

A healthy development of recent years, affecting mainly pupils in the last year of compulsory school attendance, has been day-release from school to college, usually for technical, scientific or commercial studies. The college courses are not specifically vocational, but aim at introducing pupils to a range of related techniques and skills, at the same time bridging the gap between full-time study at school and work in industry with part-time college study. They should serve as a potent form of careers guidance. The number on such 'linked courses' was about 12,000 in 1970.

Such schemes are however peripheral to the central problem. Nor is any simple solution, by division of courses between schools and colleges, practicable. Even if sixth-form colleges and the sixth forms of other secondary schools were to confine themselves to GCE work only, leaving all full-time non-GCE work to the colleges, it would still be necessary for the colleges to provide for part-time and evening-only GCE students. To attempt to assign all full-time courses to schools and all part-time to further education would be to court yet more serious difficulties. Expensive specialist accommodation and equipment would have to be provided in each institution. Many further education teachers cannot teach in the schools, since they have neither a Certificate of Education nor a degree. Dual provision is easier in heavily populated areas, where large schools and colleges serve compact catchment areas. But in rural areas colleges catering for all post-sixteen students, full- and part-time, and operating under the further education rather than the school regulations, may be the only answer. The south-west of England—Exeter, Devon, and Somerset—is pioneering experimentation with such colleges, as part of the secondary reorganization programme.

Numerically the most important post-school courses for fifteen- or sixteen-year-olds in further education colleges are those for intending office workers. They may be of only one year's duration, and aimed at improving the student's general education while giving him or her an introduction to office practice. Two-year courses, normally for sixteen-year-olds, are designed to fit students for secretarial posts or careers leading to office supervision.

In 1970 some 8,000 students were on Ordinary National Diploma (OND) courses in business studies, and as many again on other full-time non-advanced business studies courses. A large number of full-time students of the younger age-groups take one-year pre-apprenticeship courses in engineering, building, agriculture, or catering, and in these subjects too there are OND courses, on which over 9,000 students were enrolled in 1970. Not all OND students are under nineteen (in 1970 some 13,000 in all subjects), and some of them (2,000 in this age-group) take sandwich rather than full-time courses, with periods of five or sixth months spent in the appropriate industry. Sandwich courses originated about the turn of the century, but their development has been largely a postwar phenomenon.

The OND is the full-time or sandwich equivalent of the Ordinary National Certificate (ONC), gained by part-time study. Both last for two years, with an entry qualification of four or more GCE 'O' Level passes in appropriate subjects, or the same number of CSE Grade 1 passes. The full-time course has, because there is more time available, a broader subject-base than the part-time. A further two years' part-time work will take the student to the Higher

National Certificate (HNC), and two years full-time or three years sandwich to the HND. An alternative entry qualification is here one 'A' Level with four appropriate 'O' Levels. Since the system began in 1921 these courses, the areas covered by which have extended slowly, have been under the supervision of Joint Committees of the Department of Education and Science (here alone directly involved in awarding educational qualifications) and the appropriate professional institutions. They have provided a route peculiar to further education by following which through full-time study it is possible to reach a standard normally thought to be about one year's academic work short of a pass degree. In 1970 there were some 20,000 HND students (many at polytechnics), more than a doubling in seven years: the HND in business studies, and especially its sandwich version, was one of the great educational growth areas of the 1960s. Many colleges have offered (the practice is now less frequent) courses designed to top up the HND in engineering and science subjects to degree level, with the award of a college Associateship, which used often to be, and sometimes still is, accepted by professional institutions as giving exemption from their own examinations. Further, it is possible to switch from the National Certificate/Diploma to the degree route: some universities now accept ONC/D for admission to a first degree course, and CNAA treats a 'good' pass as equivalent to two 'A' Levels. Yet historically, it is the part-time route, culminating in HNC, which has been of the greatest importance. Between the wars the National Certificate, gained by evening study, was the foundation-stone upon which technical education was built. It is to part-time courses in further education that we now turn.

Most of the part-time day students in the colleges working for GCE 'O' and 'A' Level, and some of those following evening only courses, have taken employment, progress in which depends upon the attainment of these qualifications. Some of them will have some subject passes gained at school, but not enough for their purpose. Here then further education plays a quasi-remedial role.

The great majority of part-time day students in the colleges are however those on craft courses. Day-release, sometimes supplemented by evening study, is the system by which most British craftsmen are trained. The variety of craft courses is immense. While engineering and building take the lion's share, every craft industry is covered. Most such courses are in two parts from the age of sixteen, each taking two years, although three years to Part 1 will normally be allowed for those leaving school at fifteen. Some crafts also provide a Part 3 course, lasting one year.

For those who enter the colleges intent upon becoming technicians rather than craftsmen, there is a choice of routes. Some may have the GCE passes which will secure them direct entry to National Certificate courses. Others, with fewer or inappropriate GCE or CSE Grade 1 passes, may, at the discretion of the college principal, embark immediately upon the alternative route, which leads to Technician Certificates, mostly awarded by the City and Guilds of London Institute (CGLI). This was founded in 1878 by the companies of the City of London with the purpose 'of educating young artisans and others in the scientific and artistic branches of their trades'; in the course of the last century it has established craft and technician courses and examinations, now covering some 300 subjects. It has been a vehicle for the development and adoption by industries of national schemes for the integration of further education into apprenticeships and on-the-job training.[26]

Many students will not be assigned initially to either route, but will take the appropriate general course ('G' course). These are broad prognostic courses (in for example engineering, *simpliciter*, rather than in any specific branch of engineering). Examinations in them are offered by CGLI, and by the six regional examining bodies, some of which, like the Union of Lancashire and Cheshire Institutes, also have a proud history, rooted in the Mechanics Institutes of the 1830s and 1840s, which were the ultimate ancestors of today's further education colleges.[27]

A student who passes his 'G' course at a high enough level enters an ONC course, but if his performance is less good he passes directly into the second year of a CGLI technician course (a 'T' course). If he began his 'G' course when he was fifteen, he may enter instead the first year of the technician course.

Most CGLI technician courses, like craft courses and National Certificates, are of two years' study, part-time, beginning at age sixteen, leading to the Part 1 award, and then a further two years' study to Part 2. In many subjects the student may then progress to Part 3, or other more advanced work. Alternatively, some who succeed in Part 2 may be allowed to transfer to an HNC course, thus rejoining the National Certificate route. The past decade has seen a great growth in the number and range of technician courses offered by CGLI, and of the students following them. This was largely the result of the 1961 White Paper, *Better Opportunities for Technical Education*, which identified a national shortage of technicians, resulting in part from the confusion of objectives in National Certificate courses, designed to cater simultaneously for technicians and would-be technologists. Such courses had a very high wastage and failure rate: the development of CGLI courses, tailor-made for the intending technician only, and with a consequent high pass-rate, has kept in education many who before 1961 would early have been lost. In 1961 there were only two such courses: by 1970 there were over ninety.

National Certificate courses have themselves been redesigned to meet specifically technician requirements, and some of them have been combined to give a broader-based curriculum, the ONCs in the separate branches of engineering becoming for example a single ONC in engineering. Their number has however increased, with the addition of new subjects to meet changing employment prospects (statistics and computing, and medical laboratory technology are good examples). Passes in the ONC, 17,580 in 1960, reached a peak in the mid-1960s, and then declined to 14,136 in 1968, as a result of the combined effect of a smaller age-group and of the introduction of CGLI 'T' courses. Nevertheless, the success of the 1961 strategy can be seen in the pass-rate: in 1960 less than one in two entrants succeeded, and in 1968, seven out of every eleven.

There thus exist two routes to technician qualifications, with cross-links between them. Below them are the craft courses, and from them too it is possible for some to join the technician stream, via 'end on' CGLI courses, which are so called to distinguish them from the 'ab initio' courses designed for immediate school-leavers, and which are themselves designed to build upon craft-level work. (About one in six CGLI technician students follows an 'end on' course.) Above them lie the full-time HND, and CNAA degrees, to which ONC/D give entry. Further education part-time and full-time courses therefore represent a complex set of interlocking ladders; at many stages of the climb it is possible in theory at least to transfer from one ladder to another. While no single further education college may offer a comprehensive range of courses at every level, it is reasonable to claim that further education as a whole is a comprehensive system of post-school education, in which the early under-achiever or the student forced to leave school by economic circumstances can still attain the same ultimate educational level as his more fortunate co-evals.

The pattern of technician education has however clear weaknesses. The Haslegrave Committee, appointed to examine it and reporting late in 1969,[28] thought that the most serious was its complexity, with administrative arrangements which could impede educational progress.[29]

> The weight of evidence from industry and commerce on the existing administrative arrangements for technician courses and examinations [wrote the Committee] constituted a plea for simplification and standardization of the system. It was pointed out that while the basic pattern enunciated in the (1961) White Paper seemed simple enough, the actual provision of courses and examinations designed to give effect to it presents a bewildering picture of complexity to employers and students, and indeed has reached the point where even those concerned with providing and administering the courses and examinations had some difficulty in following all of its ramifications themselves.

Evidence from the education service laid the blame for this on industry, commerce, and the professions!

There was agreement that too many bodies had fingers in the technician pie, and that their efforts were unco-ordinated.[30] The CGLI 'T' and the National Certificate/Diploma patterns were developing separately, with new courses constantly added without thought of their effect on cognate provision. The integration of further education and industrial training could be planned on an *ad hoc* basis only, course by course.[31] Business education, despite the growth of the ONC in business studies, lacked a coherent pattern of courses at the technician-equivalent level.[32]

Haslegrave recommended a new unified pattern of courses constructed on the modular or block principle. School-leavers would enter a course with two main elements—material designed to complement the broad basic training requirements of technicians, and a study of the theoretical principles underlying this material. The first part of the course would be diagnostic, and some students would thereafter concentrate on the first element only. After two years they would, if successful, get a Technician Certificate. Those who continued and developed their theoretical studies would get a Technician Diploma. The distinction between qualifications gained by part-time and by full-time study would disappear, and it should be possible to convert a Certificate into a Diploma by further study. 'Bridge studies' would make possible transfer from craft to technician courses. At eighteen some diplomates might transfer to HND or degree routes, while others with the new certificates or diplomas would proceed to a Higher Technician Certificate (600 hours study) or Diploma (1,200 hours). In these courses, special subjects would be built upon a common core of studies pursued by all candidates, and Diploma courses would include the study of the principles of business operations. Certificands might by further study gain the Diploma, diplomates might proceed to a degree or professional qualification, and both could update, revamp, and extend their knowledge by studying any of a range of special subjects later in their careers.[33]

The Committee recommended that the administration and supervision of these new courses should be in the hands of two new national councils, for technician and business education, whose task would be to create a unified national pattern of provision. The CGLI should be invited to service the new councils. The existing regional examining bodies would form the nucleus of a new structure of regional bodies acting as the arms of the new councils in examination and assessment of students.[34]

The Secretary of State has agreed to the creation of the two councils recommended by Haslegrave, but otherwise little progress was made towards the reform of technician education in the three years following the presentation of the Committee's report. The desirability of greater coherence and clarity in the structure of technician education seems to be accepted: its achievement is likely to take many years. Further education sometimes seems a prisoner of its own history.

One other aspect of further education provision was subject to scrutiny and doubt in the early 1970s, day release for further education associated with industrial training.

The Industrial Training Act of 1964 gave the Secretary of State for Employment (formerly the Minister of Labour) power to set up industrial training boards (ITBs) for 'any activities of industry or commerce'.[35] The members of each board, appointed by him, comprise an equal number of employers and trade unionists from a particular industry, together with a smaller number of educationists. In 1972, there were twenty-seven boards, covering industries with fifteen million workers. The task of the boards was to secure the provision of an adequate number of training courses for employees in their respective industries, paying grant to those employers who provided approved training, and drawing a levy from all employers in order to finance their activities. Specifically, they were required 'to make recommendations about the length, nature, standard and content of training for different occupations and about the further education to be associated with the training'. The philosophy behind the Act was spelled out in a White Paper two years earlier, which argued that since the war shortage of skilled labour had been a persistent constraint on economic expansion, and that inadequate training was the primary cause of these shortages.[36] New demands must thus be made on the colleges to provide the 'associated further education'; the Henniker-Heaton Committee, established in November 1962, recommended a doubling by 1969–70 of the number of students receiving day-release from employment to college in 1962–3.[37]

No one would argue that the 1964 Act has been an unqualified success, and the Henniker-Heaton target was not achieved. The number of people aged under eighteen whose first employment was a craft apprenticeship has fallen gradually since 1965, but the total number entering employment each year has also fallen (because the age-groups have been smaller, and because a higher proportion of them stay on at school beyond the compulsory age each year), so that the proportion of under-eighteens in work falling into this category has risen slightly. At the same time new integrated courses of training and further education have been devised. The total number of people in Great Britain released from work to attend further education courses rose from 536,000 in 1961 to 718,000 in 1969, but fell back the following year to 698,000. In England and Wales the proportion of insured people under eighteen getting day-release rose from 19 per cent in 1964 to 25 per cent in 1969, with slippage in 1970 to 24 per cent. In Scotland, the growth was from 14 per cent in 1965 to 22 per cent in 1970—so that Scotland, starting from a worse position, seems to have caught up most of the leeway.

Educationists have not always been happy with the operation of the Act. There has, for example, been some suspicion of the innovations introduced by the Engineering Industry Training Board, who devised a scheme for the training of both craftsmen and technicians for the industry, based upon a common first year of broad off-the-job training and further education, and a range of training modules, each suitable for a particular craft. The Textile ITB has recommended courses of complementary education which seem little more than off-the-job training. It is the domination of the boards (and of the Central Training Council which co-ordinates their work) by the two sides of industry which makes some doubt whether the voice of further education is heard and heeded when schemes are prepared, despite the use made of Joint Advisory Committees, with educational as well as ITB representation, in planning courses. In any event, three out of four young workers still receive no further education, unless it be in their own time rather than the firm's, and in 1971 only 7·6 per cent of girl school-leavers entered apprenticeships (the largest number in hairdressing) and were thus likely to secure day-release.

Industry has as many complaints as further education about the workings of the Act, usually concerned with the effects of the levy–grant system. By 1972 change seemed inevitable. Early in the year the Department of Employment published a discussion document,[38] in which a massive expansion of vocational training and education, largely in government training establishments, and further education was proposed, side-by-side with the phasing out of levy-grant. Fears were expressed that if the financial framework of the scheme were destroyed, day-release would decline further. The Labour Party, in a discussion document of its own,[39] revived the proposal that day-release for all young workers should become compulsory. Once again therefore it seemed likely that the framework for much of the work of the further education colleges would be dismantled, and a new and perhaps grander structure erected in its place.

Further education remains the Heraclitan sector of British education, in which flux is the natural state and stability is transient or illusory. There is rarely a moment when at least one major change is not in the course of execution, and when no national committee is considering further reform. In part this is a reflection of the relative inflexibility of the sectors which overlap further education, the universities on the one hand and until recently the sixth forms on the other. In part it is a consequence of the central feature of further education provision: attendance at a further education college is in essence voluntary, whatever the spur to the individual student of ambition, whatever his thirst for knowledge. Further education lacks the prestige and attraction of the universities, and must win its students by responding to the changing demands of them and their employers. It thus has to be adaptable in order to survive.

Notes

1 7 & 8 Geo. VI, c.31.

2 1944 Education Act, s.44.

3 *15 to 18* (Report of the Central Advisory Council for Education, England) (HMSO 1959), esp. para. 300.

4 11 & 12 Geo. V, c.51.

5 Ministry of Education Circular 133, dated 19 March 1947.

6 1944 Education Act, s.42, ss.4.

7 s.8 lays upon LEAs the duty of securing sufficient schools for providing both primary and secondary education, and the latter is defined as 'full-time education suitable to the requirements of senior pupils, other than such full-time education as may be provided for senior pupils in pursuance of a scheme made under the provisions of this Act relating to further education'. s.114 defines 'senior pupil' as 'a person who has attained the age of twelve years but has not attained the age of nineteen years.'

8 S.1, 1969, no. 403.

9 Cmnd 3006.

10 s.53. Cf. The Education (Miscellaneous Provisions) Act, 1948, 11 & 12 Geo. VI, c.40, s.11 (1) and Part I of the First Schedule.

11 Physical Training and Recreation Acts, 1937 and 1958. (6 & 7 Eliz. II, c.36).

12 n.8 above.

13 *The Youth Service in England and Wales* (Report of the Committee appointed by the Minister of Education in November 1958) (HMSO 1960), generally named after the chairman of the Committee, Lady Albemarle; and *Youth and Community Work in the 70s* (HMSO 1970). On the adult education work of the WEA and university extra-mural departments, see the succession of statements issued since the mid fifties by the WEA, and official publications, especially:

(i) *Education for a Changing Society: The Role of the WEA* (Temple House 1958)

(ii) The Report of the Working Party on *Structure Organization Finance and Staffing* (WEA Temple House 1966)

(iii) *The Organization and Finance of Adult Education in England and Wales* (HMSO 1957)

(iv) *The Universities and Adult Education* (HMSO 1957)

(v) *University Adult Education in the Later Twentieth Century* (Universities Council for Adult Education 1970).

14 See below, pp. 230–9.

15 See above, pp. 11–12.

16 On the CATs and their history, see Tyrrell Burgess and John Pratt, *Policy and Practice* (Allen Lane 1970).

17 See below, pp. 240–66, esp. 252–3.

18 For the CNAA, see below, pp. 257–60; London external degrees are being phased out, often to be replaced by those of the CNAA.

19 The Dip. A.D. (Diploma in Art and Design) is accepted as a degree equivalent. The absorption into polytechnics of some art colleges offering it has been the subject of fierce controversy, some arguing that art education can take place successfully at this level only in separate and independent establishments.

20 Local Education Authorities Recoupment (Further Education) Regulations 1954, S.I., 1954, no. 815, as amended by the LEA Recoupment (Further Education) Amending Regulations 1965, S.I., 1965, no. 512. Cf.

also *Inter-authority Financial Adjustments in Respect of Further Education* (Pimlott Committee) (HMSO 1961).

21 Rate Support Grants (Pooling Arrangements) Regulations 1967, S.I., 1967, no. 467.

22 This, the machinery for the negotiation of further education salaries (settlements lasting for periods ranging from one to three years), operates in conjunction with the Burnham machinery for the settlement of schoolteachers' salaries.

23 *Size of Classes and Approval of Further Education Courses* (HMSO 1966). Cf. also Association of Teachers in Technical Institutions, *Size of Classes— Observations on the Report of the Committee on Technical College Resources*, 1967.

24 *Government and Conduct of Establishments of Further Education*, dated 14 April 1970.

25 The Principal is responsible for, among other things, the 'internal organization of the college', while the Academic Board is responsible for the academic work of the college. There seems to be an implicit overlap or conflict of functions here.

26 CGLI, which examines over 300,000 candidates a year, has over 200 Advisory Committees on the development of courses and examinations. When a request is made for a new course and examination scheme, it is considered by the Technical Education and Policy Committees of the Institute, and if it is acceptable an Exploratory Committee is then established. This Committee draws up a scheme appropriate to the educational needs of the intended students, which it submits to the Committee for Technical Education for consideration of its feasibility and educational validity. If the Policy Committee is also satisfied that the scheme accords with the broad policy of the Institute, it is adopted and published. The Exploratory Committee is then reconstituted as a Standing Advisory Committee, and becomes responsible for keeping contact with colleges running the course, recommending examiners to the Institute, moderating examination papers, and revising syllabuses.

27 The six regional examining bodies, which have an agreement with CGLI on examination provision (see DES Administration Memorandum 2/66) are:

The Union of Educational Institutions (Birmingham and West Midlands),

The Welsh Joint Education Committee,

East Midland Educational Union,

Yorkshire Council for Further Education,

Union of Lancashire and Cheshire Institutes,

Northern Counties Technical Examinations Council.

They and CGLI are represented on the Council of Technical Examining Bodies, established 'to consider any matter of common interest to member bodies, make recommendations thereon to members and to other bodies and to take such action as may be deemed necessary'.

28 *National Advisory Council on Education for Industry and Commerce* (Report of the Committee on Technician Courses and Examinations, under the chairmanship of Dr H. L. Haslegrave) (HMSO 1969).

29 para. 140.

30 para. 141.

31 paras 154–5.

32 paras 49 and 109–11.

33 Chapter 8 and Appendix 7.
34 Chapter 7.
35 1964, c.16.
36 Cmnd 1892.
37 *Day Release* (the Report of a Committee set up by the Minister of Education in November 1962) (HMSO 1964).
38 *Training for the Future—A plan for discussion* (HMSO 1972).
39 Labour's Programme for Britain, published in July 1972, Section 7, 'Education for Democratic Advance'. The document says:

> Legislation will give the *right* to continued education to all young people, whether in schools or college, and give to the Secretary of State the power to extend compulsory education at an appropriate time. It should not be necessary for any young person to continue education solely in evening classes ... The obligation to release for

education should continue until the end of the academic year in which the student reaches the age of 18. It should be open to both employers and young people to concentrate their educational commitment in block release rather than day release.

I.e., the proposal differs from the system embodied in the Acts of 1918, 1921 and 1944, but never operative, in that it would make it compulsory for employers to give release to any young worker who requested it, but would seem not to obligate the latter to request or accept release—initially, at least. Another proposal seeks to redress the imbalance between industry and education felt by some to inhere in the Industrial Training Act 1964: 'The Secretary of State (for Education) should be involved in the drafting of regulations to govern the conduct of training within firms, and Her Majesty's Inspectors should have access to such training in order to advise and assist.'

The Robbins Report of 1963, known by the name of the chairman of the committee which produced it, was a massive and well-evidenced survey of the state of British higher education (especially in the universities). The Report was supported by five Appendices, published in six additional volumes.

The establishment of the Committee early in 1961 followed a growth in concern that the expansion of British higher education was inadequate to match the rise in the numbers of those staying on into the sixth forms of the schools and becoming 'qualified' for higher education by gaining two GCE 'A' Levels or the equivalent. The Report's supporting statistics, prepared under the direction of Professor Claus Moser, demonstrated that both staff and students would be available for rapid and continuing expansion of the higher education system, raising the percentage of the age-group on full-time courses at this level from about 8 per cent to about 17 per cent by 1980. (Girls would still be under-represented, only 12 per cent of the age-group securing full-time places, compared with 22 per cent of men.)

We reprint here the brief statement the Committee gave of its view of the aims and objectives of higher education. Most of the Committee's important recommendations, and what was done about them, are discussed in the extracts from *University Development 1962–67* (HMSO, Cmnd 3820, 1968) and in other pieces in this section.

At almost the same moment as the Robbins Committee reported, one of the seminal political speeches of the decade was made by the then Leader of the Opposition, the Rt Hon. Harold Wilson, MP, addressing the Labour Party Conference at Scarborough (1 October 1963; excerpts are taken from the Report of the 62nd Annual Conference of the Labour Party, published by the Labour Party, Transport House, Smith Square, London, S W 1).

The importance of the speech lay in the fact that a year later the Labour Party won the 1964 General Election, and Mr Wilson became Prime Minister, holding office until June 1970. His Government was thus responsible for the direction of higher education in the post-Robbins period. The Conservative Government committed itself to the Robbins targets for student numbers; but they were not in power when policy was turned into practice.

Mr Wilson, in his speech, saw the expansion of higher education provision in terms not only of a wider spread of educational opportunity (in this context he relates Labour plans for the comprehensivization of secondary education to the growth of higher education), but also of the new industrial demands being forged in 'the white heat of the scientific revolution'. Thus, the universities and colleges, industry, and government must change their attitudes and their organization if we are to educate, keep and utilize properly the scientists and technologists whose work would lay the foundation of national and international prosperity. Industrial training must be similarly expanded and reorganized. The effect of these beliefs can be easily traced in the Labour Government's subsequent policies for higher education.

The speech was made in a debate on a party policy document called 'Labour and the scientific revolution', and Mr Wilson referred also to the report of a working party under the chairmanship of Lord Taylor which had outlined possible Labour policies for higher education.

36 The aims of higher education
(Extract from the Robbins Report, 1963)

To begin with aims and objectives—what purposes, what general social ends should be served by higher education?

The question is not a new one; and the answers have been many and various. But of one thing we may

Source: The Robbins Report (*Report* of the Committee appointed by the Prime Minister under the Chairmanship of Lord Robbins 1961–3), HMSO, Cmnd 2154 (October 1963), chapter 2, 6, paras 22–9.

be reasonably certain: no simple formula, no answer in terms of any single end, will suffice. There is no single aim which, if pursued to the exclusion of all others, would not leave out essential elements. Eclecticism in this sphere is not something to be despised: it is imposed by the circumstances of the case. To do justice to the complexity of things, it is necessary to acknowledge a plurality of aims.

In our submission there are at least four objectives

essential to any properly balanced system.

We begin with instruction in skills suitable to play a part in the general division of labour. We put this first, not because we regard it as the most important, but because we think that it is sometimes ignored or undervalued. Confucius said in the Analects that it was not easy to find a man who had studied for three years without aiming at pay. We deceive ourselves if we claim that more than a small fraction of students in institutions of higher education would be where they are if there were no significance for their future careers in what they hear and read; and it is a mistake to suppose that there is anything discreditable in this. Certainly this was not the attitude of the past: the ancient universities of Europe were founded to promote the training of the clergy, doctors and lawyers; and though at times there may have been many who attended for the pursuit of pure knowledge or of pleasure, they must surely have been a minority. And it must be recognized that in our own times, progress —and particularly the maintenence of a competitive position—depends to a much greater extent than ever before on skills demanding special training. A good general education, valuable though it may be, is frequently less than we need to solve many of our most pressing problems.

But, secondly, while emphasizing that there is no betrayal of values when institutions of higher education teach what will be of some practical use, we must postulate that what is taught should be taught in such a way as to promote the general powers of the mind. The aim should be to produce not mere specialists but rather cultivated men and women. And it is the distinguishing characteristic of a healthy higher education that, even where it is concerned with practical techniques, it imparts them on a plane of generality that makes possible their application to many problems—to find the one in the many, the general characteristic in the collection of particulars. It is this that the world of affairs demands of the world of learning. And it is this, and not conformity with traditional categories, that furnishes the criterion of what institutions of higher education may properly teach.

Thirdly, we must name the advancement of learning. There are controversial issues here concerning the balance between teaching and research in the various institutions of higher education and the distribution of research between these institutions and other bodies. We shall deal with these later. But the search for truth is an essential function of institutions of higher education and the process of education is itself most vital when it partakes of the nature of discovery. It would be untrue to suggest that the advancement of knowledge has been or ever will be wholly dependent on universities and other institutions of higher education. But the world, not higher education alone, will suffer if ever they cease to regard it as one of their main functions.

Finally there is a function that is more difficult to describe concisely, but that is none the less fundamental: the transmission of a common culture and common standards of citizenship. By this we do not mean the forcing of all individuality into a common mould: that would be the negation of higher education as we conceive it. But we believe that it is a proper function of higher education, as of education in schools, to provide in partnership with the family that background of culture and social habit upon which a healthy society depends. This function, important at all times, is perhaps especially important in an age that has set for itself the ideal of equality of opportunity. It is not merely by providing places for students from all classes that this ideal will be achieved, but also by providing, in the atmosphere of the institutions in which the students live and work, influences that in some measure compensate for any inequalities of home background. These influences are not limited to the student population. Universities and colleges have an important role to play in the general cultural life of the communities in which they are situated.

Institutions of higher education vary both in their functions and in the way in which they discharge them. The vocational emphasis will be more apparent in some than in others. The advancement of learning will be more prominent at the postgraduate than at the undergraduate stage. The extent of participation in the life and culture of the community will depend upon local circumstances. Our contention is that, although the extent to which each principle is realized in the various types of institution will vary, yet, ideally, there is room for at least a speck of each in all. The system as a whole must be judged deficient unless it provides adequately for all of them.

37 Extracts from a speech by the Rt Hon. Harold Wilson, MP, in the debate on 'Labour and the Scientific Revolution'

We are living perhaps in a more rapid revolution than some of us realize. The period of 15 years from the last time we were in Scarborough, in 1960, to the middle of the 1970s will embrace a period of technical change, particularly in industrial methods, greater than in the whole industrial revolution of the last 250 years. When you reckon, as it is calculated, that 97 per cent of all the scientists who have ever lived in the history of the world since the days of Euclid, Pythagoras and Archimedes, are alive and at work today, you get some idea of the rate of progress we have to face.

It is only a few years since we first in this Conference debated automation, when almost every word uttered in that debate is already as out of date today as if we had been talking about the advent of the spinning jenny ...

Let us be frank about one thing. It is no good trying to comfort ourselves with the thought that automation need not happen here; that it is going to create so many problems that we should perhaps put our heads in the sand and let it pass us by. Because there is no room for Luddites in the Socialist Party! If we try to abstract from the automative age, the only result will be that Britain will become a stagnant backwater, pitied and condemned by the rest of the world ...

The problem is this. Since technological progress left to the mechanism of private industry and private property can lead only to high profits for a few, a high rate of employment for a few, and to mass redundancies for the many, if there had never been a case for Socialism before, automation would have created it. Because only if technological progress becomes part of our national planning can that progress be directed to national ends.

So the choice is not between technological progress of the kind of easy-going world we are living in today. It is the choice between the blind imposition of technological advance, with all that means in terms of unemployment, and the conscious, planned, purposive use of scientific progress to provide undreamed of living standards and the possibility of leisure ultimately on an unbelievable scale.

That is why we must in the Labour Party, devote a lot more thought to providing facilities for the use of leisure, and this is why again, as this document suggests, we shall have to be a lot more imaginative

about the provision for retraining the workers made redundant by the development of new skills and new techniques.

Now I come to what we must do, and it is a fourfold programme. First, we must produce more scientists. Secondly. having produced them we must be a great deal more successful in keeping them in this country. Thirdly, having trained them and kept them here, we must make more intelligent use of them when they are trained than we do with those we have got. Fourthly, we must organize British industry so that it applies the results of scientific research more purposively to our national production effort. These, then, are the four tasks: first, more scientists—we are simply not training anything like enough for the nation's needs. Russia is at the present time training ten to eleven times as many scientists and technologists. And the sooner we face up to that challenge the sooner we shall realize what kind of a world we are living in.

I know, of course, that a Government Committee has said that we shall have all the scientists we need by 1965. Of course we shall—if we do not use them. We shall have all the bull-fighters we need by 1965. But to train the scientists we are going to need will mean a revolution in our attitude to education, not only higher education but at every level. I do not want to anticipate the debate on education, but it means that as a nation we cannot afford to force segregation on our children at the 11-plus stage.

As Socialists, as democrats, we oppose this system of educational apartheid, because we believe in equality of opportunity. But that is not all. We simply cannot as a nation afford to neglect the educational development of a single boy or girl. We cannot afford to cut off three-quarters or more of our children from virtually any chance of higher education. The Russians do not, the Germans do not, the Americans do not, and the Japanese do not, and we cannot afford to either. And if you want proof, only this month in part of my constituency we have a big new town where, thanks to the imagination of the Socialist authority there, every secondary school in that town is comprehensive. The children who live there have no conception of what it means to go along on a cold February morning to take an 11-plus examination or any other system of 11-plus selection either. There is a boy who, when his family lived in Liverpool, took the 11-plus examination and was not accepted for a grammar school place, but when he came to live in

Source: Given on 1 October 1963 at the 62nd Annual Conference of the Labour Party, Scarborough.

Kirby he went to the comprehensive school, and this boy who, in the conventional jargon, failed his 11-plus, is starting this morning at Liverpool University with a State scholarship in physics. And how many more are there? But we cannot afford segregation at 11-plus nor can we afford segregation at 18-plus. There are students this year who are failing to secure entry to universities . . . who possess qualifications which a year ago would have got them in, because, to quote a phrase which I read in the paper this morning by the Director of the North-Western Council of Industry . . . they are facing an increasingly severe 'rat race' in the problem of entering universities.

Last year, 1962, a quarter of those who had the necessary qualifications at A level could not get in because there were not enough places, and this year a much higher proportion than that will have been excluded, despite the fact that they have got the necessary qualifications for entry. And as the number of boys and girls reaching university age rises, as a result of the birth rate of the 1940s—facts which were known to the Government a very long time ago—as a higher and higher proportion of those boys and girls stay at school—and we are glad they are doing it—we shall have a greater number of students every year failing to get in because the places are simply not there. The Government could have foreseen this, and they could have taken the steps necessary to see that the places were there. To give students today the same chances of getting a place in the late 1960s as they had even in the late 1950s, we are going to need between 180,000 and 200,000 places in our universities, and the Government's plan provides for only 150,000—and that is only to get back to the same standards of entry as we had in the late 1950s; and in the late 1950s our rate was too small; we were near the bottom of the international league. This is why we in the Labour Party give such a high priority to plans for higher education.

I think the report of Lord Taylor's working party has been one of the most important contributions to the study of the problem of higher education in this country. They recommend, and we accept, a crash programme, first, to make fuller use of existing universities and colleges of higher education. They propose, and every one of us must accept, a tremendous building programme of new universities, and in this programme let us try and see that more of them are sited in industrial areas where they can in some way reflect the pulsating throb of local industry, where they can work in partnership with the new industries we seek to create.

Not enough thought has been given, when we fight against the problem of declining areas and the migration of population away from some of our older areas, to the establishment of new universities who, by the very nature of their industrial research, can help to revitalize areas in which they are going to be sited. As Lord Taylor said in the report, our aim must be at the earliest possible moment to provide facilities for higher education for at least 10 per cent of our young people, instead of the 5 per cent at which the Tories are tepidly aiming.

There is another thing we have got to do in the field of higher education, and this is to put an end to snobbery. Why should not the colleges of advanced technology award degrees? Why should not teachers training colleges be given more and more their proper place in the educational system? You know, what is needed here is not going to happen by chance. We are going to need a Ministry of Higher Education. You can argue about whether you link it with the existing Ministry of Education, whether you link it with the new Ministry of Science or, as may be right, constituting it as a Ministry in its own right under a Minister of Cabinet rank. You can all produce arguments. The important thing is that the Ministry of Higher Education must become the focal point of the planning of higher education in this country.

Relevant, also, to these problems are our plans for a university of the air. I repeat again that this is not a substitute for our plans for higher education, for our plans for new universities, and for our plans for extending technological education. It is not a substitute; it is a supplement to our plans. It is designed to provide an opportunity for those who, for one reason or another, have not been able to take advantage of higher education, now to do so with all that TV and radio and the State-sponsored correspondence course, and the facilities of a university for setting and marking papers and conducting examinations, in awarding degrees, can provide. Nor, may I say, do we envisage this merely as a means of providing scientists and technologists. I believe a properly planned university of the air could make an immeasurable contribution to the cultural life of our country, to the enrichment of our standard of living.

Mr Chairman, because this morning we are talking about science I have been referring so far to plans for training scientists, but of course in the whole of our university and higher education expansion programme scientists will have their place but no more than their place in the development, because the development of higher education based purely on the training of scientists and technologists would, of course, fail to meet the full human requirements of our nation. Secondly, we must hold our scientists in this country. The Royal Society has recently reported that 12 per cent of new Ph.Ds. are now leaving this country every year to go abroad. We have heard recently of universities where practically the whole scientific department has emigrated *en bloc*. Only the other day I heard of one of our most famous scientific colleges where in one particular faculty nine Ph.Ds. have been awarded this year in a field which is as relevant to the future of Britain as any subject I could think of, and of those nine, seven have already left to go to the United States. Lord Hailsham tells us that this loss of scientists is due to the deficiencies of the American educational system. His Lordship is wrong. It is due not to the deficiencies of the American educational system; it is due to the deficiencies of the British industrial system, in that we do not put a proper valuation on our trained scientists; that they are not afforded the status and the prospects to which they are entitled . . .

Scientific research in industry needs to be very purposively organized. This is one reason why we are going to establish a full Ministry of Science; not what we have today—an office of the Minister for Science, with no powers, no staff, no scientists, no clear direction of what he is about. The Labour Party has been saying for years, that we have got to get a proper organization and a proper sponsorship of scientific research in this country . . .

Mr Chairman, let me conclude with what I think the message of all this is for this Conference, because in this Conference, in all our plans for the future, we are re-defining and we are re-stating our Socialism in terms of the scientific revolution. But that revolution cannot become a reality unless we are prepared to make far-reaching changes in economic and social attitudes which permeate our whole system of society.

The Britain that is going to be forged in the white heat of this revolution will be no place for restrictive practices or for outdated methods on either side of industry. We shall need a totally new attitude to the problems of apprenticeship, of training and re-training for skill. If there is one thing where the traditional philosophy of capitalism breaks down it is in training for apprenticeship, because quite frankly it does not pay any individual firm, unless it is very altruistic or quixotic or farsighted, to train apprentices if it knows at the end of the period of training they

will be snapped up by some unscrupulous firm that makes no contribution to apprenticeship training. That is what economists mean when they talk about the difference between marginal private cost and net social cost.

So we are going to need a new attitude. In some industries we shall have to get right away from the idea of apprenticeship to a single firm. There will have to be apprenticeship with the industry as a whole, and the industry will have to take responsibility for it. Indeed, if we are going to end demarcation and snobbery in our training for skill and for science why should not these apprenticeship contracts be signed with the State itself. Then again, in the Cabinet room and the board room alike those charged with the control of our affairs must be ready to think and to speak in the language of our scientific age . . .

For those of us who have studied the formidable Soviet challenge in the education of scientists and technologists, and above all, in the ruthless application of scientific techniques in Soviet industry, know that our future lies not in military strength alone but in the efforts, the sacrifices, and above all the energies which a free people can mobilize for the future greatness of our country. Because we are democrats we reject the methods which Communist countries are deploying in applying the results of scientific research to industrial life, but because we care deeply about the future of Britain, we must use all the resources of democratic planning, all the latent and under-developed energies and skills of our people, to ensure Britain's standing in the world. That is the message which I believe will go out from this Conference to the people of Britain and to the people of the world.

Introduction to readings 38–39

The Report of the Robbins Committee in 1963 set the framework for the expansion of the British university system. The task of implementing its recommendations fell largely to the University Grants Committee (the UGC), then under the chairmanship of Sir John Wolfenden, formerly Vice-Chancellor of Reading University.

The University Grants Committee, composed of academics and others independent of government, although serviced by civil servants on secondment, has been the medium through which the government has financed the universities for more than half a century. It has been seen as the bulwark of academic freedom and university autonomy in Britain. In the post-Robbins years its role changed somewhat. In the first of the following two passages, both taken from the Committee's Report to the Secretary of State for Education and Science, *University Development 1962–67* (HMSO, Cmnd 3820, November 1968), the Committee examines its own changing role, and its relations with the universities, with government and with parliament (pp. 176–92 of the Report).

The grant made to the universities on the advice of the UGC is calculated for successive five-year periods, each known as a 'quinquennium'. One way in which the Committee informs itself of the needs of individual universities is by visiting each in the period before the grant for the next quinquennium is calculated—the 'quinquennial visitations'. In general, when a university has received its grant, it may spend it as it will; this is why it is described as a 'block grant'. Although the UGC is an on-going Committee, its membership changes, and hence its Report refers from time to time to the activities of 'our predecessors'.

References in this first extract from the Report to the transformation of the Colleges of advanced technology into universities, and to the fate of the Robbins proposal for the creation of five Special Institutions of Scientific and Technological Education and Research are explained in the second passage which we print.

The four Research Councils, charged with the support of research projects in the fields of science, medicine, agriculture and the environment, are funded through the Department of Education and Science. The Ministry of Technology, to which reference is made by the Committee, has now been absorbed into the Department of Trade and Industry. The Public Accounts Committee is a Committee of the House of Commons whose task is to examine the financial regularity, propriety and efficiency of the administration of the sums made available by parliament to government departments and agencies under headings known as 'Votes'. The accounting officer of a department, responsible for this financial administration, is normally the Permanent Under-Secretary of State, the senior civil servant of the department.

The second extract from the Report (excerpted from pp. 48–78) shows how the UGC and the government set about turning the major Robbins recommendations into policy and practice. References to the Scottish Central Institutions are explained in MacLean's article in the first section of this volume.

38　University development 1962-7

The role of the University Grants Committee

It is not quite clear who first described the University Grants Committee as a 'buffer'. In 1948, at the first Commonwealth Universities Conference held after the Second World War, Sir Walter Moberly said: 'I remember that Mr Dalton, when he was Chancellor of the Exchequer, described the function of the Committee as being to act as a buffer or shock-absorber between the Government and the Universities.'[1] This

Source: *Report of the University Grants Committee to the Secretary of State for Education and Science*, HMSO, Cmnd 3820 (November 1968).

designation has been in general use since that time; and it was repeated by the Robbins Committee[2] (with significant change of emphasis) and by Mr Quintin Hogg, as Lord President of the Council and Minister for Science, in March 1964.[3]

The fundamental purpose of the original doctrine persists and is no less important today than ever it was. Successive Governments, of whatever party, have consistently maintained, over the whole history of the relations between Government and the universities, that there should be no direct confrontation between the Government, on the one hand, and universities, individually or collectively, on the other. Occasional meetings between a Secretary of State and the Committee of Vice-Chancellors and Principals do not invalidate this principle, for these meetings, valuable as they are, are deliberative rather than operational. The doctrine has been re-affirmed as recently as 1967 by Mr Crosland, then Secretary of State for Education and Science. In the context of 'accountability', he said: 'The existence of an independent check on how the universities spend public money should serve to reassure Parliament and the public. It need not infringe the academic freedom of the universities. It does not denote any lack of confidence in the existing system whereby the University Grants Committee stands as a "buffer" between the Government and the universities. It was in this spirit that the Public Accounts Committee made its recommendations. It is in this spirit that the Government accept them.'

There is no doubt that in the early days, when relationships between the Government and the universities were being tentatively and gradually established, the 'buffer' concept was advantageous to both sides. It relieved the Government of assuming direct responsibility for the universities, and it safeguarded the universities from political interference. More positively, it was an earnest of the Government's willingness to provide money for the universities 'without strings', and it enabled the universities to enjoy public funds without the fear that the gift might turn out to be a Greek one.

For almost fifty years this principle has been observed, under Governments of many different kinds and in widely varying political and economic circumstances. Not surprisingly, there have been variations in the nuances of interpretation and in the closeness or distance, the warmth or coolness, of the relationship. But throughout these variations the principle itself has never been seriously challenged. It has been rooted and grounded in one indispensable element, reciprocal confidence between the bodies concerned. To a very considerable extent the relationships between them depend on convention rather than on prescription and therefore on behaviour by each which is regarded as reasonable by all. It is a remarkable tribute to successive Governments, to the universities themselves and to our predecessors that with very rare exceptions the fundamental principle has in practice worked—and that achievement is more to the point than legal definition or constitutional precision.

But times change. And the apparently passive function of the Committee as a buffer or shock-absorber has changed with them.

Throughout its history the Committee has shown, perhaps not always consciously, the way in which an enduring entity adapts itself to a constantly changing environment, remaining substantially and in principle the same entity while its accidental manifestations of activity gradually alter. In the course of the recent quinquennium the changes have been more marked

and more obvious than in some earlier periods, because the rate of change in the universities, in number, size and complexity, has been greatly accelerated. The Committee's activities, in relation both to the Government and to the universities, have correspondingly become more complex and more extensive. But while this is so, and must be recognized as being so, it would be wrong to minimize the element of continuity with the past in the developments which have taken place.

Lord Robbins and his colleagues recognized this when they said: 'nevertheless the University Grants Committee is not passive in regard to the policy of particular universities'.[4] The recommendations of the Robbins Committee, and the Government's acceptance of them, have themselves contributed to the swing towards an increasingly active interpretation by the University Grants Committee of its rôle. For instance the increase in the number of university institutions from 24 to 43 in the past ten years has made it all the more necessary that the Committee should exercise a more positive function. It no longer makes sense, if it ever did, that each university should seek to develop the range of its own offerings with no regard to the intentions and the practices of sister universities. Increasingly there has been recognized the need for at least the outline of a central strategy if only because of this notable increase in the size of the university family. If it be granted that neither the Government nor the Committee of Vice-Chancellors and Principals would be the right body to exercise such a strategic influence, then the responsibility falls on the University Grants Committee.

But it is not only the increase in the number of universities and in the size of the university population that has led in this direction. Very rapidly over recent years the traditional 'ivory-tower' isolationism of the universities has wasted away. They have come to see themselves as a part—a clearly distinguishable and very distinguished part, but still a part—of the nation's provision of higher education. They are surrounded by the other parts of the higher education system: they have common boundaries with them—and sometimes common problems. The movement of the former Colleges of Advanced Technology across one of those boundaries had a profound effect in this connection. Many of the established universities had practised many forms of technology for many years; it is an ingenuous mistake to suppose that the ex-CAT's introduced technology into the university world. But the arrival in the university world of a dozen institutions primarily concerned with technology, already active and flourishing in their own right, made an impact which without doubt widened both the popular and the professional notion of what universities are and are for. On another flank the closer association between the colleges of education and the universities was an influence in the same direction; and although the recommendations of the Robbins Committee in this regard were not carried out in full the strengthening of academic links between the colleges and the universities brought home to many members of university staffs the similarities as well as the differences between their own work and that of their colleagues in the colleges.

Behind this again developed an increasing interest in the place of the universities in the national life. The point of approach may have been primarily financial; since the universities spend so much public money, ought not the public to have some sort of guarantee that that money is efficiently and economically spent? So words and ideas such as 'cost-consciousness', 'plant utilization', 'unit cost' passed into normal academic thought and conversation. Some think this trend has already gone too far: others that it has not yet gone far enough. The fact to be recorded is that this kind of consideration is now familiar.

But though the immediate question might be a financial one the real question was seen to be a deeper one. In earlier days if the man in the street was conscious of the universities at all it was as rather mysterious and remote places which were the preserve of a tiny minority to which he did not belong. So questions about their relation to the nation's life hardly arose. All that is now changed. The Public, the Press, Parliament, show a deep and almost daily concern not simply with student behaviour but with the place of the universities in discussion about skilled manpower, with the 'Brain Drain', and with the proper adjustment of the provision of university places to student demand at the one end and national needs at the other.

It is perhaps not irrelevant also that throughout the national life there has been an increasing emphasis, in recent years, on organization. It has taken many forms. But right through, from direct governmental planning to increased organization of the leisure of young people, this tendency has shown itself and has become part of the background against which the universities themselves operate. Both inside each university and among the universities as a family there has emerged a felt need for more conscious and deliberate planning, organization and arrangement. And that in turn calls for a more positive or activist attitude on the part of all who are concerned with them, not least the Committee itself.

Increasingly, therefore, the University Grants Committee has come to be regarded (we are tempted to say, recognized) as having a more positive function than simply to be a buffer or a shock-absorber. It still is those things; and it is the interpreter of the Government to the universities and of the universities to the Government. But today it is more than this.

It has fallen to us, for example, to decide in practical operational detail which universities should be encouraged to develop biological studies, which should be built up to become something like the SISTERS which the Robbins Committee advocated, which should take the lead in the use of Audio-Visual Aids. More significant—and more difficult of achievement—we have felt it to be our duty to discourage particular activities in particular universities, for instance Agriculture in three.

In short, we are now inescapably involved in making positive judgments, an activity which goes far beyond the capacity of a buffer or a shock-absorber. The sheer number of universities, their decreasing homogeneity and the correspondingly increasing variety of their offerings, together with national considerations of the kind which have been mentioned, demand some central appraisal if uneconomic duplication is to be avoided and a reasonable degree of differentiation of function is to be achieved. The word 'rationalization' sounds cold and austerely functional in relation to the warm-blooded and spontaneous activities of universities. But a rational distribution of specialized function seems to be not inconsistent with clear thinking or with a sensible distribution of the financial resources which the taxpayer provides.

The Committee has not undertaken this extension of its functions inadvisedly, lightly or wantonly. There was abundant evidence during the quinquennial round of visits to the universities that a lead from the centre would be welcomed. One of the useful purposes of the quinquennial visitations is that they provide an opportunity for the Committee to make known to individual universities the current national picture of development in higher education. And by contrast with earlier rounds of visitations it was apparent that now the universities were asking for guidance. So far from resenting and resisting hints or advice about their own local developments one university after another positively asked to be given a lead. There may be some who will deplore this, as an indication that the universities no longer have faith in themselves or in their own choices: others will recognize this as a development which was bound to come as the university family grew in size and complexity. However that may be, it is perhaps a sign of the abiding strength of the underlying pattern that the universities were not reluctant or ashamed to ask the Committee for a lead and that they felt able to discuss openly, as between people who speak the same language, the particular lines of expansion or development which were in their minds.

That all this has its dangers nobody would deny. The dilemma is clear. On the one hand, if each university does that which is right in its own eyes, with no regard for the totality of university provision or for national needs, there is a clear danger that anarchy and licence, under the universally respected name of academic freedom, will result. On the other hand, if the Committee becomes too *dirigiste*, too tidy-minded and too much concerned with overall planning, there is an equally clear danger that the free growth of academic institutions will be stunted by excessive control. In this area, as in many others, the Committee's duty is to be both sensible and sensitive. Accustomed as it is to adopting a Janus-like posture, looking with one face towards the Government and with one towards the universities, in this particular situation also its duty is to be two-faced, preserving a balance between uncontrolled exuberance and repressive direction.

In this context and for these reasons it has seemed right to the Committee that they should make clear to the universities (and to the interested public) the lines along which their thoughts were moving. They therefore prepared and issued, simultaneously with the individual letters to universities in which they communicated their allocations of recurrent block grant, a Memorandum of General Guidance. This was an innovation which has been widely welcomed. The purpose of the memorandum was to sketch the general background of the Committee's thinking against which individual grant allocations had been made. Attention was called to such overall considerations as student numbers, unit costs, and national needs, as well as to the consequences, for universities' planning, of the need for collaboration with industry, the pattern of postgraduate studies and the application of these generalities to particular fields of study. It is not to be expected—certainly it was not expected by the Committee—that every one of its expressed opinions would command universal agreement in every one of 43 academic societies. But it seemed right to set out the general lines of the Committee's thinking; and the important thing is not total agreement with each of the Committee's conclusions but rather the acceptance by the universities of the proposition that it is right and proper that the Committee should so convey to universities its own thinking and conclusions. This proposition is broadly accepted.

This is not to say that the Committee aspires, still less that it should rightly aspire, to a detailed planning of each university's development or a detailed oversight of such planning. But it is to say that in the increasing complexity of university affairs there should somewhere be a broad strategic picture. And it is today regarded as the Committee's responsibility to sketch that picture.

We are well aware that there are other bodies besides ourselves who contribute to the activities of the universities. We have in mind especially the Research Councils. It is very important that there should be universal recognition and acceptance of the difference between our function and the function of the Research Councils, for otherwise there will be confusion about aims, procedures and responsibilities.

Our duty is to ensure, by our advice to the Government, that the universities, as institutions, have at their disposal adequate funds for their total and continuing activities. The Research Councils have responsibilities which are not confined to the universities. In relation to the universities the Research Councils, as we understand it, have as their basic function to ensure that supplementary funds are available for the support of individual persons (or groups or units) inside the universities who are engaged in particular research enterprises, either of 'timeliness and promise' or of specific and identifiable national importance. We, broadly speaking, support universities, as institutions, over the whole range of their activities: the Research Councils, broadly speaking, support individuals or groups or units, for purposes of research in selected fields.

These two separate functions are, or should be, complementary. It would plainly be wrong that we should arrogate to ourselves the specific and research-oriented responsibilities of the Research Councils, for our concern is with the broad canvas of a university's total activities in teaching and research. Equally, it would seem inappropriate that they should undertake responsibility for the general or basic needs of the universities, which extend beyond particular research enterprises.

This difference in functions could, in a particular case, lead quite naturally and properly to a difference in approach. What would be unfortunate would be a situation in which we and they, in taking decisions, were unmindful of our respective intentions and objectives. For many years we have maintained close contact with the Research Councils through the exchange of papers, through assessors and through our Chairman's regular meetings with their Chairmen and Secretaries. We have been at pains to exchange information with them about our general intentions as outlined in our Memorandum of General Guidance and about their own plans for the support of specific projects within their respective fields. We hope that by these means our exchange of information on policies and proposals is reasonably complete. Certainly we and they are continually concerned that there should be no misunderstandings; and we are happy to record our appreciation of the continuing and cordial meetings of minds between all the Research Councils and ourselves.

We also maintain contact with the various Government Departments which in the course of their work find it helpful to arrange research contracts with universities or to provide support for new university activities relevant to their purposes. Among these the Ministry of Technology, with its dual concern of encouraging technological and economic advance in particular sectors of industry and of improving the quality of industrial technology generally, is of special importance. The Ministry is represented by an assessor at our meetings and at those of our relevant Sub-Committees; and our officers participate in the work of the Ministry's Advisory Board on Relations with Universities.

A different area of collaboration is that between the universities themselves and industry. Here the influence we are in a position to exert is less direct. But we have made it clear beyond any doubt that we regard this field of concerted action as being of the utmost importance. Over and above general exhortation and general provision within the block grant, we have called special attention to the desirability of university/industry collaboration, and in some particular cases we have made special provision for it. Here, as is almost commonplace, we are in a dilemma. On the one hand, we desire that this form of collaboration between the universities and industry should be regarded as a normal activity of the universities and therefore as falling within the range of their normal expenditure of block grant. On the other hand, we recognize that particular enterprises may need, before they become self-supporting, a measure of 'pump-priming'. We have therefore commended this kind of activity to the universities as a normal call on their block grant and at the same time reserved certain sums to be used for specific initiatives, which might, in their early years, if this additional assistance were not available, 'lose out' in a university's internal decisions about the deployment of its block grant.

This kind of commendation of one particular activity—and there are many other examples—goes far beyond the traditional description of the Committee as a 'buffer'. This more activist function has been deliberately adopted. We have not permitted ourselves to be frightened by charges of our becoming more *dirigiste*. At the same time we continue to be the most vocal defenders of the block grant principle.

Relations with Government

From 1919 until 1963 the University Grants Committee was the direct concern of the Treasury. Its staff consisted of Treasury Civil Servants. It was always clear, and totally accepted, that once they 'came to the University Grants Committee' those Civil Servants were the servants of the Committee and not of the Treasury. But they knew the Treasury, its habits, its ways of thinking; and they knew personally the individual Treasury officials with whom they were dealing on the Committee's behalf.

Not only was this fact a source of immense strength to the Committee, through its officials and their day-by-day dealings with their Treasury colleagues. More, the authority of the Treasury was behind the Committee in its dealings both with the Government and with, for example, the Public Accounts Committee. The Treasury was deeply committed to the 'buffer' principle, and guarded most jealously the Committee's independent status. A succession of highly-placed Treasury officials, among whom the most determined was Sir Edward (now Lord) Bridges, defended with all their acumen and experience the autonomy of the universities, and of the Committee, against every attack from whatever quarter.

But as the years went by and the pattern of the machinery of government changed, the very strength of the relationship with the Treasury began to seem to involve, in the eyes of some, a subcutaneous weakness in the Committee's position. From the purely financial point of view there was a constant danger of embarrassment. The Committee's financial submissions, on behalf of the universities, were made direct to the Treasury, and Treasury Ministers were responsible for decisions upon them. With the best will in the world (and that was never in doubt) that was always a potentially embarrassing situation. The Treasury is not by nature a spending Department. If Treasury Ministers are at any time compelled to impose restraints or 'cuts' on their colleagues in other Departments the expenditure for which they are themselves responsible can hardly escape similar treatment. Indeed, in the last resort, Treasury Ministers and their senior advisers were inevitably in an ambivalent position: on the one hand, as responsible for the totality of Government expenditure, they were bound to question with full rigour the proposals for university grants; on the other, they themselves were pleading the case for those grants. That the universities were, over the years, treated as generously as they were is a great tribute to the persuasive powers of a succession of Treasury Ministers. But the whole situation had in it the marks of anomaly if not of self-contradiction.

There is another side to this besides the financial. In their relationships with the Treasury the universities, through the Committee, were in a special position from the point of view of policy. They were relatively detached from the plans and the decisions of Ministers responsible for schools, teacher training colleges and further education. No doubt the reasons for this were historically sound. But from the point of view of the development of a comprehensive national policy for higher education it began to be felt that history was not enough. No doubt also the rapidly increasing number of students in the universities, with the consequent increase in the amount of public money involved, had its effect also. But fundamentally this was an issue of policy—were the universities to remain a separate and disconnected element in the country's educational system? Or were they to be brought into connection with the whole of the rest of that system and entrusted to a policy-making Department of State?

Into an existing ferment of ideas of this kind came the Robbins Report in October 1963. It would be otiose to recapitulate here the arguments which Lord Robbins and his colleagues set out with such clarity and precision. Briefly, the choice they set before the Government was this: on the assumption that the 'buffer' University Grants Committee should continue but that the Treasury should cease to be directly responsible for it, should the university element in higher education be brigaded with Science and the Arts in a separate Ministry or should all these interests be amalgamated with the existing Ministry of Education? The Government's decision, immediately on the publication of the Robbins Report, found a third possibility. The University Grants Committee was transferred from the Treasury not to a departmental Minister but to the Lord President of the Council, who was already the Minister responsible for Science.

The immediate operational problem was the implementation of the Government's acceptance of the recommendations of the Robbins Committee. True, that acceptance stopped short of the creation of five Special Institutions of Scientific and Technological Education and Research and of bringing the teachers' training colleges inside the university system. But nevertheless there was a good deal to do. Chiefly, an expansion of the university population in accordance with the statistical projections of the Robbins Committee involved an unprecedented growth in the established universities and in those whose foundations had been laid in the preceding five years. The Lord President and his staff applied themselves to this task with vigour and gusto.

But the Robbins Committee were not concerned with the universities only. Their terms of reference were: 'To review the pattern of full-time higher education in Great Britain and in the light of national needs and resources to advise Her Majesty's Government on what principles its long-term development should be based. In particular, to advise, in the light of these principles, whether there should be any changes in that pattern, whether any new types of institution are desirable and whether any modifications should be made in the present arrangements for planning and co-ordinating the development of the various types of institution.' And they laid down as a 'guiding principle' that 'courses of higher education should be available for all those who are qualified by ability and attainment to pursue them and who wish to do so'.[5] They did not, as has often been mistakenly supposed, equate 'places in higher education' with 'places in universities', for they had a proper concern for the colleges of education and for the whole structure of higher education throughout the country.

Inevitably, therefore, plans for the expansion of the universities and plans for the expansion of other forms of higher education came to have, and to be seen to have, implications for each other. Neither could sensibly be planned without reference to the other. So the decision was taken to make both the responsibility of one Minister. It would still have been possible to remove non-university higher education from the Ministry of Education and form a new Ministry of Higher Education. But the weight of argument fell on the side of maintaining the intimate connection between the non-university sector of higher education and the rest of the national educational system. The alternative was therefore adopted of linking the university sector, together with Science,[6] with the Department responsible for education at large. The Ministry of Education was accordingly transformed into the Department of Education and Science, and ministerial responsibility for the universities passed to that Department. The transition was eased by the appointment of Mr Quintin Hogg, then Lord President of the Council, as the first Secretary of State for Education and Science and of Sir Edward Boyle, then Minister of Education, as the first Minister of State in the new Department. So while the departmental responsibility for the universities changed the persons most immediately concerned remained the same.

It would be idle to pretend that these changes were universally popular in the university world. The direct contact between the University Grants Committee and the Treasury had been cherished by the universities as a symbol of their independence of the Government; that independence had been sturdily defended over the years, by Treasury Ministers and officials, and it was not clear what advantages the universities would derive from the new arrangement to compensate them for losing what they had enjoyed under the old one. They feared, in particular, that their financial needs and claims would be in competition, within a departmental budget, with the needs and claims not only of other forms of higher education but also of the schools. In general, they feared that politics might for the first time come into their lives; for a departmental Minister is the political head of a Department in a sense in which Treasury Ministers are not, and to be attached to a 'policy' Department meant that the universities were 'latched on' to the Government in a more direct and potentially dangerous way than had been customary.

It is difficult for us to assess the extent to which these fears on the part of the universities have turned out to be justified. Only the universities themselves can say that: and to a degree their answer must be speculation, since nobody can know what would have happened if this new arrangement had not been made. From our own point of view the following comments can be made.

(1) Our connection with a 'policy' Department has in no sense introduced politics, still less Party politics, into our activities. Changes of Government have not changed the relationship between the Government and the Committee, either in theory or in practice. And so far as appointments to the Committee itself are concerned, these remain, as they have always been, non-political.

(2) No single one of the responsible Ministers or Permanent Under-Secretaries since 1963 has shown the slightest inclination to reduce the independence of the Committee or of the universities. On the contrary, they and their colleagues 'down the line' have been scrupulous in their regard for it. The words used by Mr Hogg in announcing the formation of the Department of Education and Science, in March 1964, have been strictly observed:—
'The University Grants Committee will have direct access both to the new Secretary of State and to the two Ministers of State. The only other change affecting the University Grants Committee is that, as has already been announced, its organization will be strengthened to enable it to deal with the heavier load with which it will be faced as a result of the Robbins Report. I need hardly tell the House—although perhaps I should mention it—that the

University Grants Committee will retain its traditional position in relation to the universities and to Whitehall, on the 'buffer' principle as it was called, recommended by the Robbins Committee'.

(3) From time to time the existence of the link with the Department of Education and Science has seemed, in ordinary day-to-day operational fact, to interpose another link between the Committee and the Government. Financial questions, in particular, must now be presented by the Committee to the Department and by the Department to the Treasury, instead of by the Committee to the Treasury direct. Occasionally this procedure has led to delays. Two things need to be said: (i) the Departmental officials in the relevant branch (which has been deliberately kept as small as possible) have been unfailing in their good-will and sympathetic understanding of the position of the universities and the Committee: (ii) granted that the Committee have now to substantiate their financial proposals to the Department, with all that that means in rigorous examination of details, the fact is that when the Department has been convinced of the propriety of those proposals the advocacy of Departmental Ministers in the presentation to the Treasury is invaluable. On this score the universities have reason—perhaps more than they always recognize—to be grateful to a succession of Ministers and Secretaries of State. It may well be that they have been more successful than the Committee itself would have been in direct dealings with the Treasury.

Relations with Parliament

A different area is that of relations between the Committee and Parliament. For many years the Committee of Public Accounts has expressed its concern about accountability to Parliament for the funds voted for university purposes. It is not the case, as is sometimes supposed, that these moneys were not accounted for. There has always been an Accounting Officer, formerly in the Treasury, whose duty it was to ensure 'propriety, regularity and efficiency' in the expenditure of these funds; and if the Public Accounts Committee felt it necessary to examine him the custom has always been that he was accompanied by the Secretary of the University Grants Committee in his appearance before the Public Accounts Committee.

The transfer of financial responsibility for the University Grants Committee and the universities from the Treasury to the Office of the Lord President of the Council, and subsequently to the Department of Education and Science, made no change in the principles involved, though the persons of the Accounting Officers were different. For a time there were two Permanent Under-Secretaries in the Department, one of them charged with responsibility for the Universities and Science. But finally this responsibility was merged in the existing duties of one Permanent Under-Secretary.

The major change was yet to come. In the Autumn of 1966 the Committee of Public Accounts undertook a full and specific review of the position of the Universities and Colleges Vote.

The question at issue was not accountability in itself—that had always been accepted and practised—but the degree of direct access which Parliament, through its own officers, should have to the 'books and papers' of the University Grants Committee and of the universities. Hitherto that access had been at second hand. The Committee itself had (and has) never paid out any money to any university; it had (and has) no cheque-book. Technically, the Committee makes recommendations, formerly to the Treasury now to the Department of Education and Science; the Committee itself has no authority (and never has had) to issue public funds. By custom and convention its recommendations for the payment of grant, capital or recurrent, have never been questioned, and provided that they fall within the sums voted by Parliament grants have been paid, by the relevant Government issuing authority, in accordance with those recommendations. The Comptroller and Auditor-General, as the servant of Parliament, has had access to the accounts of the Department concerned. But if any question arose—and there have been some over the years—his access, and therefore his knowledge, was confined to what could be derived from the books and papers of the Department. His knowledge, and therefore Parliament's, stopped at the stage of the issue by the Department of money to a Deposit Account from which payments were made, on the Committee's recommendation, to individual universities. The Public Accounts Committee was therefore unable to exercise any direct check on the efficiency or the economy in the spending by a university of funds which came to it from a Parliamentary Vote.

During the autumn and winter of 1966 the Public Accounts Committee undertook a special enquiry into this whole matter, as the culmination of a series of comments on it over a long period of years. Evidence was presented, written and oral, by many distinguished individuals, by the Committee of Vice-Chancellors and Principals, the Association of University Teachers and the University Grants Committee itself. The thoroughness and comprehensiveness of the enquiry are beyond doubt and the Special Report which was presented to Parliament in January 1967, will long remain the *locus classicus* on the very important and far-reaching issues involved.

In their simplest (perhaps over-simplified) form those issues are two. On the one hand, can Parliament continue to exempt from the normal procedures of public accountability the expenditure of a sum of money amounting to over £200 million a year? On the other hand, can the principles of academic freedom, cherished and defended in this country for so long, be reconciled with the normal requirements of Parliamentary scrutiny?

There were (and are) some misunderstandings and

confusions which the Special Enquiry served to dispel. First, it was never the case that money which flowed from the public purse through the University Grants Committee to the universities was 'not accounted for at all'. The books and papers of the Government Department responsible for the University Grants Committee, whichever at any one time it might be, were and always had been open to the normal procedures of scrutiny on behalf of Parliament. And from time to time, before 1966, questions had been asked of the responsible Accounting Officer about particular financial transactions in universities. The point at issue was the different one, whether the Comptroller and Auditor General should have direct access to the books and papers of the University Grants Committee and the universities and be able to satisfy himself at first hand, instead of having to rely, as in the past, on information which the relevant Accounting Officer assembled and transmitted. It was (and is) also the case that the accounts of each university are, in accordance with its Charter, examined and certified by professional Accountants of the highest standing. There was never any suggestion of irregularity. The point was to ensure that Parliament should be in a position to be satisfied, through enquiries conducted independently on its behalf, that the financial procedures and competence of the University Grants Committee and the universities were capable of handling £200 million a year of public money.

A second confusion in the minds of some related to the constitutional position of the Comptroller and Auditor General. He was sometimes regarded and described as 'the Government's financial watch-dog' and from that description were inferred dangers of governmental interference in the affairs of the universities. In fact the Comptroller and Auditor General is the servant of Parliament, not of the Government; and it could easily happen that in the course of his statutory duties he might be very critical, on behalf of Parliament, of activities carried on on behalf of the Government.

Thirdly, there was some confusion about what was to be understood by the words 'academic freedom'. At the least, a distinction should be made between the intellectual freedom of the individual academic and the institutional autonomy of an academic society. Decisions or events which might affect the one need not necessarily have any effect on the other.

The University Grants Committee's position was, in broad terms, that there was no need for a change in the existing arrangements, that Parliament's interests were sufficiently safeguarded by the obligations of the Accounting Officer, that there was an inevitable danger of closer involvement of the Accounting Officer in the affairs of the Committee and of the universities. While the universities were naturally more concerned about possible encroachments on academic freedom, the Committee's major uneasiness was lest increased attention to financial detail by the officers of the Department might erode the 'buffer'

principle on which the Committee's usefulness depends. An increase in direct governmental intervention was not expected. But there were, the Committee felt, two indirect dangers, that financial comments made by the Public Accounts Committee might lead to pressure for more direct Governmental control of the universities, and that the Committee itself might be driven to more detailed financial oversight of the universities' spending if it had to be equipped to answer detailed questions on it. Where the Public Accounts Committee was asking why the University Grants Committee and the universities should continue to enjoy exemptions from procedures which were standard in other areas of public spending, the University Grants Committee asked why the existing system, which had not been shown to be inadequate or inefficient, should be radically changed; especially they feared that the inevitably unpredictable consequences of such a change might be of a kind and a magnitude which Parliament itself did not desire. It was not easy, they felt, for the Department to confine its attention to questions of financial propriety, since the line between finance and policy is often difficult to draw, and they feared that with no malevolent intention on the part of anybody the Committee would be drawn further and further into the position of being a branch of the Department of Education and Science. (This last fear was expressed in his evidence by the Permanent Secretary of the Department himself.)

In the end the Public Accounts Committee made the following recommendations:

(1) that, with effect from the beginning of the next quinquennium (that is, from 1st August, 1967), the Comptroller and Auditor General should be given access to the books and records of the University Grants Committee and the universities;

(2) that in the meantime steps should be taken (*a*) to work out suitable conventions as to how his scrutiny will be conducted and how his queries will be handled; and (*b*) to ensure that the universities are fully informed about the nature and purposes of the Comptroller and Auditor General's scrutiny and what would be in practice involved.

The Government accepted these recommendations, with a postponement to 1st January 1968, of the date from which they should take effect.

Throughout the hearing of evidence and in the text of their Report the Public Accounts Committee were at pains to make clear that they had no intention of damaging in any way the position of the University Grants Committee or the proper autonomy of the universities. They repeated that their concern, and that of the Comptroller and Auditor General, was limited to financial regularity, propriety and efficiency, and that questions of policy, in the University Grants Committee and the universities, were outside their concern and his. They felt, in short, that the Comptroller and Auditor General's activities would be of a routine nature and could be absorbed by the University Grants Committee and the universities without any change in any other facet of the lives of either.

Despite some misgivings on this last point the University Grants Committee and the universities have accepted the new state of affairs. The Comptroller and Auditor General has himself addressed the Committee of Vice-Chancellors and Principals and the Council of the Association of University Teachers, in accordance with the Public Accounts Committee's wish that suitable conventions should be worked out as the framework of his activities. Officers of the University Grants Committee have co-operated with officers of the Department and of the Comptroller and Auditor General's staff in order to make the new procedures as smooth as possible in their initiation and operation.

Nobody can tell what the outcome will be. It is certain that there is no intention on anybody's part to disturb more than is unavoidable the relations which have hitherto existed between Parliament, the Government, the University Grants Committee and the universities. And there is in any event the positive gain that the question of the 'accountability' for the Universities and Colleges Vote, which had provoked comment from a succession of Public Accounts Committees, has now been thoroughly and definitely examined. The hope is that by bringing this whole matter into the open the Public Accounts Committee may have strengthened Parliamentary and public confidence in the University Grants Committee and the universities. The University Grants Committee's own history has been one of adapting itself to changing circumstances and changing demands, and although the need for this particular change was not accepted there will be no sparing of effort or determination to make it work. The Committee rely on the words of the Secretary of State quoted already—'The existence of an independent check on how the universities spend public money should serve to reassure Parliament and the public. It need not infringe the academic freedom of the universities.'

Relations with the universities

Relations with the Government constitute one side of the Committee's activities, the field to which one of the two Janus heads looks. The other and complementary field is that of the universities, individually and collectively.

It is sometimes thought that the Committee's relations with individual universities are confined to the formal quinquennial visitations and to official deputations from the universities to the Committee or its Chairman. That is not the case. Every day, by correspondence or telephone conversation or personal visits, Vice-Chancellors, Registrars, Finance Officers, Buildings Officers and other university officials are in direct and personal contact with the officers of the Committee, and increasingly it is becoming possible to arrange for officers to visit universities for personal discussions on the spot with their opposite numbers in the universities.

The range of these contacts is almost unlimited. A Vice-Chancellor may write a personal letter to the Chairman asking for his informal advice about the acceptance of an offered benefaction. A Registrar may come, either of his own accord or on invitation, to clear up an ambiguity in the categorization of part-time students on a post-experience course leading towards a higher degree. A Finance Officer may come to discuss a discrepancy between the university's and the Committee's estimates under a particular heading of the university's income. A Buildings Officer, with his university's Architect, may come to take the officers' and technical experts' views on the form of contract for a particular building. A Catering Officer may come for advice about the planning and equipment of a kitchen in a communal-feeding block. And so on.

These may seem to be details, and so they are. But they are important details in the efficient management of universities, and they exemplify the closeness of the working relationships between the universities and the officers of the Committee. There is every likelihood that these contacts will be deepened by the continuing activities of the subject Sub-Committees.

But there are, of course, wider questions of a university's policy which a Vice-Chancellor and his senior colleagues may wish to put forward either for preliminary discussion or, at a later stage in their thinking, for decision. Would it be sensible for University A to contemplate establishing a Medical School? How far ought University B to go in the direction of Slavonic Studies? What prospect is there that University C will be given the money to reach its objective of 10,000 students by 1985? How far would the Committee encourage University D to buy up terrace houses for conversion into student residences? Does the Committee accept University E's claim (with consequent financial help) to be regarded as a 'centre of excellence' in Engineering Studies? It is encouraging that so many Vice-Chancellors are willing to discuss their problems and their aspirations and that they appear to think that these conversations are worth their time and their journeys. At the very least there is a continuous accumulation of information and an almost daily increase in mutual knowledge.

The other aspect of the Committee's relations with the universities is not individual but corporate. It is concerned, that is, with matters of general policy which affect all universities. The sheer number of issues of this kind has inevitably increased with the size and complexity of the university family, and while the number of circular letters and questionnaires which flow from the Committee's offices necessarily put additional and regrettable burdens on the administrative staffs of universities the alternative, of confusion, uncertainty and misunderstanding, would be worse. Decisions such as those to change the system of grants for the equipping of buildings, to negotiate a provisional recurrent grant for the first year of the quinquennium, to re-assess the capital grant for residential places or to alter the ratio of senior to junior staff, have to be communicated to the universities in terms which are unambiguous.

An extremely important element in the reaching of these decisions and in the manner of their formulation is consultation with the Committee of Vice-Chancellors and Principals. And it is right to acknowledge here the help which this body and its successive Chairmen have given to us in recent years. They are in no way to be held responsible for the decisions we have reached; but it is certainly true that the form and content of many of those decisions have been greatly influenced by their advice.

The Committee of Vice-Chancellors and Principals has changed, as a body, almost beyond recognition in recent years. It began, as is well known, as an unofficial monthly meeting of Vice-Chancellors in the days when their number was small enough to enable them to meet on terms of friendly informality. Its purpose was essentially the exchange of opinion and interesting information. It did not intend or claim to make policy. There was a clear understanding that no Vice-Chancellor could commit his university to any opinion which he might express to his peers. Gradually, in the face of pressures from external forces such as wars, Governments, University Senates and plain economics, austere individualism gave place to co-operation and collaborative thinking, so that almost imperceptibly the Committee came to be regarded as the body from which 'university opinion' might be sought. This was not an easy transition, still less a complete one; for so long as the Vice-Chancellors, in monthly conclave represented nobody but themselves they were bound to speak with a rather tentative and modest voice, even when they were themselves of one mind.

Within the past two or three years this picture has substantially changed. The membership of the Committee is now fifty-two, so that its meetings are quite different from those of earlier days, both in their size and in the diversity of institutions and points of view which are represented. Even more important, the Committee has now with the approval and encouragement of the universities deliberately set itself the task of being able to represent a university view to the University Grants Committee, to Government and to the outside world. In order to do this it has introduced into its own administrative organization a pattern of functional Divisions which enables it to consider and discuss in depth a variety of business which could not possibly be brought within the bounds of one half-day meeting each month. We have established working relationships with these Divisions;

we have regular meetings, for informal exchange of views, with the Steering Committee; and successive Chairmen of the Committee meet with our own Chairman for discursive conversations at least once a month, in addition to more formal occasions. The Committee of Vice-Chancellors and Principals has moved towards a more sophisticated and articulate rôle in a way which is similar, if not parallel, to our own progress.

It will be interesting to see, over the next few years, how far these developments go. It could be argued that some of the decisions which the University Grants Committee now take could be more appropriately taken by the Committee of Vice-Chancellors and Principals. Certainly that Committee has of recent years been instrumental in setting up the Universities Central Council on Admissions, in encouraging the introduction of Organization and Methods studies and in enquiries into the use of university capacity, in ways which ten years ago would have seemed very improbable. These are fields (and there are others) where work clearly ought to be done; and for our part we much prefer that it should be done on the collective initiative of the universities than that we should have to do it ourselves. There are signs that the autonomy of each individual university is already to some extent being voluntarily surrendered in the interests of a corporate autonomy of them all. As the activities of the Committee of Vice-Chancellors and Principals develop, in reports on, for example, the utilization of university buildings or the provision of student residence by loan finance, a situation may develop in which on many subjects the universities enter into the dialogue with the University Grants Committee collectively and not individually. It is in that direction rather than in the direction of increasing individualism that recent developments in the Committee of Vice-Chancellors and Principals seem to point.

So the 'buffer' is by no means wholly passive. We have these positive and active relations with the Government, with Parliament and with the Universities individually and collectively. The question is sometimes asked 'Whose side is the University Grants Committee on?' This question misunderstands, in our view, the realities of our function. We are not on any 'side'. We are concerned to ensure that a vigorous and creative University life prospers in this country without reference from the Government of the day and at the same time to ensure that the tax-paying community, represented by Parliament and the Government, gets a proper return for its money in this field of considerable public expenditure. Nobody supposes—certainly we do not—that these twin tasks are easy to perform. But we do believe that these two objectives represent our rôle and function, and we expect that the years will see our successors develop them further in accordance with the Committee's history of organic evolutionary development.

Notes

1 *Report of Proceedings of the Sixth Congress of the Universities of the Commonwealth* (1948), 16.
2 *Higher Education*, HMSO, Cmnd 2154, paras 725–31; and App. 4, pt. I, Sect. 2.
3 Hansard, 11 March 1964.

4 Cmnd 2154, para. 730.
5 Robbins Report, para. 31.
6 Responsibility for the Arts was transferred to the Department of Education and Science in April 1965.

39 Expansion of the universities in the 1960s: problems and achievements

University development during the quinquennium was dominated by the *Report of the Robbins Committee on Higher Education*[1] and by the Government's policy statement on that Report.[2] The Robbins Report was the first comprehensive and definitive survey ever made in this country of higher education as a whole. It dealt not only with universities but with the whole structure of higher education, as it then existed, including the Colleges of Advanced Technology, the Regional and Area Technical Colleges, and the Teacher Training Colleges. It made far-reaching recommendations about the future development of higher education, in particular about the expansion of student numbers, the pattern of institutions, and the administrative structure.

Student numbers

Expansion was nothing new for the universities. The student population had increased from 50,000 in 1938–9 to 113,000 at the end of the 1957–62 quinquennium. Pre-Robbins plans had already provided for a further expansion to 150,000 by 1966–7 and to 170,000 by 1973–4. This expansion fell into three main phases.[3] First there was the immediate post-war period which saw the return of those whose university education had been interrupted or postponed by the war. The student population rose to 85,400 in 1949–1950; it included about 26,000 ex-service students, accounting for some two-thirds of the increase over 1938–9. As the wave of ex-service students spent itself, the total student population declined for a period of four years, the lowest point being reached in 1953–4 at 80,600. 1953–4 was also the year of the lowest entry (21,150) since the war.

In the second phase student entries and total student population increased steadily year by year until by 1961–2 the entry figure was 32,160 and total student numbers had reached 113,000. This increase took place in spite of the fall in the size of the 17+ age group as a result of the decline in the birth-rate in the

Source: Report of the University Grants Committee to the Secretary of State for Education and Science, HMSO, Cmnd 3820 (November 1968).

30's. Three main factors were responsible. The most important was the 'trend', that is the growing proportion of children staying on at school to 17 or 18. This proportion rose from about 6 per cent before the war to 12 per cent in 1962. Other factors were the wider availability of student awards (culminating, towards the end of this period, in the adoption of the Anderson Report[4] by the Government) and a marked increase in postgraduate studies, the number of advanced students rising from 3,094 in 1938–9 to 19,362 in 1961–2.

In the third phase—the period, broadly, of the middle 60's—a new factor supervened. This was the 'bulge', the increase in the size of the 17+ age group as the result of the rise in the birth-rate after the war. The 'bulge', coupled with the continuance and indeed the expected acceleration of the 'trend', made it evident that provision would be required for a very large expansion in the number of university places. Our predecessors started making plans for this expansion in 1955, in consultation with the Education Departments and the universities, and their plans were revised and adjusted in succeeding years . . .

In planning for this expansion our predecessors had come to the conclusion that a number of new universities would be needed to cope with the increased student demand in the late 60's and the 70's. The first of these, Sussex, was authorized by the Government in 1957. Authority was given in 1960 for the establishment of the new universities of York and East Anglia, and in 1961 for the establishment of the new universities of Essex, Kent, Lancaster and Warwick.

It was at the height of this planning, in 1961, that the Government appointed the Robbins Committee to take full stock of the existing situation and to review the pattern and future development of higher education. It is no disrespect to the Robbins Committee to say that their Report did not initiate the process of expansion in the universities, or in other sectors of higher education. What their Report did do was to establish, publicly and authoritatively, the principles which should govern the scale and pattern of higher education in this country . . .

The basic assumption in the Report was that courses

of higher education should be available for all those who were qualified by ability and attainment to pursue them and who wished to do so. The Government accepted this assumption and adopted the Robbins Committee's calculations on the number of places required, both in higher education as a whole and in institutions of University status, by 1967–8 and 1973–4 as their objectives for those years.

The targets for the number of places in institutions of university status were now set at 197,000 by 1967–8 and 218,000 by 1973–4. The institutions concerned included the ten Colleges of Advanced Technology in England and Wales and two Central Institutions in Scotland (the Scottish College of Commerce, Glasgow, and Heriot-Watt College, Edinburgh); these Colleges, as recommended in the Robbins Report, were to be given university status. The Government Statement made clear that the operation was being given a high priority. The additional resources required, both recurrent and capital, would be provided, but the greatest importance was attached to the economical use of these resources and to securing the fullest possible value for money . . .

The immediate task was to secure the short-term expansion required by 1967–8. The student target set in 1962 for the existing universities was, as already explained, 150,000 by 1966–7, followed by a further increase to 170,000 by 1973–4. The Government's decision meant that these universities had now to be asked to make a still greater effort and to achieve collectively by 1967–8 the student numbers which they had in mind for the first half of the 70's. In effect this meant trying to achieve a build-up of student numbers over the four years 1964–5 to 1967–8 to a total of 20,000 above the figure which, on former plans, would have been achieved over the three years 1964–5 to 1966–7; an increase in the average rate of growth from 8,000 a year over three years to 11,000 a year over four years.

Looking further forward to the 1973–4 situation, it seemed clear to us that the increase in student numbers proposed over the six years from 1967–8 to 1973–4 would mean a much less rapid rate of expansion and would afford the prospect of a period of relative stability and consolidation. It was the acceleration of already existing expansion programmes to meet the 'bulge' in the mid-sixties which was the really critical hurdle. If this could be surmounted, the 1973–4 target should be manageable without undue pressure . . .

In spite of difficulties the universities managed to make steady progress towards the Robbins short-term target. In 1961–2, the last year of the previous quinquennium, there were 113,000 full-time students in the existing universities and about 10,000 in the Colleges of Advanced Technology and Central Institutions which were to be given university status. To reach the new target of 197,000 for 1967–8 meant, therefore, an expansion by 74,000, or 60 per cent, over a period of six years. By 1965–6 the total number of full-time students had risen to 169,500 and by

1966–7 to 184,800. The count for the autumn term, 1967, showed a total of 200,287. The short-term Robbins target had been met, and more than met.

The changes which have taken place between 1938–9 and 1967–8 in student numbers, and in the proportions of the total student population, at university institutions in England, Wales and Scotland, and at different groups of university institutions, are shown in the Table 39.1.

Colleges of Advanced Technology and Scottish Central Institutions

The Robbins Committee recommended, and the Government agreed, that the Colleges of Advanced Technology and certain Scottish Central Institutions should have university status. There were ten Colleges of Advanced Technology:

Battersea College of Technology
Birmingham College of Advanced Technology
Bradford Institute of Technology
Bristol College of Science and Technology
Brunel College, Acton
Chelsea College of Science and Technology
Loughborough College of Technology
Northampton College of Advanced Technology, Finsbury
Royal College of Advanced Technology, Salford
Welsh College of Advanced Technology, Cardiff.

These Colleges, originally financed by local education authorities, had been placed on a direct grant basis in 1962. They were administered by independent governing bodies which received grants from the Ministry of Education both for recurrent expenses and for capital development. They had two main organs of government:

(i) a Governing Body consisting of some 25–30 members and including representatives of industry, professional and scientific bodies, universities, local authorities and of the teaching staff;
(ii) an Academic Board, consisting of Heads of Departments together with a specific number of other teaching staff, and responsible to the Governing Body for academic matters.

The Colleges had developed into national institutions, drawing students from all over the country and from overseas. Courses below university level were being progressively transferred to other colleges. The typical feature of the Colleges was the 'sandwich course'—in which academic study up to honours degree level was combined with periods of training in industry—leading to the Diploma in Technology, a national qualification at honours degree level administered by the National Council for Technological Awards.

In Scotland there were two Central Institutions involved, the Scottish College of Commerce, Glasgow, and the Heriot-Watt College, Edinburgh. Discussions

Table 39.1 Universities in Great Britain: full-time student numbers and percentages

	1938–39		1953–54		1961–62		1967–68	
	Student Numbers	Percentage	Student Numbers	Percentage	Student Numbers	Percentage	Student Numbers	Percentage
London	13,191	26·4	18,125	22·5	22,589	20·0	29,375*	14·7
Oxford and Cambridge	10,954	21·9	14,867	18·4	17,821	15·7	20,412	10·2
Other older-established universities in England	13,044	26·1	29,181	36·2	45,995	40·7	74,143	37·0
Recently-established universities in England	—		—		52	†	12,107	6·0
Former C.A.T.s in England	—		—		—		18,948	9·5
London and Manchester Business Schools	—		—		—		128	0·1
Total, England	37,189	74·4	62,173	77·1	86,457	76·4	155,113	77·5
Older Colleges of University of Wales	2,779	5·5	4,431	5·5	7,067	6·2	11,176	5·6
St David's College, Lampeter	—		—		186	0·2	292	0·1
Institute of Science and Technology	—		—		—		1,435	0·7
Total, Wales	2,779	5·5	4,431	5·5	7,253	6·4	12,903	6·4
Older Scottish Universities	10,034	20·1	13,998	17·4	19,433	17·2	30,426	15·2
Heriot-Watt	—		—		—		1,493	0·7
Stirling	—		—		—		186	0·1
Total, Scotland	10,034	20·1	13,998	17·4	19,433	17·2	32,105	16·0
Total, Great Britain	50,002	100·0	80,602	100·0	113,143	100·0	200,121	100·0

* Excluding Chelsea. † Less than 0·05 per cent.

had been going on for some time, with the support of the Committee, for the amalgamation of the College of Commerce with the Royal College of Science and Technology, Glasgow, which subsequently became the University of Strathclyde. The arrangements for amalgamation were finally completed in May, 1964.

The decision to give these institutions university status had important consequences for the work of the Committee. In the first place we had to consider the appropriate procedures for organizing the transition to university status. It was of great importance that these should be such as to ensure the confidence of the existing universities in the maintenance of academic standards. We therefore, after discussion with the Colleges, proposed to them in November 1963 that they should arrange, in consultation with us, for the appointment of Academic Advisory Committees. These Committees were to be appointed by the Colleges and would be advisory to them. It would be for the Colleges themselves to consider the reports of the Committees and to decide whether to adopt them or to put forward alternative proposals for consideration by us. The membership of the Academic Advisory Committees should be kept quite small, a Chairman and five or six other members, mainly academic but including representation from industry. The membership should include the Principal of the College con-

cerned; other names would be selected in agreement between the Colleges and ourselves . . .

The work of the Academic Advisory Committees, involving as it did the preparation of an academic and constitutional blueprint for each College (apart from day-to-day advice to the Governing Bodies on a variety of current problems), covered a very wide range. Broadly speaking, however, three main issues had to be resolved.

First there was the question whether the College concerned should become a separate, independent University or should develop in association with an existing University or other institution of higher education. In practice there was very little doubt that in the great majority of cases the right answer was for the College to seek independent University status. But there were three particular cases where the possibility of 'association' had to be seriously considered; these were the Chelsea College of Science and Technology, the Welsh College of Advanced Technology and Heriot-Watt College . . .

After discussions with us in which we made clear that, for our part, we were not in favour of independent status for the College, Chelsea entered into negotiations with the University of London with a view to becoming a grant-receiving School of the University. We assured London that, in our view, the situation of Chelsea, in particular the fact that the College had been promised university status by the Government, was sufficiently special that no other institution could legitimately draw any inference about its own future from a decision by London to admit Chelsea . . .

It was finally agreed between the University and the College that the College should become a grant-receiving School of the University from 1st August 1966.

In the case of the Welsh College of Advanced Technology at Cardiff, the promise of University status raised difficult and delicate problems about the future relationship of the College with the University of Wales and with the two existing university institutions at Cardiff—the University College of South Wales and Monmouthshire and the Welsh National School of Medicine—which were themselves within the University of Wales. The fundamental question was whether it would be sensible academically, in this situation, to establish the College of Advanced Technology as an independent University. The University of Wales had offered to enter into discussions with the College on the basis of it becoming a constituent College of the University. The College itself was attracted by the idea of establishing an independent, confederate University at Cardiff in which it would be associated with the University College and the School of Medicine; failing this, it was in favour of developing as an independent degree-giving institution and of moving to a new site outside Cardiff where it would have greater scope for expansion.

The Committee, after very full consideration, gave their advice to the Government on the academic issues involved. On 22 December 1965 Mr Crosland stated in the House of Commons that, in the light of the recent review of its constitution by the University of Wales, and after considering the advice of the University Grants Committee, the Government had concluded that they could not support the establishment of the Welsh College of Advanced Technology as a separate degree-giving University. An alternative road to University status was afforded by the invitation which the College had received from the University of Wales to become a full constituent member of the University; the Government were confident that such an arrangement would contribute to the development of the College as a centre of higher technological education. The Government had much sympathy with the idea of an association between the College of Advanced Technology, University College, Cardiff, and the Welsh National School of Medicine, but believed that this could well be worked out within the framework of the University of Wales.

Discussions followed between the University and the College, and by the end of 1966 agreement in principle had been reached on the entry of the College into the University of Wales as a fifth constituent College, with the title of the University of Wales Institute of Science and Technology; a new draft Charter was prepared by the College on this basis for submission to the Privy Council[5] . . .

In the case of Heriot-Watt College, there were discussions with Edinburgh University about the possibility of some form of association. The College eventually decided that it would wish to proceed independently to university status. This was accepted by the Committee and the Government.

The second main issue for the Academic Advisory Committees and Governing Bodies was the extent to which the Colleges, on attaining University status, should retain their technological bias, and how that bias might best be expressed. Some apprehension was being voiced at the time lest the Colleges might be tempted to diversify their activities too widely and, in an effort to present the traditional image of a University, to reduce their emphasis on technology and their close links with the industrial world, the distinctive feature of which was the sandwich-course system. In practice it became clear that the Academic Advisory Committees were whole-heartedly in favour of maintaining, and indeed improving, the technological bias of the Colleges, and that this was also the view held by the majority of College Governors and staffs. Many of the Colleges felt reluctant to consider a technological designation or to qualify the title 'University' by the addition of words which might be held in the future to restrict the scope and manner of their development. But they held firmly to the principle of the sandwich-course. And, while they had no doubt about the desirability of introducing more non-technological subjects, especially in the social sciences, in order to improve the education of technologists, they accepted in general the need to limit the development of new, independent degree courses in subjects not closely associated with, or relevant to, their primary role as technological institutions.

Thirdly there was the need to determine the future constitutional and administrative framework of the Colleges, and to give this expression in draft Charters for submission to the Privy Council. In general the Colleges decided to adopt the normal structure of university government, with executive and financial authority vested in a Council, including a majority of lay members, and academic authority vested in a Senate, including representation of the non-professorial staff. It seemed to us that it would be desirable to include, in the Charters of those Colleges which were planning to become separate universities, provision for an Academic Advisory Committee to operate for an initial period after the creation of the new university institution. We felt that such provision would be of benefit to the universities concerned, not as a form of tutelage or probation, but as strengthening the universities' own academic position and guaranteeing their standards to the university world at large; similar provision had been made in the Charters of the new university foundations. This proposal was accepted by the Colleges. In general the membership of the Academic Advisory Committees appointed under the Charters was drawn from the Advisory Committees which had been established to advise the Colleges on their development to university status. The period of existence of the Committees established under Charters was left to be decided by the Privy Council; we had in mind that a period of five years, broadly corresponding to the 1967–72 quinquennium, would be reasonable.

Considerable interest was aroused, in discussion of the Charters for the former colleges of advanced technology, in the provisions relating to student interests, and in the whole question of students' rights and student discipline. The Privy Council, after considering representations made to it by the National Union of Students and receiving advice from us, decided to put to the bodies sponsoring new Charters the desirability of including the following provisions:

1 The Senate and the Council of the new universities should be expressly empowered to establish joint committees of themselves and representatives of the student body.
2 Provision should be made whereby a procedure would be laid down for a right on the part of a student suspended or expelled to be formally heard by the Senate or by a body appointed by the Senate before the decision became final.
3 Provision should be made for an association representing the student body.

It was also established that the provisions included in a Charter were subject to the general rule of law that they should be exercised in accordance with natural justice. The obligation to observe the requirements of natural justice (for example, that a person charged should be informed of the nature of the charge and given an opportunity of defending himself) existed independently of the Charter which could not impair the ordinary legal rights of students.

The provision for joint committees of the Council or Senate and the student body reflected a general feeling that systematic arrangements should be made for consultation between university authorities and students on matters of proper concern to the students. It gave formal expression to a practice which had already developed widely, though often on an informal basis, among the existing universities. Apart from this aspect, the new Charters did not in general introduce innovations in the matter of student participation in university government. Proposals for such participation, such as those put forward by the National Union of Students for student representation on Council and Senate, seemed to us to raise a number of serious difficulties. For example, would a student nominee be a 'representative' of his nominating body? How far would he be expected, or entitled, to report back on discussions? What part would he play in confidential discussions? Was it right or proper that he should be involved in questions of the appointment or promotion of academic staff? It did not seem at all easy to answer questions such as these

or to define the proper status of a member who would be in some sense 'representative' of the students. It seemed doubtful whether in practice provision for such student representation would be as effective a means of bringing student opinion to bear as provision for matters involving student interests to be discussed by joint Council/Student and Senate/Student Committees.

On the other hand, provision for student representation on Governing Bodies already existed at Queen's University, Belfast, and at certain other universities in the Commonwealth—apart from the Rectorial arrangements of the older Scottish universities. Moreover we were agreed that it was desirable to encourage experiment in the constitution and government of new universities.

In the light of these considerations a proposal by Bradford to make provision in its Charter for the Council to include 'not more than one person who may be co-opted after considering nominations from the students' was accepted by the Privy Council, on the basis that this reflected a willingness to allow experiments rather than the adoption of a particular pattern of university government as being desirable in principle.

The titles of these universities (with their previous titles given in brackets), are as follow:

The University of Aston in Birmingham (Birmingham College of Advanced Technology).
The Bath University of Technology (Bristol College of Science and Technology).
The University of Bradford (Bradford Institute of Technology).
Brunel University (Brunel College).
The City University (Northampton College of Advanced Technology).
The Heriot-Watt University (Heriot-Watt College).
The Loughborough University of Technology (Loughborough College of Technology).
The University of Salford (Royal College of Advanced Technology, Salford).
The University of Surrey (Battersea College of Technology).

Establishment of new universities

The Robbins Committee recommended the creation of six new universities, at least one of which should be in Scotland. In making this recommendation they had in mind the probable requirement for university places by 1980, which they estimated at about 350,000; they put the maximum capacity of the existing universities (including the recently established ones) at about 300,000; and they thought it improbable that any University founded within the next few years could accommodate more than 5,000 students by 1980, that is a total of 30,000 places for the six proposed new universities. (This would still leave a gap, on their estimates, of 20,000 places; these, they suggested, might be provided by giving university status in due course to some of the colleges at present outside the university system.)

The Government Statement on the Robbins Report said:

> The proposals for the foundation of six new institutions will be considered during the formulation of the 10-year programme by the University Grants Committee and the Government. The University Grants Committee is being asked for an early report on the specific recommendation that a new University should be located in Scotland.

Some three years earlier the conclusion had been reached that, in the context of the overall target adopted at that time by the Government of 170,000 places by 1973–4, the case for a new university in Scotland was not proven. But the position had now to be reviewed in the light of the estimates used by the Robbins Committee of the potential student demand in Scotland. The rate of growth implied by these estimates was considerably higher than that implied by earlier estimates and it was clear that, whatever might be the future trend in the movement of students from England and Wales to Scotland, there would still be a substantial gap between demand and supply as contrasted with the position when we had examined it in 1960. We accordingly advised the Government that we felt satisfied about the need for a new university in Scotland . . .

We reconstituted our New Universities Sub-Committee (which had been originally established in 1959) in order to examine the various proposals in detail. Considered proposals had earlier been received from six places, Ayr, Dumfries, Falkirk, Inverness, Perth and Stirling. An additional proposal was submitted on behalf of the New Town of Cumbernauld. The Sub-Committee visited these seven areas in April and May, 1964, to discuss the proposals with the sponsoring bodies and to inspect the proposed sites. They also had discussions with the Scottish Education Department and (as regards regional planning considerations) with the Scottish Development Department.

We then considered the matter in the light of the advice of the New Universities Sub-Committee. The choice was a difficult one. Impressive evidence had been submitted by each of the sponsoring bodies; each of the possible locations offered attractions and advantages. The problem was to assess which location gave, on balance, the best combination of advantages. The main factors which we took into account were as follows.

(a) Whether the proposed location, site and sponsorship were such as to give confidence that the creation and growth of an academic institution of university standard would proceed smoothly and effectively.

(b) Whether staff of the necessary quality would be attracted in appropriate numbers.

(c) Whether the location was such as to enable the Scottish tradition of day students to be continued, while at the same time providing substantial numbers of student lodgings, to supplement any residential accommodation provided by the university.

(d) Whether the proposed site was a suitable one on which to develop a university and whether it was available on suitable terms.

(e) Whether local financial and other support was likely to be available.

(f) Whether the area offered associated industrial and research activities.

(g) Whether the location would enable specifically Scottish needs to be met and attract a suitable proportion of students from elsewhere.

After very careful thought we concluded in favour of Stirling and so advised the Government . . .

Stirling opened its doors to students with an initial entry of 188 in October 1967. It receives its Royal Charter in December 1967.

England and Wales

The question whether additional universities would be needed in England and Wales and, if so, when they would be needed raised a number of difficult problems. In the first place, we were satisfied that there was no need for any new foundations in order to reach the target of 218,000 places by 1973–4. This figure, or indeed a substantially higher figure, could be reached without difficulty by the natural growth of the existing universities and former colleges of advanced technology. Secondly, the experience of the recently-established universities suggested that the Robbins Committee had taken an unduly conservative view of the time that it took for a new university, given the necessary resources, to build up its student numbers. Moreover, in so far as new universities were expected to contribute to academic innovation and experiment, it might be supposed that the recent wave of new universities had probably exhausted the stock of new ideas for the time being. And, to the extent that new universities drew staff away from existing universities, it might seem unwise to increase the strain on the latter at a time of rapid general expansion.

On the other hand, looking further ahead, while the Government had not committed itself to the Robbins Committee's long-term estimates of demand, it had accepted 'the need for further big expansion after 1973–4'. Whatever the eventual target for 1980 might be, it seemed probable that there would be a substantial gap between that target and what could be practically and economically achieved by the existing universities and former colleges of advanced technology, and that part at least of the gap would have to be filled by the foundation of new universities. The whole purpose of the Robbins Report was to lay a basis for long-term planning and to avoid a situation (such as had occurred in the past) where measures to meet the need for university places were not put in hand until the last moment and in an atmosphere of crisis. On the question of timing, it could well be argued that the recently-established universities had gone ahead under great pressure and that it would be an advantage if the development of further new universities could be planned more deliberately and calmly and if they could become well established before the strain of renewed expansion in the seventies made itself felt.

It was not an easy matter to strike a balance between these various arguments. But the over-riding consideration, we thought, must be the prospect of our having sufficient funds put at our disposal to allow us to plan on an adequate scale both for replacement and development at the older universities and for the growth of the recently-established universities. However strong the case might be for new universities, we were convinced that it would be idle, and indeed indefensible, to encourage the foundation of new institutions as long as we were unable to meet the legitimate requirements of the existing universities and were compelled in practice (however preferentially they might be treated) to throttle back the rate of development of the seven new universities recently established.

Special technological institutions

The Robbins Committee recommended that there should be developed as quickly as possible a small number of 'Special Institutions for Scientific and Technological Education and Research' (SISTERs), comparable in scope and scale with the Massachusetts Institute of Technology and the Technical High Schools at Zurich and Delft. These should be university institutions and the centre of gravity should be in science and technology, though other related subjects such as social studies, operational research and statistics should be developed, and languages would be needed at least as ancillary subjects. The institutions should have from 3,500 to 4,500 students; there might be 1,000 in science, at least 2,000 in technology, and perhaps 1,000 or so in other subjects. There should be a strong emphasis on post-graduate studies; postgraduate students should form about half the student body. The institutions should have good staffing ratios, a liberal proportion of senior to junior posts, and adequate provision of equipment and technical assistance.

The Report recommended as the immediate aim the development of five such institutions. Three could be based on Imperial College, London, the Manchester College of Science and Technology (now the University of Manchester Institute of Science and Technology) and the Royal College of Science and Technology, Glasgow (now the University of Strathclyde). For the other two the Report recommended that:

(a) one should be established as a completely new foundation (as one of the six new universities proposed in the Report);

(b) the other should be developed from a selected College of Advanced Technology.

The Government Statement on the Robbins Report said:

> The Government strongly endorse the Report's emphasis on the building up of technological universities and the development of management studies. They are asking the University Grants Committee for an early report on the further development of Imperial College, London, the Royal College of Science and Technology, Glasgow, and the Manchester College of Science and Technology; and also on the proposal for a completely new technological university.

We had no doubt whatever about the great national importance of expanding and improving technological education (both undergraduate and postgraduate) and research in the universities and colleges of advanced technology. We agreed also that development should be selective and that the total effort should be planned in such a way as to make the most effective and economical use of the resources available in the universities and colleges, taking account of industrial needs and of the distribution of industrial facilities and support. But we saw serious academic disadvantages about the concept of SISTERs as a separate and special category of institutions all broadly similar in size, weight of faculties, and proportions of undergraduate and postgraduate students. In the first place it would tend to establish a uniform pattern of development, instead of encouraging each institution concerned to undertake those developments which grew most naturally out of its existing activities and to build on its own characteristic strengths and interests. Secondly, it would tend to stifle growth elsewhere and to draw strength away from those university institutions which already had highly developed faculties of science and engineering, with large postgraduate schools, and were already making important contributions to the national effort in this field. Thirdly, there was evidence, from representations which the Committee had received from a number of universities and colleges, that the SISTER concept would introduce unhealthy considerations of status and title into what should be conceived and planned as a coherent and balanced development of growing points in the University field as a whole.

We gave our advice to the Government in May 1964. The Government also sought the advice of the (then) Advisory Council on Scientific Policy. In his general statement on the development of higher education on 24 February 1965 the Secretary of State for Education and Science (Mr Crosland) said that the Government wholly accepted the principle of selective development and expansion of technological education at a high level. They considered, however, that this would be best achieved not by creating a separate category within institutions of university status, but by continuing the build-up of the three specialized institutions named by the Robbins Committee (Imperial College, London, the Manchester College of Science and Technology, and Strathclyde University). These would be given priority in the provision of finance, both capital and recurrent; moreover the creation of a new technological university in the North-East was being urgently examined. But the Government did not accept the recommendation to select one of the Colleges of Advanced Technology for special treatment; and they had decided, on balance, against giving any institutions a special designation as SISTERs. Mr Crosland said:

> The House will see that the Government accept the substance of the Robbins Committee's proposals on this matter. But, as to method, they prefer to encourage and expand the many promising developments in the technological departments of other universities, including colleges of advanced technology; and they wish to prevent the false impression arising that a first-class technological education is only available in a small handful of institutions.

Teacher training colleges

The Robbins Committee made a series of far-reaching recommendations about the future development and organization of the teacher training colleges. The essential features of the pattern proposed for England and Wales were as follows:

1 On the academic side, the Colleges should be enabled to provide for suitable students a four-year course leading to a university degree. The existing University Institutes of Education should be replaced by University Schools of Education (embracing the various Colleges and the University Departments of Education, and having governing bodies of their own) which would be responsible to the University Senates for the degree work done in the Colleges.
2 On the administrative side, responsibility should be transferred from the Local Authorities to the universities. The Colleges should have independent governing bodies which would be related federally to the Schools of Education and through them to the universities.
3 On the financial side, the Colleges should be supported by ear-marked grants made by the University Grants Committee through universities to the Schools of Education.

A different pattern was proposed for Scotland, where the universities did not have the same responsibility, academic or administrative, for the training of teachers. The Robbins Committee recommended that arrangements should be made between individual Universities and Colleges to enable the Colleges to offer a four-year course leading to a university degree, and that the Colleges should be financed through the University Grants Committee. But they did not propose that the Colleges should be brought under the control of universities.

The Committee, having been asked by the Government for their views, proceeded first to consult both the Committee of Vice-Chancellors and Principals and the individual universities. While a few universities made reservations, most of them were willing to accept the proposals in principle and to co-operate in their implementation. In particular they accepted the recommendation that four-year courses leading to both a B.Ed. degree and a professional qualification should be provided in the Colleges for suitable students. Universities in England and Wales were prepared, with only a few exceptions, to consider establishing Schools of Education on the lines proposed by the Robbins Committee. Some universities felt that the proposals on the academic side could be accepted only if the administrative and financial arrangements recommended by the Robbins Committee were also accepted *in toto*. But many universities did not share this view or did not feel so strongly about it.

For our part, we were not convinced that the academic, administrative and financial problems were inseparable. We saw no reason why the process of forging academic links between the Universities and the Colleges, which had already been carried a fair way as a result of the 1944 Report of the McNair Committee on Teachers and Youth Leaders, should not be extended and accelerated as a separate operation. In most areas, at least, it should be possible for universities to participate in the academic arrangements necessary to ensure the proper institution of degree courses for a proportion of students in the Colleges, without having to alter fundamentally the constitutional relationship between the bodies or the channels by which the Colleges were financed.

The administrative and financial proposals were far more controversial and raised far greater problems. It seemed to us that, at a time when the Colleges were urgently engaged in planning for expansion, it would be unwise to introduce comprehensive changes which were bound to result in prolonged local argument and upheaval, and which would alter, with effects that could not easily be foreseen, the existing distribution of responsibility for the supply of teachers. It might be that closer academic relationships would eventually produce a situation in which more radical constitutional and financial changes became necessary. But these changes could be introduced then as the natural outcome of the academic developments and by agreement between all the various bodies concerned.

On 11 December 1964 the Secretary of State for Education and Science (Mr Stewart) made the following statement in the House of Commons:

There has been widespread agreement with the Robbins proposals for closer academic links between the training colleges and the universities, including the grant of degrees. For their part the Government share the view that wider opportunities should be provided for suitable training college students to obtain a degree together with a professional teaching qualification by means of a four year course. They would think it appropriate that the relationship between the universities and training colleges already existing should be further extended in the academic sphere through the development of the present institutes of education. They are glad to know that most universities have expressed their readiness to consider making degrees available to suitable students, subject to appropriate arrangements for the safeguard of standards, and they hope that the universities will now proceed to work out with the colleges the form which such courses should take and the nature of the degrees to be awarded.

There has been far less agreement over the Robbins Committee's proposals for the administration and finance of the training colleges. The Government, after considering the advice given them by the University Grants Committee, have concluded that the academic and the administrative and financial aspects are separable, and that fundamental changes should not be made in the administrative and financial structure of the teacher training system, particularly at a time when the colleges are engaged in a very large and rapid expansion, and when the problems of teacher supply are especially difficult. They have, therefore, decided that for the present the colleges should continue to be administered by the existing maintaining bodies under the present system of overall supervision. They intend, however, to secure that the present arrangements for the internal government of colleges are reviewed by all those concerned in the light of the Robbins Committee's recommendations on this subject. The Government also agreed with the Committee that the training colleges could appropriately be renamed 'Colleges of Education'.

In the light of the Government's decision, we asked universities whether they were prepared, in principle, to go ahead with degree-granting arrangements to cover some of the students in the Colleges; and invited them to give their views on the type of arrangement which they had in mind and in particular on the question whether arrangements for granting degrees, which, in some sense and to some extent at least, would be 'external' degrees, could be applied in the case of Colleges of Education without any consequent or necessary extension to higher education institutions of other kinds. The point here was the possible effect on the work of the Council for National Academic Awards—the body set up (with strong university representation) to perform, on a national basis, the function of awarding degrees for students in non-university institutions. Indeed some universities expressed anxiety, particularly after Mr Crosland's speech on 27 April 1965, at the Woolwich Polytechnic about the dual system of higher education, lest the Government might now intend the degrees for students in Colleges of Education to be those of the CNAA. Mr Crosland, in a statement on 13 May, confirmed the Government's desire to see closer academic links between Colleges of Education and the universities, including the grant of University degrees in suitable cases, and said that he hoped that some universities would soon be in a position finally to approve such arrangements.

The replies from the universities showed that most of them regarded arrangements for the grant of B.Ed. degrees to a proportion of students in the Colleges as both practicable and desirable, subject to certain conditions, and that they saw no difficulty about drawing a distinction in this field between Colleges of Education and other non-university institutions. In the light of these replies, and of the Government's confirmation of their own attitude, the Committee, in June 1965 expressed the hope that the discussions and deliberations which the Universities had initiated would now be carried forward and that firm arrangements would be made as soon as possible for extending University degrees in suitable cases to students in the Colleges of Education . . .

Some twenty-six universities at present offer a B.Ed. degree, and a number of others are considering proposals for introducing the degree. The degree is normally based on a four-year full-time course, though special provision is made in some cases for qualified students to complete the course in three years. Practice varies as to whether the students are college-based or university-based in their fourth year; the more common practice is that they should be college-based. Some universities require students to register at the end of the first college year, with selection at the end of the third year; others select students at the end of the first year, with the final selection dependent on performance in the Certificate examination: some select in the second college year.

There is considerable variation in the content of the courses, but in general the pattern of the B.Ed. degree is that of a three-subject degree in which Education is studied in conjunction with two main academic subjects. Problems have arisen for some universities about the recognition of such subjects as crafts and physical education as academic subjects for this purpose, and varying policies have been adopted.

There is also considerable variation between universities in the status of the B.Ed. degree. In about one-third of the universities offering the degree, it will be awarded as a classified Honours degree. A rather larger number of universities will not use the term

Honours but will publish the results in a form which records categories of merit. A few universities offer the degree as a 'general' or 'ordinary' degree at a standard which is recognized as being lower than Honours, but they may allow the best students to proceed to Honours after further study . . .

Royal College of Art and College of Aeronautics

The Robbins Committee made the following recommendations:

1 The Royal College of Art had a clear claim to be treated administratively in the same way as the colleges of advanced technology, and should, like them, be financed through the future machinery for grants to universities.
2 The College of Aeronautics should also be brought within the University grants system. Higher degrees should be available for its students. But the Robbins Committee were not happy that a relatively small college of this kind should have power to award its own degrees and recommended that, if it remained at about its present size, it should form an appropriate association with a University.

The Government statement on the Robbins Report accepted the recommendation that these two Colleges should be brought within the ambit of a university grants system. It seemed to the Committee that it would be helpful to them and to the Government in considering the problems of the future development and status of these Colleges if the procedure of appointing the Academic Advisory Committee were used also in these cases. This procedure was acceptable to the Colleges.

The Academic Advisory Committee of the Royal College of Art reported in June 1965. They recommended that the College should be established by Charter as an independent university institution, with power to grant its own first and higher degrees. The Council of the College submitted the report, with their own observations on it, to the Secretary of State for Education and Science, who asked for the views of the Committee.

There was no doubt in our mind about the excellence of the work done by the College or about its very high national and international standing in the field of art education. There was no suggestion that the quality of the College's work and the standards which it operated were in any way inferior to those of an academic institution. But, as we saw it, they were different and indeed rightly different. Artistic capacity was not the same as—nor was it just one particular branch of—academic capacity. It was true that courses in Fine Arts, leading to degrees, existed in a number of universities. But these courses had been organized with academic standards in mind and they were not primarily or mainly directed to the objective of developing artistic performance and design to the highest pitch of excellence. It was this objective, however, which was the distinguishing characteristic of

the College and was essentially different from the characteristic nature of University degree work. Indeed if the College were to strive to develop curricula as rigorous and systematic in the *academic* sense as the curricula of University degree courses, there would be a very real danger of its ceasing to fulfil its true purpose.

There was a further practical consideration which weighed with us. We felt that we would not be competent to assess the financial needs, in comparison with those of the existing universities, of an institution so different from a University.

For these reasons, it seemed to us that it would not be appropriate for the College to be treated, administratively and financially, in the same way as existing university institutions. The Department of Education and Science accordingly discussed with the College the possibility of working out a special solution, other than the conferment of normal university status; and of establishing a structure of awards which would be distinctively different from the normal university degree designations. The solution which emerged from these discussions was that the College should continue to be financed by the Department as a direct-grant institution and should be empowered to grant its own degrees which would be designated B.Art (RCA) or B.Des. (RCA), with corresponding designations for higher degrees. The College received a new Royal Charter in August 1967.

In the case of the College of Aeronautics, the report of the Academic Advisory Committee, also made in June 1965, recommended that the College should become a University, concerned primarily with technological education at postgraduate level and research, independent of other institutions but having strong links with industry, and having power to grant its own degrees.

The Governing Body of the College submitted the report, with their own observations on it, to the Secretary of State for Education and Science who asked for the views of the Committee. In considering this matter the Committee had the benefit of views expressed by the Department of Education and Science, the Ministry of Technology and other Government Departments, including views on the regional development aspects.

The main difficulty was that to which the Robbins Committee had drawn attention, namely the small size of the College and the consequent restriction of the scale of its activities and academic offerings. Any substantial expansion would be very expensive and would be virtually equivalent to creating a new University in an isolated situation and on an almost totally residential basis. At the same time there was no doubt about the value of the equipment and other facilities which were available at the College and the importance of many of its activities, a high proportion of which were directed towards 'post experience' work, of value to industry, rather than 'postgraduate' work in the normal sense.

In this situation we concluded that, as in the case

of the Royal College of Art, it would not be appropriate for the College of Aeronautics to be added as a university institution to our grant list. In discussion between the Department, the Committee and the College, various suggestions were explored for enabling higher degrees to be made available through the Council for National Academic Awards, by an arrangement for sponsorship by some existing University or Universities, or by the affiliation of the College with an existing University. We consulted the Committee of Vice-Chancellors and Principals and also one or two individual universities. But, while the College was willing to be financed as a direct-grant institution by the Department of Education and Science, none of the various suggestions about the availability of higher degrees was regarded by it as satisfactory or acceptable. In February 1967 the College announced that it had decided to apply to the Privy Council for a Charter establishing an Institute of Technology, with power to grant its own degrees.

Notes

1 *Report of the Committee on Higher Education*, HMSO, Cmnd 2154, October 1963.
2 Government Statement on the *Report of the Committee on Higher Education*, HMSO, Cmnd 2165.
3 These were described in detail in the Committee's last quinquennial report, *University Development 1957–1962*, HMSO, Cmnd 2267, February 1964.
4 *Report of the Committee on Grants to Students*, HMSO, Cmnd 1051, 1960.
5 The College received its Charter in December 1967.

Introduction to readings 40–41

Reading 40, ' "Home Rule" and the Scottish universities', is taken from *Government and Nationalism in Scotland: An Enquiry by Members of the University of Edinburgh* (Edinburgh University Press, 1969). The author, R. E. Bell, was at the time of writing a lecturer in education at the University of Edinburgh, and is now a lecturer in educational studies at the Open University and one of the editors of this volume. The paper deals with the anomalous position of the Scottish universities, and suggests means by which Scottish secondary and post-secondary education might come under unified control. It is followed by a short critique by Professor W. H. Walsh, Professor of Moral Philosophy in the University of Edinburgh, who argues that it is advantageous to the Scottish universities to remain within the same system of financing as the English and Welsh.

A brief explanation of the subject-matter of these two contributions is necessary for the reader who is unfamiliar with the Scottish system. While the rest of the Scottish education system is governmentally the responsibility of the Scottish Education Department (here called SED), of which the Secretary of State for Scotland is the political head, the Scottish universities are financed through the University Grants Committee (UGC), whose funds in turn come since 1964 out of the provision made in central government for the Department of Education and Science (DES), otherwise responsible for education in England and Wales only. Student admissions are similarly made through the scheme run by the Universities' Central Council for Admissions (UCCA), and grants for scientific, environmental, medical, and agricultural research are made by the four Research Councils, again funded through DES.

Other allusions require explanation. The references to Scottish 'Highers', and the (on average) shorter period of secondary and longer period of university education which obtains in Scotland by contrast with England, are explained in MacLean's article in the first section of this book, as is that to the structure of the Scottish first degree. The 'FSSU' is the Federated Superannuation Scheme for Universities, through which pension arrangements are made for academic (and some other) university staff. The *First Book of Discipline*, published in 1560, was the major statement of policy by the Scottish Church reformers, and contained the blueprint of what eventually became the Scottish education system.

Explanations of the references to the Council for National Academic Awards (CNAA), the 'binary' policy, the 'Woolwich speech' of the Rt Hon. C. A. R. Crosland MP (then Secretary of State for Education and Science), and the Bachelor of Education (B.Ed.) degree for teachers, all developments of the mid and late sixties, will be found in other parts of this section, especially in the second extract from *University Development 1962–67* and in the group of passages on the binary system and the polytechnics.

The universities were advised by the government in 1967 to increase the fees they charged students from overseas to a higher and more 'economic' level. As the paper makes clear, this recommendation, which provoked widespread dissent in the universities, was ignored by the Northern Ireland government, and initially by the University of Oxford.

Readers are reminded that while Northern Ireland remains part of the United Kingdom, it has been responsible, through its own government and parliament, for education within the province, including Queen's University, Belfast. Trinity College Dublin, remains however a British copyright library, which means that it is entitled to receive free copies of material printed and published in the United Kingdom.

What follows is a chapter, 'The headquarters of Higher Education', from Jasper Rose and John Ziman's book, *Camford Observed* (Gollancz, 1964; pp. 217–33). In it the authors give a very personal view of education and scholarship at Oxford and Cambridge, and of the influence of these two universities upon the wider British educational world. Both Mr Rose and Dr Ziman were at the time of writing dons at Cambridge.

Readers are reminded that not only would many have dissented from some of the authors' views in 1964, but that much has changed in Oxford and Cambridge, organizationally and academically, since then. For example, new disciplines have enjoyed a new vogue, the Association of University Teachers has a much larger membership in the ancient English universities, and student admissions are made through the Universities' Central Council for Admissions (UCCA). In Oxford, the implementation of many of the recommendations of an internal Commission, under the chairmanship of Lord Franks, has radically changed the structure of university government. Nevertheless, this chapter still provides an impressionistic picture of Oxbridge in the 1960s.

Those unfamiliar with the Oxbridge system should note that both universities are collegiate. The colleges appoint their own Fellows, who are responsible for the tuition of the college's undergraduates, and who are normally also university lecturers. The colleges also admit their own undergraduates, electing some to college scholarships, awarded on the basis of an examination which the colleges normally run in groups. The faculties, on the other hand, are a university disciplinary structure. At Oxford a course culminating in an examination, on the results of which an Honours degree may be awarded, is known as an Honour School; the Cambridge equivalent is the Tripos. At Oxford 'Greats' is the name given to the Final Honour School of Literae Humaniores—students reading philosophy, ancient history, and classical languages and literature.

Fellowships tenable until the death of the incumbent ('Life Fellowships') have not been given for many years past. Such changes in Oxbridge practice since the mid-nineteenth century have flowed primarily from the work of the three royal commissions appointed to investigate the affairs of the ancient English universities in seventy years, the last in 1922. It was the first of these which removed the requirement that Fellows must be in holy orders of the established Church. 'Beak', as used in this reading, is public school slang for 'headmaster'.

40   'Home Rule' and the Scottish universities

R. E. Bell

I must emphasize at the outset that this paper is not intended to provide a detailed discussion of the financing of the Scottish universities. I avoid such a topic not only because it would be presumptuous for a non-economist to attempt such a thing but also because there is so little solid information on which to base the discussion. Indeed, to try and separate the Scottish university economy from the economy of the British universities as a whole would probably be as difficult as task as that, attempted elsewhere in this volume, of separating the general economies of Scotland and the United Kingdom, for the continuous interchange of university personnel (previously mainly of staff and research students—but, since the

arrival of UCCA, increasingly of undergraduates) and the sharing of joint services such as computers etc. make it difficult to estimate either the economic or the educational results of university investment in an 'isolated' Scotland.

In any case, the statistics of education, even when they are financial statistics, require very special handling. For example, Professor Carter of Lancaster has, in recent years, been rightly drawing attention to the inadequacy of most current methods of measuring university productivity and has counselled caution in using, for example, such crude measures (still, alas, in vogue) as the number of articles, or even pages, that a lecturer has published or the number of students or hours he has taught without taking into account the content, quality or influence of such work.[1] Indeed, it is only during the past decade, with the founding of

Source: Government and Nationalism in Scotland: an enquiry by members of the University of Edinburgh, Edinburgh University Press (1969).

such bodies as the Society for Research into Higher Education, that the study of university affairs has even begun to be put on a proper scientific footing and progress so far has been slow.

I intend then to concentrate not on the Scottish universities' financial problems but on the related matter of their formal relationships with government and the agencies of government such as the University Grants Committee and the Research Councils although in doing so I am, of course, only too aware that, in this field, formal relations with, or even representation on committees and other bodies can often mean very little. Many (perhaps most) of the major decisions in a university are made before committees even meet while, all too often, the telephone and the staff club bar may be more potent instruments of policy making than a seat for an official assessor at the quarterly meeting of a board. This is, of course, a system which, on the occasions when it favours one's own department or faculty, seems 'humane', 'flexible', 'practical', 'organic', but on less fortunate occasions, strikes one as 'undemocratic', 'inefficient', 'dictatorial' or even downright 'corrupt'! But occasionally as Lord Robbins has trained us to believe,[2] the UGC and similar bodies can act as genuine buffers between government and university and, being largely composed of university people, can often prove, as one might say, 'neutral in the universities' favour'; and while recent, apparently undue interference by ministers and other agents of government in university affairs makes one begin to doubt the complete validity of this, Robbins probably still has much right on his side.

In the circumstances, therefore, the way in which Scottish interests are represented on such bodies remains important, and, so far as the Research Councils are concerned, probably gives us little to fear. On the other hand, the position with regard to the UGC itself is more complex.

The committee is now 'overseen' (for want of a better term) by the Department of Education and Science; for the government, in rejecting Robbins's plea for a Ministry of Higher Education, insisted that such matters should be dealt with by the same department as oversees the rest of the educational system rather than by the Treasury as hitherto. Needless to say, the difficulties for Scotland in such an arrangement became quickly apparent, for the DES has no responsibility for the non-university sectors of Scottish education and there was a grave danger that in assessing any problems connected with the relationship of university and school or university and further education the Department would be unduly influenced by the English conditions more familiar to them. These difficulties were obviously considered by the Government to be of considerable importance for when Mr Willie Hamilton and Lady Megan Lloyd George raised the matter in the House of Commons in August 1965[3] the Prime Minister answered at some length, outlining a system of joint consultation between the Secretaries of State both on mutual problems connected with the relationship between the universities and the rest of the educational system and on appointments to the UGC. On the other hand, the only formal representation on the latter was by means of an assessor—and while the Secretary of State for Scotland would continue to make Regius appointments and handle parliamentary business connected with the Scottish universities, it seems clear that his role is otherwise seen to be that of a consultant rather than a major policy-maker so far as other Scottish university matters are concerned. Moreover, similar representation was provided for Welsh interests, even though Wales has not the same degree of independence in educational matters as Scotland and it looks therefore as if a main intention at that time was to safeguard Scottish interests in general rather than those of educational institutions in particular. Nevertheless the Scottish UGC assessor has always been the Secretary of the Scottish Education Department and it is of some interest in view of what I hope to say later, that he, as an administrative official should attend the UGC whereas a professional official, an inspector, attends meetings of the Council for National Academic Awards, thus suggesting, perhaps, that the Department has a more distinctly educational interest in the latter. The matter was also discussed further by the members of Parliament concerned with the framing and passage of the Scottish Universities Bill but they were apparently convinced by 'the Scottish universities' (whatever this commonly used phrase means—the Principals? the Courts? the Senates?) that the universities preferred to be 'overseen' by Whitehall rather than St Andrew's House and in subsequent discussions of the matter, such an arrangement is always said to be 'in accordance with the wishes of the universities themselves'.

On the other hand, the fate of the universities is not merely their own concern. They have a relationship to the rest of the educational system and to the national life in general and the comparatively meagre nature of such official Scottish representation provides ammunition for those, who in at least two of the parliamentary parties, demand the formation of a separate Scottish UGC more attuned to Scottish needs and conditions, and those making this demand almost always link it with a demand that greater constitutional protection should be given to what is loosely called the 'Scottish educational tradition' which, they say, is being further eroded as a result of there being a closer connection between the university planners and the DES than between the same planners and the SED.

There is, of course, alongside this, another body of opinion which says that all this is so much cant, and that, behind the scenes, things are going well for the Scottish universities, that the whole subject is too delicate and dangerous to be raised in public at all; but it seems reasonable at least to discuss such matters publicly at a time when three out of the four Scottish parliamentary parties are already committed to programmes of political devolution that would go far beyond the appointment of a Scottish UGC; for in all of these programmes a common factor is that, whatever fields are eventually put under the complete control of Edinburgh, education (whether at school or university level) is already assumed to be one of them, especially as the devolution of effective control over the non-university sectors passed from London to Edinburgh even before the building of St Andrew's House. Again, the normal justification offered for this assumption, is what is taken to be the undoubted existence of a separate and distinctive tradition of Scottish education, at the heart of which lie the old universities. Even the Dainton report, ostensibly concerned with that hard-headed United Kingdom economic issue—the need for scientists—seems to have suspended its critical faculties under the spell of this 'tradition' and it is clearly a political notion to be taken seriously.

On the other hand the opponents of such a view claim, with some justification, that, whatever the earlier Scottish university tradition *was* and, whatever the Scottish school tradition may still be, the English and Scottish universities have, for a century or more, been gradually drawing into a recognizably British (as opposed to a Scottish or English) pattern which in itself has for long been merging into a North Atlantic or even a world-wide English speaking one and while there may still be great contrasts between British universities on the one hand and those of France or Germany on the other, a distinctively Scottish pattern is disappearing (as Heriot-Watt, Strathclyde and Stirling seem finally to have proved). It is true, they admit, that (for the present, at any rate) the five old-style universities preserve 'ordinary' courses of a type unknown in most of England and that Scottish freshmen tend to be (though now only marginally) younger; equally, they agree, that a distinctively Scottish degree structure is to be found in the four ancient universities and in Dundee although, they point out, the English and, even more, the Americans, have always had differences among themselves about such matters, and a 'Scottish' degree is only one of many types in the English speaking world; they agree that the older universities have a form of university government based on different principles from that of Oxford and Cambridge but then many of the English and North American universities such as Manchester, Queen's in Ontario[4] and others originally adopted Scottish models for their constitutions, and have thus modified the national distinctiveness even in this field. Nevertheless, the Scottish tradition continues to be defended and for its defenders, the central issue tends to remain the continuance of the 'generalist' elements in the Scottish schools and first degree course, seen as a manifestation of the universal tradition of a Europe in which only 'specialist' England is out of step and they rely greatly and rightly on George Davie's eloquent exposition of this generalist tradition in *The Democratic Intellect*,[5] forgetting that the whole purpose of that book is to describe how the traditionalists eventually fought a losing battle until, in the Act of 1889, the generalist degree was only just caught by the tail before it disappeared, like the general undergraduate course in England, into the sixth forms of the remodelled Public Schools and the newly established, middle-class secondary schools such as George Watson's and George Heriot's who modelled their courses upon them.

Would the present mere relic of the old generalist university course be worth preserving? Or even the Highers? Both the Dainton and Swann reports accept the latter at their face value as a credible agency for providing a worthwhile general education yet, in an article in a recent issue of the *Universities Quarterly*,[6] A. F. McPherson makes a striking indictment of Dainton's inferences from his Scottish information and even questions the common assumption that the work of the fifth and sixth year Scottish secondary courses induces a truly generalistic outlook in the student.

Nevertheless, whether they add up to something worth the name of a living 'tradition', the many differences between English and Scottish education remain and whether they are seen as the seeds of a potential revival as many nationalists hope or merely as irritating difficulties that must be endured for the time being, they need to be taken more seriously in practical terms than they have usually been taken in the past. There has, for example, been little or no discussion at governmental level of the fact that the Scottish university Honours course is normally longer and the secondary school course normally shorter than in England and that some Goschen-type formula might take account of this by effectively moving certain resources from one sector to the other; certainly it seems reasonable that some *body* ought already to exist that could at least investigate and advise on such questions.

Indeed, the need for such a committee on the joint problems of secondary and tertiary education in Scotland grows, in any case, for other reasons—not the least of which is the lack of any properly organized central collection of higher education and other relevant data. There are great dangers in continuing to allow committees such as Dainton and Robbins to rely too heavily on the opinions of individuals or ad hoc sub-committees, however able, rather than on a regular, properly staffed committee with adequate research facilities and with the continuity of existence necessary for building up an informed body of experience. What information is collected (and upon which the UGC presumably relies heavily), is all too often collected with an English model in mind and thus Scottish factors are sometimes pushed badly out of shape in the process of collection.

However, the present proposals for more general political devolution go, of course, far beyond the creation of such an advisory committee and I want now to examine the possible consequences of some of these.

Complete political independence is naturally seen by many in the universities as spelling complete financial disaster, and they point, as an object-lesson, to the comparatively slow development of tertiary education in the other small West European countries which have gained independence in this century (the Republic of Ireland, Norway, and Iceland). In fact, none of these is as highly developed or even as densely populated as Scotland, but in any case, one must remember that in the field of educational development, it is possible to misunderstand the significance of general national prosperity. In eighteenth-century Scotland, for example, though the national prosperity and population increased and though certain educational sectors flourished as never before, other sectors declined alarmingly just as in the twentieth-century United States, although one can see educational provision at its most sophisticated, one can also see it at its crudest and least effective. There is no automatic correspondence between general wealth and educational investment. Thus in the comparatively prosperous state of Ohio, where in 1957 the average annual income was $2,255, the educational investment per pupil was $330; yet the same sum of $330 was being invested in the poorer state of Louisiana where the average income was some 30 per cent less.[7] Indeed, given certain other favourable factors, a national poverty that is not too extreme may do much to stimulate an increase in educational development, in so far as this is seen as promoting economic or administrative expansion.

There is, however, as yet no evidence that in the event, England would welcome or necessarily insist on a complete break in her relations with the Scottish universities. Since the nineteenth century these have been much more important to her than her relations with the Irish universities ever were; yet with hardly any fuss, and despite the complete political severance, the House of Commons accepted the confirmation of Trinity College, Dublin's right to remain a British copyright Library. It is important to remember how it remained natural, even after the Republic left the Commonwealth, for some Ulster students to begin their studies at the University College in Derry and then to complete them in Dublin and how the Belfast government has consistently refused to finance the provision of a Veterinary school because one is already available in Dublin. All these may be signs (and the continued support of the University of East Africa provides at least a temporary further example) of how the complete political dismemberment of a previously unified area need not necessarily involve its cultural dismemberment. To have transferred the copyright from Dublin to Belfast would eventually have saved the British and Northern Ireland exchequers the extremely large amounts now being spent on library provision for the Ulster universities while many local education authorities and industrial concerns in the United Kingdom continue to place no restriction on the holding of scholarships at universities in Dublin and elsewhere. Indeed, British industry continues to invest in research there. Thus the political severance need not end the flow even of direct financial assistance. Indeed, had the Republic not left the United Kingdom in such unpropitious circumstances, more far-reaching arrangements might have been arrived at for the further and deeper integration of University life and finances throughout these islands, for even the present, comparatively restricted interchange of staff, research students and examiners across the political frontier makes clear the potential fruitfulness of such an integration.

A more legitimate fear is that a completely independent Scotland would be excluded from the large scale research projects, particularly those requiring expensive equipment and those concerned with defence, which are obviously more easily and regularly mounted by a major government; a minor, Scottish government might well leave such projects to the vagaries of private industry in order to concentrate on an expansion of technical training at a lower level and on other ways of satisfying more immediate social need. It might indeed revert to the view of the First Book of Discipline and begin to regard the whole educational system as one unit for purposes of allocating funds so that on occasion the universities might find themselves having to give way to the primary sector, greater attention to the needs of which might, indeed, ultimately be more to the advantage of the university sector than so much of the present expenditure on prestige projects of short-term value.

However, it is too easily forgotten that even the most short-sighted and philistine of governments tends to hold the universities in an awe which seems quite remarkable to those who know them intimately, as the autonomy which they are accorded even in some of the politically darker parts of Latin America demonstrates and it is very improbable that any Scottish government would risk the decline in social standards (in such fields as medicine and law, for example) involved in any undue squeeze on universities even if the failure to squeeze meant severe economies in other areas of the national life. The attitude to be expected is perhaps nearer to that found in the relationship of the Belfast government to its universities since the establishment of home rule and their experience will perhaps also serve as a model for what might happen in the event of some lesser form of devolution taking place, whereby a central British (or other Federal) government remains in over-all control of the finance available but allows the provincial government considerable powers of discretion in general expenditure, while bodies such as the Research Councils continue to be free to operate in their own spheres, throughout the Union.

Even before the partition of Ireland and the setting

up of the two governments, the handling of Irish university finances differed from that in the remainder of the United Kingdom. Under the Irish Universities Act of 1908, their books were to be available for complete audit by the Comptroller and Auditor General (in the way now condemned in Britain as a threat to academic freedom[6]) and although it had seemed likely for a time that the UGC would perform a buffer function for Ireland as well as Britain, the establishment of a separate (though dependent) treasury in Belfast brought a return to the previous direct relationship between the state and the university, which had resulted from the fact that the Irish universities (that is, excluding Trinity) were clearly state foundations and were more heavily dependent on state grants than other British universities at that time. In 1920, before home-rule, Queen's University made a direct appeal to Westminster for help and the UGC passed judgment on this claim on behalf of the London government.[8] And this same consultative role has been essentially its role in later years. In 1930, for example, Queen's privately asked for the UGC's comments on certain aspects of its affairs,[9] though it was not until 1944 that the Stormont government asked the Committee to act as its own agent in assessing university needs.[10]

In 1945, they completed a general survey of university provision and expenditure, carried out at government request, and gave their advice on how, after the war, Northern Ireland's university and university college could be brought up to British standards and could thus remain clearly within the British academic community and career structure. (Membership of the FSSU and salary scales were typical major issues at the time.) The Government accepted virtually the entire recommendations, and, since then, the Unionist government's general policy of keeping 'step by step with Britain' on the social services (assisted by massive help from London) has normally meant that they have kept pace with developments in Britain without at any point being *bound* slavishly to follow the way outlined by the UGC or, more sinisterly, by the DES. The major example of Northern Irish dissent and thus the major demonstration of true independence of action, came in 1967 over the matter of the increase in overseas students' fees when Captain Long, then Minister of Education, obviously took pleasure in being able to back up the university authorities who, for once, viewed London's suggestions with disfavour.[11] The reasons for his stand on this issue are obscure and he readily admitted that it was made at some cost to the provincial Exchequer. It has been suggested that either a strong missionary lobby (both Protestant and Catholic) was at work or that he feared reprisals from the Republic (whom Britain had included in the increase) as Northern Ireland's students there numbered some 7–800 (in contrast with the 35–40 Republican students in Belfast)[12] and any increase in fees would have born directly and heavily on the Northern Ireland county authorities had

Dublin retaliated, though this would perhaps have involved a sinking of the Republic's constitutional principle that Northern Ireland is part of the national territory and in no sense 'foreign'. In fact, however, it seems to have been strong academic opinion (then being expressed in Britain by token strikes of both staff and students) that carried the day and the decision made clear once and for all that the UGC or the DES's advice *was* only 'advice' and not a command enforceable through Exchequer sanctions, so long as, like the university treasury at Oxford, Stormont was willing to bear the direct financial consequences of ignoring this possibility of extra revenue. However, in this connection, it should be emphasized that there appears to have been no hint that any general grant to the Belfast government was ever cut in terms of the number of individual overseas students as presumably happened in the case of grants to Oxford.

Apart from this notable exception, the system at present works much as in Britain. A full-scale quinquennium system has been established (one year out of step with Britain) and when the Ministry of Finance's support for a project seems to be in doubt, the Ministry of Education or the University finds that to have the prestige of UGC advice behind it normally carries great weight in the argument.

There is some evidence that in tendering its advice to Belfast, the UGC bears local conditions in mind. Thus it seems to have suggested a more extensive building programme than it would have authorized in so limited a time in Britain, possibly to help relieve the high local unemployment. On the other hand, its academic suggestions tend to be based on general United Kingdom, rather than local social need. Thus it has advocated an expansion in medical and engineering education at a time when both these professions are comparatively over-stocked in Northern Ireland and it could therefore, as in Scotland, be legitimately accused of encouraging the emigration of graduates from Northern Ireland in the interests of the United Kingdom as a whole.

There is, then, in this Northern Ireland experience, no sign of a provincial government developing that parochial view of university education which many fear might arise if the SED took over from the DES its general responsibility for the Scottish universities. On the other hand, Belfast could not be described as having either as long-standing a reputation for university education or as distinctive an educational tradition as Scotland. It is perhaps natural, therefore, that as part of her general search for prestige, she should follow the English models closely, hoping that some of the metropolitan glamour would thereby rub off on her. Any Scottish body, whether government or UGC, would be likely to take a more divergent and self-confident path. Yet Northern Ireland's experience does at least suggest that such a diverging could at least be well-financed, particularly if a more sophisticated federal structure had been developed than that under which Northern Ireland remains part of the United Kingdom.

Briefly, and finally, however, I want to question the all too common assumption that if none of the plans for general Home Rule come to anything, university relations with government can continue much as before. The same series of decisions that placed the UGC under the DES also led to the Crosland speech at Woolwich expounding his notion of the Binary system. Since then, the growth of the English Poly-technics, the rapid development of the activities of the CNAA and the appearance in concrete terms of the Open University, allied to the extremely severe restrictions on university expansion, both in terms of buildings and personnel, have produced a situation whereby, possibly even as early as 1975, the number of people graduating in a given year outside the univer-sities could begin to exceed (perhaps even *far* exceed) those who graduate inside. In Scotland the process might take longer, but its eventual consequences for the ordinary degree, not to mention the Scottish 'tradition' seem clear.

The way in which the Honours degree developed during the later years of the nineteenth century provides a possible model. Oxford and Cambridge gradually began to allow the taking of school courses to give exemption from a growing number of under-graduate examinations, thus satisfying the public school headmasters who wished both to improve their schools' academic status and to keep their boys until a greater age. At the same time, the universities satisfied their own desire for the introduction of a more exacting course and the attraction of a more mature type of student. In Cambridge, the Classics Tripos, for example, until the 1850s essentially a postgraduate course, was eventually moved down to undergraduate level without loss of standard, while at the same time the old undergraduate Classics examina-tions were merged into the Previous Examination and the new School Certificate which gave exemption from it.[13] Against this background and bearing in mind the immense economic and administrative advantages of the idea, it is, I feel, not too fanciful to envisage a situation in which the government might now eventually abandon the current policy of *encour-aging* universities to concentrate on undergraduates, and encourage them to abandon the undergraduate courses altogether, in order to hand them over to the twentieth-century's counterpart of the public schools, Colleges of Education and the Polytechnics, hungry for the prestige hitherto so unjustifiably denied them.

The Scottish Ordinary degree might disappear first and there are already signs of a desire for such a disappearance on the part of purist professors who resent having to provide what they regard as inferior courses for inferior, or at least only marginally interested students; but even the honours degree might eventually follow, for with all undergraduate teaching on their side of the Binary fence, the govern-ment could not only provide cheaper forms of teaching but could lower the cost of residential accommodation by discouraging students from leaving home until the postgraduate level and could give themselves much greater control over standards of entry and the nature of the training provided. Indeed the official encourage-ment of the present B.Ed. arrangements may be the first half-conscious groping towards such a policy which, if it came to full awareness, would, as a bonus, solve many of the postgraduate accommodation and research problems of the universities overnight and release many unwilling university teachers from the chores involved in the teaching of large first and second year classes.

On the other hand it would strain even more severely the present constitutional arrangements for the running of higher education in Scotland. For even with the present degree of CNAA activity in Scotland and with the growth of the B.Ed., the SED's im-mediate concern with degree teaching is immensely enlarged and its concern in this field, with the eventual growth of that sense of rivalry *vis-à-vis* the univer-sities, which some have seen developing among the relevant civil servants in England, makes the SED less and less suitable as the provider of a Scottish spokesman at the UGC, to say the least.

If this situation is to develop in a civilized and constructive way, then the appointment of a committee to advise on the general problems of Scottish Higher Education is urgently needed for reasons quite apart from those of national self-esteem and in addition to those which I outlined earlier. This is one form of home rule which seems to me necessary if we are to avoid disaster, for even if my speculations prove over-fanciful and the universities preserve an undergraduate sector, so long as the other parts of the Binary system are also providing such a sector, we need some single committee and some single body of officials to co-ordinate their efforts and to relate their plans both to the other educational sectors and to the needs of Scottish society. The present ragbag of formal and informal relationships between London, Edinburgh, the universities and the colleges cannot possibly suffice.

Notes

1 For example, in his article, 'Measuring the productivity of universities', in *The Times*, 17 May 1966.

2 Lord Robbins, *The University in the Modern World* (London: Macmillan, 1966), 36 *et passim*.

3 United Kingdom Hansard (Commons), vol. 171, col. 437–8, 5 August 1965.

4 H. B. Charlton, *Portrait of a University* (Manchester University Press, 1951), 27 ff. and D. D. Calvin, *Queen's University at Kingston* (Kingston, Ontario, 1941), 29.

5 G. E. Davie, *The Democratic Intellect* (Edinburgh University Press, 1961).

6 A. F. McPherson, 'The Dainton Report—a Scottish Dissent', *Universities Quarterly*, 22 (3) (June 1968).

7 T. Hillway, *Education in American Society* (Boston: Houghton Mifflin, 1961), 162.

8 T. W. Moody and J. C. Beckett, *Queen's, Belfast 1845–1949* (London: Faber, 1959), 465.

9 Ibid., 502.

10 Ibid., 525 ff.

11 Northern Ireland Hansard (Commons), vol. 67, col. 742–4, 17 October, 1967.

12 These approximate figures for 1967–8 were supplied in response to a personal enquiry to the Ministry of Education.

13 D. A. Winstanley, *Later Victorian Cambridge* (Cambridge University Press, 1947) deals in greater detail with this whole matter.

Discussion

PROFESSOR W. H. WALSH

Mr R. E. Bell's paper on Home Rule and the Scottish universities raises some interesting questions, but fails to mention one crucial fact: that in comparison with the rest of the United Kingdom Scotland is over-provided with universities. With about 10 per cent of the total population she has something like 17 per cent of the available student places. This proportion may diminish as the new English universities increase in size, but it is not likely to reduce to anything like 10 per cent, for there are four new foundations in Scotland too, and St Andrews wants to build up its numbers from two to three thousand in the course of the next few years. It looks as if, for quite a time ahead, Scotland will have to draw on her neighbour's resources as well as her own if she is to run her universities properly. And this fact seems to me to have an important bearing on the question how Scottish universities are to be administered. I think it rules out the kind of solution which Mr Bell favours.

But first let us get the argument about the facts straight. In what way must the Scots depend on English help in running their universities? Do the Scottish universities need English students? It is of course the case that they have numbers of English students now, but many Scotsmen think that this is a fact to be deplored. Clear out the English, and there would be places for every Scots boy or girl who attains the minimum entrance qualifications. There would, but with the consequence that degree standards would need to be lowered in a noticeable and alarming way. As things are, students who arrive with (say) two B and two C passes in Highers often have the greatest difficulty in passing their first-year examinations; students with four C passes would be almost certain failures. Are Scotsmen ready to see the level of their university degrees lowered sufficiently to make this result avoidable?

It could be argued that no such expedient is necessary: the Scottish universities could keep their English students, or as many of them as they wished, without having to remain part of the general British system. Did not something of this sort obtain in the great days of the eighteenth century, when the Scottish universities were the best in Europe? It did, but conditions are very different now. In those days a university staff consisted of nothing but a number of individual professors: a great man like Dugald Stewart could instruct a large class of students through the medium of lectures, without so much as

a professional assistant. But subjects have diversified enormously since then and teaching has become altogether more costly: 'participation' requires a large staff with a multiplicity of talents, not just a few star performers. And it seems that the Scottish universities are, at present, just not capable of producing university teachers in sufficient numbers: well-qualified Scottish applicants for posts in Arts faculties at least are disappointingly few. A glance at the list of all professors at Edinburgh will show that 40 per cent or more come from outside Scotland. And experience on appointing committees leads me to believe that something similar is true of non-professorial staff, though I have no figures here.

I infer from this that the Scottish universities need outside help if they are to be adequately staffed. But there is more to be said than this. They also need more than their share of general educational resources —of money to build laboratories, stock libraries and finance research. Just because of their favourable position in the United Kingdom university set-up they can as things are draw on central funds to a greater extent than their strict due. Now there is nothing wrong with this so long as they remain within the overall British system: the whole point of having a single organization for universities is to see that every foundation gets fairly treated. But once it is claimed that one part of the system is in a special position and needs to be administered separately, difficulties and objections could very easily arise. One can imagine the English asking why, if the Scottish universities exist apart, they should not be financed from purely Scottish resources. And it is hard to think of a convincing answer to that question.

The Scots have always valued education, and they might be willing to pay more to keep their universities going. But even if they did, could they get the staff they need once responsibility for Scottish universities was transferred from Whitehall to St Andrew's House? I am sorry to say that reflection on general educational administration in Scotland suggests that they could not. Whatever one thinks of the Scottish school system (and my own view is that its merits are much exaggerated), one cannot describe its administration as either liberal or imaginative. Scottish schools are run with a maximum of red tape and organized on lines which even their warmest defender would have to regard as hierarchical. There is very little opportunity in these circumstances for the meeting of minds or the free exchange of ideas: children are encouraged to learn, not to think, teachers to instruct, not to question themselves. It seems to me that such an atmosphere is wholly alien to a university, and that to hand over university administration to those who are used to it would have fatal effects on the recruitment of staff. Teachers who knew no better would perhaps put up with it; others would simply not come. I would therefore argue that to detach the Scottish universities from the general United Kingdom system can only conduce to their decline. I realize of course that the government in London may well decide to make just this move, as an innocuous step in the process of general devolution. But if it does the final result will, in my opinion, be to Scotland's disadvantage. Her universities in these circumstances might eventually become comparable not to the great academies of Europe and America, but rather to the inward-looking institutions of the Republic of Ireland.

41 The headquarters of Higher Education

Jasper Rose and John Ziman

For seeing the Universities are the fountains of civil and moral doctrine, from whence the preachers, and the gentry, drawing such water as they find, use to sprinkle the same (both from the pulpit and in their conversation), upon the people, there ought certainly to be great care taken, to have it pure, both from the venom of heathen politicians, and from the incantation of deceiving spirits.

HOBBES

The science of Animal Behaviour has provided a cliché: Oxbridge is at the top of the *Pecking Order* of educational institutions. It is more than that. It is a separate category. In a gentler age we would have been quicker to appreciate the distance between a Prince of the Blood and a mere Duke.

It is abundantly clear that this exalted position is due mainly to their age and descent. For many centuries they were the only English Universities. Within the English speaking world they can only be challenged by the Scottish universities—and these are at least two centuries younger. Other great universities—Harvard and Yale, Trinity College Dublin, Sydney, Cape Town, Manchester, Berkeley, Bombay —all are but daughters and grand-daughters of the mighty twins. Oxford and Cambridge are themselves; unique, mysteriously conceived in the mists of the Middle Ages, owing allegiance to none but the Universal Church and the King at Westminster, they stand a whole rank above the rest.

Nevertheless, the daughters have grown up. In a world where Pecking Orders do not always coincide with lineage, one may, presumably, look at the claims of Oxbridge to its superior position within the educational system, without fear of being set in the stocks or having one's ears cut off for blasphemy, *lèse-majesté*, or sacrilege.

First, we note that they are large Universities. With

Source: Jasper Rose and John Ziman, *Camford Observed*, Gollancz (1964), 217–33.

8,000 students each, they do not bulk half so large in human flesh as some American State Universities. Nor do they assemble under a single administrative umbrella such numbers as may be found on the books of the University of London. But American State Universities spread down and down into the most subterranean realms of the intellect, and the University of London is really four or five separate Universities, and numerous Colleges and teaching Hospitals, united and divided by a common examination system.

There was a period, perhaps ten years ago, when the talk at Redbrick was all for cosy little University Colleges, where everyone knew everyone else. It was a nostalgic sentiment. It is now pretty well agreed that only a big University—say 5,000 students—can provide sufficient variety, intellectually and educationally, to be efficient and effective. There are dangers of anonymity, of mechanical administration, of bureaucratic teaching, in big institutions; but these should be guarded against specifically—for example, by the creation of colleges—and not made an excuse for restricting size and scope. Their size alone, relative to the University population of Britain, would give the ancient Universities a fair claim to dominance. They are big enough to be complete in themselves, with every possible Faculty, with all the apparatus of scholarship and research. They are the largest coherent universities in England; for that reason alone, they might well be the best.

The quality of their students also gives them a strong claim to superiority. The scholarships and entrance examinations may be imperfect instruments of selection. We may wonder whether the man who only got a *gamma* in the Practical Exam. in Botany, and had to go to Aberystwyth, might not, in the end, have turned out quite well. We may all know of the brilliant scholar who only got a Third, and of the famous Grammar School whose ugly ducklings all grow up to be geese—and so on. Yet the system does ensure that a boy or girl of high scholastic ability gets his chance for admission if he wants it, and if his school will back him. Given that so many of the cleverest school children put Oxbridge as their first choice, and work very hard to get there, it is inevitable that the ancient Universities will find themselves with a much higher proportion of outstandingly talented students than other universities. Even those who are not outstanding in talent have been exceptionally well trained at school.

It is much more questionable whether the bulk of Oxbridge graduates in the long run turn out to be much better than those at London, or Manchester, or other good English universities. The formal standard of a degree—the sorts of questions that are asked, the sorts of answers expected—is kept very nearly uniform throughout the country. The system of external examiners, whereby a Professor from another University always participates in the final degree examinations, ensures parity of quality, if not parity of esteem. Oxbridge may be able to award more Firsts and Upper Seconds—it also shows its due proportions of Thirds and worse.

Indeed, there is some evidence that the bottom of the Oxbridge Class-lists (reproduced so faithfully, in all their tinsel, in *The Times* newspapers) contains the names of creatures who would not have been allowed into another University at all. The college admissions system is flexible. The Masters and Tutors have a free hand. They will sometimes, in pursuit of some private doctrine of excellence, or in a mood of sentimental self-indulgence, persuade themselves that the College will actually benefit by the presence of some amiable nincompoop who happens to be good at cricket, or is the son of an Earl, or who sings divinely, or who has perfectly charming manners.

These aberrations are not so worrying, or so degrading to intellectual standards, as the prejudices or processes, or connections, or influences, or skills, or whatever it is, that ensure that a high proportion of Oxbridge students are products of the Public Schools. Of course, if that is what is meant by the 'best' students, then Oxbridge has them, all right. But in purely scholastic terms the effect of excluding steady Second Class Grammar School boys in favour of Third Class Public School boys can only be deleterious. The idea that a man with a Third from Oxbridge is rather better scholastically than a graduate of any other University, is nonsense. He may have more social poise, he may come from a better family, he may articulate his vocables with more precision, he may have acquired a thick coating of spit and polish—he may have all the qualities that appealed to a Tutor, as much as they will to a Personnel Officer or a War Office Selection Board: there is no reason to suppose that he is better informed on the subject matter of his degree, or that he is naturally more intelligent, or that he is a nicer person.

Nor should it be assumed that education at Oxbridge is so much better in an academic sense than at other Universities. Contrary to common belief, the staff-student ratio is little different. The quality of the teachers is, perhaps, on the average, higher—but many of their best efforts are frustrated by the vagaries of College and Faculty organization, or by the prejudice against new methods and new ideas. Again, all we can say is that there is a tremendous range. For a good student, in a good College, in one of the old-established disciplines, the teaching may be the best in the world. Oxford Greats, the Classical Tripos, History Schools, the Mathematical Tripos—these are superb academic disciplines, the product, like College gardens, of years of attention and devotion. But put a mediocre student into a poor College, in an out of the way subject, and he may be neglected, pushed from one supervisor to another, badly lectured to, and allowed to idle his days into nothingness. There are few English Universities offering such minimal courses of study, demanding so little of the student, as some of the traditional Oxbridge courses leading to the ordinary B.A. degree. There are few institutions more dull than some of the smaller Oxbridge Colleges. There are few University teachers quite so lax, incompetent, and deleterious to their pupils as a lazy Oxbridge don.

In one respect, Oxbridge cannot claim superiority over other Universities. Like the Duke of Plaza-Toro, it leads its regiment from behind. It has been slow to introduce new subjects, to recognize the value of new methods, to build new bridges between old islands on the academic map. Bold as Oxbridge scholars may be in their research, pressing forward tirelessly into the unknown, they are intensely conservative in their teaching. The old disciplines still dominate the Faculties. History, English, Classics, Law, Philosophy, Mathematics, Physics, Chemistry, Geology, Botany, Zoology, Anatomy and Physiology—one can easily make a list of respectable subjects. But try to study Psychology, Sociology, Anthropology, Statistics, Biophysics, Oriental Studies, Archaeology, Genetics, and you will have to surmount absurd obstacles from College authorities, in order to enrol in a small, self-conscious Faculty, struggling to establish itself against prejudice and obscurantism. In many such Faculties the research effort and the intellectual quality of the staff are far higher than the numbers of students whom they are permitted to teach. By discouraging its able students from entering these new fields, Oxbridge abdicates its claim to lead.

In its attitude to new teaching methods, to new types of degree, Oxbridge is also behind, below, the level set by other English Universities. There may be good reasons why any particular experiment seems too dangerous, too expensive, unnecessary, etc. The fact is that syllabuses for the Triposes and the Honour Schools change only slowly, and that there has been almost nothing in the last twenty years to match the new schemes of education being tried at some new Universities (by ex-Oxbridge dons, in many cases) or even the great reforms of Oxbridge itself in the late nineteenth century. The patterns were set before and between the Wars; it has been impossible to do more than chip at them since.

The surest claim for the paramountcy of Oxbridge springs from the standard of its scholarship and research ... Seen from a national point of view, Oxford and Cambridge have transformed themselves into great centres of active intellectual effort. In the early nineteenth century, original science and scholarship in England were to be found anywhere but in the ancient Universities. Nowadays, Oxbridge can boast of first-rate research schools in most subjects; in some disciplines—Economics, Mathematics and Physics at Cambridge, Philosophy and Political Science at Oxford—they have some of the most important centres in the world.

How has this come about? The revolution in opinion may be difficult to trace, but the mechanism of development is simple. By their tremendous prestige, Oxford and Cambridge have been able to tempt the finest scholars from other Universities to Professorial Chairs. By the creaming process, they can skim off the brightest British schoolboys. From all over the Commonwealth, young Rutherfords, young Braggs, young Salams are drawn to the twin fountainheads of wisdom. Given the will to create research schools, given the money to finance them—money that comes nowadays from the State—Oxbridge could scarcely fail to become a great centre of scholarship. The intellectual talent of the nation, of a Commonwealth of nations, can be refracted and concentrated there as by a burning-glass.

Again, there is a great spread in quality. The achievements of the Cavendish and Clarendon Laboratories, the revolution of thought caused by Keynes and his successors, the wide influence of Leavis, of Gilbert Murray, of Wittgenstein, cannot be matched in every field. There are dim little Faculties and Departments at Oxbridge, presided over by dim and lazy professors, producing nothing, doing nothing. There are large laboratories where the work is mediocre, where the staff potter along gently, and whence the bright young men depart with their doctorates to blossom elsewhere.

Nevertheless, there is an ideal of high scholarship which is preserved and fostered. Oxbridge research has a style of its own—a style that is recognizable as its special contribution to the world of the mind. It is an aristocratic style, self-confident, alert, elegant. To the best Oxbridge scholar, research is not a labour, nor a duty—it is a game. The final results may not matter so much as the manner in which they are achieved and expounded. The era of sealing wax and string is over—but the principle that it embodies, the making of beautiful discoveries with the slenderest means, is still part of the ethos of the Oxbridge scientist. There is an aesthetic appreciation of technique, an intensely critical attitude to clumsiness. It is nearer, perhaps, to the high French academic tradition than to the German or American, except that it is more empirical, less analytical in argument.

This attitude has its weaknesses. Scholars sometimes lavish tremendous powers of mind on trivial and frivolous topics. It becomes more important to demonstrate the authorship of an obscure manuscript by brilliant deduction and clever analysis than to collate many works and establish laboriously their common features. The sort of distinction that is sometimes made between a Fellowship Dissertation and a Ph.D. thesis—the suggestion that a neat argument, a subtle notion, an elegant proof may demonstrate more 'promise' than a solid mass of detailed evidence —is often made, unconsciously, by Oxbridge scholars when they dismiss some weighty work, some elaborate monograph, as boorish and 'Germanic'. Subjects such as Sociology, or Bibliography, or Geography, where masses of material may have to be processed for dull but certain gains, are dismissed by Oxbridge dons; they seem ugly, or pedestrian.

There is also a prejudice, an aristocratic prejudice, against technology, against applied science, against Agriculture, Engineering, Tropical Medicine—against anything that is studied more for the practical importance of the problems than for their intrinsic intellectual interest. There is an air of purity, of abstraction from the real world, of devotion to higher ideals than worldly needs. The basic sciences have flourished at Oxbridge, but not their applied counterparts. Oxford, in particular, has excluded them almost entirely, except for medicine. Cambridge, with less of a bias against Science, has its big Schools of Engineering, but never deals with direct technological problems except as examples of the hypothetical, theoretical principles with which its research is mostly concerned. In the Arts Faculties, again, one does not study *Business*, or *Commerce* or *Administration*; it is always 'Economics', or 'Politics'.

The concentration on pure knowledge is perhaps inevitable, given the general prejudice against business and industry in traditional English intellectual circles. But it reinforces that prejudice, both at Oxbridge and throughout the whole academic world. Oxbridge is the ideal model of other universities in England. Technology is despised by Oxbridge; then it does not win full recognition even at Leeds or Manchester. The snobbery that denied to the Colleges of Advanced Technology the title of Universities (even whilst it acknowledged the equivalence of Dip.Tech. to an Honours B.Sc.) comes eventually from this source. High-mindedness is sometimes a cloak for arrogance.

Despite his prejudices the Oxbridge scholar has one precious asset—independence of mind. He is the citizen of a Greek Republic; it is assumed that he can think for himself. He is not subject to strong pressure, in his undergraduate or research career, to conform to particular intellectual patterns. The reform movement of the nineteenth century was high minded, and moralistic; it was also intensely liberal in its theories of knowledge and of education; the truth had only to be seen for it to prevail. The best products of the system are permeated with this sentiment. They know that they have a right to their views, and they respect the rights of others. Conformism at Oxbridge is unconscious, a habit, a careless re-echoing of accepted opinions; it is not reinforced by social action. One can be a free-thinker, a Flat Earther, a Baconian, an advocate of Free Love, a Communist—any sort of intellectual non-conformist—and no one will object, provided that it does not spoil one's manners at High Table or make nonsense of one's scholarship. Even eccentricity of social and personal behaviour is countenanced provided it is not too boring or in bad taste. Wild and angry young men are not dangerous beasts; provided they are house trained, they make amusing pets.

One can trace this attitude back to the days of Life Fellowships, to the tolerance accorded to the clergy within the Church of England, to the enormous legal obstacles to dispossessing a Fellow of his Fellowship. It was his freehold, and like any stout yeoman he could stand upon it and thumb his nose at the world. In our society there are very few such freeholds left; Oxbridge dons and Redbrick Professors are well enough paid, and secure enough in their tenure, to enjoy the self-confident independence of a nobleman, a dean, a retired admiral, or a man with £100,000 in the Funds. They are responsible to no higher authority than themselves, yet they carry no great burdens of responsibility for others. Tiresome as they may be when they quarrel and argue interminably in the government of their own affairs, they are superb in their willingness to follow new ideas without reference to their fellows, and in their courage in speaking their minds against authority.

The influence of Oxbridge scholarship and of Oxbridge men and women is felt throughout the British academic world. Naturally, when the batch of Victorian Universities were created, Oxbridge graduates were amongst their first Professors. Until the turn of the century, Oxbridge was still producing more graduates than all the rest of England, so that it is not surprising that it supplied the staff of the new institutions as they arose and expanded in London and the North. This has continued. With its strong graduate schools in the Sciences and the Arts, Oxbridge is the major source of University staff for England and the Commonwealth. This is especially true at the Professorial level. When a Chair falls vacant at Redbrick, and there is no obvious successor ready to step on to the throne, it is to Oxbridge that the electors first turn. Lecturers from Oxbridge are natural candidates for Professorships in the new universities; more senior dons may find themselves with Vice-Chancellorships. The same advantages can be felt at lower levels. An Oxford or Cambridge Ph.D. frequently walks into a Lectureship at another University; the reputation of his background may carry more weight than the actual work he has done.

In many cases, the higher academic posts in British Universities are held by men who have not taken their first degrees at Oxbridge, but who have gone there as research students, and become assimilated. It is natural enough for a brilliant graduate of Bristol or the London School of Economics to be encouraged to apply to Oxford or Cambridge to do a research degree. Indeed, this is a form of super-creaming that works strongly in favour of Oxbridge; very few of the best students from the Honour Schools or the Tripos elect to do *their* research elsewhere.

We have already mentioned the thousands of scholars who flock to England every year, of whom the best seek entry to Oxford and Cambridge. In due course many of them return to their home countries, often to their own Universities. The proportion of Oxbridge graduates on the staff of Sydney or Melbourne, Toronto or McGill, Auckland or Otago, seems almost as high as at Leeds or Manchester. The need for study abroad from Australasia may enforce the academic mobility that is often not encouraged in the provinces of Redbrick England. A Lecturer in a Commonwealth University is expected to have been to England for a few years of higher study; an Oxbridge degree is the best guarantee that he has successfully qualified.

It is not easy to decide whether the advantages of the Oxbridge graduate in the academic labour market are justified. Again, the level of a Ph.D. is fairly well standardized throughout the country, and much of the best research is done in other places. But there is something in that 'style' to which we have referred, the influence of a large and active community of scholars, the standards of excellence set in the strongly competitive intellectual atmosphere of the ancient Universities. The generally high reputation of English scholarship in Science and the Arts may be due to the fact that so many of the ablest men and women have passed at one time or another through Oxbridge, as undergraduates or research students. The formal training, the overt imparting of information, may not be well organized there, but the whole tone of academic life is a powerful influence against uncritical, careless, sloppy work.

This is not to say that the Oxbridge Ph.D. is necessarily better than his Redbrick counterpart; one must judge each man on his merits. It would be disastrous— it sometimes is disastrous—if the mere *cachet* of the Oxbridge degree prevailed. Nothing is more depressing to the morale of Redbrick research than the feeling that their best efforts may be ignored, their best men slighted, because they came from the wrong address. But the infusion of that aristocratic, self-confident yet self-critical, attitude may be an important contribution to an institution with all sorts of homespun virtues, all sorts of good intentions, all sorts of aptitudes and intelligence, except the readiness to answer back.

It is not merely in the training of staff that Oxbridge influences other Universities. As we have already remarked, it is seen as an ideal, as a model of 'the University'. It is true that the new foundations at Manchester and London in the nineteenth century were consciously reacting against the decadence and obscurantism of Oxbridge, and belong to a different strain of English life, the strain of non-conformist puritanism rather than the strain of aristocratic self-cultivation. But the reform of Oxbridge itself has made that reaction seem less needful, and the New Universities created in the past twenty years seem to owe much more to the Oxbridge model, seem to pay much more homage to Oxbridge standards, then they might care to admit.

The day of the Gothic or Classical building is over, but the idea of a small town campus, a landscape of buildings and gardens, far away from the traffic and commerce of a great city, is dominant. The choice of towns out of *Baedeker*—Brighton, York, Norwich, Canterbury—is symbolic of this attempt to keep up with the appeal of the ecclesiological and the antique. Oxbridge denies the everyday world of cities and industry; the belief that a University must, ideally, be in the Green Belt is both a cause and a consequence of the death of cities themselves as chosen centres of life.

The model of the specialized honours degree, the model of the teaching and Research Department under a powerful Professorial head may be more specifically Redbrick inventions. But the student hostels as a modest version of a College, the generally paternalistic attitude towards students, the attempts to create, artificially, the social contact between dons and undergraduates, which is a special feature of Oxbridge—these all flow out of a conscious or unconscious adoption of Oxbridge standards and Oxbridge practices.

Again, the technique of the lecture and the tutorial, mechanisms of instruction that happened accidentally to be prevalent in Victorian Oxbridge were taken as fixed and ideal, without critical analysis of their effectiveness or economy. The seminar and the small class have been treated as imperfect versions of the tutorial, cheap enough for poorer institutions that lacked the wealth of Oxbridge in staff and facilities. The essay answer, the written papers, final determining examinations at the end of the long course, have been assumed without question as the norm of University tests of achievement, regardless of alternative techniques elsewhere, such as oral examinations on the Continent, or the continuous accumulation of 'grades' in the United States.

It would be unfair to blame Oxbridge because others have slavishly imitated her ways—or to hold her to account because Redbrick lecturers have been consumed with envy of their Oxbridge colleagues. Academic life is inevitably somewhat competitive; academic preferment is properly the reward of scholarly excellence; it can truly be said that nowadays an academic career is open to any sufficiently talented man; he has himself to blame if he allows himself to eat out his heart because he was not quite lucky enough or clever enough or dexterous enough to get into the very best place. Some of the advantages and privileges of being at Oxbridge are not as great as they look to the ignorant outsider.

But one can reasonably complain that Oxbridge is not very sympathetic to other Universities. As we have seen, Oxbridge dons are very inbred; only a few have direct experience of Redbrick, and the rest do little to cure their ignorance. A year or two away as an Assistant Lecturer, between taking one's Ph.D. and returning to a Fellowship or Lectureship, is not likely to be very encouraging or instructive, and does not give time for prejudices to wear off, or roots to go down. Older men come as Professors to Oxbridge, after holding Redbrick Chairs, but they do not interact strongly with the other dons, and are already too senior, too involved with administrative and research responsibilities to affect attitudes of mind inside College Common Rooms. For the others, an occasional hurried visit, in smoke and fog, to lecture to graduate students at Manchester or Sheffield, a Ph.D. to be examined at Southampton, a stint as external examiner for Reading or Newcastle, may be all that they see of other places. They may meet their Redbrick colleagues at conferences, on committees, or at their own College Feasts, but they have little knowledge of Redbrick students, or of the Redbrick pattern of education.

This ignorance and indifference infuriates Redbrick. Oxbridge dons do not seem to exist on the same plane as Lecturers, Senior Lecturers or Readers of other Universities. A Redbrick Professor may count for something—the chances are that he is an Oxbridge man, anyway—but below that the other academic grades are treated as if they were elementary school-teachers. The Association of University Teachers, which, for all its faults, speaks as the recognized trade union of the academic profession, scarcely exists at Oxford and Cambridge. It is not considered subversive—nobody could accuse it of that—it is just thought to be plebeian.

The arrogance is even more noticeable at an institutional level. A scale of salaries for academic staff is set up nationally by the University Grants Committee—but Oxbridge claims the right to have its own private scheme because of the 'special position of the Colleges and College Fellows'. A clearing-house for University admissions is established—but cannot include Oxbridge, whose Colleges insist on putting everybody to the trouble of going through their peculiar separate mills. The College Scholarship system cuts right across the whole business of GCE 'A' levels, and completely muddles up any possibility of establishing a rational University Entrance Examination for the whole country—but the Colleges go calmly on in pursuit of their own private butterflies. There is a great national drive to expand University education; every other University agrees to grow—but Oxbridge decides that it must not in the least dilute its perfection, and each College decides independently that it would be disastrous for it, socially, to take in another few dozen undergraduates.*

*An interesting situation has now arisen. Oxbridge has been growing slowly since the War, and has certainly got a good

The fact is, paradoxically, that Oxbridge is not really interested in education. The most obvious sign of this is the position of the two Departments of Education in the Universities. The training of University graduates to become teachers has been treated as an entirely insignificant activity, about on a par with the University Air Squadron or the undergraduate Health Service. Only recently, under more dynamic leadership, is Education becoming a serious academic subject at Oxbridge.

One can observe the same phenomenon in the indifference to teaching methods, in the complete absence of curiosity about the effects of examinations, in the purely anecdotal attitude to the psychology of the educational process. Learning, scholarship, knowledge, sometimes wisdom, are things that you have, and that you try to convey to the young men by talking to them—that is all.

The only contact that Oxbridge seems to have with other branches of education is with the Public Schools. It is well known that most Public Schools will only have Oxons and Cantabs on their staff—the Prospectus does not usually state whether First, Second or Third Class. To become a Headmaster one must certainly come from the right stable; sometimes, directly from a College Fellowship, without any ordinary schoolmastering experience at all. Dons and Beaks—put them together, add a Bishop or two, and the Establishment is epitomized.

But the relationship is more complex than it used to be. Dons nowadays are not overwhelmingly ex-public-school boys. A high proportion have come the hard way, through Grammar Schools and Scholarships. If they favour the Public Schools, it is not out of pious memory but, more simply, with a tinge of honest snobbery. The Socialist MP who sends his son to Eton is a familiar prototype. The Tutor who sends his son to Uppingham or Oundle is just doing his best for him; it will not necessarily prevent his leaning over backwards in favour of the boy from Gateshead or Wolverhampton in the College Entrance Examination and interview. Oxbridge does not really care much about the Public Schools, and certainly does not see itself as the defender and maintainer of their status. The traditional connections between individual Colleges and Schools—Winchester and New College, Eton and King's, Merchant Taylors' and St John's, Westminster and Trinity, Abingdon and Pembroke—are customary courtesies rather than active partnerships. A few dons are Governors, and sit there amongst the City magnates and Colonels listening to the disquisitions of the Beak.

It is the Public Schools which care about Oxbridge. We have already discussed the efforts they make, the skills they exercise, in getting their boys into a College. For them also, Oxbridge is the fountainhead, the Sun King under whose benign rule they exist, towards whose court all their thoughts are turned. They try too hard. By their attentions they saturate the limited capacity that Oxbridge has for interest in secondary education. The fact that the Beaks and their brethren do not complain against the College Scholarship Examinations is taken as sufficient evidence that everybody else is perfectly satisfied. The fact that almost all public-school boys are taught Latin was quite enough to persuade a substantial minority of dons that all other schoolboys could also learn it if they wanted to, so that it was perfectly reasonable as a compulsory qualification for matriculation.

Of ordinary Grammar Schools, Oxbridge seems to know very little. There are small bands of devoted enthusiasts who spend frustrating hours and days governing the Local Examinations Syndicate. There are bigwigs that sit on Government Commissions and boom, in the large, about Education. There are little-wigs that wriggle about in the local education world of Oxford and Cambridge, and their surrounding villages. There are dons with views on the teaching of their subjects, who confer with schoolmasters and try to reform their syllabuses. And of course, there is all that interminable correspondence between Tutors and Heads, Heads and Tutors, about all those interminable, indescribable, not quite admissible boys and girls.

But all this adds up to nothing when one considers the enormous influence that Oxbridge has on school teaching, especially in the final years at the Grammar School. Those College Entrance Scholarships set the pattern for GCE A levels—and GCE A levels control the school syllabuses. The best schools must aim for the Scholarships, must set the path of their best pupils towards them. The other schools feel bound to compete in the same field; the weaker pupils are drawn in the same direction. The dons take pride in 'keeping up the standards in the Sixth Form' by their Scholarship papers—whilst at the same time recounting their cunning in preventing the schoolmasters from tailoring their pupils too precisely to the questions they might ask. Sometimes, Oxbridge disclaims any responsibility for school syllabuses and teaching; listen to the dons when their guard is down, and you will hear them insist that this is one of the most important functions that they perform. Yes, they say, we could easily scrap the scholarships—but the schools

share of the increases in University Grants. However, in the current quinquennium, increased grants have gone mainly to Universities willing and able to expand. Oxford and Cambridge have suddenly found themselves unable, as Universities, to make the new appointments, and put up the new buildings, on the scale which they have grown accustomed to since the War. These new appointments were, of course, the source of all those non-Fellows that the Colleges would not elect—on the grounds that they would never see the end of University expansion, etc., etc. It is the refusal of the College to increase undergraduate numbers that has held down the quinquennial grant—and stopped the expansion of University posts that the Colleges claim to fear. In the same breath, however, the Colleges ask for more University posts in the main teaching subjects, such as English and History, so that they can elect more teaching Fellows without too much cost. What they should be doing, of course, is admitting more undergraduates to read Oriental Studies, Agriculture, Veterinary Science, etc., where University staff exist—and thus earn a larger quinquennial grant to pay for more History dons etc.

must have something to work for, mustn't they?

What is so depressing is that they never bother systematically to find out. A verbal skirmish over lunch in the Common Room, a letter to the *Oxford Magazine* about the evils of specialization, a half-hearted attempt to introduce a General Knowledge paper in their own Group Exam.—that is about all the energy they can muster for thinking about it. Yet they will spend days, weeks, setting Scholarship papers, marking Scholarship papers, arguing over the relative weight to be given to different combinations of subjects, discussing how many Major Scholars the College should take, as if it were perfectly settled and agreed that this was the only ideal of education that the world could ever know. Because what they are doing is in the service of the College, because it is an exercise in the sort of fine discrimination within their subject which gives them intellectual pleasure, they go blindly, nobly, conscientiously on.

They do not go out and see what effects it has on the schools. They do not listen to a growing body of educationists who castigate the over-specialization of English schools. They do not look at the boys they admit, and ask themselves whether they have been made fit for living. They do not institute statistical analyses, to find out whether they could choose their scholars better by less elaborate techniques. They do not ask themselves whether a third year in the Sixth Form, going over in greater detail a syllabus that already overlaps some University work, is the best way of spending a sixtieth part of one's life. They do not enquire whether very difficult questions over a narrow field are more 'searching' of some ultimate quality of intellect or character than simpler questions asked over a broader front.

Here is not the place to enter in detail into these familiar controversies. The point is to emphasize that Oxbridge, by its action, pushes English education in a particular direction—a direction of specialization, of élitism, of academicism. These things have their virtues, but the time is long past when they could simply be taken for granted. If they want to bear responsibility for the school system, then the dons must go down from their cosy *châteaux* into the trenches and find out what is going on amidst the mud and muddle.

But do the dons want to bear this responsibility? In spite of receiving nine-tenths of their income in one way or another from public funds they persist in thinking of their Colleges and Universities as private enterprises. For all their Royal Charters and Royal Commissions they were never really nationalized. Instead of taking their place at the summit of a national system of education they cling to the role invented for them by the Victorian middle classes. *Tom Brown's Schooldays* had a sequel, *Tom Brown at Oxford*. The Public Schools and the reformed Universities constituted a single educational sequence for the sons of gentlemen and of others who could pay for it. From the Lower School at Rugby to Degree Day at Oxford, boys were being prepared to take their place as officers in the chain of command of a stratified society.

Your modern don may have a new vision of 'officer-like qualities'; intelligence, expertise and efficiency may now seem more important than bluff honesty and team loyalty: the meritocrat may be his version of a modern Major-General. And if the State, rather than a rich parent, is willing to pay the fees, it is all one to him: the job remains essentially the same.

Oxford and Cambridge still think of themselves as having a unique and specialized social function which it is entirely within their own province to determine. They insist upon remaining independent estates of the realm. Perhaps that is why they refuse to rub shoulders with other universities, whose business they unconsciously define as the production of reliable Warrant Officers and Technical Sergeants. Perhaps that is why they avoid contact with primary schools, secondary modern schools, comprehensive schools—all those engines for the instruction of Tommy Atkins. It irritates them to be told that they are the coping stone of an educational system for Everyman; they are reluctant to see their own special mission as part of a whole strategy.

The title of this chapter can only be read ironically. Oxbridge is, indeed, a source, a standard, of academic excellence, of devotion to learning, of pure research, of the quest for truth. It is the sun round which a great many other institutions of Lower and Higher Learning see themselves as revolving. But, like the sun, Oxbridge is profoundly indifferent to its planets. It is too busy in its own little orb, too actively contemplating its own navel. Charles I chose Oxford for *his* headquarters—and we all know what happened to *him*.

Education, in fact, in England is what the Universities choose to make it. This seems to me too great a power to be possessed by two corporations, however venerable and illustrious, especially since we know them to have grown up under very peculiar circumstances, and to be fortified by endowments against all modern influences, good or bad. I wish we had several more Universities . . . But in the meanwhile, since Education in England is, in the main, what Oxford and Cambridge makes it, how important is it that Oxford and Cambridge should disseminate just and profound views on education. There is no greater or deeper subject: there is no subject which demands more comprehensive knowledge or more fresh observation. There are general principles to be grasped, and there are particular circumstances of age and country to be noted by the men who would legislate for the education of a nation. Oxford and Cambridge legislate for us, and we may be sure that if those Universities labour at present under any serious defect of system, the whole education of the country will suffer for it.

JOHN SEELEY (1868)

The Open University grew from the concept of a 'University of the Air' first mooted by Harold Wilson, then Leader of the Opposition, in a speech at Glasgow in 1963. When the Labour Party came to power, a White Paper was published, and in September 1967 a Planning Committee was appointed, with the following terms of reference: 'To work out a comprehensive plan for an Open University, as outlined in the White Paper of February 1966, "A University of the Air" and to prepare a draft Charter and Statutes.'

The Planning Committee reported to the Secretary of State for Education and Science on 31 December 1968. The first of the two following passages consists of extracts from its Report (HMSO, 1969, pp. 2–8, 16–19). They illustrate the thinking of those who created the University.

The University began the teaching of its first course in January 1971. The second passage is an article first published in *New Society*, 27 April 1972, written by Tyrrell Burgess, Director of the Centre for Institutional Studies at North East London Polytechnic. He argues that the Open University has failed in its founders' objectives and has none of its own—and that this is simply because it is a university, in the British tradition.

42   Extracts from the Report of the Open University Planning Committee

The objects of the Open University

In the past limited opportunities for education, determined by social, economic and political factors, have resulted in a low educational attainment on the part of a vast number of individuals. This low level of attainment has been taken as firm evidence of limited innate ability, which in turn was held to justify an absence of any increase in educational provision. It is both unjust and unwise to ascribe the adventitious hazards of nurture to alleged inherited defects— unjust to the individual, and unwise for society thus to deny the greatest educational opportunity to the greatest number of its citizens. For long regarded as a privilege of the few, the opportunity to engage in higher education is at last becoming widely accepted as a basic individual right. In these changes in recent years, science and technology have proved to be most powerful catalysts of educational demand and development. Moreover, education generally, and higher education in particular is, at one and the same time, a necessary condition of a modern technological society and a defence against its abuses. The two conditions—of securing on the one hand national economic viability through increased productivity

Source: HMSO (1969), 2–8, 16–19.

and efficiency of management, and of ensuring, on the other, the personal fulfilment and happiness of individual citizens in a democratic society—these are the burden in varying measure of most, if not all, recent major educational reports—Crowther, Robbins, Newsom, Dainton, Swann, and of various other manpower reports.

The educational tasks yet to be accomplished relate not only to the present and the future, pressing and numerous though these are, but also to the past. Accurate estimates are impossible as the data are not available, but a broad comparison may be made in terms of the proportion of the 18-year-old group entering full-time higher education at the beginning and end of the last three decades, and when the Robbins Report[1] targets are reached (they are in fact likely to be exceeded) in 1980. Without doubt there has been a substantial, though slowly diminishing proportion of people able enough to enter higher education who were born too soon to reap the benefits of increasing educational opportunity. If the Robbins Report targets had applied retrospectively over the last three decades, the total number concerned could hardly be less than one million. It is not to be supposed that, of these, the majority would be both able and willing to undertake study after a gap of years, but perhaps 10 per cent (at least 100,000) might. That this is a reasonable first estimate is supported by some pilot research investigations.

Another method of making preliminary estimates of numbers is to consider the possible requirements of specialist professional groups. The teaching profession is a case in point, with about 240,000 certificated non-graduate teachers in England and Wales, and some 15,000 in Scotland, who had no opportunity to take the B.Ed. degree or otherwise gain graduate status. Again, and recent discussions with professional organizations support the view, at least 10 per cent (about 25,000) would be a reasonable first estimate. With the incentives of graduate status and a related salary allowance, and with established habits of study, such teachers are likely to prove a highly committed group of students. Preliminary enquiries have been received which indicate that there are likely to be other significant groups of professional students interested in the University's courses.

We commissioned a survey of the interest of the adult population in the Open University. This was carried out for us by the National Institute of Adult Education. A random sample of some 3,000 adults over 21 years of age was chosen from six areas and of these some 70 per cent returned the questionnaire. Each was asked to express his or her degree of interest in the Open University, having been presented with a short outline of the opportunities that it would offer and of the effort that would be involved. The degree of interest was graded; 'not interested', 'mildly interested', 'very interested', or 'I will certainly be one of the first students'. About 5 per cent fell into the 'very interested' category and about 0·9 per cent into the 'I will certainly be one of the first students' category. These proportions were consistent between the six individual areas, lending some further support to the validity of the survey.

If these proportions are applied to the whole unselected adult population of the country, they yield a figure for the possible student number of 170,000–450,000 (allowing for the limits of error of the ratio) in respect of the 'very interested', and of 34,000–150,000 in respect of those people intending to register as students. Thus the results of the survey are in general agreement with the broad calculations made by other means . . . It seems to us, therefore, that there are good grounds for expecting candidates for the Open University to come forward in substantial numbers.

It is known from experience both at home and abroad, but notably at the University of New England, Armidale, New South Wales, that adult students, whose attitudes, habits and motivation differ from those of immediate school-leavers, can and do succeed in obtaining university degrees largely by correspondence tuition. There is thus good reason to suppose that such students will succeed in the Open University, particularly as correspondence will be closely integrated with tuition by radio and television . . .

The University will provide first and higher degree courses for such adult students, but its work would not cease if the problem of past deficiencies were adequately dealt with. Social inequalities will not suddenly vanish, nor will all individuals suddenly mature at the same age in the same environment. The recent book, *All Our Future*, by J. W. B. Douglas *et al.*,[2] provides timely evidence in this regard of the large number of boys and girls who have the ability to become scientists, doctors, civil servants, teachers and managing directors, but who leave school every year at the age of fifteen. It is probable that this will still continue to be substantially true after the raising of the school leaving age to sixteen, now projected for 1972–3.

Furthermore the latest UCCA[3] Report shows that, of some 100,000 applicants for university entrance in 1966–7, just under half found places. Of the remaining 50,000 candidates, UCCA estimate that 20,000 failed to achieve the minimum entrance standard currently set by universities. Thus, some 30,000 boys and girls, all qualified to proceed to a degree course, failed to satisfy their ambition. Some, no doubt, entered other institutions of higher education, but it seems unlikely that, even with further university expansion, there will be a sudden elimination of a need for more opportunities. We do not, therefore, see the need for the Open University as a transient one, lasting only until such time as the 'backlog' of adults denied and anxious for higher education is eliminated, but as a continuing one throughout the foreseeable future.

Thus the main work of the Open University will focus upon adult students. Indeed, we believe that it is always preferable for those aged 16–21 years in employment to attend sandwich courses, block release courses, or part-time day release courses at technical colleges, and at degree level, sandwich courses at technological universities and polytechnics designate. We consider that only those whose circumstances make it impossible for them to do so should be enrolled in the courses of the Open University.

Besides providing fresh and renewed opportunities for such students as we have been discussing, the University will have an important role arising from the changes in, and the increasing rate of change within modern technological society. This is exemplified in Annex D on Technological Innovation in the Swann Report,[4] and the Report remarks: 'We have become accustomed to the idea that the career of an individual spans only one major technological phase: it is almost certain in the future that it will span two or even more such phases'.[5] Manifestly, industry cannot release all the people all the time to attend updating or refresher courses, and the University will be able to make a very special contribution through its combined services of broadcasting, correspondence courses, and residential short courses. It is intended that these courses should be developed from the outset, and that the scope should be widened to include courses for professions, which, as in commerce, though not themselves scientific or technological, are nevertheless increasingly subject to the impact of technological innovation.

Besides the necessity to keep abreast of modern developments within particular occupations, it is increasingly important to facilitate movement between occupations and movement upwards through the occupational structure, as from specialist activity to general management. 'Post experience courses' and 'conversion courses' will be required of appropriate frequency and duration, which may lead by 'credit' stages (possibly sufficient in themselves) to postgraduate qualifications—degrees, diplomas and certificates. In the design of updating, refresher courses, and of occupational conversion courses, the University will wish to take expert advice from those engaged in industry, commerce and the relevant professions.

Change in social and economic circumstances, and in personal outlook at a more mature age, will stimulate others to take courses of study. This may be purely for personal satisfaction or for new occupational opportunities as, for example, for married women whose families are growing up. With earlier marriage and smaller families, this had been until lately a much neglected educational opportunity. This is indeed one aspect only of a much wider problem, and the national statistics of further and higher education show how markedly educational opportunities have been and are currently denied to women as compared with men, and with this, occupational opportunities also. The University will have an unrivalled opportunity to rectify this long-continuing imbalance.

In summary, therefore, the objects of the Open University are to provide opportunities, at both undergraduate and postgraduate level, of higher education to all those who, for any reason, have been or are being precluded from achieving their aims through an existing institution of higher education. This does not imply competition with existing institutions, but rather an attempt on a national scale to complement their efforts; an attempt which may well increase the demands upon existing institutions, as students, stimulated by the experience of part-time study, increasingly come to want the opportunity for full-time study.

General approach to Open University education

It is no longer necessary to argue that the broadcasting media, when imaginatively used, are efficient means of instruction, since that has now been established by an adequate body of research. So far as teaching of university level is concerned, the findings of research have been amply confirmed by the experience of the universities making large-scale use of closed-circuit television in their internal teaching.

The Hale Report[6] makes it clear that the 'lecture' or other large group teaching method, rather than the seminar or tutorial class, is still quantitatively the principal mode of university teaching. Given its logistic advantages, it is seen as the simplest way of offering to the first-year student a broad and up-to-date conspectus of some field of knowledge and, at its best, of motivating a survey of new knowledge, problems and growing points. The broadcast programme has even greater economies of scale; it will be more elaborate and carefully prepared; it can employ the best academic talent; and present detail in a manner most lectures cannot. On balance it is likely to achieve results at least as good as and often better than those secured by the normal live lecture in the classroom. Once the validity of broadcasting as a means of teaching is accepted, it is possible to think in terms of drawing on a nation-wide pool of specialized teaching abilities and of providing teaching programmes available to all that exploit the unique qualities and economies of scale that characterize the broadcasting media.

Direct teaching by broadcasting supported by printed literature may provide all that is required for a short course of professional refreshment. It is, however, neither practically possible nor pedagogically sound to rely on broadcasting as the principal or exclusive means of instruction in an operation designed to provide disciplined courses of university level.

The serious student needs to make the facts and concepts that have been presented to him his own by using them. He must undertake regular written work, some of which may be self-instructional and self-correcting, some of which must be corrected so as to help him with his individual problems and errors and to permit assessment of his progress. The only method of individual instruction capable of being made available everywhere, and capable of indefinite expansion as new needs arise, is correspondence tuition, which can readily incorporate these newer techniques. It is already used in Russia as a main agent of university expansion, nearly half of all Russian students in higher education following correspondence courses under the supervision of local institutions of higher education.

In Japan, in Australia, and in other countries faced with the problem of distant and isolated communities, correspondence tuition has been developed within the context of the national system of education, and at all levels. In this country it has, in the main, been left to private enterprise, and perhaps as many as half a million students are enrolled with one or other of the fifty to sixty colleges—many of them very small—which are now operating. They include a very substantial number of students for the external degrees of the University of London; and a much larger number aiming at professional qualifications. In one instance only does London University itself undertake correspondence teaching, preparing students for the B.Sc.(Econ.) through the activities of its Commerce Degree Bureau. At least half of the external students for that degree are receiving correspondence tuition from the Bureau or from some other source.

With these facts in mind the Robbins Committee

on higher education felt able to make the specific recommendation that British universities should experiment with correspondence courses, supplemented by vacation courses and laboratory work where appropriate; they added the following rider: 'We think it likely that television, as a technique of educational communication, may be found to have considerable potential value as an ancillary both for part-time and correspondence study.'[7]

Broadcasting, then, can most effectively be used as a component part of a fully integrated teaching system which also makes use of printed material, including specially written textbooks and directions for further reading; of correspondence tuition; of part-time face-to-face teaching, and of group discussion. In the circumstances it has very obvious potentialities, viz.:

(a) Using its full range of resources it can make the initial presentation of topics with the maximum impact. It can make the best authorities and the best expositors universally available, and it can thereby serve as an incomparably rapid means for the diffusion of the newest knowledge and ideas.

(b) Although they must be designed with a single-minded concern for the enrolled student audience, many of the programmes may have a cultural value for a much larger body of viewers and listeners, an important consideration in the use of an expensive medium like television.

(c) It can allow men and women to sample the broadcast components of a course, and to measure their own capacities against its demands before enrolling as students, and may thereby open up the possibilities of higher education for many people who would not otherwise discover them.

(d) It can provide an incentive to reduce the 'fall-out' rate, which is high in many forms of adult education.

(e) For the enrolled student it means a reduction of time spent in travelling, and the disruption of family life which might be involved in attendance at more remote courses.

(f) To some extent it can help students to feel that they are members of a corporate body, and in touch with its teaching staff.

The broadcasting contribution should not be regarded merely as programmes which reproduce (though they may replace) conventional lectures. It should use and experiment with the full and highly flexible resources of the media, with a strict attention to the purpose in hand. For serious students the most important characteristics of educational programmes are those that should be common to all modes of teaching: a clear definition of aims; accuracy of focus in terms of audience level; lucidity, cogency, and firmness of structure; a proper judgment of pace, and relevant illustration.

Articulated teaching systems of this type have so far received their fullest development at levels below that of university teaching. Some of these combined operations have, indeed, much more significance for the future of higher education than those widespread forms of broadcasting which may use the label 'university', but which consist essentially of programmes of a high cultural standard calling for no long-sustained effort, integrated with no other modes of teaching, and leading to no qualifications.

Degree structure

The degree of the Open University should, we considered, be a 'general degree' in the sense that it would embrace studies over a range of subjects rather than be confined to a single narrow speciality. In our view the Open University should not set out to compete with the established universities which can so much more efficiently provide 'special' degrees for students who can spend three years of full-time study in the laboratories and libraries of their specialist schools. Rather should the Open University degree be complementary, providing for the part-time student a broadly-based higher education, for which the teaching techniques available to the Open University are particularly suited. Furthermore we were aware of the great need and demand in the country, emphasized in the Swann Report,[8] for an extension of facilities for such general degrees.

Students increasingly complain that over the years degree course structures have become too rigid. We have therefore sought to evolve a degree structure that would be as flexible as possible, allowing students a reasonable maximum choice from among courses offered.

The majority of the students of the Open University are likely to be drawn from those whose school education ended a varying number of years ago and at varying levels of attainment. We took it as axiomatic that no formal academic qualifications would be required for registration as a student. Anyone could try his or her hand, and only failure to progress adequately would be a bar to continuation of studies. The first year courses must therefore be designed to suit, as far as possible, a wide variety of preparative backgrounds. This led to the concept of 'foundation courses'.

The foundation courses are to be designed as a means of familiarizing mature students with the modern concepts of the main 'lines' of study. Thus foundation courses will be offered in:

(a) Mathematics.
(b) Understanding Science.
(c) Literature and Culture.
(d) Understanding Society.

The initial challenge that faces the academic staff is so to devise these courses that the whole of a broad field is explored in a way that will stimulate and excite students with very varied backgrounds: but that will, at the same time, make intellectual demands upon them of the same order as the demands made by any normal first-year university course.

The degree of the Open University will be obtained by the accumulation of 'credits' in individual courses, which will last for one academic year. A certificate indicating the acquisition of a credit will be issued to students who are successful in both the continuous and the final assessments of their work. Each foundation course will count as one credit and all students will normally be required to obtain two credits in foundation courses before proceeding to further study.

The programme of study after the foundation courses is based on the breakdown of each line into a number of components. Thus mathematics might be broken down into statistics, computer science, pure mathematics and so on. The number of such components will initially be limited by the availability of broadcasting time to about four in each line. Each component will be made the subject of two courses, each of one year's duration and each counting as a credit. Students could not study the second, more advanced course in any subject unless they had obtained a credit in the first course in that subject. With this exception it is intended that students should be as free as possible to choose any combination of courses from any lines that they wish. Thus one student might draw all his courses (save one foundation course) from the line of mathematics where another drew his from all the four (or later, five) lines of the University.

We propose that the degree should be awarded at two levels. All degrees should be 'general' in type, although a varying measure of specialization will be possible. We are aware that in some established universities an 'honours' degree is regarded as synonymous with a 'special' degree, and a 'pass' degree or 'ordinary' degree as synonymous with a 'general' degree. In other universities this pattern has been abandoned and degrees are now offered which are both 'general' and 'honours'. There is thus considerable semantic difficulty in the terminology. We considered the use of a complete new terminology, but decided that this would merely serve to confuse still further an already confused situation. The Open University should therefore offer its general degrees both at ordinary and at honours levels. For the ordinary degree a total of six credits will be required; for the honours degree eight credits will be needed and there may be some restriction on the choice of the last two courses in which credits are obtained. We have not, however, taken the argument further than this as it is a matter on which the Senate is bound to have its own views.

Credits may be acquired over any number of years of study. Exceptional students could complete a degree course in three years, but we imagine that four years would be the normal time and five years the median period in practice.

The determination of the success of each student in a course leading to a credit will be by a combination of continuous assessment and final examination. The latter will be an essential feature, despite its limitations, since only at that stage can standards be unequivocally established. In accordance with university practice, external examiners will be appointed for the final examinations of each course to ensure that proper academic standards are maintained.

One vital and pressing need is for degree courses for practising certificated teachers. We have been engaged in detailed discussions of this problem with representatives of the professional bodies and we hope to arrive at an early decision on this particular problem.

Course structure

Each degree course will make substantial use of correspondence course techniques which will provide the nucleus around which an integrated sequence of radio and television programmes, of discussion groups and of short residential courses can be built. The broadcasts will not necessarily form a coherent course of themselves, though there may be good grounds for offering 'study guides' and reading lists for sale. Thus members of the general public, who are not registered students, will be free to watch or listen to the broadcast programmes, and they may get considerable satisfaction and value from the series of broadcasts. It must, however, be affirmed as policy that the interests of the registered students are paramount, and that the broadcasts will be designed and produced primarily for their benefit as part of the integrated teaching/learning system of the University.

Each correspondence course will be based upon 'assignments' sent by post to each student in a form and at intervals to be determined. Initially, an assignment will comprise at least a study guide, references to the reading required, a programme of the related broadcast material, and requirements for written work to be submitted to the tutor. One of the main advantages of the normal correspondence course is the flexibility of timing that it allows; however, this flexibility is not available with the broadcast element of the course. Thus, to the extent that assignments are linked to the broadcasts, students must keep abreast of them or fall behind. This will remain inherent in the integrated course structure, until such time as recording machines for the television broadcasts become readily available and reasonably inexpensive. The same difficulty is less serious with sound broadcasts since audio tape-recorders are now cheap and familiar, and since recording on tape or disc can easily be offered for sale or on loan, once the right to do so has been negotiated. The technical development of recording devices is already very promising, and the University will give this close attention so that the work of students can be facilitated.

We have discussed the feasibility of permitting

students to begin their studies at any time of the year. This is another attractive feature of many correspondence courses, but we regard it as impracticable in the immediate future for the fully integrated courses. Thus, initially, courses will run from January to December. There are several reasons for this choice, which departs from the traditional academic year beginning in October, namely:

(a) courses may run for up to forty weeks of broadcasting and for a similar number of weeks of correspondence each year. Thus any break in the summer would tend to fall in the middle of a course and offer a chance for wider reading, revision and catching up;

(b) short-term residential courses would mainly fall mid-way through the course. They will depend upon the use of existing accommodation in other universities and educational institutions, and such accommodation is often available only during the summer months;

(c) examinations would be held in November or December. This is 'off-peak' time for both school and university examinations, so that both space and personnel should be the more readily available;

(d) because of the complex regional organization of the Open University a period of some months will be needed between the registration of students and the start of the course. Registration in September for courses beginning in January would provide the University with the interval for preparation and organization that is required, and the student with an opportunity for consulting the student counselling service about background reading in preparation for his course.

Postgraduate courses

We differentiate postgraduate courses into three main types. There is, first, the 'postgraduation' course that follows immediately after a first degree. This can, and often does, lead to a higher degree or diploma and may re-orient a student from one discipline to another in preparation for employment. Secondly there is the 'postgraduate post-experience' course, which may be of two kinds. First the courses which are required by those who, after practising their profession for some years, are called upon to make a significant change in their activities, such as from the scientific into the management side of industry. Secondly, there are 'updating' or 'refresher' courses which enable a professional man to keep up with recent advances in his own field of work, whether scientific, technological or managerial.

The University may ultimately offer courses of all these kinds, but following our discussions with a variety of professional organizations, we believe that the critical need is for both kinds of post-experience courses and these will be considered from the outset.

In very general terms we think that these postgraduate courses may depend mainly on a nucleus of a series of broadcasts, but that correspondence tuition may be essential in preparation for some advanced diplomas and higher degrees, where these are offered by the University. The extent to which the University can embark upon such courses in the early years will therefore depend upon the availability of broadcasting time at suitable hours of the day.

Notes

1 *Higher Education* (Report of the Committee under the chairmanship of Lord Robbins), (HMSO, Cmnd 2154, 1963).
2 J. W. B. Douglas, J. M. Ross and H. R. Simpson, *All Our Future*, Peter Davies, 1968.
3 Universities Central Council on Admissions, *Fifth Report, 1966–67*.
4 *The Flow into Employment of Scientists, Engineers and Technologists* (Report of the Working Group on Manpower for Scientific Growth, under the chairmanship of Professor Michael Swann), (HMSO, Cmnd 3760, 1968).
5 Page 73, para. 149.
6 *University Teaching Methods* (Report of the Committee under the chairmanship of Sir Edward Hale), (HMSO 1964), 52, para. 165 *et seq*.
7 Robbins Report, 262, para. 821.
8 Swann Report, para. 165–9, and para. 14 in 'Summary of Recommendations' (p. 92).

43 The Open University

Tyrrell Burgess

When I was in the United States last year, it seemed that the one experience all educational institutions had shared was a visit from the vice-chancellor of our Open University. From the east to the west coast people mentioned him: he had been, it seems, everywhere. Europe must by now be in a similar condition. Sales literature has gone to Scandinavia and the Low Countries and a sales team is visiting Scandinavia, South Africa, Hongkong and Singapore.

Neither is the university without honour at home. In 1970, more than 42,000 people applied for first-year places and 24,000 received them. In 1971, more than 34,000 people applied for 1972 courses and more than 21,000 were allocated places. Allowing for a margin of people who do not wish to take up their places, this year's admissions come to about 19,000 students—18 per cent of whom are taking two courses. The latest news is that more than 20,000 people have applied to study in 1973, and there are still eight weeks to go for applications.

The university can congratulate itself not only on the number of its students, but also on their performance. Naomi McIntosh, senior lecturer in research methods at the Open University, has been responsible for monitoring students' progress, and her graph (below) shows the progress of students during 1971 by course after final registration. Overall, out of every 100 students who started (provisional registration) in January last year, 81 paid all their fees and were finally registered. From here on, the university has figures for courses, not students. For every 100 initial student courses (January), 60 examinations were sat and 56 credits were awarded. For each 100 students finally registered, 75 credits were awarded. This success rate is far better than normal correspondence study and better than most people expected. There is an understandable tendency, in the university itself and to some extent outside, to claim that this is a success story and that it is time for the cavilling to cease.

But we can accept this claim only by equating activity with success. To judge the latter, we need to look at the objectives of the Open University and see how far they are being attained. I argue that the Open University is indeed becoming a university (British style), in that its objectives are swiftly becoming ever more vague and its activities more and more self-justifying. This development affects not only its policies, but its educational attitudes and processes. It means that the university can avoid serious judgment of its performance—with the consequence that it can

Source: New Society, 27 April 1972.

neither convincingly claim to have succeeded, nor rebut the view that it has failed.

Growing vagueness about objectives characterized even the pre-history of the university. Undoubtedly, it was, and still is, regarded by the Labour Party as an engine of social equality. In his speech at Glasgow in 1963, Harold Wilson defined the group who would benefit from the university to include 'technicians

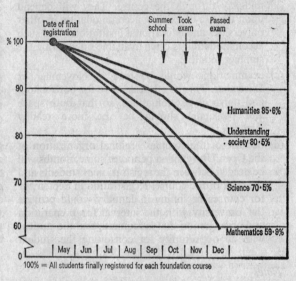

Figure 43.1 Student progress by course: 1971

and technologists who left school at 16 or 17,' and others, who had no opportunity to take GCE at 'O' or 'A' level. At Scarborough, a month later, he said the university would offer opportunity to 'those who, for one reason or another, have not been able to take advantage of higher education'. The planning committee's report said the university would 'provide opportunities, at both undergraduate and postgraduate level, of higher education to all those who, for any reason, have been or are being excluded from achieving their aims through an existing institution of higher education'.

The planning committee identified two broad groups of such people. The first consisted of those who had missed higher education in the past: 'Without doubt there has been a substantial, though slowly diminishing proportion of people able enough to enter higher education who were born too soon to reap the benefits of increased educational opportunity.' It reasonably enough foresaw continuing social inequality, based upon a reference to J. W. B. Douglas's work. And it seemed from the UCCA forms that about a third of the applicants to universities were both minimally qualified and rejected. This concern is obviously still in the egalitarian tradition, though the reference to 'able enough' people, and university rejections, suggests that the egalitarianism was already becoming limited.

The second group of potential students was identified as including those who wanted updating or refresher courses, on the one hand, and post-experience and conversion courses on the other. By definition, these courses were directed towards those who had already had some form of higher education, and so were rather short on egalitarian purpose.

The duality of purpose was reflected in the inaugural address by the chancellor, Lord Crowther, in July 1969. Echoing the findings and the concern of the educational report which bears his name, Lord Crowther said, 'The existing system, for all its expansion, misses and leaves aside a great unused, reservoir of human talent and potential ... These are our primary material. To them we offer a further opportunity.' He went on, however, 'but if this were all we could hardly call ourselves a *university*. This is not simply an educational rescue mission—though that is our first task and we do not decry it. But we also aim wider and higher. Wherever there is an unprovided need for higher education, supplementing the existing provision, there is our constituency ...'

The implications of this are interesting. Doing what the early sponsors of the Open University wanted was, of itself, insufficient. Nor did Lord Crowther pause to wonder whether aiming wider and higher would help or hinder the university in its 'first task'. He might have guessed that the determination to be a university would make this more difficult. It is true that many people capable of higher education drop out of the education system, but they tend to drop out early on. Such people are not necessarily incapable of the level and type of work associated with universities—as the early experience of the Workers Educational Association showed. But their numbers are probably small—if only because it is unreasonable to expect them to cope with the academic process, on the basis of little or no experience of it.

This means that the people most likely to apply for, enrol in and complete the Open University courses are those who have, at some stage, reached the point of entry to higher education. The table below shows the occupational analysis of applicants and the allocations for the 1972 courses, with a comparison of those for the previous year. The university's occupational groupings do not necessarily correspond with particular social classes. Even so, it is clear to what extent the Open University's students have had some form of higher education and how few are in semi-skilled or unskilled occupations.

My own view is that this was bound to happen, once it was decided to found a university. And this view is shared by the vice-chancellor. In a speech to the Royal Institution, he said: 'It is not surprising that, in this first year of its existence, the Open University has not attracted as many applicants from the educationally underprivileged groups as had been hoped.' His explanation was that: 'Many of the applicants, like the schoolteachers, came from those groups who read the sort of journals which gave maximum coverage to the new institution. To bring the Open University to the attention of the underprivileged requires publicity in the media to which they have the readiest access. This would either cost a great deal in terms of an advertising campaign—and we have no reserves for such expenditure—or would demand the sort of free publicity that might be afforded by characters in such popular series as *Coronation Street* or *The Archers* becoming students of the Open University.'

In other words, the vice-chancellor made it clear that the Open University cannot be certain of attracting those whom its originators hoped to serve. And only in an aside does he meet the objection that the university might not be a good means of meeting its stated objectives. The planning committee, he said, 'was not asked to plan an open primary school or an open secondary school, but an open university'. And, later, 'The staff of the university ... were clearly not concerned with the value judgments as to whether the Open University was the best way of extending the provision of adult tertiary education. They were appointed to do the job that way and no other.'

It is the vice-chancellor's belief that an open institution other than an open university would have stood little chance in the battle for resources, for independence or for broadcasting time.

In a later speech, he asserted that the university must achieve 'academic credibility' before it could offer remedial courses in higher education for deprived adults. He reportedly said that 'the Open University was naturally concerned about the education of deprived adults, but many of them were terribly unprepared for university-type education. It was very good to set up courses to salvage the wreckage of the elitist education system, and established universities could go in for experiments of that kind, but the Open University had first to establish its own academic credibility.'

At the same time, the vice-chancellor has been at pains to modify the crude picture presented by the table. His claim is that 'so many of our middle-class students have battled up from the working class in spite of many deprivations.' Naomi McIntosh's study, to be published later this year, will show the extent to which this is true. But of course it merely supports the assertion that the Open University does best for those who have already battled. (I would, myself, expect that the Open University, like grammar schools, does best with working class students whose mothers have married beneath them.)

It is clear, then, that from the point of view of the Labour Party and of other egalitarians, the Open

Table 43.1   Occupation of Open University students

group	01	02	03	04	05	06	07	08	09	10	11	12	13	14
	%	%	%	%	%	%	%	%	%	%	%	%	%	%
applicants 1970	9·2	1·7	6·9	35·9	11·9	8·0	7·5	1·8	2·8*		8·2	3·4	2·5	0·1
applicants 1971	11·0	1·6	4·6	30·2	12·6	4·4	11·9	3·0	2·3	1·3	9·4	4·4	3·1	0·1
men 1971	0·1	1·6	4·3	19·8	8·0	4·3	11·1	3·0	2·2	1·2	5·3	3·8	2·2	0·1
women 1971	10·9	0	0·3	10·4	4·6	0·1	0·8	0	0·1	0·1	4·1	0·6	0·9	0
target quota set	11·0	1·7	4·6	30·2	12·6	4·4	11·9	3·1	2·3	1·3	9·4	4·4	3·1	0·2
allocations 1970	9·8	2·0	5·6	34·3	10·0	9·3	9·2	2·3	3·1*		8·1	3·7	2·5	0·1
allocations 1971	10·8	1·9	4·7	29·9	12·5	4·8	12·1	3·2	2·3	1·3	9·7	4·2	3·0	0·1
number of applicants 1971	3,763	577	1,572	10,327	4,283	1,486	4,084	1,017	772	476	3,224	1,514	1,066	61
number of allocations 1971	2,270	397	999	6,306	2,630	1,009	2,555	681	491	200	1,881	895	647	24

*groups 09+10

Occupation group: 01 housewives; 02 armed forces; 03 administrators and managers; 04 teachers and lecturers; 05 the professions and the arts; 06 qualified scientists and engineers; 07 technical personnel: including data processing, draughtsmen and technicians; 08 electrical, electronic, metal and machines, engineering and allied trades; 09 farming, mining, construction and other manufacturing; 10 communications, and transport, air, sea, road, and rail; 11 clerical and office staff; 12 shopkeepers, sales, services, sport and recreation workers, fire brigade and police; 13 retired, independent means, not working (other than housewives), students; 14 in institutions (prison, chronic sick).

University is a failure. It does not, and probably will not, meet their dearest objectives. But this is only of interest in so far as the university itself proclaims that these objectives are still its own—and, as we have seen, these claims are getting rarer. There is nothing particularly odd in this—institutions set up for one purpose can quite quickly come to serve another, though the Open University has, in this respect, shown a pretty turn of speed.

The way to judge the Open University now is by reference to its own objectives, and here the difficulty is that it appears to have none. For example, chapter one of the prospectus for 1972 is supposed to be on 'background, objectives, methods and government'. Two full pages are devoted to these topics, and there is not an objective in sight. The vice-chancellor's latest report has three lines on objectives. It quotes the planning committee's statement (above) and adds that this 'has been endorsed by the council and senate on a number of occasions, and there has been little or no evidence of any change of view'. Nowhere does his report discuss success or failure in the light of these objectives, which are clearly in no way operational. When one talks to the vice-chancellor and the staff of the Open University, they tend to disclaim any attempt to speak for the institution as a whole. People differ in their objectives, and what one is given is one man's view of what these are.

People, of course, differ in any institution. The question is whether the institution itself has evolved objectives to which its energies are devoted and which its staff accept. It has to be confessed that, like most universities, the purpose of the Open University is to be the Open University. It is, therefore it succeeds. It has a headquarters and staff. It creates courses. It enrols students, sets examinations and awards degrees.

Anyone with a television set can watch the programmes. Anyone who can afford the fees can apply. With a restricted number of places, and an elaborate quota system for courses and regions, the openness of the university looks a little theoretical, but it does at least try not to demand 'A' levels. The trouble is that to the question 'what is it all for?' the only reply can be, for its own sake.

My own belief is that this lack of external objectives, plus its difficulty in attracting the deprived, derives from the very organization of the university. The fact that it is a university, establishing its credibility and operating through an inevitably complex system of technologies and procedures, means that its educational approach must be 'academic'.

It is worth recalling what is involved. As Brian Lewis, deputy director of the university's Institute of Educational Technology, says: 'Study materials will be parcelled up and sent through the post to the student, at intervals of about four to six weeks. Each package will contain a sequence of correspondence and other materials, accompanied by study notes, private exercises, and self-administered tests which the student can take to help satisfy himself that he has understood the main teaching points. Also included will be a set of written homework assignments, which the student will be expected to return, within a specified time period, for marking. So far as is possible, each package will be a self-contained entity. It will provide the student with everything that he needs, in order to advance his studies for a further four to six weeks. From time to time it may be necessary to refer the student to set books and readers which he will be expected to buy or borrow. But the study packages will, in general, constitute the core materials of the course.'

To reinforce and supplement all this, the university is collaborating with the BBC to produce a regular series of radio and television programmes. There is a network of twelve regional offices organizing 250 study centres, with associated tutorial services. There have been 50 to 60 summer schools in eight different university centres. The organization of all this from Milton Keynes amounts almost to poetry. They have the largest mail inserter in Europe and imposing systems for production, on time, of course materials.

These organizational constraints are even more important than the inevitable ones of time and money in making the university's staff acutely self-conscious of what they are doing and forcing them to face openly the problems of education at university level. This is reinforced by the fact that the results of their work emerge not in cloistered privacy, but in public. The struggle to present material for the Open University is an extraordinary attempt to make explicit the assumptions and processes of academic teaching. The Open University is doing what all university teachers should do but in fact do rarely.

The elaborate arrangements, made principally through the Institute of Educational Technology, grew, of course, out of practical difficulties. If a course team of academics sets out to produce a 36-week course, it must at least see that the early part of the course is a proper foundation for later parts. There can be no question of the course repudiating, towards its end material that has been offered at the beginning. This means that the academics must be helped to specify the structure of the material they are offering and decide on strategies for offering it. Brian Lewis talks about developing a plan of knowledge 'for talking about the structure of knowledge'. And I believe he himself accepts that all this rests upon particular assumptions about knowledge and a particular view of teaching.

All 'subjects' are constructs. We set bounds to an area of knowledge for our own convenience. But once we start from the structure of the subject, we are inevitably concerned with knowledge for its own sake.

Teaching, on this basis, must be an academic and indeed anti-educational proceeding and also encourage conservatism. The elaborate processes of the Open University, the need for an integrated course, must mean only the tried and true is viable.

There is, of course, an alternative education tradition which, to put it baldly, starts with the student not the subject. Its object is to make the student competent at something, not just to tell him things. It rests on the educational commonplace that people learn best by solving problems. It is an approach which has permeated state primary schools and was always glorified in the golden days of the Oxford tutorial. In an impoverished and limited sense, it is what is behind all those 'mere' vocational part-time courses in technical colleges. And it is precisely these courses which attract the educationally deprived in very much larger proportions than the Open University can ever aspire to. A technical college is not interested in its own credibility. It is interested in the student and the problem of improving his economic and social viability.

The Open University rejects this approach: indeed my argument is that it is bound to do so for both academic and social reasons. It must operate in the grammar school tradition of 'O' level and 'A' level, as if two or three decades of educational development had not taken place. One would indeed predict that it will go the way of the WEA, providing ornamental knowledge mainly to middle class people.

It is, of course, to the credit of the Open University that this is well understood. But understanding is not enough. The Open University was founded in this country to mitigate social inequality. It is being taken up abroad for the same reasons. Here, it can be seen to have failed and the university can avoid the sense of failure only by giving up the initial objective. The form of the university enables it to entertain, but makes it hard for it to educate. Of course, if the Open University were to succeed in educating the un-educated, either here or abroad, it would be all set to save the world; but it won't succeed.

Introduction to readings 44–49

On 27 April 1965 the Rt Hon. C. A. R. Crosland MP, then Secretary of State for Education and Science, announced in a speech at Woolwich Polytechnic the government's acceptance of a 'dual' (later usually called 'binary') system of higher education. This meant the effective rejection of the Robbins Committee proposal that some ten of the regional colleges of technology, financed through the local authorities, should be elevated to autonomous university status. Instead, the local authority, or 'technical', sector was to be strengthened, and degree work, validated through the new Council for National Academic Awards (CNAA) developed. The following year, in April, the government published a White Paper (*A Plan for Polytechnics and Other Colleges*, HMSO, Cmnd 3006) announcing its intention to designate up to thirty institutions, formed from regional colleges of technology, colleges of art or of commerce (later two colleges of education were added) as polytechnics, which would become the focal point of development at higher education level within the local authority sector.

The next four passages examine this policy. In the first ('Binary dilemmas—an American view', from *Higher Education Review*, 2 (1), 1969, 27–43), Professor Martin Trow, looking with American eyes, sees the binary policy as a solution to problems deeply rooted in a peculiarly British structure of higher education and of society. In the second (taken from *Technical Education in the United Kingdom*, OECD, Paris, 1971, 89–103), Tyrrell Burgess and John Pratt, at the time of writing members of the Higher Education Research Unit at the London School of Economics, examine the development of government policies for the polytechnics in the late nineteen-sixties, and the form of education which the new institutions seemed likely to offer. They also discuss the proposed governmental structure of the polytechnics, which was paralleled by changes in the government of colleges of education stemming from the Weaver Report (*The Government of Colleges of Education*, HMSO, February 1966). Their reference to 'maintained Colleges of Education' —colleges within the local authority sector—is explained in Mr Burgess's treatment of the colleges printed later in this section.

The third passage is an article by Anne Corbett (first published in *New Society*—of which she is education correspondent—9 December 1971, pp. 1142–4), in which she describes, and praises, the procedures of the CNAA.

Finally, Pamela Lewis, in an article called 'Finance and the fate of the polytechnics' (*Higher Education Review*, summer 1971, 23–34) examines resource provision for the polytechnics, and its effect upon their educational objectives.

The professional education of intending teachers in England and Wales takes place both in colleges of education and in university departments of education. Broadly, the former run three-year courses, leading to a certificate, or for a minority four-year, leading to the B.Ed. degree, in which personal and professional education are integrated (the 'concurrent' pattern), while the latter offer one-year postgraduate courses (the 'consecutive' pattern). Late in 1970 the Secretary of State for Education and Science appointed a committee under the chairmanship of Lord James of Rusholme to investigate the present arrangements and to make recommendations for changing them. Its Report was published on 25 January 1972. The Secretary of State had announced no decision on its recommendations at the time this volume went to press, and we have therefore ignored the James Report.

Readings 48 and 49 are concerned with the colleges of education under the pre-James arrangements.

Tyrrell Burgess, whose article 'Teacher Training within higher education' (of which part is reprinted here) first appeared in *Dear Lord James—A Critique of Teacher Education* (Penguin Books, 1971, 146–58) describes, and criticizes, the present academic and administrative structure of the colleges of education.

Ronald Goldman, now Dean of Education at La Trobe University in Australia, but formerly Principal of a college of education, questions the possibility of sound academic and educational development within the colleges while they remain under local authority control. In his article (reprinted from *The Times Educational Supplement*, 1 January 1971), he refers to the Weaver Report (*Report of the Study Group on the Government of Colleges of Education*, HMSO, February 1966), in consequence of which changes in the government of colleges were made which paralleled the system introduced for the polytechnics. (See Burgess and Pratt, on polytechnics, on pp. 250–56 in this section.) His criticism of the financing of the colleges applies *mutatis mutandis* to all local authority institutions of higher education, and for balance his article should therefore be read alongside Pamela Lewis's on 'Finance and the fate of the polytechnics'.

44 Binary dilemmas-an American view

Martin Trow

The peculiar demands of modern industrial societies for large numbers of educated people place strains on any system of higher education forced into almost continuous and rapid growth. The strains experienced in Western European countries arise chiefly out of the difficulties of changing educational systems designed for the provision of a relatively small elite for Government, the free professions and business into one producing large numbers of skilled men and women needed for new and semi-professions, for a greatly enlarged educational system, and for middle level managerial and technical positions which call for more than a secondary school education.

The forms these strains take in Great Britain resemble those in other Western European countries, but also take quite special and to my mind more difficult forms than in most others. One central policy issue in British higher education, the dispute over the 'binary' versus 'unitary' form of higher education, captures and focuses many of the basic strains in British society and culture that bear on higher education.

The present Government, contrary to the recommendation of the Robbins Committee, has decided to perpetuate the 'binary' system of higher education. The main elements in this decision are: first, that there are to be no more new universities or accessions to university status for at least ten years; and second, that the Council for National Academic Awards (CNAA), a national degree-awarding body, with headquarters in London, should grant external degrees to courses in non-autonomous institutions which can meet its rigorous criteria on curriculum, staff and amenities. This agency has no formal connections with the university sector, but is being developed as a full-blown alternative to it, with great effort being directed to building up its independent prestige. Thus, alongside the 'autonomous' universities with their UGC buffer and block grants, there is to be developed a 'non-autonomous' sector of higher education, responsible to local authorities and the Department, including a wide range of institutions offering work of varying kinds, with parts of it hooked into a degree-granting system separate from the universities, and barred from promotion to university status. This

Source: Higher Education Review (1969), **2** (1), 27–43.

is the substance of the binary system, and of Labour Government policy for higher education.

What Robbins recommended was a system which would also distinguish sharply between universities and other institutions of higher education, but which would hold out the hope to some of the latter of their someday being accepted into the circle of the elect. When the quality of their students, staff and studies seemed on a high enough level, they too could hopefully apply for a Royal Charter, or for amalgamations with an existing university, and thus come within the charmed circle of autonomous institutions under the loose 'authority' of the UGC, an authority exerted solely through its powers of persuasion and its control over the block grants it makes to the autonomous institutions under it. Moreover, crucial to Robbins was the assumption (and recommendation) that the bulk of expansion of higher education be in the university sector. By contrast the present Government appear inclined to favour a faster growth of places in the other sector of higher education.

The best Ministerial defence[1] of the policy (at least that part which can be made public) is this:

There is an ever-increasing need and demand for vocational, professional and industrially-based courses in higher education—at full-time degree level, at full-time just below degree level, at part-time advanced level, and so on. This demand cannot be fully met by the universities. It must be fully met if we are to progress as a nation in the modern technological world. In our view it therefore requires a separate sector, with a separate tradition and outlook within the higher education system.

Secondly, a system based on the ladder concept must inevitably depress and degrade both morale and standards in the non-university sector. If the universities have a 'class' monopoly of degree giving, and if every college which achieves high standards moves automatically into the University Club, then the residual public sector becomes a permanent poor relation perpetually deprived of its brightest ornaments, and with a permanently and openly inferior status. This must be bad for morale, bad for standards, and productive only of an unhealthy competitive mentality.

Thirdly, it is desirable in itself that a substantial part of the higher education system should be under social control, and directly responsive to social needs. It is further desirable that local government, responsible for the schools and having started and built up so many institutions of higher education, should maintain a reasonable stake in higher education.

Fourthly . . . we shall not survive in this world if we in Britain alone down-grade the non-university professional and technical sector.

And citing the Grandes Ecoles, the Technische Hochschule, and Leningrad Poly, he went on,

Why should we not aim at this kind of development? At a vocationally oriented non-university sector which is degree-giving and with an appropriate amount of post-graduate work with opportunities for learning comparable with those of the universities, and giving a first-class professional training. Let us now move away from our snobbish caste-ridden hierarchical obsession with university status.

And the Secretary of State added: 'For all these reasons we believe in the dual pattern. The university sector will continue to make its own unique and marvellous contribution. We want the public sector to make its own equally distinguished but separate contribution. And between them we want—and I believe we shall get—mutual understanding and healthy rivalry where their work overlaps.'

The first and third of Crosland's points have to do with numbers, growth rates, control, and (important though implicit) relative costs. The second and fourth points have to do with status, and with the relation of status to the character of institutions and their evolution. A few words on both these themes.

Control and costs

First, Crosland was clearly serious about wanting larger numbers of technologists and applied social scientists. In this respect he was really more radical and more 'American' than the great majority of both his supporters and his opponents on the binary question. When he says that 'this demand cannot be fully met by the universities' he means that it will not be met. British universities have their own strong traditions, and conceptions of what constitutes appropriate university studies. Those conceptions do not include most 'vocational' subjects. As one author has put it:

The tone of the British universities is set by the two ancient universities, Oxford and Cambridge, which 'typify the English University system, and are so singularly venerable and traditional that, in the English-speaking world, their names are almost synonymous with the word university'. They remain deeply conscious of their origin as communities of scholars, and the universities that have sprung up in England during the past hundred years tend to reflect this inherited attitude. It is their common view that a university, as Lord Douglas put it . . . is very different from a place to which you go to learn a trade, even if that trade is dignified by the name of a profession.

Though many concessions have been made, over the years, to vocational demands on education, the universities still feel, with Herbert Spencer, that 'education has for its object the formation of character'. Great stress is laid on the growth of spirit, broadening of understanding, and sharpening of intellect that can be actuated through the communal life in a university. A university's real job it has been said, 'is to turn out . . . men whose academic qualifications are an addendum to their true manhood'.[2]

The same author could shortly thereafter observe that Britain's universities, Oxford and Cambridge not excepted, became in fact, professional vocational schools. The arts education with which they primarily concerned themselves was simply the appropriate vocational training for graduates whose principal occupations would be found in the law, the church, and the administrative civil service. (ibid, pp. 156–57.) But while the universities' efforts to shape character, develop certain qualities of mind, and bring a student up to the point of being able to do original research in a special branch of one of the traditional fields of learning, may in fact also function as a kind of 'vocational training' as Payne suggests, it is not seen that way by university people. And that is important for the way they see non-university higher education as well. As Eric Ashby has observed:

'It was difficult enough for British universities to adapt themselves to scientific thought; it is proving much more difficult for them to adapt themselves to technological thought . . . Technology is of the earth, earthy; it is susceptible to pressure from industry and government departments; it is under an obligation to deliver the goods. And so the crude engineer, the mere technologist (the very adjectives are symptoms of the attitude) are tolerated in universities because the State and industry are willing to finance them. Tolerated but not yet willing to admit that technologists may have anything intrinsic to contribute to academic life.'[3]

This is less true than it was when Payne and Ashby wrote in the late 1950s, and will be even less true in the future. But it is a question of the rate of change of the British universities as compared with the rate of change in the demands for trained manpower of the economy, the occupational structure, and the welfare services. As I have suggested elsewhere, universities are not the most flexible or responsive institutions, and properly so. To a very large extent, what goes on within them is of intrinsic worth, and not merely a means to economic or politically defined ends. Their concerns with basic research, first principles and time-less questions, their very distance from the flux of events, make them a supremely important source of fundamental innovations in thought, as well as increasingly important conservators of social values and standards. But societies have immediate problems as well as long-range interests; and the immediate problems, both social and technological, increasingly call for more trained intelligence. British universities will indeed accept the elite forms of 'vocational training' as they have the handful of CATs and a few top schools of business administration. At a sufficiently lofty level, close enough to science or top industrial management, such studies are no longer even perceived as 'vocational training', and join medicine and law as appropriate studies for university men. But it is the unsanctified social and technical studies that will not find room within the British universities for all the enormous expansion that they are undergoing. These include a large part of both technological and applied social studies: social welfare, criminology, social administration, education, for example. These studies are *represented* in the universities, but are not likely to flourish and grow there. From the point of view of national needs, the Government cannot *count* on the universities to make adequate provision for research and training in these rapidly growing professions.

And they cannot be forced to do so. The genuine autonomy of the universities is protected not only by their own traditions and position in the society, but also by the UGC buffer. It is true that Government interests can be registered and will be reflected in university policy, but largely through the universities' readiness to respond to certain kinds of interests which they take to be legitimate. For example the UGC accepts the Government's interests in efficiency of operation, in non-duplication of expensive facilities, or in a shift in the distribution of students as between arts and science. But the influence of the Government on the universities is very limited, and relatively slow in operation. The Government is naturally concerned with short-run national problems —the provision of adequate numbers of teachers and engineers, for example—while the universities are concerned with scholarship and basic scientific work, whose immediate contributions to the nation's economic and social problems are relatively slight or invisible. But despite the fact that the universities get almost all their funds from the Government, both their traditions and government allow them to defend their academic freedom against short-run utilitarian criteria; and in this they have the approval, or at least the acquiescence, of all political parties, But therefore, as Crosland made clear in his Woolwich speech, despite their dependence on public funds, the 'autonomous' universities could not be considered part of 'public' higher education. When he speaks of the 'public' system of higher education 'under social control and directly responsive to social needs', he means a set of institutions whose responsiveness to the needs of their local community is assured by their being under the authority of the local and national governments who exercise their joint authority through externally appointed governing bodies, through direct control over college finances, and through the supervision of their courses of study by the Department of Education and Science, in conjunction with national boards (especially the CNAA) set up by the Department.

The transfer of an institution from local authority to the autonomous sector immediately puts it outside the direct influence of the Department and local interests. This is reason enough for both the Department and local authorities to oppose their loss of the institutions which they created and nurtured. It is also true that the Department would meet considerable opposition from the organized local educational officers, representing local authorities, if any substantial number of 'their' institutions were taken out of their control. But while the question of authority for its own sake is undoubtedly a political consideration, it is the concern with the preservation of genuinely 'vocational' institutions, that lies behind much of the feeling for the binary solution.

The question of relative costs is also involved. It is not only that the universities are by and large snobbish about vocational studies. It is also that their costs are so much higher than those of the 'non-autonomous' institutions that this alone places a real constraint on very rapid expansion within the university sector. Differences in operating costs between the universities and the institutions of 'further education' (not including teacher training colleges), can be seen in figures provided in the National Plan. For the year 1964–5 current expenditures of all types for further education in England, Wales and Scotland (including student stipends) was £126m. There were many different kinds of students in those roughly 150 institutions, but all together they were equivalent to 578,000 full-time students. The average expenditure per full-time equivalent in these non-autonomous institutions was a bit under £220. During the same year there were about 156,000 students enrolled in the 42 British universities and CATS whose operating expenses and student stipends came to £140m, an average of about £900 per student.[4]

But the question of relative costs of higher education is of course more complicated than this. One difficulty is that not all students in further education are 'advanced', that is on courses comparable with university courses. Another is how to count part-time students, the bulk of whom, of course, are in further education. The Robbins Committee, in making its rough estimates, distinguished between part-time day students in the universities, two of whom were taken as equivalent to one full-time student, and part-time day students in further education, five of whom added up to one full-time equivalent. Even on this formula, the Committee estimated the costs per student per annum for 1962–3, in different kinds of institutions, thus: universities, £660; training colleges, £255; advanced further education, £477. These differences are not nearly as great as those derived from the figures in the Plan, but are still appreciable.[5]

The status question

I do not want to minimize the questions of control and costs as factors lying behind the Department's strong defence of the binary system (which incidentally is also supported by the Tory shadow Minister for Education, Sir Edward Boyle, but for different reasons).[6] But if we look at what the 'unitary' spokesmen, notable among them being Lord Robbins himself, really want, it is not incompatible with the continued existence of a large network of sub-university institutions, remaining under the control of local authorities and the Department. Robbins talks of no more than another ten institutions promoted to university status over the next decade.[7] And he favours a larger number of 'arrangements' between colleges of technology or art or design, and a nearby university.[8] But as important in the debate as the issue of control or the higher costs of universities over further education is the principle of institutional mobility for the deserving into what would remain clearly understood to be the highest stratum of British educational institutions, the universities in the autonomous sector. For the acceptance of that principle would affect motivations and calculations and directions of development right through the system of further education, almost regardless of the actual numbers of successfully mobile. If upgrading is even remotely possible through the efforts of the institution, and if the criteria for 'advancement' would be the legitimate and universally accepted criteria of academic standards fairly applied (as they surely would be), then there is no doubt that many men and many institutions would hold the university as the model of emulation, and approach it, in so far as they were able in their curricula, their staff, their standards for admission, their institutional character and climate. And many more institutions would be affected this way than had any realistic hope of elevation: such is the nature of status systems.

It is this liberal conception of individual mobility for the deserving within a pre-established and unchallenged status system that Crosland rejected:[9]

> The Government accepts this dual system as being fundamentally the right one, with each sector making its own distinctive contribution to the whole. We infinitely prefer it to the alternative concept of a unitary system, hierarchically arranged on the 'ladder' principle, with the universities at the top and the other institutions down below. Such a system would be characterized by a continuous rat-race to reach the first or university division, a constant pressure on those below to ape the universities above, and a certain inevitable failure to achieve the diversity in higher education which contemporary society needs.

If we read that statement, and reread the second and fourth paragraphs in Crosland's statement quoted earlier, through American eyes, and with American universities in mind, we may be forgiven some confusion. Why, for example, must 'a system based on the ladder concept ... inevitably depress and degrade both morale and standards in the non-university sector'? And why should the translation of 'every college which achieves high standards ... into the University Club' leave the 'residual public sector' a 'permanent poor relation perpetually deprived of its brightest ornaments, and with a permanent and openly inferior status'? The very oddness, to the American ear, of such assertions about the psychology of British higher education, coming from such a knowledgeable and responsible source, hints at the profound differences which underlie our respective conceptions of higher education. And it points not only to differences in our educational conceptions, but also to the differing patterns of class and political relations of the two societies which shape their conceptions of education. 'Let us move away from our snobbish caste-ridden hierarchical obsession with university status,' says the chief minister of education in a Socialist Government (himself, incidentally, a winner of first class honours in the oldest of British universities). And we catch a sense of the moral and political feeling underlying this debate over what might appear to be mere administrative arrangements.

Crosland was not just attacking some proposed administrative arrangements which he found inconvenient, and proposing another set which would give him more leverage over parts of the system of higher education, to achieve such specific goals as, say, more technologists for less money. That concern is present in the binary policy, as Crosland and other defenders of the Government's policy have made clear: they are worried about further education in a unitary system being in part assimilated, in part colonized by the universities. (They clearly believe, for example, that if the teacher training colleges had been taken over by the universities, as Robbins recommended, the Government could not have got the marked increase in teacher production that it has been able to achieve in the past years.) But much more fundamentally, Crosland was attacking the status system of British higher education, a system of differential prestige and rewards that has strong historical roots, and is linked to and buttressed by the systems of prestige, power and wealth in the larger society. And his attack is not merely in words but also through deeds: he has ended, at least for the duration of the present Government, the possibility of institutional mobility into the autonomous sector; and he has established an alternative extra-university degree-granting machinery which he means to be 'comparable in standard and quality with a university course'.

The Government wants a large and growing sector of non-university institutions which will be the basis of a system of mass higher education, centring on (but not exclusively devoted to) the acquisition, application and dissemination of useful knowledge, linked both administratively and informally with private industry and local and national authorities who will employ their products, proud of its distinctive character as the 'modern' sector of higher education, no longer worshipping the false gods of the university honours degree and the university prestige. Can the effort succeed, given the distribution of power and prestige in British society? What will result from efforts to achieve it? What price will be paid, in the long and in the short run, in trying to achieve it? Is it not possible, as some opponents claim, that to bar institutional mobility will be to create just the second class system that Crosland wants to destroy, a truly and permanently second class system, with all the dingy overtones of deference, resentment, and lack of self-respect that notion conveys, and not least in British history and society?

The binary policy: conservative or radical?

The binary-unitary issue cuts across the spectrum of British political sentiment in interesting and revealing ways. The Robbins Report gained support from the great bulk of forward-looking and progressive people in both parties. Its attack was on the reactionary view that the pool of university standard talent was small and fixed, and that, as Kingsley Amis put it, 'more means worse'. This view was very widely held in the academic world itself, even after Robbins, as a current study of British university teachers shows.[10] Moreover, apart from the issue of numbers, the Robbins Report also appeared as progressive in its persuasive argument that the way to break the monopoly of prestige held by university and non-vocational studies was not by the establishment of an alternative institutional and prestige system, but by dilution, by the gradual incorporation of more vocationally oriented institutions into the university system (of which the immediate elevation of the ten CATs was symbol and example), and by the encouragement of varied and close relations between the universities and other non-U institutions. For example, Robbins urged the incorporation of training colleges into the universities as associated colleges of education, which might, in the Robbins vision, evolve toward liberal arts colleges, or broaden their work to include other forms of vocational training at a higher level. He also imagined close ties of various kinds between technical and regional colleges and nearby CATs and universities.

Robbins himself is a liberal; his support comes also from liberal Conservatives, moderate Socialists, and Liberals. Ironically, the Government's policy is supported also by quite conservative people, in part because it recognizes and makes permanent the distinction between the academic education for gentlemen provided in the universities and the vocational education for 'other ranks' offered by the institutions for further education. Lord Aberdare, a staunch Conservative Peer, and defender of the public schools, observed in a debate in the Lords that on the matter of the binary policy:[11]

> I find myself in greater sympathy with the Government than with the noble Lord, Lord Robbins ... It seems to me that, basically, there has always been a dual approach to higher education and it is really a matter of where one draws the line. In their recommendations, the Robbins Committee themselves singled out ten regional colleges for university status. This would have left many regional and area colleges with higher grade status, but still without university status. I think that one has to draw the line somewhere. The noble Lord [Robbins] himself instanced himself a number of exaggerated claims from a variety of different colleges seeking university status, and I think this points to the difficulties that there will always be wherever one draws the line; but I believe that there really are excellent arguments for preserving the technical colleges in their present set-up ... Many a student who might not have been suited in a university type education has found his way to higher education through a technical college.

And agreeing also with the Government's decision to leave control over the colleges of education in the hands of the local authorities and outside the university system, he observes that 'I do not feel that they are really academic institutions in that sense of the term. They are there for vocational study ...' This is basically a defence of the differences in status between academic studies and vocational studies, and an expression of the 'snobbish caste-ridden hierarchical obsession with University status' that Crosland attacked so spiritedly in his Woolwich speech.

This characteristic of the binary system, that from one perspective it can be seen as a defence of the academic character of the university system as the summit of the system of higher education, against the contamination of vocational studies, leaves it open to liberal attacks from Robbins and others. Robbins observes that the binary plan in part reflects misconceptions about the nature of the modern university, misconceptions that 'still drift about the corridors of the Department (of Education and Science)'.

> For instance, there still seem to be a considerable number of people who conceive of the life of a modern university as of some community of pure scholar-students pursuing their work regardless of its bearing on their subsequent careers, and of staff having the sole duty of inculcating appropriate habits of thought and advancing knowledge with no practical application ... Of course if you have this kind of conception you will wish to keep the universities free of any contamination with everyday life and anything vocational.[12]

And Robbins goes on to argue for the appropriateness of vocational studies in the university, citing the United States as a useful model in this respect. And another liberal critic, the Vice-Chancellor of the University of Aston (formerly the Birmingham CAT), argues that the binary conception:[13]

> presupposes a distinction between the vocational and the fundamental in technological education which belongs to the 19th century ... The point is not to freeze the gap between the study of science and its application but to close it. Unless those colleges placed by the Minister in the public sector are able to foster the development of fundamental science as well as its application, their graduates will never be able to anticipate new technological developments, but will become merely high-grade technicians. In this respect, over-emphasis on vocational education in a separate sector with a separate outlook would only succeed in maintaining its present deplorable lack of status.

But to this liberal criticism of the binary system the Government can reply that it is merely rhetoric which gives the impression that only it stands between the universities and their transformation into a modern comprehensive university system, offering a range of academic and vocational subjects in intimate and fruitful relation to one another. But unfortunately, it might reply, the universities have no intention of transforming themselves into American land-grant universities devoted to social service and useful skills and knowledge. It might observe that Robbins recommended the elevation of only ten additional regional colleges over the next decade, and that. with some few exceptions, the existing universities will not modify their character to throw their doors open to large numbers of vocationally oriented students and subjects.

Mr Crosland certainly conveyed a distaste for the deeply felt assumptions of superiority by the universities, and a dislike for their readiness to accept an occasional new recruit from those among the ranks who have shown themselves worthy. In his view, only if the possibilities for institutional mobility were cut off could the non-autonomous institutions settle down to defining their own character as technological and vocational institutions of high standard, and to acquiring self-respect without regard to the inappropriate standards and models of the universities. He evidently believed that the majority of university people want little or nothing to do with local institutions. And even if 'arrangements' and connections were made with institutes and colleges, the Government fears that universities would restrain their independent growth, or distort their purposes, making little contained branches of the university out of useful technical institutes. The Department may currently accept these arrangements where they are desired on both sides and made evident sense in terms of shared interests or complementary programmes, but with a notable lack of enthusiasm. So far as the colleges of technology are concerned, they are clearly concerned that such 'arrangements' will weaken the Department's efforts to make the CNAA a stable and prestigious degree. Every area and regional college, they fear, will want to become or form a university, and the CNAA will be permanently downgraded into a second class degree. Moreover, continuous pressure on the Department to allow 'promotions' would be degrading to the colleges involved, and also would create pressures very difficult to deal with, since they would involve continuous public invidious judgments of institutional quality and character.

Problems of an administered status system

But this last point raises again the spectre of academic status, and in the special and intransigent form of an administered status system. Within the binary system, so long as the 'public' sector has not yet achieved parity of esteem with the university system, there will be men and institutions that look across the divide to institutions that seem no more distinguished than they, and yet which command larger resources, higher salaries, and greater prestige. And they can believe that they are prevented from gaining entrance to the university system not by their own limitations, or the accidents of a stingy local authority or a bad location, but by the decisions of men. And that is the prescription for discontent, resentment and low morale.

The problems of administering a status system are intertwined with the functions of institutions and their costs as well. The institutions of the 'public' sector can only gain parity of esteem, in British terms, if they have parity of support, working conditions and amenities. A committee of the Association of Teachers in Technical Institutions points out reasonably enough that:

'One of the most important issues facing the CNAA is the development of higher degrees and especially of higher degrees based upon research. Higher education depends for its vitality upon the interaction of teaching and research. The teaching staff cannot keep themselves at the forefront of their own studies unless they themselves are involved to some extent in pushing the frontiers of their own subject further into the unknown. Higher education cannot be led from behind: and if the teaching staff of the regional colleges are not themselves engaged in research, they will not be able to bring professional men and women up to date in their professional knowledge or perform many of the other tasks we have envisaged for them.'[14]

That is all true; it is also very expensive. Advanced degrees and research, especially in science and technology, are immensely costly. And yet if the 'public sector' is to have a genuine parity of esteem, and escape the stigma of narrow vocational training of technicians, it must provide such facilities for at least some of its institutions. But which ones? In a publicly supported system, with common salary schedules, common levels of support, etc., there is very little room for the achievement of high distinction largely through self-help and free enterprise. The decisions about the support for higher degrees and advanced research, necessary to break the status pre-eminence of the universities, will necessarily be made by the Department—and that is to create an admin-istered status system. But on what bases, on what criteria, and with what success? The aspirations are not lacking among the technical colleges and, ironically, one of the reasons given for the binary system with its bars to promotion was the lofty and 'unrealistic' ambitions of technical colleges, and the necessity, in the national interest, of keeping those ambitions under control. Speaking of the power of 'intellectual emulation', Lord Annan, a Labour supporter in the Lords, observed:[15]

Every place wants to be a first-rate place, the kind of place which will have a department in it which might conceivably attract funds from the Research Councils; and it is this intellectual emulation which I think brings about the process that every university and every institution of higher education in the country tries to approach the level of the very highest universities in the country. As a result, we get colleges of advanced technology wanting to become as eminent as the Imperial College, in Prince Consort Road. We get regional technical colleges wishing to give university degrees, as the colleges of advanced technology will now be able to do; and there is the danger, with this, of every civic university wanting to have a social science degree of the same standard and standing as that of the London School of Economics . . .

There is a danger, also, of regional technical colleges wanting to shed their ordinary degree work and qualify for university status by teaching only for honours degrees . . . When one of the colleges of advanced technology was being transformed into a technological university . . . two-thirds of the staff petitioned the Privy Council to drop the word 'technology' from the title.

This is one of the causes why the Secretary of State is worried about breaking the binary system as it existed before the Robbins Report was issued and as it exists today.

So emulation is not only a power for raising in-stitutional standards and aspirations; it is also a powerful subversive force that makes men and institutions want to be what they are not, and to make demands for resources and statuses that will allow them to become what they wish to be. And that is not only a heavy drain on the nation's resources, but also, in this view, threatens to distract them from the necessary if humbler functions appropriate to their academic station in life.

The fear, and it is clearly based on some reality is, that the prospect or hope of promotion would lead would-be mobile technical colleges to slough off their technical and vocational courses, both because they are not part of the university model, and because they are low status, lower in repute and dignity than 'liberal studies', hopelessly stained by sweat and long association with industry and the working class. This is a constant danger in a class-linked educational system in which 'useful', despite fashionable dis-claimers, is still a pejorative term in academic circles.

But that problem is not solved by the barriers of the binary system. Even if elevation to autonomous (university) status is barred, institutions will want to climb the ladder within their own sphere. As Lord Annan noted in this same speech, the regional and area colleges that have come within the CNAA system are increasingly teaching for honours degrees: 'Here again, the tendency is always to push forward towards the very highest status in higher education, and this, of course, has effects which it seems to me every Secretary of State must consider.' Emulation, and the powerful drive to gain academic prestige, in a society in which status is enormously important, is from the Department's point of view as much a problem as a source of academic excellence.

This concern, that technical colleges would tend to develop inappropriate ambitions, is of long standing. For example, C. T. Millis, Principal of the Borough Polytechnic, wrote in 1925 complaining that 'some of the polytechnics have been allowed and encouraged to drop some of their proper work and to take up Higher and University work for which they were not intended'.[16] Behind this concern there were two quite different objections, which still persist: first, that to strive for the status and curriculum of the universities would be to subvert the true character of the technical colleges: second that these 'higher' studies are 'in-appropriate' for the lower classes. Something of both is present in Quintin Hogg's answer to the criticism that he neglected cultural subjects in his Regent Street Polytechnic: 'I do not include the subjects you men-tion for fear of attracting a class of young men of a higher educational status than those for whom the institute was intended.'[17]

Attitudes in the technical colleges towards the binary system are, predictably, mixed. Some welcome the Department's clear interest in non-university in-stitutions as an alternative 'public' sector of higher education, with its own functions and form of distinc-tion. And it is to the promises implicit in that support that the committee of the Association of Teachers in Technical Institutes, quoted above, appeal. But others in the technical colleges look at present realities and are bitter at the ending of hopes of translation to the autonomous sphere. They complain that they do not have the autonomy of the universities; their accounts and academic programmes are closely scrutinized and modified by 'minor officials' in the local authority; their salaries are lower; their teaching loads higher;

amenities poorer than in universities; they lose their best students to the universities; their staff members are stigmatized as 'tech instructors' and lose the possibility of individual mobility into the university system; and most broadly of all, that the binary system, in a hierarchical society ridden by dual systems, perpetuates a class linked duality comprising a middle and upper class university system and a working and lower middle class system of further education.

It is easy for Americans to suggest their own alternative—that is, to bring large numbers and varied kinds of institutions within the 'autonomous' fold, and allow the unseen hand, with some Government help, to sort out the kinds and varieties of courses offered and functions performed by each. This breaks the monopoly of a small group of universities on academic and social prestige by diluting the prestige of university status, on one hand, and by throwing up innumerable challengers to various kinds of preeminence. It blurs the status distinctions (and differences in function) between a low cost system of mass education and the more expensive, usually more selective, and academically more distinguished forms of higher education by creating a long continuum along which institutions are 'free' to move, and where their position is a function of many contingencies rather than the result of a set of identifiable administrative regulations and decisions. But this American pattern, which is in part a consequence of extreme decentralization of support and authority for higher education, is simply a 'non-starter' in Britain.

The British, like most continental countries, must move toward mass higher education through centralized, and visible, governmental machinery. The British universities can be thought of as the campuses of a University of Great Britain. The binary issue is in part an argument about whether there is to be one national university or two; and if two, what the relation between them will be.

The centralizing forces in British academic life take many forms in the instruments of control and finance. But they also are reflected within the academic world itself, in the defence of 'standards'. If one were to try to identify one aspect of British higher education which 'stands for' the complex of historical, institution and normative factors preventing the adoption of an American pattern of higher education in Great Britain, it might be the nature of the bachelor's degree, of high and approximately uniform standard throughout the system of higher education. It is what distinguishes the 'graduate' from everyone else, and is still a distinction of considerable importance for one's self-conception and life chances. (For example, graduates who enter teaching start at about £200 a year more than non-graduates doing the same job—and the graduates tend to get and hold better jobs.)

The defence of the degree—its significance, and its high and uniform standard—carries a great many consequences in its train. First, it means that the degree can only be awarded under certain academic conditions: a staff, equipment, amenities, of high (and expensive) standard. Moreover, the equality of institutions within each system awarding 'the degree' means that in principle (and to a high degree in practice) all institutions have an equal claim on resources, and are so treated by the UGC or the Department. Within each system, the 'autonomous' and the 'public', there is a national salary scale; a common minimum requirement for student admission; a common system of student stipends; common formulas for the provision of facilities, and so on. Of course, one university or technical college is not a carbon copy of another; and the UGC and Department reserve the right to restrict work in this special and expensive field to these institutions, denying it to those. And of course some institutions are stronger than others in this or that department, or even across the board. But the differences within each system are perhaps of the range of the differences among the campuses of the University of California, all of which occupy a narrow band in the whole spectrum of variation (in costs, quality, and performance) of all American higher education.

The supporters of a unitary system speak of a single unified system within which institutions can achieve their own level and function, and they even draw analogies with the American system. But they are as committed to the defence of the university degree as anyone, and that immediately ensures first, that the number of institutions that can actually gain university status will necessarily be small, and second, that the number of students ever gaining university entrance must continue to be relatively small.

The English are very proud of their bachelor's degree, and with reason. But they never consider the cost of maintaining an undergraduate degree of high and uniform standard. But the costs are there, and they are high. For example:

It helps prevent the emergence of a unified system of higher education, including vocational, academic and professional studies, in a wide range of standards. It is enormously expensive in staff time. This not only keeps staff-student ratios, and costs, high, thus restricting numbers. It also focuses energies and attention on undergraduate education, and contributes to the complex of factors hindering the development of post-graduate training on a large scale. That in turn inhibits the development of new subjects and subdisciplines. The focus on the first degree (and thus on undergraduate education) is a powerful conservative force in British education.

It sustains an important and divisive status symbol, ostensibly rooted in intellectual distinction and academic achievement, and thus defensible in a democratic age. University status becomes part of the machinery whereby differences in social origins translate themselves into achieved status, and thus legitimize themselves.

The commitment to the preservation of the character and standards of the university degree, and thus of the present university system, is one aspect of the problem the supporters of the unitary system do not discuss. Their liberal rhetoric, of an academic universe open to talents and self-help, is an attractive one, especially to Americans when we overlook the differences in our institutional circumstances. And the arguments that surround it are genuinely progressive and liberating in the face of a traditional system which asserts, more by practice than words, the principle of a caste system in higher education, of an unbridgeable gulf between the worlds of pure and applied studies, of scholarship and science on one hand and practice on the other, of gentlemen and players, of intellectual and 'other' kinds of talents. To Americans especially, the reduction of formal and administered distinctions, the lowering of barriers, the encouragement of institutional and individual mobility, the creation of *ad hoc* relations among varied kinds of institutions around a common interest and job, are all more attractive than the formal barriers and rigidities and inevitable absurdities and difficulties inherent in the binary system. But the principles on which the unitary position is based and the rhetoric in which it is argued are attractive only in so far as we ignore the real limitations on its application under British conditions, limitations inherent *both* in the values and commitments of its adherents and in the realities and necessities of British higher education and the society at large.

The supporters of Robbins may have the best of the arguments; the Department is left with the realities.

But the realities which justify (and perhaps require) a binary system in the short run may be creating a system which threatens to perpetuate just the caste system, just the prejudices and snobberies and hierarchies, that are Britain's greatest social handicap, and one that Crosland would most like to destroy.

His goal and the country's need is a system of higher education, of large size and varied standard, freed from class prejudice and snobbery, creating and disseminating knowledge both for its own sake and for its varied uses. The expansion of useful studies, given the costs and values of British universities, appears to require a large non-university system. To give that system a chance to find its own character, an artificial barrier to the elevation of a minority of those institutions has been raised. But the resulting system, and its degree-granting machinery, will be hard put to gain prestige and self-respect. If it does not, if it acquires (or retains) the habits of mind, the budgets, the students and staff, the deference and resentments of a second class system, then the Government, with the best of motives, may be locking the future into the institutional arrangements of the past. Yet the unitary policy for all the attractiveness of its rhetoric, accepts at the apex of its academic hierarchy a university system that has not, by and large, made generous provision for technical and vocational studies itself, has not respected the men and institutions that have, and is not likely to change very quickly in either respect. This is the Government's dilemma, and the dilemma of British higher education.

Notes

1 From the speech by the then Secretary of State for Education and Science Anthony Crosland, at Woolwich Polytechnic, 27 April 1965.

2 George L. Payne, *Britain's Scientific and Technological Manpower* (Stanford University Press 1960), 154.

3 *Technology and the Universities* (Macmillan 1958), 65, 66.

4 Figures from the *National Plan*, Cmd 2764 (HMSO 1965), chapter 21 'Education'. For a defence of the binary system on the grounds of the cost of university education, see the speech by Lord Wynne-Jones, House of Lords, 1 December 1965.

5 Robbins Report, Appendix iv, Table 17, 109.

6 See his speech in the House of Commons, 26 January 1966, and Mr Reg Prentice's speech in the same debate.

7 See, for example, Lord Robbins, *The University in the Modern World* (Macmillan 1966), 148.

8 See the discussions of the binary issue by Professor

Boris Ford and Sir Peter Venables in *Universities Quarterly* (December 1965).

9 Crosland, Woolwich.

10 A. H. Halsey and Martin Trow, *The British Academics* (Faber, 1971).

11 House of Lords, 1 December 1965.

12 *Universities Quarterly* (December 1965), 9.

13 Sir Peter Venables, quoted by Boris Ford in the *New Statesman*, 21 January 1966.

14 *The Future of Higher Education within the Further Education System* (report of the higher education panel of the Association of Teachers in Technical Institutions), March 1965, 15.

15 House of Lords, 1 December 1965.

16 Quoted by S. F. Cotgrove, *Technical Education and Social Change* (Allen & Unwin 1958), 63.

17 Ibid.

45 Polytechnics

Tyrrell Burgess and John Pratt

Numbers

The establishment of polytechnics announced in the Government's White Paper of 1966,[1] was certainly bound up with meeting the demand for places in higher education. In the six years from 1961–2 to 1967–8 the number of students in full-time higher education in Great Britain[2] grew from 193,000 to 376,000,[3] and this increase in absolute numbers was greater than in the previous century. The unprecedented expansion was a consequence of the Government's response to the demand for places after the publication of the Robbins Report[4] which had acted both as a guide to the Government and as a stimulant to both demand and the will to accommodate it. But the basis of the increased demand for places was the coincidence of what have become known as the 'bulge' (the increase in the number of young people of relevant age due to the post-war surge in births) and the 'trend' (the growing proportion of the age group getting school leaving qualifications).

When the Robbins Committee was appointed the provision of university places had for some years grown more slowly than the relevant group of school leavers, so the latter's opportunities proportionally declined. There was no clear policy on how to respond to the growing number of applicants. It was the achievement of the Robbins Committee to supply a philosophy for expansion. It said that ratio of entrants to the output of those with two or more passes at GCE 'A' level should remain constant. The Committee than translated this principle into numbers on the basis of pretty conservative assumptions. As the Committee itself thought likely, the proportion of the age group getting two or more 'A' levels rose from 6·9 in 1961 to 9·6 in 1966 not to 8·4 per cent as Robbins assumed.

So the number of leavers with relevant qualifications was 26 per cent higher than assumed, only six years from the base year. And the difference was due not so much to greater numbers in schools as to greater numbers getting two or more A levels. What is interesting is that the difference between the assumed and actual rate of growth was much greater for girls than for boys. The Government accepted the Robbins Committee's quantitative recommendations with a speed at least partly induced by the forthcoming general election. For the universities this meant a 40 per cent increase over four years to 197,000 places. The universities actually offered to accommodate

10 per cent more than required but in the event they met the target almost exactly. Unfortunately this was not enough to meet the Robbins' principle—even though it did meet the Robbins' numbers. This was because the number of qualified school leavers had risen—so the ratio of entrants to leavers fell by about 15 per cent.

In contrast to this the two other main sectors of higher education, the colleges of education (for teacher training) and the colleges of further education, have expanded remarkably. In the colleges of education the Robbins' recommendations have been exceeded by 25 per cent by 1967–8.

Our main concern here is with further education . . . This sector has in some respects always been regarded as a 'safety valve'—taking those who were able to do a course of higher education but for some reason had not got into a university. This might be because of a shortage of places or because the applicants had unacceptable qualifications. The Robbins Committee thought that as more people went to university and colleges of education, the entry rate to further education would fall. In the event it rose. In 1968 it was well above the Robbins' recommendations.

The reasons for these differences from Robbins are highly complex. One was the simple administrative point that in expansion a Government has to work on numbers, not principles. The assumptions about 'A' level were seriously falsified in 5 years, but by then the planning based on the numbers had been done. It is easy to forget now, too, that by previous standards Robbins was recommending a stunning expansion: over 80 per cent by 1973–4 for all higher education. It would be unrealistic to expect Governments to do more, even though the Committee emphasized the conservatism of its assumptions.

But there was the further factor that a change of Government in 1964 has encouraged a change of attitude. The 1966 White Paper[5] spoke of 'developing a distinctive sector of higher education within the further education system to complement the universities and colleges of education'. Once this had been decided the attempt to keep the expansion of universities in line with the Robbins' principles became, to put it mildly, much less urgent.

There were, according to the White Paper, 40,000 full-time and sandwich students on advanced courses at further education colleges in England and Wales. Of these, nearly 12,000 were working for degrees and 8,000 for HNDs. Over 100.000 students were taking advanced courses part-time, 2,500 of them for degrees and 50,000 for HNCs. All but one of the regional

Source: Technical Education in the United Kingdom, Paris, OECD (1971), 89–103.

colleges were offering full-time degree courses as were 30 of the area colleges and colleges of commerce. Some 40 colleges of art were engaged in advanced work. The volume of advanced work varied from college to college; 25 of them had more than 500 full-time students, seven had more than 1,000. Eight had more than 500 full-time degree students, nine had fewer than 50. And these figures did not include large numbers of students taking courses which were higher than 'A' level in standard but lower than degree level.

Quoting the National Plan,[6] the White Paper said that by 1969–70 there should be 70,000 full-time (including sandwich) advanced students in further education, compared with Robbins' 51,000 by 1973–4. Over 60,000 of these places were to be in England and Wales.[7] The Government would try to concentrate advanced work in 30 polytechnics ... It sought to preserve the technical college tradition, to give professional and technical education a high status, to give opportunities to part-time students, to have a sector of higher education under public administration, particularly of the local authorities, to avoid the permanent depression of the technical colleges which would follow from a single hierarchical system. The educational distinction of the colleges, that they should be 'comprehensive academic communities' accommodating students 'at all levels of higher education', will be discussed later. For the moment it is enough to say that the Government took advantage of the opportunity offered by the growing demand for higher education to introduce a new concept and new institutions.

There were to be 28 polytechnics selected,[8] of which six were single existing colleges of technology. The rest were to be made up of neighbouring colleges of technology, art, commerce and so on. The geographical spread was fair, at least so far as centres of population were concerned. (The north-east, which had failed to get a CAT, got three polytechnics). But there were places where the new polytechnics seemed to be replacing the 'lost' CATs. Manchester (Salford), Birmingham, Bristol, Treforest (Cardiff) and other places where the polytechnics were alongside new universities—Coventry (Warwick) and Brighton (Sussex). Some areas were still without polytechnics, Humberside and East Anglia, for example. Altogether, including London, just over half the polytechnics were in university towns.

These polytechnics are to be the main centres for the development of full-time higher education within the further education system, and it is not intended to add to their list for at least ten years. The object is to reduce substantially the number of colleges engaged in full-time higher education, and colleges not already engaged in higher education are not expected to embark on it. On the other hand colleges not designated as polytechnics would continue to offer full-time courses in higher education where they satisfied the criteria for their approval.

The size of individual polytechnics would necess-

arily vary, since they were made up in different ways. But the polytechnics were expected to have long-term plans for growth to at least 2,000 full-time students, plus part-time students from the areas they serve. It is of course too early to say how far the expectations of concentration and growth have been fulfilled ...

The technical colleges have traditionally attempted to accommodate the sons and daughters of manual workers and others who were rejected by the selective route to universities. Perhaps the major effort in the polytechnics was to offer substantial opportunity to part-time students. As the then Secretary of State for Education and Science said[9] 'There are tens of thousands of part-time students who need advanced courses either to supplement other qualifications or because for one reason or another they missed the full-time route. There are immense fields of talent and aspiration here; common justice and social need combine to demand that they should be harvested'.

Hitherto part-time students have been thought of as a sort of residual. The Robbins Committee was not even required to consider them by its terms of reference ...

The establishment of the polytechnics was perhaps the first official recognition of the needs of part-time students at the highest levels. It showed a determination to create institutions which would at the same time be of high standing and performance and treat part-time studies as a permanent and important part of their work in their own right.

Contents and structure of studies specialization

The major educational contribution of the polytechnics is likely to be the extension of sandwich courses and the purposes of professional education from the technologies to the social sciences. This is being achieved through the expanded CNAA. Even in 1965 the Woolwich polytechnic in London had pioneered sandwich courses in business studies at honours-degree level. The Enfield College of Technology (to be part of a polytechnic in north London) has sandwich courses in mathematics for business and in social science. For the former the students spend an integrated part of their time in industry, in the latter they go into social work, child care, national and local government offices, industry and planning departments for their 'industrial experience', according to their speciality. The notion of mathematicians and economists spending part of their course in firms is still somewhat shocking—but welcome: even the dropouts from the mathematics course are commanding high initial salaries.

A second educational contribution of the colleges is in offering courses below degree level. As Mr Crosland said:[10]

It is here that the colleges meet the needs of the thousands of young people who will occupy the all important intermediate posts in industry, business and the professions—the high-level technicians and middle managers who must support the scientists, technologists and top managers in a modern community. These students both for their own sake and for obvious social and economic reasons, must have a full share of the resources of the colleges, and not be neglected through preoccupation with the (degree level) category of student.

This, at any rate is the theory, but the Government have scarcely backed it in practice. If it was policy to accommodate this lower level work in the polytechnics one would expect the Government to encourage it in every possible way; in salaries for example. At the end of 1967, salaries of staff in further education were referred to an arbitral body after the breakdown of the Burnham negotiations. The question arose whether the salaries in polytechnics should be comparable with those in universities. The representatives of the DES and the local authorities argued that:[11]

> Higher education was not synonymous with work at university level, and a high proportion of the work in polytechnics . . . would be below degree standard. In some of the polytechnics, moreover, a certain proportion of work which was below the level of higher education would be continuing at least for some years to come. The proportion of post-graduate to undergraduate work was never likely to approach that which was commonly found in universities; nor was the amount of effort devoted to research. The comparison was not a comparison of like with like, and it was therefore reasonable that there should be differences in salaries.

The lesson was very clear. If the staff of polytechnics were to improve their salaries they must become like the universities and drop lower level work. The Government was telling them that the polytechnics' road to better salaries was to reverse Government policy. This kind of action over matters of salary is a far more effective influence on what actually happens in the colleges than any amount of policy statements and White Papers, and in this respect the Department can be said to be virtually promoting the collapse of its own policy.

A third contribution was to accommodate growing numbers of arts and social science students. This arose from the swing away from science in the sixth forms of schools, and it was reflected in the numbers of entrants to higher education. The Dainton Report[12] showed that between 1962 and 1966 entrants to arts and social science faculties of universities increased by 58 per cent and to technology faculties by 35 per cent. In the colleges of further education there was a similarly greater increase in courses other than in science and technology. The numbers entering advanced full-time (including sandwich) courses in subjects other than science and technology rose from 3,700 in 1961 to 7,900 in 1965, compared with an increase from 4,000 to 7,000 in science and technology. The non-science entrants had surpassed science entrants, and the proportion of the total taking science and technology fell from 52 per cent to 47 per cent.[13]

So far from becoming specialized institutions, the polytechnics were extending their range. Liberal and business studies were joined by sociology and economics. In a number of colleges of technology the arts and social science staff were suggesting that the 'of technology' should be dropped from the title. This caused a good deal of irritation and defensiveness among their technological colleagues.

Organizational structures

The 1966 White Paper said it would be a condition of designation for a polytechnic that the arrangements for government and academic organization were consistent with those recommended by the Secretary of State. Subsequently legislation was introduced to provide for the making by local education authorities of instruments and articles of government for the governing bodies of maintained colleges of education and of technical and other colleges of further education.[14] In *Notes for Guidance* on the government and academic organization of polytechnics the Secretary of State said[15] 'that the polytechnics should have suitably constituted governing bodies with a large measure of autonomy'.

He added that the polytechnics must of course operate within national policies and within limits set by the financial and legal responsibilities of the local education authority. The Secretary of State would determine the number of polytechnics and coordinate development throughout the system through his control of building programmes and the approval of courses; he would continue to set and enforce minimum standards. The salary and grading structures for the academic staff would also be settled under national arrangements. The local authorities, within national policies, would settle the broad range of courses to be provided. They would retain their controls in financial and administrative matters such as the approval of estimates, capital development and level of fees.

However, within limits set by national policy and dependence on public finance, the polytechnics were to be given all possible freedom in managing themselves with the minimum detailed control by the maintaining authorities.

The *Notes for Guidance* suggested that a polytechnic's governing body should be a balanced and broadly based one, composed of: representatives of the maintaining local education authority; members from neighbouring local authorities supplying part-time students; a strong representation from industry, commerce and the professions; the director[16] of the polytechnic *ex officio* and other members of the academic staff, including some members elected by the staff, other members with relevant experience including perhaps university representatives, teachers from schools and other further education colleges and other suitable individuals. The local chief education officer, though not a member should be empowered to attend or be represented and speak at all meetings of the governing body.

The articles of government should contain a clear statement of the responsibilities to be reserved to the local education authority and those to be assigned to the governing body, the director and academic board. Within the national and local limits referred to above the governing body should be responsible for the general direction of the polytechnic. It should submit the estimates of the polytechnic to the authority, and within the estimates as approved should be free to incur expenditure without further reference to the authority. In order to promote freedom of action the main subheads should be drawn widely and there should be provision for virement within them. Under the general direction of the governing body the director should be responsible for the college's internal organization, management and discipline.

The articles of government should make provision for an academic board whose membership should include the director, heads of departments, other senior officers, other members of the teaching staff chosen by the staff and co-opted members from outside, perhaps from institutions with which the polytechnic had links. Within the general policy of the college and subject to the ultimate responsibility of the governing body the responsibilities of the academic board should cover planning, co-ordination, development and oversight of all academic work including the admission and examination of students.

The articles of government should also provide for the appointment and dismissal of staff, The *Notes for Guidance* said that the director, the deputy director and chief administrative officer should be appointed by the governing body subject to confirmation by the education authority. The director should be responsible for the appointment or promotion of members of staff, but the governing body should be represented on the selection committee for the more important appointments. The articles of government should specify the arrangements for the suspension and dismissal of staff.

The *Notes for Guidance* also discussed the position of students, and said that provision should be made for the students' union to conduct and manage its own affairs and funds. Arrangements should enable representations on matters of proper concern to students to be made on their behalf to the governing body, the director or the academic board as appropriate. The power of suspending a student for misconduct should rest with the director, and the power of expulsion with the governing body. There should be a recognized procedure, with a right of appeal for such cases.

These arrangements proposed for the governing bodies for polytechnics were quite new in the public system of higher education. If one looks back at the development of the colleges of advanced technology, one sees that the local authorities retained control over the day-to-day working of the college right up to the point at which the colleges became direct-grant institutions. The governing bodies of the CATs were strengthened, they were not given effective power. The *Notes for Guidance* were an attempt to import into colleges administered by the local authorities the degree of academic independence, self-government and democracy that had hitherto been confined to universities.

This was not universally acceptable. A number of local authorities produced schemes of government which did not begin to satisfy the requirements. The length of time between the publication of the *Notes for Guidance* and approval of the first schemes for polytechnics, from April 1967 to May 1968, was attributable, partly at least, to the need to persuade some local authorities to agree.

There is no doubt that the new arrangements will give greater independence and responsibility to the academic staff of the polytechnics. This has involved a new kind of relationship between the colleges and the organs of state. This is neither the autonomy of the universities, protected by the 'buffer' of the University Grants Committee. Neither is it the former dependence of the colleges upon the local authorities for even trivial decisions. It is an attempt to import university independence into the public system of higher education. Naturally this will have important implications for the relationships between the staff themselves . . .

New relationships between principals and heads of departments and between senior staff and junior staff in the planning and organization of academic matters will now develop with all the strains that this will impose on the staff as a whole. It is not that the administrative structures now evolved are very new. The novelty is that these structures are being evolved in local authority colleges.

Teachers, teaching and research

When the colleges of advanced technology were designated they were given a salary structure which was noticeably different from that in other colleges of further education. This was done against the wishes of the staff of the majority of colleges. With the announcement about the polytechnics, the wishes of the staff associations prevailed. No special salary structure was created for the polytechnics. This contributed to the difficulties which we have already described.

The arbitral body[17] reported that the Council for National Academic Awards had often stated that the Burnham further education awards did not provide salaries sufficient to obtain the calibre of staff required for the development of the kind of course the Council hoped to recognize, and the CNAA had at least once formally argued this to the Burnham Further Education Committee. There were known to be cases where the council had had to withdraw recognition from a course because of the inability of the college to appoint staff of the required calibre.

Perhaps the most important anomaly occurred in the Arbitral Body's award to the heads of departments in polytechnics. There are several grades of head of department in technical colleges,[18] but under the award only the highest grade, Grade VI, was to carry a salary greater than the minimum of the university professor scale, and it fell several hundred pounds short of the university professor's average salary. This meant that any head of department who was able to move from a polytechnic to a professorship at a university could reasonably expect a salary increase of up to £1,000. The criterion for making a department a Grade VI one was the number of full-time degree-level students in it. It could only become Grade VI mandatorily if it had at least 300 such students. This is very much bigger than most university departments. It was hard to see how the colleges could be expected to provide an alternative but no less worthy experience of higher education unless at least a few heads of departments could expect salaries at least comparable to professors in universities.

In other words so far from there being improved salary conditions and career prospects, the polytechnics have started under a handicap compared with universities.

Research was not mentioned in the White Paper of 1966. The Secretary of State did attach four paragraphs on the subject to the *Notes for Guidance* in April 1967. In these it was held that the main responsibility of the polytechnics would be as teaching institutions, but that provision should be made for research which was essential to the proper fulfilment of the teaching function and the maintenance and development of close links with local industry. The Secretary of State hoped the polytechnics would be ready to undertake *ad hoc* research projects on behalf of industry or under contracts from the research councils and other bodies. This was to be done without prejudice to the colleges' other work and without adding to the permanent establishment unless the cost was covered by the arrangements with the sponsors.

He also hoped that suitably qualified members of the teaching staff would pursue research where it would contribute to better teaching, and he saw that some personal experience of research was necessary for teachers who were responsible for supervising the projects which formed part of some courses. But he did not envisage that it would normally be necessary for teachers to devote the whole or most of their time to research, nor would he expect full-time research assistants to be employed on any considerable scale.

On the other hand teachers should be able to keep abreast with new knowledge through having an appropriate time for private study. Where appropriate they should also be able to work for the higher degrees of universities and the CNAA and where possible of associating their research with that of an accessible university research establishment or industrial organization.

It is clear that as yet the volume of research in polytechnics is not such as to cause the problems which are normally expected to be dealt with under this section.

It is also too early to say whether the polytechnics are likely to make any major innovations in teaching. In so far as they have adopted the sandwich-course principle they are following in lines laid down by the CATs and some of their own number. In so far as they are offering fewer formal lectures and more seminars and tutorials they are accepting the fact that higher education in universities and elsewhere has normally demanded it.

Role and status of students

We have seen in the study of the CATs that in technical education students often have a different status from those in universities. A good proportion of them are older, partly because part-time courses take longer, partly because students embark on their courses later in life. Most of them have had some experience in industry and gain in status from that experience. They cannot be treated as if their course were a continuation of school and as if they themselves were inexperienced teenagers.

On the other hand, there is only one example here of the polytechnics leading to institutional innovations. Students are becoming members of both academic boards and governing bodies. The very fact that these boards were being created often for the first time, but in any case were largely reconstituted, made this move more possible. But there is some evidence that pressure came from the new and young staff who had been recruited to the polytechnics from universities. In all institutions of higher education in Britain, the younger staff have found themselves caught between the students with whom they often sympathize (and among whom they themselves were so recently) and the demands of the institution and its senior members. In the fluid situation which marked the announcement of polytechnic policy, these young staff were able to help the students to real advances. And ministers made it clear that they were not opposed to students on governing bodies—which gave a good deal of impetus to the movement in those polytechnics which were resisting it. It is always hard to follow the movements of an underground stream but the students in polytechnics were in contact with their contemporaries in universities through the National Union of Students, and it is not fanciful to suggest that part of the pressure of the demand in universities for 'student power' grew from the spreading knowledge of developments in polytechnics . . .

One major grievance of the polytechnic students is on physical accommodation. The polytechnics have been built, of course, upon existing institutions, and ones which have been very lavishly equipped in some respects and very ill-equipped in others. Their scientific and technical laboratories and workshops have been almost over-equipped. Their libraries have been scanty and places for private study almost nil. This was in some ways a hangover from the old technical college belief that knowledge should be imparted by the teacher in a lecture, the students should write it down and reproduce it in examinations. The idea that the students themselves might read and think about material for themselves is a comparatively new growth.

At the same time, the growth of student unions has been very slow in the technical colleges, and even now there has been little physical provision for them. They have to exist in the exiguous accommodation the colleges can spare from already overcrowded buildings. By comparison, the universities normally have very lavish union accommodation provided by the UGC, which the polytechnics are scarcely provided with. The fact that they are being started at a time of national economy means that they can expect little soon. Indeed, ministers have even tried to rationalize this student poverty by saying that polytechnic students are somehow different. Not surprisingly the Government has not said what it is prepared to do for polytechnic student unions, and this is a cause of great resentment among their students.

Higher education and the outside world

We have seen that one purpose of the development of polytechnics was to bring the concept of public service to industry into higher education.

In his speech at Woolwich[19] the Secretary of State for Education and Science quoted with approval a report by the Association of Teachers in Technical Institutions which said:

> The underlying assumption is that the student's primary motivation is the profession he intends to follow. He is committed to a profession from the outset and his course of study is closely integrated with his professional work. He is given direct experience of professional practice at an early stage in his course . . . He and the staff who teach him maintain close contact with the profession and, as a rule, many of his teachers have themselves spent time practising the professional occupation for which they are preparing him . . . The technical college tradition is to maintain close contact with the world of employment and to provide higher education in which education and professional experience are obtained concurrently in a single integrated course.

And he then added:

> The leading colleges must surely build on their

own proud tradition of service to industry, business and the professions, and not set out simply to duplicate the provision in the universities. As the ATTI Report points out, if they seek merely to extend the number of external degree courses they offer, they will come to be regarded as places for students who fail to get into university. Of course they should not try to be different just for the sake of being different. But they should exploit their own traditions and standards of excellence, and develop the fields in which they can make their own distinctive contribution to meeting society's needs.

It would be right to claim that the polytechnics represent a new approach to adult and continuing education. Of course, technical colleges had always offered refresher courses and had taken people into long-term courses without conventional formal qualifications. But at any rate in intention the polytechnic policy was to do more than this.

What has been called 'adult', as distinct from 'further' education has been provided in Britain by voluntary bodies like the Workers' Educational Association, and the university extra-mural departments. It is fair to say that this has been thought of as education for leisure. It has been concerned with people's interests and hobbies—and has hence always appealed most, not to the workers, but to the middle classes. A normal WEA class is composed of professional and trades people, or more likely their wives. As Eric Robinson says in his book, *The New Polytechnics*,[20] this tradition has been one of offering personal liberation and cultivation to the working classes. Vocational education has been associated with the bad old days, so the adult education has not sought to provide it. This, Mr Robinson says, has the fundamental assumption that the elite can expect to live through their work but the majority must try to live in spite of their work: liberal education for the workers is conceived as education for leisure. And the interesting thing is that this view has found most adherents among the left.

This is why the Government's policy for polytechnics is so startling. The comprehensive academic communities that the polytechnics are to be, standing at the apex of a system of professional and vocational education, represent a challenge to the old concept of adult education . . .

Evaluation and planning

The White Paper of 1966 was called *A Plan for Polytechnics and Other Colleges*,[21] but it is hard to see any planning in it. It was more a statement of intent. In outlining the present position it mentioned 'growing numbers of students of 18 and over which are above GCE Advanced level in standard but are not classified as advanced'. These students represented the most crucial development of the polytechnics: it was their inclusion which made them 'comprehensive'. Yet there was no indication in the White Paper of how many of them there were. Similarly, in the paragraph on 'future needs' it accepted the projections of the National Plan[22] which in turn derived from the scarcely planned growth of higher education since the Robbins Report.

The familiar arguments 'for concentrating on advanced work were then advanced, and it was recognized that there were also strong arguments, particularly those concerning part-time students, for allowing the growth of advanced work elsewhere than in the selected colleges. The object of the White Paper, it said:

> will be to reduce substantially the number of colleges engaged in full-time higher education but colleges not designated as polytechnics will continue to offer full-time courses of higher education where they satisfy the criteria for approval of courses in force from time to time. Existing provision for courses in specific professional fields under nationally settled arrangements will be reviewed in due course. Colleges already engaged in part-time higher education will continue with such work subject to the criteria for approval of courses in force from time to time. In the absence of exceptional circumstances colleges not already engaged in higher education will not be expected to embark on it.

In returning details of their accommodation and courses the colleges were specifically asked not to prepare development plans, but simply to say what was envisaged within the present accommodation and that known to be coming into use.

Nor did the Department of Education and Science seem anxious to use all the instruments available to it to ensure the success of its policy. We have seen how its policies for the salaries of teachers worked directly against its policies for polytechnics. The CNAA was grossly undermanned for its new task, both in terms of its permanent officials and of part-time members of its subject boards. The consequence is that colleges are finding serious administrative delays in securing the approval of new courses.

The Government has also given no indication of the resources they are prepared to put into the polytechnics. There are thus no financial implications which are specific to this innovation. It may be, however, that the Department's most serious failure will come to be seen in its inability to ensure serious academic planning in the colleges. Of course it can be argued that academic planning was the business of the individual colleges and that there was nothing to stop it. Equally, the Department has taken the view that until the polytechnics are officially set up, with their governing bodies arranged and their new directors appointed, academic planning could not reasonably be started. But in practice this has meant decisions, affecting the long-term development of the colleges, have been taken in the intervening years in the absence of overall academic plans. At all events only one college, Hatfield, has produced a serious plan, and it cannot be said that any college is showing urgency in emulating this.

Notes

1 *A Plan for Polytechnics and Other Colleges* (HMSO 1966).
2 England, Wales and Scotland.
3 These and subsequent figures are taken from a unit study, *The Impact of Robbins*, J. R. King, R. Layard and C. A. Moser (Penguin 1969).
4 *Higher Education* (HMSO 1963).
5 Op. cit.
6 *The National Plan* (HMSO 1965).
7 See below, pp. 260–6.
8 Later 30.
9 In a speech at Woolwich Polytechnic, 27 April 1965.
10 Woolwich speech, 1965.
11 Report of the Arbitral Body of Salary Scales for Teachers in Establishments of Further Education, 1965.
12 *Enquiry into the Flow of Candidates in Science and Technology into Higher Education* (HMSO 1968).
13 Ibid., Table 10.
14 The Education Act (no. 2), 1968.
15 Sent to local authorities with a copy of the Secretary of State's Parliamentary Statement, 5 April 1967.
16 A name coined for the head of a polytechnic to distinguish him from the principals of constituent colleges.
17 Op. cit.
18 Op. cit.
19 Op. cit.
20 *The New Polytechnics*, Eric E. Robinson (Cornmarket; Penguin 1968).
21 Op. cit.
22 Op. cit.

46 Degrees of esteem

Anne Corbett

'Separate but equal' has an unhappy history as an educational slogan. It was the patent inequalities between secondary modern and grammar schools which forced the change to comprehensives. Now, with separate sectors of higher education under the 'binary policy', there are pressures to make history repeat itself on behalf of the latter-day secondary mods, the non-university colleges. Universities are seen as having a privileged autonomous life on one side of the fence, while the polytechnics, further education colleges, and colleges of education, lag behind under local education authority control on the other.

Short of resources for a new higher education job, not always adequately staffed, probably in unsuitable buildings, the public sector colleges have a dingy image. They are not helped when most of their encouragement comes from the government praising them for worthy but unglamorous jobs: like providing a safety net for students, or for being socially responsive. It is rather like getting a school prize for effort, when everyone knows that it is academic achievement that counts.

The idea of the binary failure is perpetuated by many people in the colleges. And for some of the institutions not far from being able to claim an equality with universities, the feelings may be agonized. Ten or a dozen of the 30 polytechnics, which 'have the substance but not the form, must be converted into universities. If not, the young are being sold a pup,' says Terence Miller, director of the North London Polytechnic. And at the City of London Polytechnic I was told: 'Look round our staff, count our Ph.Ds. Are we different from the new universities, the ex-colleges of advanced technology, even the Open University?'

So it comes as a surprise to talk to students and to staff in polytechnics below the political level, and to find the places humming. Sure, there are the smells of today's and yesterday's lunches in some of the older buildings. There are the sites overlooking the carpark and the railway station, rather than a park or a lake. There are the staff lists with rather a lot of second-class honours. But there is also a tremendous intellectual energy coming from staff who believe that they can provide an alternative to universities without aping them.

In three polytechnics I saw—City of London, North East London and Sheffield—there seemed to be an enormous effort put into devising new and more demanding ways of teaching students and tackling

Source: New Society, 9 December 1971, 1142–4.

research. These three polytechnics are also experimenting with new patterns of courses (the City of London wants an entirely modular structure for which students wouid get credits) and with new forms of assessment, like 'open book' examinations.

But the most striking feature I saw was the effort going into devising new courses, in which it was clear that the object was to involve *all* staff teaching the course in a process of curriculum development. This was a matter of staff education, at least as much as of finding new ways of presenting material or new material to present. At the North East London Polytechnic, I watched a group of science and technology teachers being grilled by staff from other disciplines seconded to its course development unit, about what they were really trying to do in making their subject 'contribute to thinking about the major engineering, economic and social problems of our time'. How would a modular course help? What was the philosophy underlying the course, and how was this translated in curriculum terms? Were they being fair to students in suggesting that the course could be examined most effectively by two four-hour papers on the same day?

It is no accident that innovations in higher education are going on outside universities. The college staff and students are the beneficiaries of a quiet and highly effective revolution. Unlike the secondary modern schools, the colleges have a guarantor for their academic standards, the Council for National Academic Awards. It should be a guarantor for their esteem, too. The way the CNAA works could provide some lessons ... on how to validate awards and stimulate development. It might make some of the most arrant status-seekers reconsider their route to success.

The CNAA was recommended by the Robbins report, as a means of extending degree opportunities outside universities. It was set up in 1964, building on the foundations of the National Council for Technological Awards. But the CNAA differs in one important respect from the National Council. It is empowered by its charter 'to award degrees and other academic qualifications, comparable in standard with those granted by universities, to students who complete approved courses of study or research, in establishments which do not have the power to award degrees'. The National Council could award diplomas only.

The CNAA has, indeed, extended degree opportunities for non-university students by providing an alternative to the system of London external degrees. It is the largest degree-awarding body outside London University and the Open University. With 4,000 students when it started (the students it took over from the National Council for Technological Awards) it now has 25,000, including 1,000 registered for research degrees. The numbers will increase still more over the next few years, if the London external degree system is phased out after 1977, as recommended in a report now being considered by the university. Two thirds of the CNAA students are 'sandwich' students; and the overwhelming majority of the students are at the 29 polytechnics, at the four Scottish equivalents (the central institutions), at eight other further education colleges, and at three service colleges.

Their subdegree work apart, the colleges run 176 'sandwich', 101 full-time, and 24 part-time CNAA first-degree courses: and 19 postgraduate courses, ranging from technology and marketing, to modern English studies and music. Many are subjects that might be found in a university. But the difference that shows in the CNAA's annual *Compendium of Degree Courses* is not that these courses are more vocational, just that they have been devised within the last five years.

More to the point; in view of academic sceptics, the CNAA has established that its degrees are very much worth the paper they are written on, with one proviso only. They are worth it to those who have heard of them. (But here, time—if nothing else—will help, as CNAA students increase.) The CNAA has established its standards through a novel approach in British higher education.

Unlike the London external degree board, the CNAA is not a syllabus setting and examining body over which colleges have no influence. The CNAA is designed to encourage college development. Colleges take the initiative. Their staff devises the courses, and decide on teaching methods and examining techniques. They examine their students with the aid of external examiners. It is the same academic freedom as a university. But the CNAA is there to vouch that the course has an equivalent standing, too, once the hurdle of viability has been cleared. Courses have first to be approved by the Department of Education, operating through the regional advisory council for further education and the H.M. Inspectorate.

The CNAA has to approve courses and the appointment of external examiners. There are a lot of courses which do not get approved. The table shows the work of the subject boards. Last year, 131 courses were approved, 76 rejected. CNAA officials point to a growing proportion of successful submissions. Last year, 57 per cent of courses were approved; the year before that, only 48 per cent.

A first-degree course for the CNAA is approved for five years usually; a four-year course for six years; and a higher degree for three years. A few of the early courses were approved with a pinch of faith, and a few of them had a sticky time when it came to re-

validation. They have been given approval for a further year only, or they have had to revise their submission. Only one has been turned down. Re-validation is a dilemma. 'Think of students already on courses,' officials emphasize.

The CNAA works through a council. A new chairman has just been appointed. He is Michael Clapham, a deputy chairman of ICI and a man long involved in education. His fellow-members of the council are drawn from industry, from professional bodies, and from local authorities (including influential figures like Dame Kathleen Ollerenshaw; and, until recently, Sir Lionel Russell). There are also some polytechnic people (Sir Alan Richmond, director of Lanchester, and chairman of the Committee of Poly-technic Directors; and the Rev Dr George Tolley, director of Sheffield Polytechnic and the committee's secretary). And there are university academics (including Maurice Peston, Professor of Economics at Queen Mary College, London; and Donald MacRae, Professor of Sociology at the London School of Economics, who was appointed last month).

Power, however, is in the hands of the 600 or so members of the subject and area boards, and a small secretariat, whose chief officer is Frank Hornby, an ex-teacher of chemistry and the former chief officer of the National Council for Technological Awards. The 50 subject boards represent the same sorts of interests as the council, but are mostly appointed as individuals, which makes them usefully anarchic.

It is the academics who attract most of the respect, as well as most of the odium. Colleges having difficulties tend to personalize it as old X with a kink about the university way to teach the subject. But it is university people who are most frequently mentioned as being a tremendous help and flexible in their attitudes, both by college staff and by officials. They point out that academics had to bear most of the work in the early days of the area boards. Members add that, since the work is voluntary, the only pay-off is the feeling that it is worth while.

The CNAA's method is to ask, first for a submission on the degree. So far, despite the flexibility given in its charter, the CNAA has concentrated on degree work. A submission may be 40 pages or so of foolscap. (It takes a day to absorb, said one tired board member.) The submission describes the aims and origins of the course, the intended students, the entry requirements, the course structure, the proposed methods of teaching and assessment, and the teaching staff and their qualifications. It also gives a detailed description of the syllabus, usually including a reading list. While some college staff explode at having to get down to the trivia of a book list, the submissions are seen by the CNAA as giving useful information about staff quality as well as about the content of the course.

A submission has one of four fates:

1 It may be rejected outright. If so, reasons have to be given. Very often, apparently, it is because the course is too like a London external degree. Alterna-

Table 46.1 The work of the CNAA subject boards, 1969–70

subject boards	No. of courses considered	No. of visits	approved	rejected
aeronautical engineering	2	1	1	—
architecture	2	2	1	1
biological sciences	5	2	4	1
business studies	15	9	8	5
chemical engineering	1	1	1	—
chemistry	16	7	9	4
civil engineering	17	7	12	5
combined studies	13	4	1	10
economics	8	4	5	2
electrical engineering	23	12	15	7
English studies	5	1	1	4
estate management, building economics and land use	4	2	1	1
food science and dietetics	1	—	1	—
general science	4	1	3	1
geography	2	—	2	—
instrumentation and control engineering	3	3	3	—
languages	10	4	2	6
legal studies	4	1	2	1
librarianship	7	2	5	2
management studies	2	1	—	1
materials studies	4	2	3	1
maths/computer science	22	5	16	6
mech/prod engineering	25	12	15	8
music	1	—	—	—
nautical studies	1	1	—	1
naval architecture and ship technology	1	—	—	—
ophthalmic optics	1	1	1	—
pharmacy	2	—	1	1
photography	1	1	1	—
physics	12	5	11	—
printing technology	1	—	1	—
psychology	1	—	—	1
public administration	4	2	1	3
sociological studies	6	1	1	4
special (land use)	2	—	2	—
textile technology	1	—	—	—
theology and religious studies	1	—	—	—
town planning	1	1	1	—
totals, 1969–70	231	95	131	76
(totals, 1968–69)	(209)	(101)	(100)	(74)

Note: the 24 courses not classified under the last two columns were still under consideration at 30 September 1970

Source: CNAA annual report, 1969–70.

tively, the submission is seen as not concerned enough with getting the student to think, and too concerned with syllabus.

2 A college may be advised to discuss the submission further with CNAA officials. These have vast expertise on staffing implications and resources.

3 A course may be approved on the submission only. 'Oh, we know Ealing well for this, and Enfield and Newcastle for that,' members and officials say.

4 More usually, a submission is followed by a visit to assess whether there are the resources in the college to back the course. Courses may be rejected then because of the low quality of the staff and the facilities. 'Usually, though,' says a member, 'we say we'll approve on certain conditions: if the authority spends £5,000 on the library, and takes on three extra staff, or if the staff cut down the teaching hours. They usually do.'

A visiting party, which goes for a day and is usually empowered to reach a decision, has a private meeting to decide its approach. It then meets the college principal and senior staff concerned with the course. It follows this by detailed discussions with the staff actually teaching the course. It looks at the college's resources. Generally it meets students. It then meets privately again to make a decision.

It is a procedure which attracts the gamut of emotions, all the way to hate. There is a vast mythology attached to a visit. Few at the receiving end seem to have acted with the bravado of a Sheffield department which packed all its 50 members into the initial meeting as an intimidation exercise. But I was given plenty of advice on tactics for the earlier stages: on how to knock up syllabuses in an evening, and how to interpret the CNAA's scant statements of guidance.

Though rather more college staff were ready with their comments about the clammy hand of the CNAA, they could not pin down outright repression of ideas. 'Now with the necessary—the very necessary —hindsight, I see a subject board as doing a useful job in protecting students from an overloaded first year, in clarifying the relationship between subjects in a combined studies course and between year courses,' says John Salt at Sheffield. But he wiped his brow at the thought of what it was like at the time. Even at the City of London, whose director, Arthur Suddaby, has pushed the other polytechnic directors in arguing for self-validation, the staff working on the modular degree ('interdisciplinary,' they call it) feel that both they and the CNAA have progressed.

If you contrast the way the CNAA works with two scenes from university life, its revolutionary impact becomes clearer. A young philosophy lecturer boasted to me the other day that he and two colleagues had just revised their syllabus. He was, indeed, unusual among university acquaintances. 'We're lucky,' he said. 'Our professor is great. He runs an open department.' And were these proposals subjected to any outside scrutiny, which might see the possible confusions for students? 'Well, yes: the Senate. But no trouble there. It had a full agenda that day.'

The other university contrast is the working of the University Grants Committee. The UGC, unlike the CNAA, is a fund-raising body. It does not validate awards. Nevertheless, it exercises some academic controls, by allocating money on a basis which could boost particular departments and result in great national prestige for centre of excellence. The UGC has subject committees, too. The agenda for one of the UGC's recent visits, in contrast with the CNAA, gave time for a single hour's ('useless') discussion.

The CNAA's achievement shows up in three ways. It is a force for innovation in a whole college. Its expectation that all levels of staff should be involved in devising courses has gone a long way towards clearing the path for academic boards in colleges, towards increasing staff participation and towards raising the quality of staffing. It is, as a rival body, beginning to exert pressure on universities, through the academics who are involved in its work. At least one subject board chairman appoints his university members partly in the hope that they will be a 'cell' within their own universities. The CNAA has, also, been a lever for the improvement of college facilities.

As put to me by Eric Robinson, further education's greatest champion and author of *The New Polytechnics*, it is because the CNAA has exercised a 'marvellous educational detachment'. Not too cluttered by problems of planning, course distribution and what is administratively possible, it has been able to ask what is educationally desirable. University members, in particular, going into library-less colleges, have shaken technical teachers and local authorities out of the cosy assumptions that engineers do not need to read, or that a tutorial service can be provided when six members of staff share a room.

Now the CNAA is likely to move into a new phase. A model for development, it still shows a willingness to go on learning, as with its recent decision that honours and ordinary degrees should signify the difference between students, not the difference between courses. Its success is widely seen as the creation of its chief officer, Hornby, backed by able senior staff, like Jean Rossiter. Hornby retires in September, to be replaced by Edwin Kerr, at present director of Paisley Polytechnic.

One of the issues to be considered then is whether the CNAA should play a more national role. It has done a great deal for libraries locally, for instance: would this have been more effectively done nationally? Why has it had such difficulties in getting colleges to realize that the CNAA boards are concerned not with preconceived ideas, but with ideas well put? Should the CNAA do anything to fill the vacuum

in higher education planning? Fury with the regional advisory council/HMI procedure leads some to argue (against the Robinson line) that it should. It would, in fact, seem more reasonable for the CNAA to be represented, along with the UGC and local authorities on a national advisory body.

Then, how should the CNAA respond to the polytechnics' pressure for greater academic freedom? There is a widespread feeling that it *should* respond, possibly by approving colleges, not courses. Within the terms of its charter, it cannot give them the self-validation they ask for.

How should the CNAA cope with new demands like subdegree work and education courses? Apart from some early highly political incidents, education courses have not been rejected on principle. Didsbury College of Education is at present discussing how the CNAA might validate its subdegree certificate course, as well as the B.Ed. degree. Modular courses make great demands on the CNAA. And it has to come to terms with ways in which sufficiently high standards can be set for highly vocational courses like catering.

At its last council meeting, the CNAA agreed to set up a working party to look at its own future. Some of its members can be relied on to press the educational, rather than the administrative, case. They will be doing a great service if they can push the CNAA beyond the political wall of silence which has surrounded it, ever since Anthony Crosland, as Secretary for Education, mentioned it in the ill-fated Woolwich speech on the binary system. For, as effectively as anything in higher education, the CNAA shows that academic freedom can consist of the freedom to do things, not freedom from doing them.

47   Finance and the fate of the polytechnics

Pamela Lewis

Expenditure on education not only continues to rise year by year but also accounts for an ever increasing share of the national product. Higher and further education have taken a full part in this expansion of resources going to education. Indeed, in 1960 the share of GNP going to education was 3·4 per cent and by 1968 this had risen to 4·6 per cent (*National Income* 1970). These figures are somewhat inflated because transfer payments such as students' grants and non-educational expenditure (School Health Service, for example) are included along with purchases from other sectors but they do, nevertheless, illustrate the rise

Source: Higher Education Review (1971), **3** (3), 23–34.

in expenditure (Peacock 1968). In monetary terms the cost of universities and further education (including adult education) has risen from £58·1m and £75·1m respectively in 1959–60 to £200·6m and £206·3m in 1967–8 (*Statistics of Education* 1968). This means that university expenditure has risen by over 245 per cent in eight years and the cost of further education by 175 per cent in the same time. In the face of such rising costs it is hardly surprising that successive governments have been eager to keep as tight a rein as possible on the spending of the institutions of higher and further education. Consequently, because resources are one of the few variables involved in expansion that the government can monitor accurately and control, one would expect to see them being employed as an instrument in the implementation of policy. This, however, is clearly not the case in England and Wales at present. Although it is true that in general terms resources are cut here and there (and usually everywhere), it is rarely as a response to educational policy decisions but as a result of the economic strictures imposed upon the country by the government.

The polytechnic policy and finance

In 1965, the government announced its intention of creating the 30 new polytechnics as comprehensive academic communities whose goals have often been clearly explored. In what ways do the present methods of financing further and higher education, and the allocation of resources, contribute to the achieving of these goals? How far do they fall short of requirements and what are the unexpected consequences of the method of financing the polytechnics? Would any modifications improve the situation?

A glance at the official statements on the setting up, organization and designation of the polytechnics immediately makes it clear that no guidance has been given to the institutions concerned and that the DES has overlooked the potentiality of resources as an instrument of policy. In the early speeches and White Paper (White Paper 1966), it was stated that the best use of limited resources was to be made by concentrating higher education in a relatively small number of institutions, so that the advantages of large scale production could be reaped (Manchester 1968). All references to resources are vague and it was not until 1970 (Circular 7/70), when most of the polytechnics were already designated and the policy five years old, that guidance was given on the administration of resources. Even this referred only to recurrent expenditure. Finally, the speech at Leicester pays lipservice to the need for long term development plans to prevent waste (Leicester 1970). This does not mean that the polytechnics will have a great deal of financial freedom, it is that local authorities have received absolutely no guidance on the financial aspects of the new policy. Apparently, it has been assumed that resources will be administered as elsewhere in the further education sector and that there is no need to alter the method of provision although the purpose of the institutions has clearly changed from meeting local demand for industrial education and training to providing full time higher education as part of the national effort to diversify and expand educational facilities for modern youth. It will be shown that, as far as resources are concerned, such a non-policy has a negative effect on the proposed policy and that, as long as the *status quo* remains, the statements of policy are vacuous.

Before looking at the intended and unintended consequences of the method of finance and resource allocation in the polytechnics and their impact on policy, it may be helpful to summarize the structure of the distribution of resources in this sector.

The method of finance

Capital expenditure on buildings is controlled directly by the DES and in the five years since 1966–7 a limit has been fixed for the polytechnic building programme. The size of this programme depends more on the vagaries of the economic situation than on the underlying education policy. This means that the total amount of money committed to building by the polytechnics in any one year cannot exceed the sum laid down by the DES. Each college works out its plans for buildings and submits it to the controlling authority who then submit the plan to the DES. All such plans must conform to cost and standard norms stipulated by the DES. It is asserted that these do not differ greatly from those of the UGC for university building, but the treatment of such as circulation space within the ceiling for further education, but as an extra for universities, can make a considerable difference to building programmes between the two sectors. Even if approval is granted fairly promptly the college cannot begin its programme until permission to start is granted. This power of delay, together with the strict control over the projects themselves, enables a very tight hold to be kept on the colleges as far as building is concerned.

To finance capital projects, be they building or the provision of major items of equipment, the local authority must raise the money in the usual local authority way by resorting to the capital market. Loans must be raised and rates of interest paid. The cost to the college thus appears on its recurrent expenditure statement as loan repayments, debt management expenses and interest. Because the authorities must have recourse to the market, the cost of building programmes can be over 100 per cent higher than the initial capital cost. Fortunately, the DES does not count interest as part of the building programme. The full cost does not however fall exclusively on the local authority but forms part of the expenditure that may be claimed from the advanced further education 'Pool'.

The financing of recurrent expenditure is more complex than that of capital and the lines of control of the DES are less easily identified. Resources are allocated on an annual basis, the colleges usually knowing their allocation two years in advance. At the top of the hierarchy, the DES negotiates the educational component of the rate support grant with the Treasury. The DES and the Department for the Environment (the former Ministry of Housing and Local Government) in turn decide on the size of the rate support grant. This grant is then passed on to the local authorities, together with guidance on its spending from the DES and the local authority associations. On the basis of this guidance the finance committee of the local authority allocates monies to the institutions it aids. The total allocation for education is then passed on to the education committee which fixes the sums to go to individual institutions on the basis of the estimates submitted by them. In the polytechnics these estimates arrive at the education committee and the finance committee by way of the departments and the director and governing body.

The money is not allocated to the colleges under the same heads of expenditure as those included in the estimates but under 15 heads laid down by the DES (Capps 1969). The colleges thus receive a lump sum each for teaching salaries, establishment, repairs and so on. The division of these sums between departments is left entirely at the discretion of the colleges, except that they have no authority to transfer money from one of the 15 major heads to another (that is, there is no virement). The colleges then spend their allocations without further reference to the local authority but with the following provisions (Circular 7/70). There is virement within the 15 heads of expenditure but not between them. Secondly, the lump sum for teaching staff must be allocated within the numbers and grading structures for advanced further education specified in the Burnham Scales (Burnham 1968). Thirdly, the approval of the local authority is required before more than £500 is spent on an individual item of repair. Finally, for supplies that involve expenditure in excess of £100, the college is required to consult the local authority concerning the possibility of one of the authority's suppliers providing the item rather than those of the college. It is appropriate to note here that items of equipment costing more than £1,000 need the approval of the DES.

The existence of the advanced further education Pool complicates the allocation of resources in the polytechnics. Many students on advanced courses at any polytechnic will not come from the local area. For each authority with extra-area students to claim the cost of these students from the relevant local authority would be too awesome a task and so the advanced FE Pool was set up in response to the need for some sort of national clearing house for student costs. All local authorities contribute to the Pool on the basis of their school population and their non-domestic rateable value.

Contributions are therefore unrelated to the number of advanced students living or studying in the area. As the total number of advanced students in the country rises, so the contributions of every local authority rise. Authorities claim the recurrent cost of all advanced students in their area from the Pool. Capital costs appear as recurrent expenditure and as a consequence a part of these costs is similarly recouped.

Capital as an instrument

Having surveyed the financial organization of the polytechnics, it is now appropriate to turn to the consequences of such a structure. In assessing the role of capital in polytechnic policy some comparisons with the universities are valid, as they are the set of institutions competing most with the polytechnics in the higher education sector. There are two essential elements in such an examination of capital: size and method of provision. A summary of the provision for buildings in the two sectors is given in Table 47.1.

Table 47.1 Polytechnic and university building

	Polytechnics	Universities
1967–8	7·6m	35m
1968–9	4·0m	25m
1969–70	8·5m	29m
1970–71	5·2m	29m
1971–2	4·8m	50m
1972–3	7·3m	

The disparities in the sizes of the two programmes is not brought to its full significance until the number of students in the two sectors is considered. At the close of 1968 the polytechnics had 43,392 and the universities 177,668 full-time students (*Statistics of Education* 1968). Polytechnics thus had approximately one quarter of the number of full-time students in the universities but in only one year covered by the building programme did that sector receive as much as one quarter of the money received by the universities, and this at a time when the whole nature of the polytechnic sector was supposed to be undergoing change. The plight of the polytechnics becomes even more evident when it is further considered that they cater for a vast number of sandwich and part-time students, of whom sandwich students are virtually full-time when they are studying in the college. Polytechnics in 1968 had over 18,000 sandwich and over 100,000 part-time students. If part-time students are taken as one quarter of a full-time student as was done in the Robbins Report (Robbins 1963) and sandwich students as one third, then the number of full-time equivalent students in the universities and advanced further education was 181,921 and 74,668 respectively. Thus advanced further education had almost half as many full-time equivalent students as the universities but never has it received more than one third of the money allocated to the universities for building and usually less than one quarter.

In comparing the provision of capital for the polytechnics and the universities, consideration must be given both to the resource cost and its incidence. The universities receive interest free grants from the Exchequer, which means that the cost to the universities is zero and the full resource cost is met out of public funds raised in taxes. That is, in so far as taxes fall equitably on all sections of the community so does the cost of university building. The situation with the polytechnics is very different however, for no grants are received by the colleges. As explained above, the colleges raise the money for buildings in the normal local authority manner by having recourse to the capital market. This means that the full cost of the repayments and interest falls on the local authority. A percentage of the cost can be recouped from the advanced FE Pool which means that this sum is paid for by the other local authorities contributing to the Pool. Their contributions are in turn raised by local rates and a part of the rate support grant from the public purse. The payment of the balance that is not claimed from the Pool falls on the local authority coffers which are filled by local ratepayers and the country as a whole from taxes to make up the rate support grant. In summary then, it appears that the universities' buildings are paid for by the public funds and so do not fall in any sense specifically on the area local to the university or on the institution itself, whereas the financing of buildings in the polytechnics falls partly on the public purse via the rate support grant but partly on the local community. The polytechnics tend therefore to be penalized because their total building programme is not only significantly smaller than that for the universities but depends to some extent on the ability of the local authority to finance it.

There are two clear points to be drawn from the above. First, there are advantages and disadvantages with both methods of financing capital but it would not necessarily be a best solution to make a wholesale substitution of one for the other in either of the sectors. It would not be a good thing for polytechnics to have the same opportunities as the universities have had up until now. There is much evidence of waste and careless planning in the university sector and such extravagance should not be duplicated in the polytechnics. Second, it is not the *system* of finance that *necessarily* penalizes the polytechnics. If the government decided to give guidance on massive capital investment in further education and cut back the university sector, the situation could be reversed. The point is that both sectors are dependent on pressures in the DES, but the universities are a much better pressure group. That the DES permits this situation to continue emphasizes its lack of awareness of the uses to which resources can be put as an instrument of policy.

The fight for local authority resources

Universities obtain their recurring expenditure by submitting applications for funds, in the form of estimates, to the UGC. On the basis of these estimates the UGC applies to the DES for funds. The money it receives as a result, it can distribute as it wishes to the universities, which can then spend the money without regard to their estimates, if they so wish (although this may bias their supply of funds in the future). The polytechnics obtain their funds from the local authorities and are thereby much more obviously public institutions.

Thus, the universities compete with each other for funds but as a whole the sector is in competition only at the level of the Treasury and DES allocation. In the Treasury, the universities compete with every other head of government expenditure and at the DES the allocation to the universities is influenced by the policy at the time, and the degree to which they compete here will probably increase in the future. Once the allocations are clear of the DES the universities compete no more. In contrast, the polytechnics have to compete at all levels right down from the Treasury to the local authority. The decisions that affect the sum that ultimately goes to each polytechnic are: the educational component of the rate support grant determined by the Treasury and the DES; the decision of the DES and the Department for the Environment on the size of the rate support grant; the guidance of the DES and the local authority associations on the spending of the rate support grant and finally the decisions of the finance committee and the controlling authority. It is only too obvious that the polytechnics are, as it were, fighting all along the line for every penny that they get.

Within the local authority the polytechnics not only compete with other educational heads of expenditure but with other local authority expenditure heads. Once the total for education is decided, the polytechnics are perhaps at their most vulnerable. This is because up to this point the government policy on education, especially the expansion of higher education, has helped the local authorities to obtain a larger proportion of the rate support grant for education. Once the money is in the hands of the controlling authority, however, the polytechnics, and indeed further education as a whole, are likely to suffer. The majority of local authority expenditure which is not spent on further education goes to the local schools, and since schooling is compulsory, the local authorities are compelled to provide sufficient accommodation in their schools for all the children in the area. On the other hand further education is not compulsory and thus its allocation of cash is much more easily cut than that for schools (Robinson 1969).

The fact that the FE colleges may suffer at the expense of the schools when money is tight in the local authorities, which is more often than not, becomes particularly pertinent when the government changes its schools policy. The DES recognizes that when the school leaving age is raised to 16, the number of 15 year-old children in the schools will rise. To cater for these extra students the government proposes to raise the amount of money going to the schools' building programme up to 1972–3, the year scheduled for the raising of the minimum leaving age. One wonders if the DES has allowed for more students staying on to the sixth form as a result of the change in policy. If not, and also because the number of students staying on may have been underestimated, the local authorities may find themselves in a tight position if insufficient money has been allowed for the extra students. But this is not the only reason why the FE sector may be denuded of cash. In its White Paper on public expenditure (*Public Expenditure* 1970), the government assumes that in the two years following 1972–3 the number of students in FE will fall off significantly because the children who would be entering FE at this time will be staying on at school. Although this is true of a small number, the numbers are hardly significant enough to justify any cut in financial provision. Indeed, of a total of 3,152,777 students in recognized FE establishments in November 1968, only 213,096 (or 6·75 per cent) were aged 15 and of these only 9,326 (0·29 per cent) were on full-time or sandwich courses (*Statistics of Education* 1968). The financial differences that this comparatively small number of students will make at the local authority level is tiny. But if provision is reduced on the basis of such arguments the colleges could find themselves starved of funds. This problem could become particularly acute as the extra students staying on into the sixth form, a result of the raising of the leaving age, go on to the FE sector. If the DES does not recognize the need to cater for these students, cuts will again be in operation. Crampin and Armitage (Armitage 1970) have estimated that in 1980–81 there will be an extra 50,000 school leavers with five or more O levels and an extra 25,000 with two or more A levels merely as a result of raising the school leaving age. If a substantial number of these found their way into an unprepared FE sector the results could be disastrous.

One point however must be made in favour of local authority control. This is the much greater flexibility afforded to the FE sector with annual budgets than that experienced by the universities with their quinquennial system. It would seem unlikely that the FE system could have expanded as it has if the finance system had been the same as the universities. Planners had problem enough swallowing the university rate of increase. The growth of the FE sector would have presented an insuperable psychological obstacle.

The Pool as an instrument

One redeeming feature of the method of financing the polytechnics is the advanced FE Pool. It has established itself as a means of expansion for enterprising polytechnics. It permitted the unplanned meeting of demand, which was a shock because there was so much demand. It has been a success more by default than by design. This, unfortunately, has led to a certain amount of criticism and the future of the Pool now seems to be in jeopardy. As it stands at the moment, local authorities contribute to the Pool independently of the number of advanced students living or studying in their areas, and they recoup from the Pool their own recurrent expenditure on advanced students. As capital appears on the recurrent expenditure statements of the polytechnics, a percentage of capital costs can be recouped in the same way. This means that a small but enterprising authority can build up

a large, prestigious polytechnic at very little extra cost to itself. This somewhat permissive method of finance has undoubtedly aided the recent rapid increase in the student population in advanced further education. Such an expansion has given rise to a desire to contain it. The Pool thus stands in grave danger.

The validity of the arguments against the Pool, namely that some authorities expand their colleges at the expense of others, especially the large ones, may be questioned. If it is argued that the large polytechnics have expanded at the cost of the smaller ones, it must be assumed that the authorities in whose boundaries these parasitic colleges stand contribute much less to the Pool than they draw out of it. A careful study of the location of the larger polytechnics could immediately give lie to this argument. It becomes clear that most of the larger polytechnics are in fact situated in large towns or county boroughs and these are the authorities which pay most into the Pool because of their high non-domestic rateable value and school populations. It may be that such authorities pay into the Pool a sum very similar to that which they draw from it. Indeed, it is possible that they contribute more than they draw. In such a case, what is vital is that large towns and county boroughs that do not have further education colleges but have high non-domestic rateable values are probably subsidizing not the larger town and city polytechnics but the rural ones located in smaller towns with low non-domestic rateable values. Thus, instead of the rich robbing the poor for their own ends, as the popular argument says, the rich and collegeless authorities are subsidizing the poor ones. Any attempt to disband the Pool would therefore deal a blow to these authorities and cut off an easy but equitable source of finance. In fact, it is extremely difficult to prove or disprove the arguments for and against the Pool because no autonomous set of figures so far exists concerning contributions to it and withdrawals from it by the local authorities. Any arguments about disbanding the Pool are therefore vacuous and the lack of figures is an indication of the lack of understanding in the DES of the use of resources as an instrument.

There is, however, one drawback with the Pool and that is the method of recoupment. To calculate the sum to be drawn from the Pool, the colleges multiply their total expenditure on all levels of work by the proportion of the total salary bill that goes on advanced FE. This proportion is based on the number of staff hours spent on advanced, as opposed to non-advanced work. The present trend in teaching methods is towards less formal teaching and more private study by the students. If this trend continues and is carried very far, the number of hours that are spent on advanced students may fall more than proportionally to the number of hours devoted to non-advanced students, although the relative number of students remains unchanged. This means that the colleges will recoup less than their total expenditure on advanced courses from the Pool. This however is not an argument against the operation of the Pool or a justification for disbanding it. It merely brings out the errors that can occur when hours are used as bases of calculations in colleges. If some more reliable estimate of the amount of money devoted to advanced work were found, the Pool could continue to run smoothly and equitably.

The effect of local authority control

The stranglehold of the controlling authority and insistence on a lack of virement between heads of expenditure add fuel to the fire of discontent in the polytechnics and militate against the colleges' attempts to lose their status as second class institutions. The authority bases its allowance for the colleges' establishment costs on the prevailing arrangements in the local authorities. For example, it assumes that because local government officers can survive with only one secretary for about 40 staff, the polytechnics can do the same. This lack of secretarial help, and services in general, is aggravated by the fact that there is no virement between the major heads of expenditure. In many situations colleges would be pleased to exchange, for example, one lecturer for two secretaries but this is not possible because teaching staff and establishment staff are under different heads. As a consequence lecturers tend to spend a great deal of time doing trivial tasks that could be done much more cheaply and better by a secretary or office clerk. This leads to discontent among the staff, who cannot help feeling that they are much worse off than their colleagues in the universities who have, perhaps, one secretary serving six people rather than a whole department of about 40 or so lecturers.

Teaching staff are not only made to suffer by the conditions imposed upon them by the controlling authority but also by the attitude of the Burnham salary committee and its conditions of work. These provide for remuneration to depend upon the number of student hours devoted to various grades of work: degree, post A level but not reaching final degree standard, above O level, and equivalent O level (Burnham 1968). These scales would seem to provide for polytechnic teachers to be paid on a par with university staff, but this is not so, as the teachers are aware, because it is argued by the committee that as long as the degree work in polytechnics is carried on alongside sub-degree work, the institutions are not equal to the universities and the staff cannot be paid on the same scales. To the naïve, it must seem incredible that the DES should give with one hand and take away with the other, but again, it has missed a golden opportunity to use resources as an instrument to achieve the aims of its policy. Instead it has used them to destroy it.

Resources for part-time students

The fate of the part-timer is brought into question with respect to resources. More part-timers are of local origin than full-timers in the polytechnics. As the resources of the polytechnics are concentrated more and more on a few sites, which are widely dispersed, it will become more difficult for part-timers to attend advanced courses. They will either have to travel much greater distances or give up the hope of studying part-time altogether. The multi-site polytechnics are hoping to make provision for part-timers by providing a wider range of courses at each site for part-timers than for full-timers. If, for example, an engineering faculty is concentrated on one site and pure science on another, it will not be necessary for pure science part time students who live near the engineering faculty precinct to travel all the way to the other one. This is because engineering students do study a certain amount of pure science and there will be a certain number of laboratories in the engineering faculty. This may seem to be a fair solution to the problem but there is the fact that, for their main subject, the part-timers are having to make do with laboratories that are equipped for the subsidiary subjects of students studying completely different disciplines. It seems, therefore, that part-timers must travel large distances, use second rate equipment or give up the idea altogether. This is particularly true of evening only students.

This somewhat piecemeal look at the polytechnic methods of finance and their consequences with respect to the polytechnic policy cannot but make the future look black. By making no effort to adapt the financial provision for the polytechnics, the DES is encouraging them to aspire to join the university club where conditions seem to be so much more favourable. In fact, in some of its provisions the DES is positively moving towards a destruction of the polytechnic aims. It is all very well for commentators to assert that the idea of the polytechnic cannot work but at least some effort should be made before their epitaph is written. It is all too clear that the DES has made no attempt to use resources as an instrument to gain its ends. Indeed, the one institution that does at least allow the polytechnics to expand along the lines outlined by the DES (the Pool) is in danger of destruction and for what may be the wrong reasons.

This is not to say that the polytechnics should leave the local authority sector altogether because the authorities have some contribution to make. Innovation in the polytechnic sector seems to be much more likely if they remain in the hands of the local authorities than if they become autonomous institutions like the universities, which are notoriously conservative. The idea of a Polytechnic Grant Committee run along similar lines to the UGC has been mooted in many areas, not least among the polytechnics themselves. Were such an institution to see the light of day, one cannot help feeling that the death warrant of the polytechnics would be signed at the same time. If the polytechnics came to be financed and run in the same way as the universities, how could they help but be absorbed none-too-gradually into the university sector? The same administrative set up cannot be successful for two types of institutions which have very different goals. On balance it is clear that the best hope for the polytechnic lies in the field of the local authorities. After all, why take them away from a sector, which, although it has its faults, has managed the rapid expansion and development of the FE sector? Both of these aspects—expansion and development are important. The universities have certainly expanded as autonomous institutions, but how much have they developed?

If the hold of the controlling authority could be loosened a little and the colleges given more freedom

in the spending of their money and if they could be freed somewhat from the everlasting fight for funds, they will have gone a long way to being able to concentrate on becoming comprehensive academic communities. At the same time, if the DES could be persuaded that the polytechnics do need a little more capital for their expansion programmes and that their staff need to be treated more fairly with respect to the Burnham scales, we could expect to see the polytechnics moving into the areas designed for them. One cannot expect institutions to go where the DES wants when they are penalized for doing so.

References

Armitage 1970—A. Crampin and P. Armitage, 'The Pressure of numbers: speculation for the seventies', *Higher Education Review* (spring 1970), Table 4, p. 11.

Burnham 1968—Department of Education and Science, *Scales of Salaries for Teachers in Establishments for Further Education, England and Wales, 1967* (HMSO 1968), Appendix VI, Part A.

Capps 1969—Committee on the More Effective Use of Technical College Resources, *A Report on the Use of Costing and Other Financial Techniques in Technical Colleges* (HMSO 1969), 36.

Circular 7/70—Department of Education and Science, *Circular 7/70* (HMSO 14 April 1970).

Leicester 1970—Speech given by the Parliamentary Under-Secretary of State for Education and Science at Leicester Polytechnic on 2 December 1970.

Manchester 1968—Speech by Secretary of State for Education and Science to Regional Planning Seminar at Manchester on 1 March 1968.

National Income 1970—Central Statistical Office, *National Income and Expenditure 1970* (HMSO 1970).

Peacock 1968—A. Peacock, H. Glennerster and R. Lavers, *Educational Finance: its sources and uses in the United Kingdom* (Oliver & Boyd 1968).

Public Expenditure 1970—*Public Expenditure 1969–70 to 1974/75* (HMSO 1971), 36–7.

Robbins 1963—Committee on Higher Education, *Higher Education* (Robbins Committee), Appendix Two A, Annex II (HMSO 1963), 308.

Robinson 1969—E. Robinson, 'The cuts and further education', *Higher Education Review* (summer 1969), 19–26.

Statistics of further education 1968—The cost of further education and the universities is given in *Statistics of Education 1968*, **5**, *Finance* (HMSO 1970). Department of Education and Science, Table 1. The former colleges of advanced technology changed sectors in the period under consideration. The costs of these colleges are included in the 1960 figure for further education and in the 1968 figure for the universities. Further education: Department of Education and Science, *Statistics of Education 1968*, **3**, *Further Education* (HMSO 1970), Table 9 (xii). Universities: Department of Education and Science, *Statistics of Education 1968*, **6**, *Universities* (HMSO 1970), Table 1.

White Paper 1966—The two early speeches referred to are those given by the Secretary of State for Education and Science at Woolwich Polytechnic on 27 April 1965 and at Lancaster University on 20 January 1967. The White Paper is Department of Education and Science, *A Plan for Polytechnic and Other Colleges* (HMSO 1966).

48 Teacher training within higher education

Tyrrell Burgess

The administration of teacher education has its roots in history. Of course, at a time when education was carried on privately in almost family-sized groups, in the Dame schools with which the history of modern education always starts, there were no formal arrangements for training teachers at all. But this cosy situation could not continue after the 1830s, when the State began to assist the voluntary efforts of the Churches in educating people on a large scale. The problem was how to find enough teachers in a largely uneducated population. It was solved, abroad and in England, by the method known as the 'monitorial system', advocated here by Joseph Lancaster—who called it 'a new mechanical system for the use of schools'—and Andrew Bell. The system was simplicity itself: the older children in a school taught the younger. As Andrew Bell said, 'give me twenty-four pupils today and I will give you twenty-four teachers tomorrow'. The system was cheap, and it meant that the absence of teachers did not entirely mean an absence of education. It lasted for a generation because there was nothing better to be done, and attempts to establish a training college for teachers broke down because of the opposition of religious denominations. By the middle of the century, improvement became possible. The depressing state of education brought to light by the inspectors of schools led to a public outcry and the establishment in 1846 of a scheme of apprenticeship for pupil-teachers. The essence of this was that the pupil-teachers were apprenticed for five years to schools recommended by the inspectors. Both the masters taking the apprentices and the apprentices themselves were given grants. Training colleges were at last to be established to which the apprentices should go, with financial assistance; and there was a syllabus of training for them with annual examinations. The regulations laid down standards which must be achieved by both the schoolmaster and the schools if they were to take on an apprentice.

It seems to us today to have been a fairly meagre advance—but it had one important consequence. In setting up special training colleges for those who were to educate the children of the poor, the Government in the middle of the nineteenth century started a division in education which has lasted until today. The universities have not seen themselves as being concerned with the general education of teachers for the younger age groups, except in schools for the middle and upper classes. Most teachers, teaching most children, have not had a university education.

After a twenty-five-year attempt to improve the quality of school teaching by a method of 'payment by results' (in introducing the scheme in the House of Commons in 1863, Robert Lowe said 'I cannot promise the House that this system will be an economical one and I cannot promise that it will be an efficient one, but I can promise that it shall be one or the other. If it is not cheap, it shall be efficient; if it is not efficient it shall be cheap'), the Cross Commission, reporting in 1888, tried again with teacher training. Unhappily the Commission was split. A minority of eight members deplored the pupil-teacher system, calling it 'the weakest part of our educational machinery'. They agreed with one of the witnesses who said: 'It is at once the cheapest and the very worst possible system of supply' and 'It should be abolished root and branch.' The majority, on the other hand, were convinced by those who said that the pupil-teachers were 'on the whole the best as well as the main source of the supply of certificated teachers'. It was said that students in the training colleges who had been pupil-teachers had the greater practical experience.

Again, the minority wanted to lengthen the training-college course from two to three years (an objective achieved a mere seventy years later), to give training-college students some time in universities and to extend teacher training in non-residential colleges. The majority supported these ideas in principle or as experiments, but doubted if a third year was advisable, believed that the experience of university would merely cause disgruntlement, and insisted that residential training was best. And behind all this the denominational struggles echoed on, bedevilling attempts to get more Government grants for teacher training.

A consequence was that when Mr Balfour introduced his Education Act of 1902 he was forced to say:

Any child who wishes to become a teacher gets made a pupil-teacher, and when he has reached that status half his time goes to teaching and the other half . . . to learning . . . What is the result? . . . I find that 36 per cent have never got through the examination for the certificate, and that 55 per cent of the existing teachers have never been to a training college of any sort.

So it was one of the objects of the 1902 Act to provide an extensive system of teacher training.

What the 1902 Act did was to establish that the

Source: 'Teacher training within higher education', in *Dear Lord James—A Critique of Teacher Education*, Penguin Books (1971), 146–58.

preliminary education and training of teachers was a form of secondary, not elementary, education. The new local education authorities could make their secondary schools available for the education of pupil-teachers, and more and more independent pupil-teacher centres became attached to secondary schools. The minimum age for the recognition of a pupil-teacher in urban areas became sixteen, and all pupil-teachers had to be relieved from teaching for at least half their time. However, in 1907 the Board of Education's general report on the instruction and training of pupil-teachers said this system disorganized the education of the pupil-teachers and doubted whether the experience of class teaching and management which the pupil-teacher gained outweighed the disadvantages. An alternative scheme provided that pupils of sixteen and over who wished to become teachers were eligible for grants to enable them to stay at school until seventeen or eighteen when they could enter a training college or become student teachers for a year before entering college. Between the ages of twelve and sixteen a pupil might receive a scholarship from his local authority, which was usually given on condition that he undertook to become a teacher. This kind of 'pledge' became a feature of a good deal of financial support for student teachers, although the age at which the commitment had to be made was gradually raised from twelve to eighteen or later.

Another consequence of the 1902 Act depended on the power it gave to local education authorities to spend money on the training of teachers. In 1904 a new type of college, the municipal training college, was recognized. From the outset the local education authorities were able to offer better salaries and conditions of employment in their own colleges than were available in the voluntary ones. After a confused start, two familiar and tenacious patterns of training teachers emerged in the first quarter of the century: a two-year course of training at a college for teachers in elementary schools, and a one-year course following graduation for teachers in secondary schools. In the colleges the syllabuses were prescribed by the Board of Education and the final examination of the students was conducted by His Majesty's Inspectors. This system was modified after the Burnham Report of 1925, and the conduct of the final examination of students was transferred to joint boards set up by the colleges and the universities. This promising idea was briefly revived, as we shall see, by the minority on the McNair Committee whose deliberations accompanied the great debates leading to the 1944 Education Act.

The McNair Report was in many ways a substantial advance. It recommended higher salaries for teachers and said that the course of training should last three years. It recommended an end to the system whereby grants to attend a training college were available only to those who signed the 'pledge' that they would teach. It also condemned the ban on married women teachers. It was agreed that the hundred individual colleges should be grouped in areas 'to produce a coherent training service'.

But it is since the McNair Report that there has been the present division between the arrangements for the administrative and financial control of the colleges and those for the oversight of their academic development. The former is in the hands of the Department of Education and Science, the local education authorities and the governing bodies; the latter the responsibility of the Institute of Education and the colleges. Of course, there is a good deal of overlap. An expansion of the system, determined by the Department, has implications for the Institutes; and the character of courses may have a significance for teacher supply. The need for consultation is written into the Training of Teachers Regulations, 1967. The local authorities and the voluntary bodies are represented on the governing bodies of Institutes, and the Institutes are represented on college governing bodies and so on.

It is convenient to start with the academic work of the colleges. This is supervised and coordinated by Institutes (sometimes termed Schools) of Education acting as Area Training Organizations. The purpose of the ATOs is defined in the regulations as that of 'supervising the academic work of member institutions, securing cooperation among training establishments in its area, advising the Secretary of State on the approval of persons as teachers in schools, and promoting the study of education'. The Institutes are responsible for the content and standards of a college course, for approving syllabuses and for conducting examinations. They are a medium for planning the total training provision of an area and the means through which college courses are adjusted to the needs of teacher supply. They coordinate arrangements for teaching practice and they regulate the exceptional admission of students with less than or more than the required academic qualifications. They also provide libraries and in-service and other short courses.

In effect the Institutes have followed half the McNair Committee in creating an organization which brought the training colleges into a close and subordinate relationship with the universities. The McNair supporters of university Schools of Education said that they

did not believe that any area system for the training of teachers can be effective unless those who shoulder the responsibility derive their authority from a source which, because of its recognized standards and its standing in the educational world, commands the respect of all the partners concerned, and which, because of its established independence, is powerful enough to resist the encroachment of centralization. The universities embody these standards and have this standing and this independence.

They added that 'quite apart from these considerations

the universities have an obligation to the whole educational system'.

This solution was not inevitable. The other half of the McNair Committee thought there should be a development of the joint-boards scheme. In this, the university department and the training colleges would have preserved their identity and would have joined in assessing each other's students. Its supporters said that 'the joint boards scheme is more flexible than the university School of Education scheme, it involves an association of equals in the discharge of a common task instead of making the training colleges depend on the universities'. The rejection of this obvious truth has been a tragedy for teacher education.

Each Institute of Education has its governing body, whose members include representatives nominated by the senate together with those of member colleges and of the local authorities in the area. In many cases vice-chancellors preside. The governing bodies are responsible for the whole work of the Institutes, and since their ultimate authority is derived from the senate, the universities concerned assume the responsibility for the standards of work in the colleges. Below the Institutes' governing bodies there are academic or professional boards composed in the main of members of the training colleges, of the university department of education, and other university members. These are concerned with academic matters, especially syllabuses. Some members are appointed ex officio, others elected by the teaching staff of the colleges and the department of education. The director of the Institute presides. Assessors from the Department of Education and Science are present at meetings both of the governing bodies and of the academic boards of the Institutes.

Detailed work on syllabuses is carried out through a system of boards of studies composed of the college lecturers on the subject together with their opposite numbers from the university department of education, and some representatives from the relevant subject department of the university. These sometimes lay down uniform syllabuses, but they more usually consider syllabuses put up by individual colleges. The boards of studies also nominate internal and external examiners. Within the colleges themselves it is becoming normal for there to be academic boards and boards of studies in individual subjects to manage the colleges' academic work. Although these boards may comment upon administration and finance, power in these matters resides with the principal and governing body.

As far as administration and finance is concerned, training colleges are administered either by local authority or by voluntary bodies. The authorities own and maintain their colleges in the same way as their schools and other institutions. Since the Education (No. 2) Act, 1968, however, they have relinquished numerical control of governing bodies and appointment of their clerks and have given the governors power to spend under broad headings of estimates.

The voluntary colleges are direct-grant institutions getting almost 100 per cent of their recurrent expenditure from the Department of Education and Science. Their annual estimates are subject to approval by the Department, and the colleges are then free to spend within five broad heads. The Department pays 80 per cent of capital expenditure on expansion. Each college has its own governing body which is independent except so far as a parent body may control capital finance or staff be subject to the discipline of a religious order.

But behind the local authorities and the voluntary bodies is the Secretary of State and the Department of Education and Science. In contrast to its provisions on further education, the 1944 Education Act lays upon the Secretary of State for Education and Science specific duties for the training of teachers. Section 62 says that he shall

make such arrangements as he considers expedient for securing that there shall be available sufficient facilities for the training of teachers for service in schools, colleges and other establishments maintained by local education authorities, and for that purpose [he] may give to any local education authority such directions as he thinks necessary requiring them to establish, maintain or assist any training college or other institution or to provide or assist the provision of any other facilities specified in the direction.

In other words, in further education, as with schools, the initiative rests with the local education authority. So far as colleges of education are concerned, the initiative rests with the Secretary of State. Of course a number of colleges of education are owned by voluntary bodies and are aided by the local authorities. The rest have been established and maintained by the local authorities. Funnily enough, the Secretary of State has never given any specific directions about the establishment of these colleges and so the precise legal basis of the local authority colleges is somewhat vague.

The Education (No. 2) Act, 1968, laid down that in colleges of education there should be an instrument providing for the constitution of a body of governors. Such an instrument was to be made by order of the local authority with the approval of the Secretary of State. The articles of government, determining the functions to be exercised by the local authority, the body of governors, the principal and the academic board if any, were also to have the approval of the Secretary of State.

There is another kind of legal requirement which affects colleges of education. This appears in the Rate Support Grant (Pooling Arrangements) Regulations, 1967. These regulations provide for the pooling of expenditure of all local education authorities on teacher training (as well as on advanced further education and the education of pupils who do not belong to the area of any authority) and for the adjustment of the rate support grants in order to distribute the expenditure amongst all local education authorities. The aggregate amount of the actual expenditure in providing teacher training is apportioned among all local education authorities in proportion to their school population.

The Secretary of State also issues regulations governing colleges for the training of teachers: the Training of Teachers Regulations, 1967, as subsequently amended from time to time. These lay down that the initial training for a qualified teacher shall be not less than three years in a college of education, not less than one year of postgraduate training. They also provide for the supervision of the academic work of colleges by Area Training Organizations approved by the Secretary of State, and provide for representation of the universities, colleges of education and LEAs within the area. The regulations also give the Secretary of State quite detailed powers. He may give directions, after consultation, as to 'the numbers and categories of students to be admitted' to any particular college. Equally, it is the LEA that has to be satisfied about the suitability of a particular applicant for a course in a college of education. The regulations also lay down both a minimum age and the minimum qualifications of students entering the colleges.

In other words the colleges of education are subject to very many more detailed regulations involving more detailed ministerial control than are schools or colleges of further education. What is more, the Secretary of State's functions give him not only these additional powers but also the power to initiate in teacher training.

The educational consequences

These administrative arrangements have important educational consequences. First, the education of teachers takes place in 'mono-technic' institutions which are effectively isolated from the rest of higher education. Second, their vulnerability to Government demand has meant that over the years their chief preoccupation has been with accommodating ever larger numbers of students. Third, in so far as they have links, through the universities, with higher education they are subject to pressures which are irrelevant to their major purposes. These three sets of consequences are all linked, but it is convenient to take them in turn.

The isolation of the colleges is, as we have seen, explicable in historical terms though it is almost impossible to defend academically. For example, the very names 'university' and 'polytechnic' imply an educational view that it is best for students in higher education to be educated alongside others in different disciplines. Indeed it would be argued that contact between students taking different subjects is an essential part of higher education. All kinds of devices, some of them very expensive, have been evolved to encourage this, from colleges at Oxford and Cambridge to student unions and extra-curricular activities elsewhere. Until fairly recently, a concentration on even a fairly wide group of disciplines, like applied science and technology, was held to disqualify technical colleges from aspiring to full university status. When the University Grants Committee decided to inhibit the development of the social sciences in universities which had been colleges of advanced technology the victims' astonishment derived partly from the realization that they had more academic freedom when directly controlled by a Government department than they had through the UGC, but partly from what must have seemed a cavalier denial of a hundred-year-old assumption about what constituted a university.

In teacher education the isolation is especially serious, for two reasons. The first is that potential teachers may never escape from 'education'. They go from school to college and from college back to school without any contact with life outside. One need not overestimate the extent to which students in different disciplines mix and influence each other in other universities and colleges, but the possibility of doing so is there. It does not exist in a college of education.

The second defect of isolation is that it limits the intellectual contacts of the staffs of colleges of education. They come to depend academically upon the one university Institute of Education. In other words, they not only miss regular contact with university teachers in other disciplines; their relationship with university teachers, even of education, is actually impeded. In these circumstances very few of the colleges escape academic parochialism.

The second educational implication of the administrative structure is that for a decade or more the colleges have been vulnerable to Government pressure to accommodate ever increasing numbers of students. Their achievement here is astonishing. The numbers in colleges have more than doubled in the past five years alone. Much of this expansion has taken place without extra building resources. It may be argued that such responsiveness was right, in the interests of the schools, but to be quite happy about it one would need to assume that the decisions of the Department of Education and Science were rational and thoughtful and related to the interests of the students. Indeed, the staff of colleges and especially the principals had grave doubts about expansion until the salaries of both principals and vice-principals were related to a capitation grant based upon student numbers. It is becoming clear, however, that the quality of discussion within the Department has been rather low, based upon crude and misleading statistical projections about the demand for teachers . . . Certainly the Department seems to have shown only an incidental interest in the quality of teachers being produced by the colleges, whether this is measured in terms of the qualifications of entrants or of the level of work expected of them. Even the famous decision to lengthen the training-college course from two years to three was taken for reasons of supply and demand, to be rationalized later as an opportunity to increase quality. The more recent decisions to require specified subjects at O-level and to require that graduate teachers be trained can also be seen as a tentative response to a fear that we shall have 'too many teachers'.

But the preoccupation with colleges cannot, of course, be confined to administrators. The colleges themselves have been subjected to great strain. The last ten years have not been propitious for thinking deeply about the fundamental purposes of teacher education. It has been as much as most colleges can do to accommodate the extra students and educate them to something like the standards they remembered from the past. There may be other reasons for the lack of profound educational thinking in the colleges. But one of the most important has been the sheer pressure of work.

The third consequence of the administrative situation of the colleges is that their academic aspirations are determined by the universities. This is perhaps the most serious consequence of all. I have written elsewhere about the existence of two traditions in British higher education. The first, which I call the 'university tradition', is academic and exclusive. It is concerned, to put it crudely, with the preservation, extension and dissemination of knowledge 'for its own sake'. It is on the whole educationally conservative. It gives at least as high a value to research as to teaching. The other tradition I call the 'technical-college tradition'. This is inclusive or 'comprehensive'. It is concerned not with knowledge for its own sake but with vocational and professional education—even with 'mere' vocational training. It is educationally innovative: the only major innovation in higher education this century has been the sandwich course, an invention of the technical colleges. The technical college tradition is a teaching tradition: research tends to be 'applied' or even a 'service', perhaps to local industry.

It ought to have been a matter of continuous debate which of these traditions was more appropriate for colleges concerned with the training of teachers. In fact, it seems to have been assumed without question, not least by the established senior staff in the colleges themselves, that academic and other links with universities were the only obvious and desirable ones, and this despite the fact that the universities have shown themselves almost wholly inimical to the development of teacher education as a university discipline. Even university departments of education have never been accepted on terms of equality with other departments, still less the colleges, which have been kept not only in tutelage but at arm's length.

Many of the complaints which the schools make about the products of the colleges, much of the disgust which students express about their training, much of the timidity, aridity and conservatism of the colleges can be directly attributed to the influence of the academic tradition. The pursuit of knowledge for its own sake is not a good basis for professional education: at this level it is a recipe for triviality and irrelevance. Perhaps the best example of this can be seen in the development of the B.Ed. degree. It is clear that the universities see the B.Ed. not as a way of producing better teachers so much as a way of keeping college students out of the universities, or at best of attracting better people into the colleges of education—where, given many B.Ed. courses, they are promptly turned into worse teachers. In other words, for most colleges, and for most teachers in training, the university connection has been a mistake and often a disaster. The preparation of teachers can best be thought of in terms of the technical-college tradition, and if such thinking became common it would lead to a fundamental reappraisal of the training of teachers in educational terms. It is important to realize the influence which administrative arrangements have had in preventing this fundamental thinking from taking place.

As well as all these educational consequences there is one political consequence of the administrative structure surrounding colleges of education. It derives from the direct initiative which the Secretary of State enjoys—and which she does not have either in the schools or in further education. Policy is evolved and implemented almost in private. Because of the extent of her controls, the Secretary of State can make decisions and get them implemented as if they were purely administrative acts. Important educational questions like the length of course, the balance of training, the qualifications of entrants are answered almost out of the blue, and the reason is that the Secretary of State possesses such a battery of controls and such a direct method of communicating her decisions. No doubt letters to colleges are discussed in draft with the local authorities and teachers' associations, but the extent of the discussion is extremely limited.

The situation in the schools and further education is quite different. Because the Secretary of State's power of initiative is much less, the evolution of policy goes on much more in public. A decision to designate polytechnics requires a White Paper, followed by notes for guidance. A decision about class sizes in schools elicits an explanatory circular. The difference is an important one of administrative style, and it has helped to explain why public disquiet about teacher education has not been matched by public debate. The refusal of successive Secretaries of State . . . to have a full-scale inquiry into teacher education which would include questioning of their own policies and practices is both a symptom of what is wrong and an unnecessarily brutal emphasis of their determination to preserve the *status quo*. The situation of teacher education is such that an informed public discussion of its problems would entail a revolution in its administrative structures.

49 No way to run a college

Ronald Goldman

Are local authorities in Britain competent to control institutions of higher education? After 17 years working in various universities and colleges, the last three as principal of Didsbury College, one of England's largest colleges of education, my answer is firmly negative. The colleges of education situation illustrates this point well.

There are 163 colleges of education in England and Wales. Fifty are voluntary colleges run by the churches and financed directly by the Department of Education and Science. The remaining 113 are under the control of local education authorities and are financed from the teacher training pool, a levy drawn from all local authorities on the basis of pupils enrolled in the maintained schools.

A large city like Manchester may have five colleges concerned with teacher training but only about 3 per cent of the total costs are met out of the rates; the rest comes from the 'pool'. The local authorities are guardians of the public purse and in this manner control many other institutions of higher education such as colleges of art, colleges of technology and polytechnics.

My experience and that of many other principals has led me to believe that local authority control, in spite of the Weaver report, leads to considerable financial waste, inept administration, irrational interference by partisan interests and an attitude of mind totally alien to the basic assumption of higher education. To the general public the examples which follow may appear bizarre. To those involved in running the colleges, they are a daily and dismal reality.

A classical example in Manchester is the new sports hall and swimming pool now approaching completion at Didsbury College. This was offered as a capital grant project costing £60,000 in 1963 to provide for what was then to be a college of 1,200 students. With strong PE departments, the swimming pool was designed to provide courses for teachers of swimming, which the country desperately needs.

Protracted discussions began and continued for six years in governors' meetings, further education, finance, buildings and the baths and laundries committees. Argument centred on two issues—whether the pool should be on the main college campus or three-quarters of a mile away next to a secondary school, and whether the college should have a swimming pool at all.

College representatives were at some of these meet-

ings and sometimes decisions were made, and later reversed, when no representatives were present. The swimming pool became a political shuttlecock between those who claimed to represent the schools, their local constituencies, the general public and other interested parties.

Eventually, after an indication from the Department of Education and Science that if work did not begin on the project before March 1969 it would be lost, the Manchester City Council approved it by 70 votes to 31, after its rejection had been moved by the chairman of the Baths and Laundries Committee.

Meanwhile, costs had escalated from £60,000 to more than £126,000. This was pruned to £112,000, then to £105,650. The college will now have a building far less useful and with many essential features cut which may be reinstated later only at considerable expense to the taxpayer.

Some of the delays and struggles are caused by a mentality which is geared to the administration of schools. For example, the principal of a college of 850 students soon to expand to more than 1,000 was re-equipping the deputy principal's office to a reasonable standard. The governors approved a desk and chair and the usual paper-work began in June.

The principal went on holiday in late August and returned a week before the start of term. There was still no office furniture for the deputy principal. After nearly half an hour on the phone to the 'office' a clerk told him that he 'struck it off' because the chair and the desk were more expensive than the furniture allowed to a headmaster in the schools.

A newish day college ordered six microscopes. The principal was told that he could have only three because no more than three were supplied at one time to any of the authority's schools.

Some colleges are bound by catering contracts negotiated for school meals. In some cases, no consultation between the college and the l.e.a. takes place before the contracts are placed and the meals are frequently unsuitable for a residential college.

Whether certain institutions of higher education should remain under the control of local authorities is much more than a financial matter. Even if local authorities do not continually make the blunders cited here, it is questionable if there exists an adequate administrative framework or a sufficiently sympathetic appreciation of the tasks of the colleges by a local authority's officers, councillors and aldermen.

Power lies in the hands of many who are apparently unaware of the changes occurring in universities and

Source: The Times Educational Supplement, 1 January 1971.

colleges today. Three years ago it was recognized in a college of 1,400 students that a senior administrative officer was needed to attend to day-to-day administration. An appointment was delayed for three years because the salary required was not acceptable to other local authority groups and interests.

Heads of large college departments with staffs of 20 or 30 type letters and keep files because the college must conform to a staffing formula observed by the local authority although it is quite inappropriate to the needs of expanding undergraduate and postgraduate teaching programmes.

The attitude of mind is often totally alien to the basic assumption about higher education most of us hold. Officials appear to expect lecturers to be present every day from nine to five. Anything suggestive of 'research' and other activities not apparently directly involved in producing more teachers is regarded with suspicion.

After some patient negotiations for research funds, one principal reported to governors his success in gaining a first large research grant. This was accepted by the chairman with the remark: 'I don't know what we need research money for. We have our local authority officers to tell us what we want to know.'

The first suggestion for a visiting professor was met with: 'We don't need foreigners coming here and telling us about our school problems.' Permission for the head of a college department of Russian to lead a party of teachers of Russian to the Soviet Union was received with: 'Why do we have to send people there? They can't teach us anything about education.'

Such ignorance is not confined to verbal squabbles in governors' meetings. Many principals have been asked to disclose the names of colleagues whose views were misreported to narrow-minded governors as 'dangerous'. I personally refused such information since the questioners left me in no doubt that there would be interference with the rights of colleagues.

All this is contrary to the whole tradition of academic freedom. Small wonder I was advised, when reporting to such governors, not to say anything about my books (I produced two educational books while a college principal) because some members might feel I was not doing my job properly. I was also told to say little about invitations to lecture in the United States and Australia; they 'might be misunderstood'! The fact that the academic head of a large college is cautioned in this way is a sad commentary on the parochial outlook of those who control its affairs.

Officials often justify the continuance of such control by pointing out the advantages which the expertise of the finance, buildings, legal, estates, management and other departments of a city council can provide. Sometimes such expertise is of value; usually it is a nuisance, causing considerable delays and, occasionally, serious loss.

A principal of a large college secured the offer of a lease of part of a suite of buildings opposite the campus. Set in pleasant grounds, there were tutorial and lecture rooms, laboratories and workshops. He was told by the authority that its experts would secure the lease on advantageous terms within a short time.

Their negotiations were so long-winded that fifteen months later the offer was withdrawn and the premises lost to the college. Within a month, a nationalized industry had them for offices. Today the college is overcrowded and lacking in essential features, which, at a conservative estimate, it would cost more than £300,000 to provide.

In another authority in the north the principal told officials that land separating two parts of the college was available at about £2,500. After considerable delay the land was finally bought for more than £8,000.

Delays and failure to consult are excused by such statements as 'Nothing belongs to the College. It is the local authority's land and building to use as it decides.' It is often said that the authority has a total view of the educational needs of a city and is in the best position to plan wisely for the future.

But even in the limited range of planning for teacher education many cities have bungled badly. Colleges have been founded and allowed to develop piecemeal without any survey of the availability of teaching practice places in the surrounding schools.

With four l.e.a. and two voluntary colleges, Manchester opened a teacher education section for 300 students in the local college of technology, adding to the demands on the schools and preventing smaller colleges from growing to larger and more viable economic size. Availability of B.Ed. courses in most of the colleges led to small uneconomic groupings of students at a time when staffing was difficult. The authority is now aware of these problems but the time for planning wisely was five years before.

What method of government could prevent these abuses not only in colleges of education but as demonstrated so spectacularly in the Hornsey and Guildford colleges of Art, now threatening the polytechnics? If the Maud report on local government is carried out the situation may become worse. Greater size is no guarantee of greater efficiency. The alternative is to let local interests be represented on governing bodies of the colleges, but to take financial control from the local authority.

If all university-equivalent institutions within the binary system, colleges of education, colleges of art, polytechnics and others were released from the hands of local authorities and financial control were given to a joint grants committee with effective treasury control, this could create a more suitable climate.

Successive governments having chosen to reject the Robbins recommendation and having set up the binary system should play fair with the non-university sector. Apart from the issue of placing power in the hands of local political despots of both the major political parties, financial considerations alone would seem to argue for a different system.

Introduction to reading 50

In the following article (originally printed in *Higher Education Review*, spring 1970) Brian MacArthur, then education correspondent of *The Times*, and now editor of *The Times Higher Education Supplement*, gives a journalist's view of how crucial decisions for the future of British higher education come to be made. The article is now partly of historical interest only, since the Labour Government fell soon after it was written, and Mr Short and Mr Fowler ceased to be Secretary of State and Minister of State for Education and Science. No decision on the main issues discussed had been announced by the new Conservative Government by mid-1972, although a projection of student numbers in higher education up to 1981, broadly confirming the figures given by Mr MacArthur, was published by the Department of Education and Science in autumn 1970 (*Educational Planning Paper No. 2*, HMSO, 1970). The article still provides however an interesting external view of the machinery and process of planning.

The 'NUS' is the National Union of Students, and the 'AUT' the Association of University Teachers. 'DEP' were the initials by which the Department of Employment and Productivity (now 'of Employment' only) was known.

50   Who plans higher education?

Brian MacArthur

During the past five to six years the Government and the education authorities have increasingly acknowledged a duty to enable the debate about education to be conducted on an informed basis. The output of information from Curzon Street and education offices has increased enormously, and the career of the education correspondent has blossomed. There has also been a spiral effect. Newspapers recognized a public appetite for news about schools, colleges and universities by appointing education correspondents. The correspondents (whose work was pioneered by Tyrrell Burgess, Peter Preston and Willem van der Eyken) did their work impressively well. So the public appetite was still further whetted, leading to a still greater output of news from the authorities. It is a rare day now when there is no report about some aspect of education in daily newspapers, and some papers now have two correspondents.

So far, so good, but the inquiring education correspondent still faces many barriers if he wants to discover the real, as opposed to the inspired, story. The tradition of confidentiality about the disposal of millions of pounds of public money still persists; and one recent example of this has been the debate about the future of higher education. It is one in which I have been particularly involved, and it offers an object lesson in the persisting barriers to an informed public discussion of crucial issues, as well as showing how newspapers can remove them. As one insider observed, the present discussions confront the Government with a major democratic and qualitative decision. Yet until recently, that decision was being debated

Source: Higher Education Review (1970), **2** (2), 31–7.

privately by 20 or 30 academics, civil servants and Ministers. Neither the NUS nor the AUT was involved; and until now none of the names of the participants have been disclosed. All through 1969, however, the details of what was occurring seeped out slowly until by December the debate had at last become public; and it is worth considering how this happened.

January 1969: The issues were well known but the developing crisis, showing in demographic and school leaving trends, was not. It was clear that the Robbins projections would be exceeded, but not by how much. According to Robbins, 204,000 university places would be needed in 1971–2, but in 1968 the Government authorized an expansion to between 220,000 and 225,000, and the actual figure will now be some 230,000. A similar expansion was occurring outside the universities, and on an even more dramatic scale. In 1968, colleges of education and advanced FE were each about 20,000 students beyond the Robbins target. Several of the new polytechnics were on the verge of designation, and it was a year for the UGC to start its planning for the next quinquennium, 1972 to 1977.

March 24: A front page story in *The Times*, under the headlines 'Student total may double by 1982' and 'Cut-cost scheme to expand universities', announced that plans to expand universities, polytechnics and colleges of education whilst reducing student unit costs were being prepared in Whitehall. The student population, it suggested, might double from 380,000 to perhaps 750,000, and one prospect was that one in three 18 year olds would be qualified for higher education instead of the present one in four or five. One paragraph said: 'If the Treasury says that the economy in the 1970's can support only the same proportion of 18 year olds entering higher education, about 17 per cent a year, much will depend on what savings the universities can offer'. The report was dismissed at the Department of Education and Science as 'moonshine'.

March 28: Sir William Alexander, secretary of the Association of Education Committees, writing in his weekly column in *Education*, said that the announcement would come as 'something of a surprise' to education authorities because so far there had been no discussion of it with the local authority associations. He argued that it was a basic fact that demand for higher education would double and that such an expansion, on present arrangements, could not be afforded. He aired the ideas of more students attending their local universities and a worsening of the universities' staff student ratio.

May 14: Speaking at Bradford University, Shirley Williams, then Minister of State overseeing education said that an increase in places of at least two thirds would be needed if opportunities were to remain equal. 'In the present atmosphere,' she said, during a speech about student extremism, 'that is not going to be easy to achieve.' A guess from her remarks indicated a student population of about 650,000 by 1982.

April 25: The slow unfolding continued. Edward Short, Secretary of State for Education and Science, speaking to university teachers at Newcastle upon Tyne, outlined the Government's two main expectations of the universities: that their funds should be used effectively and that they should be responsible to the manpower needs of the economy. He went on: 'We cannot be certain that the proportion of GNP devoted to universities will increase at the same rate as the number of well-qualified candidates coming forward . . . and we have to be prepared to meet the situation that will arise if it does not.' He outlined two alternatives. One, for which he opted personally, was rationalization. The other, which he found unacceptable, was to reduce the proportion of the age group able to get into higher education by raising the entry qualifications.

July 24–28: The future of higher education was debated at about 3 a.m. by Mrs Williams and Sir Edward Boyle, Opposition spokesman on education, in a short Commons debate. On July 28 the front page of *The Times* reported that Mrs Williams had described a plan to save costs by introducing a six term academic year as 'most encouraging'. It would enable an expansion of student numbers by a third without any effect on the staff-student ratio or increases in spending. At that time, I quoted a student population of 630,000 as the Government's minimum target for 1980 —a figure for England and Wales which was then being used by universities, the UGC and Ministers, based on DES projections of school leavers' examination successes.

August 4: A report printed across five columns in *The Times* announced: 'No places planned for 50,000 students.' It reported an updated DES forecast suggesting that the number of sixth formers achieving two 'A' levels by 1980 would be 170,000 a year instead of the 120,000 on which the Department had based its estimate of a student population of 630,000. On the old target, student populations of 350,000 for the universities and 150,000 for the polytechnics had been projected, but the effect of the updated projection remained privy only to insiders.

September 25: A press release was put out by the DES (against, I understand, the advice of civil servants but on the insistence of Mrs Williams) after a meeting between Ministers, civil servants, the UGC and Vice-Chancellors at University College, London. Although it did not draw any conclusions or add any sums, it confirmed the earlier *Times* report. It included one crucial paragraph: 'Revised DES/SED projections show a large increase in the 1970's and 1980's in the numbers of school leavers and others who will obtain appropriate qualifications for entry to higher education, as compared with previously published projections. If assumptions similar to those embodied in the Robbins Report are applied to these revised projections, *the number of full-time places in higher education required in the mid-1970's and beyond would be some 40 per cent higher than those recommended in the Robbins Report*' (my italics).

September 26: After doing some hurried sums, *The Times* estimated on the basis of the DES information that 630,000 places would be needed in 1976 and 780,000 in 1980. Among the measures canvassed at the meeting, according to the official release and reported in the paper, were: greater selection for higher education, the more productive use of facilities and the scope for their joint use, the adoption of new forms of organization, expansion of part time and correspondence courses, a more intensive use of equipment, more economical construction of buildings, a change in the proportion of students who were residential, in lodgings or based at home, types of student support and the staff-student ratio.

October: The story, now almost confirmed by the Government, continued to grow and emerge. Volume One of 1968 *Statistics of Education*, published on October 17, confirmed the projections disclosed in the DES release. They forecast 171,600 pupils aged 17 at school in 1975, against the previous estimate of 142,000 and 238,000 in 1980 instead of 191,000. They projected 278,000 in 1990. On October 21, *The Times* at last got the real projection on which the talks were being based. This was a target of about 825,000 students, based on 720,000 for England and Wales and another 100,000 for Scotland. It added that the understanding was that universities would expand to 450,000 students and polytechnics presumably to about 250,000, but that about ten new universities would be needed if the universities were to go to 450,000. Under the heading 'Awkward shape of things to come', the debate was continued on the 24th in a leader page article in *The Times Educational Supplement* by Stuart Maclure, its editor, which ended by saying that the more Gerald Fowler, successor to Mrs Williams, could bring the argument out into the open the better.

November: After *The Times* report on September 26, the AUT (reviving under the energetic leadership of Laurie Sapper) as well as the NUS, had protested to the DES at their exclusion from the University College meeting. Now, on November 24, the AUT published a summary of a report it was preparing on the future of higher education. It was a radical document for the AUT, proposing a university population of 450,000 by 1980, an end to the binary policy and the development of the polytechnics into universities, but opposing most of the economies under discussion. On November 25, at Birmingham University, Mr Fowler made his first major speech and a Minister set out squarely for the first time the dramatic nature of the debate. It was now expected, he said, that over 20 per cent of the 18 year old age group by 1977–8 would be getting at least two 'A' levels, and he added: 'If in a decade we shall be faced with a demand for student places in higher education which is composed of over 20 per cent of the age group and still rising, we are undoubtedly moving towards a mass higher education system different from that which we have traditionally known in this country. Certainly in a period of rapid expansion we shall need to consider nationally, against the best advice we can receive, the problem of where to concentrate resources or how to divide up the resources which are available for higher education as a whole.'

December: Another front page article in *The Times* disclosed details of a document sent round the universities by the Committee of Vice-Chancellors, setting out all 13 methods suggested at the University College meeting (the most contentious of which had been omitted from the official release). Although the document had not been sent to newspapers, it represented an ambitious attempt at least to open a debate within the universities.

The story was followed up by all newspapers and it could be said at last that the debate was truly out in the open: open to teachers, students, MPs and the public.

Other events during the month were a spate of articles and letters to newspapers and questions in Parliament; separate meetings between Mr Fowler and the AUT and the NUS; the six-monthly conference of the AUT, which decided to hold a special conference on the issue in February; and the establishment, after encouragement from Sir Alan Richmond, principal of Lanchester Polytechnic who was at first

rebuffed, of a committee of polytechnic directors, or at least of a working party under R. E. Wood, director of the Leicester Polytechnic, to plan one. A vigorous and public debate was about to be joined in 1970, which had not been at all certain at the start of the academic year.

It was after the meeting with the AUT that the Department took the first major step towards promoting an open debate. It issued the following admirable press notice:

FUTURE STUDENT NUMBERS IN HIGHER EDUCATION
1. The latest projection by the Department of Education and Science suggests that the number of school leavers with qualifications for entry into higher education will grow even more markedly during the 1970's than previous projections had implied. The new forecast of school leavers with two or more 'A' level passes in 1981 is in the case of boys over 25 per cent higher, and in the case of girls over 50 per cent higher, than the most recently published estimate.[1]
2. The table below sets out, on the Robbins basis of relating higher education to numbers of qualified school leavers and other potential entrants, numbers of full-time students (undergraduate and post-graduate) in higher education as a whole in *England and Wales*. The Robbins figures are given for comparisons.

STUDENTS IN FULL-TIME HIGHER EDUCATION,
ENGLAND AND WALES

	(THOUSANDS)	
	DES	ROBBINS
1962–3	185	188
	(actual)	(recommendation)
1967–8	331	281
	(actual)	(recommendation)
1971–2 projection	437	305
1976–7 projection	557	388
1981–2 projection	727	510

If the figures for the colleges of education, the size of whose entry is determined by other considerations, are subtracted from the DES figures, the remaining figure is of the order of 433,000 in 1976–7 and 597,000 in 1981–2.
3. Whether places should in fact be found for all these numbers, and if so how they should be distributed between universities and advanced further education, are being considered in the Department. If in 1981 the universities were to take about 53 per cent of all school leavers with two or more 'A' levels, which was the proportion in 1963, and if allowance is made for entrants otherwise than from school and for numbers in Scottish universities, the number of university students in *Great Britain* in 1981–2 would be over 450,000.
4. The Department hopes to publish in the early part of 1970 a detailed account of its projections

of student numbers in higher education, and of the assumptions on which they are based.

Department of Education and Science

5 December 1969

Some of the principal developments during 1970 can already be predicted ... University vice-chancellors will presumably be informing UGC and the Government about university reactions to the 13 proposals, and the UGC will then inform the Government of its own conclusions about the two next quinquennia. A decision should be reached during the summer. But will this represent simply another leap in the dark, a hunch, or will it be based on the most informed advice and projections available to *all* the parties?

So far as the UGC is concerned, especially under Kenneth Berrill, the new chairman and an expert on public expenditure, it will be sophisticated, as, indeed, it should be with the expertise and experience at the Committee's disposal. Surveys both of sites and of the capacity of existing universities have been made, suggesting, I believe, that present universities could expand, if pushed, to up to about 420,000, but that new universities would be needed to meet a target of 450,000. As the university building programme for the next quinquennium must be got in hand this year, the urgency of the decision, especially if new universities are to be created, can be appreciated.

At the DES, however (perhaps understandably in view of the UGC's admitted expertise and the alleged role as a buffer between universities and Government), it seems that no work at all on estimating the costs of all the various alternatives open to Ministers had started until quite recently.

Against this, the Committee of Vice-Chancellors has been developing its own special inquiries and expanding its own work, so that in some areas it is now better informed than the UGC as well as better able to offer necessary interpretation in others on some matters. Surveys have been made of the use and capacity of buildings, alternative arrangements of the academic year and of any savings, almost nil it turned out, if more students lived at home.

Advising the main committee are four divisions, dealing respectively with university capital considera-

tions, recurrent grants and fees, academic matters and student matters, under the chairmanship respectively of Lord Annan, Charles Carter, Dr T. A. S. Noble and James Drever.

Who are the principal participants in the inside debate, and who will eventually take the major decision? The major bodies, of course, will be the Committee of Vice-Chancellors, the committee of polytechnic directors if it establishes itself in time, the UGC, the branches of DES dealing with finance, planning, colleges of education and polytechnics, and Mr Fowler and Mr Short. If the members of the University College meeting on September 25 offer any clue, the small group which will decide the future of the universities will be formed from the six vice-chancellors who attended (Sir Eric Ashby, Sir Derman Christopherson, Lord Annan, J. B. Butterworth, Mr Carter and Dr F. S. Dainton); Kenneth Berrill and Sir Robert Aitken from the UGC; and Toby Weaver, R. Toomey, N. T. Hardyman and Philip Redfern, all senior civil servants—and Mr Fowler and Mr Short.

Their conclusions will probably go to the education programmes committee in Whitehall (chaired by the DES, with representation from Scotland, Wales, the Treasury, the Technology Ministry and the DEP), to the Social Services Committee of the Cabinet, and then to the Cabinet itself. After that the university building programme for 1972–7 will be announced, which should offer a clue to the decision that has been reached.

Even so, however splendid the attempt to draw up a coherent national plan for higher education, any decision this year should be considered only as provisional. All past experience has shown the need for constant upward revision of the projections of student demand. Two factors whose effect cannot yet be estimated, for example, are universal comprehensivization and the raising of the school-leaving age. ... At least, however, on this occasion, a serious attempt is being made to get the broad outlines for development correct. All that an education correspondent could ask is that newspapers should be able to sustain a serious debate on the statistical and other factors which affect the eventual decision.

Note

1 *Statistics of Education, 1967,* **2** (HMSO 1969), Table 34.

Appendix Statements on education in the general election manifestos of the three major British political parties 1959–70

1 Conservative manifestos

1959

EDUCATION. During the next five years we shall concentrate on producing a massive enlargement of educational opportunity at every level. The necessary work is already in hand. Four programmes, each the biggest of its kind ever undertaken in Britain, are gathering momentum.

Training colleges for teachers, which will now provide a three-year course, are being expanded by nearly two-thirds so as to get rid of over-large classes; the number of students at universities is to be further increased by at least one-third; new technical college buildings are opening at the rate of one a week; and we shall spend some £400 million by 1965 to improve the quality of our school buildings.

We shall defend the grammar schools against doctrinaire Socialist attack, and see that they are further developed. We shall bring the modern schools up to the same high standard. Then the choice of schooling for children can be more flexible and less worrying for parents. This is the right way to deal with the problem of the 'eleven-plus'. Already, up and down the country, hundreds of new modern schools are showing the shape of things to come. Our programme will open up the opportunities that they provide for further education and better careers to every boy and girl; and by 1965 we expect that at least 40 per cent will be staying on after fifteen.

We have appointed a Committee to review the system of awards to students from public funds, including the present 'means test', and improvements will be made when it has reported.

1964

BUILDINGS AND TEACHERS. The building of new schools and the modernizing of existing ones will be pressed ahead. The rising school population will put heavy pressure on our resources, but we are determined to devote a share of each year's programme to improving conditions in the older primary schools.

The training colleges will be producing by 1970 three times as many new teachers as in 1958, and the larger numbers going on to higher education will mean more teachers later on. We shall sustain our successful campaign for the return of qualified married women to teaching. Improved machinery will be established for the negotiation of teachers' salaries.

RESEARCH AND ORGANIZATION. We shall continue to encourage educational research and provide extra funds for this purpose.

Of the many different forms of secondary school organization which now exist, none has established itself as exclusively right. The Socialist plan to impose the comprehensive principle, regardless of the wishes of parents, teachers and authorities, is therefore foolishly doctrinaire. Their leader may protest that grammar schools will be abolished 'over his dead body', but abolition would be the inevitable and disastrous consequence of the policy to which they are committed. Conservative policy, by contrast, is to encourage provision, in good schools of every description, of opportunities for all children to go forward to the limit of their capacity.

THE YOUTH SERVICE. Beyond the gates of school, college and factory young people need ample facilities for social activity and outlets for adventure and service.

As we promised in 1959, the Youth Service has been rejuvenated through the building of new clubs and the training of capable leaders. We shall press forward with this work, encourage more courses of the 'Outward Bound' type and foster schemes whereby young people can assist the elderly.

Opportunity for youth

Education is the most rapidly developing feature of

our social outlay. Its share of the expanded national wealth has risen since 1951 from 3 per cent to 5 per cent, and will go on rising. This reflects our view of education as at once a right of the child, a need of society, and a condition of economic efficiency. It also matches a tremendous upsurge in educational ambition and attainment.

EDUCATIONAL EXPANSION. Our aim is to see that suitable education or training is available to every boy and girl up to at least eighteen. These are the steps we shall take:

1. The minimum school-leaving age will be raised to sixteen for all who enter secondary school after the summer of 1967. This, which we looked forward to in the 1944 Education Act, is not to be just 'another year at school'. The whole school course will be refashioned to give a wider and deeper education.

2. More and more who have the ability to benefit will stay on to seventeen and eighteen and go forward to higher education. This will be made possible by our plans for the universities colleges of advanced technology, higher technical institutions and teacher training colleges. There will be places for 100,000 extra students by 1968, and for a steadily growing number after that.

3. For those leaving school to start work at once, we shall further develop the Youth Employment Service and encourage the appointment by schools of careers advisers of high calibre, as well as improving industrial apprenticeship and training. Steps will be taken to increase the number of industrial workers under eighteen who are released during the day to attend technical and other courses. We shall continue our great expansion of technical colleges.

1966

TO PROVIDE BETTER EDUCATION. Get more teachers especially for the primary schools by expanding the Colleges of Education, enabling part-time teachers to qualify for pension, and giving more encouragement to married women who want to return to teaching.

See that more teaching aids are made available.

Give back to local authorities the freedom to make small improvements, for example, an extra classroom or better sanitation.

Encourage local education authorities to provide as full a range of courses as possible in all their secondary schools.

Judge proposals for reorganization on their educational merits. Strongly oppose hasty and makeshift plans, especially in the big cities, for turning good grammar and secondary modern schools into comprehensive schools.

Give improvements to primary school accommodation priority over projects for building new comprehensive schools where adequate secondary accommodation already exists.

Give parents as much choice as possible by having diversity in the pattern of education. Give independent

schools of high standing the opportunity to become direct grant schools, thus narrowing the gap between State schools and fee paying schools.

Establish an Educational Television Centre to encourage the best use of television—broadcast and closed circuit—in schools, colleges and universities.

Restore the university and further education buildings programmes cut by the Labour Government.

1970

BETTER EDUCATION. In education above all the problem of resources is crucial. The number of children in the schools is rising. More and more are qualifying to go on to colleges, polytechnics and universities. That they should be able to develop their abilities to the full is not only right in itself but a vital national investment in the future.

Within the education budget itself, we shall shift the emphasis in favour of primary schools—the foundation on which all later education and training is built.

We also recognize the need for expansion of nursery education. This is especially important in areas of social handicap, such as the poorer parts of our large cities, where it is so vital to give children a better start.

In secondary education, a number of different patterns have developed over the years, including many types of comprehensive school. We will maintain the existing rights of local education authorities to decide what is best for their area.

They will take into account the general acceptance that in most cases the age of eleven is too early to make final decisions which might affect a child's whole future. Many of the most imaginative new schemes abolishing the eleven-plus have been introduced by Conservative councils.

Local councils must ensure that the education they provide is the best for the children, taking into account the suitability of the buildings, the supply of staff, the travelling distances involved, the advice of teachers, and the wishes of parents and local electors. And they must be certain that they provide properly for the late developer. And they will naturally be slow to make irrevocable changes to any good school unless they are sure that the alternative is better.

We believe that the proper role of the central government is to satisfy itself that every local education authority provides education which will enable a child's talents and abilities to be developed to the full, at whatever age these may appear. All children must have the opportunity of getting to 'O' level and beyond if they are capable of doing so.

We therefore believe that Labour's attempt to insist on compulsory reorganization on rigid lines is contrary to local democracy and contrary to the best interests of the children.

We will raise the school leaving age to sixteen as planned. Opportunities should be given to some children, under the authority of their head teacher, to take advantage in their final year of the facilities available in colleges of further education.

We will encourage the direct grant schools. Many of these schools have an excellent record and provide opportunities which may not otherwise be available for children of academic ability, regardless of their parents' income.

Parents must have the freedom to send their children to independent schools if they wish.

The demand for higher and further education in universities, polytechnics and other colleges will increase during the 1970's. We will expand the number of places available.

Concern about teacher training is widespread. We will institute an inquiry into teacher training, as the Plowden Committee recommended. We wish the teaching profession to have a career structure which will attract recruits of high quality into the profession, and retain them.

2 Labour manifestos

1959

EDUCATION. Money spent on education is an investment for the future. We propose, therefore, a great drive to abolish slum schools, to reduce the size of classes to 30 in primary and secondary schools, and to expand facilities for technical and other higher education.

One of the greatest barriers to equality of opportunity in our schools is the segregation of our children into grammar and other types of school at the age of 11. This is why we shall get rid of the 11-plus examination. The Tories say this means abolishing the grammar schools. On the contrary, it means that grammar-school education will be open to all who can benefit by it. In our system of comprehensive education we do not intend to impose one uniform pattern of school. Local authorities will have the right to decide how best to apply the comprehensive principle.

At present, children whose parents cannot pay fees often suffer from an unfair disadvantage in secondary education. By improving the system of maintenance grants, we shall make sure that no child is deprived of secondary schooling by the parents' lack of money. In the same way we shall ensure that any student accepted by a university will receive a really adequate State scholarship.

1964

EDUCATION. Our country's 'investment in people' is still tragically inadequate. The nation needs and Labour will carry through a revolution in our educational system.

(i) Labour will cut down our overcrowded classes in both primary and secondary schools; the aim is to reduce all classes to 30 at the earliest possible moment.

(ii) Labour will get rid of the segregation of children into separate schools caused by 11 plus selection: secondary education will be reorganized on comprehensive lines. Within the new system, grammar school education will be extended: in future no child will be denied the opportunity of benefiting from it through arbitrary selection at the age of eleven. This reform will make it possible to provide a worthwhile extra year of education by raising the school-leaving age to 16.

(iii) To minimize the effects of the postponement of school leaving on the large family, Labour will replace inadequate maintenance grants with reorganized family allowances, graduated according to the age of the child, with a particularly steep rise for those remaining at school after the statutory leaving age.

(iv) As the first step to part-time education for the first two years after leaving school, Labour will extend compulsory day and block release.

(v) Labour will carry out a programme of massive expansion in higher, further and university education. To stop the 'brain drain' Labour will grant to the universities and colleges of advanced technology the funds necessary for maintaining research standards in a period of rapid student expansion.

(vi) Labour will set up an educational trust to advise on the best way of integrating the public schools into the state system of education.

The modernization of our school system will require time and money and manpower. In order to get the priorities right Labour will work out a phased and costed plan for the whole of education. To assure the funds, Labour will restore the percentage grant and transfer the larger part of the cost of teachers' salaries from the rates to the Exchequer. Finally—and most important—since everything depends on teachers, Labour will give to teacher supply a special priority in its first years in office, negotiating a new salary structure including a new superannuation scheme favourable to part-time and elderly teachers, encouraging more entrants to teaching and winning back the thousands of women lost by marriage.

The whole future of our education depends on the success of a crash programme for teacher recruitment which appeals not merely to boys and girls at school but to adults with experience of practical life that will give an edge to their teaching.

1966

EDUCATIONAL OPPORTUNITIES FOR ALL. Our educational aims are two-fold: to give the highest possible standard of education to all children, and to ensure that those with special abilities have the opportunity to develop them to the full.

These aims have to be achieved against an inheritance of acute teacher shortage, oversized classes, old and inadequate school buildings, and a chronically overstrained system of higher education.

SCHOOLS. Our first priority is to reduce the size of classes. We shall intensify our efforts to increase the recruitment of teachers, and improve their status in society.

We must also make the most effective use of teachers, by encouraging the use of audio-visual aids and programmed learning; and by providing the teacher with the ancillary help which he increasingly needs.

We shall carry out the largest school building programme in our history. The National Plan shows that the programme will be increased from £84 million in the last year of Tory rule to £138 million in 1969/70.

Equally important, we shall press ahead with our plans to abolish the 11-plus—that barrier to educational opportunity—and re-organize secondary education on comprehensive lines. We have appointed the Public Schools Commission, to recommend the best ways of integrating the Public Schools into the State sector.

NEW DEAL FOR THE SCHOOL LEAVER. Far too many of our young people still leave school at 15, enter jobs with no training prospects and break off all contact with education. We plan to transform this situation by the early 1970's.

The school leaving age will be raised to 16. The new Schools Council is studying ways of making this extra year at school the greatest success.

Industrial Training Boards will increase the range of training opportunities for school leavers. They are not just concerned with the traditional craft skills. They will deal with the office, the shop, and the farm as well as the factory; with girls as well as boys.

There will be a big increase of day-release and block release courses at local colleges of further education. It will become normal, rather than exceptional, for young workers to have part-time education up to the age of at least 18.

There will also be radical improvements in the Youth Employment Service, and in careers advice at school, in accordance with the Albemarle Report.

Finally, a new Minister is energetically creating, through regional sports councils, a new approach to the provision of facilities for sport.

HIGHER EDUCATION. We shall expand higher education provision in the universities, the colleges of education, and the leading technical colleges.

The universities are being assisted to make a growing contribution in science, technology and social studies.

The colleges of education will benefit from our new plans to liberalize their systems of government, giving more academic freedom. We shall encourage the growth of arrangements between the colleges and the universities, to enable more students to take a B.Ed. degree.

In the leading technical colleges we shall rationalize the provision of higher courses, so that there can be a very large expansion with very high quality.

THE OPEN UNIVERSITY. We shall establish the University of the Air. By using TV and radio, communal facilities, high grade correspondence courses and new teaching techniques, this open University will enormously extend the best teaching facilities and give everyone the opportunity of study for a full degree.

It will mean genuine equality of opportunity for millions of people for the first time. Moreover, even for those who prefer not to take a full course, it will bring the widest and best contribution possible to their general level of knowledge and breadth of interests.

1970

EDUCATION AND SOCIAL EQUALITY. Britain is now spending more on education than ever before. This has brought improvements in the quality of education —more teachers and better schools—and the rapid enlargement of opportunity in our secondary schools, our colleges of education and in higher education as a whole.

This increased expenditure reflects our belief that all children can benefit from a broader and deeper education; that the rich variety of talent that exists must be given the widest possible chance to develop; and that it will make a major contribution to the welfare, quality and happiness of our society.

Our first priority has been to end the system under which 80 per cent of our nation's children were, at the age of eleven, largely denied the opportunity of a broad secondary education with the chance of higher education beyond.

Comprehensive reorganization has been vigorously pursued. In the past six years 129 of the 163 English and Welsh local education authorities have agreed plans for reorganizing their secondary schools.

This progress must not be checked; it must go forward. We shall legislate to require the minority of Tory education authorities who have so far resisted change to abandon eleven plus selection in England and Wales. We have legislated to end fee-paying in Scotland, and we intend to legislate further to ensure that no local authority in Scotland can maintain an area of privilege which destroys the full benefit of comprehensive reorganization for its children.

School building has proceeded at a record level; 13 new schools a week have been completed in the first five years of the Labour Government, compared with less than 9 in the last five years of Tory rule.

In the next five years, we shall put more resources, both teachers and building, into the primary schools and expand nursery schools provision both in, and outside, the educational priority areas.

We intend to make further progress, now that the supply of teachers has been increased, towards our aim of reducing to 30 the size of all classes in our schools.

We shall introduce for England and Wales a new Education Bill to replace the 1944 and subsequent Acts. One of our aims will be to bring parents and teachers into a closer partnership in the running of our schools.

In 1972 we shall raise the school leaving age to 16.

Preparations for this—increasing the supply of teachers, extending the school building programme, and planning a new course for the extra year—are now well advanced.

We shall still further expand higher education. Already since 1964 the number of young people in full time higher education, including the universities, has almost doubled. We are in transition to a new era where higher education, traditionally the preserve of a small educational élite, could become available to a wider section of the community. This expansion will require very careful planning. We shall undertake an early review of the whole field, including universities, polytechnics, higher further education and the colleges of education.

We have never believed that education and educational opportunity should stop at the school leaving age; nor that further education should be confined to full-time students in colleges and universities.

The capacity of people to learn and their desire to learn continues at all ages. It is, therefore, essential that provisions should be made for people, for adults of all ages, to re-enter the education system. To provide such an opportunity for those who have missed higher education, we have created the Open University, which will commence next year, with 25,000 students— almost half the annual intake of all our other universities together.

Social Equality. The widening and extension of education is the best preparation that we can make for our people and our country for the world of tomorrow. Investment in people is also the best way of developing a society based on tolerance, co-operation and greater social equality.

The education system itself must not perpetuate educational and social inequalities; that is one reason why full integration of secondary education is essential.

But progress in the field of education must be accompanied by measures to deal with social and economic inequalities elsewhere.

Until Labour came to power, those living off capital gains or land profits were allowed to substantially escape the net of taxation. We have dealt with this, and similar problems, through the Capital Gains Tax, Land Levy, Expense Accounts, Gaming Levy and by removing some loopholes in covenants and in Estate Duty. We shall continue to close loopholes.

There is much more to do to achieve a fairer distribution of wealth in our community. A Labour Government will continue its work to create a fairer tax system: we shall ensure that tax burdens are progressively eased from those least able to bear them and that there is a greater contribution to the National Revenue from the rich.

3 Liberal manifestos

INVEST IN EDUCATION. People Count . . . and so do their children.

Britain's future as a nation lies with the children.

More teachers and more schools are needed. Secondary schools come first. Then the primary schools must be improved. There is room for public, grammar, comprehensive and independent schools in our system. Remember Russia spends seven times as much per head on education as we do. America spends twice as much. A big extension of University education is needed. The means test on University education should be ended.

1964

INVEST IN PEOPLE. Education decides the country's economic future and shapes our children's lives.

Here priorities are all important. The crux of our educational problem is the teacher shortage, and the first priority is to bring about a massive expansion of teacher training.

Liberals propose to double full time places in higher education in the next ten years. Then the men and women will be available to reduce the size of classes and eliminate the slum schools. Special attention will be given to the primary and infant schools, where neglect has been worst.

Teaching as a career must be made more attractive by an improved salary structure, service conditions and pensions. New methods of teaching must be developed and financial rewards given to teachers who improve their skills. The setting up of new machinery for negotiating teachers' pay to replace the broken Burnham system is overdue.

The 11-plus exam must go. It is socially divisive and unfair in its results. We will encourage forms of nonselective secondary education, ranging from the campus system to the Leicestershire type schemes and the comprehensive school. This cannot be left to local authorities alone. The Government must help, especially with cash for buildings.

1966

WHAT ARE YOUR CHILD'S CHANCES? Although Conservative and Labour Governments have always expressed a desire to increase educational opportunity, in times of financial difficulty it is always education that they cut. Instead of setting up a proper building research group for Universities in order to bring down their costs, the Labour Government has simply imposed a six months' stop on building for Further and Higher Education thus throwing carefully phased plans into chaos.

We must get our plans and priorities right and then stick to them. Liberals recognize that education is the most important investment we can make.

Schools. Priority in school building must be given to bring our slum primary schools, urban and rural, up to a decent standard and to prepare for raising the school-leaving age. This means more generous support for minor works; special grants for depressed areas; and a willingness by Local Authorities to accept large scale industrial building.

Eleven Plus. Liberals regard the abolition of all

selection at eleven plus not as a dogmatic principle, but as a necessary and long overdue reform. We accept the need for detailed consultation at local level and we realize that not every area in the country can go 'fully comprehensive' immediately, nor do we regard the 'all-through, purpose-built eleven to nineteen comprehensive' as necessarily the best solution. We are fighting for reform in the interests of all the children, not in the interests of dogma or special privilege.

Higher Education. We reject the Labour Government's long-term aim of two separate systems, one 'autonomous' under the University Grants Committee and the other 'public' under the Local Authorities. The links between Universities and other institutions of higher education should be drawn closer together by exercising public control through Regional Councils rather than the 160 different Local Authorities.

If the teacher shortage is to be conquered, there must be new methods of part-time training and retraining for teachers. In this connection we regret the Government's failure in this Parliament to establish the University of the Air, proposed originally by the Liberals and promised in the last Labour Manifesto.

Teachers. All professional teachers should be professionally trained and their salaries, working conditions and pensions improved. This could be done if many sub-professional jobs in schools were taken over by ancillary staff.

Cost. The necessary improvements in our education cannot be made without expenditure of a higher proportion of the national income. We would oppose any plan to abolish all individual fee-paying schools although the role of the direct grant, grammar and independent schools must be re-examined.

1970

THE YOUNG. Children are not a pressure group either. Everyone is agreed that they deserve the best possible start in life. The emphasis should be on the improvement of primary schools and the provision of nursery schools. Secondary education should be non-selective. Age eleven to eighteen comprehensive schools have an important part to play in this. But they are not the only means to a non-selective system. They should not be hastily imposed where the buildings, staff and facilities are not suitable. There should be greater opportunities for further education outside the Universities.

Index